10/13 2

50 Best Jobs® for Your Personality

Part of JIST's Best Jobs® Series

Third Edition

Laurence Shatkin, Ph.D.

JIST Works
America's Career Publisher®

HF
5381
.15
F3618
2012

50 Best Jobs for Your Personality, Third Edition

© 2012 by JIST Publishing

Published by JIST Works, an imprint of JIST Publishing
875 Montreal Way
St. Paul, MN 55102

E-mail: info@jist.com   Website: www.jist.com

Some Other Books by Laurence Shatkin, PhD

2011 Career Plan	200 Best Jobs Through Apprenticeships
The Sequel	50 Best Jobs for Your Personality
Best Jobs for the 21st Century	40 Best Fields for Your Career
200 Best Jobs for College Graduates	225 Best Jobs for Baby Boomers
300 Best Jobs Without a Four-Year Degree	250 Best-Paying Jobs
150 Best Federal Jobs	150 Best Jobs for a Better World
150 Best Jobs for a Secure Future	200 Best Jobs for Introverts

Visit www.jist.com for information on JIST, free job search tips, tables of contents, sample pages, and ordering information on our many products.

Acquisitions Editor: Susan Pines
Development Editor: Grant E. Mabie
Production Editor: Jeanne Clark
Cover and Interior Designer: Aleata Halbig
Cover Photo: iStockphoto®
Cover Design: Aleata Halbig
Interior Layout: Julie Johnston
Proofreader: Susan Capecchi
Indexer: Cheryl Ann Lenser

Printed in the United States of America

18 17 16 15 14 13 12   9 8 7 6 5 4 3 2 1

Library of Congress Cataloging-in-Publication Data is on file with the Library of Congress.

This Is a Big Book, But It Is Very Easy to Use

Psychologists have long understood a principle that many of us consider just common sense: that people have an aspect called personality that makes them feel more comfortable in some situations than in others. People who have a certain personality feel more capable of doing certain things and dealing with certain problems; they also feel more accepted when they are among people with personalities similar to their own.
This is especially true for one place where people spend a major portion of their time: at work. People want to feel that they fit in with the people and with the activities where they work.

If personality is the key to this feeling of fitting in, then you need to consider this question: *What kind of personality do you have?* Maybe you can come up with a few ways to describe yourself, such as "sunny," "energetic," "conscientious," "loyal," "outgoing," "funny," or "competitive." But what do those terms suggest for the kind of work you might enjoy and do well? What terms might be more useful?

Some Things You Can Do with This Book

This book can help you think about your personality in terms that have proven relevance to the world of work. You'll learn about the personality types that many psychologists and career development practitioners use to describe people and jobs. You'll take a quick assessment to help you clarify your dominant personality type. Then you'll dig into a gold mine of facts about the jobs that are the best fit for your personality type—and that are the best for other reasons, too, such as their wages and job openings. The lists of "best jobs" will help you zero in on promising careers, and the descriptive profiles of the jobs will open your eyes to career choices that previously you may not have known much about.

We all want to fit in somewhere. And there are probably several different careers in which each of us could find a comfortable niche. But why not do it in a *really good job?* That's what this book can help you choose.

Credits and Acknowledgments: While the author created this book, it is based on the work of many others. The occupational information is based on data obtained from the U.S. Department of Labor and the U.S. Department of Education. These sources provide the most authoritative occupational information available.

Table of Contents

Summary of Major Sections

Introduction. A short overview to help you better understand and use the book. *Starts on Page 1.*

Part I: Overview of Personality and Career. Part I is an overview of personality and of personality types. This section also explores the relationship between personality and career. *Starts on page 19.*

Part II: What's Your Personality Type? Take an Assessment. This part helps you discover your personality type with a short, easy-to-complete assessment. *Starts on page 27.*

Part III: The Best Jobs Lists: Jobs for Each of the Six Personality Types. The 131 lists in Part III show you the best jobs in terms of high salaries, fast growth, and plentiful job openings for each of the six personality types. Further lists classify the jobs according to education and training required and several other features, such as jobs with the highest percentage of women and of men and jobs with high rates of self-employment. Although there are a lot of lists, they are easy to understand because they have clear titles and are organized into groupings of related lists. *Starts on page 37.*

Part IV: Descriptions of the 50 Best Jobs for Each Personality Type. This part provides a brief but information-packed description of the 50 jobs from each personality type that met the criteria for this book. Each description contains information on earnings, projected growth, education and training required, job duties, skills, related job titles, related knowledge and courses, and many other details. The descriptions are presented in alphabetical order within each personality type. This structure makes it easy to look up a job that you've identified in a list from Part III and that you want to learn more about. *Starts on page 147.*

Part V: Appendixes. Appendix A contains a list of occupations in this book and their two-letter personality codes. Appendix B defines the skills and the types of knowledge listed in the job descriptions in Part IV. Appendix C identifies resources for further career exploration. *Starts on page 451.*

Detailed Table of Contents

Introduction

Before you get started finding the best jobs for your personality type, here are a few things you may want to know about the information in this book and how it is organized.

Where the Information Comes From

The information I used in creating this book comes from three major government sources.

The U.S. Department of Labor. I used several data sources to construct the information I put into this book. I started with the jobs included in the U.S. Department of Labor's O*NET database. The O*NET is now the primary source of detailed information on occupations and includes personality information on about 900 occupations. The Labor Department updates the O*NET on a regular basis, and I used the most recent one available, release 16.

Because I also wanted to include figures for earnings, growth, and number of openings—information not included in the O*NET—I used sources at the U.S. Department of Labor's Bureau of Labor Statistics (BLS). The Occupational Employment Statistics survey provided the most reliable figures on earnings I could obtain, and the Employment Projections program provided the nation's best figures on job growth and openings. These two BLS programs use a slightly different system of job titles than the O*NET does, but I was able to link the BLS data with most of the O*NET data I used to develop this book.

Information about the level of education or training required for each occupation is taken mostly from a table on the website of the Office of Occupational Statistics and Employment Projections (www.bls.gov/emp/ep_table_112.htm). For recently emerged job specializations not included in that table, I relied on other sources of information, such as professional associations.

The U.S. Census Bureau. Data on the demographic characteristics of workers came from the Current Population Survey (CPS), conducted by the U.S. Census Bureau. This includes the information about the proportion of workers in each job who are men and women and in various age brackets. As with the BLS data, I had to match slightly different sets of job titles, but I was able to identify CPS data for almost all the jobs included in this book.

The U.S. Department of Education. I used the Classification of Instructional Programs, a system developed by the U.S. Department of Education, to cross-reference the educational or training programs related to each job. I linked programs to jobs by following the crosswalk developed jointly by the BLS and the National Center for Education Statistics (NCES). I modified the names of some education and training programs so that they would be more easily understood. In 11 cases, I abbreviated the listing of related programs for the sake of space; such entries end with "others." The Office of Vocational and Adult Education (OVAE) provided information about the career clusters and pathways linked to each occupation.

As you can see, this information came from numerous databases housed in various government agencies. In its original database format, the information would have been disjointed and sometimes confusing, so I did many things to connect related data and present it to you in a form that is easy to understand.

How the Jobs in This Book Were Selected

Here is the procedure I followed to select the jobs I included in this book:

1. I began by creating my own database from the O*NET, the BLS, the Census Bureau, and other sources to include the information that I wanted. The one classification system that all of these sources have in common is the Standard Occupational Classification (SOC), so this system of job titles is the one I chose for my best jobs lists.

2. However, I also had to consider the other organizing principle of the lists: the six RIASEC personality types. RIASEC data is available only for O*NET occupations. I used several methods to link SOC titles with the RIASEC data available in the O*NET database. First, 675 SOC titles are each linked to a single O*NET title that has RIASEC ratings, so it was easy to identify the dominant RIASEC type for each of these occupations.

3. On the other hand, many SOC titles are linked to two or more O*NET occupations with RIASEC ratings. Fortunately, in 40 cases, all the linked O*NET occupations have the same dominant RIASEC type. For example, the SOC job Accountants and Auditors combines two O*NET jobs, as the title indicates, and both have Conventional as their dominant personality type. So for my second step, I assigned the shared personality type to these 40 homogeneous SOC occupations.

4. Some 37 SOC occupations, however, represent such diverse collections of workers that their component O*NET titles do not share the same dominant RIASEC type. A good example is Compliance Officers, which subsumes the O*NET titles Environmental Compliance Inspectors (Conventional), Equal Opportunity Representatives and Officers (Social), and Coroners (Investigative). In such cases, I assigned the SOC occupation to all the dominant RIASEC types of the linked O*NET titles. Compliance Officers thus went into the pools of job titles to be sorted for three different lists of best jobs. At this point, the six pools of jobs ranged in size from 33 for Artistic through 339 for Realistic.

5. Because I wanted to identify 50 best jobs for each personality type, I needed a pool of more than 33 jobs for the Artistic type. Therefore, I added to this pool another 42 SOC jobs for which Artistic is the highest-rated *secondary* personality type. (I determined the secondary personality types for SOC jobs by averaging the RIASEC ratings for all O*NET jobs linked to each SOC job. I followed the procedures of the O*NET developers for ordering the secondary personality types.) As a result, you'll find that some jobs listed as Artistic also appear on lists for another RIASEC type. Some examples are Advertising and Promotions Managers (which has Enterprising as its dominant RIASEC type), Training and Development Specialists (Social), and Camera Operators, Television, Video, and Motion Picture (Realistic).

6. At this point, the pool of jobs included 745 unique titles. When I connected these jobs to the economic information that I needed to sort them, I found the complete set of data for only 725 titles. I eliminated 59 jobs that are expected to employ fewer than 500 workers per year and to shrink rather than grow in workforce size. I also removed an additional 42 jobs because they have annual earnings of less than $22,150, which means that 75 percent of workers earn more than the workers in these jobs. At this point, I had a pool of 624 unique occupations.

7. Next, I ranked each of the six RIASEC-based pools of jobs three times, based on these major criteria: median annual earnings, projected growth through 2018, and number of job openings projected per year.

8. I then added the three numerical rankings for each job to calculate its overall score.

9. To emphasize jobs that tend to pay more, are likely to grow more rapidly, and have more job openings, I selected the 50 job titles with the best total scores for each of the six RIASEC types. Because some jobs appear on multiple lists, a total of 264 jobs (rather than 300) appear on the Part III lists, and they are the focus of this book.

For example, Accountants and Auditors is the Conventional job with the highest combined score for earnings, growth, and number of job openings, so Accountants and Auditors is listed first in the "50 Best Conventional Jobs" list even though it is not the best-paying Conventional job (which is Financial Managers), the fastest-growing

Conventional job (which is Dental Assistants), or the Conventional job with the most openings (which is Office Clerks, General).

Why This Book Has More Than 50 Job Descriptions for Each Personality Type

I didn't think you would mind that this book actually provides information on more than 50 jobs for each personality type. As this introduction explains, the jobs on the Part III lists are based on the SOC job classification system, but in Part IV I also describe the related O*NET jobs under the heading "Job Specialization." This means that, although I used 264 SOC job titles to construct the lists, Part IV actually describes an additional 197 job specializations.

Understand the Limits of the Data in This Book

In this book, I use the most reliable and up-to-date information available on earnings, projected growth, number of openings, and other topics. As you look at the figures, keep in mind that they are estimates. They give you a general idea about the number of workers employed, annual earnings, rate of job growth, and annual job openings.

Understand that a problem with such data is that it describes an average. Just as there is no precisely average person, there is no such thing as a statistically average example of a particular job. I say this because data, while helpful, can also be misleading.

Take, for example, the way I assign the jobs to the six personality types. I follow the ratings assigned by the O*NET database, which are based on analysis of the occupation's definition, core work tasks, types of knowledge used, and other information about the job. But workers with the same occupation title often work in different settings and have varying work duties, use varying kinds of knowledge, and vary in other ways that should influence the RIASEC type one would assign to their job. For example, Librarians who do research for a corporation have considerably different work tasks from the Librarians who work in a public library. Therefore, although the O*NET assigns Librarians to the Conventional personality type, you should keep in mind that Librarians can also find niches within their profession that are compatible with other personality types. One way to uncover such niche work roles is to note any secondary personality types assigned to the occupation. These are listed in the Part IV description of the job, where you'll find Librarians identified as Conventional-Social-Enterprising. Some of the Part III lists also include RIASEC codes—for example, CSE for Librarians.

Salary figures, which seem so precise, likewise summarize a great amount of variation. The yearly earnings information in this book is based on highly reliable data obtained from a very large U.S. working population sample by the Bureau of Labor Statistics. It tells us the average annual pay received as of May 2010 by people in various job titles (actually, it is the median annual pay, which means that half earned more and half less).

This sounds great, except that half of all people in that occupation earned less than that amount. For example, people who are new to the occupation or with only a few years of work experience often earn much less than the median amount. People who live in rural areas or who work for smaller employers typically earn less than those who do similar work in cities (where the cost of living is higher) or for bigger employers. People in certain areas of the country earn less than those in others. Other factors also influence how much you are likely to earn in a given job in your area.

The earnings data from the OES survey is reported under the SOC system of job titles. As noted earlier in this introduction, the SOC system collapses some O*NET job titles, such as Accountants and Auditors. Accountants probably do not have the same average earnings as Auditors, but only one figure ($61,690) is available for the combined occupation.

Also keep in mind that the figures for job growth and number of openings are projections by labor economists—their best estimates of what we can expect between now and 2018. Those projections are not guarantees. A catastrophic economic downturn, war, or technological breakthrough could change the actual outcome. The projections are also averages over a ten-year period. During economic slow-downs, you can expect job growth and openings to be lower; during recoveries, both will be higher.

Finally, don't forget that the job market consists of both job openings and job *seekers*. The figures on job growth and openings don't tell you how many people will be competing with you to be hired. The Department of Labor does not publish figures on the supply of job candidates, so I can't provide a number that tells you how much competition you can expect. Competition is an important issue that you should research for any tentative career goal. Each job description in Part IV includes a brief statement about outlook that may include a comment about competition. You can find additional discussion in the *Occupational Outlook Handbook*. You also should speak to people who educate or train tomorrow's workers; they probably have a good idea of how many graduates find rewarding employment and how quickly. People in the workforce can provide insights into this issue as well. Use your critical thinking skills to evaluate what people tell you. For example, educators or trainers may be trying to recruit you, whereas people in the workforce may be trying to discourage you from competing. Get a variety of opinions to balance out possible biases.

So, in reviewing the information in this book, please understand the limitations of the data. You need to use common sense in career decision making as in most other things in life. I hope that, by using that approach, you find the information helpful and interesting.

Data Complexities

If you are curious about details, the following section explains some of the complexities inherent in the sources of information I used and what I did to make sense of them. You don't need to know this to use the book, so jump to the section about "How This Book Is Organized" if you are bored with details.

I selected the jobs partly on the basis of economic data, and I include information on earnings, projected growth, and number of job openings for each job throughout this book. I think this information is important to most people, but getting it for each job is not a simple task.

Earnings

The employment security agency of each state gathers information on earnings for various jobs and forwards it to the U.S. Bureau of Labor Statistics. This information is organized in standardized ways by a BLS program called Occupational Employment Statistics (OES). To keep the earnings for the various jobs and regions comparable, the OES screens out certain types of earnings and includes others, so the OES earnings I use in this book represent straight-time gross pay exclusive of premium pay. More specifically, the OES earnings include the job's base rate; cost-of-living allowances; guaranteed pay; hazardous-duty pay; incentive pay, including commissions and production bonuses; on-call pay; and tips. They do not include back pay, jury duty pay, overtime pay, severance pay, shift differentials, nonproduction bonuses, or tuition reimbursements. The earnings of self-employed workers also are not included.

For each job described in Part IV, you'll find two facts related to earnings, both based on the OES survey:

❊ The Annual Earnings figure shows the median earnings (half earn more, half earn less).

❊ The Earnings Growth Potential figure represents the ratio between the 10th percentile and the median. This information answers the question, "If I compared the wages of the low earners to the median, how much of a pay difference (in percentage terms) would I find?" If the difference is large, the job has great potential for increasing your earnings as you gain experience and skills. If the difference is small, you probably will need to move on to another occupation to improve your earnings substantially. Because a percentage figure would be hard to interpret, I also provide an easy-to-understand verbal tag that expresses the Earnings Growth Potential: "very low" when the percentage is 25 percent or less, "low" for 26 percent to 35 percent, "medium" for 36 percent to 40 percent, "high" for 41 percent to 50 percent, and "very high" for any figure 51 percent or higher.

The median earnings for all workers in all occupations were $33,840 in May 2010. The 264 SOC jobs in this book were chosen partly on the basis of good earnings, so their average is a respectable $58,850. (This is a weighted average, which means that jobs with larger workforces are given greater weight in the computation. It also is based on the assumption that a job with income reported as "more than $166,400" pays exactly $166,400, so the actual average is somewhat higher.) One-quarter of the jobs in the book have earnings less than $43,520, compared to $22,150 across all occupations. One-quarter of the jobs in the book have earnings greater than $77,610, compared to $54,250 across all occupations.

Projected Growth and Number of Job Openings

This information comes from the Office of Occupational Statistics and Employment Projections, a program within the Bureau of Labor Statistics that develops information about projected trends in the nation's labor market for the next ten years. The most recent projections available cover the years from 2008 to 2018. The projections are based on information about people moving into and out of occupations. The BLS uses data from various sources in projecting the growth and number of openings for each job title: Some data comes from the Census Bureau's Current Population Survey, and some comes from an OES survey. The BLS economists assumed a steady economy unaffected by a major war, depression, or other upheaval. They also assumed that recessions may occur during the decade covered by these projections, as would be consistent with the pattern of business cycles we have experienced for several decades. However, because their projections cover 10 years, the figures for job growth and openings are intended to provide an average of both the good times and the bad times.

Like the earnings figures, the figures on projected growth and job openings are reported according to the SOC classification. So, to continue the example I used earlier, the Department of Labor projects growth (21.6%) and openings (49,750) for one SOC occupation called Accountants and Auditors, and I can't tell you whether Accountants are growing faster or more slowly than Auditors.

The Department of Labor provides a single figure (15.1%) for the projected growth of 38 postsecondary teaching jobs and also provides a single figure (55,290) for the projected annual job openings for these 38 jobs. Because these college-teaching jobs are related to three different RIASEC types—Investigative, Artistic, and Social—and because separate *earnings* figures are available for each of the 38 jobs, I thought you'd appreciate having these jobs appear separately in the lists in this book. If the trends of the last several years continue, none of these jobs can be expected to grow or take on workers at a much faster rate than the other 37. Therefore, in preparing the Part III lists and the Part IV descriptions, I assumed that all of these college-teaching jobs share the same rate of projected job growth, 15.1%, and I computed a figure for their projected job openings by dividing the total (55,290) into 38 parts, each of which is proportional in size to the current workforce of the job.

On the other hand, I collapsed eight jobs for medical doctors into one occupation called Physicians and Surgeons. Recent trends indicate that the various medical specializations are growing at different rates, but I could obtain projected growth and job openings figures only for this combined occupation.

While salary figures are fairly straightforward, you may not know what to make of job-growth figures. For example, is projected growth of 15 percent good or bad? Keep in mind that the average (mean) growth projected for all occupations by the Bureau of Labor Statistics is 10.1 percent. One-quarter of the SOC occupations have a growth projection of 0.3 percent or lower. Growth of 9.1 percent is the median, meaning that half of the occupations have more, half less. Only one-quarter of the occupations have growth projected at more than 15.4 percent.

Because the jobs in this book were selected as "best" partly on the basis of job growth, their mean growth is 15.0 percent, which compares favorably to the mean for all jobs. Among the jobs in this book, one-quarter have projected growth of 22.0 percent or more, the job at the median has projected growth of 15.0 percent, and only one-quarter of the jobs have a projected growth of less than 12.0 percent.

The number of job openings for the 283 best jobs is slightly lower than the national average for all occupations. The Bureau of Labor statistics projects an average of about 35,000 job openings per year for the 750 occupations that it studies, but for the 264 SOC occupations included in this book, the average is about 9,600 openings. One-quarter of the jobs are projected to have more than 11,200 annual openings, the job ranked 132nd (the median) has about 4,200 openings projected, and one-quarter of the jobs have fewer than 1,600 openings projected.

Don't be concerned about the fact that the occupations in this book are projected to offer fewer job openings than is the average for all occupations in the economy. Many of the occupations with the largest number of openings are low-skill, low-wage jobs with rapid turnover of workers, such as in fast food. I'm confident that you would not be interested in such jobs as long-term career goals.

Perhaps you're wondering why I present figures on both job growth *and* number of openings. Aren't these two ways of saying the same thing? Actually, you need to know both. Consider the occupation Biomedical Engineers, which is projected to grow at the astounding rate of 72.0 percent. There should be lots of opportunities in such a fast-growing job, right? Not exactly. This is a tiny occupation, with only about 16,000 people currently employed. So, even though it is growing rapidly, it will not create many new jobs (about 1,500 per year). Now consider Secretaries and Administrative Assistants, Except Legal, Medical, and Executive. This occupation is growing at the lackluster rate of 4.6 percent now that many secretarial tasks are being handled by word processors, voice mail, and other kinds of office automation. Nevertheless, this is a huge occupation that employs two million workers. So, even though its growth rate is unimpressive, it is expected to take on about 37,000 new workers each year as existing workers retire, die, or move on to other jobs. That's why I based my selection of the best jobs on both of these economic indicators and why you should pay attention to both when you scan the lists of best jobs.

Education or Training Required

One set of lists in Part III organizes jobs on the basis of the amount of education or training that they typically require for entry. In Part IV, each job description includes a statement of the education or training requirements.

You should keep in mind that some people working in these jobs may have credentials that differ considerably from the level listed here. For example, although a bachelor's degree is considered the appropriate preparation for Cost Estimators, more than one-quarter of these workers have no college background at all. Conversely, although Registered Nurses can begin working after earning an associate degree, more than half have a bachelor's, and in fact career opportunities without the bachelor's are considerably more limited.

Some workers who have more than the minimum required education for their job have earned a higher degree *after* being hired, but others entered the job with this educational credential, and the more advanced degree may have given them an advantage over other job vseekers with less education. Some workers with *less* than the normal minimum requirement may have been hired on the basis of their work experience in a similar job. So don't assume that the one-line "Education Required" statement in the Part IV job descriptions gives a complete picture of how best to prepare for the job. If you're considering the job seriously, you need to investigate this topic in greater detail. Consider using some of the resources listed in Appendix C for further career exploration.

Other Job Characteristics

Some of the figures used to create the lists of jobs in this book are shared by more than one job title. This is particularly the case for demographic information about occupations that are so small that the BLS does not track separate statistics for them. For example, the occupation Sound Engineering Technicians has a total workforce of only about 19,000 workers, so the BLS does not report a specific figure for the percentage of women workers. In this case, I had to use the figure that BLS reports for a group of occupations it calls Broadcast and Sound Engineering Technicians and Radio Operators. I relied on this same figure for three other jobs: Audio and Video Equipment Technicians, Broadcast Technicians, and Radio Operators. You may notice similar figure-sharing among related jobs where I list the percentages of workers in specific age brackets.

Information in the Job Descriptions

I used a variety of government and other sources to compile the job descriptions I provide in Part IV. Details on these various sources are mentioned later in this introduction under the heading "Part IV: Descriptions of the 50 Best Jobs for Each Personality Type."

How This Book Is Organized

The information in this book moves from the general to the highly specific. It starts by explaining how personality relates to career choice and presents a widely used model for making that connection. An assessment helps you focus on your dominant personality type (or types), and then you can consult a wealth of lists that itemize the best jobs for your personality type. These lists let you look at the jobs from several different perspectives—for example, which jobs pay the best, which jobs employ the most young people, and which jobs require an associate degree for entry. Finally, you can get highly detailed information about any of these career choices in the fact-packed job descriptions that make up the last part of the book.

Part I. Overview of Personality and Career

Part I is an overview of how personality relates to careers—the basic theory, plus the six personality types that were originally described by John Holland and have since become the basis of many guidance resources. This section may clear up some misunderstandings you have about what personality means in the context of career choice, and it will help you understand a useful way of looking at yourself and the world of work.

Part II. What's Your Personality Type? Take an Assessment

You probably are not reading this book simply to educate yourself about career development theory. Rather, the odds are that you have a more practical goal: making a career choice. To guide you, I've included a paper-and-pencil assessment that can help you clarify your dominant personality type or types. The Personality Type Inventory usually takes about 20 or 30 minutes to complete, but there is no time limit, nor are there any right or wrong answers.

After taking the Personality Type Inventory, you can use what you've learned about your personality type to identify a job that suits you well. This book makes that task easy because all of the information about jobs is grouped by the dominant personality type of the jobs. That means you don't have to waste time exploring jobs that are unlikely to be a good match for your personality. Also, because this book focuses on the 50 most rewarding jobs for each personality type, you don't have to complicate your search by considering jobs with low earnings or highly limited odds of being employed.

Part III. The Best Jobs Lists: Jobs for Each of the Six Personality Types

For many people, the 131 lists in Part III are the most interesting section of the book. Here you can see which jobs for each personality type are best in terms of high salaries, fast growth, and plentiful job openings and best when these three factors are combined. Other lists break out the best of each personality type according to the level of education or training required and several other features of the jobs and of the people who hold them. Look in the Table of Contents for a complete list of the lists. Although there are a lot of lists, they are not difficult to understand because they have clear titles and are organized into groupings of related lists.

People who prefer to think about careers in terms of economic rewards will want to browse the lists that show the best jobs in terms of earnings, growth, and openings. On the other hand, some people think first in terms of opportunities for young people or representation of women, and these readers will find other useful lists that reflect these interests.

I suggest that you use the lists that make the most sense for you. Following are the names of each group of lists along with short comments on each group. You will find additional information in a brief introduction provided at the beginning of each group of lists in Part III.

Best Jobs Overall for Each Personality Type: Jobs with the Highest Pay, Fastest Growth, and Most Openings

This group has four sets of six lists, and they are the ones that most people want to see first. The first set of lists presents, for each personality type, all 50 jobs that are included in this book in order of their total scores for earnings, growth, and number of job openings. These jobs are used in the more-specialized lists that follow and in the descriptions in Part IV. Three more sets of lists in this group present, for each personality type, specialized lists of jobs extracted from the best 50 overall: the 20 best-paying, the 20 fastest-growing, and the 20 with the most openings.

The Best Jobs for Each Personality Type with a High Percentage of Workers Age 16–24

This section provides lists of the jobs for each personality type that have the highest percentage of workers age 16–24. Each list is then re-sorted to present these youthful jobs in order of their total combined scores for earnings, growth, and number of openings. Thus, there is a total of 12 lists in this section.

The Best Jobs for Each Personality Type with a High Percentage of Workers Age 55 and Over

The 12 lists in this section were assembled in the same manner as the lists in the previous section, except that these jobs have a high percentage of workers age 55 and over.

The Best Jobs for Each Personality Type with a High Percentage of Self-Employed Workers

The 12 lists in this section show you the jobs that have the highest percentage of self-employed workers. Once again, the lists for the six personality types are re-sorted in order of the jobs' total combined scores for earnings, growth, and number of openings.

Best Jobs for Each Personality Type with a High Percentage of Women and of Men

For each personality type, you can see the jobs that have the highest percentage of workers who are women and workers who are men. In addition, each of the lists is re-sorted to show these predominantly-male or predominantly-female jobs ordered by their overall ranking on earnings, growth, and openings. That makes a total of 24 lists.

Best Jobs for Each Personality Type with a High Percentage of Urban and Rural Workers

The 24 lists in this section show you, for each personality type, the jobs that are concentrated in big cities and in areas without big cities. Jobs are sorted by how highly concentrated they are in these geographical areas and by the usual three economic criteria.

The Best Jobs for Each Personality Type Sorted by Education or Training Required

When considering a career choice, many people put a lot of emphasis on how long it takes to prepare for the job and what kind of preparation is appropriate—education, training, work experience. Just as it's important to choose a job that suits your personality, it can be helpful to choose learning goals that suit your preferences and abilities. Your financial circumstances also may shape your plans for career preparation because higher education can be expensive (even with financial aid) and the years you spend in college will postpone the years in which you will earn a salary. This set of lists sorts the jobs linked to each personality type into groups according to what preparation method is the fastest route to career entry. Within each group, the jobs are sorted by their overall ranking on earnings, growth, and openings.

Bonus Lists: Best Jobs That May Appeal to Other Aspects of Your Personality

The six RIASEC types are not the only way you can look at the relationship between your personality and work. For this set of lists, I analyzed the 264 jobs included in this book in terms of 11 other characteristics that may be considered personality traits. For each list, I identified the 50 jobs that score highest on one of these traits and then extracted the 20 jobs that have the best combination of earnings, job growth, and openings. You'll find lists of the best jobs for introverts, extroverts, persistent people, sensitive people, people with self-control, stress-tolerant people, flexible people, detail-oriented people, innovators, analytical thinkers, and people who don't like working behind a desk.

Part IV. Descriptions of the 50 Best Jobs for Each Personality Type

This part of the book provides a brief but information-packed description of each of the 264 best jobs that met my criteria for this book. The descriptions are divided into six groups, one for each personality type, and are presented in alphabetical order within each group. This structure makes it easy to look up a job that you've identified in a list from Part III or Appendix A and that you want to learn more about.

Note that some of the jobs in the Part III lists don't have the same primary RIASEC type as most of the other jobs in that list, as explained earlier in this introduction. Recreational Therapists is one such job; its dominant RIASEC type is actually Social, but it also appears on Artistic lists in Part III. If you should look it up in the Artistic section of Part IV, you will find a note there telling you to look for Recreational Therapists in the Social section of Part IV instead.

As I explained earlier in this introduction, the job titles used in the lists are based on the Standard Occupational Classification (SOC), but in Part IV the information is partly derived from the O*NET database. Sometimes the O*NET information is listed under "Job Specialization" headings that are subsumed under the SOC title used in the Part III lists.

Although I've tried to make the descriptions easy to understand, the sample that follows—with an explanation of each of its parts—may help you better understand and use the descriptions.

Job Title →

First-Line Supervisors of Fire Fighting and Prevention Workers

Data Elements →

❀ Personality Type: Enterprising-Realistic
❀ Annual Earnings: $68,240
❀ Earnings Growth Potential: Medium (39.3%)
❀ Growth: 8.2%
❀ Annual Job Openings: 3,250
❀ Self-Employed: 0.0%

Considerations for Job Outlook →

Considerations for Job Outlook: Most job growth will stem from the conversion of volunteer fire fighting positions into paid positions. Job-seekers are expected to face keen competition. Those who have completed some fire fighter education at a community college and have EMT or paramedic certification should have the best prospects.

Job Specialization (not all profiles have) →

Job Specialization: Forest Fire Fighting and Prevention Supervisors

Summary Description and Tasks →

Supervise fire fighters who control and suppress fires in forests or vacant public land. Communicate fire details to superiors, subordinates, and interagency dispatch centers, using two-way radios. Serve as working leader of an engine, hand, helicopter, or prescribed fire crew of three or more firefighters. Maintain fire suppression equipment in good condition, checking equipment periodically to ensure that it is ready for use. Evaluate size, location, and condition of forest fires in order to request and dispatch crews and position equipment so fires can be contained safely and effectively. Operate wildland fire engines and hoselays. Direct and supervise prescribed burn projects, and prepare post-burn reports analyzing burn conditions and results. Monitor prescribed burns to ensure that they are conducted safely and effectively. Identify staff training and development needs to ensure that appropriate training can be arranged. Maintain knowledge of forest fire laws and fire prevention techniques and tactics. Recommend equipment modifications or new equipment purchases. Perform administrative duties such as compiling and maintaining records, completing forms, preparing reports, and composing correspondence. Recruit and hire forest fire-fighting personnel. Train workers in such skills as parachute jumping, fire suppression, aerial observation, and radio communication, both in the classroom and on the job. Review and evaluate employee performance.

Education/Training Required: Work experience in a related occupation. **Education and Training Programs:** Fire Prevention and Safety Technology/Technician; Fire Services Administration. **Knowledge/Courses:** Public Safety and Security; Building and Construction; Mechanical Devices; Customer and Personal Service; Personnel and Human Resources; Transportation.

Personality Type: Enterprising-Realistic-Conventional. **Career Cluster:** 12 Law, Public Safety, Corrections, and Security. **Career Pathway:** 12.2 Emergency and Fire Management Services.

Skills: Operations Analysis; Equipment Maintenance; Operation and Control; Management of Personnel Resources; Coordination; Operation Monitoring; Monitoring; Equipment Selection.

Work Environment: Outdoors; standing; walking and running; using hands; noise; very hot or cold; bright or inadequate lighting; contaminants; cramped work space; hazardous equipment; minor burns, cuts, bites, or stings.

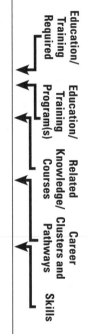

← **Education/Training Required**
← **Education/Training Program(s)**
← **Related Knowledge/Courses**
← **Career Clusters and Pathways**
← **Skills**

↑
Work Environment

Here are some details on each of the major parts of the job descriptions you will find in Part IV:

❋ **Job Title:** This is the job title for the job as defined by the Standard Occupational Classification (SOC) taxonomy.

❋ **Data Elements:** This information comes from various databases, mostly from the U.S. Department of Labor, as explained elsewhere in this introduction.

❋ **Summary Description and Tasks:** The boldfaced sentence provides a summary description of the occupation. It is followed by a listing of tasks generally performed by people who work in this job. This information comes from the O*NET database but, where necessary, has been edited to avoid exceeding 2,000 characters.

❋ **Considerations for Job Outlook:** This information, derived from the Employment Projections Office of the Department of Labor, explains some factors that are expected to affect opportunities for job seekers. Note that these comments apply to the period of time from 2008 to 2018.

❋ **Education/Training Required:** Based mostly on information from the BLS, this phrase identifies the most common level of education or training that is required of workers entering the career. Understand that a higher level of preparation may sometimes be beneficial, either to make you more competitive against other job-seekers or to allow you to enter the job at a more responsible and better-paying level. On the other hand, if the demand for workers is high, it sometimes may be possible for you to enter the career with a lower level of preparation.

❋ **Education/Training Program(s):** This part provides the names of one or more programs for preparing for the job. The titles are based on the U.S. Department of Education *Classification of Instructional Programs*. A particular college major or training program may not have the identical title—for example, there probably is no college that offers a major called "Political Science and Government, General," but you are likely to find a major called "Political Science" or "Government." I derived this information from a crosswalk created by the National Crosswalk Service Center to connect information in the Classification of Instructional Programs (CIP) to O*NET job titles. I modified the names of some educational and training programs so they would be more easily understood. In 25 cases, I abbreviated the listing of related programs for the sake of space; such entries end with "others."

❋ **Related Knowledge/Courses:** This entry can help you understand the most important knowledge areas that are required for a job and the types of courses or programs you will likely need to take to prepare for it. I used information in the O*NET database for this entry. For each job, I identified any knowledge area with a rating that was higher than the average rating for that knowledge area for all jobs; then I listed as many as six in descending order. You'll find a definition for each knowledge area in Appendix B.

❋ **Career Clusters and Pathways:** This information cross-references the scheme of career clusters and pathways that was created by the U.S. Department of Education's Office of Vocational and Adult Education in 1999 and is now used by many states to organize career-oriented programs and career information. In identifying a career cluster and pathway for the job (sometimes more than one), I followed the assignments of the online O*NET database. Your state might assign this job to a different career pathway or even a different cluster.

❋ **Skills:** For each job, I included the skills whose level-of-performance scores exceeded the average for all jobs by the greatest amount and whose ratings on the importance scale were higher than very low. I included as many as eight such skills for each job, and I ranked them by the extent to which their rating exceeds the average. You'll find a definition for each skill in Appendix B.

❋ **Work Environment:** I included any work condition with a rating that exceeds the midpoint of the rating scale. The order does not indicate any condition's frequency on the job. Consider whether you like these conditions and whether any of these conditions would make you uncomfortable. Keep in mind that, when hazards are present (for example, contaminants), protective equipment and procedures are provided to keep you safe.

Getting all the information I used in the job descriptions was not a simple process, and it is not always perfect. Even so, I used the best and most recent sources of data I could find, and I think that my efforts will be helpful to many people.

How to Use This Book

This is a book that you can dive right into:

❋ **If you don't know much about what personality types are,** you'll want to read Part I, which is an overview of the theory behind using personality types as a way of making career choices. You'll also see definitions of the six personality types that are used in this book.

❋ **If you want to understand your own personality type,** you'll want to do the assessment in Part II. It takes only 20 or 30 minutes to complete and can guide you to jobs that suit you.

❋ **If you like lists and want an easy way to compare jobs,** you should turn to Part III. Here you can browse lists showing the 50 jobs for each personality type with the best pay, the fastest growth, and the most job openings. You can see these "best jobs" lists broken down in various ways, such as by amount of education or training required.

❀ **For detailed information about jobs,** turn to Part IV and read the profiles of the jobs. I include 264 jobs and 197 job specializations, itemizing their major tasks, their top skills, their educational or training programs, and other facts you won't learn from the lists in Part III.

On the other hand, **if you like to do things in a methodical way,** you may want to read the sections in order:

1. Part I will give you useful background on how personality type can be a guide in choosing a career.

2. The assessment in Part II will help you identify your dominant personality type.

3. With a clearer understanding of your personality type, you can browse the appropriate lists of "best jobs" in Part III and take notes on the jobs that have the greatest appeal for you.

4. Then you can look up the descriptions of these jobs in Part IV and narrow down your list. Ask yourself, Do the work tasks interest me? Does the required education or training discourage me?

Part I

Overview of Personality and Career

Why Use Personality to Choose a Career?

Many psychological theorists and practicing career counselors believe that you will be most satisfied and productive in a career if it suits your personality. Two main aspects of a job determine whether it is a good fit:

❋ The nature of the work tasks and the skills and knowledge you use on the job must be a good match for the things you like to do and the subjects that interest you. For example, if you like to help other people and promote learning and personal development and if you like communication more than working with things or ideas, then a career in social work might be one that you would enjoy and do well in.

❋ The people you work with must share your personality traits so that you feel comfortable and can accomplish good work in their company. For an example of the opposite, think of how a person who enjoys following set procedures and working with data and detail might feel if forced to work with a group of conceptual artists who constantly seek self-expression and the inspiration for unconventional new artistic ideas.

Personality theorists believe that people with similar personality types naturally tend to associate with one another in the workplace (among other places). As they do so, they create a working environment that is hospitable to their personality type. For example, a workplace with a lot of Artistic types tends to reward creative thinking and behavior. Therefore, your personality type not only predicts how well your skills will match the demands of the work tasks in a particular job; it also predicts how well you will fit in with the culture of the work site as shaped by the people who will surround you and interact with you. Your personality type thus affects your satisfaction with the job, your productivity in it, and the likelihood that you will persist in this type of work.

One of the advantages of using personality as a key to career choice is that it is *economical*—it provides a tidy summary of many aspects of people and of careers. Consider how knotty a career decision could get if you were to break down the components of the work environment into highly specific aspects and reflect on how well you fit them. For example, you could focus on the skills required and your ability to meet them. Next you could analyze the kinds of knowledge that are used on the job and decide how much you enjoy working with those topics. Then you could consider a broad array of satisfactions, such as variety, creativity, and independence; for each one, you would evaluate its importance to you and then determine the potential of various career options to satisfy this need. You can see that, when looked at under a microscope like this, career choice gets extremely complex.

But the personality-based approach allows you to view the career alternatives from 40,000 feet. When you compare yourself or a job to certain basic personality types, you encounter much less complexity. With fewer ideas and facts to sort through and consider, the task of deciding becomes much easier.

Describing Personality Types

You probably have heard many labels that describe people's personalities: "He's a perfectionist." "She's a control freak." "He's a go-getter." "She's very self-confident." "He's pushy." "She's wishy-washy." "He has a short fuse." "She's a drama queen." The list could go on and on.

These everyday terms for personality types have some bearing on work, but they are not very useful for several reasons: They don't differentiate well between jobs (for example, self-confidence is useful in just about every job); some of them are too specific (for example, "control freak" focuses on one small aspect of how a person functions at work); and, worst of all, most of them are too negative for people to want to apply to themselves.

Now that it's clear what kinds of personality labels you *wouldn't* want to use, consider the characteristics of a useful set of personality types:

- They should differentiate well between kinds of work.
- They should differentiate well between people.
- They should be broad enough that a small number of these categories can cover the whole universe of jobs and people.
- They should have neutral connotations, neither negative nor positive.

The RIASEC Personality Types

During the 1950s, the career guidance researcher John L. Holland tried to find a meaningful new way to arrange the output of an interest inventory and relate it to occupations. He devised a set of six personality types that would meet the criteria listed in the previous section, and he called them Realistic, Investigative, Artistic, Social, Enterprising, and Conventional. (The acronym *RIASEC* is a convenient way to remember them.)

The following table shows how these labels apply to both people and work:

Personality Type	How It Applies to People	How It Applies to Work
Realistic	Realistic personalities like work activities that include practical, hands-on problems and solutions. They enjoy dealing with plants, animals, and real-world materials like wood, tools, and machinery. They enjoy outside work. Often they do not like occupations that mainly involve doing paperwork or working closely with others.	Realistic occupations frequently involve work activities that include practical, hands-on problems and solutions. They often deal with plants, animals, and real-world materials like wood, tools, and machinery. Many of the occupations require working outside and do not involve a lot of paperwork or working closely with others.
Investigative	Investigative personalities like work activities that have to do with ideas and thinking more than with physical activity. They like to search for facts and figure out problems mentally rather than to persuade or lead people.	Investigative occupations frequently involve working with ideas and require an extensive amount of thinking. These occupations can involve searching for facts and figuring out problems mentally.
Artistic	Artistic personalities like work activities that deal with the artistic side of things, such as forms, designs, and patterns. They like self-expression in their work. They prefer settings where work can be done without following a clear set of rules.	Artistic occupations frequently involve working with forms, designs, and patterns. They often require self-expression, and the work can be done without following a clear set of rules.
Social	Social personalities like work activities that assist others and promote learning and personal development. They prefer to communicate more than to work with objects, machines, or data. They like to teach, to give advice, to help, or otherwise to be of service to people.	Social occupations frequently involve working with, communicating with, and teaching people. These occupations often involve helping or providing service to others.
Enterprising	Enterprising personalities like work activities having to do with starting up and carrying out projects, especially business ventures. They like persuading and leading people and making decisions. They like taking risks for profit. These personalities prefer action rather than thought.	Enterprising occupations frequently involve starting up and carrying out projects. These occupations can involve leading people and making many decisions. They sometimes require risk taking and often deal with business.

Conventional	Conventional personalities like work activities that follow set procedures and routines. They prefer working with data and details rather than with ideas. They prefer work in which there are precise standards rather than work in which you have to judge things by yourself. These personalities like working where the lines of authority are clear.	Conventional occupations frequently involve following set procedures and routines. These occupations can include working with data and details more than with ideas. Usually there is a clear line of authority to follow.

Holland went further by arranging these six personality types on a hexagon:

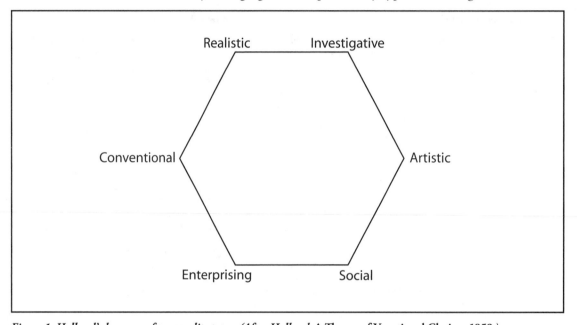

Figure 1: Holland's hexagon of personality types. (After Holland, A Theory of Vocational Choice, 1959.)

He used this diagram to explain that people tend to resemble one type primarily, but they may also have aspects of one or more adjacent types. Each personality type tends to have aspects of the types on the adjacent sides of the hexagon, but little in common with the type on the opposite side. Therefore, for example, a person might be primarily Realistic, with an additional but smaller resemblance to the Conventional type. Such a person would be described by the two-letter code RC and might be well suited to work as a Boilermaker or a Roofer (both coded RC). This person would have little in common with a Social personality type and likely would not be very happy or productive as a Special Education Teacher (coded SA). But this person could get along well with both Realistic and Conventional personalities and, to a lesser extent, with Investigative personalities.

The existence of secondary personality types helps explain how a workplace may have lots of people with the same dominant personality type, yet they don't all think alike. That's helpful, because too much similarity of personalities would lead to "groupthink," a situation where nobody has original or divergent ideas. Successful workplaces have a dominant culture but also value diversity.

Although Holland originally applied his hexagonal model to academic advising, he soon extended it to the larger question of career choice. Since then, hundreds of researchers and practitioners have investigated the RIASEC framework and have applied it to real-life decisions and situations. Researchers have even found it useful for predicting who will have the most traffic accidents or what kinds of drug abuse people are likely to engage in. More relevant to the theme of this book, however, is the fact that a number of career decision-making assessments have been developed to help people determine what personality type best describes them (and perhaps an additional adjacent type or types that are also important). You can find one such assessment in Part II of this book.

Although the RIASEC scheme does a good job of covering the whole world of work, the symmetrical hexagon shape used to illustrate it may be a little misleading because when you count the different jobs in our economy and the number of people working in those jobs, you'll find that some sectors of the hexagon are much more heavily populated than others. Here is a breakdown of the 732 occupations in the Department of Labor's SOC classification scheme for which I could find both RIASEC codes and figures for workforce size:

Personality Type	Number of Occupations	Number of Workers 2008
Realistic	319	43,804,320
Investigative	86	7,580,000
Artistic	32	2,641,090
Social	106	24,049,950
Enterprising	91	27,462,910
Conventional	98	36,233,060

As the United States shifts from a manufacturing economy to an information economy, employment in the Realistic sector is declining and employment in the Investigative sector is growing, but a large imbalance is likely to continue for the foreseeable future.

The six sectors are asymmetrical in other ways, too. As you'll see when you look at the lists in Part III, Social jobs employ a lot more women than Realistic jobs do. Enterprising jobs employ a lot more men than Conventional jobs do. Likewise, there are differences when you consider where large numbers of young people and older people work.

The differences get really significant when you look at the amounts of education or training required by jobs linked to the various personality types. For example, the most common entry route for Realistic and Conventional jobs is on-the-job training, whereas a college degree is usually needed for Investigative jobs. John Holland and other researchers have explained that these differences reflect the different levels of cognitive complexity to be found in the jobs. Realistic jobs deal mainly with manipulating things physically—moving them, cleaning them, repairing them, and so forth. Conventional jobs deal mainly with data at the level of organizing it according to pre-determined patterns—filing it, keying it in, and so forth. Investigative jobs, on the other hand, deal mainly with ideas and solving problems mentally, so the level of cognitive complexity is high and a college education becomes a necessity.

You should not be troubled by this lack of symmetry in the RIASEC model (even if you are an Artistic type). It does not indicate a weakness in the theory. But it does create some problems for a book like this. Although I have attempted to give equal coverage to each of the six personality types, you will notice that some of the sets of lists in Part III are not of equal size. Also, since I identified the "50 Best Artistic Jobs" out of a pool of only 75 jobs (some of which have Artistic as a *secondary* personality type), when you scan that list you may want to concentrate on the higher-ranked choices. On the other hand, to create the list of the "50 Best Realistic Jobs," I started with a pool of 339 jobs, so all the best 50 represent the upper crust of that large group. These differences simply reflect the nature of the United States workforce.

No theory can perfectly describe the infinite variety of personalities to be found in our culture and the messy distribution of jobs that a free economy produces. You should be aware that Holland's RIASEC scheme for describing personality types is not the only one that is used in career decision-making. However, it is the most popular and most thoroughly researched one, so it is the most appropriate one to use in this book.

Other Assessments with RIASEC Output

Apart from the assessment in Part II of this book, you may want to use any of these free assessments to explore your personality type in RIASEC terms:

❋ **The O*NET Computerized Interest Profiler** (the assessment in Part II is based on it). You can take it as an interactive assessment at www.mynextmove.org/explore/ip. If your browser supports Flash animation, go to www.careerzone.org/flash/assessments.html and click "Interest Profiler."

❋ **The University of Missouri's Career Center Career Interests Game** at http://career.missouri.edu/students/majors-careers/skills-interests/career-interest-game.

You also have a number of options if you are willing to pay a fee. For example, you can access John Holland's own *Self-Directed Search* at www.self-directed-search.com.

Keep in mind that, although all of these assessments produce outputs with RIASEC codes and some of them also link these codes to occupations, they will not necessarily produce the exact same output. Assessment of personality is not as exact a science as, say, chemistry. Neither is the task of linking personality types to occupations.

You should not regard the output of *any* personality assessment as the final word on what career will suit you best. Use a variety of approaches to decide what kind of person you are and narrow down the kinds of work you enjoy. Actual work experience is probably the best way to test a tentative choice.

Part II

What's Your Personality Type? Take an Assessment

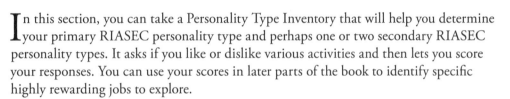

In this section, you can take a Personality Type Inventory that will help you determine your primary RIASEC personality type and perhaps one or two secondary RIASEC personality types. It asks if you like or dislike various activities and then lets you score your responses. You can use your scores in later parts of the book to identify specific highly rewarding jobs to explore.

It's easy to use the Personality Type Inventory—just turn the page and follow the directions beginning with Step 1. This is not a test, so there are no right or wrong answers. There is also no time limit for completing this inventory.

If someone else will be using this book, you should photocopy the inventory pages and mark your responses on the photocopy.

Note: This inventory is based on the O*NET Interest Profiler, Version 3.0, developed by the U.S. Department of Labor (DOL). A few items in the inventory have been updated to reflect changes in technology or terminology. The DOL's edition consists of several components, including the Interest Profiler Instrument, Interest Profiler Score Report, and Interest Profiler O*NET Occupations Master List. The DOL provides a separate Interest Profiler User's Guide with information on the Profiler's development and validity as well as tips for professionals using it in career counseling. Additional information on these items is available at www.onetcenter.org, which is maintained by the DOL. This Personality Type Inventory is a version of the DOL's O*NET Interest Profiler that uses its work activity items and scoring system but has shorter directions, format changes, and additional content.

Restrictions for use: This and any other form of the O*NET Interest Profiler should be used for career exploration, career planning, and vocational counseling purposes only, and no other use has been authorized or is valid. Results should not be used for employment or hiring decisions or for applicant screening for jobs or training programs. Please see the DOL's separate "O*NET User Agreement" at www.onetcenter.org/agree/ tools for additional details on restrictions and use. The word "O*NET" is a trademark of the U.S. Department of Labor, Employment and Training Administration.

JIST Publishing offers a color foldout version of this assessment. It is called the *O*NET Career Interests Inventory* and is sold in packages of 25.

Step 1: Respond to the Statements

Carefully read each work activity (items 1 through 180). For each item, fill in just one of the three circles as follows:

If you think you would LIKE the activity, fill in the circle containing the L, like this:

If you think you would DISLIKE the activity, fill in the circle containing the D, like this:

If you are UNSURE whether you would like the activity, fill in the circle with the ?, like this:

As you respond to each activity, don't consider whether you have the education or training needed for it or how much money you might earn if it were part of your job. Simply fill in the circle based on whether you would like, would dislike, or aren't sure about the activity.

After you respond to all 180 activities, you'll score your responses in Step 2.

Would you LIKE the activity or DISLIKE the activity, or are you UNSURE?

1. Build kitchen cabinets   (L)   (?)   (D)
2. Guard money in an armored car   (L)   (?)   (D)
3. Operate a dairy farm   (L)   (?)   (D)
4. Lay brick or tile   (L)   (?)   (D)
5. Monitor a machine on an assembly line   (L)   (?)   (D)
6. Repair household appliances   (L)   (?)   (D)
7. Drive a taxicab   (L)   (?)   (D)
8. Install flooring in houses   (L)   (?)   (D)
9. Raise fish in a fish hatchery   (L)   (?)   (D)
10. Build a brick walkway   (L)   (?)   (D)
11. Assemble electronic parts   (L)   (?)   (D)
12. Drive a truck to deliver packages to offices and homes   (L)   (?)   (D)
13. Paint houses   (L)   (?)   (D)
14. Enforce fish and game laws   (L)   (?)   (D)
15. Operate a grinding machine in a factory   (L)   (?)   (D)
16. Work on an offshore oil-drilling rig   (L)   (?)   (D)
17. Perform lawn care services   (L)   (?)   (D)
18. Assemble products in a factory   (L)   (?)   (D)
19. Catch fish as a member of a fishing crew   (L)   (?)   (D)
20. Refinish furniture   (L)   (?)   (D)
21. Fix a broken faucet   (L)   (?)   (D)
22. Do cleaning or maintenance work   (L)   (?)   (D)
23. Maintain the grounds of a park   (L)   (?)   (D)
24. Install an array of solar panels   (L)   (?)   (D)
25. Spray trees to prevent the spread of harmful insects   (L)   (?)   (D)
26. Test the quality of parts before shipment   (L)   (?)   (D)
27. Operate a motorboat to carry passengers   (L)   (?)   (D)
28. Repair and install locks   (L)   (?)   (D)
29. Set up and operate machines to make products   (L)   (?)   (D)
30. Put out forest fires   (L)   (?)   (D)

____ **Page Score for R**

Would you LIKE the activity or DISLIKE the activity, or are you UNSURE?

		L	?	D
31.	Study space travel	L	?	D
32.	Make a map of the bottom of an ocean	L	?	D
33.	Study the history of past civilizations	L	?	D
34.	Study animal behavior	L	?	D
35.	Develop a new medicine	L	?	D
36.	Plan a research study	L	?	D
37.	Study ways to reduce water pollution	L	?	D
38.	Develop a new medical treatment or procedure	L	?	D
39.	Determine the infection rate of a new disease	L	?	D
40.	Study rocks and minerals	L	?	D
41.	Diagnose and treat sick animals	L	?	D
42.	Study the personalities of world leaders	L	?	D
43.	Conduct chemical experiments	L	?	D
44.	Conduct biological research	L	?	D
45.	Study the population growth of a city	L	?	D
46.	Study whales and other types of marine life	L	?	D
47.	Investigate crimes	L	?	D
48.	Study the movement of planets	L	?	D
49.	Examine blood samples using a microscope	L	?	D
50.	Investigate the cause of a fire	L	?	D
51.	Study the structure of the human body	L	?	D
52.	Develop psychological profiles of criminals	L	?	D
53.	Develop a new way to better predict the weather	L	?	D
54.	Work in a biology lab	L	?	D
55.	Invent a replacement for sugar	L	?	D
56.	Study genetics	L	?	D
57.	Study the governments of different countries	L	?	D
58.	Do research on plants or animals	L	?	D
59.	Do laboratory tests to identify diseases	L	?	D
60.	Study weather conditions	L	?	D

____ **Page Score for I**

Would you LIKE the activity or DISLIKE the activity, or are you UNSURE?

		L	?	D
61.	Conduct a symphony orchestra	L	?	D
62.	Write stories or articles for magazines	L	?	D
63.	Direct a play	L	?	D
64.	Create dance routines for a show	L	?	D
65.	Write books or plays	L	?	D
66.	Play a musical instrument	L	?	D
67.	Perform comedy routines in front of an audience	L	?	D
68.	Perform as an extra in movies, plays, or television shows	L	?	D
69.	Write reviews of books or plays	L	?	D
70.	Compose or arrange music	L	?	D
71.	Act in a movie	L	?	D
72.	Dance in a Broadway show	L	?	D
73.	Draw pictures	L	?	D
74.	Sing professionally	L	?	D
75.	Perform stunts for a movie or television show	L	?	D
76.	Create special effects for movies	L	?	D
77.	Conduct a musical choir	L	?	D
78.	Act in a play	L	?	D
79.	Paint sets for plays	L	?	D
80.	Audition singers and musicians for a musical show	L	?	D
81.	Design sets for plays	L	?	D
82.	Announce a radio show	L	?	D
83.	Write scripts for movies or television shows	L	?	D
84.	Write a song	L	?	D
85.	Perform jazz or tap dance	L	?	D
86.	Direct a movie	L	?	D
87.	Sing in a band	L	?	D
88.	Design artwork for magazines	L	?	D
89.	Edit movies	L	?	D
90.	Pose for a photographer	L	?	D

____ **Page Score for A**

Would you LIKE the activity or DISLIKE the activity, or are you UNSURE?

91. Teach an individual an exercise routine	Ⓛ	⍰	Ⓓ
92. Perform nursing duties in a hospital	Ⓛ	⍰	Ⓓ
93. Give CPR to someone who has stopped breathing	Ⓛ	⍰	Ⓓ
94. Help people with personal or emotional problems	Ⓛ	⍰	Ⓓ
95. Teach children how to read	Ⓛ	⍰	Ⓓ
96. Work with children with developmental disabilities	Ⓛ	⍰	Ⓓ
97. Teach an elementary school class	Ⓛ	⍰	Ⓓ
98. Give career guidance to people	Ⓛ	⍰	Ⓓ
99. Supervise the activities of children at a camp	Ⓛ	⍰	Ⓓ
100. Help people with family-related problems	Ⓛ	⍰	Ⓓ
101. Perform rehabilitation therapy	Ⓛ	⍰	Ⓓ
102. Do volunteer work at a nonprofit organization	Ⓛ	⍰	Ⓓ
103. Help elderly people with their daily activities	Ⓛ	⍰	Ⓓ
104. Teach children how to play sports	Ⓛ	⍰	Ⓓ
105. Help disabled people improve their daily living skills	Ⓛ	⍰	Ⓓ
106. Teach sign language to people with hearing disabilities	Ⓛ	⍰	Ⓓ
107. Help people who have problems with drugs or alcohol	Ⓛ	⍰	Ⓓ
108. Help conduct a group therapy session	Ⓛ	⍰	Ⓓ
109. Help families care for ill relatives	Ⓛ	⍰	Ⓓ
110. Provide massage therapy to people	Ⓛ	⍰	Ⓓ
111. Plan exercises for disabled students	Ⓛ	⍰	Ⓓ
112. Counsel people who have a life-threatening illness	Ⓛ	⍰	Ⓓ
113. Teach disabled people work and living skills	Ⓛ	⍰	Ⓓ
114. Organize activities at a recreational facility	Ⓛ	⍰	Ⓓ
115. Take care of children at a day-care center	Ⓛ	⍰	Ⓓ
116. Organize field trips for disabled people	Ⓛ	⍰	Ⓓ
117. Assist doctors in treating patients	Ⓛ	⍰	Ⓓ
118. Work with juveniles on probation	Ⓛ	⍰	Ⓓ
119. Provide physical therapy to people recovering from an injury	Ⓛ	⍰	Ⓓ
120. Teach a high school class	Ⓛ	⍰	Ⓓ

_____ **Page Score for S**

Would you LIKE the activity or DISLIKE the activity, or are you UNSURE?

121.	Buy and sell stocks and bonds	(L)	(?)	(D)
122.	Manage a retail store	(L)	(?)	(D)
123.	Sell cell phones and other communication equipment	(L)	(?)	(D)
124.	Operate a beauty salon or barbershop	(L)	(?)	(D)
125.	Sell merchandise over the telephone	(L)	(?)	(D)
126.	Run a stand that sells newspapers and magazines	(L)	(?)	(D)
127.	Give a presentation about a product you are selling	(L)	(?)	(D)
128.	Buy and sell land	(L)	(?)	(D)
129.	Sell furniture at a home furnishings store	(L)	(?)	(D)
130.	Run a toy store	(L)	(?)	(D)
131.	Manage the operations of a hotel	(L)	(?)	(D)
132.	Sell houses	(L)	(?)	(D)
133.	Sell candy and popcorn at sports events	(L)	(?)	(D)
134.	Manage a supermarket	(L)	(?)	(D)
135.	Manage a department within a large company	(L)	(?)	(D)
136.	Sell a soft drink product line to stores and restaurants	(L)	(?)	(D)
137.	Sell refreshments at a movie theater	(L)	(?)	(D)
138.	Sell hair-care products to stores and salons	(L)	(?)	(D)
139.	Start your own business	(L)	(?)	(D)
140.	Negotiate business contracts	(L)	(?)	(D)
141.	Represent a client in a lawsuit	(L)	(?)	(D)
142.	Negotiate contracts for professional athletes	(L)	(?)	(D)
143.	Be responsible for the operation of a company	(L)	(?)	(D)
144.	Market a new line of clothing	(L)	(?)	(D)
145.	Sell newspaper advertisements	(L)	(?)	(D)
146.	Sell merchandise at a department store	(L)	(?)	(D)
147.	Sell automobiles	(L)	(?)	(D)
148.	Manage a clothing store	(L)	(?)	(D)
149.	Sell restaurant franchises to individuals	(L)	(?)	(D)
150.	Sell computer equipment in a store	(L)	(?)	(D)

___ **Page Score for E**

Would you LIKE the activity or DISLIKE the activity, or are you UNSURE?

		L	?	D
151.	Develop a spreadsheet using computer software	L	?	D
152.	Proofread records or forms	L	?	D
153.	Use a computer program to generate customer bills	L	?	D
154.	Schedule conferences for an organization	L	?	D
155.	Keep accounts payable/receivable for an office	L	?	D
156.	Load computer software into a large computer network	L	?	D
157.	Transfer funds between banks using a computer	L	?	D
158.	Organize and schedule office meetings	L	?	D
159.	Use a word processor to edit and format documents	L	?	D
160.	Operate a calculator	L	?	D
161.	Direct or transfer phone calls for a large organization	L	?	D
162.	Perform office filing tasks	L	?	D
163.	Compute and record statistical and other numerical data	L	?	D
164.	Generate the monthly payroll checks for an office	L	?	D
165.	Take notes during a meeting	L	?	D
166.	Keep shipping and receiving records	L	?	D
167.	Calculate the wages of employees	L	?	D
168.	Assist senior-level accountants in performing bookkeeping tasks	L	?	D
169.	Take information from visitors at a building's front desk	L	?	D
170.	Inventory supplies using a hand-held computer	L	?	D
171.	Develop an office filing system	L	?	D
172.	Keep records of financial transactions for an organization	L	?	D
173.	Record information from customers applying for charge accounts	L	?	D
174.	Photocopy letters and reports	L	?	D
175.	Record rent payments	L	?	D
176.	Enter information into a database	L	?	D
177.	Keep inventory records	L	?	D
178.	Maintain employee records	L	?	D
179.	Stamp, sort, and distribute mail for an organization	L	?	D
180.	Handle customers' bank transactions	L	?	D

____ **Page Score for C**

Step 2: Score Your Responses

Do the following to score your responses:

1. **Score the responses on each page.** On each page of responses, go from top to bottom and add the number of "L's you filled in. Then write that number in the "Page Score" box at the bottom of the page. Go on to the next page and do the same there.

2. **Determine your primary interest area.** Which Page Score has your highest score: R, I, A, S, E, or C? Enter the letter for that personality type on the following line.

My Primary Personality Type: ___

You will use your Primary Personality Type *first* to explore careers. (If two Page Scores are tied for the highest scores or are within 5 points of each other, use both of them for your Primary Personality Type. You are equally divided between two types.)

❋ R = Realistic

❋ I = Investigative

❋ A = Artistic

❋ S = Social

❋ E = Enterprising

❋ C = Conventional

3. **Determine your secondary interest areas.** Which Page Score has your next highest score? Which has your third highest score? Enter the letters for those areas on the following lines.

My Secondary Personality Types: ___ ___

(If you do not find many occupations that you like using your Primary Personality Type, you can use your Secondary Personality Types to look at more career options.)

Step 3: Find Jobs That Suit Your Personality Type

Start with your Primary Personality Type. Turn to Part III and look at the Best Jobs lists for your type. Find lists that suit your particular priorities and see what job titles appear there. Don't rule out a job just because the title is not familiar to you.

When you find job titles that interest you or that you want to learn more about, turn to Part IV. The job descriptions there are grouped by Primary Personality Type and are listed alphabetically within each type. Of course, you can also look at jobs that are linked to one of your Secondary Personality Types.

If you want to find jobs that *combine* your Primary Personality Type and a Secondary Personality Type, turn to Appendix A. All 442 O*NET jobs described in Part IV of this book are listed there by their one-, two-, or three-letter personality codes. For example, if your Primary Personality Type is Social and your Secondary Personality Type is Enterprising, you would look in Appendix A for the letter S and then for jobs coded SE, such as Personal Financial Advisors and Training and Development Specialists.

You may discover that you can't find an appealing job in your Primary Personality Type that *also* is coded for one of your Secondary Personality Types. That is not necessarily a problem. John Holland himself has remarked, "You cannot expect a single job to satisfy all aspects of your personality." This is why we have hobbies. Use recreational time for activities related to your Secondary Personality Types. Volunteer work can be another outlet for these interests and abilities.

Part III

The Best Jobs Lists: Jobs for Each of the Six Personality Types

This part contains a lot of interesting lists, and it's a good place for you to start using the book. Here are some suggestions for using the lists to explore career options:

❋ The table of contents at the beginning of this book presents a complete listing of the list titles in this section. You can browse the lists or use the table of contents to find those that interest you most.

❋ I gave the lists clear titles, so most require little explanation. I provide comments for each group of lists.

❋ As you review the lists of jobs, one or more of the jobs may appeal to you enough that you want to seek additional information. As this happens, mark that job (or, if someone else will be using this book, write it on a separate sheet of paper) so that you can look up the description of the job in Part IV.

❋ Keep in mind that all jobs in these lists meet my basic criteria for being included in this book, as explained in the introduction. All lists, therefore, emphasize jobs that have high pay, high growth, and/or large numbers of openings. These measures are easily quantified and are often presented in lists of best jobs in the newspapers and other media. Although earnings, growth, and openings are important, you also should consider other factors in your career planning. The job's suitability for your personality type is obviously an important concern, but you may also want to consider matters such as location, physical demands, and amount of opportunity to be creative. Many other factors that may help define the ideal job for you are difficult or impossible to quantify and thus aren't used in this book, so you will need to consider the importance of these issues yourself. The resources listed in Appendix C may help you research these issues.

✵ All data used to create these lists comes from the U.S. Department of Labor and the Census Bureau. The earnings figures are based on the average annual pay received by full-time workers. Because the earnings represent the national averages, actual pay rates can vary greatly by location, amount of previous work experience, and other factors. Even lists that focus on a particular type of worker (for example, rural workers) use earnings figures based on the national averages.

Some Details on the Lists

The sources of the information I used in constructing these lists are presented in this book's introduction. Here are some additional details on how I created the lists:

✵ A few jobs may appear on lists that surprise you. For example, what is Registered Nurses doing on the lists of Enterprising jobs? The reason is that Clinical Nurse Specialists manage patient care and thus serve a businesslike role. Many other job specializations involve work activities that you may be unaware of.

✵ Some jobs have the same scores for one or more data elements. For example, in the category of fastest-growing Realistic jobs, two jobs (Commercial Pilots and Firefighters) are expected to grow at the same rate, 18.5 percent. Therefore I ordered these two jobs alphabetically, and their order in relation to each other has no other significance. Avoiding these ties was impossible, so understand that the difference of several positions on a list may not mean as much as it seems.

✵ Likewise, it is unwise to place too much emphasis on small differences in outlook information: projections for job growth and job openings. For example, Photographers are projected to have 4,800 job openings per year, whereas 4,680 openings are projected for Architects, Except Landscape and Naval. This is a difference of only 120 jobs spread over the entire United States, and of course, it is only a projection. Before 2007, the Bureau of Labor Statistics rounded these projections to the nearest 1,000 and would have assigned these two occupations the same figure (5,000), which would have given Architects the higher rank on the basis of alphabetical ordering. So, again, keep in mind that small differences of position on a list aren't very significant.

Best Jobs Overall for Each Personality Type: Jobs with the Highest Pay, Fastest Growth, and Most Openings

The four sets of lists that follow are the most important lists in this book. The first set of lists presents, for each personality type, the jobs with the highest combined scores for pay, growth, and number of openings. These are very appealing lists because they represent jobs with the highest quantifiable measures from our labor market. The 264 jobs in these six lists are the ones that are described in detail in Part IV.

The three additional sets of lists present, for each personality type, jobs with the highest scores in each of three economic measures: annual earnings, projected percentage growth, and largest number of openings.

The 50 Best Jobs for Each Personality Type

These are the lists that most people want to see first. For each personality type, you can see the jobs that have the highest overall combined ratings for earnings, projected growth, and number of openings. (The "How the Jobs in This Book Were Selected" section in the Introduction explains in detail how I rated jobs to assemble this list.)

Although each list covers one personality type, you'll notice a wide variety of jobs on the list. For example, among the top 50 Investigative jobs are some in the fields of high technology, medicine, education, and business. Among the top 50 Conventional jobs are some in the financial, legal, technology, and health-care industries. The lists include each job's personality code, which indicates its primary and secondary (if any) personality types.

This personality code may help you understand why some jobs appear on the list of Artistic jobs even though they may not seem very artsy to you. As I noted in the introduction, because of the small number of jobs with Artistic as their primary personality type, I had to include in the Artistic list several occupations with that as their secondary type. Biochemists and Biophysicists (IAR), Self-Enrichment Education Teachers (SAE), and Sociologists (IAS) are some examples. Workers in many of these jobs do college teaching or other work that requires creativity; some do research that requires them to search for patterns or write up their findings in articles.

A look at one list will clarify how I ordered the jobs—take the Realistic list as an example. Civil Engineers is on the top of the list because it was the occupation with the best total score. The second-place job, Surveyors, has somewhat better projected job growth, but it has fewer projected job openings and considerably lower earnings, so its total score was lower than that for Civil Engineers. The other occupations follow in descending order based on their total scores. Many jobs had tied scores and were simply listed one after another, so there are often only very small or even no differences between the scores of jobs that are near each other on the list. All other job lists in this book use these lists as their source. You can find descriptions for each of these jobs in Part IV, beginning on page 147.

The 50 Best Realistic Jobs

Job	Personality Code	Annual Earnings	Percent Growth	Annual Openings
1. Civil Engineers	RIC	$77,560	24.3%	11,460
2. Physician Assistants	SIR	$86,410	39.0%	4,280
3. Business Operations Specialists, All Other	CER	$62,450	11.5%	36,830
4. Radiologic Technologists	RS	$54,340	17.2%	6,800
5. Heating, Air Conditioning, and Refrigeration Mechanics and Installers	RC	$42,530	28.1%	13,620
6. Firefighters	RS	$45,250	18.5%	15,280
7. Plumbers, Pipefitters, and Steamfitters	RC	$46,660	15.3%	17,550
8. Computer User Support Specialists	RIC	$46,260	13.8%	23,460
9. Electricians	RIC	$48,250	11.9%	25,090
10. Commercial Pilots	RIE	$67,500	18.5%	2,060
11. Construction and Building Inspectors	RCI	$52,360	16.8%	3,970
12. Medical and Clinical Laboratory Technologists	IRC	$56,130	11.9%	5,330
13. Police and Sheriff's Patrol Officers	ERS	$53,540	8.7%	22,790
14. Captains, Mates, and Pilots of Water Vessels	REC	$64,180	17.3%	1,950
15. Surgical Technologists	RSC	$39,920	25.3%	4,630
16. Water and Wastewater Treatment Plant and System Operators	RC	$40,770	19.8%	4,690
17. Carpenters	RCI	$39,530	12.9%	32,540
18. Cardiovascular Technologists and Technicians	RIS	$49,410	24.0%	1,910
19. Surveyors	RCI	$54,880	14.9%	2,330
20. Civil Engineering Technicians	RCI	$46,290	16.9%	3,280
21. Brickmasons and Blockmasons	RCI	$46,930	11.5%	5,000
22. Heavy and Tractor-Trailer Truck Drivers	RC	$37,770	12.9%	55,460
23. Medical Equipment Repairers	RIC	$44,490	27.2%	2,320
24. Engineers, All Other	IR	$90,270	6.7%	5,020
25. Operating Engineers and Other Construction Equipment Operators	RCI	$40,400	12.0%	11,820
26. Biological Technicians	RIC	$39,020	17.6%	4,190
27. Transportation Inspectors	RCI	$57,640	18.3%	1,130
28. Airline Pilots, Copilots, and Flight Engineers	RCI	$103,210	8.4%	3,250
29. Health Technologists and Technicians, All Other	RIC	$38,460	18.7%	3,200
30. Security and Fire Alarm Systems Installers	RC	$38,500	24.8%	2,780
31. Life, Physical, and Social Science Technicians, All Other	RC	$43,350	13.3%	3,640
32. Medical and Clinical Laboratory Technicians	RIC	$36,280	16.1%	5,460
33. Surveying and Mapping Technicians	CR	$37,900	20.4%	2,940
34. Correctional Officers and Jailers	REC	$39,040	9.4%	14,360

The 50 Best Realistic Jobs

Job	Personality Code	Annual Earnings	Percent Growth	Annual Openings
35. Ship Engineers	RCE	$65,880	18.6%	700
36. Refuse and Recyclable Material Collectors	RC	$32,640	18.6%	7,110
37. Boilermakers	RC	$54,640	18.8%	810
38. Architectural and Civil Drafters	RCA	$46,430	9.1%	3,620
39. Construction Laborers	RC	$29,280	20.5%	33,940
40. Cement Masons and Concrete Finishers	RE	$35,450	12.9%	7,640
41. Electrical Power-Line Installers and Repairers	RIC	$58,030	4.5%	4,550
42. Cartographers and Photogrammetrists	RCI	$54,510	26.8%	640
43. Environmental Engineering Technicians	RIC	$43,390	30.1%	1,040
44. Mobile Heavy Equipment Mechanics, Except Engines	RC	$44,830	8.6%	3,770
45. Drywall and Ceiling Tile Installers	RC	$37,320	13.5%	3,700
46. Industrial Machinery Mechanics	RIC	$45,420	7.3%	6,240
47. Maintenance and Repair Workers, General	RCI	$34,730	10.9%	35,750
48. Audio and Video Equipment Technicians	RIC	$40,540	12.6%	2,370
49. Tile and Marble Setters	RCA	$38,110	14.3%	3,070
50. Physical Scientists, All Other	RI	$94,780	11.1%	1,010

The 50 Best Investigative Jobs

Job	Personality Code	Annual Earnings	Percent Growth	Annual Openings
1. Physicians and Surgeons	ISR	$165,279	21.8%	26,050
2. Software Developers, Systems Software	ICR	$94,180	30.4%	15,340
3. Software Developers, Applications	IRC	$87,790	34.0%	21,840
4. Computer Network Architects	ICR	$75,660	53.4%	20,830
5. Pharmacists	ICS	$111,570	17.0%	10,580
6. Management Analysts	IEC	$78,160	23.9%	30,650
7. Medical Scientists, Except Epidemiologists	IRA	$76,700	40.3%	6,620
8. Veterinarians	IR	$82,040	33.0%	3,020
9. Dentists, General	IRS	$141,040	15.3%	5,180
10. Optometrists	ISR	$94,990	24.4%	2,010
11. Computer Systems Analysts	ICR	$77,740	20.3%	22,280
12. Environmental Engineers	IRC	$78,740	30.6%	2,790
13. Computer and Information Research Scientists	IRC	$100,660	24.2%	1,320

(continued)

(continued)

The 50 Best Investigative Jobs

Job	Personality Code	Annual Earnings	Percent Growth	Annual Openings
14. Biomedical Engineers	IR	$81,540	72.0%	1,490
15. Biochemists and Biophysicists	IAR	$79,390	37.4%	1,620
16. Network and Computer Systems Administrators	IRC	$69,160	23.2%	13,550
17. Compliance Officers	CEI	$58,720	31.0%	10,850
18. Market Research Analysts and Marketing Specialists	IEC	$60,570	28.1%	13,730
19. Petroleum Engineers	IRC	$114,080	18.4%	860
20. Environmental Scientists and Specialists, Including Health	IRC	$61,700	27.9%	4,840
21. Operations Research Analysts	ICE	$70,960	22.0%	3,220
22. Orthodontists	IRS	$166,500+	19.8%	360
23. Social Scientists and Related Workers, All Other	ICR	$74,620	22.4%	2,380
24. Computer Occupations, All Other	ICR	$79,240	13.1%	7,260
25. Logisticians	CEI	$70,800	19.5%	4,190
26. Industrial Engineers	ICE	$76,100	14.2%	8,540
27. Prosthodontists	IR	$118,400	27.7%	30
28. Geoscientists, Except Hydrologists and Geographers	IR	$82,500	17.5%	1,540
29. Physicists	IR	$106,370	15.9%	690
30. Political Scientists	IAS	$107,420	19.5%	280
31. Engineers, All Other	IR	$90,270	6.7%	5,020
32. Engineering Teachers, Postsecondary	SIR	$89,670	15.1%	1,000
33. Mathematicians	ICA	$99,380	22.5%	150
34. Aerospace Engineers	IR	$97,480	10.4%	2,230
35. Industrial-Organizational Psychologists	IEA	$87,330	26.3%	130
36. Environmental Science and Protection Technicians, Including Health	IRC	$41,380	28.9%	2,520
37. Computer Hardware Engineers	IRC	$98,810	3.8%	2,350
38. Electronics Engineers, Except Computer	IR	$90,170	0.3%	3,340
39. Mechanical Engineers	IRC	$78,160	6.0%	7,570
40. Biological Scientists, All Other	IRA	$68,220	18.8%	1,610
41. Psychologists, All Other	ISA	$89,900	14.4%	680
42. Electrical Engineers	IR	$84,540	1.7%	3,890
43. Diagnostic Medical Sonographers	ISR	$64,380	18.3%	1,650
44. Clinical, Counseling, and School Psychologists	ISA	$66,810	11.1%	5,990
45. Nuclear Engineers	IRC	$99,920	10.9%	540
46. Audiologists	IS	$66,660	25.0%	580

The 50 Best Investigative Jobs

Job	Personality Code	Annual Earnings	Percent Growth	Annual Openings
47. Atmospheric and Space Scientists	IR	$87,780	14.7%	330
48. Survey Researchers	ICE	$36,050	30.4%	1,340
49. Urban and Regional Planners	IEA	$63,040	19.0%	1,470
50. Geographers	IRA	$72,800	26.2%	100

The 50 Best Artistic Jobs

Job	Personality Code	Annual Earnings	Percent Growth	Annual Openings
1. Public Relations Specialists	EAS	$52,090	24.0%	13,130
2. Training and Development Specialists	SAC	$54,160	23.3%	10,710
3. Architects, Except Landscape and Naval	AI	$72,550	16.2%	4,680
4. Biochemists and Biophysicists	IAR	$79,390	37.4%	1,620
5. Elementary School Teachers, Except Special Education	SAC	$51,660	15.8%	59,650
6. Middle School Teachers, Except Special and Career/Technical Education	SA	$51,960	15.3%	25,110
7. Special Education Teachers, Middle School	SA	$53,440	18.1%	4,410
8. Writers and Authors	AEI	$55,420	14.8%	5,420
9. Technical Writers	AIC	$63,280	18.2%	1,680
10. Self-Enrichment Education Teachers	SAE	$36,340	32.0%	12,030
11. Art, Drama, and Music Teachers, Postsecondary	SA	$62,040	15.1%	2,500
12. Landscape Architects	AIR	$62,090	19.7%	980
13. Art Directors	AE	$80,630	11.7%	2,870
14. Kindergarten Teachers, Except Special Education	SA	$48,800	15.0%	6,300
15. Producers and Directors	EAC	$68,440	9.8%	4,040
16. Public Relations and Fundraising Managers	EA	$91,810	12.9%	2,060
17. English Language and Literature Teachers, Postsecondary	SAI	$60,400	15.1%	2,000
18. Interior Designers	AE	$46,280	19.4%	3,590
19. Political Scientists	IAS	$107,420	19.5%	280
20. Education Teachers, Postsecondary	SAI	$59,140	15.1%	1,800
21. Secondary School Teachers, Except Special and Career/Technical Education	SAE	$53,230	8.9%	41,240
22. Substance Abuse and Behavioral Disorder Counselors	SAI	$38,120	21.0%	3,550

(continued)

(continued)

The 50 Best Artistic Jobs

Job	Personality Code	Annual Earnings	Percent Growth	Annual Openings
23. Sociologists	IAS	$72,360	21.9%	200
24. Interpreters and Translators	AS	$43,300	22.2%	2,340
25. Multimedia Artists and Animators	AI	$58,510	14.1%	2,890
26. Adult Basic and Secondary Education and Literacy Teachers and Instructors	SAE	$46,530	15.1%	2,920
27. Anthropologists and Archeologists	IA	$54,230	28.1%	450
28. Hairdressers, Hairstylists, and Cosmetologists	AES	$22,760	20.1%	21,950
29. Preschool Teachers, Except Special Education	SA	$25,700	19.0%	17,830
30. Foreign Language and Literature Teachers, Postsecondary	SAI	$59,080	15.1%	900
31. Communications Teachers, Postsecondary	SA	$60,300	15.1%	800
32. Graphic Designers	ARE	$43,500	12.9%	12,480
33. Astronomers	IAR	$87,260	16.0%	70
34. Philosophy and Religion Teachers, Postsecondary	SAI	$62,330	15.1%	600
35. Architecture Teachers, Postsecondary	SA	$73,500	15.1%	200
36. Commercial and Industrial Designers	AER	$58,230	9.0%	1,760
37. Architectural and Civil Drafters	RCA	$46,430	9.1%	3,620
38. Museum Technicians and Conservators	RA	$37,310	25.5%	610
39. Advertising and Promotions Managers	EAC	$83,890	−1.7%	1,050
40. Recreational Therapists	SA	$39,410	14.6%	1,160
41. Set and Exhibit Designers	AR	$46,680	16.6%	510
42. Photographers	AR	$29,130	11.5%	4,800
43. Editors	AEC	$51,470	−0.3%	3,390
44. Film and Video Editors	AEI	$50,930	11.9%	930
45. Music Directors and Composers	AE	$45,970	9.9%	1,620
46. Marriage and Family Therapists	SAI	$45,720	14.4%	950
47. Fashion Designers	AER	$64,530	0.8%	720
48. Makeup Artists, Theatrical and Performance	AR	$38,130	16.9%	90
49. Merchandise Displayers and Window Trimmers	AER	$25,960	7.1%	3,220
50. Camera Operators, Television, Video, and Motion Picture	RA	$40,390	9.2%	890

The 50 Best Social Jobs

Job	Personality Code	Annual Earnings	Percent Growth	Annual Openings
1. Physicians and Surgeons	ISR	$165,279	21.8%	26,050
2. Physician Assistants	SIR	$86,410	39.0%	4,280
3. Physical Therapists	SIR	$76,310	30.3%	7,860
4. Dental Hygienists	SRC	$68,250	36.1%	9,840
5. Registered Nurses	SI	$64,690	22.2%	103,900
6. Occupational Therapists	SI	$72,320	25.6%	4,580
7. Compliance Officers	CEI	$58,720	31.0%	10,850
8. Health Specialties Teachers, Postsecondary	SI	$85,270	15.1%	4,000
9. Speech-Language Pathologists	SIA	$66,920	18.5%	4,380
10. Training and Development Specialists	SAC	$54,160	23.3%	10,710
11. Instructional Coordinators	SIA	$58,830	23.2%	6,060
12. Elementary School Teachers, Except Special Education	SAC	$51,660	15.8%	59,650
13. Radiation Therapists	SRC	$74,980	27.1%	690
14. Self-Enrichment Education Teachers	SAE	$36,340	32.0%	12,030
15. Licensed Practical and Licensed Vocational Nurses	SR	$40,380	20.6%	39,130
16. Medical Assistants	SCR	$28,860	33.9%	21,780
17. Middle School Teachers, Except Special and Career/Technical Education	SA	$51,960	15.3%	25,110
18. Healthcare Social Workers	SI	$47,230	22.4%	6,590
19. Business Teachers, Postsecondary	SEI	$73,760	15.1%	2,000
20. Chiropractors	SIR	$67,200	19.5%	1,820
21. Fitness Trainers and Aerobics Instructors	SRE	$31,090	29.4%	12,380
22. Physical Therapist Assistants	SRI	$49,690	33.3%	3,050
23. Respiratory Therapists	SIR	$54,280	20.9%	4,140
24. Biological Science Teachers, Postsecondary	SI	$72,700	15.1%	1,700
25. Customer Service Representatives	SEC	$30,460	17.7%	110,840
26. Special Education Teachers, Middle School	SA	$53,440	18.1%	4,410
27. Coaches and Scouts	SRE	$28,340	24.8%	9,920
28. Kindergarten Teachers, Except Special Education	SA	$48,800	15.0%	6,300
29. Computer Science Teachers, Postsecondary	SIC	$70,300	15.1%	1,000
30. Mental Health Counselors	SIA	$38,150	24.0%	5,010
31. Law Teachers, Postsecondary	SIE	$94,260	15.1%	400
32. Mental Health and Substance Abuse Social Workers	SIA	$38,600	19.5%	6,130
33. Probation Officers and Correctional Treatment Specialists	SEC	$47,200	19.3%	4,180

(continued)

(continued)

The 50 Best Social Jobs

Job	Personality Code	Annual Earnings	Percent Growth	Annual Openings
34. Art, Drama, and Music Teachers, Postsecondary	SA	$62,040	15.1%	2,500
35. Economics Teachers, Postsecondary	SI	$83,370	15.1%	400
36. Psychology Teachers, Postsecondary	SIA	$67,330	15.1%	1,000
37. Occupational Therapy Assistants	SR	$51,010	29.8%	1,180
38. Physics Teachers, Postsecondary	SI	$77,610	15.1%	400
39. Preschool Teachers, Except Special Education	SA	$25,700	19.0%	17,830
40. English Language and Literature Teachers, Postsecondary	SAI	$60,400	15.1%	2,000
41. Mathematical Science Teachers, Postsecondary	SIA	$65,710	15.1%	1,000
42. Chemistry Teachers, Postsecondary	SIR	$70,520	15.1%	600
43. Atmospheric, Earth, Marine, and Space Sciences Teachers, Postsecondary	SI	$82,840	15.1%	300
44. Agricultural Sciences Teachers, Postsecondary	SIR	$78,370	15.1%	300
45. Political Science Teachers, Postsecondary	SEA	$70,540	15.1%	500
46. Nursing Instructors and Teachers, Postsecondary	SI	$62,390	15.1%	1,500
47. Athletic Trainers	SRI	$41,600	36.9%	1,150
48. Vocational Education Teachers, Postsecondary	SR	$48,210	15.1%	4,000
49. Rehabilitation Counselors	SI	$32,350	18.9%	5,070
50. Education Teachers, Postsecondary	SAI	$59,140	15.1%	1,800

The 50 Best Enterprising Jobs

Job	Personality Code	Annual Earnings	Percent Growth	Annual Openings
1. Computer and Information Systems Managers	ECI	$115,780	16.9%	9,710
2. Lawyers	EI	$112,760	13.0%	24,040
3. Registered Nurses	SI	$64,690	22.2%	103,900
4. Construction Managers	ERC	$83,860	17.2%	13,770
5. Sales Managers	EC	$98,530	14.9%	12,660
6. Medical and Health Services Managers	ECS	$84,270	16.0%	9,940
7. Marketing Managers	EC	$112,800	12.5%	5,970
8. Personal Financial Advisors	ECS	$64,750	30.1%	8,530
9. Supervisors of Construction and Extraction Workers	ERC	$58,680	15.4%	24,220
10. Financial Managers	EC	$103,910	7.6%	13,820
11. Public Relations Specialists	EAS	$52,090	24.0%	13,130

The 50 Best Enterprising Jobs

Job	Personality Code	Annual Earnings	Percent Growth	Annual Openings
12. Managers, All Other	EC	$96,450	7.3%	29,750
13. Business Operations Specialists, All Other	CER	$62,450	11.5%	36,830
14. Human Resources Specialists	ESC	$52,690	27.9%	11,230
15. Administrative Services Managers	EC	$77,890	12.5%	8,660
16. Sales Representatives, Wholesale and Manufacturing, Technical and Scientific Products	EC	$73,710	9.7%	14,230
17. Detectives and Criminal Investigators	ECR	$68,820	16.6%	4,160
18. Natural Sciences Managers	EI	$116,020	15.4%	2,010
19. Sales Representatives, Services, All Other	EC	$50,620	13.9%	22,810
20. Education Administrators, Elementary and Secondary School	ESC	$86,970	8.6%	8,880
21. Customer Service Representatives	SEC	$30,460	17.7%	110,840
22. General and Operations Managers	ECS	$94,400	–0.1%	50,220
23. Securities, Commodities, and Financial Services Sales Agents	EC	$70,190	9.3%	12,680
24. Human Resources Managers	ESC	$99,180	9.6%	4,140
25. Financial Examiners	EC	$74,940	41.2%	1,600
26. Chief Executives	EC	$165,080	–1.4%	11,250
27. Public Relations and Fundraising Managers	EA	$91,810	12.9%	2,060
28. Writers and Authors	AEI	$55,420	14.8%	5,420
29. Police and Sheriff's Patrol Officers	ERS	$53,540	8.7%	22,790
30. First-Line Supervisors of Office and Administrative Support Workers	ECS	$47,460	11.0%	48,900
31. Real Estate Sales Agents	EC	$40,030	16.2%	12,830
32. Architectural and Engineering Managers	ERI	$119,260	6.2%	4,870
33. Air Traffic Controllers	EC	$108,040	13.0%	1,230
34. Insurance Sales Agents	ECS	$46,770	11.9%	15,260
35. Social and Community Service Managers	ES	$57,950	13.8%	4,820
36. Captains, Mates, and Pilots of Water Vessels	REC	$64,180	17.3%	1,950
37. First-Line Supervisors of Non-Retail Sales Workers	ECS	$68,880	4.8%	12,950
38. Sales Engineers	ERI	$87,390	8.8%	3,500
39. First-Line Supervisors of Police and Detectives	ESC	$78,260	8.1%	5,050
40. Producers and Directors	EAC	$68,440	9.8%	4,040
41. Agents and Business Managers of Artists, Performers, and Athletes	ES	$63,130	22.4%	1,010
42. First-Line Supervisors of Personal Service Workers	ECS	$35,290	15.4%	9,080
43. Financial Specialists, All Other	CIE	$60,980	10.5%	4,320

(continued)

(continued)

The 50 Best Enterprising Jobs

Job	Personality Code	Annual Earnings	Percent Growth	Annual Openings
44. First-Line Supervisors of Landscaping, Lawn Service, and Groundskeeping Workers	ERC	$41,860	14.9%	5,600
45. Training and Development Managers	ES	$89,170	11.9%	1,010
46. First-Line Supervisors of Mechanics, Installers, and Repairers	ECR	$59,150	4.3%	13,650
47. Compensation and Benefits Managers	ECS	$89,270	8.5%	1,210
48. Property, Real Estate, and Community Association Managers	EC	$51,480	8.4%	7,800
49. Farmers, Ranchers, and Other Agricultural Managers	ERC	$60,750	5.9%	6,490
50. First-Line Supervisors of Fire Fighting and Prevention Workers	ER	$68,240	8.2%	3,250

The 50 Best Conventional Jobs

Job	Personality Code	Annual Earnings	Percent Growth	Annual Openings
1. Accountants and Auditors	CEI	$61,690	21.6%	49,750
2. Compliance Officers	CEI	$58,720	31.0%	10,850
3. Financial Analysts	CIE	$74,350	19.8%	9,520
4. Cost Estimators	CE	$57,860	25.3%	10,360
5. Business Operations Specialists, All Other	CER	$62,450	11.5%	36,830
6. Paralegals and Legal Assistants	CIE	$46,680	28.1%	10,400
7. Managers, All Other	EC	$96,450	7.3%	29,750
8. Compensation, Benefits, and Job Analysis Specialists	CE	$57,000	23.6%	6,050
9. Database Administrators	CI	$73,490	20.3%	4,440
10. Computer Occupations, All Other	ICR	$79,240	13.1%	7,260
11. Financial Managers	EC	$103,910	7.6%	13,820
12. Logisticians	CEI	$70,800	19.5%	4,190
13. Purchasing Agents, Except Wholesale, Retail, and Farm Products	CE	$56,580	13.9%	11,860
14. Executive Secretaries and Executive Administrative Assistants	CE	$43,520	12.8%	41,920
15. Dental Assistants	CRS	$33,470	35.8%	16,100
16. Detectives and Criminal Investigators	ECR	$68,820	16.6%	4,160

The 50 Best Conventional Jobs

Job	Personality Code	Annual Earnings	Percent Growth	Annual Openings
17. Sales Representatives, Wholesale and Manufacturing, Except Technical and Scientific Products	CE	$52,440	6.6%	45,790
18. Legal Secretaries	CE	$41,500	18.4%	8,380
19. Medical Secretaries	CS	$30,530	26.6%	18,900
20. Actuaries	CIE	$87,650	21.4%	1,000
21. Claims Adjusters, Examiners, and Investigators	CE	$58,620	7.1%	9,560
22. Pharmacy Technicians	CR	$28,400	30.6%	18,200
23. Loan Officers	CES	$56,490	10.1%	6,880
24. Budget Analysts	CEI	$68,200	15.1%	2,230
25. Financial Specialists, All Other	CIE	$60,980	10.5%	4,320
26. Bill and Account Collectors	CE	$31,310	19.3%	15,690
27. Credit Analysts	CE	$58,850	15.0%	2,430
28. Cargo and Freight Agents	CE	$37,150	23.9%	4,030
29. Billing and Posting Clerks	CE	$32,170	15.3%	16,760
30. Bookkeeping, Accounting, and Auditing Clerks	CE	$34,030	10.3%	46,040
31. Social and Human Service Assistants	CSE	$28,200	22.6%	15,390
32. Medical Records and Health Information Technicians	CE	$32,350	20.3%	7,030
33. Librarians	CSE	$54,500	7.8%	5,450
34. Receptionists and Information Clerks	CES	$25,240	15.2%	48,020
35. Surveying and Mapping Technicians	CR	$37,900	20.4%	2,940
36. Postal Service Mail Carriers	CR	$53,860	−1.1%	10,720
37. Tax Examiners and Collectors, and Revenue Agents	CE	$49,360	13.0%	3,520
38. Statisticians	CI	$72,830	13.1%	960
39. Office Clerks, General	CER	$26,610	11.9%	77,090
40. Police, Fire, and Ambulance Dispatchers	CRE	$35,370	17.8%	3,840
41. Life, Physical, and Social Science Technicians, All Other	RC	$43,350	13.3%	3,640
42. Interviewers, Except Eligibility and Loan	CES	$28,820	15.6%	9,210
43. Court Reporters	CE	$47,700	18.3%	710
44. Production, Planning, and Expediting Clerks	CE	$42,220	1.5%	7,410
45. Secretaries and Administrative Assistants, Except Legal, Medical, and Executive	CE	$30,830	4.6%	36,550
46. Social Science Research Assistants	CI	$37,230	17.8%	1,270
47. Insurance Underwriters	CEI	$59,290	−4.1%	3,000
48. Judicial Law Clerks	CI	$39,780	13.9%	1,080
49. Court, Municipal, and License Clerks	CE	$34,390	8.2%	4,460
50. Occupational Health and Safety Technicians	CR	$45,330	14.4%	520

The 20 Best-Paying Jobs for Each Personality Type

In the following six lists you'll find the 20 best-paying jobs for each personality type that met my criteria for this book. These are popular lists, for obvious reasons.

I sorted the jobs based on their annual median earnings from highest to lowest. *Median earnings* means that half of all workers in each of these jobs earn more than that amount and half earn less. Keep in mind that the earnings reflect the national average for all workers in the occupation. This is an important consideration, because starting pay in the job is usually much less than the pay that workers can earn with several years of experience. (To get an idea of how much difference this might make, see the statement about earnings growth potential in the Part IV description of the job.) Earnings also vary significantly by region of the country, so actual pay in your area could be substantially different.

The 20 Best-Paying Realistic Jobs

Job	Annual Earnings
1. Airline Pilots, Copilots, and Flight Engineers	$103,210
2. Physical Scientists, All Other	$94,780
3. Engineers, All Other	$90,270
4. Physician Assistants	$86,410
5. Civil Engineers	$77,560
6. Commercial Pilots	$67,500
7. Ship Engineers	$65,880
8. Captains, Mates, and Pilots of Water Vessels	$64,180
9. Business Operations Specialists, All Other	$62,450
10. Electrical Power-Line Installers and Repairers	$58,030
11. Transportation Inspectors	$57,640
12. Medical and Clinical Laboratory Technologists	$56,130
13. Surveyors	$54,880
14. Boilermakers	$54,640
15. Cartographers and Photogrammetrists	$54,510
16. Radiologic Technologists	$54,340
17. Police and Sheriff's Patrol Officers	$53,540
18. Construction and Building Inspectors	$52,360
19. Cardiovascular Technologists and Technicians	$49,410
20. Electricians	$48,250

The 20 Best-Paying Investigative Jobs

Job	Annual Earnings
1. Orthodontists	$166,500+
2. Physicians and Surgeons	$165,279
3. Dentists, General	$141,040
4. Prosthodontists	$118,400
5. Petroleum Engineers	$114,080
6. Pharmacists	$111,570
7. Political Scientists	$107,420
8. Physicists	$106,370
9. Computer and Information Research Scientists	$100,660
10. Nuclear Engineers	$99,920
11. Mathematicians	$99,380
12. Computer Hardware Engineers	$98,810
13. Aerospace Engineers	$97,480
14. Optometrists	$94,990
15. Software Developers, Systems Software	$94,180
16. Engineers, All Other	$90,270
17. Electronics Engineers, Except Computer	$90,170
18. Psychologists, All Other	$89,900
19. Engineering Teachers, Postsecondary	$89,670
20. Software Developers, Applications	$87,790

The 20 Best-Paying Artistic Jobs

Job	Annual Earnings
1. Political Scientists	$107,420
2. Public Relations and Fundraising Managers	$91,810
3. Astronomers	$87,260
4. Advertising and Promotions Managers	$83,890
5. Art Directors	$80,630
6. Biochemists and Biophysicists	$79,390
7. Architecture Teachers, Postsecondary	$73,500
8. Architects, Except Landscape and Naval	$72,550
9. Sociologists	$72,360
10. Producers and Directors	$68,440
11. Fashion Designers	$64,530
12. Technical Writers	$63,280

(continued)

(continued)

The 20 Best-Paying Artistic Jobs

Job	Annual Earnings
13. Philosophy and Religion Teachers, Postsecondary	$62,330
14. Landscape Architects	$62,090
15. Art, Drama, and Music Teachers, Postsecondary	$62,040
16. English Language and Literature Teachers, Postsecondary	$60,400
17. Communications Teachers, Postsecondary	$60,300
18. Education Teachers, Postsecondary	$59,140
19. Foreign Language and Literature Teachers, Postsecondary	$59,080
20. Multimedia Artists and Animators	$58,510

The 20 Best-Paying Social Jobs

Job	Annual Earnings
1. Physicians and Surgeons	$165,279
2. Law Teachers, Postsecondary	$94,260
3. Physician Assistants	$86,410
4. Health Specialties Teachers, Postsecondary	$85,270
5. Economics Teachers, Postsecondary	$83,370
6. Atmospheric, Earth, Marine, and Space Sciences Teachers, Postsecondary	$82,840
7. Agricultural Sciences Teachers, Postsecondary	$78,370
8. Physics Teachers, Postsecondary	$77,610
9. Physical Therapists	$76,310
10. Radiation Therapists	$74,980
11. Business Teachers, Postsecondary	$73,760
12. Biological Science Teachers, Postsecondary	$72,700
13. Occupational Therapists	$72,320
14. Political Science Teachers, Postsecondary	$70,540
15. Chemistry Teachers, Postsecondary	$70,520
16. Computer Science Teachers, Postsecondary	$70,300
17. Dental Hygienists	$68,250
18. Psychology Teachers, Postsecondary	$67,330
19. Chiropractors	$67,200
20. Speech-Language Pathologists	$66,920

The 20 Best-Paying Enterprising Jobs

Job	Annual Earnings
1. Chief Executives	$165,080
2. Architectural and Engineering Managers	$119,260
3. Natural Sciences Managers	$116,020
4. Computer and Information Systems Managers	$115,780
5. Marketing Managers	$112,800
6. Lawyers	$112,760
7. Air Traffic Controllers	$108,040
8. Financial Managers	$103,910
9. Human Resources Managers	$99,180
10. Sales Managers	$98,530
11. Managers, All Other	$96,450
12. General and Operations Managers	$94,400
13. Public Relations and Fundraising Managers	$91,810
14. Compensation and Benefits Managers	$89,270
15. Training and Development Managers	$89,170
16. Sales Engineers	$87,390
17. Education Administrators, Elementary and Secondary School	$86,970
18. Medical and Health Services Managers	$84,270
19. Construction Managers	$83,860
20. First-Line Supervisors of Police and Detectives	$78,260

The 20 Best-Paying Conventional Jobs

Job	Annual Earnings
1. Financial Managers	$103,910
2. Managers, All Other	$96,450
3. Actuaries	$87,650
4. Computer Occupations, All Other	$79,240
5. Financial Analysts	$74,350
6. Database Administrators	$73,490
7. Statisticians	$72,830
8. Logisticians	$70,800
9. Detectives and Criminal Investigators	$68,820
10. Budget Analysts	$68,200
11. Business Operations Specialists, All Other	$62,450
12. Accountants and Auditors	$61,690

(continued)

(continued)

The 20 Best-Paying Conventional Jobs

Job	Annual Earnings
13. Financial Specialists, All Other	$60,980
14. Insurance Underwriters	$59,290
15. Credit Analysts	$58,850
16. Compliance Officers	$58,720
17. Claims Adjusters, Examiners, and Investigators	$58,620
18. Cost Estimators	$57,860
19. Compensation, Benefits, and Job Analysis Specialists	$57,000
20. Purchasing Agents, Except Wholesale, Retail, and Farm Products	$56,580

The 20 Fastest-Growing Jobs for Each Personality Type

From the six lists of 50 jobs that met my criteria for this book, these six lists show the 20 for each personality type that are projected to have the highest percentage increase in the numbers of people employed through 2018.

The 20 Fastest-Growing Realistic Jobs

Job	Percent Growth
1. Physician Assistants	39.0%
2. Environmental Engineering Technicians	30.1%
3. Heating, Air Conditioning, and Refrigeration Mechanics and Installers	28.1%
4. Cartographers and Photogrammetrists	26.8%
5. Medical Equipment Repairers	27.2%
6. Security and Fire Alarm Systems Installers	24.8%
7. Surgical Technologists	25.3%
8. Civil Engineers	24.3%
9. Cardiovascular Technologists and Technicians	24.0%
10. Construction Laborers	20.5%
11. Surveying and Mapping Technicians	20.4%
12. Water and Wastewater Treatment Plant and System Operators	19.8%
13. Refuse and Recyclable Material Collectors	18.6%
14. Health Technologists and Technicians, All Other	18.7%
15. Boilermakers	18.8%
16. Commercial Pilots	18.5%

The 20 Fastest-Growing Realistic Jobs

Job	Percent Growth
17. Firefighters	18.5%
18. Ship Engineers	18.6%
19. Biological Technicians	17.6%
20. Transportation Inspectors	18.3%

The 20 Fastest-Growing Investigative Jobs

Job	Percent Growth
1. Biomedical Engineers	72.0%
2. Computer Network Architects	53.4%
3. Medical Scientists, Except Epidemiologists	40.3%
4. Biochemists and Biophysicists	37.4%
5. Software Developers, Applications	34.0%
6. Veterinarians	33.0%
7. Environmental Engineers	30.6%
8. Compliance Officers	31.0%
9. Software Developers, Systems Software	30.4%
10. Survey Researchers	30.4%
11. Environmental Science and Protection Technicians, Including Health	28.9%
12. Prosthodontists	27.7%
13. Environmental Scientists and Specialists, Including Health	27.9%
14. Market Research Analysts and Marketing Specialists	28.1%
15. Geographers	26.2%
16. Industrial-Organizational Psychologists	26.3%
17. Audiologists	25.0%
18. Optometrists	24.4%
19. Computer and Information Research Scientists	24.2%
20. Management Analysts	23.9%

The 20 Fastest-Growing Artistic Jobs

Job	Percent Growth
1. Biochemists and Biophysicists	37.4%
2. Self-Enrichment Education Teachers	32.0%
3. Anthropologists and Archeologists	28.1%
4. Museum Technicians and Conservators	25.5%
5. Public Relations Specialists	24.0%
6. Training and Development Specialists	23.3%
7. Sociologists	21.9%
8. Interpreters and Translators	22.2%
9. Substance Abuse and Behavioral Disorder Counselors	21.0%
10. Hairdressers, Hairstylists, and Cosmetologists	20.1%
11. Landscape Architects	19.7%
12. Political Scientists	19.5%
13. Preschool Teachers, Except Special Education	19.0%
14. Interior Designers	19.4%
15. Special Education Teachers, Middle School	18.1%
16. Technical Writers	18.2%
17. Makeup Artists, Theatrical and Performance	16.9%
18. Set and Exhibit Designers	16.6%
19. Architects, Except Landscape and Naval	16.2%
20. Elementary School Teachers, Except Special Education	15.8%

The 20 Fastest-Growing Social Jobs

Job	Percent Growth
1. Athletic Trainers	36.9%
2. Dental Hygienists	36.1%
3. Medical Assistants	33.9%
4. Physical Therapist Assistants	33.3%
5. Self-Enrichment Education Teachers	32.0%
6. Compliance Officers	31.0%
7. Occupational Therapy Assistants	29.8%
8. Physical Therapists	30.3%
9. Fitness Trainers and Aerobics Instructors	29.4%
10. Radiation Therapists	27.1%
11. Occupational Therapists	25.6%
12. Coaches and Scouts	24.8%

The 20 Fastest-Growing Social Jobs

Job	Percent Growth
13. Mental Health Counselors	24.0%
14. Training and Development Specialists	23.3%
15. Instructional Coordinators	23.2%
16. Physicians and Surgeons	21.8%
17. Registered Nurses	22.2%
18. Healthcare Social Workers	22.4%
19. Licensed Practical and Licensed Vocational Nurses	20.6%
20. Respiratory Therapists	20.9%

The 20 Fastest-Growing Enterprising Jobs

Job	Percent Growth
1. Financial Examiners	41.2%
2. Personal Financial Advisors	30.1%
3. Human Resources Specialists	27.9%
4. Public Relations Specialists	24.0%
5. Agents and Business Managers of Artists, Performers, and Athletes	22.4%
6. Registered Nurses	22.2%
7. Customer Service Representatives	17.7%
8. Computer and Information Systems Managers	16.9%
9. Construction Managers	17.2%
10. Captains, Mates, and Pilots of Water Vessels	17.3%
11. Detectives and Criminal Investigators	16.6%
12. Medical and Health Services Managers	16.0%
13. Real Estate Sales Agents	16.2%
14. First-Line Supervisors of Landscaping, Lawn Service, and Groundskeeping Workers	14.9%
15. Sales Managers	14.9%
16. Supervisors of Construction and Extraction Workers	15.4%
17. First-Line Supervisors of Personal Service Workers	15.4%
18. Writers and Authors	14.8%
19. Natural Sciences Managers	15.4%
20. Sales Representatives, Services, All Other	13.9%

The 20 Fastest-Growing Conventional Jobs

Job	Percent Growth
1. Dental Assistants	35.8%
2. Pharmacy Technicians	30.6%
3. Compliance Officers	31.0%
4. Paralegals and Legal Assistants	28.1%
5. Medical Secretaries	26.6%
6. Cost Estimators	25.3%
7. Cargo and Freight Agents	23.9%
8. Compensation, Benefits, and Job Analysis Specialists	23.6%
9. Social and Human Service Assistants	22.6%
10. Accountants and Auditors	21.6%
11. Actuaries	21.4%
12. Logisticians	19.5%
13. Medical Records and Health Information Technicians	20.3%
14. Surveying and Mapping Technicians	20.4%
15. Financial Analysts	19.8%
16. Database Administrators	20.3%
17. Bill and Account Collectors	19.3%
18. Social Science Research Assistants	17.8%
19. Court Reporters	18.3%
20. Police, Fire, and Ambulance Dispatchers	17.8%

The 20 Jobs with the Most Openings for Each Personality Type

From the six lists of 50 jobs that met my criteria for this book, this list shows the 20 jobs for each personality type that are projected to have the largest number of job openings per year through 2018.

Jobs with many openings present several advantages that may be attractive to you. Because there are many openings, these jobs can be easier to obtain, particularly for those just entering the job market. These jobs may also offer more opportunities to move from one employer to another with relative ease. Though some of these jobs have average or below-average pay, some also pay quite well and can provide good long-term career opportunities or the ability to move up to more responsible roles.

It is interesting but not surprising that job openings are much more scarce in the Artistic list than in the other five lists; this is a category in which keen competition for nonteaching jobs is the rule. The two personality types with outstanding figures for job openings are Conventional and Social.

On all the lists, the jobs that are expected to have the greatest number of openings tend to be those that require hands-on or in-person work—for example, truck drivers, teachers, construction workers, or salespeople. These workers are less likely to be replaced by technology or by overseas workers.

The 20 Realistic Jobs with the Most Openings

Job	Annual Openings
1. Heavy and Tractor-Trailer Truck Drivers	55,460
2. Business Operations Specialists, All Other	36,830
3. Maintenance and Repair Workers, General	35,750
4. Construction Laborers	33,940
5. Carpenters	32,540
6. Electricians	25,090
7. Computer User Support Specialists	23,460
8. Police and Sheriff's Patrol Officers	22,790
9. Plumbers, Pipefitters, and Steamfitters	17,550
10. Firefighters	15,280
11. Correctional Officers and Jailers	14,360
12. Heating, Air Conditioning, and Refrigeration Mechanics and Installers	13,620
13. Operating Engineers and Other Construction Equipment Operators	11,820
14. Civil Engineers	11,460
15. Cement Masons and Concrete Finishers	7,640
16. Refuse and Recyclable Material Collectors	7,110
17. Radiologic Technologists	6,800
18. Industrial Machinery Mechanics	6,240
19. Medical and Clinical Laboratory Technicians	5,460
20. Medical and Clinical Laboratory Technologists	5,330

The 20 Investigative Jobs with the Most Openings

Job	Annual Openings
1. Management Analysts	30,650
2. Physicians and Surgeons	26,050
3. Computer Systems Analysts	22,280
4. Software Developers, Applications	21,840
5. Computer Network Architects	20,830
6. Software Developers, Systems Software	15,340
7. Market Research Analysts and Marketing Specialists	13,730
8. Network and Computer Systems Administrators	13,550
9. Compliance Officers	10,850
10. Pharmacists	10,580
11. Industrial Engineers	8,540
12. Mechanical Engineers	7,570
13. Computer Occupations, All Other	7,260
14. Medical Scientists, Except Epidemiologists	6,620
15. Clinical, Counseling, and School Psychologists	5,990
16. Dentists, General	5,180
17. Engineers, All Other	5,020
18. Environmental Scientists and Specialists, Including Health	4,840
19. Logisticians	4,190
20. Electrical Engineers	3,890

The 20 Artistic Jobs with the Most Openings

Job	Annual Openings
1. Elementary School Teachers, Except Special Education	59,650
2. Secondary School Teachers, Except Special and Career/Technical Education	41,240
3. Middle School Teachers, Except Special and Career/Technical Education	25,110
4. Hairdressers, Hairstylists, and Cosmetologists	21,950
5. Preschool Teachers, Except Special Education	17,830
6. Public Relations Specialists	13,130
7. Graphic Designers	12,480
8. Self-Enrichment Education Teachers	12,030
9. Training and Development Specialists	10,710
10. Kindergarten Teachers, Except Special Education	6,300
11. Writers and Authors	5,420

The 20 Artistic Jobs with the Most Openings

Job	Annual Openings
12. Photographers	4,800
13. Architects, Except Landscape and Naval	4,680
14. Special Education Teachers, Middle School	4,410
15. Producers and Directors	4,040
16. Architectural and Civil Drafters	3,620
17. Interior Designers	3,590
18. Substance Abuse and Behavioral Disorder Counselors	3,550
19. Editors	3,390
20. Merchandise Displayers and Window Trimmers	3,220

The 20 Social Jobs with the Most Openings

Job	Annual Openings
1. Customer Service Representatives	110,840
2. Registered Nurses	103,900
3. Elementary School Teachers, Except Special Education	59,650
4. Licensed Practical and Licensed Vocational Nurses	39,130
5. Physicians and Surgeons	26,050
6. Middle School Teachers, Except Special and Career/Technical Education	25,110
7. Medical Assistants	21,780
8. Preschool Teachers, Except Special Education	17,830
9. Fitness Trainers and Aerobics Instructors	12,380
10. Self-Enrichment Education Teachers	12,030
11. Compliance Officers	10,850
12. Training and Development Specialists	10,710
13. Coaches and Scouts	9,920
14. Dental Hygienists	9,840
15. Physical Therapists	7,860
16. Healthcare Social Workers	6,590
17. Kindergarten Teachers, Except Special Education	6,300
18. Mental Health and Substance Abuse Social Workers	6,130
19. Instructional Coordinators	6,060
20. Rehabilitation Counselors	5,070

The 20 Enterprising Jobs with the Most Openings

Job	Annual Openings
1. Customer Service Representatives	110,840
2. Registered Nurses	103,900
3. General and Operations Managers	50,220
4. First-Line Supervisors of Office and Administrative Support Workers	48,900
5. Business Operations Specialists, All Other	36,830
6. Managers, All Other	29,750
7. Supervisors of Construction and Extraction Workers	24,220
8. Lawyers	24,040
9. Sales Representatives, Services, All Other	22,810
10. Police and Sheriff's Patrol Officers	22,790
11. Insurance Sales Agents	15,260
12. Sales Representatives, Wholesale and Manufacturing, Technical and Scientific Products	14,230
13. Financial Managers	13,820
14. Construction Managers	13,770
15. First-Line Supervisors of Mechanics, Installers, and Repairers	13,650
16. Public Relations Specialists	13,130
17. First-Line Supervisors of Non-Retail Sales Workers	12,950
18. Real Estate Sales Agents	12,830
19. Securities, Commodities, and Financial Services Sales Agents	12,680
20. Sales Managers	12,660

The 20 Conventional Jobs with the Most Openings

Job	Annual Openings
1. Office Clerks, General	77,090
2. Accountants and Auditors	49,750
3. Receptionists and Information Clerks	48,020
4. Bookkeeping, Accounting, and Auditing Clerks	46,040
5. Sales Representatives, Wholesale and Manufacturing, Except Technical and Scientific Products	45,790
6. Executive Secretaries and Executive Administrative Assistants	41,920
7. Business Operations Specialists, All Other	36,830
8. Secretaries and Administrative Assistants, Except Legal, Medical, and Executive	36,550
9. Managers, All Other	29,750
10. Medical Secretaries	18,900
11. Pharmacy Technicians	18,200
12. Billing and Posting Clerks	16,760
13. Dental Assistants	16,100
14. Bill and Account Collectors	15,690
15. Social and Human Service Assistants	15,390
16. Financial Managers	13,820
17. Purchasing Agents, Except Wholesale, Retail, and Farm Products	11,860
18. Compliance Officers	10,850
19. Postal Service Mail Carriers	10,720
20. Paralegals and Legal Assistants	10,400

Best Jobs Lists by Demographic

Different types of jobs attract different types of workers. It's interesting to consider which jobs have the highest percentage of men or young workers. I'm not saying that men or young people should consider these jobs over others based solely on this information, but it is useful information to know.

In some cases, these lists can give you ideas for jobs to consider that you might otherwise overlook. For example, perhaps women should consider some jobs that traditionally have high percentages of men in them. Or older workers might consider some jobs typically held by young people. Although these aren't obvious ways of using these lists, the lists may give you some good ideas of jobs to consider. The lists may also help you identify jobs that work well for others like you—for example, jobs with plentiful opportunities for self-employment, if that's a work arrangement that appeals to you.

I used the same process to create all the lists in this section. First, I sorted the 50 best jobs for each personality type using the primary criterion for each set of lists. I eliminated jobs that scored low on the primary criterion and created an initial list of jobs for each personality type ordered from highest to lowest percentage of the criterion. For example, when I sorted the jobs based on the percentage of workers age 16 to 24, I set the cutoff point at 7.5 percent and produced a list of 22 Realistic jobs. For other criteria, such as number of self-employed workers or female workers, I used other cutoff levels.

From this initial list of jobs with a high percentage of each type of worker, I created a second list of the best jobs for each personality type, based on their combined scores for earnings, growth rate, and number of openings. Note that the economic figures I used to sort the jobs are based on the averages for *all* workers, not just workers who match the particular demographic group. For example, it was not possible to obtain earnings figures that applied specifically to young people or to women, although it is known that they tend to earn less on average. Similarly, it was not possible to obtain separate percentage figures for job growth in urban or rural areas.

The Best Jobs for Each Personality Type with a High Percentage of Workers Age 16–24

In the following lists, I sorted the 50 best jobs for each personality type and included only those that employ the highest percentage of workers age 16–24. Workers in this age bracket make up 14.1 percent of the workforce, and jobs in the lists that follow include at least 7.5 percent of these workers. (I was unable to obtain age data for workers in two occupations, Computer User Support Specialists and Judicial Law Clerks.)

Though young workers are employed in virtually all major occupations, and therefore in settings associated with all six personality types, you may notice that the jobs for the Realistic, Conventional, and Artistic personality types are considerably "younger" than those for the Investigative and Enterprising personality types. This largely reflects the fact that careers in the Investigative and Enterprising categories often require a lot of prior education or time spent rising through the ranks to a supervisory role, whereas on-the-job training requiring less commitment of time may be sufficient preparation for many jobs for the other personality types.

Keep in mind that the young people who hold the jobs listed in this section may not stay in those jobs, or even in jobs related to the same personality type, for a whole career. Some people are "late bloomers" who do not recognize at an early age what their personality type is and how to find a job appropriate to that type. Others may take a job related to an inappropriate personality type because it offers the opportunity to enter the labor market, earn some money, gain basic job skills, and acquire the experience necessary for moving up to a job that is a better fit.

Realistic Jobs with the Highest Percentage of Workers Age 16–24

Job	Percent Workers Age 16–24
1. Life, Physical, and Social Science Technicians, All Other	23.8%
2. Surgical Technologists	21.5%
3. Construction Laborers	18.3%
4. Biological Technicians	18.3%
5. Drywall and Ceiling Tile Installers	15.9%
6. Refuse and Recyclable Material Collectors	15.5%
7. Surveying and Mapping Technicians	12.9%
8. Tile and Marble Setters	12.9%
9. Health Technologists and Technicians, All Other	12.1%
10. Audio and Video Equipment Technicians	11.6%
11. Security and Fire Alarm Systems Installers	11.2%
12. Carpenters	9.8%
13. Heating, Air Conditioning, and Refrigeration Mechanics and Installers	9.5%
14. Plumbers, Pipefitters, and Steamfitters	9.5%
15. Electrical Power-Line Installers and Repairers	9.5%
16. Brickmasons and Blockmasons	9.5%
17. Electricians	9.1%
18. Medical and Clinical Laboratory Technicians	9.0%
19. Medical and Clinical Laboratory Technologists	9.0%
20. Cement Masons and Concrete Finishers	8.9%
21. Firefighters	7.6%
22. Architectural and Civil Drafters	7.5%

Best Realistic Jobs Overall Employing 7.5 Percent or More Workers Age 16–24

Job	Percent Workers Age 16–24	Annual Earnings	Percent Growth	Annual Openings
1. Heating, Air Conditioning, and Refrigeration Mechanics and Installers	9.5%	$42,530	28.1%	13,620
2. Firefighters	7.6%	$45,250	18.5%	15,280
3. Plumbers, Pipefitters, and Steamfitters	9.5%	$46,660	15.3%	17,550
4. Electricians	9.1%	$48,250	11.9%	25,090
5. Surgical Technologists	21.5%	$39,920	25.3%	4,630

(continued)

(continued)

Best Realistic Jobs Overall Employing 7.5 Percent or More Workers Age 16–24

Job	Percent Workers Age 16–24	Annual Earnings	Percent Growth	Annual Openings
6. Construction Laborers	18.3%	$29,280	20.5%	33,940
7. Carpenters	9.8%	$39,530	12.9%	32,540
8. Medical and Clinical Laboratory Technologists	9.0%	$56,130	11.9%	5,330
9. Brickmasons and Blockmasons	9.5%	$46,930	11.5%	5,000
10. Biological Technicians	18.3%	$39,020	17.6%	4,190
11. Electrical Power-Line Installers and Repairers	9.5%	$58,030	4.5%	4,550
12. Refuse and Recyclable Material Collectors	15.5%	$32,640	18.6%	7,110
13. Security and Fire Alarm Systems Installers	11.2%	$38,500	24.8%	2,780
14. Medical and Clinical Laboratory Technicians	9.0%	$36,280	16.1%	5,460
15. Health Technologists and Technicians, All Other	12.1%	$38,460	18.7%	3,200
16. Life, Physical, and Social Science Technicians, All Other	23.8%	$43,350	13.3%	3,640
17. Surveying and Mapping Technicians	12.9%	$37,900	20.4%	2,940
18. Cement Masons and Concrete Finishers	8.9%	$35,450	12.9%	7,640
19. Architectural and Civil Drafters	7.5%	$46,430	9.1%	3,620
20. Drywall and Ceiling Tile Installers	15.9%	$37,320	13.5%	3,700
21. Audio and Video Equipment Technicians	11.6%	$40,540	12.6%	2,370
22. Tile and Marble Setters	12.9%	$38,110	14.3%	3,070

Investigative Jobs with the Highest Percentage of Workers Age 16–24 Percent Workers

Job	Percent Workers Age 16–24
1. Mathematicians	27.3%
2. Environmental Science and Protection Technicians, Including Health	23.8%
3. Nuclear Engineers	11.4%
4. Social Scientists and Related Workers, All Other	8.2%
5. Geographers	8.2%
6. Political Scientists	8.2%
7. Engineering Teachers, Postsecondary	7.6%
8. Survey Researchers	7.5%
9. Market Research Analysts and Marketing Specialists	7.5%

Best Investigative Jobs Overall Employing 7.5 Percent or More Workers Age 16–24

Job	Percent Workers Age 16–24	Annual Earnings	Percent Growth	Annual Openings
1. Market Research Analysts and Marketing Specialists	7.5%	$60,570	28.1%	13,730
2. Environmental Science and Protection Technicians, Including Health	23.8%	$41,380	28.9%	2,520
3. Social Scientists and Related Workers, All Other	8.2%	$74,620	22.4%	2,380
4. Survey Researchers	7.5%	$36,050	30.4%	1,340
5. Political Scientists	8.2%	$107,420	19.5%	280
6. Mathematicians	27.3%	$99,380	22.5%	150
7. Engineering Teachers, Postsecondary	7.6%	$89,670	15.1%	1,000
8. Nuclear Engineers	11.4%	$99,920	10.9%	540
9. Geographers	8.2%	$72,800	26.2%	100

Artistic Jobs with the Highest Percentage of Workers Age 16–24

Job	Percent Workers Age 16–24
1. Camera Operators, Television, Video, and Motion Picture	16.9%
2. Film and Video Editors	16.9%
3. Adult Basic and Secondary Education and Literacy Teachers and Instructors	16.7%
4. Self-Enrichment Education Teachers	16.7%
5. Hairdressers, Hairstylists, and Cosmetologists	13.6%
6. Photographers	13.4%
7. Recreational Therapists	12.7%
8. Makeup Artists, Theatrical and Performance	12.6%
9. Kindergarten Teachers, Except Special Education	11.1%
10. Preschool Teachers, Except Special Education	11.1%
11. Music Directors and Composers	10.6%
12. Public Relations Specialists	10.2%
13. Producers and Directors	9.4%
14. Marriage and Family Therapists	8.9%
15. Substance Abuse and Behavioral Disorder Counselors	8.9%
16. Political Scientists	8.2%
17. Anthropologists and Archeologists	8.2%
18. Graphic Designers	7.9%
19. Commercial and Industrial Designers	7.9%

(continued)

(continued)

Artistic Jobs with the Highest Percentage of Workers Age 16–24

Job	Percent Workers Age 16–24
20. Set and Exhibit Designers	7.9%
21. Interior Designers	7.9%
22. Merchandise Displayers and Window Trimmers	7.9%
23. Fashion Designers	7.9%
24. English Language and Literature Teachers, Postsecondary	7.6%
25. Art, Drama, and Music Teachers, Postsecondary	7.6%
26. Communications Teachers, Postsecondary	7.6%
27. Education Teachers, Postsecondary	7.6%
28. Foreign Language and Literature Teachers, Postsecondary	7.6%
29. Architecture Teachers, Postsecondary	7.6%
30. Philosophy and Religion Teachers, Postsecondary	7.6%
31. Architectural and Civil Drafters	7.5%

Best Artistic Jobs Overall Employing 7.5 Percent or More Workers Age 16–24

Job	Percent Workers Age 16–24	Annual Earnings	Percent Growth	Annual Openings
1. Public Relations Specialists	10.2%	$52,090	24.0%	13,130
2. Art, Drama, and Music Teachers, Postsecondary	7.6%	$62,040	15.1%	2,500
3. Self-Enrichment Education Teachers	16.7%	$36,340	32.0%	12,030
4. English Language and Literature Teachers, Postsecondary	7.6%	$60,400	15.1%	2,000
5. Interior Designers	7.9%	$46,280	19.4%	3,590
6. Political Scientists	8.2%	$107,420	19.5%	280
7. Education Teachers, Postsecondary	7.6%	$59,140	15.1%	1,800
8. Hairdressers, Hairstylists, and Cosmetologists	13.6%	$22,760	20.1%	21,950
9. Producers and Directors	9.4%	$68,440	9.8%	4,040
10. Kindergarten Teachers, Except Special Education	11.1%	$48,800	15.0%	6,300
11. Preschool Teachers, Except Special Education	11.1%	$25,700	19.0%	17,830
12. Adult Basic and Secondary Education and Literacy Teachers and Instructors	16.7%	$46,530	15.1%	2,920
13. Substance Abuse and Behavioral Disorder Counselors	8.9%	$38,120	21.0%	3,550
14. Anthropologists and Archeologists	8.2%	$54,230	28.1%	450
15. Architecture Teachers, Postsecondary	7.6%	$73,500	15.1%	200

Best Artistic Jobs Overall Employing 7.5 Percent or More Workers Age 16–24

Job	Percent Workers Age 16–24	Annual Earnings	Percent Growth	Annual Openings
16. Communications Teachers, Postsecondary	7.6%	$60,300	15.1%	800
17. Graphic Designers	7.9%	$43,500	12.9%	12,480
18. Foreign Language and Literature Teachers, Postsecondary	7.6%	$59,080	15.1%	900
19. Philosophy and Religion Teachers, Postsecondary	7.6%	$62,330	15.1%	600
20. Set and Exhibit Designers	7.9%	$46,680	16.6%	510
21. Architectural and Civil Drafters	7.5%	$46,430	9.1%	3,620
22. Commercial and Industrial Designers	7.9%	$58,230	9.0%	1,760
23. Film and Video Editors	16.9%	$50,930	11.9%	930
24. Photographers	13.4%	$29,130	11.5%	4,800
25. Fashion Designers	7.9%	$64,530	0.8%	720
26. Marriage and Family Therapists	8.9%	$45,720	14.4%	950
27. Music Directors and Composers	10.6%	$45,970	9.9%	1,620
28. Recreational Therapists	12.7%	$39,410	14.6%	1,160
29. Makeup Artists, Theatrical and Performance	12.6%	$38,130	16.9%	90
30. Merchandise Displayers and Window Trimmers	7.9%	$25,960	7.1%	3,220
31. Camera Operators, Television, Video, and Motion Picture	16.9%	$40,390	9.2%	890

Social Jobs with the Highest Percentage of Workers Age 16–24

Job	Percent Workers Age 16–24
1. Coaches and Scouts	33.7%
2. Fitness Trainers and Aerobics Instructors	30.3%
3. Customer Service Representatives	21.6%
4. Physical Therapist Assistants	21.6%
5. Medical Assistants	18.6%
6. Self-Enrichment Education Teachers	16.7%
7. Occupational Therapy Assistants	13.3%
8. Preschool Teachers, Except Special Education	11.1%
9. Kindergarten Teachers, Except Special Education	11.1%
10. Probation Officers and Correctional Treatment Specialists	9.5%
11. Rehabilitation Counselors	8.9%
12. Mental Health Counselors	8.9%

(continued)

(continued)

Social Jobs with the Highest Percentage of Workers Age 16–24

Job	Percent Workers Age 16–24
13. Business Teachers, Postsecondary	7.6%
14. Art, Drama, and Music Teachers, Postsecondary	7.6%
15. Education Teachers, Postsecondary	7.6%
16. Vocational Education Teachers, Postsecondary	7.6%
17. Nursing Instructors and Teachers, Postsecondary	7.6%
18. Political Science Teachers, Postsecondary	7.6%
19. Agricultural Sciences Teachers, Postsecondary	7.6%
20. Atmospheric, Earth, Marine, and Space Sciences Teachers, Postsecondary	7.6%
21. Chemistry Teachers, Postsecondary	7.6%
22. English Language and Literature Teachers, Postsecondary	7.6%
23. Biological Science Teachers, Postsecondary	7.6%
24. Health Specialties Teachers, Postsecondary	7.6%
25. Computer Science Teachers, Postsecondary	7.6%
26. Physics Teachers, Postsecondary	7.6%
27. Law Teachers, Postsecondary	7.6%
28. Psychology Teachers, Postsecondary	7.6%
29. Economics Teachers, Postsecondary	7.6%
30. Mathematical Science Teachers, Postsecondary	7.6%

Best Social Jobs Overall Employing 7.5 Percent or More Workers Age 16–24

Job	Percent Workers Age 16–24	Annual Earnings	Percent Growth	Annual Openings
1. Medical Assistants	18.6%	$28,860	33.9%	21,780
2. Self-Enrichment Education Teachers	16.7%	$36,340	32.0%	12,030
3. Physical Therapist Assistants	21.6%	$49,690	33.3%	3,050
4. Fitness Trainers and Aerobics Instructors	30.3%	$31,090	29.4%	12,380
5. Health Specialties Teachers, Postsecondary	7.6%	$85,270	15.1%	4,000
6. Agricultural Sciences Teachers, Postsecondary	7.6%	$78,370	15.1%	300
7. Biological Science Teachers, Postsecondary	7.6%	$72,700	15.1%	1,700
8. Business Teachers, Postsecondary	7.6%	$73,760	15.1%	2,000
9. Atmospheric, Earth, Marine, and Space Sciences Teachers, Postsecondary	7.6%	$82,840	15.1%	300
10. Customer Service Representatives	21.6%	$30,460	17.7%	110,840
11. Mental Health Counselors	8.9%	$38,150	24.0%	5,010

Best Social Jobs Overall Employing 7.5 Percent or More Workers Age 16–24

Job	Percent Workers Age 16–24	Annual Earnings	Percent Growth	Annual Openings
12. Coaches and Scouts	33.7%	$28,340	24.8%	9,920
13. Preschool Teachers, Except Special Education	11.1%	$25,700	19.0%	17,830
14. Probation Officers and Correctional Treatment Specialists	9.5%	$47,200	19.3%	4,180
15. Art, Drama, and Music Teachers, Postsecondary	7.6%	$62,040	15.1%	2,500
16. Occupational Therapy Assistants	13.3%	$51,010	29.8%	1,180
17. Economics Teachers, Postsecondary	7.6%	$83,370	15.1%	400
18. Rehabilitation Counselors	8.9%	$32,350	18.9%	5,070
19. Law Teachers, Postsecondary	7.6%	$94,260	15.1%	400
20. Chemistry Teachers, Postsecondary	7.6%	$70,520	15.1%	600
21. Computer Science Teachers, Postsecondary	7.6%	$70,300	15.1%	1,000
22. Kindergarten Teachers, Except Special Education	11.1%	$48,800	15.0%	6,300
23. Education Teachers, Postsecondary	7.6%	$59,140	15.1%	1,800
24. English Language and Literature Teachers, Postsecondary	7.6%	$60,400	15.1%	2,000
25. Nursing Instructors and Teachers, Postsecondary	7.6%	$62,390	15.1%	1,500
26. Physics Teachers, Postsecondary	7.6%	$77,610	15.1%	400
27. Mathematical Science Teachers, Postsecondary	7.6%	$65,710	15.1%	1,000
28. Political Science Teachers, Postsecondary	7.6%	$70,540	15.1%	500
29. Psychology Teachers, Postsecondary	7.6%	$67,330	15.1%	1,000
30. Vocational Education Teachers, Postsecondary	7.6%	$48,210	15.1%	4,000

Enterprising Jobs with the Highest Percentage of Workers Age 16–24

Job	Percent Workers Age 16–24
1. Customer Service Representatives	21.6%
2. Agents and Business Managers of Artists, Performers, and Athletes	11.0%
3. Sales Representatives, Services, All Other	11.0%
4. Public Relations Specialists	10.2%
5. Air Traffic Controllers	9.9%
6. Producers and Directors	9.4%
7. Financial Specialists, All Other	8.2%

Best Enterprising Jobs Overall Employing 7.5 Percent or More Workers Age 16–24

Job	Percent Workers Age 16–24	Annual Earnings	Percent Growth	Annual Openings
1. Public Relations Specialists	10.2%	$52,090	24.0%	13,130
2. Customer Service Representatives	21.6%	$30,460	17.7%	110,840
3. Agents and Business Managers of Artists, Performers, and Athletes	11.0%	$63,130	22.4%	1,010
4. Air Traffic Controllers	9.9%	$108,040	13.0%	1,230
5. Sales Representatives, Services, All Other	11.0%	$50,620	13.9%	22,810
6. Financial Specialists, All Other	8.2%	$60,980	10.5%	4,320
7. Producers and Directors	9.4%	$68,440	9.8%	4,040

Conventional Jobs with the Highest Percentage of Workers Age 16–24

Job	Percent Workers Age 16–24
1. Social Science Research Assistants	23.8%
2. Life, Physical, and Social Science Technicians, All Other	23.8%
3. Receptionists and Information Clerks	22.6%
4. Pharmacy Technicians	21.5%
5. Office Clerks, General	19.5%
6. Bill and Account Collectors	18.4%
7. Dental Assistants	17.6%
8. Surveying and Mapping Technicians	12.9%
9. Interviewers, Except Eligibility and Loan	12.8%
10. Cargo and Freight Agents	12.6%
11. Social and Human Service Assistants	9.5%
12. Court Reporters	8.7%
13. Police, Fire, and Ambulance Dispatchers	8.3%
14. Financial Specialists, All Other	8.2%
15. Production, Planning, and Expediting Clerks	8.0%
16. Medical Records and Health Information Technicians	7.9%
17. Librarians	7.6%

Best Conventional Jobs Overall Employing 7.5 Percent or More Workers Age 16–24

Job	Percent Workers Age 16–24	Annual Earnings	Percent Growth	Annual Openings
1. Dental Assistants	17.6%	$33,470	35.8%	16,100
2. Pharmacy Technicians	21.5%	$28,400	30.6%	18,200
3. Cargo and Freight Agents	12.6%	$37,150	23.9%	4,030
4. Bill and Account Collectors	18.4%	$31,310	19.3%	15,690
5. Medical Records and Health Information Technicians	7.9%	$32,350	20.3%	7,030
6. Social and Human Service Assistants	9.5%	$28,200	22.6%	15,390
7. Financial Specialists, All Other	8.2%	$60,980	10.5%	4,320
8. Surveying and Mapping Technicians	12.9%	$37,900	20.4%	2,940
9. Court Reporters	8.7%	$47,700	18.3%	710
10. Librarians	7.6%	$54,500	7.8%	5,450
11. Production, Planning, and Expediting Clerks	8.0%	$42,220	1.5%	7,410
12. Interviewers, Except Eligibility and Loan	12.8%	$28,820	15.6%	9,210
13. Life, Physical, and Social Science Technicians, All Other	23.8%	$43,350	13.3%	3,640
14. Office Clerks, General	19.5%	$26,610	11.9%	77,090
15. Police, Fire, and Ambulance Dispatchers	8.3%	$35,370	17.8%	3,840
16. Receptionists and Information Clerks	22.6%	$25,240	15.2%	48,020
17. Social Science Research Assistants	23.8%	$37,230	17.8%	1,270

The Best Jobs for Each Personality Type with a High Percentage of Workers Age 55 and Over

In the following lists, I sorted the 50 best jobs for each personality type and included only those that employ the highest percentage of workers age 55 and over. Workers in this age bracket make up roughly 15 percent of the workforce. I included occupations in the lists if the percentage of workers 55 and over was 20 percent or higher.

One use for these lists is to help you identify jobs that might be interesting to you as you decide to change careers or approach retirement. Some jobs are on the lists because they are attractive to older workers wanting part-time work to supplement their retirement income—for example, Real Estate Sales Agents. Other occupations on the lists, such as several jobs in writing (Artistic), medicine and science (Investigative), counseling (Social), and college teaching (several personality types), take many years of training and experience. People who are established in such careers often have many incentives to continue working at ages when workers in other fields are ready to retire. These jobs also may not be as physically demanding as some other jobs, especially compared to those linked to the Realistic personality type, and therefore may be easier for older workers to perform.

Realistic Jobs with the Highest Percentage of Workers Age 55 and Over

Job	Percent Workers Age 55 and Over
1. Construction and Building Inspectors	40.1%
2. Transportation Inspectors	31.3%
3. Medical Equipment Repairers	29.3%
4. Maintenance and Repair Workers, General	24.6%
5. Business Operations Specialists, All Other	24.2%
6. Heavy and Tractor-Trailer Truck Drivers	24.1%
7. Medical and Clinical Laboratory Technicians	23.4%
8. Medical and Clinical Laboratory Technologists	23.4%
9. Water and Wastewater Treatment Plant and System Operators	23.1%
10. Captains, Mates, and Pilots of Water Vessels	22.8%
11. Civil Engineering Technicians	22.5%
12. Environmental Engineering Technicians	22.5%
13. Cartographers and Photogrammetrists	22.3%
14. Surveyors	22.3%
15. Operating Engineers and Other Construction Equipment Operators	21.9%
16. Civil Engineers	21.8%
17. Industrial Machinery Mechanics	21.6%

Realistic Jobs with the Highest Percentage of Workers Age 55 and Over

Job	Percent Workers Age 55 and Over
18. Physical Scientists, All Other	21.5%
19. Engineers, All Other	21.4%
20. Architectural and Civil Drafters	20.5%

Best Realistic Jobs Overall Employing 20 Percent or More Workers Age 55 and Over

Job	Percent Workers Age 55 and Over	Annual Earnings	Percent Growth	Annual Openings
1. Civil Engineers	21.8%	$77,560	24.3%	11,460
2. Business Operations Specialists, All Other	24.2%	$62,450	11.5%	36,830
3. Captains, Mates, and Pilots of Water Vessels	22.8%	$64,180	17.3%	1,950
4. Construction and Building Inspectors	40.1%	$52,360	16.8%	3,970
5. Medical and Clinical Laboratory Technologists	23.4%	$56,130	11.9%	5,330
6. Transportation Inspectors	31.3%	$57,640	18.3%	1,130
7. Engineers, All Other	21.4%	$90,270	6.7%	5,020
8. Cartographers and Photogrammetrists	22.3%	$54,510	26.8%	640
9. Heavy and Tractor-Trailer Truck Drivers	24.1%	$37,770	12.9%	55,460
10. Medical Equipment Repairers	29.3%	$44,490	27.2%	2,320
11. Water and Wastewater Treatment Plant and System Operators	23.1%	$40,770	19.8%	4,690
12. Civil Engineering Technicians	22.5%	$46,290	16.9%	3,280
13. Surveyors	22.3%	$54,880	14.9%	2,330
14. Environmental Engineering Technicians	22.5%	$43,390	30.1%	1,040
15. Operating Engineers and Other Construction Equipment Operators	21.9%	$40,400	12.0%	11,820
16. Medical and Clinical Laboratory Technicians	23.4%	$36,280	16.1%	5,460
17. Physical Scientists, All Other	21.5%	$94,780	11.1%	1,010
18. Industrial Machinery Mechanics	21.6%	$45,420	7.3%	6,240
19. Maintenance and Repair Workers, General	24.6%	$34,730	10.9%	35,750
20. Architectural and Civil Drafters	20.5%	$46,430	9.1%	3,620

Investigative Jobs with the Highest Percentage
of Workers Age 55 and Over

Job	Percent Workers Age 55 and Over
1. Clinical, Counseling, and School Psychologists	41.9%
2. Industrial-Organizational Psychologists	41.9%
3. Psychologists, All Other	41.9%
4. Orthodontists	36.1%
5. Dentists, General	36.1%
6. Prosthodontists	36.1%
7. Nuclear Engineers	34.3%
8. Physicists	33.8%
9. Urban and Regional Planners	33.8%
10. Management Analysts	32.3%
11. Optometrists	30.6%
12. Engineering Teachers, Postsecondary	30.1%
13. Audiologists	28.7%
14. Physicians and Surgeons	26.3%
15. Environmental Scientists and Specialists, Including Health	24.6%
16. Geoscientists, Except Hydrologists and Geographers	24.6%
17. Compliance Officers	23.2%
18. Pharmacists	23.2%
19. Industrial Engineers	23.0%
20. Aerospace Engineers	22.0%
21. Engineers, All Other	21.4%

Best Investigative Jobs Overall Employing
20 Percent or More Workers Age 55 and Over

Job	Percent Workers Age 55 and Over	Annual Earnings	Percent Growth	Annual Openings
1. Physicians and Surgeons	26.3%	$165,279	21.8%	26,050
2. Pharmacists	23.2%	$111,570	17.0%	10,580
3. Management Analysts	32.3%	$78,160	23.9%	30,650
4. Dentists, General	36.1%	$141,040	15.3%	5,180
5. Compliance Officers	23.2%	$58,720	31.0%	10,850
6. Optometrists	30.6%	$94,990	24.4%	2,010
7. Prosthodontists	36.1%	$118,400	27.7%	30
8. Orthodontists	36.1%	$166,500+	19.8%	360

Best Investigative Jobs Overall Employing 20 Percent or More Workers Age 55 and Over

Job	Percent Workers Age 55 and Over	Annual Earnings	Percent Growth	Annual Openings
9. Environmental Scientists and Specialists, Including Health	24.6%	$61,700	27.9%	4,840
10. Physicists	33.8%	$106,370	15.9%	690
11. Geoscientists, Except Hydrologists and Geographers	24.6%	$82,500	17.5%	1,540
12. Industrial Engineers	23.0%	$76,100	14.2%	8,540
13. Industrial-Organizational Psychologists	41.9%	$87,330	26.3%	130
14. Aerospace Engineers	22.0%	$97,480	10.4%	2,230
15. Engineers, All Other	21.4%	$90,270	6.7%	5,020
16. Audiologists	28.7%	$66,660	25.0%	580
17. Engineering Teachers, Postsecondary	30.1%	$89,670	15.1%	1,000
18. Clinical, Counseling, and School Psychologists	41.9%	$66,810	11.1%	5,990
19. Urban and Regional Planners	33.8%	$63,040	19.0%	1,470
20. Nuclear Engineers	34.3%	$99,920	10.9%	540
21. Psychologists, All Other	41.9%	$89,900	14.4%	680

Artistic Jobs with the Highest Percentage of Workers Age 55 and Over

Job	Percent Workers Age 55 and Over
1. Museum Technicians and Conservators	39.0%
2. Multimedia Artists and Animators	35.0%
3. Art Directors	35.0%
4. Astronomers	33.8%
5. Music Directors and Composers	32.3%
6. Writers and Authors	31.9%
7. Architecture Teachers, Postsecondary	30.1%
8. Art, Drama, and Music Teachers, Postsecondary	30.1%
9. Communications Teachers, Postsecondary	30.1%
10. Foreign Language and Literature Teachers, Postsecondary	30.1%
11. English Language and Literature Teachers, Postsecondary	30.1%
12. Education Teachers, Postsecondary	30.1%
13. Philosophy and Religion Teachers, Postsecondary	30.1%
14. Technical Writers	28.6%
15. Landscape Architects	25.5%

(continued)

(continued)

Artistic Jobs with the Highest Percentage of Workers Age 55 and Over

Job	Percent Workers Age 55 and Over
16. Architects, Except Landscape and Naval	25.5%
17. Secondary School Teachers, Except Special and Career/Technical Education	24.8%
18. Substance Abuse and Behavioral Disorder Counselors	24.4%
19. Marriage and Family Therapists	24.4%
20. Self-Enrichment Education Teachers	24.1%
21. Adult Basic and Secondary Education and Literacy Teachers and Instructors	24.1%
22. Editors	23.7%
23. Interpreters and Translators	23.6%
24. Middle School Teachers, Except Special and Career/Technical Education	23.4%
25. Public Relations and Fundraising Managers	23.4%
26. Elementary School Teachers, Except Special Education	23.4%
27. Special Education Teachers, Middle School	22.4%
28. Advertising and Promotions Managers	21.0%
29. Photographers	20.9%
30. Architectural and Civil Drafters	20.5%

Best Artistic Jobs Overall Employing 20 Percent or More Workers Age 55 and Over

Job	Percent Workers Age 55 and Over	Annual Earnings	Percent Growth	Annual Openings
1. Architects, Except Landscape and Naval	25.5%	$72,550	16.2%	4,680
2. Elementary School Teachers, Except Special Education	23.4%	$51,660	15.8%	59,650
3. Special Education Teachers, Middle School	22.4%	$53,440	18.1%	4,410
4. Writers and Authors	31.9%	$55,420	14.8%	5,420
5. Middle School Teachers, Except Special and Career/Technical Education	23.4%	$51,960	15.3%	25,110
6. Technical Writers	28.6%	$63,280	18.2%	1,680
7. Self-Enrichment Education Teachers	24.1%	$36,340	32.0%	12,030
8. Art, Drama, and Music Teachers, Postsecondary	30.1%	$62,040	15.1%	2,500
9. Landscape Architects	25.5%	$62,090	19.7%	980
10. Astronomers	33.8%	$87,260	16.0%	70
11. English Language and Literature Teachers, Postsecondary	30.1%	$60,400	15.1%	2,000
12. Public Relations and Fundraising Managers	23.4%	$91,810	12.9%	2,060

Best Artistic Jobs Overall Employing 20 Percent or More Workers Age 55 and Over

Job	Percent Workers Age 55 and Over	Annual Earnings	Percent Growth	Annual Openings
13. Substance Abuse and Behavioral Disorder Counselors	24.4%	$38,120	21.0%	3,550
14. Art Directors	35.0%	$80,630	11.7%	2,870
15. Education Teachers, Postsecondary	30.1%	$59,140	15.1%	1,800
16. Adult Basic and Secondary Education and Literacy Teachers and Instructors	24.1%	$46,530	15.1%	2,920
17. Architecture Teachers, Postsecondary	30.1%	$73,500	15.1%	200
18. Interpreters and Translators	23.6%	$43,300	22.2%	2,340
19. Philosophy and Religion Teachers, Postsecondary	30.1%	$62,330	15.1%	600
20. Secondary School Teachers, Except Special and Career/Technical Education	24.8%	$53,230	8.9%	41,240
21. Communications Teachers, Postsecondary	30.1%	$60,300	15.1%	800
22. Multimedia Artists and Animators	35.0%	$58,510	14.1%	2,890
23. Foreign Language and Literature Teachers, Postsecondary	30.1%	$59,080	15.1%	900
24. Advertising and Promotions Managers	21.0%	$83,890	−1.7%	1,050
25. Museum Technicians and Conservators	39.0%	$37,310	25.5%	610
26. Architectural and Civil Drafters	20.5%	$46,430	9.1%	3,620
27. Photographers	20.9%	$29,130	11.5%	4,800
28. Editors	23.7%	$51,470	−0.3%	3,390
29. Marriage and Family Therapists	24.4%	$45,720	14.4%	950
30. Music Directors and Composers	32.3%	$45,970	9.9%	1,620

Social Jobs with the Highest Percentage of Workers Age 55 and Over

Job	Percent Workers Age 55 and Over
1. Instructional Coordinators	31.9%
2. Agricultural Sciences Teachers, Postsecondary	30.1%
3. Art, Drama, and Music Teachers, Postsecondary	30.1%
4. Atmospheric, Earth, Marine, and Space Sciences Teachers, Postsecondary	30.1%
5. Biological Science Teachers, Postsecondary	30.1%
6. Business Teachers, Postsecondary	30.1%
7. Chemistry Teachers, Postsecondary	30.1%

(continued)

(continued)

Social Jobs with the Highest Percentage of Workers Age 55 and Over

Job	Percent Workers Age 55 and Over
8. Computer Science Teachers, Postsecondary	30.1%
9. Economics Teachers, Postsecondary	30.1%
10. Education Teachers, Postsecondary	30.1%
11. English Language and Literature Teachers, Postsecondary	30.1%
12. Health Specialties Teachers, Postsecondary	30.1%
13. Law Teachers, Postsecondary	30.1%
14. Mathematical Science Teachers, Postsecondary	30.1%
15. Nursing Instructors and Teachers, Postsecondary	30.1%
16. Physics Teachers, Postsecondary	30.1%
17. Political Science Teachers, Postsecondary	30.1%
18. Psychology Teachers, Postsecondary	30.1%
19. Vocational Education Teachers, Postsecondary	30.1%
20. Occupational Therapy Assistants	26.8%
21. Physicians and Surgeons	26.3%
22. Respiratory Therapists	24.6%
23. Mental Health Counselors	24.4%
24. Rehabilitation Counselors	24.4%
25. Athletic Trainers	24.1%
26. Self-Enrichment Education Teachers	24.1%
27. Elementary School Teachers, Except Special Education	23.4%
28. Middle School Teachers, Except Special and Career/Technical Education	23.4%
29. Compliance Officers	23.2%
30. Registered Nurses	23.2%
31. Licensed Practical and Licensed Vocational Nurses	22.7%
32. Special Education Teachers, Middle School	22.4%
33. Healthcare Social Workers	20.6%
34. Mental Health and Substance Abuse Social Workers	20.6%
35. Chiropractors	20.4%

Best Social Jobs Overall Employing 20 Percent or More Workers Age 55 and Over

Job	Percent Workers Age 55 and Over	Annual Earnings	Percent Growth	Annual Openings
1. Physicians and Surgeons	26.3%	$165,279	21.8%	26,050
2. Registered Nurses	23.2%	$64,690	22.2%	103,900
3. Compliance Officers	23.2%	$58,720	31.0%	10,850
4. Health Specialties Teachers, Postsecondary	30.1%	$85,270	15.1%	4,000
5. Instructional Coordinators	31.9%	$58,830	23.2%	6,060
6. Self-Enrichment Education Teachers	24.1%	$36,340	32.0%	12,030
7. Business Teachers, Postsecondary	30.1%	$73,760	15.1%	2,000
8. Elementary School Teachers, Except Special Education	23.4%	$51,660	15.8%	59,650
9. Healthcare Social Workers	20.6%	$47,230	22.4%	6,590
10. Licensed Practical and Licensed Vocational Nurses	22.7%	$40,380	20.6%	39,130
11. Chiropractors	20.4%	$67,200	19.5%	1,820
12. Middle School Teachers, Except Special and Career/Technical Education	23.4%	$51,960	15.3%	25,110
13. Respiratory Therapists	24.6%	$54,280	20.9%	4,140
14. Biological Science Teachers, Postsecondary	30.1%	$72,700	15.1%	1,700
15. Law Teachers, Postsecondary	30.1%	$94,260	15.1%	400
16. Mental Health Counselors	24.4%	$38,150	24.0%	5,010
17. Art, Drama, and Music Teachers, Postsecondary	30.1%	$62,040	15.1%	2,500
18. Economics Teachers, Postsecondary	30.1%	$83,370	15.1%	400
19. Special Education Teachers, Middle School	22.4%	$53,440	18.1%	4,410
20. Mental Health and Substance Abuse Social Workers	20.6%	$38,600	19.5%	6,130
21. English Language and Literature Teachers, Postsecondary	30.1%	$60,400	15.1%	2,000
22. Computer Science Teachers, Postsecondary	30.1%	$70,300	15.1%	1,000
23. Occupational Therapy Assistants	26.8%	$51,010	29.8%	1,180
24. Physics Teachers, Postsecondary	30.1%	$77,610	15.1%	400
25. Athletic Trainers	24.1%	$41,600	36.9%	1,150
26. Atmospheric, Earth, Marine, and Space Sciences Teachers, Postsecondary	30.1%	$82,840	15.1%	300
27. Psychology Teachers, Postsecondary	30.1%	$67,330	15.1%	1,000
28. Agricultural Sciences Teachers, Postsecondary	30.1%	$78,370	15.1%	300
29. Chemistry Teachers, Postsecondary	30.1%	$70,520	15.1%	600

(continued)

(continued)

Best Social Jobs Overall Employing 20 Percent or More Workers Age 55 and Over

Job	Percent Workers Age 55 and Over	Annual Earnings	Percent Growth	Annual Openings
30. Nursing Instructors and Teachers, Postsecondary	30.1%	$62,390	15.1%	1,500
31. Political Science Teachers, Postsecondary	30.1%	$70,540	15.1%	500
32. Education Teachers, Postsecondary	30.1%	$59,140	15.1%	1,800
33. Mathematical Science Teachers, Postsecondary	30.1%	$65,710	15.1%	1,000
34. Rehabilitation Counselors	24.4%	$32,350	18.9%	5,070
35. Vocational Education Teachers, Postsecondary	30.1%	$48,210	15.1%	4,000

Enterprising Jobs with the Highest Percentage of Workers Age 55 and Over

Job	Percent Workers Age 55 and Over
1. Farmers, Ranchers, and Other Agricultural Managers	54.9%
2. Real Estate Sales Agents	35.7%
3. Chief Executives	35.5%
4. Property, Real Estate, and Community Association Managers	35.4%
5. Education Administrators, Elementary and Secondary School	32.2%
6. Administrative Services Managers	31.9%
7. Writers and Authors	31.9%
8. Social and Community Service Managers	30.8%
9. Lawyers	29.4%
10. Architectural and Engineering Managers	28.8%
11. Medical and Health Services Managers	28.7%
12. Insurance Sales Agents	27.7%
13. Managers, All Other	25.1%
14. Construction Managers	24.6%
15. Business Operations Specialists, All Other	24.2%
16. Personal Financial Advisors	24.1%
17. Natural Sciences Managers	23.9%
18. First-Line Supervisors of Non-Retail Sales Workers	23.7%
19. First-Line Supervisors of Office and Administrative Support Workers	23.6%
20. Public Relations and Fundraising Managers	23.4%
21. First-Line Supervisors of Mechanics, Installers, and Repairers	23.2%
22. Registered Nurses	23.2%

Enterprising Jobs with the Highest Percentage of Workers Age 55 and Over

Job	Percent Workers Age 55 and Over
23. Compensation and Benefits Managers	22.9%
24. Training and Development Managers	22.9%
25. Human Resources Managers	22.9%
26. Captains, Mates, and Pilots of Water Vessels	22.8%
27. Sales Representatives, Wholesale and Manufacturing, Technical and Scientific Products	21.6%
28. Securities, Commodities, and Financial Services Sales Agents	21.1%
29. Supervisors of Construction and Extraction Workers	21.0%
30. General and Operations Managers	20.8%

Best Enterprising Jobs Overall Employing 20 Percent or More Workers Age 55 and Over

Job	Percent Workers Age 55 and Over	Annual Earnings	Percent Growth	Annual Openings
1. Lawyers	29.4%	$112,760	13.0%	24,040
2. Registered Nurses	23.2%	$64,690	22.2%	103,900
3. Construction Managers	24.6%	$83,860	17.2%	13,770
4. Medical and Health Services Managers	28.7%	$84,270	16.0%	9,940
5. Managers, All Other	25.1%	$96,450	7.3%	29,750
6. Natural Sciences Managers	23.9%	$116,020	15.4%	2,010
7. Supervisors of Construction and Extraction Workers	21.0%	$58,680	15.4%	24,220
8. General and Operations Managers	20.8%	$94,400	–0.1%	50,220
9. Personal Financial Advisors	24.1%	$64,750	30.1%	8,530
10. Business Operations Specialists, All Other	24.2%	$62,450	11.5%	36,830
11. Sales Representatives, Wholesale and Manufacturing, Technical and Scientific Products	21.6%	$73,710	9.7%	14,230
12. Administrative Services Managers	31.9%	$77,890	12.5%	8,660
13. Public Relations and Fundraising Managers	23.4%	$91,810	12.9%	2,060
14. Chief Executives	35.5%	$165,080	–1.4%	11,250
15. Education Administrators, Elementary and Secondary School	32.2%	$86,970	8.6%	8,880
16. First-Line Supervisors of Office and Administrative Support Workers	23.6%	$47,460	11.0%	48,900
17. Human Resources Managers	22.9%	$99,180	9.6%	4,140

(continued)

(continued)

Best Enterprising Jobs Overall Employing 20 Percent or More Workers Age 55 and Over

Job	Percent Workers Age 55 and Over	Annual Earnings	Percent Growth	Annual Openings
18. Real Estate Sales Agents	35.7%	$40,030	16.2%	12,830
19. Architectural and Engineering Managers	28.8%	$119,260	6.2%	4,870
20. Securities, Commodities, and Financial Services Sales Agents	21.1%	$70,190	9.3%	12,680
21. Captains, Mates, and Pilots of Water Vessels	22.8%	$64,180	17.3%	1,950
22. Insurance Sales Agents	27.7%	$46,770	11.9%	15,260
23. Training and Development Managers	22.9%	$89,170	11.9%	1,010
24. Writers and Authors	31.9%	$55,420	14.8%	5,420
25. First-Line Supervisors of Non-Retail Sales Workers	23.7%	$68,880	4.8%	12,950
26. Compensation and Benefits Managers	22.9%	$89,270	8.5%	1,210
27. Social and Community Service Managers	30.8%	$57,950	13.8%	4,820
28. First-Line Supervisors of Mechanics, Installers, and Repairers	23.2%	$59,150	4.3%	13,650
29. Farmers, Ranchers, and Other Agricultural Managers	54.9%	$60,750	5.9%	6,490
30. Property, Real Estate, and Community Association Managers	35.4%	$51,480	8.4%	7,800

Conventional Jobs with the Highest Percentage of Workers Age 55 and Over

Job	Percent Workers Age 55 and Over
1. Librarians	41.8%
2. Cost Estimators	30.9%
3. Court, Municipal, and License Clerks	29.3%
4. Bookkeeping, Accounting, and Auditing Clerks	28.9%
5. Executive Secretaries and Executive Administrative Assistants	28.4%
6. Legal Secretaries	28.4%
7. Medical Secretaries	28.4%
8. Secretaries and Administrative Assistants, Except Legal, Medical, and Executive	28.4%
9. Tax Examiners and Collectors, and Revenue Agents	26.4%
10. Managers, All Other	25.1%
11. Interviewers, Except Eligibility and Loan	24.8%
12. Statisticians	24.4%

Conventional Jobs with the Highest Percentage of Workers Age 55 and Over

Job	Percent Workers Age 55 and Over
13. Business Operations Specialists, All Other	24.2%
14. Postal Service Mail Carriers	24.0%
15. Compliance Officers	23.2%
16. Receptionists and Information Clerks	23.2%
17. Office Clerks, General	22.4%
18. Sales Representatives, Wholesale and Manufacturing, Except Technical and Scientific Products	21.6%
19. Accountants and Auditors	21.2%
20. Production, Planning, and Expediting Clerks	21.2%
21. Purchasing Agents, Except Wholesale, Retail, and Farm Products	20.5%
22. Occupational Health and Safety Technicians	20.3%
23. Police, Fire, and Ambulance Dispatchers	20.0%

Best Conventional Jobs Overall Employing 20 Percent or More Workers Age 55 and Over

Job	Percent Workers Age 55 and Over	Annual Earnings	Percent Growth	Annual Openings
1. Accountants and Auditors	21.2%	$61,690	21.6%	49,750
2. Compliance Officers	23.2%	$58,720	31.0%	10,850
3. Cost Estimators	30.9%	$57,860	25.3%	10,360
4. Business Operations Specialists, All Other	24.2%	$62,450	11.5%	36,830
5. Purchasing Agents, Except Wholesale, Retail, and Farm Products	20.5%	$56,580	13.9%	11,860
6. Managers, All Other	25.1%	$96,450	7.3%	29,750
7. Executive Secretaries and Executive Administrative Assistants	28.4%	$43,520	12.8%	41,920
8. Medical Secretaries	28.4%	$30,530	26.6%	18,900
9. Receptionists and Information Clerks	23.2%	$25,240	15.2%	48,020
10. Sales Representatives, Wholesale and Manufacturing, Except Technical and Scientific Products	21.6%	$52,440	6.6%	45,790
11. Statisticians	24.4%	$72,830	13.1%	960
12. Legal Secretaries	28.4%	$41,500	18.4%	8,380
13. Office Clerks, General	22.4%	$26,610	11.9%	77,090

(continued)

(continued)

Best Conventional Jobs Overall Employing 20 Percent or More Workers Age 55 and Over

Job	Percent Workers Age 55 and Over	Annual Earnings	Percent Growth	Annual Openings
14. Bookkeeping, Accounting, and Auditing Clerks	28.9%	$34,030	10.3%	46,040
15. Police, Fire, and Ambulance Dispatchers	20.0%	$35,370	17.8%	3,840
16. Interviewers, Except Eligibility and Loan	24.8%	$28,820	15.6%	9,210
17. Librarians	41.8%	$54,500	7.8%	5,450
18. Tax Examiners and Collectors, and Revenue Agents	26.4%	$49,360	13.0%	3,520
19. Occupational Health and Safety Technicians	20.3%	$45,330	14.4%	520
20. Postal Service Mail Carriers	24.0%	$53,860	−1.1%	10,720
21. Secretaries and Administrative Assistants, Except Legal, Medical, and Executive	28.4%	$30,830	4.6%	36,550
22. Court, Municipal, and License Clerks	29.3%	$34,390	8.2%	4,460
23. Production, Planning, and Expediting Clerks	21.2%	$42,220	1.5%	7,410

The Best Jobs for Each Personality Type with a High Percentage of Self-Employed Workers

About 8 percent of all working people are self-employed or own their own business. This substantial part of our workforce gets little mention in most career books.

The jobs in the lists in this section are selected from the 50 best jobs for each personality type, and all have 8 percent or more self-employed workers. Many jobs in these lists, such as the various types of artists, are held by people who operate one- or two-person businesses and who may also do this work part time. Those in other occupations, such as Carpenters, often work on a per-job basis under the supervision of others.

As you will see from these lists, self-employed people hold a wide range of jobs at all levels of pay and skill. Many are in the arts (Artistic), construction (Realistic), or health-care (Investigative) professions, but many other fields are also represented. Also, while the lists do not include data on age and gender, older workers and women make up a rapidly growing part of the self-employed population. For example, some highly experienced older workers set up consulting and other small businesses following a layoff or as an alternative to full retirement. Large numbers of women are forming small businesses or creating self-employment opportunities as an alternative to traditional employment.

Where the following lists give earnings estimates, keep in mind that these figures are based on a survey that *doesn't include self-employed workers*. The median earnings for self-employed workers in these occupations may be significantly higher or lower.

Realistic Jobs with the Highest Percentage of Self-Employed Workers

Job	Percent Self-Employed Workers
1. Tile and Marble Setters	35.1%
2. Carpenters	32.0%
3. Brickmasons and Blockmasons	27.3%
4. Construction Laborers	21.3%
5. Drywall and Ceiling Tile Installers	18.8%
6. Medical Equipment Repairers	16.4%
7. Heating, Air Conditioning, and Refrigeration Mechanics and Installers	15.5%
8. Audio and Video Equipment Technicians	12.4%
9. Plumbers, Pipefitters, and Steamfitters	12.3%
10. Commercial Pilots	12.0%
11. Refuse and Recyclable Material Collectors	11.8%
12. Physical Scientists, All Other	10.9%
13. Electricians	9.3%
14. Heavy and Tractor-Trailer Truck Drivers	8.3%

Best Realistic Jobs Overall with 8 Percent or More Self-Employed Workers

Job	Percent Self-Employed Workers	Annual Earnings	Percent Growth	Annual Openings
1. Heating, Air Conditioning, and Refrigeration Mechanics and Installers	15.5%	$42,530	28.1%	13,620
2. Plumbers, Pipefitters, and Steamfitters	12.3%	$46,660	15.3%	17,550
3. Commercial Pilots	12.0%	$67,500	18.5%	2,060
4. Construction Laborers	21.3%	$29,280	20.5%	33,940
5. Electricians	9.3%	$48,250	11.9%	25,090
6. Medical Equipment Repairers	16.4%	$44,490	27.2%	2,320
7. Carpenters	32.0%	$39,530	12.9%	32,540
8. Heavy and Tractor-Trailer Truck Drivers	8.3%	$37,770	12.9%	55,460
9. Brickmasons and Blockmasons	27.3%	$46,930	11.5%	5,000
10. Refuse and Recyclable Material Collectors	11.8%	$32,640	18.6%	7,110
11. Tile and Marble Setters	35.1%	$38,110	14.3%	3,070
12. Audio and Video Equipment Technicians	12.4%	$40,540	12.6%	2,370
13. Drywall and Ceiling Tile Installers	18.8%	$37,320	13.5%	3,700
14. Physical Scientists, All Other	10.9%	$94,780	11.1%	1,010

Investigative Jobs with the Highest Percentage of Self-Employed Workers

Job	Percent Self-Employed Workers
1. Clinical, Counseling, and School Psychologists	34.1%
2. Industrial-Organizational Psychologists	33.6%
3. Psychologists, All Other	32.8%
4. Orthodontists	28.1%
5. Dentists, General	28.0%
6. Prosthodontists	27.9%
7. Management Analysts	25.8%
8. Optometrists	24.6%
9. Computer Network Architects	19.4%
10. Physicians and Surgeons	11.7%

Best Investigative Jobs Overall with 8 Percent or More Self-Employed Workers

Job	Percent Self-Employed Workers	Annual Earnings	Percent Growth	Annual Openings
1. Physicians and Surgeons	11.7%	$165,279	21.8%	26,050
2. Computer Network Architects	19.4%	$75,660	53.4%	20,830
3. Management Analysts	25.8%	$78,160	23.9%	30,650
4. Optometrists	24.6%	$94,990	24.4%	2,010
5. Dentists, General	28.0%	$141,040	15.3%	5,180
6. Orthodontists	28.1%	$166,500+	19.8%	360
7. Prosthodontists	27.9%	$118,400	27.7%	30
8. Industrial-Organizational Psychologists	33.6%	$87,330	26.3%	130
9. Psychologists, All Other	32.8%	$89,900	14.4%	680
10. Clinical, Counseling, and School Psychologists	34.1%	$66,810	11.1%	5,990

Artistic Jobs with the Highest Percentage of Self-Employed Workers

Job	Percent Self-Employed Workers
1. Writers and Authors	69.4%
2. Art Directors	60.2%
3. Multimedia Artists and Animators	60.1%
4. Photographers	60.1%
5. Hairdressers, Hairstylists, and Cosmetologists	43.5%
6. Music Directors and Composers	36.2%
7. Makeup Artists, Theatrical and Performance	32.1%
8. Fashion Designers	26.8%
9. Commercial and Industrial Designers	26.7%
10. Interior Designers	26.7%
11. Merchandise Displayers and Window Trimmers	26.7%
12. Film and Video Editors	26.3%
13. Graphic Designers	26.3%
14. Camera Operators, Television, Video, and Motion Picture	26.2%
15. Set and Exhibit Designers	26.2%
16. Interpreters and Translators	26.1%
17. Landscape Architects	21.3%
18. Architects, Except Landscape and Naval	21.2%
19. Adult Basic and Secondary Education and Literacy Teachers and Instructors	20.4%
20. Producers and Directors	20.1%
21. Self-Enrichment Education Teachers	17.3%
22. Advertising and Promotions Managers	16.6%
23. Editors	12.1%

Best Artistic Jobs Overall with 8 Percent or More Self-Employed Workers

Job	Percent Self-Employed Workers	Annual Earnings	Percent Growth	Annual Openings
1. Architects, Except Landscape and Naval	21.2%	$72,550	16.2%	4,680
2. Writers and Authors	69.4%	$55,420	14.8%	5,420
3. Self-Enrichment Education Teachers	17.3%	$36,340	32.0%	12,030
4. Hairdressers, Hairstylists, and Cosmetologists	43.5%	$22,760	20.1%	21,950
5. Interior Designers	26.7%	$46,280	19.4%	3,590
6. Landscape Architects	21.3%	$62,090	19.7%	980

(continued)

(continued)

Best Artistic Jobs Overall with 8 Percent or More Self-Employed Workers

Job	Percent Self-Employed Workers	Annual Earnings	Percent Growth	Annual Openings
7. Producers and Directors	20.1%	$68,440	9.8%	4,040
8. Art Directors	60.2%	$80,630	11.7%	2,870
9. Graphic Designers	26.3%	$43,500	12.9%	12,480
10. Multimedia Artists and Animators	60.1%	$58,510	14.1%	2,890
11. Adult Basic and Secondary Education and Literacy Teachers and Instructors	20.4%	$46,530	15.1%	2,920
12. Interpreters and Translators	26.1%	$43,300	22.2%	2,340
13. Photographers	60.1%	$29,130	11.5%	4,800
14. Set and Exhibit Designers	26.2%	$46,680	16.6%	510
15. Advertising and Promotions Managers	16.6%	$83,890	−1.7%	1,050
16. Commercial and Industrial Designers	26.7%	$58,230	9.0%	1,760
17. Editors	12.1%	$51,470	−0.3%	3,390
18. Film and Video Editors	26.3%	$50,930	11.9%	930
19. Fashion Designers	26.8%	$64,530	0.8%	720
20. Music Directors and Composers	36.2%	$45,970	9.9%	1,620
21. Makeup Artists, Theatrical and Performance	32.1%	$38,130	16.9%	90
22. Merchandise Displayers and Window Trimmers	26.7%	$25,960	7.1%	3,220
23. Camera Operators, Television, Video, and Motion Picture	26.2%	$40,390	9.2%	890

Social Jobs with the Highest Percentage of Self-Employed Workers

Job	Percent Self-Employed Workers
1. Chiropractors	44.5%
2. Self-Enrichment Education Teachers	17.3%
3. Coaches and Scouts	16.2%
4. Physicians and Surgeons	11.7%
5. Fitness Trainers and Aerobics Instructors	9.2%
6. Speech-Language Pathologists	9.0%
7. Physical Therapists	8.0%

Best Social Jobs Overall with 8 Percent or More Self-Employed Workers

Job	Percent Self-Employed Workers	Annual Earnings	Percent Growth	Annual Openings
1. Physicians and Surgeons	11.7%	$165,279	21.8%	26,050
2. Physical Therapists	8.0%	$76,310	30.3%	7,860
3. Self-Enrichment Education Teachers	17.3%	$36,340	32.0%	12,030
4. Fitness Trainers and Aerobics Instructors	9.2%	$31,090	29.4%	12,380
5. Coaches and Scouts	16.2%	$28,340	24.8%	9,920
6. Chiropractors	44.5%	$67,200	19.5%	1,820
7. Speech-Language Pathologists	9.0%	$66,920	18.5%	4,380

Enterprising Jobs with the Highest Percentage of Self-Employed Workers

Job	Percent Self-Employed Workers
1. Writers and Authors	69.4%
2. Construction Managers	60.9%
3. Real Estate Sales Agents	58.3%
4. Managers, All Other	57.1%
5. First-Line Supervisors of Landscaping, Lawn Service, and Groundskeeping Workers	50.4%
6. Property, Real Estate, and Community Association Managers	45.9%
7. Agents and Business Managers of Artists, Performers, and Athletes	45.8%
8. First-Line Supervisors of Non-Retail Sales Workers	45.6%
9. First-Line Supervisors of Personal Service Workers	37.8%
10. Personal Financial Advisors	29.3%
11. Lawyers	26.2%
12. Insurance Sales Agents	22.4%
13. Chief Executives	21.6%
14. Producers and Directors	20.1%
15. Supervisors of Construction and Extraction Workers	19.0%
16. Securities, Commodities, and Financial Services Sales Agents	15.4%

Best Enterprising Jobs Overall with 8 Percent or More Self-Employed Workers

Job	Percent Self-Employed Workers	Annual Earnings	Percent Growth	Annual Openings
1. Construction Managers	60.9%	$83,860	17.2%	13,770
2. Lawyers	26.2%	$112,760	13.0%	24,040
3. Supervisors of Construction and Extraction Workers	19.0%	$58,680	15.4%	24,220
4. Managers, All Other	57.1%	$96,450	7.3%	29,750
5. Personal Financial Advisors	29.3%	$64,750	30.1%	8,530
6. Securities, Commodities, and Financial Services Sales Agents	15.4%	$70,190	9.3%	12,680
7. Chief Executives	21.6%	$165,080	−1.4%	11,250
8. Real Estate Sales Agents	58.3%	$40,030	16.2%	12,830
9. Agents and Business Managers of Artists, Performers, and Athletes	45.8%	$63,130	22.4%	1,010
10. First-Line Supervisors of Non-Retail Sales Workers	45.6%	$68,880	4.8%	12,950
11. Insurance Sales Agents	22.4%	$46,770	11.9%	15,260
12. Writers and Authors	69.4%	$55,420	14.8%	5,420
13. First-Line Supervisors of Personal Service Workers	37.8%	$35,290	15.4%	9,080
14. First-Line Supervisors of Landscaping, Lawn Service, and Groundskeeping Workers	50.4%	$41,860	14.9%	5,600
15. Producers and Directors	20.1%	$68,440	9.8%	4,040
16. Property, Real Estate, and Community Association Managers	45.9%	$51,480	8.4%	7,800

Conventional Jobs with the Highest Percentage of Self-Employed Workers

Job	Percent Self-Employed Workers
1. Managers, All Other	57.1%
2. Court Reporters	14.0%
3. Judicial Law Clerks	14.0%
4. Accountants and Auditors	8.1%

Best Conventional Jobs Overall with 8 Percent or More Self-Employed Workers

Job	Percent Self-Employed Workers	Annual Earnings	Percent Growth	Annual Openings
1. Accountants and Auditors	8.1%	$61,690	21.6%	49,750
2. Managers, All Other	57.1%	$96,450	7.3%	29,750
3. Court Reporters	14.0%	$47,700	18.3%	710
4. Judicial Law Clerks	14.0%	$39,780	13.9%	1,080

Best Jobs for Each Personality Type with a High Percentage of Women and of Men

Please don't misunderstand the following lists of best jobs with high percentages of men and women. The lists are not meant to restrict women or men from considering job options—in fact, one reason I include these lists is exactly the opposite. I hope the lists will help people see possibilities that they might not otherwise have considered. For example, I suggest that women browse the lists of jobs that employ high percentages of men. Many of these occupations pay quite well, and women who want to do them and are willing to undertake the education or training should consider them.

To create the lists, I sorted the jobs of each personality type that met the criteria for this book and included only those employing 70 percent or more of women or men. For the Realistic, Investigative, and Enterprising personality types, the list of predominantly male jobs is much longer than the list of predominantly female jobs. For the Social and Conventional personality types, you'll find the opposite to be true. For the Artistic personality type, the lists are roughly equal.

Like the other demographic-based sets of lists, this set includes "best overall" lists sorted by their combined ranking in terms of annual earnings, percent growth, and annual job openings. If you compare the occupations employing a high percentage of women with those employing a high percentage of men, you may notice some distinct differences beyond the obvious. For example, you may notice that the jobs with a high percentage of women are growing somewhat faster than those with a high percentage of men. I've done the math and discovered that the difference is an average growth rate of 18.3 percent for the jobs that employ mostly women versus an average rate of 13.3 percent for the jobs that employ mostly men. The number of annual job openings shows a similar pattern. Occupations with a high percentage of men average 8,491 openings per year, while more than double that number of openings, 18,416, are projected on average for occupations with a high percentage of women.

This discrepancy reflects the trend that men have had more problems than women in adapting to an economy dominated by service and information-based jobs. Many women may simply be better prepared for these jobs, possessing more appropriate skills for the jobs that are now growing rapidly and have more job openings.

On the other hand, you may notice that on average the jobs with a high percentage of men have higher wages (an average of $61,734) than do the jobs with a high percentage of women ($43,529). This gap, although it has been shrinking, suggest that women interested in improving their earnings may want to consider jobs traditionally dominated by men. A longstanding gender imbalance is not always a barrier to women. Some employers are seeking female recruits to counterbalance a traditional male dominance.

Note that some of the jobs listed here as having 100 percent men probably include a few women but have such a small total workforce that the sample queried by the Census Bureau's Current Population Survey did not include any female workers.

Realistic Jobs with the Highest Percentage of Women

Job	Percent Women
1. Surgical Technologists	77.6%
2. Medical and Clinical Laboratory Technicians	71.9%
3. Medical and Clinical Laboratory Technologists	71.9%
4. Cardiovascular Technologists and Technicians	71.1%
5. Radiologic Technologists	71.1%

Best Realistic Jobs Overall Employing 70 Percent or More Women

Job	Percent Women	Annual Earnings	Percent Growth	Annual Openings
1. Radiologic Technologists	71.1%	$54,340	17.2%	6,800
2. Medical and Clinical Laboratory Technologists	71.9%	$56,130	11.9%	5,330
3. Surgical Technologists	77.6%	$39,920	25.3%	4,630
4. Cardiovascular Technologists and Technicians	71.1%	$49,410	24.0%	1,910
5. Medical and Clinical Laboratory Technicians	71.9%	$36,280	16.1%	5,460

Realistic Jobs with the Highest Percentage of Men

Job	Percent Men
1. Captains, Mates, and Pilots of Water Vessels	100.0%
2. Brickmasons and Blockmasons	100.0%
3. Ship Engineers	100.0%
4. Cement Masons and Concrete Finishers	99.6%
5. Heating, Air Conditioning, and Refrigeration Mechanics and Installers	99.4%
6. Operating Engineers and Other Construction Equipment Operators	99.1%
7. Plumbers, Pipefitters, and Steamfitters	99.0%
8. Mobile Heavy Equipment Mechanics, Except Engines	98.6%
9. Electrical Power-Line Installers and Repairers	98.4%
10. Security and Fire Alarm Systems Installers	98.4%
11. Drywall and Ceiling Tile Installers	98.2%
12. Carpenters	98.1%
13. Construction Laborers	97.7%
14. Electricians	97.5%
15. Commercial Pilots	97.4%
16. Airline Pilots, Copilots, and Flight Engineers	97.4%
17. Maintenance and Repair Workers, General	97.3%
18. Industrial Machinery Mechanics	97.0%
19. Tile and Marble Setters	96.6%
20. Heavy and Tractor-Trailer Truck Drivers	96.3%
21. Boilermakers	95.7%
22. Firefighters	95.5%
23. Construction and Building Inspectors	94.4%
24. Surveying and Mapping Technicians	93.5%
25. Refuse and Recyclable Material Collectors	93.2%
26. Water and Wastewater Treatment Plant and System Operators	93.0%
27. Audio and Video Equipment Technicians	91.8%
28. Civil Engineers	91.7%
29. Transportation Inspectors	91.5%
30. Medical Equipment Repairers	89.4%
31. Engineers, All Other	86.4%
32. Police and Sheriff's Patrol Officers	85.4%
33. Civil Engineering Technicians	83.0%
34. Environmental Engineering Technicians	83.0%
35. Surveyors	78.3%
36. Cartographers and Photogrammetrists	78.3%

(continued)

(continued)

Realistic Jobs with the Highest Percentage of Men

Job	Percent Men
37. Architectural and Civil Drafters	75.4%
38. Computer User Support Specialists	74.2%
39. Correctional Officers and Jailers	73.6%

Best Realistic Jobs Overall Employing 70 Percent or More Men

Job	Percent Men	Annual Earnings	Percent Growth	Annual Openings
1. Civil Engineers	91.7%	$77,560	24.3%	11,460
2. Heating, Air Conditioning, and Refrigeration Mechanics and Installers	99.4%	$42,530	28.1%	13,620
3. Firefighters	95.5%	$45,250	18.5%	15,280
4. Plumbers, Pipefitters, and Steamfitters	99.0%	$46,660	15.3%	17,550
5. Computer User Support Specialists	74.2%	$46,260	13.8%	23,460
6. Commercial Pilots	97.4%	$67,500	18.5%	2,060
7. Electricians	97.5%	$48,250	11.9%	25,090
8. Construction Laborers	97.7%	$29,280	20.5%	33,940
9. Construction and Building Inspectors	94.4%	$52,360	16.8%	3,970
10. Police and Sheriff's Patrol Officers	85.4%	$53,540	8.7%	22,790
11. Cartographers and Photogrammetrists	78.3%	$54,510	26.8%	640
12. Ship Engineers	100.0%	$65,880	18.6%	700
13. Water and Wastewater Treatment Plant and System Operators	93.0%	$40,770	19.8%	4,690
14. Captains, Mates, and Pilots of Water Vessels	100.0%	$64,180	17.3%	1,950
15. Engineers, All Other	86.4%	$90,270	6.7%	5,020
16. Boilermakers	95.7%	$54,640	18.8%	810
17. Carpenters	98.1%	$39,530	12.9%	32,540
18. Medical Equipment Repairers	89.4%	$44,490	27.2%	2,320
19. Transportation Inspectors	91.5%	$57,640	18.3%	1,130
20. Civil Engineering Technicians	83.0%	$46,290	16.9%	3,280
21. Heavy and Tractor-Trailer Truck Drivers	96.3%	$37,770	12.9%	55,460
22. Surveyors	78.3%	$54,880	14.9%	2,330
23. Brickmasons and Blockmasons	100.0%	$46,930	11.5%	5,000
24. Environmental Engineering Technicians	83.0%	$43,390	30.1%	1,040
25. Airline Pilots, Copilots, and Flight Engineers	97.4%	$103,210	8.4%	3,250
26. Refuse and Recyclable Material Collectors	93.2%	$32,640	18.6%	7,110

Best Realistic Jobs Overall Employing 70 Percent or More Men

Job	Percent Men	Annual Earnings	Percent Growth	Annual Openings
27. Security and Fire Alarm Systems Installers	98.4%	$38,500	24.8%	2,780
28. Electrical Power-Line Installers and Repairers	98.4%	$58,030	4.5%	4,550
29. Operating Engineers and Other Construction Equipment Operators	99.1%	$40,400	12.0%	11,820
30. Surveying and Mapping Technicians	93.5%	$37,900	20.4%	2,940
31. Maintenance and Repair Workers, General	97.3%	$34,730	10.9%	35,750
32. Correctional Officers and Jailers	73.6%	$39,040	9.4%	14,360
33. Architectural and Civil Drafters	75.4%	$46,430	9.1%	3,620
34. Industrial Machinery Mechanics	97.0%	$45,420	7.3%	6,240
35. Cement Masons and Concrete Finishers	99.6%	$35,450	12.9%	7,640
36. Mobile Heavy Equipment Mechanics, Except Engines	98.6%	$44,830	8.6%	3,770
37. Drywall and Ceiling Tile Installers	98.2%	$37,320	13.5%	3,700
38. Tile and Marble Setters	96.6%	$38,110	14.3%	3,070
39. Audio and Video Equipment Technicians	91.8%	$40,540	12.6%	2,370

Investigative Jobs with the Highest Percentage of Women

Job	Percent Women
1. Audiologists	77.8%
2. Diagnostic Medical Sonographers	71.1%

Best Investigative Jobs Overall Employing 70 Percent or More Women

Job	Percent Women	Annual Earnings	Percent Growth	Annual Openings
1. Audiologists	77.8%	$66,660	25.0%	580
2. Diagnostic Medical Sonographers	71.1%	$64,380	18.3%	1,650

Investigative Jobs with the Highest Percentage of Men

Job	Percent Men
1. Nuclear Engineers	100.0%
2. Mechanical Engineers	95.0%
3. Electronics Engineers, Except Computer	91.3%
4. Electrical Engineers	91.3%
5. Computer Hardware Engineers	90.4%
6. Aerospace Engineers	88.9%
7. Biomedical Engineers	88.2%
8. Engineers, All Other	86.4%
9. Industrial Engineers	82.1%
10. Atmospheric and Space Scientists	80.0%
11. Petroleum Engineers	78.9%
12. Software Developers, Systems Software	78.7%
13. Software Developers, Applications	78.7%
14. Network and Computer Systems Administrators	78.4%
15. Computer Network Architects	77.5%
16. Physicists	75.0%
17. Computer Systems Analysts	72.2%
18. Computer and Information Research Scientists	72.2%
19. Computer Occupations, All Other	71.0%
20. Environmental Scientists and Specialists, Including Health	70.4%
21. Geoscientists, Except Hydrologists and Geographers	70.4%
22. Environmental Engineers	70.0%

Best Investigative Jobs Overall Employing 70 Percent or More Men

Job	Percent Men	Annual Earnings	Percent Growth	Annual Openings
1. Software Developers, Applications	78.7%	$87,790	34.0%	21,840
2. Software Developers, Systems Software	78.7%	$94,180	30.4%	15,340
3. Computer Network Architects	77.5%	$75,660	53.4%	20,830
4. Computer and Information Research Scientists	72.2%	$100,660	24.2%	1,320
5. Computer Systems Analysts	72.2%	$77,740	20.3%	22,280
6. Petroleum Engineers	78.9%	$114,080	18.4%	860
7. Biomedical Engineers	88.2%	$81,540	72.0%	1,490
8. Environmental Engineers	70.0%	$78,740	30.6%	2,790
9. Network and Computer Systems Administrators	78.4%	$69,160	23.2%	13,550
10. Physicists	75.0%	$106,370	15.9%	690
11. Engineers, All Other	86.4%	$90,270	6.7%	5,020
12. Aerospace Engineers	88.9%	$97,480	10.4%	2,230
13. Computer Occupations, All Other	71.0%	$79,240	13.1%	7,260
14. Environmental Scientists and Specialists, Including Health	70.4%	$61,700	27.9%	4,840
15. Computer Hardware Engineers	90.4%	$98,810	3.8%	2,350
16. Geoscientists, Except Hydrologists and Geographers	70.4%	$82,500	17.5%	1,540
17. Industrial Engineers	82.1%	$76,100	14.2%	8,540
18. Nuclear Engineers	100.0%	$99,920	10.9%	540
19. Electronics Engineers, Except Computer	91.3%	$90,170	0.3%	3,340
20. Mechanical Engineers	95.0%	$78,160	6.0%	7,570
21. Electrical Engineers	91.3%	$84,540	1.7%	3,890
22. Atmospheric and Space Scientists	80.0%	$87,780	14.7%	330

Artistic Jobs with the Highest Percentage of Women

Job	Percent Women
1. Kindergarten Teachers, Except Special Education	98.4%
2. Preschool Teachers, Except Special Education	98.4%
3. Hairdressers, Hairstylists, and Cosmetologists	87.0%
4. Special Education Teachers, Middle School	85.0%
5. Recreational Therapists	83.3%
6. Elementary School Teachers, Except Special Education	81.3%
7. Middle School Teachers, Except Special and Career/Technical Education	81.3%
8. Makeup Artists, Theatrical and Performance	78.6%

Best Artistic Jobs Overall Employing 70 Percent or More Women

Job	Percent Women	Annual Earnings	Percent Growth	Annual Openings
1. Elementary School Teachers, Except Special Education	81.3%	$51,660	15.8%	59,650
2. Middle School Teachers, Except Special and Career/Technical Education	81.3%	$51,960	15.3%	25,110
3. Special Education Teachers, Middle School	85.0%	$53,440	18.1%	4,410
4. Hairdressers, Hairstylists, and Cosmetologists	87.0%	$22,760	20.1%	21,950
5. Preschool Teachers, Except Special Education	98.4%	$25,700	19.0%	17,830
6. Kindergarten Teachers, Except Special Education	98.4%	$48,800	15.0%	6,300
7. Makeup Artists, Theatrical and Performance	78.6%	$38,130	16.9%	90
8. Recreational Therapists	83.3%	$39,410	14.6%	1,160

Artistic Jobs with the Highest Percentage of Men

Job	Percent Men
1. Film and Video Editors	85.7%
2. Camera Operators, Television, Video, and Motion Picture	85.7%
3. Architects, Except Landscape and Naval	75.8%
4. Landscape Architects	75.8%
5. Architectural and Civil Drafters	75.4%
6. Astronomers	75.0%
7. Art Directors	73.4%
8. Multimedia Artists and Animators	73.4%
9. Music Directors and Composers	70.4%

Best Artistic Jobs Overall Employing 70 Percent or More Men

Job	Percent Men	Annual Earnings	Percent Growth	Annual Openings
1. Architects, Except Landscape and Naval	75.8%	$72,550	16.2%	4,680
2. Art Directors	73.4%	$80,630	11.7%	2,870
3. Landscape Architects	75.8%	$62,090	19.7%	980
4. Astronomers	75.0%	$87,260	16.0%	70
5. Multimedia Artists and Animators	73.4%	$58,510	14.1%	2,890
6. Architectural and Civil Drafters	75.4%	$46,430	9.1%	3,620
7. Film and Video Editors	85.7%	$50,930	11.9%	930
8. Music Directors and Composers	70.4%	$45,970	9.9%	1,620
9. Camera Operators, Television, Video, and Motion Picture	85.7%	$40,390	9.2%	890

Social Jobs with the Highest Percentage of Women

Job	Percent Women
1. Kindergarten Teachers, Except Special Education	98.4%
2. Preschool Teachers, Except Special Education	98.4%
3. Speech-Language Pathologists	97.7%
4. Dental Hygienists	96.1%
5. Licensed Practical and Licensed Vocational Nurses	91.4%
6. Registered Nurses	90.7%
7. Medical Assistants	90.4%
8. Athletic Trainers	88.9%
9. Special Education Teachers, Middle School	85.0%
10. Occupational Therapists	81.7%
11. Healthcare Social Workers	81.5%
12. Mental Health and Substance Abuse Social Workers	81.5%
13. Elementary School Teachers, Except Special Education	81.3%
14. Middle School Teachers, Except Special and Career/Technical Education	81.3%
15. Physical Therapist Assistants	78.6%
16. Occupational Therapy Assistants	77.8%
17. Instructional Coordinators	77.4%

Best Social Jobs Overall Employing 70 Percent or More Women

Job	Percent Women	Annual Earnings	Percent Growth	Annual Openings
1. Dental Hygienists	96.1%	$68,250	36.1%	9,840
2. Registered Nurses	90.7%	$64,690	22.2%	103,900
3. Occupational Therapists	81.7%	$72,320	25.6%	4,580
4. Instructional Coordinators	77.4%	$58,830	23.2%	6,060
5. Medical Assistants	90.4%	$28,860	33.9%	21,780
6. Elementary School Teachers, Except Special Education	81.3%	$51,660	15.8%	59,650
7. Licensed Practical and Licensed Vocational Nurses	91.4%	$40,380	20.6%	39,130
8. Middle School Teachers, Except Special and Career/Technical Education	81.3%	$51,960	15.3%	25,110
9. Healthcare Social Workers	81.5%	$47,230	22.4%	6,590
10. Physical Therapist Assistants	78.6%	$49,690	33.3%	3,050
11. Occupational Therapy Assistants	77.8%	$51,010	29.8%	1,180
12. Speech-Language Pathologists	97.7%	$66,920	18.5%	4,380
13. Athletic Trainers	88.9%	$41,600	36.9%	1,150
14. Special Education Teachers, Middle School	85.0%	$53,440	18.1%	4,410
15. Preschool Teachers, Except Special Education	98.4%	$25,700	19.0%	17,830
16. Mental Health and Substance Abuse Social Workers	81.5%	$38,600	19.5%	6,130
17. Kindergarten Teachers, Except Special Education	98.4%	$48,800	15.0%	6,300

Social Jobs with the Highest Percentage of Men

Job	Percent Men
1. Coaches and Scouts	84.0%
2. Chiropractors	70.0%

Best Social Jobs Overall Employing 70 Percent or More Men

Job	Percent Men	Annual Earnings	Percent Growth	Annual Openings
1. Coaches and Scouts	84.0%	$28,340	24.8%	9,920
2. Chiropractors	70.0%	$67,200	19.5%	1,820

Enterprising Jobs with the Highest Percentage of Women

Job	Percent Women
1. Registered Nurses	90.7%

Best Enterprising Jobs Overall Employing 70 Percent or More Women

Job	Percent Women	Annual Earnings	Percent Growth	Annual Openings
1. Registered Nurses	90.7%	$64,690	22.2%	103,900

Enterprising Jobs with the Highest Percentage of Men

Job	Percent Men
1. Captains, Mates, and Pilots of Water Vessels	100.0%
2. Supervisors of Construction and Extraction Workers	97.4%
3. First-Line Supervisors of Landscaping, Lawn Service, and Groundskeeping Workers	95.8%
4. Construction Managers	93.6%
5. First-Line Supervisors of Fire Fighting and Prevention Workers	92.3%
6. Architectural and Engineering Managers	91.2%
7. First-Line Supervisors of Mechanics, Installers, and Repairers	90.6%
8. Sales Engineers	90.3%
9. First-Line Supervisors of Police and Detectives	88.0%
10. Farmers, Ranchers, and Other Agricultural Managers	87.1%
11. Police and Sheriff's Patrol Officers	85.4%
12. Air Traffic Controllers	76.7%
13. Chief Executives	75.9%
14. Detectives and Criminal Investigators	74.4%
15. Sales Representatives, Wholesale and Manufacturing, Technical and Scientific Products	73.2%
16. Securities, Commodities, and Financial Services Sales Agents	73.0%
17. Computer and Information Systems Managers	72.3%
18. General and Operations Managers	71.4%

Best Enterprising Jobs Overall Employing 70 Percent or More Men

Job	Percent Men	Annual Earnings	Percent Growth	Annual Openings
1. Computer and Information Systems Managers	72.3%	$115,780	16.9%	9,710
2. Construction Managers	93.6%	$83,860	17.2%	13,770
3. Sales Representatives, Wholesale and Manufacturing, Technical and Scientific Products	73.2%	$73,710	9.7%	14,230
4. General and Operations Managers	71.4%	$94,400	−0.1%	50,220
5. Supervisors of Construction and Extraction Workers	97.4%	$58,680	15.4%	24,220
6. Detectives and Criminal Investigators	74.4%	$68,820	16.6%	4,160
7. Securities, Commodities, and Financial Services Sales Agents	73.0%	$70,190	9.3%	12,680
8. Chief Executives	75.9%	$165,080	−1.4%	11,250
9. Air Traffic Controllers	76.7%	$108,040	13.0%	1,230
10. Architectural and Engineering Managers	91.2%	$119,260	6.2%	4,870
11. Police and Sheriff's Patrol Officers	85.4%	$53,540	8.7%	22,790
12. Sales Engineers	90.3%	$87,390	8.8%	3,500
13. Captains, Mates, and Pilots of Water Vessels	100.0%	$64,180	17.3%	1,950
14. First-Line Supervisors of Police and Detectives	88.0%	$78,260	8.1%	5,050
15. First-Line Supervisors of Landscaping, Lawn Service, and Groundskeeping Workers	95.8%	$41,860	14.9%	5,600
16. First-Line Supervisors of Mechanics, Installers, and Repairers	90.6%	$59,150	4.3%	13,650
17. Farmers, Ranchers, and Other Agricultural Managers	87.1%	$60,750	5.9%	6,490
18. First-Line Supervisors of Fire Fighting and Prevention Workers	92.3%	$68,240	8.2%	3,250

Conventional Jobs with the Highest Percentage of Women

Job	Percent Women
1. Executive Secretaries and Executive Administrative Assistants	96.8%
2. Legal Secretaries	96.8%
3. Medical Secretaries	96.8%
4. Secretaries and Administrative Assistants, Except Legal, Medical, and Executive	96.8%
5. Dental Assistants	96.7%
6. Receptionists and Information Clerks	92.4%
7. Bookkeeping, Accounting, and Auditing Clerks	90.0%

Conventional Jobs with the Highest Percentage of Women

Job	Percent Women
8. Billing and Posting Clerks	89.6%
9. Occupational Health and Safety Technicians	88.9%
10. Medical Records and Health Information Technicians	88.4%
11. Paralegals and Legal Assistants	86.7%
12. Interviewers, Except Eligibility and Loan	84.4%
13. Office Clerks, General	82.2%
14. Librarians	79.0%
15. Pharmacy Technicians	77.6%
16. Court Reporters	76.8%
17. Judicial Law Clerks	76.8%
18. Court, Municipal, and License Clerks	73.3%
19. Tax Examiners and Collectors, and Revenue Agents	72.2%
20. Bill and Account Collectors	71.2%

Best Conventional Jobs Overall Employing 70 Percent or More Women

Job	Percent Women	Annual Earnings	Percent Growth	Annual Openings
1. Paralegals and Legal Assistants	86.7%	$46,680	28.1%	10,400
2. Dental Assistants	96.7%	$33,470	35.8%	16,100
3. Executive Secretaries and Executive Administrative Assistants	96.8%	$43,520	12.8%	41,920
4. Medical Secretaries	96.8%	$30,530	26.6%	18,900
5. Legal Secretaries	96.8%	$41,500	18.4%	8,380
6. Pharmacy Technicians	77.6%	$28,400	30.6%	18,200
7. Bill and Account Collectors	71.2%	$31,310	19.3%	15,690
8. Bookkeeping, Accounting, and Auditing Clerks	90.0%	$34,030	10.3%	46,040
9. Court Reporters	76.8%	$47,700	18.3%	710
10. Billing and Posting Clerks	89.6%	$32,170	15.3%	16,760
11. Medical Records and Health Information Technicians	88.4%	$32,350	20.3%	7,030
12. Receptionists and Information Clerks	92.4%	$25,240	15.2%	48,020
13. Tax Examiners and Collectors, and Revenue Agents	72.2%	$49,360	13.0%	3,520
14. Librarians	79.0%	$54,500	7.8%	5,450
15. Office Clerks, General	82.2%	$26,610	11.9%	77,090
16. Occupational Health and Safety Technicians	88.9%	$45,330	14.4%	520

(continued)

(continued)

Best Conventional Jobs Overall Employing 70 Percent or More Women

Job	Percent Women	Annual Earnings	Percent Growth	Annual Openings
17. Interviewers, Except Eligibility and Loan	84.4%	$28,820	15.6%	9,210
18. Judicial Law Clerks	76.8%	$39,780	13.9%	1,080
19. Secretaries and Administrative Assistants, Except Legal, Medical, and Executive	96.8%	$30,830	4.6%	36,550
20. Court, Municipal, and License Clerks	73.3%	$34,390	8.2%	4,460

Conventional Jobs with the Highest Percentage of Men

Job	Percent Men
1. Surveying and Mapping Technicians	93.5%
2. Cost Estimators	85.6%
3. Detectives and Criminal Investigators	74.4%
4. Sales Representatives, Wholesale and Manufacturing, Except Technical and Scientific Products	73.2%
5. Cargo and Freight Agents	72.2%
6. Computer Occupations, All Other	71.0%
7. Postal Service Mail Carriers	70.3%

Best Conventional Jobs Overall Employing 70 Percent or More Men

Job	Percent Men	Annual Earnings	Percent Growth	Annual Openings
1. Cost Estimators	85.6%	$57,860	25.3%	10,360
2. Computer Occupations, All Other	71.0%	$79,240	13.1%	7,260
3. Detectives and Criminal Investigators	74.4%	$68,820	16.6%	4,160
4. Sales Representatives, Wholesale and Manufacturing, Except Technical and Scientific Products	73.2%	$52,440	6.6%	45,790
5. Postal Service Mail Carriers	70.3%	$53,860	−1.1%	10,720
6. Cargo and Freight Agents	72.2%	$37,150	23.9%	4,030
7. Surveying and Mapping Technicians	93.5%	$37,900	20.4%	2,940

Best Jobs for Each Personality Type with a High Percentage of Urban or Rural Workers

Some people have a strong preference for an urban setting. They want to live and work where there's more energy and excitement, more access to the arts, more diversity, more really good restaurants, and better public transportation. On the other hand, some prefer the open spaces, closeness to nature, quiet, and inexpensive housing of rural locations. If you are strongly attracted to either setting, you'll be interested in the following lists.

For each personality type, I identified urban jobs as those for which 30 percent or more of the workforce is located in the 38 most populous metropolitan areas of the United States. These 38 metro areas—the most populous 10 percent of all U.S. metro areas, according to the Census Bureau—consist primarily of built-up communities, unlike smaller metro areas, which consist of a core city surrounded by a lot of countryside. In the following lists of urban jobs, you'll see a figure called the "urban ratio" for each job. It represents the percentage of the total U.S. workforce for the job that is located in those 38 huge metro areas.

The Census Bureau also identifies 173 nonmetropolitan areas—areas that have no city of 50,000 people and a total population of less than 100,000. For each of the best jobs, I computed the percentage of the total U.S. workforce that is located in nonmetropolitan areas—a figure I call the "rural ratio"—and compiled lists of those jobs with 10 percent or higher.

The "best overall" lists of both urban and rural jobs are ordered by the usual three economic measures: earnings, growth, and openings.

Realistic Jobs with the Highest Percentage of Urban Workers

Job	Urban Ratio
1. Medical Equipment Repairers	50.5%
2. Environmental Engineering Technicians	46.5%
3. Cartographers and Photogrammetrists	46.1%
4. Ship Engineers	39.5%
5. Transportation Inspectors	37.9%
6. Tile and Marble Setters	36.7%
7. Surveyors	33.0%
8. Commercial Pilots	32.6%
9. Physical Scientists, All Other	30.5%

Best Realistic Jobs Overall Employing 30 Percent or More of Urban Workers

Job	Urban Ratio	Annual Earnings	Percent Growth	Annual Openings
1. Commercial Pilots	32.6%	$67,500	18.5%	2,060
2. Medical Equipment Repairers	50.5%	$44,490	27.2%	2,320
3. Surveyors	33.0%	$54,880	14.9%	2,330
4. Environmental Engineering Technicians	46.5%	$43,390	30.1%	1,040
5. Ship Engineers	39.5%	$65,880	18.6%	700
6. Transportation Inspectors	37.9%	$57,640	18.3%	1,130
7. Cartographers and Photogrammetrists	46.1%	$54,510	26.8%	640
8. Physical Scientists, All Other	30.5%	$94,780	11.1%	1,010
9. Tile and Marble Setters	36.7%	$38,110	14.3%	3,070

Realistic Jobs with the Highest Percentage of Rural Workers

Job	Rural Ratio
1. Water and Wastewater Treatment Plant and System Operators	28.1%
2. Electrical Power-Line Installers and Repairers	26.0%
3. Mobile Heavy Equipment Mechanics, Except Engines	18.3%
4. Refuse and Recyclable Material Collectors	18.2%
5. Operating Engineers and Other Construction Equipment Operators	17.4%
6. Industrial Machinery Mechanics	16.0%
7. Surveying and Mapping Technicians	15.3%
8. Cement Masons and Concrete Finishers	13.7%
9. Radiologic Technologists	13.6%
10. Surveyors	13.0%
11. Firefighters	12.9%
12. Civil Engineering Technicians	12.6%
13. Heating, Air Conditioning, and Refrigeration Mechanics and Installers	12.2%
14. Captains, Mates, and Pilots of Water Vessels	11.3%
15. Carpenters	11.2%
16. Brickmasons and Blockmasons	11.1%
17. Police and Sheriff's Patrol Officers	10.7%
18. Medical and Clinical Laboratory Technicians	10.4%
19. Electricians	10.3%
20. Plumbers, Pipefitters, and Steamfitters	10.3%

Best Realistic Jobs Overall Employing 10 Percent or More of Rural Workers

Job	Rural Ratio	Annual Earnings	Percent Growth	Annual Openings
1. Firefighters	12.9%	$45,250	18.5%	15,280
2. Heating, Air Conditioning, and Refrigeration Mechanics and Installers	12.2%	$42,530	28.1%	13,620
3. Radiologic Technologists	13.6%	$54,340	17.2%	6,800
4. Electricians	10.3%	$48,250	11.9%	25,090
5. Plumbers, Pipefitters, and Steamfitters	10.3%	$46,660	15.3%	17,550
6. Police and Sheriff's Patrol Officers	10.7%	$53,540	8.7%	22,790
7. Captains, Mates, and Pilots of Water Vessels	11.3%	$64,180	17.3%	1,950
8. Carpenters	11.2%	$39,530	12.9%	32,540
9. Water and Wastewater Treatment Plant and System Operators	28.1%	$40,770	19.8%	4,690
10. Civil Engineering Technicians	12.6%	$46,290	16.9%	3,280
11. Surveyors	13.0%	$54,880	14.9%	2,330
12. Refuse and Recyclable Material Collectors	18.2%	$32,640	18.6%	7,110
13. Brickmasons and Blockmasons	11.1%	$46,930	11.5%	5,000
14. Operating Engineers and Other Construction Equipment Operators	17.4%	$40,400	12.0%	11,820
15. Electrical Power-Line Installers and Repairers	26.0%	$58,030	4.5%	4,550
16. Surveying and Mapping Technicians	15.3%	$37,900	20.4%	2,940
17. Cement Masons and Concrete Finishers	13.7%	$35,450	12.9%	7,640
18. Medical and Clinical Laboratory Technicians	10.4%	$36,280	16.1%	5,460
19. Industrial Machinery Mechanics	16.0%	$45,420	7.3%	6,240
20. Mobile Heavy Equipment Mechanics, Except Engines	18.3%	$44,830	8.6%	3,770

Investigative Jobs with the Highest Percentage of Urban Workers

Job	Urban Ratio
1. Biomedical Engineers	56.0%
2. Psychologists, All Other	47.9%
3. Audiologists	42.6%
4. Mathematicians	42.4%
5. Biological Scientists, All Other	40.1%
6. Environmental Science and Protection Technicians, Including Health	40.1%
7. Optometrists	36.3%
8. Survey Researchers	34.0%
9. Urban and Regional Planners	33.2%
10. Atmospheric and Space Scientists	32.2%
11. Industrial-Organizational Psychologists	31.0%
12. Diagnostic Medical Sonographers	30.7%

Best Investigative Jobs Overall Employing 30 Percent or More of Urban Workers

Job	Urban Ratio	Annual Earnings	Percent Growth	Annual Openings
1. Optometrists	36.3%	$94,990	24.4%	2,010
2. Biomedical Engineers	56.0%	$81,540	72.0%	1,490
3. Environmental Science and Protection Technicians, Including Health	40.1%	$41,380	28.9%	2,520
4. Biological Scientists, All Other	40.1%	$68,220	18.8%	1,610
5. Mathematicians	42.4%	$99,380	22.5%	150
6. Industrial-Organizational Psychologists	31.0%	$87,330	26.3%	130
7. Survey Researchers	34.0%	$36,050	30.4%	1,340
8. Audiologists	42.6%	$66,660	25.0%	580
9. Diagnostic Medical Sonographers	30.7%	$64,380	18.3%	1,650
10. Psychologists, All Other	47.9%	$89,900	14.4%	680
11. Urban and Regional Planners	33.2%	$63,040	19.0%	1,470
12. Atmospheric and Space Scientists	32.2%	$87,780	14.7%	330

Investigative Jobs with the Highest Percentage of Rural Workers

Job	Rural Ratio
1. Pharmacists	13.5%
2. Veterinarians	12.0%
3. Biological Scientists, All Other	10.9%
4. Compliance Officers	10.9%
5. Clinical, Counseling, and School Psychologists	10.1%
6. Industrial Engineers	10.1%

Best Investigative Jobs Overall Employing 10 Percent or More of Rural Workers

Job	Rural Ratio	Annual Earnings	Percent Growth	Annual Openings
1. Pharmacists	13.5%	$111,570	17.0%	10,580
2. Veterinarians	12.0%	$82,040	33.0%	3,020
3. Compliance Officers	10.9%	$58,720	31.0%	10,850
4. Industrial Engineers	10.1%	$76,100	14.2%	8,540
5. Biological Scientists, All Other	10.9%	$68,220	18.8%	1,610
6. Clinical, Counseling, and School Psychologists	10.1%	$66,810	11.1%	5,990

Artistic Jobs with the Highest Percentage of Urban Workers

Job	Urban Ratio
1. Landscape Architects	58.6%
2. Museum Technicians and Conservators	45.9%
3. Philosophy and Religion Teachers, Postsecondary	44.1%
4. Set and Exhibit Designers	41.6%
5. Astronomers	40.8%
6. Camera Operators, Television, Video, and Motion Picture	40.2%
7. Sociologists	40.2%
8. Art Directors	39.6%
9. Advertising and Promotions Managers	39.0%
10. Communications Teachers, Postsecondary	37.2%
11. Multimedia Artists and Animators	36.4%
12. Recreational Therapists	35.9%
13. Music Directors and Composers	34.4%

(continued)

(continued)

Artistic Jobs with the Highest Percentage of Urban Workers

Job	Urban Ratio
14. Interpreters and Translators	33.7%
15. Writers and Authors	32.9%
16. Commercial and Industrial Designers	32.8%
17. Interior Designers	32.8%
18. Foreign Language and Literature Teachers, Postsecondary	31.9%
19. Architecture Teachers, Postsecondary	31.4%
20. Technical Writers	30.9%

Best Artistic Jobs Overall Employing 30 Percent or More of Urban Workers

Job	Urban Ratio	Annual Earnings	Percent Growth	Annual Openings
1. Technical Writers	30.9%	$63,280	18.2%	1,680
2. Interior Designers	32.8%	$46,280	19.4%	3,590
3. Art Directors	39.6%	$80,630	11.7%	2,870
4. Landscape Architects	58.6%	$62,090	19.7%	980
5. Writers and Authors	32.9%	$55,420	14.8%	5,420
6. Interpreters and Translators	33.7%	$43,300	22.2%	2,340
7. Sociologists	40.2%	$72,360	21.9%	200
8. Astronomers	40.8%	$87,260	16.0%	70
9. Multimedia Artists and Animators	36.4%	$58,510	14.1%	2,890
10. Architecture Teachers, Postsecondary	31.4%	$73,500	15.1%	200
11. Foreign Language and Literature Teachers, Postsecondary	31.9%	$59,080	15.1%	900
12. Advertising and Promotions Managers	39.0%	$83,890	–1.7%	1,050
13. Communications Teachers, Postsecondary	37.2%	$60,300	15.1%	800
14. Philosophy and Religion Teachers, Postsecondary	44.1%	$62,330	15.1%	600
15. Commercial and Industrial Designers	32.8%	$58,230	9.0%	1,760
16. Museum Technicians and Conservators	45.9%	$37,310	25.5%	610
17. Recreational Therapists	35.9%	$39,410	14.6%	1,160
18. Set and Exhibit Designers	41.6%	$46,680	16.6%	510
19. Music Directors and Composers	34.4%	$45,970	9.9%	1,620
20. Camera Operators, Television, Video, and Motion Picture	40.2%	$40,390	9.2%	890

Artistic Jobs with the Highest Percentage of Rural Workers

Job	Rural Ratio
1. Kindergarten Teachers, Except Special Education	16.2%
2. Music Directors and Composers	12.5%
3. Special Education Teachers, Middle School	12.5%
4. Substance Abuse and Behavioral Disorder Counselors	12.2%
5. Adult Basic and Secondary Education and Literacy Teachers and Instructors	11.9%
6. Preschool Teachers, Except Special Education	10.2%

Best Artistic Jobs Overall Employing 10 Percent or More of Rural Workers

Job	Rural Ratio	Annual Earnings	Percent Growth	Annual Openings
1. Special Education Teachers, Middle School	12.5%	$53,440	18.1%	4,410
2. Kindergarten Teachers, Except Special Education	16.2%	$48,800	15.0%	6,300
3. Preschool Teachers, Except Special Education	10.2%	$25,700	19.0%	17,830
4. Substance Abuse and Behavioral Disorder Counselors	12.2%	$38,120	21.0%	3,550
5. Adult Basic and Secondary Education and Literacy Teachers and Instructors	11.9%	$46,530	15.1%	2,920
6. Music Directors and Composers	12.5%	$45,970	9.9%	1,620

Social Jobs with the Highest Percentage of Urban Workers

Job	Urban Ratio
1. Political Science Teachers, Postsecondary	48.7%
2. Economics Teachers, Postsecondary	45.9%
3. Physics Teachers, Postsecondary	45.2%
4. Chiropractors	42.3%
5. Occupational Therapy Assistants	42.0%
6. Athletic Trainers	41.6%
7. Law Teachers, Postsecondary	41.6%
8. Chemistry Teachers, Postsecondary	41.1%
9. Radiation Therapists	38.8%

(continued)

(continued)

Social Jobs with the Highest Percentage of Urban Workers

Job	Urban Ratio
10. Atmospheric, Earth, Marine, and Space Sciences Teachers, Postsecondary	36.7%
11. Psychology Teachers, Postsecondary	35.1%
12. Computer Science Teachers, Postsecondary	33.1%
13. Mathematical Science Teachers, Postsecondary	30.5%

Best Social Jobs Overall Employing 30 Percent or More of Urban Workers

Job	Urban Ratio	Annual Earnings	Percent Growth	Annual Openings
1. Chiropractors	42.3%	$67,200	19.5%	1,820
2. Radiation Therapists	38.8%	$74,980	27.1%	690
3. Law Teachers, Postsecondary	41.6%	$94,260	15.1%	400
4. Occupational Therapy Assistants	42.0%	$51,010	29.8%	1,180
5. Athletic Trainers	41.6%	$41,600	36.9%	1,150
6. Computer Science Teachers, Postsecondary	33.1%	$70,300	15.1%	1,000
7. Economics Teachers, Postsecondary	45.9%	$83,370	15.1%	400
8. Psychology Teachers, Postsecondary	35.1%	$67,330	15.1%	1,000
9. Physics Teachers, Postsecondary	45.2%	$77,610	15.1%	400
10. Chemistry Teachers, Postsecondary	41.1%	$70,520	15.1%	600
11. Mathematical Science Teachers, Postsecondary	30.5%	$65,710	15.1%	1,000
12. Political Science Teachers, Postsecondary	48.7%	$70,540	15.1%	500
13. Atmospheric, Earth, Marine, and Space Sciences Teachers, Postsecondary	36.7%	$82,840	15.1%	300

Social Jobs with the Highest Percentage of Rural Workers

Job	Rural Ratio
1. Kindergarten Teachers, Except Special Education	16.2%
2. Physical Therapist Assistants	14.4%
3. Rehabilitation Counselors	14.0%
4. Mental Health and Substance Abuse Social Workers	13.9%
5. Probation Officers and Correctional Treatment Specialists	13.2%

Social Jobs with the Highest Percentage of Rural Workers

Job	Rural Ratio
6. Special Education Teachers, Middle School	12.5%
7. Speech-Language Pathologists	12.4%
8. Coaches and Scouts	12.3%
9. Mental Health Counselors	12.1%
10. Dental Hygienists	12.0%
11. Vocational Education Teachers, Postsecondary	11.3%
12. Physical Therapists	11.2%
13. Healthcare Social Workers	11.0%
14. Compliance Officers	10.9%
15. Respiratory Therapists	10.7%
16. Instructional Coordinators	10.6%
17. Preschool Teachers, Except Special Education	10.2%

Best Social Jobs Overall Employing 10 Percent or More of Rural Workers

Job	Rural Ratio	Annual Earnings	Percent Growth	Annual Openings
1. Dental Hygienists	12.0%	$68,250	36.1%	9,840
2. Compliance Officers	10.9%	$58,720	31.0%	10,850
3. Physical Therapists	11.2%	$76,310	30.3%	7,860
4. Instructional Coordinators	10.6%	$58,830	23.2%	6,060
5. Coaches and Scouts	12.3%	$28,340	24.8%	9,920
6. Healthcare Social Workers	11.0%	$47,230	22.4%	6,590
7. Physical Therapist Assistants	14.4%	$49,690	33.3%	3,050
8. Speech-Language Pathologists	12.4%	$66,920	18.5%	4,380
9. Preschool Teachers, Except Special Education	10.2%	$25,700	19.0%	17,830
10. Respiratory Therapists	10.7%	$54,280	20.9%	4,140
11. Mental Health and Substance Abuse Social Workers	13.9%	$38,600	19.5%	6,130
12. Mental Health Counselors	12.1%	$38,150	24.0%	5,010
13. Kindergarten Teachers, Except Special Education	16.2%	$48,800	15.0%	6,300
14. Special Education Teachers, Middle School	12.5%	$53,440	18.1%	4,410
15. Rehabilitation Counselors	14.0%	$32,350	18.9%	5,070
16. Probation Officers and Correctional Treatment Specialists	13.2%	$47,200	19.3%	4,180
17. Vocational Education Teachers, Postsecondary	11.3%	$48,210	15.1%	4,000

Enterprising Jobs with the Highest Percentage of Urban Workers

Job	Urban Ratio
1. Training and Development Managers	46.2%
2. Financial Examiners	38.1%
3. Compensation and Benefits Managers	36.5%
4. Air Traffic Controllers	36.2%
5. Writers and Authors	32.9%
6. Agents and Business Managers of Artists, Performers, and Athletes	30.5%

Best Enterprising Jobs Overall Employing 30 Percent or More of Urban Workers

Job	Urban Ratio	Annual Earnings	Percent Growth	Annual Openings
1. Financial Examiners	38.1%	$74,940	41.2%	1,600
2. Air Traffic Controllers	36.2%	$108,040	13.0%	1,230
3. Writers and Authors	32.9%	$55,420	14.8%	5,420
4. Agents and Business Managers of Artists, Performers, and Athletes	30.5%	$63,130	22.4%	1,010
5. Compensation and Benefits Managers	36.5%	$89,270	8.5%	1,210
6. Training and Development Managers	46.2%	$89,170	11.9%	1,010

Enterprising Jobs with the Highest Percentage of Rural Workers

Job	Rural Ratio
1. Education Administrators, Elementary and Secondary School	18.2%
2. First-Line Supervisors of Mechanics, Installers, and Repairers	14.2%
3. Social and Community Service Managers	14.2%
4. First-Line Supervisors of Police and Detectives	13.6%
5. First-Line Supervisors of Landscaping, Lawn Service, and Groundskeeping Workers	13.0%
6. Supervisors of Construction and Extraction Workers	12.8%
7. Medical and Health Services Managers	12.6%
8. Chief Executives	11.7%
9. Captains, Mates, and Pilots of Water Vessels	11.3%
10. Insurance Sales Agents	11.3%
11. First-Line Supervisors of Personal Service Workers	11.1%
12. Detectives and Criminal Investigators	10.9%
13. Police and Sheriff's Patrol Officers	10.7%

Best Enterprising Jobs Overall Employing 10 Percent or More of Rural Workers

Job	Rural Ratio	Annual Earnings	Percent Growth	Annual Openings
1. Medical and Health Services Managers	12.6%	$84,270	16.0%	9,940
2. Supervisors of Construction and Extraction Workers	12.8%	$58,680	15.4%	24,220
3. Detectives and Criminal Investigators	10.9%	$68,820	16.6%	4,160
4. Chief Executives	11.7%	$165,080	–1.4%	11,250
5. Education Administrators, Elementary and Secondary School	18.2%	$86,970	8.6%	8,880
6. Captains, Mates, and Pilots of Water Vessels	11.3%	$64,180	17.3%	1,950
7. Police and Sheriff's Patrol Officers	10.7%	$53,540	8.7%	22,790
8. Insurance Sales Agents	11.3%	$46,770	11.9%	15,260
9. First-Line Supervisors of Mechanics, Installers, and Repairers	14.2%	$59,150	4.3%	13,650
10. First-Line Supervisors of Personal Service Workers	11.1%	$35,290	15.4%	9,080
11. First-Line Supervisors of Landscaping, Lawn Service, and Groundskeeping Workers	13.0%	$41,860	14.9%	5,600
12. First-Line Supervisors of Police and Detectives	13.6%	$78,260	8.1%	5,050
13. Social and Community Service Managers	14.2%	$57,950	13.8%	4,820

Conventional Jobs with the Highest Percentage of Urban Workers

Job	Urban Ratio
1. Actuaries	54.6%
2. Statisticians	40.1%
3. Occupational Health and Safety Technicians	35.3%
4. Judicial Law Clerks	35.1%

Best Conventional Jobs Overall Employing 30 Percent or More of Urban Workers

Job	Urban Ratio	Annual Earnings	Percent Growth	Annual Openings
1. Actuaries	54.6%	$87,650	21.4%	1,000
2. Judicial Law Clerks	35.1%	$39,780	13.9%	1,080
3. Occupational Health and Safety Technicians	35.3%	$45,330	14.4%	520
4. Statisticians	40.1%	$72,830	13.1%	960

Conventional Jobs with the Highest Percentage of Rural Workers

Job	Rural Ratio
1. Police, Fire, and Ambulance Dispatchers	22.4%
2. Court, Municipal, and License Clerks	20.8%
3. Librarians	16.1%
4. Postal Service Mail Carriers	15.9%
5. Surveying and Mapping Technicians	15.3%
6. Pharmacy Technicians	14.6%
7. Medical Records and Health Information Technicians	13.3%
8. Social and Human Service Assistants	12.9%
9. Loan Officers	12.6%
10. Dental Assistants	11.9%
11. Compliance Officers	10.9%
12. Detectives and Criminal Investigators	10.9%
13. Billing and Posting Clerks	10.7%
14. Production, Planning, and Expediting Clerks	10.2%

Best Conventional Jobs Overall Employing 10 Percent or More of Rural Workers

Job	Rural Ratio	Annual Earnings	Percent Growth	Annual Openings
1. Compliance Officers	10.9%	$58,720	31.0%	10,850
2. Dental Assistants	11.9%	$33,470	35.8%	16,100
3. Pharmacy Technicians	14.6%	$28,400	30.6%	18,200
4. Detectives and Criminal Investigators	10.9%	$68,820	16.6%	4,160
5. Loan Officers	12.6%	$56,490	10.1%	6,880
6. Social and Human Service Assistants	12.9%	$28,200	22.6%	15,390

Best Conventional Jobs Overall Employing 10 Percent or More of Rural Workers

Job	Rural Ratio	Annual Earnings	Percent Growth	Annual Openings
7. Billing and Posting Clerks	10.7%	$32,170	15.3%	16,760
8. Medical Records and Health Information Technicians	13.3%	$32,350	20.3%	7,030
9. Librarians	16.1%	$54,500	7.8%	5,450
10. Postal Service Mail Carriers	15.9%	$53,860	−1.1%	10,720
11. Production, Planning, and Expediting Clerks	10.2%	$42,220	1.5%	7,410
12. Surveying and Mapping Technicians	15.3%	$37,900	20.4%	2,940
13. Police, Fire, and Ambulance Dispatchers	22.4%	$35,370	17.8%	3,840
14. Court, Municipal, and License Clerks	20.8%	$34,390	8.2%	4,460

The Best Jobs for Each Personality Type Sorted by Education or Training Required

On average, there's a clear relationship between education and earnings: The more education or training you have, the more you are likely to earn. The lists that follow arrange all the jobs that met my criteria for inclusion in this book (see the Introduction) by level of education, training, and work experience. These are the levels typically required for a new entrant to begin work in each occupation.

You can use these lists in various ways. For example, they can help you identify a job that has higher potential than a job you now hold that requires a similar level of education.

You can also use these lists to figure out additional job possibilities that would open up if you were to get additional training, education, or work experience. For example, maybe you are a high school graduate working in a job associated with the Social personality type. There are many jobs in this field at all levels of education, but especially at higher levels. You can identify the job you're interested in and the related training you need (you'll find more details in Part IV) so you can move ahead while still working in jobs that are well suited to the Social personality type.

These lists should also help you when you're planning your education or training. For example, you might be thinking about a job within the Realistic personality type, but you aren't sure what kind of work you want to do. The lists show that Carpenters need to get long-term on-the-job training and earn an average of $39,530, whereas Operating Engineers and Other Construction Equipment Operators need only moderate-term on-the-job training and earn an average of $40,400. If you want higher earnings without lengthy training, this information might make a difference in your choice.

Within each list, the jobs are ordered by their combined ranking on annual earnings, percent growth, and annual job openings.

The Education Levels

The U.S. Department of Labor recognizes 11 levels of education or training and this book covers 6 personality types, so you might expect to find 66 lists here. Actually, some personality types are not well represented at certain levels of education or training. For example, I found no best jobs for the Investigative personality type that require only short-term or moderate-term on-the-job training. I also found no Realistic best jobs that require a doctoral or professional degree.

Therefore, rather than offer you different sets of lists for each personality type, I decided to create only 11 lists—one for each level of education and training—and combine all the personality types on each list. Next to the name of each job on a list, you can see the one-, two-, or three-letter RIASEC code that indicates the personality type of the job.

You may find an education-personality combination that works for you by considering a secondary personality type. For example, although none of the 31 doctoral-level jobs has Realistic as its primary type, nine of them have Realistic as a secondary type.

Nineteen of the occupations appear on more than one list. For example, the occupation Statisticians appears on two lists because it is linked to two job specializations (O*NET-SOC titles) that usually require a master's degree, Biostatisticians and Statisticians, and one that usually requires only a bachelor's degree, Clinical Data Managers.

Following are the definitions of the training and education levels that I used to construct the lists in this section. Use these descriptions as guidelines that can inform you about what is generally required by the jobs on each list, but understand that you will need to learn more about specific requirements before you make a decision on one career over another.

* **Short-term on-the-job training:** It is possible to work in these occupations and achieve an average level of performance within a few days or weeks through on-the-job training.

* **Moderate-term on-the-job training:** Occupations requiring this type of training can be performed adequately after a one- to twelve-month period of combined on-the-job and informal training. Typically, untrained workers observe experienced workers performing tasks and are gradually moved into progressively more difficult assignments.

- **Long-term on-the-job training:** This training requires more than 12 months of on-the-job training or combined work experience and formal classroom instruction. This includes occupations that use formal apprenticeships for training workers that may take up to four years. It also includes intensive occupation-specific, employer-sponsored training, such as police academies. Furthermore, it includes occupations that require natural talent that must be developed over many years.

- **Work experience in a related occupation:** This type of job requires experience in a related occupation. For example, police detectives are selected based on their experience as police patrol officers.

- **Postsecondary vocational training:** This requirement can vary from training that involves a few months to usually less than one year. In a few instances, as many as four years of training may be required.

- **Associate degree:** This degree usually requires two years of full-time academic work beyond high school.

- **Bachelor's degree:** This degree requires approximately four to five years of full-time academic work beyond high school.

- **Work experience plus degree:** Many jobs in this category are management-related and require some experience in a related nonmanagerial position. Others require completion of a specific formal training program.

- **Master's degree:** Completion of a master's degree usually requires one to two years of full-time study beyond the bachelor's degree.

- **Doctoral degree:** This degree normally requires two or more years of full-time academic work beyond the bachelor's degree.

- **First professional degree:** This type of degree normally requires a minimum of two years of education beyond the bachelor's degree and frequently requires three years.

Another Warning About the Data

I warned you in the introduction to use caution in interpreting the data in this book, and I want to do it again here. The occupational data I use is the most accurate available anywhere, but it has its limitations. The education or training requirements for entry into a job are those typically required as a minimum, but some people working in those jobs may have considerably more or different credentials. For example, although a bachelor's degree is considered the usual requirement for Construction Managers, more than one-third of the people working in this occupation have no formal education beyond high school. On the other hand, Fitness Trainers and Aerobics Instructors usually need to have completed only postsecondary vocational training, but more than half of these workers have college degrees.

You also need to be cautious about assuming that more education or training always leads to higher income. It is true that people with jobs that require long-term on-the-job training typically earn more than people with jobs that require short-term on-the-job training. (For the jobs in this book, the average annual difference is $19,082.) However, some people with short-term on-the-job training earn more than the average for the highest-paying occupations listed in this book; furthermore, some people with long-term on-the-job training earn much less than the average shown in this book—this is particularly true of people just beginning in these careers.

So as you browse the following lists, please use them as a way to be encouraged rather than discouraged. Education and training are very important for success in the labor market of the future, but so are ability, drive, initiative, and—yes—luck.

Having said this, I encourage you to get as much education and training as you can. You used to be able to get your schooling and then close the schoolbooks forever, but this isn't a good attitude to have now. You will probably need to continue learning new things throughout your working life. This can be done by going back to school, which is a good thing for many people. But other workers may learn through workshops, adult education programs, certification programs, employer training, professional conferences, Internet training, or reading related books and magazines. Upgrading your computer skills—and other technical skills—is particularly important in our rapidly changing workplace, and you avoid doing so at your peril.

Best Jobs Requiring Short-Term On-the-Job Training

Job	Personality Code	Annual Earnings	Percent Growth	Annual Openings
1. Bill and Account Collectors	CE	$31,310	19.3%	15,690
2. Refuse and Recyclable Material Collectors	RC	$32,640	18.6%	7,110
3. Office Clerks, General	CER	$26,610	11.9%	77,090
4. Postal Service Mail Carriers	CR	$53,860	–1.1%	10,720
5. Interviewers, Except Eligibility and Loan	CES	$28,820	15.6%	9,210
6. Receptionists and Information Clerks	CES	$25,240	15.2%	48,020
7. Court, Municipal, and License Clerks	CE	$34,390	8.2%	4,460

Best Jobs Requiring Moderate-Term On-the-Job Training

Job	Personality Code	Annual Earnings	Percent Growth	Annual Openings
1. Heavy and Tractor-Trailer Truck Drivers	RC	$37,770	12.9%	55,460
2. Dental Assistants	CRS	$33,470	35.8%	16,100
3. Customer Service Representatives	SEC	$30,460	17.7%	110,840
4. Medical Assistants	SCR	$28,860	33.9%	21,780
5. Medical Secretaries	CS	$30,530	26.6%	18,900
6. Cargo and Freight Agents	CE	$37,150	23.9%	4,030
7. Construction Laborers	RC	$29,280	20.5%	33,940
8. Pharmacy Technicians	CR	$28,400	30.6%	18,200
9. Bookkeeping, Accounting, and Auditing Clerks	CE	$34,030	10.3%	46,040
10. Maintenance and Repair Workers, General	RCI	$34,730	10.9%	35,750
11. Operating Engineers and Other Construction Equipment Operators	RCI	$40,400	12.0%	11,820
12. Life, Physical, and Social Science Technicians, All Other	RC	$43,350	13.3%	3,640
13. Billing and Posting Clerks	CE	$32,170	15.3%	16,760
14. Surveying and Mapping Technicians	CR	$37,900	20.4%	2,940
15. Correctional Officers and Jailers	REC	$39,040	9.4%	14,360
16. Cement Masons and Concrete Finishers	RE	$35,450	12.9%	7,640
17. Police, Fire, and Ambulance Dispatchers	CRE	$35,370	17.8%	3,840
18. Drywall and Ceiling Tile Installers	RC	$37,320	13.5%	3,700
19. Social and Human Service Assistants	CSE	$28,200	22.6%	15,390
20. Production, Planning, and Expediting Clerks	CE	$42,220	1.5%	7,410
21. Secretaries and Administrative Assistants, Except Legal, Medical, and Executive	CE	$30,830	4.6%	36,550
22. Merchandise Displayers and Window Trimmers	AER	$25,960	7.1%	3,220

Best Jobs Requiring Long-Term On-the-Job Training

Job	Personality Code	Annual Earnings	Percent Growth	Annual Openings
1. Compliance Officers	CEI	$58,720	31.0%	10,850
2. Purchasing Agents, Except Wholesale, Retail, and Farm Products	CE	$56,580	13.9%	11,860
3. Plumbers, Pipefitters, and Steamfitters	RC	$46,660	15.3%	17,550
4. Firefighters	RS	$45,250	18.5%	15,280
5. Heating, Air Conditioning, and Refrigeration Mechanics and Installers	RC	$42,530	28.1%	13,620

(continued)

(continued)

Best Jobs Requiring Long-Term On-the-Job Training

Job	Personality Code	Annual Earnings	Percent Growth	Annual Openings
6. Electricians	RIC	$48,250	11.9%	25,090
7. Police and Sheriff's Patrol Officers	ERS	$53,540	8.7%	22,790
8. Carpenters	RCI	$39,530	12.9%	32,540
9. Air Traffic Controllers	EC	$108,040	13.0%	1,230
10. Claims Adjusters, Examiners, and Investigators	CE	$58,620	7.1%	9,560
11. Coaches and Scouts	SRE	$28,340	24.8%	9,920
12. Boilermakers	RC	$54,640	18.8%	810
13. Producers and Directors	EAC	$68,440	9.8%	4,040
14. Brickmasons and Blockmasons	RCI	$46,930	11.5%	5,000
15. Water and Wastewater Treatment Plant and System Operators	RC	$40,770	19.8%	4,690
16. Interpreters and Translators	AS	$43,300	22.2%	2,340
17. Electrical Power-Line Installers and Repairers	RIC	$58,030	4.5%	4,550
18. Industrial Machinery Mechanics	RIC	$45,420	7.3%	6,240
19. Tile and Marble Setters	RCA	$38,110	14.3%	3,070
20. Audio and Video Equipment Technicians	RIC	$40,540	12.6%	2,370
21. Photographers	AR	$29,130	11.5%	4,800
22. Mobile Heavy Equipment Mechanics, Except Engines	RC	$44,830	8.6%	3,770

Best Jobs Requiring Work Experience in a Related Job

Job	Personality Code	Annual Earnings	Percent Growth	Annual Openings
1. Compliance Officers	CEI	$58,720	31.0%	10,850
2. Managers, All Other	EC	$96,450	7.3%	29,750
3. Supervisors of Construction and Extraction Workers	ERC	$58,680	15.4%	24,220
4. Business Operations Specialists, All Other	CER	$62,450	11.5%	36,830
5. Detectives and Criminal Investigators	ECR	$68,820	16.6%	4,160
6. Computer Occupations, All Other	ICR	$79,240	13.1%	7,260
7. Natural Sciences Managers	EI	$116,020	15.4%	2,010
8. Sales Representatives, Wholesale and Manufacturing, Technical and Scientific Products	EC	$73,710	9.7%	14,230
9. Self-Enrichment Education Teachers	SAE	$36,340	32.0%	12,030
10. Ship Engineers	RCE	$65,880	18.6%	700
11. Captains, Mates, and Pilots of Water Vessels	REC	$64,180	17.3%	1,950

Best Jobs Requiring Work Experience in a Related Job

Job	Personality Code	Annual Earnings	Percent Growth	Annual Openings
12. First-Line Supervisors of Office and Administrative Support Workers	ECS	$47,460	11.0%	48,900
13. Sales Representatives, Services, All Other	EC	$50,620	13.9%	22,810
14. Executive Secretaries and Executive Administrative Assistants	CE	$43,520	12.8%	41,920
15. Computer User Support Specialists	RIC	$46,260	13.8%	23,460
16. First-Line Supervisors of Non-Retail Sales Workers	ECS	$68,880	4.8%	12,950
17. First-Line Supervisors of Police and Detectives	ESC	$78,260	8.1%	5,050
18. Sales Representatives, Wholesale and Manufacturing, Except Technical and Scientific Products	CE	$52,440	6.6%	45,790
19. Construction and Building Inspectors	RCI	$52,360	16.8%	3,970
20. Transportation Inspectors	RCI	$57,640	18.3%	1,130
21. Financial Specialists, All Other	CIE	$60,980	10.5%	4,320
22. First-Line Supervisors of Personal Service Workers	ECS	$35,290	15.4%	9,080
23. First-Line Supervisors of Landscaping, Lawn Service, and Groundskeeping Workers	ERC	$41,860	14.9%	5,600
24. Vocational Education Teachers, Postsecondary	SR	$48,210	15.1%	4,000
25. First-Line Supervisors of Mechanics, Installers, and Repairers	ECR	$59,150	4.3%	13,650
26. First-Line Supervisors of Fire Fighting and Prevention Workers	ER	$68,240	8.2%	3,250
27. Farmers, Ranchers, and Other Agricultural Managers	ERC	$60,750	5.9%	6,490

Best Jobs Requiring Postsecondary Vocational Training

Job	Personality Code	Annual Earnings	Percent Growth	Annual Openings
1. Licensed Practical and Licensed Vocational Nurses	SR	$40,380	20.6%	39,130
2. Business Operations Specialists, All Other	CER	$62,450	11.5%	36,830
3. Computer Occupations, All Other	ICR	$79,240	13.1%	7,260
4. Surgical Technologists	RSC	$39,920	25.3%	4,630
5. Commercial Pilots	RIE	$67,500	18.5%	2,060
6. Fitness Trainers and Aerobics Instructors	SRE	$31,090	29.4%	12,380

(continued)

(continued)

Best Jobs Requiring Postsecondary Vocational Training

Job	Personality Code	Annual Earnings	Percent Growth	Annual Openings
7. Hairdressers, Hairstylists, and Cosmetologists	AES	$22,760	20.1%	21,950
8. Preschool Teachers, Except Special Education	SA	$25,700	19.0%	17,830
9. Real Estate Sales Agents	EC	$40,030	16.2%	12,830
10. Security and Fire Alarm Systems Installers	RC	$38,500	24.8%	2,780
11. Life, Physical, and Social Science Technicians, All Other	RC	$43,350	13.3%	3,640
12. Court Reporters	CE	$47,700	18.3%	710
13. Health Technologists and Technicians, All Other	RIC	$38,460	18.7%	3,200
14. Architectural and Civil Drafters	RCA	$46,430	9.1%	3,620
15. Camera Operators, Television, Video, and Motion Picture	RA	$40,390	9.2%	890
16. Makeup Artists, Theatrical and Performance	AR	$38,130	16.9%	90

Best Jobs Requiring an Associate Degree

Job	Personality Code	Annual Earnings	Percent Growth	Annual Openings
1. Dental Hygienists	SRC	$68,250	36.1%	9,840
2. Registered Nurses	SI	$64,690	22.2%	103,900
3. Paralegals and Legal Assistants	CIE	$46,680	28.1%	10,400
4. Computer Occupations, All Other	ICR	$79,240	13.1%	7,260
5. Physical Therapist Assistants	SRI	$49,690	33.3%	3,050
6. Business Operations Specialists, All Other	CER	$62,450	11.5%	36,830
7. Respiratory Therapists	SIR	$54,280	20.9%	4,140
8. Radiation Therapists	SRC	$74,980	27.1%	690
9. Radiologic Technologists	RS	$54,340	17.2%	6,800
10. Occupational Therapy Assistants	SR	$51,010	29.8%	1,180
11. Legal Secretaries	CE	$41,500	18.4%	8,380
12. Cardiovascular Technologists and Technicians	RIS	$49,410	24.0%	1,910
13. Diagnostic Medical Sonographers	ISR	$64,380	18.3%	1,650
14. Medical and Clinical Laboratory Technologists	IRC	$56,130	11.9%	5,330
15. Interior Designers	AE	$46,280	19.4%	3,590
16. Medical Equipment Repairers	RIC	$44,490	27.2%	2,320
17. Environmental Science and Protection Technicians, Including Health	IRC	$41,380	28.9%	2,520
18. Environmental Engineering Technicians	RIC	$43,390	30.1%	1,040

Best Jobs Requiring an Associate Degree

Job	Personality Code	Annual Earnings	Percent Growth	Annual Openings
19. Medical Records and Health Information Technicians	CE	$32,350	20.3%	7,030
20. Civil Engineering Technicians	RCI	$46,290	16.9%	3,280
21. Health Technologists and Technicians, All Other	RIC	$38,460	18.7%	3,200
22. Life, Physical, and Social Science Technicians, All Other	RC	$43,350	13.3%	3,640
23. Medical and Clinical Laboratory Technicians	RIC	$36,280	16.1%	5,460
24. Fashion Designers	AER	$64,530	0.8%	720
25. Social Science Research Assistants	CI	$37,230	17.8%	1,270

Best Jobs Requiring a Bachelor's Degree

Job	Personality Code	Annual Earnings	Percent Growth	Annual Openings
1. Software Developers, Applications	IRC	$87,790	34.0%	21,840
2. Software Developers, Systems Software	ICR	$94,180	30.4%	15,340
3. Computer Network Architects	ICR	$75,660	53.4%	20,830
4. Computer Systems Analysts	ICR	$77,740	20.3%	22,280
5. Civil Engineers	RIC	$77,560	24.3%	11,460
6. Accountants and Auditors	CEI	$61,690	21.6%	49,750
7. Construction Managers	ERC	$83,860	17.2%	13,770
8. Market Research Analysts and Marketing Specialists	IEC	$60,570	28.1%	13,730
9. Network and Computer Systems Administrators	IRC	$69,160	23.2%	13,550
10. Personal Financial Advisors	ECS	$64,750	30.1%	8,530
11. Financial Analysts	CIE	$74,350	19.8%	9,520
12. Environmental Engineers	IRC	$78,740	30.6%	2,790
13. Biomedical Engineers	IR	$81,540	72.0%	1,490
14. Cost Estimators	CE	$57,860	25.3%	10,360
15. Managers, All Other	EC	$96,450	7.3%	29,750
16. Human Resources Specialists	ESC	$52,690	27.9%	11,230
17. Database Administrators	CI	$73,490	20.3%	4,440
18. Public Relations Specialists	EAS	$52,090	24.0%	13,130
19. Financial Examiners	EC	$74,940	41.2%	1,600
20. Instructional Coordinators	SIA	$58,830	23.2%	6,060
21. Industrial Engineers	ICE	$76,100	14.2%	8,540

(continued)

(continued)

Best Jobs Requiring a Bachelor's Degree

Job	Personality Code	Annual Earnings	Percent Growth	Annual Openings
22. Logisticians	CEI	$70,800	19.5%	4,190
23. Business Operations Specialists, All Other	CER	$62,450	11.5%	36,830
24. Compensation, Benefits, and Job Analysis Specialists	CE	$57,000	23.6%	6,050
25. Computer Occupations, All Other	ICR	$79,240	13.1%	7,260
26. Elementary School Teachers, Except Special Education	SAC	$51,660	15.8%	59,650
27. Architects, Except Landscape and Naval	AI	$72,550	16.2%	4,680
28. Petroleum Engineers	IRC	$114,080	18.4%	860
29. Middle School Teachers, Except Special and Career/Technical Education	SA	$51,960	15.3%	25,110
30. Customer Service Representatives	SEC	$30,460	17.7%	110,840
31. Securities, Commodities, and Financial Services Sales Agents	EC	$70,190	9.3%	12,680
32. Healthcare Social Workers	SI	$47,230	22.4%	6,590
33. Engineers, All Other	IR	$90,270	6.7%	5,020
34. Mechanical Engineers	IRC	$78,160	6.0%	7,570
35. Airline Pilots, Copilots, and Flight Engineers	RCI	$103,210	8.4%	3,250
36. Special Education Teachers, Middle School	SA	$53,440	18.1%	4,410
37. Writers and Authors	AEI	$55,420	14.8%	5,420
38. Secondary School Teachers, Except Special and Career/Technical Education	SAE	$53,230	8.9%	41,240
39. Sales Engineers	ERI	$87,390	8.8%	3,500
40. Technical Writers	AIC	$63,280	18.2%	1,680
41. Aerospace Engineers	IR	$97,480	10.4%	2,230
42. Atmospheric and Space Scientists	IR	$87,780	14.7%	330
43. Landscape Architects	AIR	$62,090	19.7%	980
44. Budget Analysts	CEI	$68,200	15.1%	2,230
45. Social and Community Service Managers	ES	$57,950	13.8%	4,820
46. Kindergarten Teachers, Except Special Education	SA	$48,800	15.0%	6,300
47. Electrical Engineers	IR	$84,540	1.7%	3,890
48. Computer Hardware Engineers	IRC	$98,810	3.8%	2,350
49. Insurance Sales Agents	ECS	$46,770	11.9%	15,260
50. Physical Scientists, All Other	RI	$94,780	11.1%	1,010
51. Credit Analysts	CE	$58,850	15.0%	2,430
52. Electronics Engineers, Except Computer	IR	$90,170	0.3%	3,340

Best Jobs Requiring a Bachelor's Degree

Job	Personality Code	Annual Earnings	Percent Growth	Annual Openings
53. Cartographers and Photogrammetrists	RCI	$54,510	26.8%	640
54. Nuclear Engineers	IRC	$99,920	10.9%	540
55. Probation Officers and Correctional Treatment Specialists	SEC	$47,200	19.3%	4,180
56. Financial Specialists, All Other	CIE	$60,980	10.5%	4,320
57. Loan Officers	CES	$56,490	10.1%	6,880
58. Medical and Clinical Laboratory Technologists	IRC	$56,130	11.9%	5,330
59. Graphic Designers	ARE	$43,500	12.9%	12,480
60. Athletic Trainers	SRI	$41,600	36.9%	1,150
61. Substance Abuse and Behavioral Disorder Counselors	SAI	$38,120	21.0%	3,550
62. Biological Technicians	RIC	$39,020	17.6%	4,190
63. Multimedia Artists and Animators	AI	$58,510	14.1%	2,890
64. Surveyors	RCI	$54,880	14.9%	2,330
65. Statisticians	CI	$72,830	13.1%	960
66. Survey Researchers	ICE	$36,050	30.4%	1,340
67. Property, Real Estate, and Community Association Managers	EC	$51,480	8.4%	7,800
68. Adult Basic and Secondary Education and Literacy Teachers and Instructors	SAE	$46,530	15.1%	2,920
69. Tax Examiners and Collectors, and Revenue Agents	CE	$49,360	13.0%	3,520
70. Museum Technicians and Conservators	RA	$37,310	25.5%	610
71. Commercial and Industrial Designers	AER	$58,230	9.0%	1,760
72. Insurance Underwriters	CEI	$59,290	–4.1%	3,000
73. Recreational Therapists	SA	$39,410	14.6%	1,160
74. Set and Exhibit Designers	AR	$46,680	16.6%	510
75. Editors	AEC	$51,470	–0.3%	3,390
76. Film and Video Editors	AEI	$50,930	11.9%	930
77. Occupational Health and Safety Technicians	CR	$45,330	14.4%	520

Best Jobs Requiring Work Experience Plus Degree

Job	Personality Code	Annual Earnings	Percent Growth	Annual Openings
1. Computer and Information Systems Managers	ECI	$115,780	16.9%	9,710
2. Sales Managers	EC	$98,530	14.9%	12,660
3. Management Analysts	IEC	$78,160	23.9%	30,650
4. Marketing Managers	EC	$112,800	12.5%	5,970
5. Medical and Health Services Managers	ECS	$84,270	16.0%	9,940
6. Financial Managers	EC	$103,910	7.6%	13,820
7. Natural Sciences Managers	EI	$116,020	15.4%	2,010
8. Chief Executives	EC	$165,080	−1.4%	11,250
9. Managers, All Other	EC	$96,450	7.3%	29,750
10. Training and Development Specialists	SAC	$54,160	23.3%	10,710
11. General and Operations Managers	ECS	$94,400	−0.1%	50,220
12. Business Operations Specialists, All Other	CER	$62,450	11.5%	36,830
13. Computer Occupations, All Other	ICR	$79,240	13.1%	7,260
14. Administrative Services Managers	EC	$77,890	12.5%	8,660
15. Architectural and Engineering Managers	ERI	$119,260	6.2%	4,870
16. Human Resources Managers	ESC	$99,180	9.6%	4,140
17. Public Relations and Fundraising Managers	EA	$91,810	12.9%	2,060
18. Detectives and Criminal Investigators	ECR	$68,820	16.6%	4,160
19. Actuaries	CIE	$87,650	21.4%	1,000
20. Education Administrators, Elementary and Secondary School	ESC	$86,970	8.6%	8,880
21. Agents and Business Managers of Artists, Performers, and Athletes	ES	$63,130	22.4%	1,010
22. Art Directors	AE	$80,630	11.7%	2,870
23. Health Technologists and Technicians, All Other	RIC	$38,460	18.7%	3,200
24. Training and Development Managers	ES	$89,170	11.9%	1,010
25. Compensation and Benefits Managers	ECS	$89,270	8.5%	1,210
26. Financial Specialists, All Other	CIE	$60,980	10.5%	4,320
27. Producers and Directors	EAC	$68,440	9.8%	4,040
28. Farmers, Ranchers, and Other Agricultural Managers	ERC	$60,750	5.9%	6,490
29. Music Directors and Composers	AE	$45,970	9.9%	1,620
30. Advertising and Promotions Managers	EAC	$83,890	−1.7%	1,050

Best Jobs Requiring a Master's Degree

Job	Personality Code	Annual Earnings	Percent Growth	Annual Openings
1. Physical Therapists	SIR	$76,310	30.3%	7,860
2. Physician Assistants	SIR	$86,410	39.0%	4,280
3. Computer Systems Analysts	ICR	$77,740	20.3%	22,280
4. Registered Nurses	SI	$64,690	22.2%	103,900
5. Occupational Therapists	SI	$72,320	25.6%	4,580
6. Environmental Scientists and Specialists, Including Health	IRC	$61,700	27.9%	4,840
7. Industrial-Organizational Psychologists	IEA	$87,330	26.3%	130
8. Instructional Coordinators	SIA	$58,830	23.2%	6,060
9. Social Scientists and Related Workers, All Other	ICR	$74,620	22.4%	2,380
10. Operations Research Analysts	ICE	$70,960	22.0%	3,220
11. Political Scientists	IAS	$107,420	19.5%	280
12. Geographers	IRA	$72,800	26.2%	100
13. Geoscientists, Except Hydrologists and Geographers	IR	$82,500	17.5%	1,540
14. Mental Health Counselors	SIA	$38,150	24.0%	5,010
15. Mental Health and Substance Abuse Social Workers	SIA	$38,600	19.5%	6,130
16. Speech-Language Pathologists	SIA	$66,920	18.5%	4,380
17. Psychologists, All Other	ISA	$89,900	14.4%	680
18. Sociologists	IAS	$72,360	21.9%	200
19. Anthropologists and Archeologists	IA	$54,230	28.1%	450
20. Rehabilitation Counselors	SI	$32,350	18.9%	5,070
21. Urban and Regional Planners	IEA	$63,040	19.0%	1,470
22. Librarians	CSE	$54,500	7.8%	5,450
23. Statisticians	CI	$72,830	13.1%	960
24. Financial Specialists, All Other	CIE	$60,980	10.5%	4,320
25. Recreational Therapists	SA	$39,410	14.6%	1,160
26. Marriage and Family Therapists	SAI	$45,720	14.4%	950

Best Jobs Requiring a Doctoral Degree

Job	Personality Code	Annual Earnings	Percent Growth	Annual Openings
1. Medical Scientists, Except Epidemiologists	IRA	$76,700	40.3%	6,620
2. Computer and Information Research Scientists	IRC	$100,660	24.2%	1,320
3. Health Specialties Teachers, Postsecondary	SI	$85,270	15.1%	4,000
4. Biochemists and Biophysicists	IAR	$79,390	37.4%	1,620
5. Engineering Teachers, Postsecondary	SIR	$89,670	15.1%	1,000
6. Physicists	IR	$106,370	15.9%	690
7. Business Teachers, Postsecondary	SEI	$73,760	15.1%	2,000
8. Biological Science Teachers, Postsecondary	SI	$72,700	15.1%	1,700
9. Biological Scientists, All Other	IRA	$68,220	18.8%	1,610
10. Mathematicians	ICA	$99,380	22.5%	150
11. Art, Drama, and Music Teachers, Postsecondary	SA	$62,040	15.1%	2,500
12. Computer Science Teachers, Postsecondary	SIC	$70,300	15.1%	1,000
13. Economics Teachers, Postsecondary	SI	$83,370	15.1%	400
14. English Language and Literature Teachers, Postsecondary	SAI	$60,400	15.1%	2,000
15. Psychology Teachers, Postsecondary	SIA	$67,330	15.1%	1,000
16. Astronomers	IAR	$87,260	16.0%	70
17. Atmospheric, Earth, Marine, and Space Sciences Teachers, Postsecondary	SI	$82,840	15.1%	300
18. Nursing Instructors and Teachers, Postsecondary	SI	$62,390	15.1%	1,500
19. Education Teachers, Postsecondary	SAI	$59,140	15.1%	1,800
20. Mathematical Science Teachers, Postsecondary	SIA	$65,710	15.1%	1,000
21. Physics Teachers, Postsecondary	SI	$77,610	15.1%	400
22. Agricultural Sciences Teachers, Postsecondary	SIR	$78,370	15.1%	300
23. Chemistry Teachers, Postsecondary	SIR	$70,520	15.1%	600
24. Audiologists	IS	$66,660	25.0%	580
25. Political Science Teachers, Postsecondary	SEA	$70,540	15.1%	500
26. Architecture Teachers, Postsecondary	SA	$73,500	15.1%	200
27. Psychologists, All Other	ISA	$89,900	14.4%	680
28. Clinical, Counseling, and School Psychologists	ISA	$66,810	11.1%	5,990
29. Communications Teachers, Postsecondary	SA	$60,300	15.1%	800
30. Philosophy and Religion Teachers, Postsecondary	SAI	$62,330	15.1%	600
31. Foreign Language and Literature Teachers, Postsecondary	SAI	$59,080	15.1%	900

Best Jobs Requiring a First Professional Degree

Job	Personality Code	Annual Earnings	Percent Growth	Annual Openings
1. Physicians and Surgeons	ISR	$165,279	21.8%	26,050
2. Dentists, General	IRS	$141,040	15.3%	5,180
3. Veterinarians	IR	$82,040	33.0%	3,020
4. Optometrists	ISR	$94,990	24.4%	2,010
5. Orthodontists	IRS	$166,500+	19.8%	360
6. Pharmacists	ICS	$111,570	17.0%	10,580
7. Prosthodontists	IR	$118,400	27.7%	30
8. Lawyers	EI	$112,760	13.0%	24,040
9. Chiropractors	SIR	$67,200	19.5%	1,820
10. Law Teachers, Postsecondary	SIE	$94,260	15.1%	400
11. Judicial Law Clerks	CI	$39,780	13.9%	1,080

Bonus Lists: Best Jobs that May Appeal to Other Aspects of Your Personality

The six RIASEC types provide a convenient way of describing personalities, but most of us are familiar with other aspects of personality, many of which are arguably relevant to career choice. The O*NET database provides ratings that allowed me to compile several lists based on these other dimensions of personality. All of the following lists are based on 263 of the 264 unique jobs that met the criteria for being listed in this book. (For the job characteristics I use to select the occupations in these lists, I was unable to obtain O*NET ratings for Sales Representatives, Services, All Other.) For each job in these lists, I also list the one-, two-, or three-letter codes for the RIASEC types that characterize the jobs, but I put it in the rightmost column because the RIASEC scheme is not the organizing principle of these lists.

Best Jobs for Introverts and Extroverts

The psychologist Carl Jung described two kinds of people: **extroverts,** whose psychic energy flows inward, gained from other people, and **introverts,** whose psychic energy flows outward, gained from solitude. Nowadays the concept of psychic energy is not taken literally, but psychologists continue to recognize that some people are stimulated by social settings and feel most comfortable there, whereas others are more energetic and productive when they can escape distractions caused by other people. So psychologists still speak of introverts and extroverts, and in the field of career development it can be useful to consider whether you lean toward one of these personality types.

For example, if you are an introvert, you are likely to fit better in a job where you can focus on the task without being distracted by ringing telephones, office chit-chat, and frequent meetings. On the other hand, if you are an extrovert, you probably don't mind multitasking and enjoy chatting up your coworkers and clients. (For a detailed look at introversion and its relationship to career choice, see *200 Best Jobs for Introverts* from JIST Publishing.)

These two personality types align with the six RIASEC types to some extent: Extroverts have much in common with Social personalities and introverts have much in common with Realistic personalities.

The O*NET database does not rate jobs for extroversion and introversion as it does for the six RIASEC types. Nevertheless, I was able to compute extroversion and introversion ratings for jobs by looking at the O*NET ratings for two aspects of the jobs: the work style Social Orientation, which is defined as preferring to work with others rather than alone and being personally connected with others on the job, and the work-context feature called Contact with Others, which represents how much the job requires workers to be in contact with others—face-to-face, by telephone, or otherwise. O*NET provides ratings for both features on a scale of 1 to 5, so to compute an extroversion score, I took the average of the two ratings and then represented that average on a scale from 0 to 100. For an introversion score, I subtracted the extroversion score from 100.

These scores enabled me to identify the 50 most introverted jobs and the 50 most extroverted jobs out of the jobs included in this book. I then used the three standard economic measures to rank each set of jobs and produce the following two lists of the best 20 jobs. If you tend toward introversion or extroversion, the jobs on one of these lists may appeal to you.

Best Jobs for Introverts

Job	Rating for Introversion	Annual Earnings	Percent Growth	Annual Openings	Personality Code
1. Software Developers, Applications	41.0	$87,790	34.0%	21,840	IRC
2. Software Developers, Systems Software	35.8	$94,180	30.4%	15,340	ICR
3. Computer Network Architects	39.0	$75,660	53.4%	20,830	ICR
4. Civil Engineers	38.7	$77,560	24.3%	11,460	RIC
5. Market Research Analysts and Marketing Specialists	37.0	$60,570	28.1%	13,730	IEC
6. Accountants and Auditors	35.9	$61,690	21.6%	49,750	CEI
7. Cost Estimators	39.8	$57,860	25.3%	10,360	CE
8. Biomedical Engineers	48.1	$81,540	72.0%	1,490	IR
9. Computer Occupations, All Other	43.7	$79,240	13.1%	7,260	ICR

Best Jobs for Introverts

Job	Rating for Introversion	Annual Earnings	Percent Growth	Annual Openings	Personality Code
10. Operations Research Analysts	43.6	$70,960	22.0%	3,220	ICE
11. Mathematicians	57.8	$99,380	22.5%	150	ICA
12. Political Scientists	40.4	$107,420	19.5%	280	IAS
13. Actuaries	48.1	$87,650	21.4%	1,000	CIE
14. Geoscientists, Except Hydrologists and Geographers	36.3	$82,500	17.5%	1,540	IR
15. Physicists	42.9	$106,370	15.9%	690	IR
16. Engineers, All Other	39.4	$90,270	6.7%	5,020	IR
17. Writers and Authors	39.6	$55,420	14.8%	5,420	AEI
18. Biological Scientists, All Other	44.0	$68,220	18.8%	1,610	IRA
19. Geographers	36.5	$72,800	26.2%	100	IRA
20. Construction and Building Inspectors	38.4	$52,360	16.8%	3,970	RCI

Best Jobs for Extroverts

Job	Rating for Extroversion	Annual Earnings	Percent Growth	Annual Openings	Personality Code
1. Dental Hygienists	87.6	$68,250	36.1%	9,840	SRC
2. Human Resources Specialists	86.0	$52,690	27.9%	11,230	ESC
3. Veterinarians	86.3	$82,040	33.0%	3,020	IR
4. Occupational Therapists	87.9	$72,320	25.6%	4,580	SI
5. Instructional Coordinators	90.3	$58,830	23.2%	6,060	SIA
6. Elementary School Teachers, Except Special Education	91.9	$51,660	15.8%	59,650	SAC
7. Medical Assistants	87.4	$28,860	33.9%	21,780	SCR
8. Licensed Practical and Licensed Vocational Nurses	94.0	$40,380	20.6%	39,130	SR
9. Middle School Teachers, Except Special and Career/Technical Education	90.5	$51,960	15.3%	25,110	SA
10. Medical Secretaries	87.5	$30,530	26.6%	18,900	CS
11. Dentists, General	88.0	$141,040	15.3%	5,180	IRS
12. Fitness Trainers and Aerobics Instructors	93.3	$31,090	29.4%	12,380	SRE
13. Physical Therapist Assistants	91.6	$49,690	33.3%	3,050	SRI
14. Radiation Therapists	86.8	$74,980	27.1%	690	SRC

(continued)

(continued)

Best Jobs for Extroverts

Job	Rating for Extroversion	Annual Earnings	Percent Growth	Annual Openings	Personality Code
15. Healthcare Social Workers	91.6	$47,230	22.4%	6,590	SI
16. Chief Executives	85.8	$165,080	−1.4%	11,250	EC
17. Secondary School Teachers, Except Special and Career/Technical Education	89.6	$53,230	8.9%	41,240	SAE
18. Speech-Language Pathologists	94.0	$66,920	18.5%	4,380	SIA
19. Education Administrators, Elementary and Secondary School	88.5	$86,970	8.6%	8,880	ESC
20. Orthodontists	92.5	$166,500+	19.8%	360	IRS

Best Jobs for Persistent People

Some people tend to stick to a task even in the face of obstacles. Whether you call them dedicated or pig-headed, they seem to represent a distinct personality type. Because the O*NET database rates jobs on Persistence (as a work style), I was able to identify the 50 jobs most hospitable to persistent people. I then ranked these jobs by the usual three economic criteria to produce the following list of the 20 best.

Best Jobs for Persistent People

Job	Rating for Persistence	Annual Earnings	Percent Growth	Annual Openings	Personality Code
1. Physicians and Surgeons	84.6	$165,279	21.8%	26,050	ISR
2. Management Analysts	84.3	$78,160	23.9%	30,650	IEC
3. Medical Scientists, Except Epidemiologists	94.8	$76,700	40.3%	6,620	IRA
4. Sales Managers	85.8	$98,530	14.9%	12,660	EC
5. Dentists, General	87.5	$141,040	15.3%	5,180	IRS
6. Veterinarians	87.5	$82,040	33.0%	3,020	IR
7. Financial Analysts	90.0	$74,350	19.8%	9,520	CIE
8. Computer and Information Research Scientists	90.8	$100,660	24.2%	1,320	IRC
9. Lawyers	90.3	$112,760	13.0%	24,040	EI
10. Biochemists and Biophysicists	89.5	$79,390	37.4%	1,620	IAR
11. Personal Financial Advisors	84.5	$64,750	30.1%	8,530	ECS
12. Prosthodontists	88.5	$118,400	27.7%	30	IR
13. Health Specialties Teachers, Postsecondary	88.3	$85,270	15.1%	4,000	SI

Best Jobs for Persistent People

Job	Rating for Persistence	Annual Earnings	Percent Growth	Annual Openings	Personality Code
14. Architects, Except Landscape and Naval	84.3	$72,550	16.2%	4,680	AI
15. Elementary School Teachers, Except Special Education	85.3	$51,660	15.8%	59,650	SAC
16. Chief Executives	90.3	$165,080	−1.4%	11,250	EC
17. Physicists	89.8	$106,370	15.9%	690	IR
18. Speech-Language Pathologists	84.8	$66,920	18.5%	4,380	SIA
19. Instructional Coordinators	86.3	$58,830	23.2%	6,060	SIA
20. Coaches and Scouts	85.3	$28,340	24.8%	9,920	SRE

Best Jobs for Sensitive People

Another work style used to rate jobs in the O*NET database is Concern for Others, which is defined as being sensitive to others' needs and feelings and being understanding and helpful on the job. I used these ratings to identify the 50 jobs most suited to sensitive people. Then I ranked this set of jobs by their earnings, job growth, and job openings and produced the following list of the 20 best.

As you might expect, the sensitive personality type has a lot in common with the Social personality type, and all the jobs listed here have Social as a primary or secondary type and involve health care or education.

Best Jobs for Sensitive People

Job	Rating for Sensitivity	Annual Earnings	Percent Growth	Annual Openings	Personality Code
1. Physicians and Surgeons	89.3	$165,279	21.8%	26,050	ISR
2. Physical Therapists	88.5	$76,310	30.3%	7,860	SIR
3. Physician Assistants	90.5	$86,410	39.0%	4,280	SIR
4. Registered Nurses	92.2	$64,690	22.2%	103,900	SI
5. Occupational Therapists	96.4	$72,320	25.6%	4,580	SI
6. Optometrists	88.5	$94,990	24.4%	2,010	ISR
7. Dental Assistants	87.8	$33,470	35.8%	16,100	CRS
8. Instructional Coordinators	89.5	$58,830	23.2%	6,060	SIA
9. Medical Assistants	91.3	$28,860	33.9%	21,780	SCR
10. Dentists, General	92.8	$141,040	15.3%	5,180	IRS
11. Licensed Practical and Licensed Vocational Nurses	94.5	$40,380	20.6%	39,130	SR

(continued)

(continued)

Best Jobs for Sensitive People

Job	Rating for Sensitivity	Annual Earnings	Percent Growth	Annual Openings	Personality Code
12. Medical Secretaries	88.8	$30,530	26.6%	18,900	CS
13. Fitness Trainers and Aerobics Instructors	92.8	$31,090	29.4%	12,380	SRE
14. Elementary School Teachers, Except Special Education	91.8	$51,660	15.8%	59,650	SAC
15. Radiation Therapists	90.5	$74,980	27.1%	690	SRC
16. Speech-Language Pathologists	97.8	$66,920	18.5%	4,380	SIA
17. Healthcare Social Workers	97.0	$47,230	22.4%	6,590	SI
18. Education Administrators, Elementary and Secondary School	90.0	$86,970	8.6%	8,880	ESC
19. Middle School Teachers, Except Special and Career/Technical Education	94.5	$51,960	15.3%	25,110	SA
20. Physical Therapist Assistants	95.5	$49,690	33.3%	3,050	SRI

Best Jobs for People with Self-Control

The O*NET database rates jobs on a work style called Self-Control, which is defined as maintaining composure, keeping emotions in check, controlling anger, and avoiding aggressive behavior, even in very difficult situations. This tendency to stay as cool as the other side of the pillow may be regarded as a personality type, so I thought it would be interesting to see which jobs are a good fit.

I identified the 50 jobs rated highest on Self-Control, then sorted them by the three usual economic measures to produce the following list of the 20 best . It's a mix of all six RIASEC types.

Best Jobs for People with Self-Control

Job	Rating for Self-Control	Annual Earnings	Percent Growth	Annual Openings	Personality Code
1. Registered Nurses	90.6	$64,690	22.2%	103,900	SI
2. Occupational Therapists	89.3	$72,320	25.6%	4,580	SI
3. Veterinarians	91.3	$82,040	33.0%	3,020	IR
4. Human Resources Specialists	88.8	$52,690	27.9%	11,230	ESC
5. Instructional Coordinators	88.5	$58,830	23.2%	6,060	SIA
6. Licensed Practical and Licensed Vocational Nurses	95.3	$40,380	20.6%	39,130	SR
7. Medical Assistants	92.8	$28,860	33.9%	21,780	SCR

Best Jobs for People with Self-Control

Job	Rating for Self-Control	Annual Earnings	Percent Growth	Annual Openings	Personality Code
8. Medical Secretaries	89.5	$30,530	26.6%	18,900	CS
9. Radiation Therapists	89.0	$74,980	27.1%	690	SRC
10. Speech-Language Pathologists	92.0	$66,920	18.5%	4,380	SIA
11. Elementary School Teachers, Except Special Education	93.3	$51,660	15.8%	59,650	SAC
12. Education Administrators, Elementary and Secondary School	90.0	$86,970	8.6%	8,880	ESC
13. Healthcare Social Workers	94.5	$47,230	22.4%	6,590	SI
14. Middle School Teachers, Except Special and Career/Technical Education	93.3	$51,960	15.3%	25,110	SA
15. Physical Therapist Assistants	90.5	$49,690	33.3%	3,050	SRI
16. Chiropractors	89.8	$67,200	19.5%	1,820	SIR
17. Commercial Pilots	91.5	$67,500	18.5%	2,060	RIE
18. Detectives and Criminal Investigators	90.1	$68,820	16.6%	4,160	ECR
19. Surgical Technologists	91.0	$39,920	25.3%	4,630	RSC
20. Coaches and Scouts	90.3	$28,340	24.8%	9,920	SRE

Best Jobs for Stress-Tolerant People

Workplace stress can be emotionally draining and can even have serious consequences for your health. But some people have a personality that allows them to tolerate stressful work situations, and I thought that they deserve a list of jobs especially suitable for them. (I also thought that the rest of us deserve a whole book about careers that *lack* these pressures: *150 Best Low-Stress Jobs,* from JIST Publishing.)

To create the list, I identified the 50 jobs that are rated highest on the O*NET work style Stress Tolerance, which is defined as accepting criticism and dealing calmly and effectively with high-stress situations. The three jobs rated highest for requiring stress tolerance were Police, Fire, and Ambulance Dispatchers; Air Traffic Controllers; and Police and Sheriff's Patrol Officers—not at all surprising when you think about what these workers do. As in the other lists in this section, I ordered the 50 highest-rated jobs by three economic criteria and extracted the 20 best overall.

Best Jobs for Stress-Tolerant People

Job	Rating for Stress Tolerance	Annual Earnings	Percent Growth	Annual Openings	Personality Code
1. Physicians and Surgeons	88.1	$165,279	21.8%	26,050	ISR
2. Management Analysts	86.5	$78,160	23.9%	30,650	IEC
3. Registered Nurses	90.9	$64,690	22.2%	103,900	SI
4. Medical Scientists, Except Epidemiologists	88.3	$76,700	40.3%	6,620	IRA
5. Lawyers	90.8	$112,760	13.0%	24,040	EI
6. Financial Analysts	91.5	$74,350	19.8%	9,520	CIE
7. Medical and Health Services Managers	88.0	$84,270	16.0%	9,940	ECS
8. Veterinarians	86.8	$82,040	33.0%	3,020	IR
9. Elementary School Teachers, Except Special Education	90.0	$51,660	15.8%	59,650	SAC
10. Licensed Practical and Licensed Vocational Nurses	89.5	$40,380	20.6%	39,130	SR
11. Medical Assistants	92.8	$28,860	33.9%	21,780	SCR
12. Middle School Teachers, Except Special and Career/Technical Education	86.5	$51,960	15.3%	25,110	SA
13. Chief Executives	93.8	$165,080	−1.4%	11,250	EC
14. Education Administrators, Elementary and Secondary School	90.5	$86,970	8.6%	8,880	ESC
15. Healthcare Social Workers	90.8	$47,230	22.4%	6,590	SI
16. Detectives and Criminal Investigators	88.0	$68,820	16.6%	4,160	ECR
17. Radiation Therapists	87.3	$74,980	27.1%	690	SRC
18. Commercial Pilots	89.3	$67,500	18.5%	2,060	RIE
19. Secondary School Teachers, Except Special and Career/Technical Education	88.5	$53,230	8.9%	41,240	SAE
20. Surgical Technologists	89.3	$39,920	25.3%	4,630	RSC

Best Jobs for Flexible People

Our rapidly changing economy has made flexibility a very useful personality trait in the workplace. Some jobs are particularly demanding of flexibility, and the O*NET database provides guidance on this matter by rating all occupations on a work style called Adaptability/Flexibility. This trait is defined as being open to change (positive or negative) and to considerable variety in the workplace. Using these ratings, I was able to identify the 50 jobs with the highest need for flexible people. The following list features the 20 best jobs, based on their economic rewards.

Best Jobs for Flexible People

Job	Rating for Flexibility	Annual Earnings	Percent Growth	Annual Openings	Personality Code
1. Management Analysts	88.3	$78,160	23.9%	30,650	IEC
2. Computer Systems Analysts	90.0	$77,740	20.3%	22,280	ICR
3. Network and Computer Systems Administrators	91.0	$69,160	23.2%	13,550	IRC
4. Registered Nurses	87.3	$64,690	22.2%	103,900	SI
5. Occupational Therapists	90.0	$72,320	25.6%	4,580	SI
6. Computer and Information Systems Managers	92.8	$115,780	16.9%	9,710	ECI
7. Human Resources Specialists	86.8	$52,690	27.9%	11,230	ESC
8. Financial Analysts	89.3	$74,350	19.8%	9,520	CIE
9. Public Relations Specialists	86.8	$52,090	24.0%	13,130	EAS
10. Computer and Information Research Scientists	86.3	$100,660	24.2%	1,320	IRC
11. Medical and Health Services Managers	87.0	$84,270	16.0%	9,940	ECS
12. Training and Development Specialists	84.5	$54,160	23.3%	10,710	SAC
13. Medical Assistants	85.0	$28,860	33.9%	21,780	SCR
14. Industrial-Organizational Psychologists	88.0	$87,330	26.3%	130	IEA
15. Chief Executives	87.0	$165,080	–1.4%	11,250	EC
16. Instructional Coordinators	84.8	$58,830	23.2%	6,060	SIA
17. Radiation Therapists	84.5	$74,980	27.1%	690	SRC
18. Education Administrators, Elementary and Secondary School	92.0	$86,970	8.6%	8,880	ESC
19. Elementary School Teachers, Except Special Education	89.3	$51,660	15.8%	59,650	SAC
20. Speech-Language Pathologists	89.8	$66,920	18.5%	4,380	SIA

Best Jobs for Detail-Oriented People

Some workers tend to be careful about detail and thorough in completing work tasks. These workers are attracted to jobs where it is important to get the fine points right. Such jobs can be identified in the O*NET database by their high ratings on a work style called Attention to Detail, so I used these ratings to extract the 50 jobs that are most detail-oriented.

Dentists, General, is the job with the highest rating on Attention to Detail, which should reassure you the next time you're in the dentist's chair. Like the other lists in this section, this one is ordered to show the 20 jobs that are best in terms of economic criteria.

Best Jobs for Detail-Oriented People

Job	Rating for Attention to Detail	Annual Earnings	Percent Growth	Annual Openings	Personality Code
1. Physicians and Surgeons	93.3	$165,279	21.8%	26,050	ISR
2. Computer Systems Analysts	93.5	$77,740	20.3%	22,280	ICR
3. Accountants and Auditors	94.1	$61,690	21.6%	49,750	CEI
4. Pharmacists	93.3	$111,570	17.0%	10,580	ICS
5. Veterinarians	97.0	$82,040	33.0%	3,020	IR
6. Financial Analysts	99.0	$74,350	19.8%	9,520	CIE
7. Environmental Engineers	97.0	$78,740	30.6%	2,790	IRC
8. Cost Estimators	94.8	$57,860	25.3%	10,360	CE
9. Dentists, General	99.3	$141,040	15.3%	5,180	IRS
10. Paralegals and Legal Assistants	97.5	$46,680	28.1%	10,400	CIE
11. Medical Assistants	94.8	$28,860	33.9%	21,780	SCR
12. Licensed Practical and Licensed Vocational Nurses	96.3	$40,380	20.6%	39,130	SR
13. Prosthodontists	95.8	$118,400	27.7%	30	IR
14. Health Specialties Teachers, Postsecondary	94.0	$85,270	15.1%	4,000	SI
15. Architects, Except Landscape and Naval	94.3	$72,550	16.2%	4,680	AI
16. Orthodontists	99.0	$166,500+	19.8%	360	IRS
17. Radiation Therapists	93.0	$74,980	27.1%	690	SRC
18. Biological Scientists, All Other	95.6	$68,220	18.8%	1,610	IRA
19. Commercial Pilots	95.0	$67,500	18.5%	2,060	RIE
20. Surgical Technologists	93.5	$39,920	25.3%	4,630	RSC

Best Jobs for Innovators

Some workers like to develop new ideas and solve work-related problems by thinking in creative and unorthodox ways. This tendency is considered to be an aspect of the Artistic personality type, but it also can be useful in the scientific and business fields. I used the O*NET database to discover the 50 jobs with the highest ratings for the work style Innovation. Then I ordered the jobs by earnings, job growth, and job openings to produce the following list of the 20 best. It comes as no surprise that Artistic jobs are more prominent in this list than in any other list in this section.

Best Jobs for Innovators

Job	Rating for Innovation	Annual Earnings	Percent Growth	Annual Openings	Personality Code
1. Computer Systems Analysts	82.0	$77,740	20.3%	22,280	ICR
2. Medical Scientists, Except Epidemiologists	80.5	$76,700	40.3%	6,620	IRA
3. Biochemists and Biophysicists	85.5	$79,390	37.4%	1,620	IAR
4. Operations Research Analysts	85.3	$70,960	22.0%	3,220	ICE
5. Speech-Language Pathologists	84.0	$66,920	18.5%	4,380	SIA
6. Architects, Except Landscape and Naval	81.0	$72,550	16.2%	4,680	AI
7. Orthodontists	79.3	$166,500+	19.8%	360	IRS
8. Geoscientists, Except Hydrologists and Geographers	82.5	$82,500	17.5%	1,540	IR
9. Mathematicians	90.8	$99,380	22.5%	150	ICA
10. Self-Enrichment Education Teachers	80.0	$36,340	32.0%	12,030	SAE
11. Business Teachers, Postsecondary	83.3	$73,760	15.1%	2,000	SEI
12. Chief Executives	80.5	$165,080	−1.4%	11,250	EC
13. Engineering Teachers, Postsecondary	90.5	$89,670	15.1%	1,000	SIR
14. Fitness Trainers and Aerobics Instructors	81.3	$31,090	29.4%	12,380	SRE
15. Middle School Teachers, Except Special and Career/Technical Education	84.3	$51,960	15.3%	25,110	SA
16. Hairdressers, Hairstylists, and Cosmetologists	87.5	$22,760	20.1%	21,950	AES
17. Public Relations and Fundraising Managers	80.3	$91,810	12.9%	2,060	EA
18. Aerospace Engineers	85.5	$97,480	10.4%	2,230	IR
19. Biological Science Teachers, Postsecondary	79.8	$72,700	15.1%	1,700	SI
20. Interior Designers	94.5	$46,280	19.4%	3,590	AE

Best Jobs for Analytical Thinkers

Maybe you know someone who likes to analyze information and use logic to address work-related issues and problems. This trait is one aspect of the Investigative personality type but, according to the O*NET database, it also characterizes some jobs that attract Enterprising and Conventional workers. I isolated the 50 jobs rated highest on the measure Analytical Thinking and sorted them by the usual economic criteria. Here are the 20 best jobs from that subset:

Best Jobs for Analytical Thinkers

Job	Rating for Analytical Thinking	Annual Earnings	Percent Growth	Annual Openings	Personality Code
1. Physicians and Surgeons	88.7	$165,279	21.8%	26,050	ISR
2. Medical Scientists, Except Epidemiologists	91.5	$76,700	40.3%	6,620	IRA
3. Veterinarians	89.3	$82,040	33.0%	3,020	IR
4. Civil Engineers	89.9	$77,560	24.3%	11,460	RIC
5. Computer Systems Analysts	91.5	$77,740	20.3%	22,280	ICR
6. Lawyers	94.3	$112,760	13.0%	24,040	EI
7. Financial Analysts	89.3	$74,350	19.8%	9,520	CIE
8. Market Research Analysts and Marketing Specialists	91.8	$60,570	28.1%	13,730	IEC
9. Network and Computer Systems Administrators	90.5	$69,160	23.2%	13,550	IRC
10. Health Specialties Teachers, Postsecondary	91.3	$85,270	15.1%	4,000	SI
11. Actuaries	96.3	$87,650	21.4%	1,000	CIE
12. Orthodontists	90.3	$166,500+	19.8%	360	IRS
13. Operations Research Analysts	96.3	$70,960	22.0%	3,220	ICE
14. Physicists	92.8	$106,370	15.9%	690	IR
15. Architects, Except Landscape and Naval	89.8	$72,550	16.2%	4,680	AI
16. Mathematicians	95.3	$99,380	22.5%	150	ICA
17. Political Scientists	89.3	$107,420	19.5%	280	IAS
18. Engineering Teachers, Postsecondary	96.0	$89,670	15.1%	1,000	SIR
19. Geoscientists, Except Hydrologists and Geographers	93.0	$82,500	17.5%	1,540	IR
20. Industrial-Organizational Psychologists	93.3	$87,330	26.3%	130	IEA

Best Jobs Not Behind a Desk

Some people have what might be called an antsy personality. They don't like being stuck behind a desk, and they enjoy work that involves physical activity. I created an entire book for these people, *175 Best Jobs Not Behind a Desk,* based on the O*NET ratings for Physical Activity and (lack of) Time Spent Sitting. The following list identifies the 20 best jobs, based on the usual economic criteria, out of the 50 with the highest level of activity.

It's worth noting that the average activity rating for the jobs on this list is only 67 on a scale of 0 to 100. Several jobs on the list are rated in the high 50s. We live in an information-based economy, with much of the growth in Dilbert-type settings, so any list of the best jobs includes many options that are not highly active. Nevertheless, a list such as the following can help you avoid the most sedentary choices.

Best Jobs Not Behind a Desk

Job	Rating for Activity	Annual Earnings	Percent Growth	Annual Openings	Personality Code
1. Physical Therapists	65.7	$76,310	30.3%	7,860	SIR
2. Veterinarians	59.9	$82,040	33.0%	3,020	IR
3. Supervisors of Construction and Extraction Workers	60.4	$58,680	15.4%	24,220	ERC
4. Heating, Air Conditioning, and Refrigeration Mechanics and Installers	72.2	$42,530	28.1%	13,620	RC
5. Licensed Practical and Licensed Vocational Nurses	59.7	$40,380	20.6%	39,130	SR
6. Physical Therapist Assistants	67.4	$49,690	33.3%	3,050	SRI
7. Firefighters	77.0	$45,250	18.5%	15,280	RS
8. Respiratory Therapists	66.3	$54,280	20.9%	4,140	SIR
9. Plumbers, Pipefitters, and Steamfitters	75.8	$46,660	15.3%	17,550	RC
10. Self-Enrichment Education Teachers	57.0	$36,340	32.0%	12,030	SAE
11. Pharmacy Technicians	62.0	$28,400	30.6%	18,200	CR
12. Radiation Therapists	65.6	$74,980	27.1%	690	SRC
13. Electricians	84.4	$48,250	11.9%	25,090	RIC
14. Chiropractors	64.6	$67,200	19.5%	1,820	SIR
15. Construction Laborers	75.1	$29,280	20.5%	33,940	RC
16. Occupational Therapy Assistants	61.6	$51,010	29.8%	1,180	SR
17. Fitness Trainers and Aerobics Instructors	78.1	$31,090	29.4%	12,380	SRE
18. Construction and Building Inspectors	58.7	$52,360	16.8%	3,970	RCI
19. Surgical Technologists	69.2	$39,920	25.3%	4,630	RSC
20. Captains, Mates, and Pilots of Water Vessels	59.6	$64,180	17.3%	1,950	REC

Best World-Improving Jobs

Some people want to do work that makes the world a better place by easing suffering, increasing knowledge, promoting safety and security, improving the natural environment, or creating things of beauty. The O*NET database does not provide ratings that are useful in identifying world-improving jobs, but the editors at JIST used the criteria in the previous sentence to create a list that became the centerpiece of the book *150 Best Jobs for a Better World*. I used this same list to identify the world-improving jobs in this book; 102 met these criteria. I then sorted these jobs by their economic potential and produced the following list of the 20 highest-ranking jobs. Health-care occupations dominate this list.

Best World-Improving Jobs

Job	Annual Earnings	Percent Growth	Annual Openings	Personality Code
1. Medical Scientists, Except Epidemiologists	$76,700	40.3%	6,620	IRA
2. Physical Therapists	$76,310	30.3%	7,860	SIR
3. Dental Hygienists	$68,250	36.1%	9,840	SRC
4. Physician Assistants	$86,410	39.0%	4,280	SIR
5. Personal Financial Advisors	$64,750	30.1%	8,530	ECS
6. Pharmacists	$111,570	17.0%	10,580	ICS
7. Registered Nurses	$64,690	22.2%	103,900	SI
8. Veterinarians	$82,040	33.0%	3,020	IR
9. Compliance Officers	$58,720	31.0%	10,850	CEI
10. Occupational Therapists	$72,320	25.6%	4,580	SI
11. Optometrists	$94,990	24.4%	2,010	ISR
12. Dentists, General	$141,040	15.3%	5,180	IRS
13. Environmental Scientists and Specialists, Including Health	$61,700	27.9%	4,840	IRC
14. Instructional Coordinators	$58,830	23.2%	6,060	SIA
15. Dental Assistants	$33,470	35.8%	16,100	CRS
16. Medical Assistants	$28,860	33.9%	21,780	SCR
17. Self-Enrichment Education Teachers	$36,340	32.0%	12,030	SAE
18. Pharmacy Technicians	$28,400	30.6%	18,200	CR
19. Architects, Except Landscape and Naval	$72,550	16.2%	4,680	AI
20. Health Specialties Teachers, Postsecondary	$85,270	15.1%	4,000	SI

Part IV

Descriptions of the 50 Best Jobs for Each Personality Type

This part provides descriptions for all the jobs included in one or more of the lists in Part III. The book's introduction gives more details on how to use and interpret the job descriptions, but here are the highlights, along with some additional information.

* The job descriptions that follow met my criteria for inclusion in this book, as I explain in the Introduction. The jobs in this book scored among the 50 highest in one or more of the personality types for earnings, projected growth, and number of job openings. Many good jobs do not meet one or more of these criteria, but I think the jobs that do are the best ones to consider in your career planning.

* The job descriptions are arranged by personality type and in alphabetical order by job title within each personality type. This approach allows you to find a description quickly if you know its title from one of the lists in Part III. If you have not browsed the lists in Part III, consider spending some time there. The lists are interesting and will help you identify job titles that you can look up in the descriptions that follow.

* In some cases a job title is linked to two or more different personality types in Part III. For this reason, when you look for the job among the descriptions for one personality type, you may find a note there telling you to look for the description under a different personality type. I did this to avoid redundancy and save space.

* Refer to the Introduction, beginning on page 1, for details on interpreting the job descriptions' content.

* The section with career cluster and pathway information includes a subsection titled Other Jobs in This Pathway to help you identify similar jobs. They all belong to the same primary personality type as the job being described, but many are not among the best jobs.

✸ When reviewing the descriptions, keep in mind that the jobs meet my criteria for being among the top 50 jobs for each personality type based on their total scores for earnings, growth, and number of openings—but one or more of these measures may not be among the highest. For example, an occupation that has high pay may be included, even though growth rate and number of job openings are below average.

"Well," you might ask, "doesn't this mean that at least some 'bad' jobs are described in this part?" My answer is yes and no. Some jobs with high scores for all measures, such as Computer and Information Systems Managers—the Enterprising job with the best total for pay, growth, and number of openings—would be a very bad job for people who dislike or are not good at that sort of work. On the other hand, many people would love working as Compensation and Benefits Managers even though that job has lower earnings, a lower projected growth rate, and fewer openings. Descriptions for both jobs are included in this book.

Possibly somewhere a former computer systems manager works as a compensation and benefits manager and loves it. This person may even have figured out how to make more money (say, by getting hired in a very large business), have a more flexible schedule, have more fun, or have other advantages not available to some computer systems managers.

The point is that each job is right for somebody, perhaps at a certain time in their lives. We are all likely to change careers and jobs several times, and it's not always money that motivates us. So browse the job descriptions that follow and know that somewhere there is a good place for you. I hope you find it.

Use the job descriptions in this section as one step in a continuing process of career exploration. When you find a job that interests you, turn to Appendix B for definitions of the skills and fields of knowledge in the job description. Also consult Appendix C for suggestions about resources for further exploration.

Realistic Occupations

Airline Pilots, Copilots, and Flight Engineers

- ❋ Personality Type: Realistic-Conventional-Investigative
- ❋ Annual Earnings: $103,210
- ❋ Earnings Growth Potential: High (46.7%)
- ❋ Growth: 8.4%
- ❋ Annual Job Openings: 3,250
- ❋ Self-Employed: 0.0%

Considerations for Job Outlook: Population growth and economic expansion are expected to boost demand for air travel. Regional airlines and low-cost carriers should have the best opportunities; pilots vying for jobs with major airlines face strong competition.

Pilot and navigate the flight of multi-engine aircraft in regularly scheduled service for the transport of passengers and cargo. Requires Federal Air Transport rating and certification in specific aircraft type used. Use instrumentation to guide flights when visibility is poor. Respond to and report in-flight emergencies and malfunctions. Work as part of a flight team with other crew members, especially during takeoffs and landings. Contact control towers for takeoff clearances, arrival instructions, and other information, using radio equipment. Steer aircraft along planned routes with the assistance of autopilot and flight management computers. Monitor gauges, warning devices, and control panels to verify aircraft performance and to regulate engine speed. Start engines, operate controls, and pilot airplanes to transport passengers, mail, or freight while adhering to flight plans, regulations, and procedures. Inspect aircraft for defects and malfunctions according to preflight checklists. Check passenger and cargo distributions and fuel amounts to ensure that weight and balance specifications are met. Monitor engine operation, fuel consumption, and functioning of aircraft systems during flights. Confer with flight dispatchers and weather forecasters to keep abreast of flight conditions. Coordinate flight activities with ground crews and air-traffic control and inform crew members of flight and test procedures. Order changes in fuel supplies, loads, routes, or schedules to ensure safety of flights. Choose routes, altitudes, and speeds that will provide the fastest, safest, and smoothest flights. Direct activities of aircraft crews during flights.

Education/Training Required: Bachelor's degree. **Education and Training Programs:** Airline/Commercial/Professional Pilot and Flight Crew Training; Flight Instructor Training. **Knowledge/Courses:** Transportation; Geography; Physics; Public Safety and Security; Psychology; Mechanical Devices.

Career Cluster: 16 Transportation, Distribution, and Logistics. **Career Pathway:** 16.1 Transportation Operations.

Skills: Operation and Control; Operation Monitoring; Science; Troubleshooting; Instructing; Judgment and Decision Making; Quality Control Analysis; Mathematics.

Work Environment: More often indoors than outdoors; sitting; using hands; noise; very hot or cold; bright or inadequate lighting; contaminants; cramped work space; exposed to radiation.

Architectural and Civil Drafters

- ❋ Personality Type: Realistic-Conventional-Artistic
- ❋ Annual Earnings: $46,430
- ❋ Earnings Growth Potential: Low (35.4%)
- ❋ Growth: 9.1%
- ❋ Annual Job Openings: 3,620
- ❋ Self-Employed: 2.9%

Considerations for Job Outlook: Employment growth of drafters is expected to fall as computer-aided drafting systems allow other workers to complete tasks previously performed by drafters.

Opportunities should be best for job-seekers who have at least two years of postsecondary training, strong technical skills, and experience with computer-aided drafting and design systems.

Job Specialization: Architectural Drafters

Prepare detailed drawings of architectural designs and plans for buildings and structures according to specifications provided by architect. Analyze building codes, by-laws, space and site requirements, and other technical documents and reports to determine their effect on architectural designs. Operate computer-aided drafting (CAD) equipment or conventional drafting station to produce designs, working drawings, charts, forms, and records. Coordinate structural, electrical, and mechanical designs and determine a method of presentation to graphically represent building plans. Obtain and assemble data to complete architectural designs, visiting job sites to compile measurements as necessary. Lay out and plan interior room arrangements for commercial buildings, using computer-assisted drafting (CAD) equipment and software. Draw rough and detailed scale plans for foundations, buildings, and structures based on preliminary concepts, sketches, engineering calculations, specification sheets, and other data. Supervise, coordinate, and inspect the work of draftspersons, technicians, and technologists on construction projects. Represent architect on construction site, ensuring builder compliance with design specifications and advising on design corrections under architect's supervision. Check dimensions of materials to be used and assign numbers to lists of materials. Determine procedures and instructions to be followed according to design specifications and quantity of required materials. Analyze technical implications of architect's design concept, calculating weights, volumes, and stress factors.

Education/Training Required: Postsecondary vocational training. **Education and Training Programs:** Architectural Drafting and Architectural CAD/CADD; Architectural Technology/Technician; CAD/CADD Drafting and/or Design Technology/Technician; Civil Drafting and Civil Engineering CAD/CADD; Drafting and Design Technology/Technician, General. **Knowledge/Courses:** Design; Building and Construction; Engineering and Technology; Fine Arts; Computers and Electronics; Law and Government.

Personality Type: Artistic-Realistic-Investigative. **Career Cluster:** 02 Architecture and Construction. **Career Pathway:** 02.1 Design/Pre-Construction.

Skills: Mathematics; Programming; Systems Analysis; Quality Control Analysis; Operations Analysis; Management of Financial Resources; Management of Material Resources; Time Management.

Work Environment: Indoors; sitting; using hands; repetitive motions.

Job Specialization: Civil Drafters

Prepare drawings and topographical and relief maps used in civil engineering projects such as highways, bridges, pipelines, flood control projects, and water and sewerage control systems. Produce drawings by using computer-assisted drafting systems (CAD) or drafting machines or by hand, using compasses, dividers, protractors, triangles, and other drafting devices. Draw maps, diagrams, and profiles, using cross-sections and surveys, to represent elevations, topographical contours, subsurface formations, and structures. Draft plans and detailed drawings for structures, installations, and construction projects such as highways, sewage disposal systems, and dikes, working from sketches or notes. Determine the order of work and method of presentation such as orthographic or isometric drawing. Finish and duplicate drawings and documentation packages according to required mediums and specifications for reproduction, using blueprinting, photography, or other duplication methods. Review rough sketches, drawings, specifications, and other engineering data received from civil engineers to ensure that they conform to design concepts. Calculate excavation tonnage and prepare graphs and fill-hauling diagrams for use in earth-moving operations. Supervise and train other technologists, technicians, and drafters. Correlate, interpret, and modify data obtained from topographical surveys, well logs, and geophysical prospecting reports. Determine quality, cost, strength, and quantity of required materials and enter figures on materials lists. Locate and identify symbols located on topographical surveys to denote geological and geophysical formations or oil field installations.

Education/Training Required: Postsecondary vocational training. **Education and Training Programs:** Architectural Drafting and Architectural CAD/CADD; Architectural Technology/Technician; CAD/CADD Drafting and/or Design Technology/Technician; Civil Drafting and Civil Engineering CAD/CADD; Drafting and Design Technology/Technician, General. **Knowledge/Courses:** Design; Engineering and Technology; Building and Construction; Geography; Mathematics; Physics.

Personality Type: Realistic-Conventional-Investigative. **Career Cluster:** 02 Architecture and Construction. **Career Pathway:** 02.1 Design/Pre-Construction.

Skills: Mathematics; Operations Analysis; Quality Control Analysis; Science; Systems Evaluation; Systems Analysis; Reading Comprehension; Management of Personnel Resources.

Work Environment: Indoors; sitting; using hands; repetitive motions.

Audio and Video Equipment Technicians

- ❋ Personality Type: Realistic-Investigative-Conventional
- ❋ Annual Earnings: $40,540
- ❋ Earnings Growth Potential: High (43.6%)
- ❋ Growth: 12.6%
- ❋ Annual Job Openings: 2,370
- ❋ Self-Employed: 12.4%

Considerations for Job Outlook: Employment growth is expected to vary. Demand for audio-visual equipment is growing, which should lead to employment increases for audio and video equipment technicians. But labor productivity increases and broadcast industry consolidation are expected to limit growth in broadcasting. Job prospects should be best in small cities and towns.

Set up or set up and operate audio and video equipment, including microphones, sound speakers, video screens, projectors, video monitors, recording equipment, connecting wires and cables, sound and mixing boards, and related electronic equipment, for concerts, sports events, meetings and conventions, presentations, and news conferences. May also set up and operate associated spotlights and other custom lighting systems. Notify supervisors when major equipment repairs are needed. Monitor incoming and outgoing pictures and sound feeds to ensure quality; notify directors of any possible problems. Mix and regulate sound inputs and feeds or coordinate audio feeds with television pictures. Install, adjust, and operate electronic used to record, edit, and transmit radio and television programs, cable programs, and motion pictures. Design layouts of audio and video equipment and perform upgrades and maintenance. Perform minor repairs and routine cleaning of audio and video equipment. Diagnose and resolve media system problems in classrooms. Switch sources of video input from one camera or studio to another, from film to live programming, or from network to local programming. Meet with directors and senior members of camera crews to discuss assignments and determine filming sequences, camera movements, and picture composition. Construct and position properties, sets, lighting equipment, and other equipment. Compress, digitize, duplicate, and store audio and video data. Obtain, set up, and load videotapes for scheduled productions or broadcasts. Edit videotapes by erasing and removing portions of programs and adding video or sound as required. Direct and coordinate activities of assistants and other personnel during production. Plan and develop pre-production ideas into outlines, scripts, storyboards, and graphics, using own ideas or specifications of assignments.

Education/Training Required: Long-term on-the-job training. **Education and Training Programs:** Agricultural Communication/Journalism; Photographic and Film/Video Technology/Technician and Assistant; Recording Arts Technology/Technician. **Knowledge/Courses:** Telecommunications; Communications and Media; Fine Arts; Computers and Electronics; Engineering and Technology; Production and Processing.

Career Cluster: 03 Arts, Audio/Video Technology, and Communications. **Career Pathways:** 03.3 Visual Arts; 03.5 Journalism and Broadcasting.

Skills: Installation; Troubleshooting; Equipment Selection; Operation and Control; Repairing; Operation Monitoring; Equipment Maintenance; Quality Control Analysis.

Work Environment: Indoors; sitting; using hands; repetitive motions.

Biological Technicians

- ❋ Personality Type: Realistic-Investigative-Conventional
- ❋ Annual Earnings: $39,020
- ❋ Earnings Growth Potential: Medium (36.1%)
- ❋ Growth: 17.6%
- ❋ Annual Job Openings: 4,190
- ❋ Self-Employed: 0.3%

Considerations for Job Outlook: The continued growth of scientific and medical research and the development and manufacturing of technical products are expected to drive employment growth for these workers. Opportunities are expected to be best for graduates of applied science technology programs who are knowledgeable about equipment used in laboratories or production facilities.

Assist biological and medical scientists in laboratories. Set up, operate, and maintain laboratory instruments and equipment; monitor experiments; make observations; and calculate and record results. May analyze organic substances, such as blood, food, and drugs. Keep detailed logs of all work-related activities. Monitor laboratory work to ensure compliance with set standards. Isolate, identify, and prepare specimens for examination. Use computers, computer-interfaced equipment, robotics, or high-technology industrial applications to perform work duties. Conduct research or assist in the conduct of research, including the collection of information and samples such as blood, water, soil, plants, and animals. Set up, adjust, calibrate, clean, maintain, and troubleshoot laboratory and field equipment. Provide technical support and services for scientists and engineers working in fields such as agriculture, environmental science, resource management, biology, and health sciences. Clean, maintain, and prepare supplies and work areas. Participate in the research, development, or manufacturing of medicinal and pharmaceutical preparations. Conduct standardized biological, microbiological, or biochemical tests and laboratory analyses to evaluate the quantity or quality of physical or chemical substances in food or other products. Analyze experimental data and interpret results to write reports and summaries of findings. Measure or weigh compounds and solutions for use in testing or animal feed. Monitor and observe experiments, recording production and test data for evaluation by research personnel. Examine animals and specimens to detect the presence of disease or other problems.

Education/Training Required: Bachelor's degree. **Education and Training Program:** Biology Technician/Biotechnology Laboratory Technician Training. **Knowledge/Courses:** Biology; Chemistry; Computers and Electronics; Mathematics; Mechanical Devices; Engineering and Technology.

Career Cluster: 13 Manufacturing. **Career Pathway:** 13.3 Maintenance, Installation, and Repair.

Skills: Science; Programming; Troubleshooting; Mathematics; Reading Comprehension; Quality

Control Analysis; Operation and Control; Equipment Maintenance.

Work Environment: Indoors; sitting; using hands; repetitive motions; contaminants.

Boilermakers

- ❋ Personality Type: Realistic-Conventional
- ❋ Annual Earnings: $54,640
- ❋ Earnings Growth Potential: High (44.3%)
- ❋ Growth: 18.8%
- ❋ Annual Job Openings: 810
- ❋ Self-Employed: 0.0%

Considerations for Job Outlook: Projected employment growth will be driven by the need to maintain and upgrade existing boilers and install equipment that is less harmful to the environment. Job prospects should be favorable.

Construct, assemble, maintain, and repair stationary steam boilers and boiler house auxiliaries. Align structures or plate sections to assemble boiler frame tanks or vats, following blueprints. Work involves use of hand and power tools, plumb bobs, levels, wedges, dogs, or turnbuckles. Assist in testing assembled vessels. Direct cleaning of boilers and boiler furnaces. Inspect and repair boiler fittings, such as safety valves, regulators, automatic-control mechanisms, water columns, and auxiliary machines. Examine boilers, pressure vessels, tanks, and vats to locate defects such as leaks, weak spots, and defective sections so that they can be repaired. Bolt or arc-weld pressure vessel structures and parts together, using wrenches and welding equipment. Inspect assembled vessels and individual components, such as tubes, fittings, valves, controls, and auxiliary mechanisms, to locate any defects. Repair or replace defective pressure vessel parts, such as safety valves and regulators, using torches, jacks, caulking hammers, power saws, threading dies, welding equipment, and metalworking machinery. Attach rigging and signal crane or hoist operators to lift heavy frame and plate sections

and other parts into place. Bell, bead with power hammers, or weld pressure vessel tube ends in order to ensure leakproof joints. Lay out plate, sheet steel, or other heavy metal, and locate and mark bending and cutting lines, using protractors, compasses, and drawing instruments or templates. Install manholes, handholes, taps, tubes, valves, gauges, and feedwater connections in drums of water tube boilers, using hand tools. Study blueprints to determine locations, relationships, and dimensions of parts. Straighten or reshape bent pressure vessel plates and structure parts, using hammers, jacks, and torches.

Education/Training Required: Long-term on-the-job training. **Education and Training Program:** Boilermaking/Boilermaker. **Knowledge/Courses:** Building and Construction; Mechanical Devices; Engineering and Technology; Design; Physics; Transportation.

Career Cluster: 02 Architecture and Construction. **Career Pathway:** 02.2 Construction.

Skills: Repairing; Equipment Maintenance; Operation and Control; Troubleshooting; Equipment Selection; Quality Control Analysis; Operation Monitoring; Installation.

Work Environment: Outdoors; standing; using hands; noise; very hot or cold; bright or inadequate lighting; contaminants; cramped work space; high places; hazardous conditions; hazardous equipment; minor burns, cuts, bites, or stings.

Brickmasons and Blockmasons

- ❋ Personality Type: Realistic-Conventional-Investigative
- ❋ Annual Earnings: $46,930
- ❋ Earnings Growth Potential: Medium (38.7%)
- ❋ Growth: 11.5%
- ❋ Annual Job Openings: 5,000
- ❋ Self-Employed: 27.3%

Realistic-B

Considerations for Job Outlook: Employment growth is expected to be driven by a growing population's need for many types of new structures. These workers will also be needed to renovate older buildings and increase their energy efficiency.

Lay and bind building materials, such as brick, structural tile, concrete block, cinderblock, glass block, and terra-cotta block, with mortar and other substances to construct or repair walls, partitions, arches, sewers, and other structures. Construct corners by fastening in plumb position a corner pole or building a corner pyramid of bricks and filling in between the corners, using a line from corner to corner to guide each course, or layer, of brick. Measure distance from reference points and mark guidelines to lay out work, using plumb bobs and levels. Fasten or fuse brick or other building material to structure with wire clamps, anchor holes, torch, or cement. Calculate angles and courses, and determine vertical and horizontal alignment of courses. Break or cut bricks, tiles, or blocks to size, using trowel edge, hammer, or power saw. Remove excess mortar with trowels and hand tools and finish mortar joints with jointing tools for a sealed, uniform appearance. Interpret blueprints and drawings to determine specifications and to calculate the materials required. Apply and smooth mortar or other mixture over work surface. Mix specified amounts of sand, clay, dirt, or mortar powder with water to form refractory mixtures. Examine brickwork or structure to determine need for repair. Clean working surface to remove scale, dust, soot, or chips of brick and mortar, using broom, wire brush, or scraper. Lay and align bricks, blocks, or tiles to build or repair structures or high-temperature equipment, such as cupola, kilns, ovens, or furnaces. Remove burned or damaged brick or mortar, using sledgehammer, crowbar, chipping gun, or chisel.

Education/Training Required: Long-term on-the-job training. **Education and Training Program:** Masonry/Mason Training. **Knowledge/Courses:** Building and Construction; Design; Engineering and Technology; Production and Processing; Physics; Public Safety and Security.

Career Cluster: 02 Architecture and Construction. **Career Pathway:** 02.2 Construction.

Skills: Repairing; Mathematics; Equipment Maintenance; Equipment Selection; Quality Control Analysis; Operation and Control; Management of Material Resources; Troubleshooting.

Work Environment: Outdoors; standing; walking and running; using hands; bending or twisting the body; repetitive motions; noise; very hot or cold; contaminants; cramped work space; high places; hazardous equipment; minor burns, cuts, bites, or stings.

Business Operations Specialists, All Other

Look for the job description among the Conventional jobs.

Camera Operators, Television, Video, and Motion Picture

Look for the job description among the Artistic jobs.

Captains, Mates, and Pilots of Water Vessels

- ❋ Personality Type: Realistic-Enterprising-Conventional
- ❋ Annual Earnings: $64,180
- ❋ Earnings Growth Potential: Very high (52.2%)
- ❋ Growth: 17.3%
- ❋ Annual Job Openings: 1,950
- ❋ Self-Employed: 7.2%

Considerations for Job Outlook: Job growth is expected to stem from increasing tourism and from growth in offshore oil and gas production. Employment is also projected to increase in and around major port cities due to growing international trade. Opportunities should be excellent as the need to replace workers, particularly officers, generates many job openings.

Job Specialization: Mates—Ship, Boat, and Barge

Supervise and coordinate activities of crew aboard ships, boats, barges, or dredges. Determine geographical position of ship, using lorans, azimuths of celestial bodies, or computers, and use this information to determine the course and speed of the ship. Observe water from ship's masthead to advise on navigational direction. Supervise crews in cleaning and maintaining decks, superstructures, and bridges. Supervise crew members in the repair or replacement of defective gear and equipment. Steer vessels, using navigational devices such as compasses and sextants and navigational aids such as lighthouses and buoys. Inspect equipment such as cargo-handling gear, life-saving equipment, visual-signaling equipment, and fishing, towing, or dredging gear to detect problems. Arrange for ships to be stocked, fueled, and repaired. Assume command of vessel in the event that ship's master becomes incapacitated. Participate in activities related to maintenance of vessel security. Stand watches on vessel during specified periods while vessel is under way. Observe loading and unloading of cargo and equipment to ensure that handling and storage are performed according to specifications.

Education/Training Required: Work experience in a related occupation. **Education and Training Programs:** Commercial Fishing; Marine Science/Merchant Marine Officer; Marine Transportation Services, Other. **Knowledge/Courses:** Transportation; Geography; Public Safety and Security; Telecommunications; Personnel and Human Resources; Mechanical Devices.

Personality Type: Enterprising-Realistic-Conventional **Career Cluster:** 16 Transportation, Distribution, and Logistics. **Career Pathway:** 16.1 Transportation Operations.

Skills: Repairing; Equipment Maintenance; Operation and Control; Troubleshooting; Operation Monitoring; Equipment Selection; Quality Control Analysis; Management of Personnel Resources.

Work Environment: More often outdoors than indoors; standing; balancing; using hands; noise; very hot or cold; bright or inadequate lighting; contaminants; cramped work space; whole-body vibration; high places; hazardous conditions; hazardous equipment; minor burns, cuts, bites, or stings.

Job Specialization: Pilots, Ship

Command ships to steer them into and out of harbors, estuaries, straits, and sounds and on rivers, lakes, and bays. Must be licensed by U.S. Coast Guard with limitations indicating class and tonnage of vessels for which licenses are valid and routes and waters that may be piloted. Maintain and repair boats and equipment. Give directions to crew members who are steering ships. Make nautical maps. Set ships' courses to avoid reefs, outlying shoals, and other hazards, using navigational aids such as lighthouses and buoys. Report to appropriate authorities any violations of federal or state pilotage laws. Relieve crew members on tugs and launches. Provide assistance to vessels approaching or leaving seacoasts, navigating harbors, and docking and undocking. Provide assistance in maritime rescue operations. Prevent ships under their navigational control from engaging in unsafe operations. Operate amphibious craft during troop landings. Maintain ships' logs. Learn to operate new technology systems and procedures, through the use of instruction, simulators, and models. Advise ships' masters on harbor rules and customs procedures. Steer ships into and out of berths, or signal tugboat captains to berth and unberth ships. Serve as vessels' docking masters upon arrival at a port and when at a berth. Operate ship-to-shore radios to exchange information needed for ship operations. Consult maps, charts, weather reports, and navigation equipment to determine and direct ship movements. Direct courses and speeds of ships, based on specialized knowledge of local

Realistic-C

winds, weather, water depths, tides, currents, and hazards. Oversee cargo storage on or below decks.

Education/Training Required: Work experience in a related occupation. **Education and Training Programs:** Commercial Fishing; Marine Science/ Merchant Marine Officer; Marine Transportation Services, Other. **Knowledge/Courses:** Transportation; Geography; Public Safety and Security; Telecommunications; Mechanical Devices; Law and Government.

Personality Type: Realistic-Conventional-Investigative. **Career Cluster:** 16 Transportation, Distribution, and Logistics. **Career Pathway:** 16.1 Transportation Operations.

Skills: Operation and Control; Operation Monitoring; Troubleshooting; Equipment Maintenance; Management of Personnel Resources; Repairing; Quality Control Analysis; Complex Problem Solving.

Work Environment: More often outdoors than indoors; standing; using hands; noise; very hot or cold; bright or inadequate lighting; contaminants; whole-body vibration; hazardous conditions.

Job Specialization: Ship and Boat Captains

Command vessels in oceans, bays, lakes, rivers, and coastal waters. Assign watches and living quarters to crew members. Sort logs, form log booms, and salvage lost logs. Perform various marine duties such as checking for oil spills or other pollutants around ports and harbors, and patrolling beaches. Contact buyers to sell cargo such as fish. Tow and maneuver barges, or signal for tugboats to tow barges to destinations. Signal passing vessels, using whistles, flashing lights, flags, and radios. Resolve questions or problems with customs officials. Read gauges to verify sufficient levels of hydraulic fluid, air pressure, and oxygen. Purchase supplies and equipment. Measure depths of water, using depth-measuring equipment. Maintain boats and equipment on board, such as engines, winches, navigational systems, fire extinguish-

ers, and life preservers. Collect fares from customers, or signal ferryboat helpers to collect fares. Arrange for ships to be fueled, restocked with supplies, and/ or repaired. Signal crew members or deckhands to rig tow lines, open or close gates and ramps, and pull guard chains across entries. Maintain records of daily activities, personnel reports, ship positions and movements, ports of call, weather and sea conditions, pollution control efforts, and/or cargo and passenger statuses. Inspect vessels to ensure efficient and safe operation of vessels and equipment, as well as conformance to regulations.

Education/Training Required: Work experience in a related occupation. **Education and Training Programs:** Commercial Fishing; Marine Science/ Merchant Marine Officer; Marine Transportation Services, Other. **Knowledge/Courses:** Transportation; Public Safety and Security; Geography; Telecommunications; Mechanical Devices; Psychology.

Personality Type: Enterprising-Realistic. **Career Cluster:** 16 Transportation, Distribution, and Logistics. **Career Pathway:** 16.1 Transportation Operations.

Skills: Operation and Control; Repairing; Management of Material Resources; Management of Financial Resources; Equipment Maintenance; Troubleshooting; Operation Monitoring; Equipment Selection.

Work Environment: More often outdoors than indoors; standing; using hands; repetitive motions; noise; very hot or cold; bright or inadequate lighting; contaminants; whole-body vibration; hazardous equipment; minor burns, cuts, bites, or stings.

Cardiovascular Technologists and Technicians

* Personality Type: Realistic-Social-Investigative
* Annual Earnings: $49,410
* Earnings Growth Potential: High (46.1%)
* Growth: 24.1%

❋ Annual Job Openings: 1,910
❋ Self-Employed: 0.8%

Considerations for Job Outlook: An aging population and the continued prevalence of heart disease will drive employment growth for cardiovascular technologists and technicians. Prospects should be the best for job-seekers who have multiple credentials.

Conduct tests on pulmonary or cardiovascular systems of patients for diagnostic purposes. May conduct or assist in electrocardiograms, cardiac catheterizations, pulmonary functions, lung capacity, and similar tests. Monitor patients' blood pressures and heart rates, using electrocardiogram (EKG) equipment during diagnostic and therapeutic procedures to notify physicians if something appears wrong. Explain testing procedures to patients to obtain cooperation and reduce anxiety. Observe gauges, recorders, and video screens of data analysis systems during imaging of cardiovascular systems. Monitor patients' comfort and safety during tests, alerting physicians to abnormalities or changes in patient responses. Obtain and record patients' identities, medical histories, or test results. Attach electrodes to patients' chests, arms, and legs; connect electrodes to leads from electrocardiogram (EKG) machines; and operate EKG machines to obtain readings. Adjust equipment and controls according to physicians' orders or established protocol. Prepare and position patients for testing. Check, test, and maintain cardiology equipment, making minor repairs when necessary, to ensure proper operation. Supervise and train other cardiology technologists and students. Perform general administrative tasks, such as scheduling appointments or ordering supplies and equipment. Maintain a proper sterile field during surgical procedures. Assist physicians in the diagnosis and treatment of cardiac and peripheral vascular treatments, such as implanting pacemakers or assisting with balloon angioplasties to treat blood vessel blockages. Inject contrast medium into patients' blood vessels.

Education/Training Required: Associate degree

Education and Training Programs: Cardiopulmonary Technology/Technologist; Cardiovascular Technology/Technologist; Electrocardiograph Technology/Technician; Perfusion Technology/Perfusionist. **Knowledge/Courses:** Medicine and Dentistry; Biology; Psychology; Customer and Personal Service; Sociology and Anthropology; Chemistry.

Career Cluster: 08 Health Science. **Career Pathway:** 08.2 Diagnostics Services.

Skills: Science; Equipment Maintenance; Operation and Control; Repairing; Operation Monitoring; Service Orientation; Equipment Selection; Troubleshooting.

Work Environment: Indoors; standing; walking and running; using hands; repetitive motions; exposed to radiation; exposed to disease or infections.

Carpenters

❋ Personality Type: Realistic-Conventional-Investigative
❋ Annual Earnings: $39,530
❋ Earnings Growth Potential: Medium (37.6%)
❋ Growth: 12.9%
❋ Annual Job Openings: 32,540
❋ Self-Employed: 32.0%

Considerations for Job Outlook: New construction projects are expected to increase employment for carpenters. Opportunities should be best for job-seekers who prepare through an apprenticeship or other formal training.

Job Specialization: Construction Carpenters

Construct, erect, install, and repair structures and fixtures of wood, plywood, and wallboard, using carpenter's hand tools and power tools. Measure and mark cutting lines on materials, using ruler, pencil, chalk, and marking gauge. Follow established safety rules and regulations, and maintain a safe and clean environment. Verify trueness of structure using plumb bob and level. Shape or cut materials to specified measurements using hand tools, machines, or power saw. Study specifications in blueprints, sketches, or building plans to prepare project layout and determine dimensions and materials required. Assemble and fasten materials to make framework or props using hand tools and wood screws, nails, dowel pins, or glue. Build or repair cabinets, doors, frameworks, floors, and other wooden fixtures included in buildings using woodworking machines, carpenter's hand tools, and power tools. Erect scaffolding and ladders for assembling structures above ground level. Remove damaged or defective parts or sections of structures, and repair or replace using hand tools. Install structures and fixtures, such as windows, frames, floorings, and trim, or hardware, using carpenter's hand and power tools. Select and order lumber and other required materials. Maintain records, document actions, and present written progress reports. Finish surfaces of woodwork or wallboard in houses and buildings using paint, hand tools, and paneling. Prepare cost estimates for clients or employers. Arrange for subcontractors to deal with special areas such as heating and electrical wiring work.

Education/Training Required: Long-term on-the-job training. **Education and Training Program:** Carpentry/Carpenter. **Knowledge/Courses:** Building and Construction; Design; Mechanical Devices; Engineering and Technology; Production and Processing; Mathematics.

Personality Type: Realistic-Conventional-Investigative. **Career Cluster:** 02 Architecture and Construction. **Career Pathway:** 02.2 Construction.

Skills: Repairing; Equipment Selection; Installation; Quality Control Analysis; Equipment Maintenance; Operation and Control; Troubleshooting; Management of Material Resources.

Work Environment: Outdoors; standing; walking and running; kneeling, crouching, stooping, or crawling; using hands; bending or twisting the body; repetitive motions; noise; very hot or cold; bright or inadequate lighting; contaminants; cramped work space; high places; hazardous equipment; minor burns, cuts, bites, or stings.

Job Specialization: Rough Carpenters

Build rough wooden structures, such as concrete forms, scaffolds, tunnel, bridge, or sewer supports, billboard signs, and temporary frame shelters, according to sketches, blueprints, or oral instructions. Study blueprints and diagrams to determine dimensions of structure or form to be constructed. Measure materials or distances, using square, measuring tape, or rule to lay out work. Cut or saw boards, timbers, or plywood to required size, using handsaw, power saw, or woodworking machine. Assemble and fasten material together to construct wood or metal framework of structure, using bolts, nails, or screws. Anchor and brace forms and other structures in place, using nails, bolts, anchor rods, steel cables, planks, wedges, and timbers. Mark cutting lines on materials, using pencil and scriber. Erect forms, framework, scaffolds, hoists, roof supports, or chutes, using hand tools, plumb rule, and level. Install rough door and window frames, subflooring, fixtures, or temporary supports in structures undergoing construction or repair. Examine structural timbers and supports to detect decay and replace timbers as required, using hand tools, nuts, and bolts. Bore boltholes in timber, masonry, or concrete walls, using power drill. Fabricate parts, using woodworking and metalworking machines. Dig or direct digging of post holes and set poles to support structures. Build sleds from logs and timbers for use in hauling camp buildings and machinery through wooded areas. Build chutes for pouring concrete.

Education/Training Required: Long-term on-the-job training. **Education and Training Program:** Carpentry/Carpenter. **Knowledge/Courses:** Building and Construction; Design; Mechanical Devices; Production and Processing; Public Safety and Security; Mathematics.

Personality Type: Realistic-Conventional-Investigative. **Career Cluster:** 02 Architecture and Construction. **Career Pathway:** 02.2 Construction.

Skills: Repairing; Equipment Maintenance; Troubleshooting; Operation and Control; Installation; Mathematics; Operation Monitoring; Coordination.

Work Environment: Outdoors; standing; walking and running; kneeling, crouching, stooping, or crawling; balancing; using hands; bending or twisting the body; repetitive motions; noise; very hot or cold; contaminants; cramped work space; high places; hazardous equipment; minor burns, cuts, bites, or stings.

Cartographers and Photogrammetrists

- ❋ Personality Type: Realistic-Conventional-Investigative
- ❋ Annual Earnings: $54,510
- ❋ Earnings Growth Potential: Medium (39.0%)
- ❋ Growth: 26.8%
- ❋ Annual Job Openings: 640
- ❋ Self-Employed: 2.5%

Considerations for Job Outlook: Increasing demand for geographic information should be the main source of employment growth. Job-seekers with a bachelor's degree and strong technical skills should have favorable prospects.

Collect, analyze, and interpret geographic information provided by geodetic surveys, aerial photographs, and satellite data. Research, study, and prepare maps and other spatial data in digital or graphic form for legal, social, political, educational, and design purposes. May work with Geographic Information Systems (GIS). May design and evaluate algorithms, data structures, and user interfaces for GIS and mapping systems. Identify, scale, and orient geodetic points, elevations, and other planimetric or topographic features, applying standard mathematical formulas. Collect information about specific features of the Earth, using aerial photography and other digital remote sensing techniques. Revise existing maps and charts, making all necessary corrections and adjustments. Compile data required for map preparation, including aerial photographs, survey notes, records, reports, and original maps. Inspect final compositions to ensure completeness and accuracy. Determine map content and layout as well as production specifications such as scale, size, projection, and colors, and direct production to ensure that specifications are followed. Examine and analyze data from ground surveys, reports, aerial photographs, and satellite images to prepare topographic maps, aerial-photograph mosaics, and related charts. Select aerial photographic and remote sensing techniques and plotting equipment needed to meet required standards of accuracy. Delineate aerial photographic detail such as control points, hydrography, topography, and cultural features, using precision stereoplotting apparatus or drafting instruments. Build and update digital databases. Prepare and alter trace maps, charts, tables, detailed drawings, and three-dimensional optical models of terrain, using stereoscopic plotting and computer graphics equipment. Determine guidelines that specify which source material is acceptable for use.

Education/Training Required: Bachelor's degree. **Education and Training Programs:** Geographic Information Science and Cartography; Surveying Technology/Surveying. **Knowledge/Courses:** Geography; Design; Computers and Electronics; Mathematics; Production and Processing.

Career Clusters: 02 Architecture and Construction; 15 Science, Technology, Engineering, and Mathematics. **Career Pathways:** 02.1 Design/Pre-Construction; 15.2 Science and Mathematics.

Skills: Mathematics; Systems Analysis; Writing; Programming; Reading Comprehension; Learning Strategies; Instructing; Technology Design.

Work Environment: Indoors; sitting; using hands; repetitive motions.

Cement Masons and Concrete Finishers

- ❋ Personality Type: Realistic-Enterprising
- ❋ Annual Earnings: $35,450
- ❋ Earnings Growth Potential: Low (34.8%)
- ❋ Growth: 12.9%
- ❋ Annual Job Openings: 7,640
- ❋ Self-Employed: 4.7%

Considerations for Job Outlook: Expected employment growth should result from new construction projects and from the need to repair and renovate existing highways, bridges, and other structures. Entry-level opportunities should be good.

Smooth and finish surfaces of poured concrete, such as floors, walks, sidewalks, roads, or curbs, using a variety of hand and power tools. Align forms for sidewalks, curbs, or gutters; patch voids; and use saws to cut expansion joints. Check the forms that hold the concrete to see that they are properly constructed. Set the forms that hold concrete to the desired pitch and depth, and align them. Spread, level, and smooth concrete, using rake, shovel, hand or power trowel, hand or power screed, and float. Mold expansion joints and edges using edging tools, jointers, and straightedge. Monitor how the wind, heat, or cold affect the curing of the concrete throughout the entire process. Signal truck driver to position truck to facilitate pouring concrete and move chute to direct concrete on forms. Produce rough concrete surface, using broom. Operate power vibrator to compact concrete. Direct the casting of the concrete and supervise laborers who use shovels or special tools to spread it. Mix cement, sand, and water to produce concrete, grout, or slurry, using hoe, trowel, tamper, scraper, or concrete-mixing machine. Cut out damaged areas, drill holes for reinforcing rods, and position reinforcing rods to repair concrete using power saw and drill. Wet surface to prepare for bonding, fill holes and cracks with grout or slurry, and smooth using trowel. Wet concrete surface and rub with stone to smooth surface and obtain specified finish. Clean chipped area using wire brush, and feel and observe surface to determine if it is rough or uneven. Apply hardening and sealing compounds to cure surface of concrete and waterproof or restore surface.

Education/Training Required: Moderate-term on-the-job training. **Education and Training Program:** Concrete Finishing/Concrete Finisher. **Knowledge/Courses:** Building and Construction; Mechanical Devices; Engineering and Technology; Design; Chemistry; Physics.

Career Cluster: 02 Architecture and Construction. **Career Pathway:** 02.2 Construction.

Skills: Operation and Control; Mathematics; Quality Control Analysis; Equipment Selection; Installation; Coordination.

Work Environment: Outdoors; standing; walking and running; kneeling, crouching, stooping, or crawling; using hands; bending or twisting the body; repetitive motions; noise; very hot or cold; bright or inadequate lighting; contaminants; whole-body vibration; hazardous equipment; minor burns, cuts, bites, or stings.

Civil Engineering Technicians

- ❋ Personality Type: Realistic-Conventional-Investigative
- ❋ Annual Earnings: $46,290
- ❋ Earnings Growth Potential: Medium (37.2%)
- ❋ Growth: 16.9%
- ❋ Annual Job Openings: 3,280
- ❋ Self-Employed: 0.7%

Considerations for Job Outlook: Labor-saving efficiencies and the automation of many engineering support activities will limit the need for new engineering technicians. In general, opportunities should be best for job-seekers who have an associate degree or other postsecondary training in engineering technology.

Apply theory and principles of civil engineering in planning, designing, and overseeing construction and maintenance of structures and facilities under the direction of engineering staff or physical scientists. Calculate dimensions, square footage, profile and component specifications, and material quantities using calculator or computer. Draft detailed dimensional drawings, and design layouts for projects and to ensure conformance to specifications. Analyze proposed site factors, and design maps, graphs, tracings, and diagrams to illustrate findings. Read and review project blueprints and structural specifications to determine dimensions of structure or system and material requirements. Prepare reports, and document project activities and data. Confer with supervisor to determine project details such as plan preparation, acceptance testing, and evaluation of field conditions. Inspect project site, and evaluate contractor work to detect design malfunctions and ensure conformance to design specifications and applicable codes. Plan and conduct field surveys to locate new sites, and analyze details of project sites. Develop plans and estimate costs for installation of systems, utilization of facilities, or construction of structures. Report maintenance problems occurring at project site to supervisor, and negotiate changes to resolve system conflicts. Conduct materials test and analysis using tools and equipment and applying engineering knowledge. Respond to public suggestions and complaints. Evaluate facility to determine suitability for occupancy and square footage availability.

Education/Training Required: Associate degree. **Education and Training Programs:** Civil Engineering Technology/Technician; Construction Engineering Technology/Technician. **Knowledge/Courses:** Building and Construction; Engineering and Technology; Design; Geography; Transportation; Physics.

Career Clusters: 02 Architecture and Construction; 13 Manufacturing. **Career Pathways:** 02.1 Design/Pre-Construction; 13.3 Maintenance, Installation, and Repair.

Skills: Operations Analysis; Operation Monitoring; Operation and Control; Mathematics; Science;

Management of Financial Resources; Management of Material Resources; Active Listening.

Work Environment: More often indoors than outdoors; sitting; using hands; repetitive motions.

Civil Engineers

* Personality Type: Realistic-Investigative-Conventional
* Annual Earnings: $77,560
* Earnings Growth Potential: Low (34.8%)
* Growth: 24.3%
* Annual Job Openings: 11,460
* Self-Employed: 4.3%

Considerations for Job Outlook: Civil engineers are expected to have employment growth of 24 percent from 2008 to 2018, much faster than the average for all occupations. Spurred by general population growth and the related need to improve the nation's infrastructure, more civil engineers will be needed to design and construct or expand transportation, water supply, and pollution-control systems as well as buildings and building complexes. They also will be needed to repair or replace existing roads, bridges, and other public structures. Because construction industries and architectural, engineering, and related services employ many civil engineers, employment opportunities will vary by geographic area and may decrease during economic slowdowns, when construction is often curtailed.

Perform engineering duties in planning, designing, and overseeing construction and maintenance of building structures and facilities such as roads, railroads, airports, bridges, harbors, channels, dams, irrigation projects, pipelines, power plants, water and sewage systems, and waste disposal units. Includes architectural, structural, traffic, ocean, and geo-technical engineers. Manage and direct staff members and construction, operations, or maintenance activities at project site. Provide technical advice regarding design, construction, or program modifications and structural repairs

Realistic-C

to industrial and managerial personnel. Inspect project sites to monitor progress and ensure conformance to design specifications and safety or sanitation standards. Estimate quantities and cost of materials, equipment, or labor to determine project feasibility. Test soils and materials to determine the adequacy and strength of foundations, concrete, asphalt, or steel. Compute load and grade requirements, water flow rates, and material stress factors to determine design specifications. Plan and design transportation or hydraulic systems and structures, following construction and government standards and using design software and drawing tools. Analyze survey reports, maps, drawings, blueprints, aerial photography, and other topographical or geologic data to plan projects. Prepare or present public reports on topics such as bid proposals, deeds, environmental-impact statements, or property and right-of-way descriptions. Direct or participate in surveying to lay out installations, and establish reference points, grades, and elevations to guide construction. Conduct studies of traffic patterns or environmental conditions to identify engineering problems and assess the potential impact of projects.

Education/Training Required: Bachelor's degree. **Education and Training Programs:** Civil Engineering, General; Civil Engineering, Other; Transportation and Highway Engineering; Water Resources Engineering. **Knowledge/Courses:** Engineering and Technology; Building and Construction; Design; Physics; Transportation; Mathematics.

Career Cluster: 15 Science, Technology, Engineering, and Mathematics. **Career Pathway:** 15.1 Engineering and Technology.

Skills: Operations Analysis; Mathematics; Science; Management of Financial Resources; Management of Material Resources; Programming; Systems Evaluation; Systems Analysis.

Work Environment: Indoors; sitting.

Job Specialization: Transportation Engineers

Develop plans for surface transportation projects according to established engineering standards and state or federal construction policy. Prepare plans, estimates, or specifications to design transportation facilities. Plan alterations and modifications of existing streets, highways, or freeways to improve traffic flow. Prepare data, maps, or other information at construction-related public hearings and meetings. Review development plans to determine potential traffic impact. Prepare administrative, technical, or statistical reports on traffic-operation matters, such as accidents, safety measures, and pedestrian volume and practices. Evaluate transportation systems or traffic control devices and lighting systems to determine need for modification or expansion. Evaluate traffic control devices or lighting systems to determine need for modification or expansion. Develop, or assist in the development of, transportation-related computer software or computer processes. Prepare project budgets, schedules, or specifications for labor and materials. Prepare final project-layout drawings that include details such as stress calculations. Plan alteration and modification of existing transportation structures to improve safety or function. Participate in contract bidding, negotiation, or administration. Model transportation scenarios to evaluate the impact of activities such as new development or to identify possible solutions to transportation problems. Investigate traffic problems, and recommend methods to improve traffic flow and safety. Investigate or test specific construction-project materials to determine compliance to specifications or standards. Inspect completed transportation projects to ensure safety or compliance with applicable standards or regulations.

Education/Training Required: Bachelor's degree. **Education and Training Programs:** Civil Engineering, General; Civil Engineering, Other; Transportation and Highway Engineering; Water Resources Engineering. **Knowledge/Courses:** Engineering and Technology; Design; Transportation; Building and Construction; Physics; Geography.

Personality Type: Realistic-Investigative. **Career Cluster:** 15 Science, Technology, Engineering, and Mathematics. **Career Pathway:** 15.1 Engineering and Technology.

Skills: Management of Financial Resources; Management of Material Resources; Mathematics; Programming; Operations Analysis; Technology Design; Systems Analysis; Science.

Work Environment: Indoors; sitting.

Commercial Pilots

- ❀ Personality Type: Realistic-Investigative-Enterprising
- ❀ Annual Earnings: $67,500
- ❀ Earnings Growth Potential: High (48.4%)
- ❀ Growth: 18.6%
- ❀ Annual Job Openings: 2,060
- ❀ Self-Employed: 12.0%

Considerations for Job Outlook: Population growth and economic expansion are expected to boost demand for air travel. Regional airlines and low-cost carriers should have the best opportunities; pilots vying for jobs with major airlines face strong competition.

Pilot and navigate the flight of small fixed- or rotary-winged aircraft primarily for the transport of cargo and passengers. Requires commercial rating. Check aircraft prior to flights to ensure that the engines, controls, instruments, and other systems are functioning properly. Start engines, operate controls, and pilot airplanes to transport passengers, mail, or freight while adhering to flight plans, regulations, and procedures. Contact control towers for takeoff clearances, arrival instructions, and other information, using radio equipment. Monitor engine operation, fuel consumption, and functioning of aircraft systems during flights. Consider airport altitudes, outside temperatures, plane weights, and wind speeds and directions to calculate the speed needed to become airborne. Order changes in fuel supplies, loads, routes, or schedules to ensure safety of flights.

Obtain and review data such as load weights, fuel supplies, weather conditions, and flight schedules to determine flight plans and to see if changes might be necessary. Plan flights, following government and company regulations, using aeronautical charts and navigation instruments. Use instrumentation to pilot aircraft when visibility is poor. Check baggage or cargo to ensure that it has been loaded correctly. Request changes in altitudes or routes as circumstances dictate. Choose routes, altitudes, and speeds that will provide the fastest, safest, and smoothest flights. Coordinate flight activities with ground crews and air-traffic control, and inform crew members of flight and test procedures.

Education/Training Required: Postsecondary vocational training. **Education and Training Programs:** Airline/Commercial/Professional Pilot and Flight Crew Training; Flight Instructor Training. **Knowledge/Courses:** Transportation; Geography; Mechanical Devices; Physics; Telecommunications; Psychology.

Career Cluster: 16 Transportation, Distribution, and Logistics. **Career Pathway:** 16.1 Transportation Operations.

Skills: Operation and Control; Operation Monitoring; Science; Instructing; Troubleshooting; Operations Analysis; Judgment and Decision Making; Complex Problem Solving.

Work Environment: Outdoors; sitting; using hands; noise; very hot or cold; contaminants; cramped work space.

Computer User Support Specialists

- ❀ Personality Type: Realistic-Investigative-Conventional
- ❀ Annual Earnings: $46,260
- ❀ Earnings Growth Potential: Medium (38.8%)
- ❀ Growth: 13.8%
- ❀ Annual Job Openings: 23,460
- ❀ Self-Employed: 1.2%

Realistic-C

Considerations for Job Outlook: As technology becomes more complex and has wider applications, these workers will be needed to resolve problems. Prospects should be good; job-seekers with a bachelor's degree and relevant work experience should have the best opportunities.

Provide technical assistance to computer users. Answer questions or resolve computer problems for clients in person, via telephone, or electronically. May provide assistance concerning the use of computer hardware and software, including printing, installation, word processing, electronic mail, and operating systems. Answer user inquiries regarding computer software or hardware operation to resolve problems. Enter commands and observe system functioning to verify correct operations and detect errors. Install and perform minor repairs to hardware, software, or peripheral equipment, following design or installation specifications. Oversee the daily performance of computer systems. Set up equipment for employee use, performing or ensuring proper installation of cables, operating systems, or appropriate software. Maintain records of daily data communication transactions, problems and remedial actions taken, or installation activities. Read technical manuals, confer with users, or conduct computer diagnostics to investigate and resolve problems or to provide technical assistance and support. Confer with staff, users, and management to establish requirements for new systems or modifications. Develop training materials and procedures, or train users in the proper use of hardware or software. Refer major hardware or software problems or defective products to vendors or technicians for service. Prepare evaluations of software or hardware, and recommend improvements or upgrades. Read trade magazines and technical manuals, or attend conferences and seminars to maintain knowledge of hardware and software. Inspect equipment and read order sheets to prepare for delivery to users. Modify and customize commercial programs for internal needs.

Education/Training Required: Work experience in a related occupation. **Education and Training Program:** Computer Support Specialist Training.

Knowledge/Courses: Computers and Electronics; Telecommunications; Engineering and Technology; Clerical Practices; Customer and Personal Service; Communications and Media.

Career Cluster: 11 Information Technology. **Career Pathway:** 11.2 Information Support Services.

Skills: Troubleshooting; Equipment Maintenance; Installation; Repairing; Programming; Quality Control Analysis; Operation and Control; Operations Analysis.

Work Environment: Indoors; sitting; using hands.

Construction and Building Inspectors

- ❋ Personality Type: Realistic-Conventional-Investigative
- ❋ Annual Earnings: $52,360
- ❋ Earnings Growth Potential: Medium (38.9%)
- ❋ Growth: 16.8%
- ❋ Annual Job Openings: 3,970
- ❋ Self-Employed: 7.5%

Considerations for Job Outlook: Employment growth is expected to be driven by desires for safety and improved quality of construction. Prospects should be best for workers who have some college education, certification, and construction experience.

Inspect structures using engineering skills to determine structural soundness and compliance with specifications, building codes, and other regulations. Inspections may be general in nature or may be limited to a specific area, such as electrical systems or plumbing. Issue violation notices and stop-work orders, conferring with owners, violators, and authorities to explain regulations and recommend rectifications. Inspect bridges, dams, highways, buildings, wiring, plumbing, electrical circuits, sewers, heating systems, and foundations during and after construction for structural quality, general safety, and conformance to specifications and codes. Approve and sign plans that meet required specifications. Review and interpret plans, blueprints, site layouts, specifications, and construction methods to ensure compliance to legal requirements and safety regulations. Monitor installation of plumbing, wiring, equipment, and appliances to ensure that installation is performed properly and is in compliance with applicable regulations. Inspect and monitor construction sites to ensure adherence to safety standards, building codes, and specifications. Measure dimensions and verify level, alignment, and elevation of structures and fixtures to ensure compliance to building plans and codes. Maintain daily logs, and supplement inspection records with photographs. Use survey instruments, metering devices, tape measures, and test equipment such as concrete strength measurers to perform inspections. Train, direct, and supervise other construction inspectors. Issue permits for construction, relocation, demolition, and occupancy.

Education/Training Required: Work experience in a related occupation. **Education and Training Program:** Building/Home/Construction Inspection/Inspector. **Knowledge/Courses:** Building and Construction; Engineering and Technology; Design; Physics; Public Safety and Security; Mechanical Devices.

Career Cluster: 02 Architecture and Construction. **Career Pathway:** 02.2 Construction.

Skills: Science; Quality Control Analysis; Operation and Control; Systems Evaluation; Mathematics; Systems Analysis; Operation Monitoring; Troubleshooting.

Work Environment: More often outdoors than indoors; standing; noise; very hot or cold; bright or inadequate lighting; contaminants; cramped work space; high places.

Construction Laborers

- Personality Type: Realistic-Conventional
- Annual Earnings: $29,280
- Earnings Growth Potential: Medium (36.6%)
- Growth: 20.5%
- Annual Job Openings: 33,940
- Self-Employed: 21.3%

Considerations for Job Outlook: Employment of these workers is projected to increase because of additional government spending on infrastructure repair and reconstruction. Opportunities will vary based on job-seekers' experience, training, and willingness to relocate.

Perform tasks involving physical labor at building, highway, and heavy construction projects; tunnel and shaft excavations; and demolition sites. May operate hand and power tools of all types: air hammers, earth tampers, cement mixers, small mechanical hoists, surveying and measuring equipment, and various other types of equipment and instruments. May clean and prepare sites; dig trenches; set braces to support the sides of excavations; erect scaffolding; clean up rubble and debris; and remove asbestos, lead, and other hazardous waste materials. May assist other craft workers. Clean and prepare construction sites to eliminate possible hazards. Read and interpret plans, instructions, and specifications to determine work activities. Control traffic passing near, in, and around work zones. Signal equipment operators to facilitate alignment, movement, and adjustment of machinery, equipment, and materials. Dig ditches or trenches, backfill excavations, and compact and level earth to grade specifications, using picks, shovels, pneumatic tampers, and rakes. Measure, mark, and record openings and distances to lay out areas where construction work will be performed. Position, join, align, and seal structural components such as concrete wall sections and pipes. Load, unload, and identify building materials, machinery, and tools, and distribute them to the appropriate locations ac-

Realistic-C

cording to project plans and specifications. Erect and disassemble scaffolding, shoring, braces, traffic barricades, ramps, and other temporary structures. Build and position forms for pouring concrete, and dismantle forms after use, using saws, hammers, nails, or bolts. Lubricate, clean, and repair machinery, equipment, and tools. Operate jackhammers and drills to break up concrete or pavement. Smooth and finish freshly poured cement or concrete using floats, trowels, screeds, or powered cement-finishing tools. Operate, read, and maintain air-monitoring and other sampling devices in confined or hazardous environments.

Education/Training Required: Moderate-term on-the-job training. **Education and Training Program:** Construction Trades, Other. **Knowledge/Courses:** Building and Construction; Design; Mechanical Devices; Transportation; Public Safety and Security; Engineering and Technology.

Career Cluster: 02 Architecture and Construction. **Career Pathway:** 02.2 Construction.

Skills: Operation and Control; Equipment Selection; Installation; Equipment Maintenance; Operation Monitoring; Troubleshooting; Repairing; Quality Control Analysis.

Work Environment: Outdoors; standing; using hands; bending or twisting the body; repetitive motions; noise; very hot or cold; bright or inadequate lighting; contaminants; whole-body vibration; hazardous equipment; minor burns, cuts, bites, or stings.

Correctional Officers and Jailers

* Personality Type: Realistic-Enterprising-Conventional
* Annual Earnings: $39,040
* Earnings Growth Potential: Low (33.3%)
* Growth: 9.4%
* Annual Job Openings: 14,360
* Self-Employed: 0.0%

Considerations for Job Outlook: Employment growth is expected to stem from population increases and a corresponding rise in the prison population. Favorable job opportunities are expected.

Guard inmates in penal or rehabilitative institution in accordance with established regulations and procedures. May guard prisoners in transit between jail, courtroom, prison, or other point. Includes deputy sheriffs and police who spend the majority of their time guarding prisoners in correctional institutions. Conduct head counts to ensure that each prisoner is present. Monitor conduct of prisoners in housing unit or during work or recreational activities according to established policies, regulations, and procedures to prevent escape or violence. Inspect conditions of locks, window bars, grills, doors, and gates at correctional facilities to ensure security and help prevent escapes. Record information such as prisoner identification, charges, and incidences of inmate disturbance, and keep daily logs of prisoner activities. Search prisoners and vehicles and conduct shakedowns of cells for valuables and contraband such as weapons or drugs. Use weapons, handcuffs, and physical force to maintain discipline and order among prisoners. Guard facility entrances to screen visitors. Inspect mail for the presence of contraband. Maintain records of prisoners' identification and charges. Process or book convicted individuals into prison. Settle disputes between inmates. Conduct fire, safety, and sanitation inspections. Provide to supervisors oral and written reports of the quality and quantity of work performed by inmates, inmate disturbances and rule violations, and unusual occurrences. Participate in required job training. Take prisoners into custody, and escort them to locations within and outside of facility, such as visiting room, courtroom, or airport. Serve meals, distribute commissary items, and dispense prescribed medications to prisoners.

Education/Training Required: Moderate-term on-the-job training. **Education and Training Programs:** Corrections; Corrections and Criminal Justice, Other; Juvenile Corrections. **Knowledge/Courses:** Public Safety and Security; Psychology;

Therapy and Counseling; Law and Government; Medicine and Dentistry; Sociology and Anthropology.

Career Cluster: 12 Law, Public Safety, Corrections, and Security. **Career Pathways:** 12.2 Emergency and Fire Management Services; 12.4 Law Enforcement Services.

Skills: Negotiation; Persuasion; Social Perceptiveness; Service Orientation; Monitoring; Instructing; Coordination; Operation Monitoring.

Work Environment: Indoors; more often sitting than standing; walking and running; using hands; repetitive motions; noise; bright or inadequate lighting; contaminants; exposed to disease or infections.

Drywall and Ceiling Tile Installers

❋ Personality Type: Realistic-Conventional
❋ Annual Earnings: $37,320
❋ Earnings Growth Potential: Low (34.4%)
❋ Growth: 13.5%
❋ Annual Job Openings: 3,700
❋ Self-Employed: 18.8%

Considerations for Job Outlook: Projected employment growth is likely to stem from increases in new construction and remodeling. Overall job prospects are expected to be good, especially for experienced workers.

Apply plasterboard or other wallboard to ceilings or interior walls of buildings. Apply or mount acoustical tiles or blocks, strips, or sheets of shock-absorbing materials to ceilings and walls of buildings to reduce or reflect sound. Materials may be of decorative quality. Includes lathers who fasten wooden, metal, or rockboard lath to walls, ceilings, or partitions of buildings to provide support base for plaster, fireproofing, or acoustical material. Inspect furrings, mechanical mountings, and masonry surface for plumbness and level, using spirit or water levels. Install metal lath where plaster applications will be exposed to weather or water or

for curved or irregular surfaces. Install blanket insulation between studs, and tack plastic moisture barriers over insulation. Coordinate work with drywall finishers who cover the seams between drywall panels. Trim rough edges from wallboard to maintain even joints using knives. Seal joints between ceiling tiles and walls. Scribe and cut edges of tile to fit walls where wall molding is not specified. Read blueprints and other specifications to determine methods of installation, work procedures, and material and tool requirements. Nail channels or wood furring strips to surfaces to provide mounting for tile. Mount tile by using adhesives or by nailing, screwing, stapling, or wire-tying lath directly to structural frameworks. Measure and mark surfaces to lay out work according to blueprints and drawings using tape measures, straightedges or squares, and marking devices. Hang drywall panels on metal frameworks of walls and ceilings in offices, schools, and other large buildings using lifts or hoists to adjust panel heights when necessary. Install horizontal and vertical metal or wooden studs to frames so that wallboard can be attached to interior walls.

Education/Training Required: Moderate-term on-the-job training. **Education and Training Program:** Drywall Installation/Drywaller. **Knowledge/Courses:** Building and Construction; Design; Mechanical Devices; Mathematics; Production and Processing; Public Safety and Security.

Career Cluster: 02 Architecture and Construction. **Career Pathway:** 02.2 Construction.

Skills: Repairing; Equipment Maintenance; Installation; Operation and Control; Troubleshooting; Equipment Selection; Quality Control Analysis; Operation Monitoring.

Work Environment: More often outdoors than indoors; standing; climbing; walking and running; kneeling, crouching, stooping, or crawling; balancing; using hands; bending or twisting the body; repetitive motions; noise; very hot or cold; bright or inadequate lighting; contaminants; cramped work space; high places; hazardous equipment; minor burns, cuts, bites, or stings.

Realistic-D

Electrical Power-Line Installers and Repairers

* Personality Type: Realistic-Investigative-Conventional
* Annual Earnings: $58,030
* Earnings Growth Potential: High (42.0%)
* Growth: 4.5%
* Annual Job Openings: 4,550
* Self-Employed: 1.4%

Considerations for Job Outlook: Slow decline in employment is projected.

Install or repair cables or wires used in electrical power or distribution systems. May erect poles and light- or heavy-duty transmission towers. Adhere to safety practices and procedures, such as checking equipment regularly and erecting barriers around work areas. Open switches or attach grounding devices to remove electrical hazards from disturbed or fallen lines or to facilitate repairs. Climb poles or use truck-mounted buckets to access equipment. Place insulating or fireproofing materials over conductors and joints. Install, maintain, and repair electrical distribution and transmission systems, including conduits; cables; wires; and related equipment such as transformers, circuit breakers, and switches. Identify defective sectionalizing devices, circuit breakers, fuses, voltage regulators, transformers, switches, relays, or wiring, using wiring diagrams and electrical-testing instruments. Drive vehicles equipped with tools and materials to job sites. Coordinate work-assignment preparation and completion with other workers. String wire conductors and cables between poles, towers, trenches, pylons, and buildings, setting lines in place and using winches to adjust tension. Inspect and test power lines and auxiliary equipment to locate and identify problems, using reading and testing instruments. Test conductors according to electrical diagrams and specifications to identify corresponding conductors and to prevent incorrect connections. Replace damaged poles with new poles, and straighten the poles. Install watt-hour meters, and connect service drops between power lines and consumers' facilities.

Education/Training Required: Long-term on-the-job training. **Education and Training Programs:** Electrical and Power Transmission Installation/Installer, General; Electrical and Power Transmission Installers, Other; Lineworker. **Knowledge/Courses:** Building and Construction; Mechanical Devices; Customer and Personal Service; Engineering and Technology; Transportation; Design.

Career Cluster: 02 Architecture and Construction. **Career Pathway:** 02.2 Construction.

Skills: Repairing; Troubleshooting; Equipment Maintenance; Operation and Control; Quality Control Analysis; Operation Monitoring; Installation; Equipment Selection.

Work Environment: Outdoors; standing; walking and running; using hands; bending or twisting the body; repetitive motions; noise; very hot or cold; bright or inadequate lighting; contaminants; cramped work space; high places; hazardous conditions; hazardous equipment; minor burns, cuts, bites, or stings.

Electricians

* Personality Type: Realistic-Investigative-Conventional
* Annual Earnings: $48,250
* Earnings Growth Potential: Medium (39.1%)
* Growth: 11.9%
* Annual Job Openings: 25,090
* Self-Employed: 9.3%

Considerations for Job Outlook: Population growth is expected to spur increases in construction, which in turn will increase employment of electricians. The need to update the electrical systems of existing buildings should also drive employment growth. Opportunities should be good.

Install, maintain, and repair electrical wiring, equipment, and fixtures. Ensure that work is in accordance with relevant codes. May install or

service street lights, intercom systems, or electrical control systems. Maintain current electrician's license or identification card to meet governmental regulations. Connect wires to circuit breakers, transformers, or other components. Repair or replace wiring, equipment, and fixtures, using hand tools and power tools. Assemble, install, test, and maintain electrical or electronic wiring, equipment, appliances, apparatus, and fixtures, using hand tools and power tools. Test electrical systems and continuity of circuits in electrical wiring, equipment, and fixtures, using testing devices such as ohmmeters, voltmeters, and oscilloscopes, to ensure compatibility and safety of system. Use a variety of tools and equipment such as power construction equipment, measuring devices, power tools, and testing equipment, including oscilloscopes, ammeters, and test lamps. Plan layout and installation of electrical wiring, equipment, and fixtures based on job specifications and local codes. Inspect electrical systems, equipment, and components to identify hazards, defects, and the need for adjustment or repair and to ensure compliance with codes. Direct and train workers to install, maintain, or repair electrical wiring, equipment, and fixtures. Diagnose malfunctioning systems, apparatus, and components, using test equipment and hand tools, to locate the cause of a breakdown and correct the problem. Prepare sketches or follow blueprints to determine the location of wiring and equipment and to ensure conformance to building and safety codes.

Education/Training Required: Long-term on-the-job training. **Education and Training Program:** Electrician. **Knowledge/Courses:** Building and Construction; Mechanical Devices; Design; Physics; Telecommunications; Engineering and Technology.

Career Cluster: 02 Architecture and Construction. **Career Pathway:** 02.2 Construction.

Skills: Installation; Repairing; Equipment Maintenance; Troubleshooting; Equipment Selection; Quality Control Analysis; Operation and Control; Management of Financial Resources.

Work Environment: More often outdoors than indoors; standing; climbing; walking and running; us-

ing hands; bending or twisting the body; repetitive motions; noise; very hot or cold; bright or inadequate lighting; contaminants; cramped work space; high places; hazardous conditions; hazardous equipment; minor burns, cuts, bites, or stings.

Environmental Engineering Technicians

- ❀ Personality Type: Realistic-Investigative-Conventional
- ❀ Annual Earnings: $43,390
- ❀ Earnings Growth Potential: Low (35.5%)
- ❀ Growth: 30.1%
- ❀ Annual Job Openings: 1,040
- ❀ Self-Employed: 0.7%

Considerations for Job Outlook: Labor-saving efficiencies and the automation of many engineering-support activities will limit the need for new engineering technicians. In general, opportunities should be best for job-seekers who have an associate degree or other postsecondary training in engineering technology.

Apply theory and principles of environmental engineering to modify, test, and operate equipment and devices used in the prevention, control, and remediation of environmental pollution, including waste treatment and site remediation. May assist in the development of environmental pollution remediation devices under direction of engineer. Receive, set up, test, and decontaminate equipment. Maintain project logbook records and computer program files. Perform environmental quality work in field and office settings. Conduct pollution surveys, collecting and analyzing samples such as air and groundwater. Review technical documents to ensure completeness and conformance to requirements. Perform laboratory work such as logging numerical and visual observations, preparing and packaging samples, recording test results, and performing photo documentation. Review work plans to schedule activities. Obtain product information, identify vendors and suppliers, and order materials and equipment to maintain inventory. Arrange for the disposal of lead, asbestos, and other hazardous materials. Inspect facilities to monitor compliance with regulations governing substances such as asbestos, lead, and wastewater. Provide technical engineering support in the planning of projects such as wastewater treatment plants to ensure compliance with environmental regulations and policies. Improve chemical processes to reduce toxic emissions. Oversee support staff. Assist in the cleanup of hazardous material spills. Produce environmental assessment reports, tabulating data and preparing charts, graphs, and sketches. Maintain process parameters, and evaluate process anomalies. Work with customers to assess the environmental impact of proposed construction and to develop pollution prevention programs.

Education/Training Required: Associate degree. **Education and Training Programs:** Environmental Engineering Technology/Environmental Technology; Hazardous Materials Information Systems Technology/Technician. **Knowledge/Courses:** Biology; Building and Construction; Physics; Chemistry; Engineering and Technology; Design.

Career Clusters: 01 Agriculture, Food, and Natural Resources; 13 Manufacturing. **Career Pathways:** 01.6 Environmental Service Systems; 13.4 Quality Assurance.

Skills: Science; Mathematics; Equipment Maintenance; Quality Control Analysis; Management of Material Resources; Equipment Selection; Troubleshooting; Repairing.

Work Environment: Indoors.

Firefighters

- ❋ Personality Type: Realistic-Social
- ❋ Annual Earnings: $45,250
- ❋ Earnings Growth Potential: High (49.1%)
- ❋ Growth: 18.5%
- ❋ Annual Job Openings: 15,280
- ❋ Self-Employed: 0.2%

Considerations for Job Outlook: Most job growth will stem from the conversion of volunteer fire fighting positions into paid positions. Job-seekers are expected to face keen competition. Those who have completed some fire fighter education at a community college and have EMT or paramedic certification should have the best prospects.

Job Specialization: Forest Firefighters

Control and suppress fires in forests or vacant public land. Maintain contact with fire dispatchers at all times to notify them of the need for additional firefighters and supplies or to detail any difficulties encountered. Rescue fire victims, and administer emergency medical aid. Collaborate with other firefighters as a member of a firefighting crew. Patrol burned areas after fires to locate and eliminate hot spots that may restart fires. Extinguish flames and embers to suppress fires using shovels or engine- or hand-driven water or chemical pumps. Fell trees, cut and clear brush, and dig trenches to create firelines using axes, chain saws, or shovels. Maintain knowledge of current firefighting practices by participating in drills and by attending seminars, conventions, and conferences. Operate pumps connected to high-pressure hoses. Participate in physical training to maintain high levels of physical fitness. Establish water supplies, connect hoses, and direct water onto fires. Maintain fire equipment and firehouse living quarters. Inform and educate the public about fire prevention. Take action to contain any hazardous chemicals that could catch fire, leak, or spill. Organize fire caches, positioning equipment for the most effective response. Transport personnel and cargo to and from fire areas. Participate in fire-prevention and inspection programs. Perform forest-maintenance and improvement tasks such as cutting brush, planting trees, building trails, and marking timber.

Education/Training Required: Long-term on-the-job training. **Education and Training Programs:** Fire Protection, Other; Fire Science/Firefighting. **Knowledge/Courses:** Geography; Building and Construction; Telecommunications; Mechanical

Devices; Public Safety and Security; Customer and Personal Service.

Personality Type: Realistic-Social. **Career Cluster:** 12 Law, Public Safety, Corrections, and Security. **Career Pathways:** 12.2 Emergency and Fire Management Services; 12.3 Security and Protective Services.

Skills: Repairing; Equipment Maintenance; Equipment Selection; Operation and Control; Troubleshooting; Quality Control Analysis; Operation Monitoring; Coordination.

Work Environment: Outdoors; standing; walking and running; using hands; bending or twisting the body; repetitive motions; noise; very hot or cold; bright or inadequate lighting; contaminants; hazardous conditions; hazardous equipment; minor burns, cuts, bites, or stings.

Job Specialization: Municipal Firefighters

Control and extinguish municipal fires, protect life and property, and conduct rescue efforts. Administer first aid and cardiopulmonary resuscitation to injured persons. Rescue victims from burning buildings and accident sites. Search burning buildings to locate fire victims. Drive and operate fire fighting vehicles and equipment. Move toward the source of a fire, using knowledge of types of fires, construction design, building materials, and physical layout of properties. Dress with equipment such as fire-resistant clothing and breathing apparatus. Position and climb ladders to gain access to upper levels of buildings or to rescue individuals from burning structures. Take action to contain hazardous chemicals that might catch fire, leak, or spill. Assess fires and situations, and report conditions to superiors to receive instructions using two-way radios. Respond to fire alarms and other calls for assistance such as automobile and industrial accidents. Operate pumps connected to high-pressure hoses. Select and attach hose nozzles, depending on fire type, and direct streams of water or chemicals onto fires. Create openings in buildings for ventilation or entrance, using axes, chisels, crowbars, electric saws, or core cutters. Inspect fire sites after flames have been extinguished to ensure that there is no further danger. Lay hose lines, and connect them to water supplies. Protect property from water and smoke using waterproof salvage covers, smoke ejectors, and deodorants. Participate in physical training activities to maintain a high level of physical fitness.

Education/Training Required: Long-term on-the-job training. **Education and Training Programs:** Fire Protection, Other; Fire Science/Firefighting. **Knowledge/Courses:** Building and Construction; Public Safety and Security; Mechanical Devices; Customer and Personal Service; Physics; Geography.

Personality Type: Realistic-Social-Enterprising. **Career Cluster:** 12 Law, Public Safety, Corrections, and Security. **Career Pathway:** 12.2 Emergency and Fire Management Services.

Skills: Equipment Maintenance; Repairing; Troubleshooting; Operation and Control; Equipment Selection; Science; Operation Monitoring; Quality Control Analysis.

Work Environment: More often outdoors than indoors; standing; using hands; noise; very hot or cold; bright or inadequate lighting; contaminants; cramped work space; exposed to disease or infections; hazardous conditions; hazardous equipment; minor burns, cuts, bites, or stings.

Health Technologists and Technicians, All Other

- ❋ Personality Type: Realistic-Investigative-Conventional
- ❋ Annual Earnings: $38,460
- ❋ Earnings Growth Potential: Low (33.5%)
- ❋ Growth: 18.7%
- ❋ Annual Job Openings: 3,200
- ❋ Self-Employed: 5.7%

Considerations for Job Outlook: Faster than average employment growth is projected.

This occupation includes all health technologists and technicians not listed separately. Because this is a highly diverse occupation, no data is available for some information topics.

Education/Training Required: Postsecondary vocational training. **Education and Training Program:** Allied Health Diagnostic, Intervention, and Treatment Professions, Other.

Career Cluster: 08 Health Science. **Career Pathways:** 08.1 Therapeutic Services; 08.2 Diagnostics Services.

Job Specialization: Neurodiagnostic Technologists

Conduct electroneurodiagnostic (END) tests such as electroencephalograms, evoked potentials, polysomnograms, or electronystagmograms. May perform nerve conduction studies. Attach electrodes to patients using adhesives. Summarize technical data to assist physicians to diagnose brain, sleep, or nervous system disorders. Conduct tests or studies such as electroencephalography (EEG), polysomnography (PSG), nerve conduction studies (NCS), electromyography (EMG), and intraoperative monitoring (IOM). Calibrate, troubleshoot, or repair equipment, and correct malfunctions as needed. Conduct tests to determine cerebral death, the absence of brain activity, or the probability of recovery from a coma. Measure visual, auditory, or somatosensory evoked potentials (EPs) to determine responses to stimuli. Indicate artifacts or interferences derived from sources outside of the brain, such as poor electrode contact or patient movement, on electroneurodiagnostic recordings. Measure patients' body parts, and mark locations where electrodes are to be placed. Monitor patients during tests or surgeries, using electroencephalographs (EEG), evoked potential (EP) instruments, or video recording equipment. Set up, program, or record montages or electrical combinations when testing peripheral nerve, spinal cord, subcortical, or cortical responses. Adjust equipment to optimize viewing of the nervous system. Collect patients' medical information needed to customize tests. Submit reports to physicians summarizing test results. Assist in training technicians, medical students, residents, or other staff members.

Education/Training Required: Associate degree. **Education and Training Program:** Electro-neurodiagnostic/Electroencephalographic Technology/Technologist. **Knowledge/Courses:** Medicine and Dentistry; Biology; Psychology; Computers and Electronics; Customer and Personal Service; Clerical Practices.

Personality Type: Realistic-Investigative. **Career Cluster:** 08 Health Science. **Career Pathway:** 08.2 Diagnostics Services.

Skills: Repairing; Troubleshooting; Equipment Maintenance; Operation and Control; Quality Control Analysis; Operation Monitoring; Science; Learning Strategies.

Work Environment: Indoors; sitting; using hands; contaminants; exposed to disease or infections.

Job Specialization: Ophthalmic Medical Technologists

Assist ophthalmologists by performing ophthalmic clinical functions and ophthalmic photography. Provide instruction and supervision to other ophthalmic personnel. Assist with minor surgical procedures, applying aseptic techniques and preparing instruments. May perform eye exams, administer eye medications, and instruct patients in care and use of corrective lenses. Administer topical ophthalmic or oral medications. Assess abnormalities of color vision, such as amblyopia. Assess refractive condition of eyes, using retinoscope. Assist physicians in performing ophthalmic procedures, including surgery. Calculate corrections for refractive errors. Collect ophthalmic measurements or other diagnostic information, using ultrasound equipment, such as A-scan ultrasound biometry or B-scan ultrasonography equipment. Conduct binocular disparity tests to assess depth perception. Conduct ocular motility tests to measure function of eye muscles. Conduct tests, such as the Amsler Grid test, to measure central visual field used in the early diagnosis of macular degeneration, glaucoma, or diseases of the eye. Conduct tonometry or tonography tests to measure intraocular pressure. Conduct visual field tests to measure field of vision. Create three-dimensional images of the eye, using computed tomography (CT). Measure and record lens power, using lensometers. Measure corneal curvature with keratometers or ophthalmometers to aid in the diagnosis of conditions such as astigmatism. Measure corneal thickness using pachymeter or contact ultrasound methods. Measure the thickness of the retinal nerve using scanning laser polarimetry techniques to aid in diagnosis of glaucoma. Measure visual acuity, including near, distance, pinhole, or dynamic visual acuity, using appropriate tests.

Education/Training Required: Associate degree. **Education and Training Program:** Ophthalmic Technician/Technologist Training. **Knowledge/Courses:** No data available.

Personality Type: No data available. **Career Cluster:** 08 Health Science. **Career Pathway:** 08.1 Therapeutic Services.

Skills: No data available.

Work Environment: No data available.

Job Specialization: Radiologic Technicians

Maintain and use equipment and supplies necessary to demonstrate portions of the human body on X-ray film or fluoroscopic screen for diagnostic purposes. Use beam-restrictive devices and patient-shielding techniques to minimize radiation exposure to patient and staff. Position x-ray equipment and adjust controls to set exposure factors, such as time and distance. Position patient on examining table, and set up and adjust equipment to obtain optimum view of specific body area as requested by physician. Determine patients' X-ray needs by reading requests or instructions from physicians. Make exposures necessary for the requested procedures, rejecting and repeating work that does not meet es-

tablished standards. Process exposed radiographs using film processors or computer-generated methods. Explain procedures to patients to reduce anxieties and obtain cooperation. Perform procedures such as linear tomography, mammography, sonograms, joint and cyst aspirations, routine contrast studies, routine fluoroscopy, and examinations of the head, trunk, and extremities under supervision of physician. Prepare and set up X-ray room for patient. Provide assistance to physicians or other technologists in the performance of more complex procedures. Provide students and other technologists with suggestions of additional views, alternate positioning or improved techniques to ensure the images produced are of the highest quality. Coordinate work of other technicians or technologists when procedures require more than one person.

Education/Training Required: Associate degree. **Education and Training Program:** Medical Radiologic Technology/Science—Radiation Therapist. **Knowledge/Courses:** Physics; Medicine and Dentistry; Psychology; Biology; Chemistry; Customer and Personal Service.

Personality Type: Realistic-Conventional-Social. **Career Cluster:** 08 Health Science. **Career Pathways:** 08.1 Therapeutic Services; 08.2 Diagnostics Services.

Skills: Operation and Control; Science; Operation Monitoring; Service Orientation; Troubleshooting; Technology Design; Coordination; Quality Control Analysis.

Work Environment: Indoors; standing; walking and running; using hands; bending or twisting the body; repetitive motions; contaminants; exposed to radiation; exposed to disease or infections.

Job Specialization: Surgical Assistants

Assist surgeons during surgery by performing duties such as tissue retraction, insertion of tubes and intravenous lines, or closure of surgical wounds. Perform preoperative and postoperative duties to facilitate patient care. Adjust and maintain operating room temperature, humidity, or lighting, according to surgeon's specifications. Apply sutures, staples, clips, or other materials to close skin, fascia, or subcutaneous wound layers. Assess skin integrity or other body conditions upon completion of the procedure to determine if damage has occurred from body positioning. Assist in the insertion, positioning, or suturing of closed-wound drainage systems. Assist members of surgical team with gowning or gloving. Clamp, ligate, or cauterize blood vessels to control bleeding during surgical entry using hemostatic clamps, suture ligatures, or electrocautery equipment. Coordinate or participate in the positioning of patients using body-stabilizing equipment or protective padding to provide appropriate exposure for the procedure or to protect against nerve damage or circulation impairment. Coordinate with anesthesia personnel to maintain patient temperature. Discuss with surgeon the nature of the surgical procedure, including operative consent, methods of operative exposure, diagnostic or laboratory data, or patient-advanced directives or other needs. Incise tissue layers in lower extremities to harvest veins. Maintain an unobstructed operative field using surgical retractors, sponges, or suctioning and irrigating equipment. Monitor and maintain aseptic technique throughout procedures. Monitor patient's intra-operative status, including patient position, vital signs, or volume or color of blood.

Education/Training Required: Work experience plus degree. **Education and Training Program:** Surgical Technology/Technologist. **Knowledge/Courses:** No data available.

Personality Type: No data available. **Career Cluster:** 08 Health Science. **Career Pathway:** 08.1 Therapeutic Services.

Skills: No data available.

Work Environment: No data available.

Heating, Air Conditioning, and Refrigeration Mechanics and Installers

- ❋ Personality Type: Realistic-Conventional
- ❋ Annual Earnings: $42,530
- ❋ Earnings Growth Potential: Medium (37.7%)
- ❋ Growth: 28.1%
- ❋ Annual Job Openings: 13,620
- ❋ Self-Employed: 15.5%

Considerations for Job Outlook: Demand for better energy management is expected to create jobs for workers who replace older systems in existing homes and buildings with newer, more efficient units. Prospects should be excellent, particularly for jobseekers who have completed accredited training programs or formal apprenticeships.

Job Specialization: Heating and Air Conditioning Mechanics and Installers

Install, service, and repair heating and air conditioning systems in residences and commercial establishments. Obtain and maintain required certifications. Comply with all applicable standards, policies, and procedures, including safety procedures and the maintenance of a clean work area. Repair or replace defective equipment, components, or wiring. Test electrical circuits and components for continuity, using electrical test equipment. Reassemble and test equipment following repairs. Inspect and test system to verify system compliance with plans and specifications and to detect and locate malfunctions. Discuss heating-cooling system malfunctions with users to isolate problems or to verify that malfunctions have been corrected. Test pipe or tubing joints and connections for leaks, using pressure gauge or soap-and-water solution. Record and report all faults, deficiencies, and other unusual occurrences, as well as the time and materials expended on work orders. Adjust system controls to setting recommended by manufacturer to balance system, using hand tools. Recommend, develop, and perform preventive and general-maintenance procedures such as cleaning, power-washing, and vacuuming equipment; oiling parts; and changing filters. Lay out and connect electrical wiring between controls and equipment according to wiring diagram, using electrician's hand tools. Install auxiliary components to heating-cooling equipment, such as expansion and discharge valves, air ducts, pipes, blowers, dampers, flues, and stokers, following blueprints.

Education/Training Required: Long-term on-the-job training. **Education and Training Programs:** Heating, Air Conditioning, Ventilation, and Refrigeration Maintenance Technology/Technician (HAC, HACR, HVAC, HVACR); Heating, Ventilation, Air Conditioning, and Refrigeration Engineering Technology/Technician; Solar Energy Technology/Technician. **Knowledge/Courses:** Mechanical Devices; Building and Construction; Physics; Chemistry; Design; Engineering and Technology.

Personality Type: Realistic-Conventional-Investigative. **Career Cluster:** 02 Architecture and Construction. **Career Pathways:** 02.2 Construction; 02.3 Maintenance/Operations.

Skills: Installation; Repairing; Equipment Maintenance; Troubleshooting; Equipment Selection; Operation and Control; Quality Control Analysis; Mathematics.

Work Environment: More often outdoors than indoors; standing; walking and running; kneeling, crouching, stooping, or crawling; using hands; bending or twisting the body; noise; very hot or cold; bright or inadequate lighting; contaminants; cramped work space; high places; hazardous conditions; hazardous equipment; minor burns, cuts, bites, or stings.

Job Specialization: Refrigeration Mechanics and Installers

Install and repair industrial and commercial refrigerating systems. Braze or solder parts to repair defective joints and leaks. Observe and test system operation, using gauges and instruments. Test lines, components, and connections for leaks. Dismantle malfunctioning systems, and test components using electrical, mechanical, and pneumatic testing equipment. Adjust or replace worn or defective mechanisms and parts, and reassemble repaired systems. Read blueprints to determine location, size, capacity, and type of components needed to build refrigeration system. Supervise and instruct assistants. Perform mechanical overhauls and refrigerant reclaiming. Install wiring to connect components to an electric power source. Cut, bend, thread, and connect pipe to functional components and water, power, or refrigeration system. Adjust valves according to specifications, and charge system with proper type of refrigerant by pumping the specified gas or fluid into the system. Estimate, order, pick up, deliver, and install materials and supplies needed to maintain equipment in good working condition. Install expansion and control valves using acetylene torches and wrenches. Mount compressor, condenser, and other components in specified locations on frames using hand tools and acetylene welding equipment. Keep records of repairs and replacements made and causes of malfunctions. Schedule work with customers, and initiate work orders, house requisitions, and orders from stock.

Education/Training Required: Long-term on-the-job training. **Education and Training Programs:** Heating, Air Conditioning, Ventilation, and Refrigeration Maintenance Technology/Technician (HAC, HACR, HVAC, HVACR); Heating, Ventilation, Air Conditioning, and Refrigeration Engineering Technology/Technician. **Knowledge/Courses:** Mechanical Devices; Physics; Building and Construction; Engineering and Technology; Design; Chemistry.

Personality Type: Realistic-Conventional-Enterprising. **Career Cluster:** 02 Architecture and Construction. **Career Pathways:** 02.2 Construction; 02.3 Maintenance/Operations.

Skills: Installation; Repairing; Equipment Maintenance; Troubleshooting; Equipment Selection; Operation and Control; Quality Control Analysis; Management of Material Resources.

Work Environment: More often outdoors than indoors; standing; walking and running; kneeling, crouching, stooping, or crawling; using hands; bending or twisting the body; repetitive motions; noise; very hot or cold; bright or inadequate lighting; contaminants; cramped work space; high places; hazardous conditions; hazardous equipment; minor burns, cuts, bites, or stings.

Heavy and Tractor-Trailer Truck Drivers

- ⊛ Personality Type: Realistic-Conventional
- ⊛ Annual Earnings: $37,770
- ⊛ Earnings Growth Potential: Low (34.5%)
- ⊛ Growth: 12.9%
- ⊛ Annual Job Openings: 55,460
- ⊛ Self-Employed: 8.3%

Considerations for Job Outlook: Employment growth for these workers is expected to correspond to overall economic growth. Job opportunities should be favorable, especially for long-haul drivers.

Drive a tractor-trailer combination or a truck with a capacity of at least 26,000 GVW to transport and deliver goods, livestock, or materials in liquid, loose, or packaged form. May be required to unload truck. May require use of automated routing equipment. Requires commercial drivers' license. Follow appropriate safety procedures when transporting dangerous goods. Check vehicles before driving them to ensure that mechanical, safety, and emergency equipment is in good working order. Maintain logs of working hours and of vehicle service and repair status, following applicable state and federal regulations. Obtain receipts or signatures when loads are delivered, and collect payment for services when required. Check all load-related documentation to ensure that it is complete and accurate. Maneuver trucks into loading or unloading positions, following signals from loading crew as needed; check that vehicle position is correct and any special loading equipment is properly positioned. Drive trucks with capacities greater than three tons, including tractor-trailer combinations, to transport and deliver products, livestock, or other materials. Secure cargo for transport, using ropes, blocks, chain, binders, or covers. Read bills of lading to determine assignment details. Report vehicle defects, accidents, traffic violations, or damage to the vehicles. Read and interpret maps to determine vehicle routes. Couple and uncouple trailers by changing trailer jack positions, connecting or disconnecting air and electrical lines, and manipulating fifth-wheel locks. Collect delivery instructions from appropriate sources, verifying instructions and routes. Drive trucks to weigh stations before and after loading and along routes to document weights and to comply with state regulations.

Education/Training Required: Moderate-term on-the-job training. **Education and Training Program:** Truck and Bus Driver Training/Commercial Vehicle Operator and Instructor Training. **Knowledge/Courses:** Transportation; Food Production; Mechanical Devices; Building and Construction; Design; Personnel and Human Resources.

Career Cluster: 16 Transportation, Distribution, and Logistics. **Career Pathway:** 16.1 Transportation Operations.

Skills: Repairing; Operation and Control; Equipment Maintenance; Troubleshooting; Operation Monitoring; Equipment Selection; Quality Control Analysis; Installation.

Work Environment: Outdoors; sitting; using hands; repetitive motions; noise; very hot or cold; bright or inadequate lighting; contaminants; cramped work space; hazardous equipment.

Industrial Machinery Mechanics

* Personality Type: Realistic-Investigative-Conventional
* Annual Earnings: $45,420
* Earnings Growth Potential: Low (34.2%)
* Growth: 7.3%
* Annual Job Openings: 6,240
* Self-Employed: 2.2%

Considerations for Job Outlook: The increasing reliance on machinery in manufacturing is expected to lead to employment growth for these maintenance and installation workers. Favorable job prospects are expected.

Repair, install, adjust, or maintain industrial production and processing machinery or refinery and pipeline distribution systems. Disassemble machinery and equipment to remove parts and make repairs. Repair and replace broken or malfunctioning components of machinery and equipment. Repair and maintain the operating condition of industrial production and processing machinery and equipment. Examine parts for defects such as breakage and excessive wear. Reassemble equipment after completion of inspections, testing, or repairs. Observe and test the operation of machinery and equipment to diagnose malfunctions, using voltmeters and other testing devices. Operate newly repaired machinery and equipment to verify the adequacy of repairs. Clean, lubricate, and adjust parts, equipment, and machinery. Analyze test results, machine error messages, and information obtained from operators to diagnose equipment problems. Record repairs and maintenance performed. Study blueprints and manufacturers' manuals to determine correct installation and operation of machinery. Record parts and materials used, ordering or requisitioning new parts and materials as necessary. Cut and weld metal to repair broken metal parts, fabricate new parts, and assemble new equipment. Demonstrate equipment functions and features to machine operators. Enter codes and instructions to program computer-controlled machinery.

Education/Training Required: Long-term on-the-job training. **Education and Training Programs:** Heavy/Industrial Equipment Maintenance Technologies, Other; Industrial Mechanics and Maintenance Technology. **Knowledge/Courses:** Mechanical Devices; Engineering and Technology; Building and Construction; Design; Chemistry; Physics.

Career Cluster: 13 Manufacturing. **Career Pathway:** 13.3 Maintenance, Installation, and Repair.

Skills: Repairing; Equipment Maintenance; Troubleshooting; Installation; Operation Monitoring; Equipment Selection; Operation and Control; Quality Control Analysis.

Work Environment: Standing; walking and running; kneeling, crouching, stooping, or crawling; using hands; bending or twisting the body; repetitive motions; noise; very hot or cold; contaminants; cramped work space; high places; hazardous conditions; hazardous equipment; minor burns, cuts, bites, or stings.

Life, Physical, and Social Science Technicians, All Other

* Personality Type: Realistic-Conventional-Investigative
* Annual Earnings: $43,350
* Earnings Growth Potential: Medium (40.9%)
* Growth: 13.3%
* Annual Job Openings: 3,640
* Self-Employed: 1.6%

Considerations for Job Outlook: About average employment growth is projected.

This occupation includes all life, physical, and social science technicians not listed separately. Because this is a highly diverse occupation, no data is available for some information topics.

Realistic-L

Education/Training Required: Associate degree. **Education and Training Program:** Science Technologies/Technicians, Other.

Career Clusters: 08 Health Science; 13 Manufacturing. **Career Pathways:** 08.1 Therapeutic Services; 13.2 Manufacturing Production Process Development.

Job Specialization: Precision Agriculture Technicians

Apply geospatial technologies, including geographic information systems (GIS) and Global Positioning System (GPS), to agricultural production and management activities, such as pest scouting, site-specific pesticide application, yield mapping, and variable-rate irrigation. May use computers to develop and analyze maps and remote sensing images to compare physical topography with data on soils, fertilizer, pests, or weather. Collect information about soil and field attributes, yield data, or field boundaries, using field data recorders and basic geographic information systems (GIS). Create, layer, and analyze maps showing precision agricultural data such as crop yields, soil characteristics, input applications, terrain, drainage patterns and field management history. Document and maintain records of precision agriculture information. Compile and analyze geospatial data to determine agricultural implications of factors such as soil quality, terrain, field productivity, fertilizers, and weather conditions. Divide agricultural fields into georeferenced zones based on soil characteristics and production potentials. Develop soil-sampling grids or identify sampling sites, using geospatial technology, for soil testing on characteristics such as nitrogen, phosphorus, and potassium content; pH; and micronutrients. Compare crop-yield maps with maps of soil-test data, chemical-application patterns, or other information to develop site-specific crop-management plans. Apply knowledge of government regulations when making agricultural recommendations. Recommend best crop varieties and seeding rates for specific field areas, based on analysis of geospatial data. Draw and read maps such as soil, contour, and plat maps. Process and analyze data from harvester monitors to develop yield maps.

Education/Training Required: Moderate-term on-the-job training. **Education and Training Program:** Agricultural Mechanics and Equipment/Machine Technology. **Knowledge/Courses:** Food Production; Geography; Biology; Chemistry; Sales and Marketing; Mechanical Devices.

Personality Type: Realistic-Investigative-Conventional. **Career Cluster:** 01 Agriculture, Food, and Natural Resources. **Career Pathways:** 01.2 Plant Systems; 01.3 Animal Systems.

Skills: Equipment Maintenance; Repairing; Science; Troubleshooting; Equipment Selection; Operations Analysis; Quality Control Analysis; Operation and Control.

Work Environment: Outdoors; very hot or cold.

Job Specialization: Quality Control Analysts

Conduct tests to determine quality of raw materials as well as bulk intermediate and finished products. May conduct stability sample tests. Train other analysts to perform laboratory procedures and assays. Perform visual inspections of finished products. Serve as a technical liaison between quality control and other departments, vendors, or contractors. Participate in internal assessments and audits as required. Identify and troubleshoot equipment problems. Evaluate new technologies and methods to make recommendations regarding their use. Ensure that lab cleanliness and safety standards are maintained. Develop and qualify new testing methods. Coordinate testing with contract laboratories and vendors. Write technical reports or documentation such as deviation reports, testing protocols, and trend analyses. Write or revise standard quality control operating procedures. Supply quality control data necessary for regulatory submissions. Receive and inspect raw materials. Review data from contract laboratories to ensure accuracy and regulatory compliance. Prepare or review required method transfer documentation, including technical transfer protocols or reports. Perform validations or transfers of analytical methods in accordance with applicable policies or guidelines. Participate in out-of-specification and failure investigations, and recommend corrective actions. Monitor testing procedures to ensure that all tests are performed according to established item specifications, standard test methods, or protocols. Investigate or report questionable test results.

Education/Training Required: Postsecondary vocational training. **Education and Training Program:** Quality Control Technology/Technician. **Knowledge/Courses:** No data available.

Personality Type: Conventional-Investigative-Realistic. **Career Cluster:** 13 Manufacturing. **Career Pathway:** 13.2 Manufacturing Production Process Development.

Skills: No data available.

Work Environment: No data available.

Job Specialization: Remote Sensing Technicians

Apply remote sensing technologies to assist scientists in areas such as natural resources, urban planning, and homeland security. May prepare flight plans and sensor configurations for flight trips. Participate in the planning and development of mapping projects. Maintain records of survey data. Document methods used, and write technical reports containing information collected. Develop specialized computer software routines to customize and integrate image analysis. Collect verification data on the ground using equipment such as global positioning receivers, digital cameras, and notebook computers. Verify integrity and accuracy of data contained in remote sensing image analysis systems. Prepare documentation and presentations including charts, photos, or graphs. Operate airborne remote sensing equipment such as survey cameras, sensors, and scanners. Monitor raw data quality during collection, and make equipment corrections as necessary. Merge scanned images or build photo mosa-

ics of large areas using image processing software. Integrate remotely sensed data with other geospatial data. Evaluate remote sensing project requirements to determine the types of equipment or computer software necessary to meet project requirements such as specific image types and output resolutions. Develop and maintain geospatial information databases. Correct raw data for errors due to factors such as skew and atmospheric variation. Calibrate data collection equipment. Consult with remote sensing scientists, surveyors, cartographers, or engineers to determine project needs.

Education/Training Required: Associate degree. **Education and Training Programs:** Geographic Information Science and Cartography; Signal/Geospatial Intelligence. **Knowledge/Courses:** No data available.

Personality Type: Realistic-Investigative-Conventional. **Career Cluster:** 11 Information Technology. **Career Pathway:** 11.2 Information Support Services.

Skills: No data available.

Work Environment: No data available.

Maintenance and Repair Workers, General

- Personality Type: Realistic-Conventional-Investigative
- Annual Earnings: $34,730
- Earnings Growth Potential: Medium (40.1%)
- Growth: 10.9%
- Annual Job Openings: 35,750
- Self-Employed: 1.1%

Considerations for Job Outlook: Employment is related to the extent of building stock and the amount of equipment needing maintenance and repair. Opportunities should be excellent, especially for job-seekers with experience or certification.

Perform work involving the skills of two or more maintenance or craft occupations to keep machines, mechanical equipment, or the structure of an establishment in repair. Duties may involve pipe fitting; boiler making; insulating; welding; machining; carpentry; repairing electrical or mechanical equipment; installing, aligning, and balancing new equipment; and repairing buildings, floors, or stairs. Repair or replace defective equipment parts, using hand tools and power tools, and reassemble equipment. Perform routine preventive maintenance to ensure that machines continue to run smoothly, building systems operate efficiently, or the physical condition of buildings does not deteriorate. Inspect drives, motors, and belts, check fluid levels, replace filters, or perform other maintenance actions, following checklists. Use tools ranging from common hand and power tools, such as hammers, hoists, saws, drills, and wrenches, to precision measuring instruments and electrical and electronic testing devices. Assemble, install, or repair wiring, electrical and electronic components, pipe systems and plumbing, machinery, and equipment. Diagnose mechanical problems, and determine how to correct them, checking blueprints, repair manuals, and parts catalogs as necessary. Inspect, operate, and test machinery and equipment to diagnose machine malfunctions. Record type and cost of maintenance or repair work. Clean and lubricate shafts, bearings, gears, and other parts of machinery. Dismantle devices to access and remove defective parts using hoists, cranes, hand tools, and power tools. Plan and lay out repair work using diagrams, drawings, blueprints, maintenance manuals, and schematic diagrams. Order parts, supplies, and equipment from catalogs and suppliers, or obtain them from storerooms.

Education/Training Required: Moderate-term on-the-job training. **Education and Training Program:** Industrial Mechanics and Maintenance Technology. **Knowledge/Courses:** Building and Construction; Mechanical Devices; Design; Public Safety and Security; Physics; Engineering and Technology.

Career Cluster: 02 Architecture and Construction. **Career Pathway:** 02.2 Construction.

Skills: Repairing; Equipment Maintenance; Installation; Equipment Selection; Troubleshooting; Operation and Control; Quality Control Analysis; Operation Monitoring.

Work Environment: Outdoors; standing; walking and running; kneeling, crouching, stooping, or crawling; using hands; bending or twisting the body; noise; very hot or cold; contaminants; cramped work space; hazardous equipment; minor burns, cuts, bites, or stings.

Medical and Clinical Laboratory Technicians

* Personality Type: Realistic-Investigative-Conventional
* Annual Earnings: $36,280
* Earnings Growth Potential: Low (33.3%)
* Growth: 16.1%
* Annual Job Openings: 5,460
* Self-Employed: 0.2%

Considerations for Job Outlook: Employment of these workers is expected to rise as the volume of laboratory tests continues to increase with population growth and the development of new tests. Excellent opportunities are expected.

Perform routine medical laboratory tests for the diagnosis, treatment, and prevention of disease. May work under the supervision of a medical technologist. Conduct chemical analyses of bodily fluids, such as blood and urine, using microscope or automatic analyzer to detect abnormalities or diseases, and enter findings into computer. Set up, adjust, maintain, and clean medical laboratory equipment. Analyze the results of tests and experiments to ensure conformity to specifications, using special mechanical and electrical devices. Analyze and record test data to issue reports that use charts, graphs, and narratives. Conduct blood tests for transfusion purposes, and perform blood counts. Perform medical research to further control and cure disease. Obtain specimens, cultivating, isolating, and identifying microorganisms for analysis. Examine cells stained with dye to locate abnormalities. Collect blood or tissue samples from patients, observing principles of asepsis to obtain blood sample. Consult with a pathologist to determine a final diagnosis when abnormal cells are found. Inoculate fertilized eggs, broths, or other bacteriological media with organisms. Cut, stain, and mount tissue samples for examination by pathologists. Supervise and instruct other technicians and laboratory assistants. Prepare standard volumetric solutions and reagents to be combined with samples, following standardized formulas or experimental procedures. Prepare vaccines and serums by standard laboratory methods, testing for virus inactivity and sterility.

Education/Training Required: Associate degree. **Education and Training Programs:** Blood Bank Technology Specialist Training; Clinical/Medical Laboratory Assistant Training; Clinical/Medical Laboratory Technician; Hematology Technology/Technician; Histologic Technician Training. **Knowledge/Courses:** Chemistry; Medicine and Dentistry; Biology; Mechanical Devices; Computers and Electronics; Production and Processing.

Career Cluster: 08 Health Science. **Career Pathways:** 08.1 Therapeutic Services; 08.2 Diagnostics Services.

Skills: Science; Equipment Maintenance; Equipment Selection; Troubleshooting; Repairing; Operation and Control; Quality Control Analysis; Operation Monitoring.

Work Environment: Indoors; standing; walking and running; using hands; repetitive motions; noise; contaminants; exposed to disease or infections; hazardous conditions.

Medical Equipment Repairers

- ❀ Personality Type: Realistic-Investigative-Conventional
- ❀ Annual Earnings: $44,490
- ❀ Earnings Growth Potential: High (41.5%)
- ❀ Growth: 27.2%
- ❀ Annual Job Openings: 2,320
- ❀ Self-Employed: 16.4%

Considerations for Job Outlook: An increased demand for health-care services and the growing complexity of medical equipment are projected to result in greater need for these repairers. Excellent job prospects are expected. Job-seekers who have an associate degree should have the best prospects.

Test, adjust, or repair biomedical or electromedical equipment. Inspect and test malfunctioning medical and related equipment following manufacturers' specifications, using test and analysis instruments. Examine medical equipment and facility's structural environment, and check for proper use of equipment to protect patients and staff from electrical or mechanical hazards and to ensure compliance with safety regulations. Disassemble malfunctioning equipment, and remove, repair, and replace defective parts such as motors, clutches, or transformers. Keep records of maintenance, repair, and required updates of equipment. Perform preventive maintenance or service such as cleaning, lubricating, and adjusting equipment. Test and calibrate components and equipment, following manufacturers' manuals and troubleshooting techniques and using hand tools, power tools, and measuring devices. Explain and demonstrate correct operation and preventive maintenance of medical equipment to personnel. Study technical manuals and attend training sessions provided by equipment manufacturers to maintain current knowledge. Plan and carry out work assignments, using blueprints, schematic drawings, technical manuals, wiring diagrams, and liquid and air flow sheets, following prescribed regulations, directives, and other instructions as required. Solder loose connections, using soldering iron. Test, evaluate, and classify excess or in-use medical equipment, and determine serviceability, condition, and disposition in accordance with regulations.

Education/Training Required: Associate degree. **Education and Training Program:** Biomedical Technology/Technician. **Knowledge/Courses:** Mechanical Devices; Engineering and Technology; Physics; Telecommunications; Computers and Electronics; Chemistry.

Realistic-M

Career Cluster: 13 Manufacturing. **Career Pathway:** 13.3 Maintenance, Installation, and Repair.

Skills: Equipment Maintenance; Repairing; Troubleshooting; Equipment Selection; Quality Control Analysis; Operation and Control; Installation; Operation Monitoring.

Work Environment: Indoors; standing; using hands; noise; bright or inadequate lighting; contaminants; cramped work space; exposed to disease or infections; hazardous conditions; hazardous equipment; minor burns, cuts, bites, or stings.

Mobile Heavy Equipment Mechanics, Except Engines

- ❋ Personality Type: Realistic-Conventional
- ❋ Annual Earnings: $44,830
- ❋ Earnings Growth Potential: Low (33.7%)
- ❋ Growth: 8.7%
- ❋ Annual Job Openings: 3,770
- ❋ Self-Employed: 5.8%

Considerations for Job Outlook: Continued expansion of the industries that use heavy mobile equipment, such as agriculture as well as energy exploration and mining, should lead to additional jobs for these workers. Opportunities should be good for job-seekers who have experience or formal training.

Diagnose, adjust, repair, or overhaul mobile mechanical, hydraulic, and pneumatic equipment, such as cranes, bulldozers, graders, and conveyors, used in construction, logging, and surface mining. Test mechanical products and equipment after repair or assembly to ensure proper performance and compliance with manufacturers' specifications. Repair and replace damaged or worn parts. Diagnose faults or malfunctions to determine required repairs, using engine diagnostic equipment such as computerized test equipment and calibration devices. Operate and inspect machines or heavy equipment to diagnose defects. Dismantle and reassemble heavy equipment, using hoists and hand tools. Clean, lubricate, and perform other routine maintenance work

on equipment and vehicles. Examine parts for damage or excessive wear, using micrometers and gauges. Read and understand operating manuals, blueprints, and technical drawings. Schedule maintenance for industrial machines and equipment, and keep equipment service records. Overhaul and test machines or equipment to ensure operating efficiency. Assemble gear systems, and align frames and gears. Fit bearings to adjust, repair, or overhaul mobile mechanical, hydraulic, and pneumatic equipment. Weld or solder broken parts and structural members, using electric or gas welders and soldering tools. Clean parts by spraying them with grease solvent or immersing them in tanks of solvent. Adjust, maintain, and repair or replace subassemblies, such as transmissions and crawler heads, using hand tools, jacks, and cranes. Adjust and maintain industrial machinery, using control and regulating devices. Fabricate needed parts or items from sheet metal.

Education/Training Required: Long-term on-the-job training. **Education and Training Programs:** Agricultural Mechanics and Equipment/Machine Technology; Heavy Equipment Maintenance Technology/Technician. **Knowledge/Courses:** Mechanical Devices; Physics; Building and Construction; Engineering and Technology; Design; Transportation.

Career Clusters: 01 Agriculture, Food, and Natural Resources; 13 Manufacturing. **Career Pathways:** 01.4 Power Structure and Technical Systems; 13.3 Maintenance, Installation, and Repair.

Skills: Repairing; Equipment Maintenance; Troubleshooting; Installation; Equipment Selection; Quality Control Analysis; Operation and Control; Operation Monitoring.

Work Environment: Outdoors; standing; walking and running; kneeling, crouching, stooping, or crawling; using hands; bending or twisting the body; repetitive motions; noise; very hot or cold; bright or inadequate lighting; contaminants; cramped work space; whole-body vibration; high places; hazardous conditions; hazardous equipment; minor burns, cuts, bites, or stings.

Operating Engineers and Other Construction Equipment Operators

* Personality Type: Realistic-Conventional-Investigative
* Annual Earnings: $40,400
* Earnings Growth Potential: Low (34.5%)
* Growth: 12.0%
* Annual Job Openings: 11,820
* Self-Employed: 3.4%

Considerations for Job Outlook: Increased government spending on infrastructure is expected to generate employment growth for these workers. Operators who have varied expertise are expected to have the best prospects.

Operate one or several types of power construction equipment, such as motor graders, bulldozers, scrapers, compressors, pumps, derricks, shovels, tractors, or front-end loaders, to excavate, move, and grade earth; erect structures; or pour concrete or other hard-surface pavement. May repair and maintain equipment in addition to other duties. Learn and follow safety regulations. Take actions to avoid potential hazards and obstructions such as utility lines, other equipment, other workers, and falling objects. Adjust handwheels and depress pedals to control attachments such as blades, buckets, scrapers, and swing booms. Start engines; move throttles, switches, and levers; and depress pedals to operate machines such as bulldozers, trench excavators, road graders, and backhoes. Locate underground services, such as pipes and wires, prior to beginning work. Monitor operations to ensure that health and safety standards are met. Align machines, cutterheads, or depth gauge makers with reference stakes and guidelines, or ground or position equipment by following hand signals of other workers. Load and move dirt, rocks, equipment, and materials, using trucks, crawler tractors, power cranes, shovels, graders, and related equipment. Drive and maneuver equipment outfitted with blades in successive passes over working areas to remove topsoil, vegetation, and rocks and to distribute and level earth or terrain. Coordinate machine actions with other activities, positioning or moving loads in response to hand or audio signals from crew members. Operate tractors and bulldozers to perform such tasks as clearing land, mixing sludge, trimming backfills, and building roadways and parking lots. Repair and maintain equipment, making emergency adjustments or assisting with major repairs as necessary.

Education/Training Required: Moderate-term on-the-job training. **Education and Training Programs:** Construction/Heavy Equipment/Earth-moving Equipment Operation; Mobile Crane Operation/Operator. **Knowledge/Courses:** Building and Construction; Mechanical Devices; Engineering and Technology; Design; Production and Processing; Public Safety and Security.

Career Clusters: 02 Architecture and Construction; 16 Transportation, Distribution, and Logistics. **Career Pathways:** 02.2 Construction; 16.1 Transportation Operations.

Skills: Operation and Control; Repairing; Equipment Maintenance; Troubleshooting; Operation Monitoring; Quality Control Analysis; Equipment Selection; Installation.

Work Environment: Outdoors; sitting; using hands; repetitive motions; noise; very hot or cold; bright or inadequate lighting; contaminants; whole-body vibration; hazardous equipment; minor burns, cuts, bites, or stings.

Physical Scientists, All Other

* Personality Type: Realistic-Investigative
* Annual Earnings: $94,780
* Earnings Growth Potential: High (49.2%)
* Growth: 11.1%
* Annual Job Openings: 1,010
* Self-Employed: 10.9%

Considerations for Job Outlook: About average employment growth is projected.

This occupation includes all physical scientists not listed separately. Because this is a highly diverse occupation, no data is available for some information topics.

Education/Training Required: Bachelor's degree. **Education and Training Program:** Physical Sciences, Other.

Career Clusters: 08 Health Science; 15 Science, Technology, Engineering, and Mathematics. **Career Pathways:** 08.2 Diagnostics Services; 15.2 Science and Mathematics.

Job Specialization: Remote Sensing Scientists and Technologists

Apply remote sensing principles and methods to analyze data and solve problems in areas such as natural resource management, urban planning, and homeland security. May develop new analytical techniques and sensor systems or develop new applications for existing systems. Analyze data acquired from aircraft, satellites, or ground-based platforms using statistical analysis software, image analysis software, or Geographic Information Systems (GIS). Manage or analyze data obtained from remote sensing systems to obtain meaningful results. Process aerial and satellite imagery to create products such as landcover maps. Develop and build databases for remote sensing and related geospatial project information. Monitor quality of remote sensing data-collection operations to determine if procedural or equipment changes are necessary. Attend meetings or seminars and read current literature to maintain knowledge of developments in the field of remote sensing. Prepare and deliver reports and presentations of geospatial project information. Conduct research into the application and enhancement of remote sensing technology. Discuss project goals, equipment requirements, and methodologies with colleagues and team members. Integrate other geospatial data sources into projects. Organize and maintain geospatial data and associated documentation. Participate in fieldwork as required. Design

and implement strategies for collection, analysis, or display of geographic data. Collect supporting data such as climatic and field survey data to corroborate remote sensing data analyses. Develop new analytical techniques or sensor systems. Train technicians in the use of remote sensing technology.

Education/Training Required: Bachelor's degree. **Education and Training Programs:** Geographic Information Science and Cartography; Signal/Geospatial Intelligence. **Knowledge/Courses:** Geography; Biology; Physics; Computers and Electronics; Engineering and Technology; Mathematics.

Personality Type: Realistic-Investigative. **Career Clusters:** 11 Information Technology; 12 Law, Public Safety, Corrections, and Security. **Career Pathways:** 11.2 Information Support Services; 12.4 Law Enforcement Services.

Skills: Science; Operations Analysis; Mathematics; Writing; Systems Evaluation; Systems Analysis; Reading Comprehension; Complex Problem Solving.

Work Environment: Indoors; sitting.

Physician Assistants

Look for the job description among the Social jobs.

Plumbers, Pipefitters, and Steamfitters

* Personality Type: Realistic-Conventional
* Annual Earnings: $46,660
* Earnings Growth Potential: Medium (40.9%)
* Growth: 15.3%
* Annual Job Openings: 17,550
* Self-Employed: 12.3%

Considerations for Job Outlook: Employment of these workers is projected to increase due to new construction and renovation projects, as well as maintenance of existing pipe systems. Increasing emphasis on water conservation should require retrofitting to conserve water, leading to employment growth for plumbers. Workers with welding experience should have especially good opportunities.

Job Specialization: Plumbers

Assemble, install, and repair pipes, fittings, and fixtures of heating, water, and drainage systems according to specifications and plumbing codes. Measure, cut, thread, and bend pipe to required angles, using hand and power tools or machines such as pipe cutters, pipe-threading machines, and pipe-bending machines. Study building plans and inspect structures to assess material and equipment needs to establish the sequence of pipe installations and to plan installation around obstructions such as electrical wiring. Locate and mark the position of pipe installations, connections, passage holes, and fixtures in structures, using measuring instruments such as rulers and levels. Assemble pipe sections, tubing, and fittings, using couplings, clamps, screws, bolts, cement, plastic solvent, caulking, or soldering, brazing, and welding equipment. Fill pipes or plumbing fixtures with water or air and observe pressure gauges to detect and locate leaks. Install pipe assemblies, fittings, valves, appliances such as dishwashers and water heaters, and fixtures such as sinks and toilets, using hand and power tools. Direct workers engaged in pipe cutting and preassembly and installation of plumbing systems and components. Cut openings in structures to accommodate pipes and pipe fittings, using hand and power tools. Review blueprints as well as building codes and specifications to determine work details and procedures. Install underground storm, sanitary, and water piping systems, and extend piping to connect fixtures and plumbing to these systems.

Education/Training Required: Long-term on-the-job training. **Education and Training Programs:** Pipefitting/Pipefitter and Sprinkler Fitter; Plumbing and Related Water Supply Services, Other; Plumbing Technology/Plumber. **Knowledge/Courses:** Building and Construction; Mechanical Devices; Physics; Design; Engineering and Technology; Customer and Personal Service.

Personality Type: Realistic-Conventional-Investigative. **Career Cluster:** 02 Architecture and Construction. **Career Pathway:** 02.2 Construction.

Skills: Repairing; Equipment Maintenance; Installation; Troubleshooting; Equipment Selection; Operation and Control; Operation Monitoring; Quality Control Analysis.

Work Environment: More often outdoors than indoors; standing; walking and running; kneeling, crouching, stooping, or crawling; using hands; bending or twisting the body; repetitive motions; noise; very hot or cold; bright or inadequate lighting; contaminants; cramped work space; whole-body vibration; hazardous equipment; minor burns, cuts, bites, or stings.

Job Specialization: Pipe Fitters and Steamfitters

Lay out, assemble, install, and maintain pipe systems, pipe supports, and related hydraulic and pneumatic equipment for steam, hot water, heating, cooling, lubricating, sprinkling, and industrial production and processing systems. Cut, thread, and hammer pipe to specifications, using tools such as saws, cutting torches, and pipe threaders and benders. Assemble and secure pipes, tubes, fittings, and related equipment according to specifications by welding, brazing, cementing, soldering, and threading joints. Attach pipes to walls, structures, and fixtures, such as radiators or tanks, using brackets, clamps, tools, or welding equipment. Inspect, examine, and test installed systems and pipelines, using pressure gauge, hydrostatic testing, observation, or other methods. Measure and mark pipes for cutting and threading. Lay out full-scale drawings of pipe systems, supports, and related equipment, following blueprints. Plan pipe-system layout, installation, or repair according to specifications. Select pipe

Realistic-P

sizes and types and related materials, such as supports, hangers, and hydraulic cylinders, according to specifications. Cut and bore holes in structures such as bulkheads, decks, walls, and mains prior to pipe installation, using hand and power tools. Modify, clean, and maintain pipe systems, units, fittings, and related machines and equipment, following specifications and using hand and power tools. Install automatic controls used to regulate pipe systems. Turn valves to shut off steam, water, or other gases or liquids from pipe sections, using valve keys or wrenches. Remove and replace worn components. Prepare cost estimates for clients.

Education/Training Required: Long-term on-the-job training. **Education and Training Programs:** Pipefitting/Pipefitter and Sprinkler Fitter; Plumbing and Related Water Supply Services, Other; Plumbing Technology/Plumber. **Knowledge/Courses:** Building and Construction; Mechanical Devices; Physics; Design; Engineering and Technology; Chemistry.

Personality Type: Realistic-Conventional. **Career Cluster:** 02 Architecture and Construction. **Career Pathway:** 02.2 Construction.

Skills: Repairing; Equipment Maintenance; Installation; Troubleshooting; Operation and Control; Quality Control Analysis; Operation Monitoring; Equipment Selection.

Work Environment: More often outdoors than indoors; standing; using hands; bending or twisting the body; repetitive motions; noise; very hot or cold; bright or inadequate lighting; contaminants; cramped work space; high places; hazardous conditions; hazardous equipment; minor burns, cuts, bites, or stings.

Police and Sheriff's Patrol Officers

Look for the job description among the Enterprising jobs.

Radiologic Technologists

❋ Personality Type: Realistic-Social
❋ Annual Earnings: $54,340
❋ Earnings Growth Potential: Low (32.8%)
❋ Growth: 17.2%
❋ Annual Job Openings: 6,800
❋ Self-Employed: 0.8%

Considerations for Job Outlook: As the population grows and ages, demand for diagnostic imaging is expected to increase. Job-seekers who have knowledge of multiple technologies should have the best prospects.

Take X-rays and CAT scans or administer nonradioactive materials into patient's bloodstream for diagnostic purposes. Includes technologists who specialize in other modalities, such as computed tomography and magnetic resonance. Includes workers whose primary duties are to demonstrate portions of the human body on X-ray film or fluoroscopic screen. Review and evaluate developed X-rays, video tape, or computer-generated information to determine whether images are satisfactory for diagnostic purposes. Use radiation safety measures and protection devices to comply with government regulations and to ensure safety of patients and staff. Explain procedures and observe patients to ensure safety and comfort during scan. Operate or oversee operation of radiologic and magnetic imaging equipment to produce images of the body for diagnostic purposes. Position and immobilize patient on examining table. Position imaging equipment, and adjust controls to set exposure time and distance, according to specification of examination. Key commands and data into computer to document and specify scan sequences, adjust transmitters and receivers, or photograph certain images. Monitor video display of area being scanned, and adjust density or contrast to improve picture quality. Monitor patients' conditions and reactions, reporting abnormal signs to physician. Set up examination rooms, ensuring that all necessary equipment is ready. Prepare and administer oral or injected contrast media to patients. Take thorough and accurate patient medical histories. Remove and process film. Record, process, and maintain patient data and treatment records, and prepare reports. Coordinate work with clerical personnel or other technologists. Demonstrate new equipment, procedures, and techniques to staff members, and provide technical assistance.

Education/Training Required: Associate degree. **Education and Training Programs:** Allied Health Diagnostic, Intervention, and Treatment Professions, Other; Medical Radiologic Technology/Science—Radiation Therapist; Radiologic Technology/Science—Radiographer. **Knowledge/Courses:** Medicine and Dentistry; Physics; Customer and Personal Service; Biology; Psychology; Chemistry.

Career Cluster: 08 Health Science. **Career Pathways:** 08.1 Therapeutic Services; 08.2 Diagnostics Services.

Skills: Science; Operation and Control; Service Orientation; Quality Control Analysis; Operation Monitoring; Programming; Instructing; Social Perceptiveness.

Work Environment: Indoors; standing; walking and running; using hands; bending or twisting the body; repetitive motions; contaminants; exposed to radiation; exposed to disease or infections.

Refuse and Recyclable Material Collectors

- ❋ Personality Type: Realistic-Conventional
- ❋ Annual Earnings: $32,640
- ❋ Earnings Growth Potential: High (42.6%)
- ❋ Growth: 18.6%
- ❋ Annual Job Openings: 7,110
- ❋ Self-Employed: 11.8%

Considerations for Job Outlook: Improvements in technology are expected to increase productivity, holding employment stable. Good job prospects are expected from the need to replace the many workers leaving these occupations.

Collect and dump refuse or recyclable materials from containers into truck. May drive truck. Inspect trucks prior to beginning routes to ensure safe operating condition. Refuel trucks, and add other necessary fluids, such as oil. Fill out any needed reports for defective equipment. Drive to disposal sites to empty trucks that have been filled. Drive trucks along established routes through residential streets and alleys or through business and industrial areas. Operate equipment that compresses the collected refuse. Operate automated or semi-automated hoisting devices that raise refuse bins and dump contents into openings in truck bodies. Dismount garbage trucks to collect garbage, and remount trucks to ride to the next collection point. Communicate with dispatchers concerning delays, unsafe sites, accidents, equipment breakdowns, and other maintenance problems. Keep informed of road and weather conditions to determine how routes will be affected. Tag garbage or recycling containers to inform customers of problems such as excess garbage or inclusion of items that are not permitted. Clean trucks and compactor bodies after routes have been completed. Sort items set out for recycling, and throw materials into designated truck compartments. Organize schedules for refuse collection. Provide quotations for refuse collection contracts.

Education/Training Required: Short-term on-the-job training. **Education and Training Programs:** No related CIP programs; this job is learned through informal short-term on-the-job training. **Knowledge/Courses:** Transportation; Customer and Personal Service.

Career Cluster: 01 Agriculture, Food, and Natural Resources. **Career Pathway:** 01.5 Natural Resources Systems.

Skills: Equipment Maintenance; Repairing; Operation and Control; Troubleshooting; Equipment Selection; Operation Monitoring; Quality Control Analysis.

Work Environment: Outdoors; more often sitting than standing; walking and running; using hands; bending or twisting the body; repetitive motions;

Realistic-R

noise; very hot or cold; contaminants; exposed to disease or infections; hazardous equipment; minor burns, cuts, bites, or stings.

Security and Fire Alarm Systems Installers

- ❋ Personality Type: Realistic-Conventional
- ❋ Annual Earnings: $38,500
- ❋ Earnings Growth Potential: Low (35.4%)
- ❋ Growth: 24.8%
- ❋ Annual Job Openings: 2,780
- ❋ Self-Employed: 6.3%

Considerations for Job Outlook: Much better than average employment growth is projected.

Install, program, maintain, and repair security and fire alarm wiring and equipment. Ensure that work is in accordance with relevant codes. Examine systems to locate problems such as loose connections or broken insulation. Test backup batteries, keypad programming, sirens, and all security features in order to ensure proper functioning, and to diagnose malfunctions. Mount and fasten control panels, door and window contacts, sensors, and video cameras, and attach electrical and telephone wiring in order to connect components. Install, maintain, or repair security systems, alarm devices, and related equipment, following blueprints of electrical layouts and building plans. Inspect installation sites and study work orders, building plans, and installation manuals in order to determine materials requirements and installation procedures. Feed cables through access holes, roof spaces, and cavity walls to reach fixture outlets; then position and terminate cables, wires and strapping. Adjust sensitivity of units based on room structures and manufacturers' recommendations, using programming keypads. Test and repair circuits and sensors, following wiring and system specifications. Drill holes for wiring in wall studs, joists, ceilings, and floors. Demonstrate systems for customers, and explain details such as the causes and consequences of false alarms. Consult with clients to assess risks and to determine security requirements. Keep informed of new products and developments. Mount raceways and conduits, and fasten wires to wood framing, using staplers. Prepare documents such as invoices and warranties.

Education/Training Required: Postsecondary vocational training. **Education and Training Programs:** Electrician; Security System Installation, Repair, and Inspection Technology/Technician. **Knowledge/Courses:** Telecommunications; Building and Construction; Mechanical Devices; Computers and Electronics; Public Safety and Security; Design.

Career Cluster: 02 Architecture and Construction. **Career Pathways:** 02.2 Construction; 02.3 Maintenance/Operations.

Skills: Installation; Repairing; Equipment Maintenance; Troubleshooting; Operation and Control; Equipment Selection; Quality Control Analysis; Operation Monitoring.

Work Environment: More often indoors than outdoors; standing; climbing; using hands; repetitive motions; noise; very hot or cold; bright or inadequate lighting; contaminants; cramped work space; high places.

Ship Engineers

- ❋ Personality Type: Realistic-Conventional-Enterprising
- ❋ Annual Earnings: $65,880
- ❋ Earnings Growth Potential: High (42.1%)
- ❋ Growth: 18.6%
- ❋ Annual Job Openings: 700
- ❋ Self-Employed: 0.0%

Considerations for Job Outlook: Job growth is expected to stem from increasing tourism and from growth in offshore oil and gas production. Employment is also projected to increase in and around major port cities due to growing international trade. Opportunities should be excellent as the need to replace workers, particularly officers, generates many job openings.

Supervise and coordinate activities of crew engaged in operating and maintaining engines; boilers; deck machinery; and electrical, sanitary, and refrigeration equipment aboard ship. Record orders for changes in ship speed and direction, and note gauge readings and test data, such as revolutions per minute and voltage output, in engineering logs and bellbooks. Install engine controls, propeller shafts, and propellers. Perform and participate in emergency drills as required. Fabricate engine replacement parts such as valves, stay rods, and bolts, using metalworking machinery. Operate and maintain off-loading liquid pumps and valves. Maintain and repair engines, electric motors, pumps, winches, and other mechanical and electrical equipment, or assist other crew members with maintenance and repair duties. Maintain electrical power, heating, ventilation, refrigeration, water, and sewerage. Monitor and test operations of engines and other equipment so that malfunctions and their causes can be identified. Monitor engine, machinery, and equipment indicators when vessels are underway, and report abnormalities to appropriate shipboard staff. Start engines to propel ships, and regulate engines and power transmissions to control speeds of ships, according to directions from captains or bridge computers. Order and receive engine rooms' stores such as oil and spare parts; maintain inventories and record usage of supplies. Act as liaison between ships' captains and shore personnel to ensure that schedules and budgets are maintained and that ships are operated safely and efficiently. Clean engine parts, and keep engine rooms clean.

Education/Training Required: Work experience in a related occupation. **Education and Training Program:** Marine Maintenance/Fitter and Ship Repair Technology/Technician. **Knowledge/Courses:** Mechanical Devices; Building and Construction; Engineering and Technology; Transportation; Chemistry; Public Safety and Security.

Career Cluster: 16 Transportation, Distribution, and Logistics. **Career Pathway:** 16.1 Transportation Operations.

Skills: Repairing; Equipment Maintenance; Troubleshooting; Equipment Selection; Operation and Control; Operation Monitoring; Quality Control Analysis; Science.

Work Environment: Outdoors; standing; using hands; noise; very hot or cold; bright or inadequate lighting; contaminants; cramped work space; whole-body vibration; high places; hazardous conditions; hazardous equipment; minor burns, cuts, bites, or stings.

Surgical Technologists

* Personality Type: Realistic-Social-Conventional
* Annual Earnings: $39,920
* Earnings Growth Potential: Low (29.6%)
* Growth: 25.3%
* Annual Job Openings: 4,630
* Self-Employed: 0.2%

Considerations for Job Outlook: Employment expansion for these workers is expected as a growing and aging population has more surgeries and as advances allow technologists to assist surgeons more often. Job opportunities should be best for technologists who are certified.

Assist in operations under the supervision of surgeons, registered nurses, or other surgical personnel. May help set up operating rooms; prepare and transport patients for surgery; adjust lights and equipment; pass instruments and other supplies to surgeons and surgeons' assistants; hold retractors; cut sutures; and help count sponges, needles, supplies, and instruments. Count sponges, needles, and instruments before and after operations. Maintain a proper sterile field during surgical procedures. Hand instruments and supplies to surgeons and surgeons' assistants, hold retractors, cut sutures, and perform other tasks as directed by surgeons during operations. Prepare patients for surgery, including positioning patients on operating tables and covering them with sterile surgical drapes to prevent exposure. Scrub arms and hands, and assist surgical teams to scrub and put on gloves, masks, and surgical clothing. Wash and sterilize equipment, using germicides and sterilizers. Monitor and continually assess operating room conditions, including needs of the patient and the surgical team. Prepare dressings or bandages, and apply or assist with their application following surgeries. Clean and restock operating rooms, gathering and placing equipment and supplies and arranging instruments according to instructions such as those found on a preference card. Operate, assemble, adjust, or monitor sterilizers, lights, suction machines, and diagnostic equipment to ensure proper operation. Prepare, care for, and dispose of tissue specimens taken for laboratory analysis. Provide technical assistance to surgeons, surgical nurses, and anesthesiologists. Maintain supply of fluids such as plasma, saline, blood, and glucose for use during operations. Maintain files and records of surgical procedures. Observe patients' vital signs to assess physical condition.

Education/Training Required: Postsecondary vocational training. **Education and Training Programs:** Pathology/Pathologist Assistant Training; Surgical Technology/Technologist. **Knowledge/Courses:** Medicine and Dentistry; Biology; Psychology; Chemistry; Therapy and Counseling; Customer and Personal Service.

Career Cluster: 08 Health Science. **Career Pathway:** 08.2 Diagnostics Services.

Skills: Equipment Maintenance; Equipment Selection; Operation Monitoring; Repairing; Quality Control Analysis; Operation and Control; Management of Material Resources; Coordination.

Work Environment: Indoors; standing; using hands; bending or twisting the body; repetitive motions; contaminants; exposed to radiation; exposed to disease or infections; hazardous conditions; hazardous equipment; minor burns, cuts, bites, or stings.

Surveying and Mapping Technicians

Look for the job description among the Conventional jobs.

Surveyors

❀ Personality Type: Realistic-Conventional-Investigative
❀ Annual Earnings: $54,880
❀ Earnings Growth Potential: High (43.9%)
❀ Growth: 14.9%
❀ Annual Job Openings: 2,330
❀ Self-Employed: 2.5%

Considerations for Job Outlook: Increasing demand for geographic information should be the main source of employment growth. Job-seekers with a bachelor's degree and strong technical skills should have favorable prospects.

Make exact measurements and determine property boundaries. Provide data relevant to the shape, contour, gravitation, location, elevation, or dimension of land or land features on or near Earth's surface for engineering, mapmaking, mining, land evaluation, construction, and other purposes. Verify the accuracy of survey data including measurements and calculations conducted at survey sites. Calculate heights, depths, relative positions, property lines, and other characteristics of terrain. Search legal records, survey records, and land titles to obtain information about property boundaries in areas to be surveyed. Prepare and maintain sketches, maps, reports, and legal descriptions of surveys to describe, certify, and assume liability for work performed. Direct or conduct surveys to establish legal boundaries for properties, based on legal deeds and titles. Prepare or supervise preparation of all data, charts, plots, maps, records, and documents related to surveys. Write descriptions of property boundary surveys for use in deeds, leases, or other legal documents. Compute geodetic measurements and interpret survey data to determine positions, shapes, and elevations of geomorphic and topographic features. Determine longitudes and latitudes of important features and boundaries in survey areas using theodolites, transits, levels, and satellite-based global positioning systems (GPS). Record the results of surveys including the shape, contour, location, elevation, and dimensions of land or land features. Coordinate findings with the work of engineering and architectural personnel, clients, and others concerned with projects. Establish fixed points for use in making maps, using geodetic and engineering instruments.

Education/Training Required: Bachelor's degree. **Education and Training Program:** Surveying Technology/Surveying. **Knowledge/Courses:** Geography; Design; Building and Construction; History and Archeology; Engineering and Technology; Mathematics.

Career Cluster: 02 Architecture and Construction. **Career Pathway:** 02.1 Design/Pre-Construction.

Skills: Science; Equipment Selection; Mathematics; Repairing; Equipment Maintenance; Management of Personnel Resources; Quality Control Analysis; Operation Monitoring.

Work Environment: More often outdoors than indoors; standing; walking and running; using hands; noise; very hot or cold; hazardous equipment; minor burns, cuts, bites, or stings.

Job Specialization: Geodetic Surveyors

Measure large areas of Earth's surface, using satellite observations, global navigation satellite systems (GNSS), light detection and ranging (LIDAR), or related sources. Review existing standards, controls, or equipment used, recommending changes or upgrades as needed. Provide training and interpretation in the use of methods or procedures for observing and checking controls for geodetic and plane coordinates. Plan or direct the work of geodetic surveying staff, providing technical consultation as needed. Distribute compiled geodetic data to government agencies or the general public. Read current literature, talk with colleagues, continue education, or participate in professional organizations or conferences to keep abreast of developments in technology, equipment, or systems. Verify the mathematical correctness of newly collected survey data. Request additional survey data when field collection errors

occur or engineering surveying specifications are not maintained. Prepare progress or technical reports. Maintain databases of geodetic and related information including coordinate, descriptive, or quality assurance data. Compute, retrace, or adjust existing surveys of features such as highway alignments, property boundaries, utilities, control, and other surveys to match the ground elevation dependent grids, geodetic grids, or property boundaries and to ensure accuracy. Compute horizontal and vertical coordinates of control networks using direct leveling or other geodetic survey techniques such as triangulation, trilateration, and traversing to establish features of the earth's surface.

Education/Training Required: Bachelor's degree. **Education and Training Program:** Surveying Technology/Surveying. **Knowledge/Courses:** Geography; Physics; Mathematics; Engineering and Technology; Computers and Electronics; Design.

Personality Type: Investigative-Conventional-Realistic. **Career Cluster:** 02 Architecture and Construction. **Career Pathway:** 02.1 Design/Pre-Construction.

Skills: Mathematics; Programming; Science; Equipment Selection; Quality Control Analysis; Operation and Control; Management of Personnel Resources; Writing.

Work Environment: More often outdoors than indoors; standing; using hands; very hot or cold.

Tile and Marble Setters

- ❀ Personality Type: Realistic-Conventional-Artistic
- ❀ Annual Earnings: $38,110
- ❀ Earnings Growth Potential: High (43.0%)
- ❀ Growth: 14.3%
- ❀ Annual Job Openings: 3,070
- ❀ Self-Employed: 35.1%

Considerations for Job Outlook: Expected employment gains for these workers will arise from growing population and resulting increases in build-

Realistic-T

ing and renovating structures. Job openings are also expected from the need to replace workers who leave the occupations permanently.

Apply hard tile, marble, and wood tile to walls, floors, ceilings, and roof decks. Align and straighten tile, using levels, squares, and straightedges. Determine and implement the best layout to achieve a desired pattern. Cut and shape tile to fit around obstacles and into odd spaces and corners, using vhand- and power-cutting tools. Finish and dress the joints and wipe excess grout from between tiles, using damp sponge. Apply mortar to tile back, position the tile, and press or tap with trowel handle to affix tile to base. Mix, apply, and spread plaster, concrete, mortar, cement, mastic, glue, or other adhesives to form a bed for the tiles, using brush, trowel, and screed. Prepare cost and labor estimates based on calculations of time and materials needed for project. Measure and mark surfaces to be tiled, following blueprints. Level concrete, and allow to dry. Build underbeds, and install anchor bolts, wires, and brackets. Prepare surfaces for tiling by attaching lath or waterproof paper or by applying a cement mortar coat onto a metal screen. Study blueprints and examine surface to be covered to determine amount of material needed. Cut, surface, polish, and install marble and granite or install pre-cast terrazzo, granite, or marble units. Install and anchor fixtures in designated positions, using hand tools. Cut tile backing to required size, using shears. Remove any old tile, grout, and adhesive, using chisels and scrapers, and clean the surface carefully. Lay and set mosaic tiles to create decorative wall, mural, and floor designs.

Education/Training Required: Long-term on-the-job training. **Education and Training Program:** Masonry/Mason Training. **Knowledge/Courses:** Building and Construction; Design; Mechanical Devices.

Career Cluster: 02 Architecture and Construction. **Career Pathway:** 02.2 Construction.

Skills: Equipment Maintenance; Equipment Selection; Repairing; Troubleshooting; Operation

and Control; Mathematics; Operation Monitoring; Quality Control Analysis.

Work Environment: Standing; kneeling, crouching, stooping, or crawling; using hands; bending or twisting the body; repetitive motions; noise; very hot or cold; bright or inadequate lighting; contaminants; cramped work space; hazardous equipment; minor burns, cuts, bites, or stings.

Transportation Inspectors

* Personality Type: Realistic-Conventional-Investigative
* Annual Earnings: $57,640
* Earnings Growth Potential: High (46.3%)
* Growth: 18.4%
* Annual Job Openings: 1,130
* Self-Employed: 4.2%

Considerations for Job Outlook: Faster than average employment growth is projected.

Job Specialization: Aviation Inspectors

Inspect aircraft, maintenance procedures, air navigational aids, air traffic controls, and communications equipment to ensure conformance with federal safety regulations. Inspect work of aircraft mechanics performing maintenance, modification, or repair and overhaul of aircraft and aircraft mechanical systems to ensure adherence to standards and procedures. Start aircraft and observe gauges, meters, and other instruments to detect evidence of malfunctions. Examine aircraft access plates and doors for security. Examine landing gear, tires, and exteriors of fuselage, wings, and engines for evidence of damage or corrosion and to determine whether repairs are needed. Prepare and maintain detailed repair, inspection, investigation, and certification records and reports. Inspect new, repaired, or modified aircraft to identify damage or defects and to assess airworthiness and conformance to standards, using checklists, hand tools, and test instruments. Examine maintenance records and flight logs to determine if service and maintenance checks and overhauls were performed at prescribed intervals. Recommend replacement, repair, or modification of aircraft equipment. Recommend changes in rules, policies, standards, and regulations based on knowledge of operating conditions, aircraft improvements, and other factors. Issue pilots' licenses to individuals meeting standards. Investigate air accidents and complaints to determine causes. Observe flight activities of pilots to assess flying skills and to ensure conformance to flight and safety regulations.

Education/Training Required: Work experience in a related occupation. **Education and Training Program:** Aircraft Powerplant Technology/Technician. **Knowledge/Courses:** Mechanical Devices; Physics; Transportation; Chemistry; Design; Law and Government.

Personality Type: Realistic-Conventional-Investigative. **Career Cluster:** 16 Transportation, Distribution, and Logistics. **Career Pathways:** 16.1 Transportation Operations; 16.5 Transportation Systems/Infrastructure Planning, Management, and Regulation.

Skills: Science; Equipment Maintenance; Troubleshooting; Repairing; Operation and Control; Equipment Selection; Quality Control Analysis; Operation Monitoring.

Work Environment: More often indoors than outdoors; sitting; noise.

Job Specialization: Freight and Cargo Inspectors

Inspect the handling, storage, and stowing of freight and cargoes. Prepare and submit reports after completion of freight shipments. Inspect shipments to ensure that freight is securely braced and blocked. Record details about freight conditions, handling of freight, and any problems encountered. Advise crews in techniques of stowing dangerous and heavy cargo. Observe loading of freight to ensure that crews comply with procedures. Recommend remedial procedures to correct any violations found during inspec-

tions. Inspect loaded cargo, cargo lashed to decks or in storage facilities, and cargo-handling devices to determine compliance with health and safety regulations and need for maintenance. Measure ships' holds and depths of fuel and water in tanks, using sounding lines and tape measures. Notify workers of any special treatment required for shipments. Direct crews to reload freight or to insert additional bracing or packing as necessary. Check temperatures and humidities of shipping and storage areas to ensure that they are at appropriate levels to protect cargo. Determine cargo transportation capabilities by reading documents that set forth cargo-loading and securing procedures, capacities, and stability factors. Read draft markings to determine depths of vessels in water. Issue certificates of compliance for vessels without violations. Write certificates of admeasurement that list details such as designs, lengths, depths, and breadths of vessels, and methods of propulsion.

Education/Training Required: Work experience in a related occupation. **Education and Training Programs:** No related CIP programs; this job is learned through work experience in a related occupation. **Knowledge/Courses:** Transportation; Engineering and Technology; Public Safety and Security; Physics; Geography; Mechanical Devices.

Personality Type: Realistic-Conventional. **Career Cluster:** 16 Transportation, Distribution, and Logistics. **Career Pathways:** 16.1 Transportation Operations; 16.5 Transportation Systems/Infrastructure Planning, Management, and Regulation.

Skills: Operation and Control; Quality Control Analysis; Operation Monitoring; Science; Management of Personnel Resources; Troubleshooting; Writing; Judgment and Decision Making.

Work Environment: More often outdoors than indoors; standing; noise; very hot or cold; bright or inadequate lighting; contaminants; cramped work space; high places; hazardous equipment.

Realistic-T

Job Specialization: Transportation Vehicle, Equipment and Systems Inspectors, Except Aviation

Inspect and monitor transportation equipment, vehicles, or systems to ensure compliance with regulations and safety standards. Conduct vehicle or transportation equipment tests, using diagnostic equipment. Investigate and make recommendations on carrier requests for waiver of federal standards. Prepare reports on investigations or inspections and actions taken. Issue notices and recommend corrective actions when infractions or problems are found. Investigate incidents or violations such as delays, accidents, and equipment failures. Investigate complaints regarding safety violations. Inspect repairs to transportation vehicles and equipment to ensure that repair work was performed properly. Examine transportation vehicles, equipment, or systems to detect damage, wear, or malfunction. Inspect vehicles and other equipment for evidence of abuse, damage, or mechanical malfunction. Examine carrier operating rules, employee qualification guidelines, and carrier training and testing programs for compliance with regulations or safety standards. Inspect vehicles or equipment to ensure compliance with rules, standards, or regulations.

Education/Training Required: Work experience in a related occupation. **Education and Training Programs:** No related CIP programs; this job is learned through work experience in a related occupation. **Knowledge/Courses:** Mechanical Devices; Transportation; Public Safety and Security; Engineering and Technology; Administration and Management; Physics.

Personality Type: Realistic-Conventional-Investigative. **Career Cluster:** 16 Transportation, Distribution, and Logistics. **Career Pathways:** 16.1 Transportation Operations; 16.5 Transportation Systems/Infrastructure Planning, Management, and Regulation.

Skills: Equipment Maintenance; Repairing; Troubleshooting; Science; Operation and Control; Quality Control Analysis; Operation Monitoring; Equipment Selection.

Work Environment: Outdoors; standing; walking and running; using hands; bending or twisting the body; repetitive motions; noise; very hot or cold; bright or inadequate lighting; contaminants; cramped work space; hazardous equipment; minor burns, cuts, bites, or stings.

Water and Wastewater Treatment Plant and System Operators

* Personality Type: Realistic-Conventional
* Annual Earnings: $40,770
* Earnings Growth Potential: Medium (39.0%)
* Growth: 19.8%
* Annual Job Openings: 4,690
* Self-Employed: 0.0%

Considerations for Job Outlook: Growth in the population, especially in suburban areas, is expected to boost demand for water and wastewater-treatment services. Job opportunities should be excellent.

Operate or control an entire process or system of machines, often through the use of control boards, to transfer or treat water or liquid waste. Add chemicals such as ammonia, chlorine, or lime to disinfect and deodorize water and other liquids. Operate and adjust controls on equipment to purify and clarify water, process or dispose of sewage, and generate power. Inspect equipment or monitor operating conditions, meters, and gauges to determine load requirements and detect malfunctions. Collect and test water and sewage samples, using test equipment and color-analysis standards. Record operational data, personnel attendance, or meter and gauge readings on specified forms. Maintain, repair, and lubricate equipment, using hand tools and power tools. Clean and maintain tanks and filter beds, using hand tools and power tools. Direct and coordinate plant workers engaged in routine operations and maintenance activities.

Education/Training Required: Long-term on-the-job training. **Education and Training Program:** Water Quality and Wastewater Treatment Management and Recycling Technology/Technician. **Knowledge/Courses:** Physics; Building and Construction; Mechanical Devices; Biology; Chemistry; Engineering and Technology.

Career Cluster: 01 Agriculture, Food, and Natural Resources. **Career Pathway:** 01.6 Environmental Service Systems.

Skills: Repairing; Equipment Maintenance; Operation and Control; Troubleshooting; Equipment Selection; Operation Monitoring; Quality Control Analysis; Systems Evaluation.

Work Environment: Outdoors; standing; climbing; walking and running; kneeling, crouching, stooping, or crawling; using hands; bending or twisting the body; repetitive motions; noise; very hot or cold; bright or inadequate lighting; contaminants; cramped work space; exposed to disease or infections; hazardous conditions; hazardous equipment; minor burns, cuts, bites, or stings.

Realistic-W

Investigative Occupations

Aerospace Engineers

- ❋ Personality Type: Investigative-Realistic
- ❋ Annual Earnings: $97,480
- ❋ Earnings Growth Potential: Medium (37.8%)
- ❋ Growth: 10.4%
- ❋ Annual Job Openings: 2,230
- ❋ Self-Employed: 3.3%

Considerations for Job Outlook: Aerospace engineers are expected to have 10 percent growth in employment from 2008 to 2018, about as fast as the average for all occupations. New technologies and new designs for commercial and military aircraft and spacecraft produced during the next decade should spur demand for aerospace engineers. The employment outlook for aerospace engineers appears favorable. Although the number of degrees granted in aerospace engineering has begun to increase after many years of declines, new graduates continue to be needed to replace aerospace engineers who retire or leave the occupation for other reasons.

Perform a variety of engineering work in designing, constructing, and testing aircraft, missiles, and spacecraft. May conduct basic and applied research to evaluate adaptability of materials and equipment to aircraft design and manufacture. May recommend improvements in testing equipment and techniques. Formulate conceptual design of aeronautical or aerospace products or systems to meet customer requirements. Direct and coordinate activities of engineering or technical personnel designing, fabricating, modifying, or testing aircraft or aerospace products. Develop design criteria for aeronautical or aerospace products or systems, including testing methods, production costs, quality standards, and completion dates. Plan and conduct experimental, environmental, operational, and stress tests on models and prototypes of aircraft and aerospace systems and equipment. Evaluate product data and design from inspections and reports for conformance to engineering principles, customer requirements, and quality standards. Formulate mathematical models or other methods of computer analysis to develop, evaluate, or modify design according to customer engineering requirements. Write technical reports and other documentation, such as handbooks and bulletins, for use by engineering staff, management, and customers. Analyze project requests and proposals and engineering data to determine feasibility, productibility, cost, and production time of aerospace or aeronautical product. Review performance reports and documentation from customers and field engineers, and inspect malfunctioning or damaged products to determine problem. Direct research and development programs. Evaluate and approve selection of vendors by study of past performance and new advertisements.

Education/Training Required: Bachelor's degree. **Education and Training Program:** Aerospace, Aeronautical, and Astronautical/Space Engineering. **Knowledge/Courses:** Engineering and Technology; Physics; Design; Mechanical Devices; Mathematics; Production and Processing.

Career Cluster: 15 Science, Technology, Engineering, and Mathematics. **Career Pathway:** 15.1 Engineering and Technology.

Skills: Science; Operations Analysis; Technology Design; Mathematics; Quality Control Analysis; Reading Comprehension; Systems Analysis; Writing.

Work Environment: Indoors; sitting.

Anthropologists and Archeologists

Look for the job description among the Artistic occupations.

Astronomers

Look for the job description among the Artistic occupations.

Atmospheric and Space Scientists

- ❋ Personality Type: Investigative-Realistic
- ❋ Annual Earnings: $87,780
- ❋ Earnings Growth Potential: High (48.7%)
- ❋ Growth: 14.6%
- ❋ Annual Job Openings: 330
- ❋ Self-Employed: 0.0%

Considerations for Job Outlook: As research leads to continuing improvements in weather forecasting, employment of these workers is projected to grow, especially in private firms that provide weather consulting services to climate-sensitive industries such as farming or insurance. Atmospheric scientists face keen competition.

Investigate atmospheric phenomena and interpret meteorological data gathered by surface and air stations, satellites, and radar to prepare reports and forecasts for public and other uses. Study and interpret data, reports, maps, photographs, and charts to predict long- and short-range weather conditions, using computer models and knowledge of climate theory, physics, and mathematics. Broadcast weather conditions, forecasts, and severe weather warnings to the public via television, radio, and the Internet or provide this information to the news media. Gather data from sources such as surface and upper-air stations, satellites, weather bureaus, and radar for use in meteorological reports and forecasts. Prepare forecasts and briefings to meet the needs of industry, business, government, and other groups. Apply meteorological knowledge to problems in areas including agriculture, pollution control, and water management and to issues such as global warming or ozone depletion. Conduct basic or applied meteorological research into the processes and determinants of atmospheric phenomena, weather, and climate. Operate computer graphic equipment to produce weather reports and maps for analysis, distribution, or use in weather broadcasts. Measure wind, temperature, and humidity in the upper atmosphere, using weather balloons. Develop and use weather forecasting tools such as mathematical and computer models. Direct forecasting services at weather stations or at radio or television broadcasting facilities. Research and analyze the impact of industrial projects and pollution on climate, air quality, and weather phenomena.

Education/Training Required: Bachelor's degree. **Education and Training Programs:** Atmospheric Chemistry and Climatology; Atmospheric Physics and Dynamics; Atmospheric Sciences and Meteorology, General; Atmospheric Sciences and Meteorology, Other; Meteorology. **Knowledge/Courses:** Geography; Physics; Mathematics; Computers and Electronics; Communications and Media; Customer and Personal Service.

Career Cluster: 15 Science, Technology, Engineering, and Mathematics. **Career Pathway:** 15.2 Science and Mathematics.

Skills: Science; Operations Analysis; Reading Comprehension; Mathematics; Active Learning; Writing; Systems Analysis; Speaking.

Work Environment: Indoors; sitting; repetitive motions; noise.

Audiologists

- ❋ Personality Type: Investigative-Social
- ❋ Annual Earnings: $66,660
- ❋ Earnings Growth Potential: Medium (36.1%)
- ❋ Growth: 25.0%
- ❋ Annual Job Openings: 580
- ❋ Self-Employed: 1.3%

Considerations for Job Outlook: Employment of audiologists is expected to grow as the population ages and more care is needed for the elderly, who often have problems with hearing and balance. Job prospects should be favorable for job-seekers who have a doctorate in audiology.

Assess and treat persons with hearing and related disorders. May fit hearing aids and provide auditory training. May perform research related to hearing problems. Examine and clean patients' ear canals. Educate and supervise audiology students and health-care personnel. Develop and supervise hearing screening programs. Counsel and instruct patients and their families in techniques to improve hearing and communication related to hearing loss. Evaluate hearing and balance disorders to determine diagnoses and courses of treatment. Program and monitor cochlear implants to fit the needs of patients. Participate in conferences or training to update or share knowledge of new hearing or balance-disorder treatment methods or technologies. Conduct or direct research on hearing or balance topics and report findings to help in the development of procedures, technology, or treatments. Plan and conduct treatment programs for patients' hearing or balance problems, consulting with educators, physicians, nurses, psychologists, speech-language pathologists, and other health-care personnel as necessary. Administer hearing tests and examine patients to collect information on type and degree of impairment, using specialized instruments and electronic equipment. Engage in marketing activities, such as developing marketing plans, to promote business for private practices. Recommend assistive devices according to patients' needs or nature of impairments. Fit, dispense, and repair assistive devices, such as hearing aids. Advise educators or other medical staff on hearing or balance topics. Provide information to the public on hearing or balance topics.

Education/Training Required: Doctoral degree. **Education and Training Programs:** Audiology/Audiologist; Audiology/Audiologist and Speech-Language Pathology/Pathologist; Communication Disorders Sciences and Services, Other; Communication Disorders, General; Communication Sciences and Disorders, General. **Knowledge/Courses:** Therapy and Counseling;

Medicine and Dentistry; Sales and Marketing; Psychology; Biology; Sociology and Anthropology.

Career Cluster: 08 Health Science. **Career Pathway:** 08.1 Therapeutic Services.

Skills: Science; Repairing; Equipment Selection; Reading Comprehension; Technology Design; Troubleshooting; Active Learning; Learning Strategies.

Work Environment: Indoors; sitting; using hands; exposed to disease or infections.

Biochemists and Biophysicists

* Personality Type: Investigative-Artistic-Realistic
* Annual Earnings: $79,390
* Earnings Growth Potential: High (45.8%)
* Growth: 37.4%
* Annual Job Openings: 1,620
* Self-Employed: 2.7%

Considerations for Job Outlook: Biotechnological research and development should continue to drive job growth. Doctoral degree holders are expected to face competition for research positions in academia.

Study the chemical composition and physical principles of living cells and organisms and their electrical and mechanical energy and related phenomena. May conduct research in order to further understanding of the complex chemical combinations and reactions involved in metabolism, reproduction, growth, and heredity. May determine the effects of foods, drugs, serums, hormones, and other substances on tissues and vital processes of living organisms. Design and perform experiments with equipment such as lasers, accelerators, and mass spectrometers. Analyze brain functions, such as learning, thinking, and memory, and analyze the dynamics of seeing and hearing. Share research findings by writing scientific articles and by making presentations at scientific conferences. Develop and test new drugs and medications intended for commercial distribution. Develop methods to process, store, and use foods, drugs, and chemical compounds. Develop new methods to study the mechanisms of biological processes. Examine the molecular and chemical aspects of immune system functioning. Investigate the nature, composition, and expression of genes, and research how genetic engineering can impact these processes. Determine the three-dimensional structure of biological macromolecules. Prepare reports and recommendations based upon research outcomes. Design and build laboratory equipment needed for special research projects. Isolate, analyze, and synthesize vitamins, hormones, allergens, minerals, and enzymes, and determine their effects on body functions. Research cancer treatment, using radiation and nuclear particles. Research transformations of substances in cells, using atomic isotopes. Study how light is absorbed in processes such as photosynthesis or vision. Analyze foods to determine their nutritional values and the effects of cooking, canning, and processing on these values.

Education/Training Required: Doctoral degree. **Education and Training Programs:** Biochemistry; Biochemistry and Molecular Biology; Biophysics; Cell/Cellular Biology and Anatomical Sciences, Other; Molecular Biochemistry; Molecular Biophysics; Soil Chemistry and Physics; Soil Microbiology. **Knowledge/Courses:** Biology; Chemistry; Physics; Engineering and Technology; Medicine and Dentistry; Mechanical Devices.

Career Clusters: 01 Agriculture, Food, and Natural Resources; 15 Science, Technology, Engineering, and Mathematics. **Career Pathways:** 01.2 Plant Systems; 15.2 Science and Mathematics.

Skills: Science; Programming; Active Learning; Technology Design; Mathematics; Learning Strategies; Reading Comprehension; Writing.

Work Environment: Indoors; sitting; using hands; exposed to disease or infections.

Biological Scientists, All Other

* Personality Type: Investigative-Realistic-Artistic
* Annual Earnings: $68,220
* Earnings Growth Potential: High (43.2%)
* Growth: 18.8%
* Annual Job Openings: 1,610
* Self-Employed: 2.5%

Considerations for Job Outlook: Biotechnological research and development should continue to drive job growth. Doctoral degree holders are expected to face competition for research positions in academia.

This occupation includes all biological scientists not listed separately. Because this is a highly diverse occupation, no data is available for some information topics.

Education/Training Required: Doctoral degree. **Education and Training Program:** Biological and Biomedical Sciences, Other.

Career Clusters: 08 Health Science; 15 Science, Technology, Engineering, and Mathematics. **Career Pathways:** 08.5 Biotechnology Research and Development; 15.2 Science and Mathematics.

Job Specialization: Bioinformatics Scientists

Conduct research using bioinformatics theory and methods in areas such as pharmaceuticals, medical technology, biotechnology, computational biology, proteomics, computer information science, biology, and medical informatics. May design databases and develop algorithms for processing and analyzing genomic information, or other biological information. Recommend new systems and processes to improve operations. Keep abreast of new biochemistries, instrumentation, or software by reading scientific literature and attending professional conferences. Confer with departments such as marketing, business development, and operations to coordinate product development

Investigative–B

or improvement. Collaborate with software developers in the development and modification of commercial bioinformatics software. Test new and updated bioinformatics tools and software. Provide statistical and computational tools for biologically based activities such as genetic analysis, measurement of gene expression, and gene function determination. Prepare summary statistics of information regarding human genomes. Instruct others in the selection and use of bioinformatics tools. Improve user interfaces to bioinformatics software and databases. Direct the work of technicians and information technology staff applying bioinformatics tools or applications in areas such as proteomics, transcriptomics, metabolomics, and clinical bioinformatics. Develop new software applications or customize existing applications to meet specific scientific project needs. Develop data models and databases. Create or modify web-based bioinformatics tools. Design and apply bioinformatics algorithms including unsupervised and supervised machine learning, dynamic programming, or graphic algorithms. Create novel computational approaches and analytical tools as required by research goals.

Education/Training Required: Doctoral degree. **Education and Training Program:** Bioinformatics. **Knowledge/Courses:** No data available.

Personality Type: Investigative-Conventional-Realistic. **Career Clusters:** 11 Information Technology; 15 Science, Technology, Engineering, and Mathematics. **Career Pathways:** 11.4 Programming and Software Development; 15.2 Science and Mathematics.

Skills: No data available.

Work Environment: No data available.

Job Specialization: Geneticists

Research and study the inheritance of traits at the molecular, organism, or population level. May evaluate or treat patients with genetic disorders. Write grants and papers or attend fundraising events to seek research funds. Verify that cytogenetic, molecular genetic, and related equipment and instrumentation is maintained in working condition to ensure accuracy and quality of experimental results. Plan curatorial programs for species collections that include acquisition, distribution, maintenance, or regeneration. Participate in the development of endangered-species breeding programs or species-survival plans. Maintain laboratory-safety programs and train personnel in laboratory-safety techniques. Instruct medical students, graduate students, or others in methods or procedures for diagnosis and management of genetic disorders. Evaluate, diagnose, or treat genetic diseases. Design and maintain genetics computer databases. Confer with information technology specialists to develop computer applications for genetic data analysis. Collaborate with biologists and other professionals to conduct appropriate genetic and biochemical analyses. Attend clinical and research conferences and read scientific literature to keep abreast of technological advances and current genetic research findings. Supervise or direct the work of other geneticists, biologists, technicians, or biometricians working on genetics research projects. Review, approve, or interpret genetic laboratory results. Search scientific literature to select and modify methods and procedures most appropriate for genetic research goals.

Education/Training Required: Doctoral degree. **Education and Training Programs:** Animal Genetics; Genetics, General; Genetics, Other; Genome Sciences/Genomics; Human/Medical Genetics; Microbial and Eukaryotic Genetics; Molecular Genetics; Plant Genetics. **Knowledge/Courses:** Biology; Chemistry; Medicine and Dentistry; Education and Training; English Language; Mathematics.

Personality Type: Investigative-Artistic-Realistic. **Career Clusters:** 01 Agriculture, Food, and Natural Resources; 15 Science, Technology, Engineering, and Mathematics. **Career Pathways:** 01.2 Plant Systems; 01.3 Animal Systems; 15.2 Science and Mathematics.

Skills: Science; Mathematics; Writing; Reading Comprehension; Learning Strategies; Instructing; Systems Analysis; Management of Material Resources.

Work Environment: Indoors; sitting; using hands.

Job Specialization: Molecular and Cellular Biologists

Research and study cellular molecules and organelles to understand cell function and organization. Verify all financial, physical, and human resources assigned to research or development projects are used as planned. Participate in all levels of bio-product development including proposing new products, performing market analyses, designing and performing experiments, and collaborating with operations and quality-control teams during product launches. Evaluate new supplies and equipment to ensure operability in specific laboratory settings. Develop guidelines for procedures such as the management of viruses. Coordinate molecular or cellular research activities with scientists specializing in other fields. Confer with vendors to evaluate new equipment or reagents or to discuss the customization of product lines to meet user requirements. Supervise technical personnel and postdoctoral research fellows. Prepare reports, manuscripts, and meeting presentations. Provide scientific direction for project teams regarding the evaluation or handling of devices, drugs, or cells for in vitro and in vivo disease models. Perform laboratory procedures following protocols including deoxyribonucleic acid (DNA) sequencing, cloning and extraction, ribonucleic acid (RNA) purification, or gel electrophoresis. Monitor or operate specialized equipment such as gas chromatographs and high pressure liquid chromatographs, electrophoresis units, thermocyclers, fluorescence-activated cell sorters, and phosphoimagers. Maintain accurate laboratory records and data.

Education/Training Required: Doctoral degree. **Education and Training Program:** Cell/Cellular Biology and Histology. **Knowledge/Courses:** Biology; Chemistry; English Language; Medicine and Dentistry; Computers and Electronics; Mathematics.

Personality Type: Investigative-Realistic-Artistic. **Career Cluster:** 15 Science, Technology, Engineering, and Mathematics. **Career Pathway:** 15.2 Science and Mathematics.

Skills: Science; Programming; Reading Comprehension; Active Learning; Mathematics; Management of Financial Resources; Writing; Learning Strategies.

Work Environment: Indoors; sitting; using hands; hazardous conditions.

Biomedical Engineers

* Personality Type: Investigative-Realistic
* Annual Earnings: $81,540
* Earnings Growth Potential: Medium (39.1%)
* Growth: 72.0%
* Annual Job Openings: 1,490
* Self-Employed: 3.3%

Considerations for Job Outlook: Biomedical engineers are expected to have employment growth of 72 percent from 2008 to 2018, much faster than the average for all occupations. The aging of the population and a growing focus on health issues will drive demand for better medical devices and equipment designed by biomedical engineers. Along with the demand for more sophisticated medical equipment and procedures, an increased concern for cost-effectiveness will boost demand for biomedical engineers, particularly in pharmaceutical manufacturing and related industries. Because of the growing interest in this field, the number of degrees granted in biomedical engineering has increased greatly. Many biomedical engineers, particularly those employed in research laboratories, need a graduate degree.

Apply knowledge of engineering, biology, and biomechanical principles to the design, development, and evaluation of biological and health systems and products, such as artificial organs, prostheses, instrumentation, medical information systems, and health-management and care-delivery systems. Evaluate the safety, efficiency, and effectiveness of biomedical equipment. Install, adjust, maintain, and/or repair biomedical equipment. Advise hospital administrators on the planning, acquisition, and use of medical equipment.

Investigative-B

Advise and assist in the application of instrumentation in clinical environments. Develop models or computer simulations of human bio-behavioral systems in order to obtain data for measuring or controlling life processes. Research new materials to be used for products such as implanted artificial organs. Design and develop medical diagnostic and clinical instrumentation, equipment, and procedures, utilizing the principles of engineering and bio-behavioral sciences. Conduct research, along with life scientists, chemists, and medical scientists, on the engineering aspects of the biological systems of humans and animals. Teach biomedical engineering or disseminate knowledge about the field through writing or consulting. Design and deliver technology to assist people with disabilities. Diagnose and interpret bioelectric data, using signal-processing techniques. Adapt or design computer hardware or software for medical science uses. Analyze new medical procedures in order to forecast likely outcomes. Develop new applications for energy sources, such as using nuclear power for biomedical implants.

Education/Training Required: Bachelor's degree. **Education and Training Program:** Bioengineering and Biomedical Engineering. **Knowledge/Courses:** Biology; Engineering and Technology; Physics; Design; Medicine and Dentistry; Chemistry.

Career Cluster: 15 Science, Technology, Engineering, and Mathematics. **Career Pathway:** 15.1 Engineering and Technology.

Skills: Science; Technology Design; Programming; Installation; Operations Analysis; Mathematics; Troubleshooting; Equipment Selection.

Work Environment: Indoors; sitting.

Clinical, Counseling, and School Psychologists

- ❀ Personality Type: Investigative-Social-Artistic
- ❀ Annual Earnings: $66,810
- ❀ Earnings Growth Potential: High (41.6%)
- ❀ Growth: 11.1%
- ❀ Annual Job Openings: 5,990
- ❀ Self-Employed: 34.1%

Considerations for Job Outlook: Employment growth is expected due to increased emphasis on mental health in a variety of specializations, including school counseling, depression, and substance abuse. Job-seekers with a doctoral degree should have the best opportunities.

Job Specialization: Clinical Psychologists

Diagnose or evaluate mental and emotional disorders of individuals through observation, interview, and psychological tests, and formulate and administer programs of treatment. Identify psychological, emotional, or behavioral issues, and diagnose disorders, using information obtained from interviews, tests, records, and reference materials. Develop and implement individual treatment plans, specifying type, frequency, intensity, and duration of therapy. Interact with clients to assist them in gaining insight, defining goals, and planning action to achieve effective personal, social, educational, and vocational development and adjustment. Discuss the treatment of problems with clients. Utilize a variety of treatment methods such as psychotherapy, hypnosis, behavior modification, stress-reduction therapy, psychodrama, and play therapy. Counsel individuals and groups regarding problems such as stress, substance abuse, and family situations to modify behavior or to improve personal, social, and vocational adjustment. Write reports on clients and maintain required paperwork. Evaluate the effectiveness of counseling or treatments and the accuracy and completeness of diagnoses; then modify plans and diagnoses as necessary. Obtain and study medical, psychological, social, and family histories by interviewing individuals, couples, or families and by reviewing records. Consult reference material such as textbooks, manuals, and journals to identify symptoms, make diagnoses, and develop approaches to treatment. Maintain current knowledge of relevant research.

Education/Training Required: Doctoral degree. **Education and Training Programs:** Psychoanalysis and Psychotherapy; Psychology, General. **Knowledge/Courses:** Therapy and Counseling; Psychology; Sociology and Anthropology; Philosophy and Theology; Customer and Personal Service; Medicine and Dentistry.

Personality Type: Investigative-Social-Artistic. **Career Clusters:** 08 Health Science; 10 Human Services. **Career Pathways:** 08.1 Therapeutic Services; 08.3 Health Informatics; 10.2 Counseling and Mental Health Services.

Skills: Science; Social Perceptiveness; Active Listening; Operations Analysis; Learning Strategies; Speaking; Service Orientation; Reading Comprehension.

Work Environment: Indoors; sitting.

Job Specialization: Counseling Psychologists

Assess and evaluate individuals' problems through the use of case history, interview, and observation, and provide individual or group counseling services to assist individuals in achieving more effective personal, social, educational, and vocational development and adjustment. Collect information about individuals or clients, using interviews, case histories, observational techniques, and other assessment methods. Counsel individuals, groups, or families to help them understand problems, define goals, and develop realistic action plans. Develop therapeutic and treatment plans based on clients' interests, abilities, and needs. Consult with other professionals to discuss therapies, treatments, counseling resources, or techniques and to share

occupational information. Analyze data such as interview notes, test results, and reference manuals in order to identify symptoms and to diagnose the nature of clients' problems. Advise clients on how they could be helped by counseling. Evaluate the results of counseling methods to determine the reliability and validity of treatments. Provide consulting services to schools, social service agencies, and businesses. Refer clients to specialists or to other institutions for non-counseling treatment of problems. Select, administer, and interpret psychological tests to assess intelligence, aptitudes, abilities, or interests. Conduct research to develop or improve diagnostic or therapeutic counseling techniques.

Education/Training Required: Doctoral degree. **Education and Training Programs:** Psychoanalysis and Psychotherapy; Psychology, General. **Knowledge/Courses:** Therapy and Counseling; Philosophy and Theology; Sociology and Anthropology; Psychology; English Language; Customer and Personal Service.

Personality Type: Social-Investigative-Artistic. **Career Clusters:** 08 Health Science; 10 Human Services. **Career Pathways:** 08.1 Therapeutic Services; 10.2 Counseling and Mental Health Services.

Skills: Social Perceptiveness; Science; Negotiation; Active Listening; Operations Analysis; Service Orientation; Learning Strategies; Speaking.

Work Environment: Indoors; sitting.

Job Specialization: School Psychologists

Investigate processes of learning and teaching, and develop psychological principles and techniques applicable to educational problems. Compile and interpret students' test results, along with information from teachers and parents, to diagnose conditions and to help assess eligibility for special services. Report any pertinent information to the proper authorities in cases of child endangerment, neglect, or abuse. Assess an individual child's needs, limitations, and potential, using observation, review of school records, and consultation with par-

Investigative–C

ents and school personnel. Select, administer, and score psychological tests. Provide consultation to parents, teachers, administrators, and others on topics such as learning styles and behavior-modification techniques. Promote an understanding of child development and its relationship to learning and behavior. Collaborate with other educational professionals to develop teaching strategies and school programs. Counsel children and families to help solve conflicts and problems in learning and adjustment. Develop individualized educational plans in collaboration with teachers and other staff members. Maintain student records, including special education reports, confidential records, records of services provided, and behavioral data. Serve as a resource to help families and schools deal with crises, such as separation and loss. Attend workshops, seminars, or professional meetings to remain informed of new developments in school psychology. Design classes and programs to meet the needs of special students.

Education/Training Required: Doctoral degree. **Education and Training Programs:** Psychoanalysis and Psychotherapy; Psychology, General. **Knowledge/Courses:** Therapy and Counseling; Psychology; Sociology and Anthropology; Education and Training; Foreign Language; Mathematics.

Personality Type: Investigative-Social. **Career Clusters:** 08 Health Science; 10 Human Services. **Career Pathways:** 08.1 Therapeutic Services; 10.2 Counseling and Mental Health Services.

Skills: Social Perceptiveness; Learning Strategies; Writing; Judgment and Decision Making; Negotiation; Reading Comprehension; Active Listening; Systems Evaluation.

Work Environment: Indoors; sitting.

Compliance Officers

Look for the job description among the Conventional jobs.

Computer and Information Research Scientists

- ❋ Personality Type: Investigative-Realistic-Conventional
- ❋ Annual Earnings: $100,660
- ❋ Earnings Growth Potential: High (42.7%)
- ❋ Growth: 24.2%
- ❋ Annual Job Openings: 1,320
- ❋ Self-Employed: 4.6%

Considerations for Job Outlook: Employment is expected to increase because of high demand for sophisticated technological research. Job prospects should be excellent.

Conduct research into fundamental computer and information science as theorists, designers, or inventors. Solve or develop solutions to problems in the field of computer hardware and software. Analyze problems to develop solutions involving computer hardware and software. Assign or schedule tasks in order to meet work priorities and goals. Evaluate project plans and proposals to assess feasibility issues. Apply theoretical expertise and innovation to create or apply new technology, such as adapting principles for applying computers to new uses. Consult with users, management, vendors, and technicians to determine computing needs and system requirements. Meet with managers, vendors, and others to solicit cooperation and resolve problems. Conduct logical analyses of business, scientific, engineering, and other technical problems, formulating mathematical models of problems for solution by computers. Develop and interpret organizational goals, policies, and procedures. Participate in staffing decisions, and direct training of subordinates. Develop performance standards, and evaluate work in light of established standards. Design computers and the software that runs them. Maintain network hardware and software, direct network security measures, and monitor networks to ensure availability to system users. Participate in multidisciplinary projects in areas such as virtual reality, human-computer interaction, or robotics. Approve, prepare, monitor, and adjust operational budgets. Direct daily operations of departments, coordinating project activities with other departments.

Education/Training Required: Doctoral degree. **Education and Training Programs:** Computer Graphics; Computer Science; Computer Software and Media Applications, Other; Computer Systems Networking and Telecommunications; Data Modeling/Warehousing and Database Administration; Modeling, Virtual Environments and Simulation; Web Page, Digital/Multimedia, and Information Resources Design. **Knowledge/Courses:** Computers and Electronics; Telecommunications; Engineering and Technology; Mathematics; Design; Education and Training.

Career Cluster: 08 Health Science; 11 Information Technology. **Career Pathways:** 08.3 Health Informatics; 11.1 Network Systems; 11.2 Information Support Services; 11.3 Interactive Media; 11.4 Programming and Software Development.

Skills: Programming; Technology Design; Systems Evaluation; Management of Financial Resources; Mathematics; Systems Analysis; Operations Analysis; Science.

Work Environment: Indoors; sitting; using hands; repetitive motions.

Computer Hardware Engineers

- ❋ Personality Type: Investigative-Realistic-Conventional
- ❋ Annual Earnings: $98,810
- ❋ Earnings Growth Potential: Medium (37.9%)
- ❋ Growth: 3.8%
- ❋ Annual Job Openings: 2,350
- ❋ Self-Employed: 1.3%

Considerations for Job Outlook: Computer hardware engineers are expected to have employment growth of 4 percent from 2008 to 2018, slower than the average for all occupations. Although the use of information technology continues to expand rapidly, the manufacture of computer hardware is expected to be adversely affected by intense foreign competition. As computer and semiconductor manufacturers contract out more of their engineering needs to both domestic and foreign design firms, much of the growth in employment of hardware engineers is expected to take place in the computer systems design and related services industry.

Research, design, develop, and test computer or computer-related equipment for commercial, industrial, military, or scientific use. May supervise the manufacturing and installation of computer or computer-related equipment and components. Update knowledge and skills to keep up with rapid advancements in computer technology. Provide technical support to designers, marketing and sales departments, suppliers, engineers, and other team members throughout the product-development and implementation process. Test and verify hardware and support peripherals to ensure that they meet specifications and requirements, analyzing and recording test data. Monitor functioning of equipment, and make necessary modifications to ensure system operates in conformance with specifications. Analyze information to determine, recommend, and plan layout, including type of computers and peripheral equipment modifications. Build, test, and modify product prototypes, using working models or theoretical models constructed using computer simulation. Analyze user needs, and recommend appropriate hardware. Direct technicians, engineering designers, or other technical support personnel as needed. Confer with engineering staff and consult specifications to evaluate interface between hardware and software and operational and performance requirements of overall system. Select hardware and material, assuring compliance with specifications and product requirements. Store, retrieve, and manipulate data for analysis of system capabilities and requirements. Write detailed functional specifications that document the hardware-development process and support hardware introduction.

Investigative-C

Education/Training Required: Bachelor's degree. **Education and Training Programs:** Computer Engineering, General; Computer Hardware Engineering. **Knowledge/Courses:** Computers and Electronics; Engineering and Technology; Telecommunications; Design; Physics; Communications and Media.

Career Clusters: 11 Information Technology; 15 Science, Technology, Engineering, and Mathematics. **Career Pathways:** 11.4 Programming and Software Development; 15.1 Engineering and Technology.

Skills: Troubleshooting; Science; Programming; Operations Analysis; Systems Evaluation; Quality Control Analysis; Equipment Maintenance; Complex Problem Solving.

Work Environment: Indoors; sitting.

Job Specialization: Telecommunications Engineering Specialists

Design or configure voice, video, and data communications systems. Supervise installation and post-installation service and maintenance. Keep abreast of changes in industry practices and emerging telecommunications technology by reviewing current literature, talking with colleagues, participating in educational programs, attending meetings or workshops, or participating in professional organizations or conferences. Estimate costs for system or component implementation and operation. Develop, maintain, or implement telecommunications disaster-recovery plans to ensure business continuity. Test and evaluate hardware and software to determine efficiency, reliability, or compatibility with existing systems. Supervise maintenance of telecommunications equipment. Review and evaluate requests from engineers, managers, and technicians for system modifications. Provide user support by diagnosing network and device problems and implementing technical or procedural solutions. Prepare system activity and performance reports. Prepare purchase requisitions for computer hardware and software, networking and telecommunications equipment, test equipment, cabling, or tools. Use computer-aided design (CAD) software to prepare or evaluate network diagrams, floor plans, or site configurations for existing facilities, renovations, or new systems. Order or maintain inventory of telecommunications equipment, including telephone sets, headsets, cellular phones, switches, trunks, printed circuit boards, network routers, and cabling. Monitor and analyze system performance, such as network traffic, security, and capacity.

Education/Training Required: Bachelor's degree. **Education and Training Program:** Computer Systems Networking and Telecommunications. **Knowledge/Courses:** No data available.

Personality Type: No data available. **Career Clusters:** 11 Information Technology; 15 Science, Technology, Engineering, and Mathematics. **Career Pathway:** 11.4 Programming and Software Development; 15.1 Engineering and Technology.

Skills: No data available.

Work Environment: No data available.

Computer Network Architects

- ✻ Personality Type: Investigative-Conventional-Realistic
- ✻ Annual Earnings: $75,660
- ✻ Earnings Growth Potential: High (42.9%)
- ✻ Growth: 53.4%
- ✻ Annual Job Openings: 20,830
- ✻ Self-Employed: 19.4%

Considerations for Job Outlook: Employment of these workers should grow as organizations increasingly use network technologies. Job prospects are expected to be excellent.

Design and implement computer and information networks, such as local area networks (LAN), wide area networks (WAN), intranets, extranets, and other data communications networks. Perform network modeling, analysis, and planning. May also design network and comput-

er-security measures. **May research and recommend network and data communications hardware and software.** Adjust network sizes to meet volume or capacity demands. Communicate with customers, sales staff, or marketing staff to determine customer needs. Communicate with system users to ensure accounts are set up properly or to diagnose and solve operational problems. Coordinate installation of new equipment. Coordinate network operations, maintenance, repairs, or upgrades. Coordinate network or design activities with designers of associated networks. Design, build, or operate equipment configuration prototypes, including network hardware, software, servers, or server operation systems. Design, organize, and deliver product awareness, skills transfer, or product education sessions for staff or suppliers. Determine specific network hardware or software requirements, such as platforms, interfaces, bandwidths, or routine schemas. Develop and implement solutions for network problems. Develop and write procedures for installation, use, or troubleshooting of communications hardware or software. Develop conceptual, logical, or physical network designs. Develop disaster-recovery plans. Develop network-related documentation. Develop or maintain project-reporting systems. Develop or recommend network security measures, such as firewalls, network security audits, or automated security probes. Develop plans or budgets for network equipment replacement. Develop procedures to track, project, or report network availability, reliability, capacity, or utilization.

Education/Training Required: Bachelor's degree. **Education and Training Program:** Computer Systems Networking and Telecommunications. **Knowledge/Courses:** Telecommunications; Computers and Electronics; Design; Engineering and Technology; Communications and Media; Clerical Practices.

Career Cluster: 11 Information Technology. **Career Pathway:** 11.4 Programming and Software Development.

Skills: Programming; Technology Design; Equipment Selection; Operations Analysis; Equipment Maintenance; Quality Control Analysis; Troubleshooting; Repairing.

Work Environment: Indoors; sitting.

Computer Occupations, All Other

- ✱ Personality Type: Investigative-Conventional-Realistic
- ✱ Annual Earnings: $79,240
- ✱ Earnings Growth Potential: High (47.4%)
- ✱ Growth: 13.1%
- ✱ Annual Job Openings: 7,260
- ✱ Self-Employed: 3.9%

Considerations for Job Outlook: Employment of these workers should grow as organizations increasingly use network technologies and collect and organize data. Job prospects are expected to be excellent.

This occupation includes all computer occupations not listed separately. Because this is a highly diverse occupation, no data is available for some information topics.

Education/Training Required: No data available. **Education and Training Program:** Computer and Information Sciences and Support Services, Other.

Career Cluster: 11 Information Technology. **Career Pathways:** 11.2 Information Support Services; 11.3 Interactive Media; 11.4 Programming and Software Development.

Job Specialization: Business Intelligence Analysts

Produce financial and market intelligence by querying data repositories and generating periodic reports. Devise methods for identifying data patterns and trends in available information sources. Provide technical support for existing reports, dashboards, or other tools. Maintain library of model documents, templates, or other reusable knowledge assets. Identify or monitor current and potential customers, using business intelligence tools. Create or review technical design documentation to ensure the accurate development of reporting solutions. Communicate with customers, competitors, suppliers, professional organizations, or others to stay abreast of industry or business trends. Maintain or update business intelligence tools, databases, dashboards, systems, or methods. Manage timely flow of business intelligence information to users. Identify and analyze industry or geographic trends with business-strategy implications. Document specifications for business intelligence or information technology (IT) reports, dashboards, or other outputs. Disseminate information regarding tools, reports, or metadata enhancements. Create business intelligence tools or systems, including design of related databases, spreadsheets, or outputs. Conduct or coordinate tests to ensure that intelligence is consistent with defined needs. Collect business intelligence data from available industry reports, public information, field reports, or purchased sources. Analyze technology trends to identify markets for future product development or to improve sales of existing products. Analyze competitive market strategies through analysis of related product, market, or share trends.

Education/Training Required: Work experience plus degree. **Education and Training Program:** Computer and Information Sciences and Support Services, Other. **Knowledge/Courses:** No data available.

Personality Type: No data available. **Career Cluster:** 11 Information Technology. **Career Pathway:** 11.2 Information Support Services.

Skills: No data available.

Work Environment: No data available.

Job Specialization: Computer Systems Engineers/Architects

Design and develop solutions to complex applications problems, system administration issues, or network concerns. Perform systems management and integration functions. Communicate with staff or clients to understand specific system requirements. Provide advice on project costs, design concepts, or design changes. Document design specifications, installation instructions, and other system-related information. Verify stability, interop-

erability, portability, security, or scalability of system architecture. Collaborate with engineers or software developers to select appropriate design solutions or ensure the compatibility of system components. Evaluate current or emerging technologies to consider factors such as cost, portability, compatibility, or usability. Provide technical guidance or support for the development or troubleshooting of systems. Identify system data, hardware, or software components required to meet user needs. Provide guidelines for implementing secure systems to customers or installation teams. Monitor system operation to detect potential problems. Direct the analysis, development, and operation of complete computer systems. Investigate system component suitability for specified purposes, and make recommendations regarding component use. Perform ongoing hardware and software maintenance operations, including installing or upgrading hardware or software. Configure servers to meet functional specifications. Develop or approve project plans, schedules, or budgets. Define and analyze objectives, scope, issues, or organizational impact of information systems.

Education/Training Required: Bachelor's degree. **Education and Training Programs:** Computer Engineering, General; Data Modeling/Warehousing and Database Administration. **Knowledge/Courses:** Computers and Electronics; Telecommunications; Engineering and Technology; Design; Mathematics; Sales and Marketing.

Personality Type: Investigative-Realistic-Conventional. **Career Cluster:** 11 Information Technology. **Career Pathway:** 11.4 Programming and Software Development.

Skills: Programming; Operations Analysis; Science; Systems Evaluation; Quality Control Analysis; Management of Financial Resources; Equipment Maintenance; Equipment Selection.

Work Environment: Indoors; sitting; repetitive motions.

Job Specialization: Data Warehousing Specialists

Design, model, or implement corporate data warehousing activities. Program and configure warehouses of database information, and provide support to warehouse users. Test software systems or applications for software enhancements or new products. Review designs, codes, test plans, or documentation to ensure quality. Provide or coordinate troubleshooting support for data warehouses. Prepare functional or technical documentation for data warehouses. Write new programs or modify existing programs to meet customer requirements, using current programming languages and technologies. Verify the structure, accuracy, or quality of warehouse data. Select methods, techniques, or criteria for data warehousing evaluative procedures. Perform system analysis, data analysis, or programming, using a variety of computer languages and procedures. Map data between source systems, data warehouses, and data marts. Implement business rules via stored procedures, middleware, or other technologies. Develop and implement data-extraction procedures from other systems, such as administration, billing, or claims. Develop or maintain standards, such as organization, structure, or nomenclature, for the design of data warehouse elements, such as data architectures, models, tools, and databases. Design and implement warehouse database structures. Create supporting documentation, such as metadata and diagrams of entity relationships, business processes, and process flow. Create plans, test files, and scripts for data warehouse testing, ranging from unit to integration testing. Create or implement metadata processes and frameworks.

Education/Training Required: Bachelor's degree. **Education and Training Program:** Data Modeling/ Warehousing and Database Administration. **Knowledge/Courses:** No data available.

Personality Type: No data available. **Career Cluster:** 11 Information Technology. **Career Pathway:** 11.2 Information Support Services.

Skills: No data available.

Work Environment: No data available.

Job Specialization: Database Architects

Design strategies for enterprise database systems, and set standards for operations, programming, and security. Design and construct large relational databases. Integrate new systems with existing warehouse structure, and refine system performance and functionality. Test changes to database applications or systems. Provide technical support to junior staff or clients. Set up database clusters, backup, or recovery processes. Identify, evaluate, and recommend hardware or software technologies to achieve desired database performance. Plan and install upgrades of database management system software to enhance database performance. Monitor and report systems resource consumption trends to assure production systems meet availability requirements and hardware enhancements are scheduled appropriately. Identify and correct deviations from database development standards. Document and communicate database schemas, using accepted notations. Develop or maintain archived procedures, procedural codes, or queries for applications. Develop load-balancing processes to eliminate down time for backup processes. Develop data models for applications, metadata tables, views or related database structures. Design databases to support business applications, ensuring system scalability, security, performance, and reliability. Design database applications, such as interfaces, data transfer mechanisms, global temporary tables, data partitions, and function-based indexes, to enable efficient access of the generic database structure. Demonstrate database technical functionality, such as performance, security, and reliability. Create and enforce database development standards.

Education/Training Required: Bachelor's degree. **Education and Training Program:** Data Modeling/ Warehousing and Database Administration. **Knowledge/Courses:** No data available.

Personality Type: No data available. **Career Cluster:** 11 Information Technology. **Career Pathway:** 11.4 Programming and Software Development.

Skills: No data available.

Work Environment: No data available.

Investigative-C

Job Specialization: Document Management Specialists

Implement and administer enterprise-wide document management procedures for the capture, storage, retrieval, sharing, and destruction of electronic records and documents. Keep abreast of developments in document management by reviewing current literature, talking with colleagues, participating in educational programs, attending meetings or workshops, or participating in professional organizations or conferences. Monitor regulatory activity to maintain compliance with records and document management laws. Write, review, or execute plans for testing new or established document management systems. Search electronic sources, such as databases or repositories, or manual sources for information. Retrieve electronic assets from a repository for distribution to users, collecting and returning to the repository, if necessary. Propose recommendations for improving content-management system capabilities. Prepare support documentation and training materials for end users of document management systems. Prepare and record changes to official documents, and confirm changes with legal and compliance management staff. Exercise security surveillance over document processing, reproduction, distribution, storage, or archiving. Implement scanning or other automated data entry procedures, using imaging devices and document imaging software. Document technical functions and specifications for new or proposed content-management systems. Develop, document, or maintain standards, best practices, or system usage procedures. Consult with end users regarding problems in accessing electronic content.

Education/Training Required: Associate degree. **Education and Training Program:** Computer and Information Sciences and Support Services, Other. **Knowledge/Courses:** No data available.

Personality Type: No data available. **Career Cluster:** 11 Information Technology. **Career Pathway:** 11.2 Information Support Services.

Skills: No data available.

Work Environment: No data available.

Job Specialization: Geographic Information Systems Technicians

Assist scientists, technologists, and related professionals in building, maintaining, modifying, and using Geographic Information Systems (GIS) databases. May also perform some custom application development and provide user support. Recommend procedures and equipment or software upgrades to increase data accessibility or ease of use. Provide technical support to users or clients regarding the maintenance, development, or operation of GIS databases, equipment, or applications. Read current literature, talk with colleagues, continue education, or participate in professional organizations or conferences to keep abreast of developments in GIS technology, equipment, or systems. Confer with users to analyze, configure, or troubleshoot applications. Select cartographic elements needed for effective presentation of information. Transfer or rescale information from original photographs onto maps or other photographs. Review existing or incoming data for currency, accuracy, usefulness, quality, or completeness of documentation. Interpret aerial or ortho photographs. Analyze GIS data to identify spatial relationships or display results of analyses using maps, graphs, or tabular data. Perform geospatial data building, modeling, or analysis using advanced spatial analysis, data manipulation, or cartography software. Maintain or modify existing GIS databases.

Education/Training Required: Associate degree. **Education and Training Program:** Geographic Information Science and Cartography. **Knowledge/Courses:** Geography; Design; Computers and Electronics; Engineering and Technology; Mathematics; Biology.

Personality Type: Investigative-Realistic-Conventional. **Career Cluster:** 11 Information Technology. **Career Pathway:** 11.4 Programming and Software Development.

Skills: Programming; Technology Design; Mathematics; Science; Operations Analysis; Reading Comprehension; Equipment Selection; Systems Evaluation.

Work Environment: Indoors; sitting; using hands; repetitive motions.

Job Specialization: Geospatial Information Scientists and Technologists

Research and develop geospatial technologies. May produce databases, perform applications programming, or coordinate projects. May specialize in areas such as agriculture, mining, health care, retail trade, urban planning, or military intelligence. Perform integrated and computerized Geographic Information Systems (GIS) analyses to address scientific problems. Develop specialized computer software routines, Internet-based GIS databases or business applications to customize geographic information. Provide technical support for computer-based GIS mapping software. Create visual representations of geospatial data using complex procedures such as analytical modeling, three-dimensional renderings, and plot creation. Perform computer programming, data analysis, or software development for GIS applications, including the maintenance of existing systems or research and development for future enhancements. Assist users in formulating GIS requirements or understanding the implications of alternatives. Collect, compile, or integrate GIS data such as remote sensing and cartographic data for inclusion in map manuscripts. Conduct or coordinate research, data analysis, systems design, or support for software such as GIS or Global Positioning Systems (GPS) mapping software. Design, program, or model GIS applications or procedures. Document, design, code, or test GIS models, Internet mapping solutions, or other applications.

Education/Training Required: Bachelor's degree. **Education and Training Program:** Geographic Information Science and Cartography. **Knowledge/ Courses:** Geography; Computers and Electronics; Design; Engineering and Technology; Mathematics; Education and Training.

Personality Type: Investigative-Realistic-Conventional. **Career Cluster:** 11 Information Technology. **Career Pathway:** 11.4 Programming and Software Development.

Skills: Science; Programming; Operations Analysis; Systems Evaluation; Systems Analysis; Technology Design; Mathematics; Reading Comprehension.

Work Environment: Indoors; sitting; using hands; repetitive motions.

Job Specialization: Information Technology Project Managers

Plan, initiate, and manage information technology (IT) projects. Lead and guide the work of technical staff. Serve as liaison between business and technical aspects of projects. Plan project stages, and assess business implications for each stage. Monitor progress to assure deadlines, standards, and cost targets are met. Perform risk assessments to develop response strategies. Submit project deliverables, ensuring adherence to quality standards. Monitor the performance of project team members, providing and documenting performance feedback. Confer with project personnel to identify and resolve problems. Assess current or future customer needs and priorities through communicating directly with customers, conducting surveys, or other methods. Schedule and facilitate meetings related to IT projects. Monitor or track project milestones and deliverables. Negotiate with project stakeholders or suppliers to obtain resources or materials. Initiate, review, or approve modifications to project plans. Identify, review, or select vendors or consultants to meet project needs. Establish and execute a project communication plan. Identify need for initial or supplemental project resources. Direct or coordinate activities of project personnel. Develop implementation plans that include analyses such as cost-benefit or return on investment (ROI). Coordinate recruitment or selection of project personnel. Develop and manage annual budgets for IT projects. Assign du-

Investigative–C

ties, responsibilities, and spans of authority to project personnel. Prepare project status reports by collecting, analyzing, and summarizing information and trends. Manage project execution to ensure adherence to budget, schedule, and scope.

Education/Training Required: Work experience in a related occupation. **Education and Training Program:** Information Technology Project Management. **Knowledge/Courses:** No data available.

Personality Type: No data available. **Career Clusters:** 11 Information Technology. **Career Pathway:** 11.4 Programming and Software Development.

Skills: No data available.

Work Environment: No data available.

Job Specialization: Search Marketing Strategists

Employ search marketing tactics to increase visibility and engagement with content, products, or services in Internet-enabled devices or interfaces. Examine search query behaviors on general or specialty search engines or other Internet-based content. Analyze research, data, or technology to understand user intent and measure outcomes for ongoing optimization. Keep abreast of government regulations and emerging Web technology to ensure regulatory compliance by reviewing current literature, talking with colleagues, participating in educational programs, attending meetings or workshops, or participate in professional organizations or conferences. Resolve product availability problems in collaboration with customer service staff. Implement online customer service processes to ensure positive and consistent user experiences. Identify, evaluate, or procure hardware or software for implementing online marketing campaigns. Identify methods for interfacing Web application technologies with enterprise resource planning or other system software. Define product requirements based on market research analysis in collaboration with design and engineering staff. Assist in the evaluation and negotia-

tion of contracts with vendors and online partners. Propose online or multiple-sales-channel campaigns to marketing executives. Assist in the development of online transactional and security policies. Prepare electronic commerce designs and prototypes, such as storyboards, mock-ups, and other content, using graphic design software. Participate in the development of online marketing strategy. Identify and develop commercial or technical specifications to promote transactional website functionality, including usability, pricing, checkout, or data security.

Education/Training Required: Bachelor's degree. **Education and Training Program:** Web Page, Digital/Multimedia, and Information Resources Design. **Knowledge/Courses:** No data available.

Personality Type: No data available. **Career Clusters:** 11 Information Technology; 14 Marketing, Sales, and Service. **Career Pathway:** 11.4 Programming and Software Development; 14.2 Professional Sales and Marketing.

Skills: No data available.

Work Environment: No data available.

Job Specialization: Software Quality Assurance Engineers and Testers

Develop and execute software test plans in order to identify software problems and their causes. Design test plans, scenarios, scripts, or procedures. Test system modifications to prepare for implementation. Develop testing programs that address areas such as database impacts, software scenarios, regression testing, negative testing, error or bug retests, or usability. Document software defects, using a bug tracking system, and report defects to software developers. Identify, analyze, and document problems with program function, output, online screen, or content. Monitor bug resolution efforts, and track successes. Create or maintain databases of known test defects. Plan test schedules or strategies in accordance with project scope or delivery dates. Participate in product design reviews to provide input on functional requirements, product designs, schedules, or potential problems. Review software documentation to ensure technical accuracy, compliance, or completeness, or to mitigate risks. Document test procedures to ensure replicability and compliance with standards. Develop or specify standards, methods, or procedures to determine product quality or release readiness. Update automated test scripts to ensure currency. Investigate customer problems referred by technical support. Install, maintain, or use software testing programs. Provide feedback and recommendations to developers on software usability and functionality. Monitor program performance to ensure efficient and problem-free operations.

Education/Training Required: Bachelor's degree. **Education and Training Program:** Computer Engineering, General. **Knowledge/Courses:** Computers and Electronics; Engineering and Technology; Design; English Language; Mathematics; Clerical Practices.

Personality Type: Investigative-Conventional-Realistic. **Career Cluster:** 11 Information Technology. **Career Pathway:** 11.4 Programming and Software Development.

Skills: Programming; Installation; Operations Analysis; Technology Design; Troubleshooting; Science; Quality Control Analysis; Systems Evaluation.

Work Environment: Indoors; sitting; using hands; repetitive motions.

Job Specialization: Video Game Designers

Design core features of video games. Specify innovative game and role-play mechanics, storylines, and character biographies. Create and maintain design documentation. Guide and collaborate with production staff to produce games as designed. Review or evaluate competitive products, film, music, television, and other art forms to generate new game design ideas. Provide test specifications to quality assurance staff. Keep abreast of game design technology and techniques, industry trends, or audience interests, reactions, and needs by reviewing current literature, talking with colleagues, participating in educational programs, attending meetings or workshops, or participating in professional organizations or conferences. Create gameplay test plans for internal and external test groups. Provide feedback to designers and other colleagues regarding game design features. Balance and adjust gameplay experiences to ensure the critical and commercial success of the product. Write or supervise the writing of game text and dialogue. Solicit, obtain, and integrate feedback from design and technical staff into original game design. Provide feedback to production staff regarding technical game qualities or adherence to original design. Prepare two-dimensional concept layouts or three-dimensional mock-ups. Present new game-design concepts to management and technical colleagues, including artists, animators, and programmers. Prepare and revise initial game sketches using two- and three-dimensional graphic design software. Oversee gameplay testing to ensure intended gaming experience and game adherence to original vision. Guide design discussions between development teams.

Education/Training Required: Postsecondary vocational training. **Education and Training Program:** Game and Interactive Media Design. **Knowledge/Courses:** No data available.

Personality Type: No data available. **Career Clusters:** 03 Arts, Audio/Video Technology, and Communications; 11 Information Technology. **Career Pathway:** 3.1 Audio and Video Technology and Film; 11.4 Programming and Software Development.

Skills: No data available.

Work Environment: No data available.

Investigative-C

Job Specialization: Web Administrators

Manage Web environment design, deployment, development, and maintenance activities. Perform testing and quality assurance of websites and Web applications. Back up or modify applications and related data to provide for disaster recovery. Determine sources of webpage or server problems, and take action to correct such problems. Review or update webpage content or links in a timely manner, using appropriate tools. Monitor systems for intrusions or denial of service attacks, and report security breaches to appropriate personnel. Implement website security measures, such as firewalls or message encryption. Administer Internet/intranet infrastructure, including components such as Web, file transfer protocol (FTP), news, and mail servers. Collaborate with development teams to discuss, analyze, or resolve usability issues. Test backup or recovery plans regularly, and resolve any problems. Monitor Web developments through continuing education, reading, or participation in professional conferences, workshops, or groups. Implement updates, upgrades, and patches in a timely manner to limit loss of service. Identify or document backup or recovery plans. Collaborate with Web developers to create and operate internal and external websites, or to manage projects, such as e-marketing campaigns. Install or configure Web server software or hardware to ensure that directory structure is well-defined, logical, and secure, and that files are named properly. Gather, analyze, or document user feedback to locate or resolve sources of problems. Develop website performance metrics. Identify or address interoperability requirements.

Education/Training Required: Bachelor's degree. **Education and Training Programs:** Computer and Information Systems Security/Information Assurance; Network and System Administration/Administrator; System, Networking, and LAN/WAN Management/Manager; Web/Multimedia Management and Webmaster Training. **Knowledge/Courses:** Computers and Electronics; Telecommunications; Design; Communications and Media; Sales and Marketing; Clerical Practices.

Personality Type: Conventional-Enterprising-Investigative. **Career Cluster:** 11 Information Technology. **Career Pathway:** 11.4 Programming and Software Development.

Skills: Programming; Operations Analysis; Troubleshooting; Science; Technology Design; Quality Control Analysis; Installation; Systems Evaluation.

Work Environment: Indoors; sitting; using hands; repetitive motions.

Computer Systems Analysts

- ❈ Personality Type: Investigative-Conventional-Realistic
- ❈ Annual Earnings: $77,740
- ❈ Earnings Growth Potential: Medium (37.8%)
- ❈ Growth: 20.3%
- ❈ Annual Job Openings: 22,280
- ❈ Self-Employed: 5.7%

Considerations for Job Outlook: Employment growth is projected as organizations continue to adopt the most efficient technologies and as the need for information security grows. Job prospects should be excellent.

Analyze science, engineering, business, and all other data-processing problems for application to electronic data-processing systems. Analyze user requirements, procedures, and problems to automate or improve existing systems, and review computer system capabilities, workflow, and scheduling limitations. May analyze or recommend commercially available software. May supervise computer programmers. Provide staff and users with assistance solving computer-related problems, such as malfunctions and program problems. Test, maintain, and monitor computer programs and systems, including coordinating the installation of computer programs and systems. Use object-oriented programming languages, as well as client and server applications development processes and multimedia and Internet technology. Confer with clients regarding the nature of the information processing or computation needs a computer program is to address. Coordinate and link the computer systems within an organization to increase compatibility and to share information. Consult with management to ensure agreement on system principles. Expand or modify the system to serve new purposes or improve work flow. Interview or survey workers, observe job performance, or perform the job to determine what information is processed and how it is processed. Determine computer software or hardware needed to set up or alter system. Train staff and users to work with computer systems and programs. Analyze information processing or computation needs, and plan and design computer systems, using techniques such as structured analysis, data modeling, and information engineering. Assess the usefulness of pre-developed application packages, and adapt them to a user environment. Define the goals of the system, and devise flow charts and diagrams describing logical operational steps of programs.

Education/Training Required: Bachelor's degree. **Education and Training Programs:** Computer Systems Analysis/Analyst; Information Science/Studies. **Knowledge/Courses:** Computers and Electronics; Engineering and Technology; Mathematics; Telecommunications; Clerical Practices; English Language.

Career Cluster: 11 Information Technology. **Career Pathways:** 11.2 Information Support Services; 11.3 Interactive Media; 11.4 Programming and Software Development.

Skills: Programming; Technology Design; Troubleshooting; Quality Control Analysis; Systems Evaluation; Operations Analysis; Systems Analysis; Mathematics.

Work Environment: Indoors; sitting; using hands; repetitive motions; noise.

Job Specialization: Informatics Nurse Specialists

Apply knowledge of nursing and informatics to assist in the design, development, and ongoing modification of computerized health-care systems. May educate staff and assist in problem solving to promote the implementation of the health-care system. Design, develop, select, test, implement, and evaluate new or modified informatics solutions, data structures, and decision-support mechanisms to support patients, health-care professionals, and their information management and human-computer and human-technology interactions within health-care contexts. Disseminate information about nursing informatics science and practice to the profession, other health-care professions, nursing students, and the public. Translate nursing practice information between nurses and systems engineers, analysts, or designers using object-oriented models or other techniques. Plan, install, repair, or troubleshoot telehealth-technology applications or systems in homes. Use informatics science to design or implement health information technology applications to resolve clinical or health-care administrative problems. Develop, implement, or evaluate health information technology applications, tools, processes, or structures to assist nurses with data management. Analyze and interpret patient, nursing, or information systems data to improve nursing services. Analyze computer and information technologies to determine applicability to nursing practice, education, administration, and research. Apply knowledge of computer science, information science, nursing, and informatics theory to nursing practice, education, administration, or research, in collaboration with other health informatics specialists.

Education/Training Required: Master's degree. **Education and Training Programs:** Computer Systems Analysis/Analyst; Information Science/Studies. **Knowledge/Courses:** Medicine and Dentistry; Sociology and Anthropology; Education and Training; Engineering and Technology; Computers and Electronics; Clerical Practices.

Investigative-C

Personality Type: Social-Investigative. **Career Clusters:** 08 Health Science; 11 Information Technology. **Career Pathway:** 08.1 Therapeutic Services; 11.2 Information Support Services.

Skills: Programming; Technology Design; Science; Systems Evaluation; Operations Analysis; Systems Analysis; Equipment Selection; Active Learning.

Work Environment: Indoors; sitting; using hands; repetitive motions.

Dentists, General

- ✺ Personality Type: Investigative-Realistic-Social
- ✺ Annual Earnings: $141,040
- ✺ Earnings Growth Potential: High (49.4%)
- ✺ Growth: 15.3%
- ✺ Annual Job Openings: 5,180
- ✺ Self-Employed: 28.0%

Considerations for Job Outlook: An increase in the elderly population who often need complicated dental work and expanded insurance coverage for dental procedures are expected to create job growth. Good prospects are expected from the need to replace the large number of dentists who are retiring.

Diagnose and treat diseases, injuries, and malformations of teeth and gums and related oral structures. May treat diseases of nerve, pulp, and other dental tissues affecting vitality of teeth. Use masks, gloves, and safety glasses to protect themselves and their patients from infectious diseases. Administer anesthetics to limit the amount of pain experienced by patients during procedures. Examine teeth, gums, and related tissues, using dental instruments, X-rays, and other diagnostic equipment, to evaluate dental health, diagnose diseases or abnormalities, and plan appropriate treatments. Formulate plan of treatment for patient's teeth and mouth tissue. Use air turbine and hand instruments, dental appliances, and surgical

implements. Advise and instruct patients regarding preventive dental care, the causes and treatment of dental problems, and oral health-care services. Design, make, and fit prosthodontic appliances such as space maintainers, bridges, and dentures, or write fabrication instructions or prescriptions for denturists and dental technicians. Diagnose and treat diseases, injuries, and malformations of teeth, gums, and related oral structures, and provide preventive and corrective services. Fill pulp chamber and canal with endodontic materials. Write prescriptions for antibiotics and other medications. Analyze and evaluate dental needs to determine changes and trends in patterns of dental disease. Treat exposure of pulp by pulp capping, removal of pulp from pulp chamber, or root canal, using dental instruments. Eliminate irritating margins of fillings and correct occlusions, using dental instruments. Perform oral and periodontal surgery on the jaw or mouth.

Education/Training Required: First professional degree. **Education and Training Programs:** Advanced General Dentistry (Cert., MS, PhD); Dental Public Health and Education (Cert., MS/MPH, PhD/DPH); Dental Public Health Specialty; Dentistry (DDS, DMD); Pediatric Dentistry Residency Program; Pediatric Dentistry/Pedodontics (Cert., MS, PhD). **Knowledge/Courses:** Medicine and Dentistry; Biology; Psychology; Chemistry; Economics and Accounting; Customer and Personal Service.

Career Cluster: 08 Health Science. **Career Pathway:** 08.1 Therapeutic Services.

Skills: Science; Management of Financial Resources; Management of Material Resources; Active Learning; Reading Comprehension; Operation and Control; Judgment and Decision Making; Complex Problem Solving.

Work Environment: Indoors; sitting; using hands; bending or twisting the body; repetitive motions; noise; contaminants; exposed to disease or infections.

Diagnostic Medical Sonographers

- Personality Type: Investigative-Social-Realistic
- Annual Earnings: $64,380
- Earnings Growth Potential: Low (30.3%)
- Growth: 18.3%
- Annual Job Openings: 1,650
- Self-Employed: 0.8%

Considerations for Job Outlook: The aging population's need for safe and cost-effective diagnostic imaging treatment is expected to spur employment growth. Prospects should be good for job-seekers who have multiple professional credentials.

Produce ultrasonic recordings of internal organs for use by physicians. Provide sonograms and oral or written summaries of technical findings to physicians for use in medical diagnosis. Decide which images to include, looking for differences between healthy and pathological areas. Operate ultrasound equipment to produce and record images of the motion, shape, and composition of blood, organs, tissues, and bodily masses such as fluid accumulations. Select appropriate equipment settings and adjust patient positions to obtain the best sites and angles. Observe screens during scans to ensure that images produced are satisfactory for diagnostic purposes, making adjustments to equipment as required. Prepare patients for exams by explaining procedures, transferring them to ultrasound tables, scrubbing skin and applying gel, and positioning them properly. Observe and care for patients throughout examinations to ensure their safety and comfort. Obtain and record accurate patient histories, including prior test results and information from physical examinations. Determine whether scope of exams should be extended, based on findings. Maintain records that include patient information; sonographs and interpretations; files of correspondence; publications and regulations; or quality assurance records such as pathology, biopsy, or post-operative reports. Record and store suitable images, using camera unit connected to the ultrasound equipment.

Education/Training Required: Associate degree. **Education and Training Programs:** Allied Health Diagnostic, Intervention, and Treatment Professions, Other; Diagnostic Medical Sonography/Sonographer and Ultrasound Technician Training. **Knowledge/Courses:** Medicine and Dentistry; Physics; Biology; Customer and Personal Service; Psychology; Clerical Practices.

Career Cluster: 08 Health Science. **Career Pathways:** 08.1 Therapeutic Services; 08.2 Diagnostics Services.

Skills: Science; Equipment Maintenance; Equipment Selection; Repairing; Operation and Control; Troubleshooting; Operation Monitoring; Quality Control Analysis.

Work Environment: Indoors; more often sitting than standing; using hands; bending or twisting the body; repetitive motions; contaminants; exposed to disease or infections.

Electrical Engineers

- Personality Type: Investigative-Realistic
- Annual Earnings: $84,540
- Earnings Growth Potential: Medium (36.1%)
- Growth: 1.7%
- Annual Job Openings: 3,890
- Self-Employed: 1.6%

Considerations for Job Outlook: Electrical engineers are expected to have employment growth of 2 percent from 2008 to 2018. Although strong demand for electrical devices—including electric power generators, wireless phone transmitters, high-density batteries, and navigation systems—should spur job growth, international competition and the use of engineering services performed in other countries will limit employment growth. Electrical engineers working in firms providing engineering expertise and design services to manufacturers should have better job prospects.

Investigative-E

50 Best Jobs for Your Personality © JIST Works

217

Design, develop, test, or supervise the manufacturing and installation of electrical equipment, components, or systems for commercial, industrial, military, or scientific use. Confer with engineers, customers, and others to discuss existing or potential engineering projects and products. Design, implement, maintain, and improve electrical instruments, equipment, facilities, components, products, and systems for commercial, industrial, and domestic purposes. Operate computer-assisted engineering and design software and equipment to perform engineering tasks. Direct and coordinate manufacturing, construction, installation, maintenance, support, documentation, and testing activities to ensure compliance with specifications, codes, and customer requirements. Perform detailed calculations to compute and establish manufacturing, construction, and installation standards and specifications. Inspect completed installations and observe operations to ensure conformance to design and equipment specifications and compliance with operational and safety standards. Plan and implement research methodology and procedures to apply principles of electrical theory to engineering projects. Prepare specifications for purchase of materials and equipment. Supervise and train project team members as necessary. Investigate and test vendors' and competitors' products. Oversee project production efforts to assure projects are completed satisfactorily, on time, and within budget. Prepare and study technical drawings, specifications of electrical systems, and topographical maps to ensure that installation and operations conform to standards and customer requirements.

Education/Training Required: Bachelor's degree. **Education and Training Program:** Electrical and Electronics Engineering. **Knowledge/Courses:** Design; Engineering and Technology; Physics; Mechanical Devices; Mathematics; Computers and Electronics.

Career Cluster: 15 Science, Technology, Engineering, and Mathematics. **Career Pathway:** 15.1 Engineering and Technology.

Skills: Science; Troubleshooting; Operations Anal

ysis; Repairing; Mathematics; Equipment Maintenance; Operation Monitoring; Technology Design.

Work Environment: Indoors; sitting; noise.

Electronics Engineers, Except Computer

- ❋ Personality Type: Investigative-Realistic
- ❋ Annual Earnings: $90,170
- ❋ Earnings Growth Potential: Low (35.8%)
- ❋ Growth: 0.3%
- ❋ Annual Job Openings: 3,340
- ❋ Self-Employed: 1.6%

Considerations for Job Outlook: Electronics engineers, except computer, are expected to experience little to no employment change from 2008 to 2018. Although rising demand for electronic goods—including communications equipment, defense-related equipment, medical electronics, and consumer products—should continue to increase demand for electronics engineers, foreign competition in electronic products development and the use of engineering services performed in other countries will limit employment growth. Growth is expected to be fastest in service-providing industries—particularly in firms that provide engineering and design services.

Research, design, develop, and test electronic components and systems for commercial, industrial, military, or scientific use, utilizing knowledge of electronic theory and materials properties. Design electronic circuits and components for use in fields such as telecommunications, aerospace guidance and propulsion control, acoustics, or instruments and controls. Design electronic components, software, products, or systems for commercial, industrial, medical, military, or scientific applications. Provide technical support and instruction to staff or customers regarding equipment standards, assisting with specific, difficult in-service engineering. Operate computer-assisted engineering and design software and equipment to perform engineering tasks. Analyze system requirements, capacity, cost, and customer needs to determine feasibility of project, and develop system plan. Confer with engineers, customers, vendors, or others to discuss existing and potential engineering projects or products. Review and evaluate work of others inside and outside the organization to ensure effectiveness, technical adequacy, and compatibility in the resolution of complex engineering problems. Determine material and equipment needs, and order supplies. Inspect electronic equipment, instruments, products, and systems to ensure conformance to specifications, safety standards, and applicable codes and regulations. Evaluate operational systems, prototypes, and proposals, and recommend repair or design modifications based on factors such as environment, service, cost, and system capabilities. Prepare documentation containing information such as confidential descriptions and specifications of proprietary hardware and software, product development and introduction schedules, product costs, and information about product performance weaknesses.

Education/Training Required: Bachelor's degree. **Education and Training Program:** Electrical and Electronics Engineering. **Knowledge/Courses:** Design; Engineering and Technology; Physics; Computers and Electronics; Mathematics; Production and Processing.

Career Cluster: 15 Science, Technology, Engineering, and Mathematics. **Career Pathway:** 15.1 Engineering and Technology.

Skills: Programming; Repairing; Technology Design; Equipment Selection; Equipment Maintenance; Troubleshooting; Operation and Control; Quality Control Analysis.

Work Environment: Indoors; sitting; using hands.

Job Specialization: Radio Frequency Identification Device Specialists

Design and implement radio frequency identification device (RFID) systems used to track shipments or goods. Verify compliance of developed applications with architectural standards and established practices. Read current literature, attend meetings or conferences, or talk with colleagues to stay abreast of industry research about new technologies. Provide technical support for RFID technology. Perform systems analysis or programming of RFID technology. Document equipment or process details of RFID technology. Train users in details of system operation. Analyze RFID-related supply chain data. Test tags or labels to ensure readability. Test RFID software to ensure proper functioning. Select appropriate RFID tags, and determine placement locations. Perform site analyses to determine system configurations, processes to be impacted, or on-site obstacles to technology implementation. Perform acceptance testing on newly installed or updated systems. Identify operational requirements for new systems to inform selection of technological solutions. Determine usefulness of new RFID technologies. Develop process flows, work instructions, or standard operating procedures for RFID systems.

Education/Training Required: Bachelor's degree. **Education and Training Program:** Electrical and Electronics Engineering. **Knowledge/Courses:** No data available.

Personality Type: Realistic-Investigative-Conventional. **Career Cluster:** 15 Science, Technology, Engineering, and Mathematics. **Career Pathway:** 15.1 Engineering and Technology.

Skills: No data available.

Work Environment: No data available.

Investigative-E

Engineers, All Other

- ❀ Personality Type: Investigative-Realistic
- ❀ Annual Earnings: $90,270
- ❀ Earnings Growth Potential: High (45.1%)
- ❀ Growth: 6.7%
- ❀ Annual Job Openings: 5,020
- ❀ Self-Employed: 6.4%

Considerations for Job Outlook: Competitive pressures and advancing technology are expected to result in businesses hiring more engineers. Overall, job opportunities are expected to be good. Professional, scientific, and technical-services industries should generate most of the employment growth.

This occupation includes all engineers not listed separately. Because this is a highly diverse occupation, no data is available for some information topics.

Education/Training Required: Bachelor's degree. **Education and Training Program:** Engineering, Other.

Career Clusters: 02 Architecture and Construction; 08 Health Science; 15 Science, Technology, Engineering, and Mathematics. **Career Pathways:** 02.1 Design/Pre-Construction; 08.3 Health Informatics; 15.1 Engineering and Technology.

Job Specialization: Biochemical Engineers

Apply knowledge of biology, chemistry, and engineering to develop usable, tangible products. Solve problems related to materials, systems, and processes that interact with humans, plants, animals, microorganisms, and biological materials. Read current scientific and trade literature to stay abreast of scientific, industrial, or technological advances. Prepare technical reports, data summary documents, or research articles for scientific publication, regulatory submissions, or patent applications. Prepare project plans for equipment or facility improvements, including time lines, budgetary estimates, or capital spending requests. Participate in equipment or process validation activities. Communicate with suppliers regarding the design and specifications of production equipment, instrumentation, or materials. Communicate with regulatory authorities regarding licensing or compliance responsibilities, such as good manufacturing practices. Collaborate in the development or delivery of biochemical manufacturing training materials. Prepare piping and instrumentation diagrams or other schematics for proposed process improvements, using computer-aided design software. Modify and control biological systems to replace, augment, or sustain chemical and mechanical processes. Maintain databases of experiment characteristics and results. Lead studies to examine or recommend changes in process sequences or operation protocols. Direct experimental or developmental activities at contracted laboratories. Develop statistical models or simulations of biochemical production, using statistical or modeling software. Consult with chemists and biologists to develop or evaluate novel technologies.

Education/Training Required: Bachelor's degree. **Education and Training Program:** Biochemical Engineering. **Knowledge/Courses:** Biology; Chemistry; Engineering and Technology; Physics; Production and Processing; Design.

Personality Type: Investigative-Realistic. **Career Cluster:** 15 Science, Technology, Engineering, and Mathematics. **Career Pathway:** 15.1 Engineering and Technology.

Skills: Science; Operations Analysis; Mathematics; Quality Control Analysis; Systems Analysis; Technology Design; Reading Comprehension; Active Learning.

Work Environment: Indoors; sitting; contaminants.

Job Specialization: Energy Engineers

Design, develop, and evaluate energy-related projects and programs to reduce energy costs or improve energy efficiency during the designing, building, or remodeling stages of construc-

tion. **May specialize in electrical systems; heating, ventilation, and air-conditioning (HVAC) systems; green buildings; lighting; air quality; or energy procurement.** Identify energy-savings opportunities, and make recommendations to achieve more energy-efficient operation. Manage the development, design, or construction of energy conservation projects to ensure acceptability of budgets and time lines, conformance to federal and state laws, or adherence to approved specifications. Conduct energy audits to evaluate energy use, costs, or conservation measures. Monitor and analyze energy consumption. Perform energy modeling, measurement, verification, commissioning, or retro-commissioning. Oversee design or construction aspects related to energy such as energy engineering, energy management, and sustainable design. Conduct jobsite observations, field inspections, or sub-metering to collect data for energy conservation analyses. Review architectural, mechanical, or electrical plans and specifications to evaluate energy efficiency or determine economic, service, or engineering feasibility. Inspect or monitor energy systems including heating, ventilation, and air conditioning (HVAC), or daylighting systems to determine energy use or potential energy savings. Evaluate construction design information such as detail and assembly drawings, design calculations, system layouts and sketches, or specifications. Direct the work of contractors or staff in the implementation of energy-management projects. Prepare project reports and other program or technical documentation. Make recommendations regarding energy fuel selection.

Education/Training Required: Bachelor's degree. **Education and Training Program:** Engineering, Other. **Knowledge/Courses:** Engineering and Technology; Building and Construction; Physics; Design; Economics and Accounting; Mechanical Devices.

Personality Type: Investigative-Realistic. **Career Cluster:** 15 Science, Technology, Engineering, and Mathematics. **Career Pathway:** 15.1 Engineering and Technology.

Skills: Science; Operations Analysis; Systems Analysis; Mathematics; Reading Comprehension; Complex Problem Solving; Writing; Systems Evaluation.

Work Environment: Indoors; sitting.

Job Specialization: Manufacturing Engineers

Apply knowledge of materials and engineering theory and methods to design, integrate, and improve manufacturing systems or related processes. May work with commercial or industrial designers to refine product designs to increase producibility and decrease costs. Identify opportunities or implement changes to improve products or reduce costs using knowledge of fabrication processes, tooling and production equipment, assembly methods, quality control standards, or product design, materials and parts. Provide technical expertise or support related to manufacturing. Determine root causes of failures using statistical methods, and recommend changes in designs, tolerances, or processing methods. Incorporate new methods and processes to improve existing operations. Supervise technicians, technologists, analysts, administrative staff, or other engineers. Troubleshoot new and existing product problems involving designs, materials, or processes. Review product designs for manufacturability and completeness. Train production personnel in new or existing methods. Communicate manufacturing capabilities, production schedules, or other information to facilitate production processes. Design, install, or troubleshoot manufacturing equipment. Prepare documentation for new manufacturing processes or engineering procedures. Apply continuous improvement methods such as lean manufacturing to enhance manufacturing quality, reliability, or cost-effectiveness. Investigate or resolve operational problems such as material use variances and bottlenecks. Estimate costs, production times, or staffing requirements for new designs. Evaluate manufactured products according to specifications and quality standards. Purchase equipment, materials, or parts.

Education/Training Required: Bachelor's degree. **Education and Training Program:** Manufacturing Engineering. **Knowledge/Courses:** Engineering and Technology; Design; Physics; Production and Processing; Mechanical Devices; Chemistry.

Personality Type: Realistic-Investigative. **Career Cluster:** 15 Science, Technology, Engineering, and Mathematics. **Career Pathway:** 15.1 Engineering and Technology.

Skills: Technology Design; Equipment Selection; Installation; Troubleshooting; Management of Financial Resources; Equipment Maintenance; Programming; Management of Material Resources.

Work Environment: Indoors; sitting; noise; contaminants; hazardous equipment.

Job Specialization: Mechatronics Engineers

Apply knowledge of mechanical, electrical, and computer engineering theory and methods to the design of automation, intelligent systems, smart devices, or industrial systems control. Publish engineering reports documenting design details and qualification test results. Provide consultation or training on topics such as mechatronics and automated control. Oversee the work of contractors in accordance with project requirements. Create mechanical design documents for parts, assemblies, or finished products. Maintain technical project files. Analyze existing development or manufacturing procedures, and suggest improvements. Implement and test design solutions. Research, select, and apply sensors, communication technologies, or control devices for motion control, position sensing, pressure sensing, or electronic communication. Identify and select materials appropriate for mechatronic system designs. Design, develop, or implement control circuits and algorithms for electromechanical and pneumatic devices or systems. Design engineering systems for the automation of industrial tasks. Design advanced electronic control systems for mechanical systems. Create embedded software design programs. Create mechanical models and tolerance analyses to simulate mechatronic design concepts. Conduct studies to determine the feasibility, costs, or performance benefits of new mechatronic equip-

ment. Upgrade the design of existing devices by adding mechatronic elements. Develop electronic, mechanical, or computerized processes to perform tasks in dangerous situations such as underwater exploration and extraterrestrial mining.

Education/Training Required: Bachelor's degree. **Education and Training Program:** Mechatronics, Robotics, and Automation Engineering. **Knowledge/Courses:** No data available.

Personality Type: Investigative-Realistic-Conventional. **Career Cluster:** 15 Science, Technology, Engineering, and Mathematics. **Career Pathway:** 15.1 Engineering and Technology.

Skills: No data available.

Work Environment: No data available.

Job Specialization: Microsystems Engineers

Apply knowledge of electronic and mechanical engineering theory and methods, as well as specialized manufacturing technologies, to design and develop microelectromechanical systems (MEMS) devices. Manage new product introduction projects to ensure effective deployment of MEMS devices and applications. Plan or schedule engineering research or development projects involving MEMS technology. Develop or implement MEMS processing tools, fixtures, gauges, dies, molds, and trays. Identify, procure, or develop test equipment, instrumentation, and facilities for characterization of MEMS applications. Develop and verify customer documentation, such as performance specifications, training manuals, and operating instructions. Develop and file intellectual property and patent disclosure or application documents related to MEMS devices, products, and systems. Develop and communicate operating characteristics or performance experience to other engineers and designers for training or new product-development purposes. Demonstrate miniaturized systems that contain components such as microsensors, microactuators, or integrated electronic circuits fabricated on silicon or silicon carbide wafers. Create or maintain formal engineering documents, such as schematics, bill of materials, components and materials specifications, and packaging requirements.

Education/Training Required: Bachelor's degree. **Education and Training Program:** Nanotechnology. **Knowledge/Courses:** No data available.

Personality Type: Investigative-Realistic-Conventional. **Career Cluster:** 15 Science, Technology, Engineering, and Mathematics. **Career Pathway:** 15.1 Engineering and Technology.

Skills: No data available.

Work Environment: No data available.

Job Specialization: Nanosystems Engineers

Design, develop, and supervise the production of materials, devices, and systems of unique molecular or macromolecular composition, applying principles of nanoscale physics and electrical, chemical, and biological engineering. Write proposals to secure external funding or to partner with other companies. Supervise technologists or technicians engaged in nanotechnology research or production. Synthesize, process, or characterize nanomaterials, using advanced tools and techniques. Identify new applications for existing nanotechnologies. Prov ide technical guidance and support to customers on topics such as nanosystem start-up, maintenance, or use. Generate high-resolution images or measure force-distance curves, using techniques such as atomic force microscopy. Prepare reports, deliver presentations, or participate in program review activities to communicate engineering results and recommendations. Prepare nanotechnology-related invention disclosures or patent applications. Develop processes or identify equipment needed for pilot or commercial nanoscale scale production. Provide scientific or technical guidance and expertise to scientists, engineers, technologists, technicians, or others using knowledge of chemical, analytical, or biological processes as applied to micro and nanoscale

systems. Engineer production processes for specific nanotechnology applications, such as electroplating, nanofabrication, or epoxy. Design or conduct tests of new nanotechnology products, processes, or systems. Coordinate or supervise the work of suppliers or vendors in the designing, building, or testing of nanosystem devices, such as lenses or probes.

Education/Training Required: Bachelor's degree. **Education and Training Program:** Nanotechnology. **Knowledge/Courses:** No data available.

Personality Type: No data available. **Career Cluster:** 15 Science, Technology, Engineering, and Mathematics. **Career Pathway:** 15.1 Engineering and Technology.

Skills: No data available.

Work Environment: No data available.

Job Specialization: Photonics Engineers

Apply knowledge of engineering and mathematical theory and methods to design technologies specializing in light information and light energy. Design, integrate, or test photonics systems and components. Develop optical or imaging systems such as optical imaging products, optical components, image processes, signal process technologies, and optical systems. Analyze system performance or operational requirements. Write reports, or research proposals. Assist in the transition of photonic prototypes to production. Develop and test photonic prototypes or models. Conduct testing to determine functionality and optimization or to establish limits of photonics systems or components. Design electro-optical sensing or imaging systems. Read current literature, talk with colleagues, continue education, or participate in professional organizations or conferences to keep abreast of developments in the field. Conduct research on new photonics technologies. Determine applications of photonics appropriate to meet product objectives and features. Document design processes including objectives, issues, and out-

Investigative–E

comes. Oversee or provide expertise on manufacturing, assembly, or fabrication processes. Train operators, engineers, or other personnel. Determine commercial, industrial, scientific, or other uses for electro-optical applications or devices. Design gas lasers, solid state lasers, infrared, or other light-emitting or light-sensitive devices. Analyze, fabricate, or test fiber-optic links. Create or maintain photonic design histories. Develop laser-processed designs such as laser-cut medical devices.

Education/Training Required: Bachelor's degree. **Education and Training Program:** Engineering, Other. **Knowledge/Courses:** Physics; Engineering and Technology; Design; Mathematics; Mechanical Devices; Computers and Electronics.

Personality Type: Investigative-Realistic-Conventional. **Career Cluster:** 15 Science, Technology, Engineering, and Mathematics. **Career Pathway:** 15.1 Engineering and Technology.

Skills: Technology Design; Equipment Selection; Mathematics; Science; Programming; Repairing; Quality Control Analysis; Troubleshooting.

Work Environment: Indoors; sitting.

Job Specialization: Robotics Engineers

Research, design, develop, and test robotic applications. Supervise technicians, technologists, or other engineers. Integrate robotics with peripherals such as welders, controllers, or other equipment. Provide technical support for robotic systems. Review or approve designs, calculations, or cost estimates. Make system device lists and event timing charts. Document robotic application development, maintenance, or changes. Write algorithms and programming code for ad hoc robotic applications. Create back-ups of robot programs or parameters. Process and interpret signals or sensor data. Plan mobile robot paths, and teach path plans to robots. Investigate mechanical failures or unexpected maintenance problems. Install, calibrate, operate, or maintain robots. Debug robotics programs. Design

end-of-arm tooling. Conduct research on robotic technology to create new robotic systems or system capabilities. Automate assays on laboratory robotics. Conduct research into the feasibility, design, operation, or performance of robotic mechanisms, components, or systems such as planetary rovers, multiple mobile robots, reconfigurable robots, and man-machine interactions. Analyze and evaluate robotic systems or prototypes. Design automated robotic systems to increase production volume and precision in high-throughput operations such as automated ribonucleic acid (RNA) analysis; or sorting, moving, and stacking production materials. Design software to control robotic systems for applications such as military defense and manufacturing.

Education/Training Required: Bachelor's degree. **Education and Training Program:** Mechatronics, Robotics, and Automation Engineering. **Knowledge/Courses:** Engineering and Technology; Design; Physics; Mechanical Devices; Computers and Electronics; Production and Processing.

Personality Type: Investigative-Realistic-Conventional. **Career Cluster:** 15 Science, Technology, Engineering, and Mathematics. **Career Pathway:** 15.1 Engineering and Technology.

Skills: Equipment Selection; Installation; Programming; Technology Design; Equipment Maintenance; Repairing; Troubleshooting; Mathematics.

Work Environment: Indoors; sitting; using hands; noise; hazardous equipment.

Job Specialization: Solar Energy Systems Engineers

Perform site-specific engineering analysis or evaluation of energy efficiency and solar projects involving residential, commercial, or industrial customers. Design solar domestic hot water and space heating systems for new and existing structures, applying knowledge of structural energy requirements, local climates, solar technology, and thermodynamics. Test or evaluate photovoltaic (PV) cells or modules. Review specifications, and recommend engineering or manufacturing changes to achieve solar design objectives. Perform thermal, stress, or cost-reduction analyses for solar systems. Develop standard operation procedures and quality or safety standards for solar installation work. Design or develop vacuum tube collector systems for solar applications. Provide technical direction or support to installation teams during installation, start-up, testing, system commissioning, or performance monitoring. Perform computer simulation of solar PV generation system performance or energy production to optimize efficiency. Develop design specifications and functional requirements for residential, commercial, or industrial solar energy systems or components. Create plans for solar energy system development, monitoring, and evaluation activities. Create electrical single-line diagrams, panel schedules, or connection diagrams for solar electric systems using computer-aided design (CAD) software. Create checklists for review or inspection of completed solar installation projects. Design or coordinate design of PV or solar thermal systems, including system components, for residential and commercial buildings. Conduct engineering site audits to collect structural, electrical, and related site information for use in the design of residential or commercial solar power systems.

Education/Training Required: Bachelor's degree. **Education and Training Program:** Engineering, Other. **Knowledge/Courses:** No data available.

Personality Type: No data available. **Career Cluster:** 15 Science, Technology, Engineering, and Mathematics. **Career Pathway:** 15.1 Engineering and Technology.

Skills: No data available.

Work Environment: No data available.

Job Specialization: Validation Engineers

Design and plan protocols for equipment and processes to produce products meeting internal and external purity, safety, and quality requirements. Analyze validation test data to determine whether systems or processes have met validation criteria and to identify root causes of production problems. Prepare validation and performance qualification protocols for new or modified manufacturing processes, systems, or equipment for pharmaceutical, electronics, and other types of production. Coordinate the implementation or scheduling of validation testing with affected departments and personnel. Study product characteristics or customer requirements and confer with management to determine validation objectives and standards. Prepare, maintain, or review validation and compliance documentation such as engineering change notices, schematics, and protocols. Resolve testing problems by modifying testing methods or revising test objectives and standards. Create, populate, or maintain databases for tracking validation activities, test results, or validated systems. Prepare detailed reports, and design statements based on results of validation and qualification tests or reviews of procedures and protocols. Identify deviations from established product or process standards, and provide recommendations for resolving deviations. Direct validation activities such as protocol creation or testing. Develop validation master plans, process flow diagrams, test cases, or standard operating procedures. Communicate with regulatory agencies regarding compliance documentation or validation results.

Education/Training Required: Bachelor's degree. **Education and Training Program:** Engineering, Other. **Knowledge/Courses:** Engineering and Technology; Design; Production and Processing; Chemistry; Physics; Mathematics.

Personality Type: Investigative-Realistic-Conventional. **Career Cluster:** 15 Science, Technology, Engineering, and Mathematics. **Career Pathway:** 15.1 Engineering and Technology.

Skills: Science; Operations Analysis; Mathematics; Systems Analysis; Operation Monitoring; Systems Evaluation; Reading Comprehension; Writing.

Work Environment: Indoors; sitting.

Job Specialization: Wind Energy Engineers

Design underground or overhead wind farm collector systems, and prepare and develop site specifications. Write reports to document wind farm collector system test results. Oversee the work activities of wind farm consultants or subcontractors. Recommend process or infrastructure changes to improve wind turbine performance, reduce operational costs, or comply with regulations. Investigate experimental wind turbines or wind turbine technologies for properties such as aerodynamics, production, noise, and load. Test wind turbine equipment to determine effects of stress or fatigue. Test wind turbine components, using mechanical or electronic testing equipment. Provide engineering technical support to designers of prototype wind turbines. Perform root cause analysis on wind turbine tower component failures. Monitor wind farm construction to ensure compliance with regulatory standards or environmental requirements. Direct balance of plant (BOP) construction, generator installation, testing, commissioning, or supervisory control and data acquisition (SCADA) to ensure compliance with specifications. Develop specifications for wind technology components, such as gearboxes, blades, generators, frequency converters, and pad transformers. Develop active control algorithms, electronics, software, electromechanical, or electrohydraulic systems for wind turbines. Create or maintain wind farm layouts, schematics, or other visual documentation for wind farms.

Education/Training Required: Bachelor's degree. **Education and Training Program:** Engineering, Other. **Knowledge/Courses:** No data available.

Personality Type: No data available. **Career Cluster:** 15 Science, Technology, Engineering, and Mathematics. **Career Pathway:** 15.1 Engineering and Technology.

Skills: No data available.

Work Environment: No data available.

Environmental Engineers

- ✵ Personality Type: Investigative-Realistic-Conventional
- ✵ Annual Earnings: $78,740
- ✵ Earnings Growth Potential: Medium (37.8%)
- ✵ Growth: 30.6%
- ✵ Annual Job Openings: 2,790
- ✵ Self-Employed: 0.6%

Considerations for Job Outlook: Environmental engineers are expected to have employment growth of 31 percent from 2008 to 2018, much faster than the average for all occupations. More environmental engineers will be needed to help companies comply with environmental regulations and to develop methods of cleaning up environmental hazards. A shift in emphasis toward preventing problems rather than controlling those which already exist, as well as increasing public health concerns resulting from population growth, also are expected to spur demand for environmental engineers. Because of this employment growth, job opportunities should be favorable.

Design, plan, or perform engineering duties in the prevention, control, and remediation of environmental health hazards, using various engineering disciplines. Work may include waste treatment, site remediation, or pollution control technology. Collaborate with environmental scientists, planners, hazardous waste technicians, engineers, and other specialists and experts in law and business to address environmental problems. Inspect industrial and municipal facilities and programs to evaluate operational effectiveness and ensure compliance with environmental regulations. Prepare, review, and update environmental investigation and recommendation reports. Design and supervise the development of systems processes or equipment for control, management, or remediation of water, air, or soil quality. Provide environmental engineering assistance in network analysis, regulatory analysis, and planning or reviewing database development. Obtain, update, and maintain plans, permits, and standard operating procedures. Provide technical-level support for environmental remediation and litigation projects, including remediation system design and determination of regulatory applicability. Monitor progress of environmental improvement programs. Inform company employees and other interested parties of environmental issues. Advise corporations and government agencies of procedures to follow in cleaning up contaminated sites to protect people and the environment. Develop proposed project objectives and targets, and report to management on progress in attaining them. Request bids from suppliers or consultants. Advise industries and government agencies about environmental policies and standards.

Education/Training Required: Bachelor's degree. **Education and Training Program:** Environmental/Environmental Health Engineering. **Knowledge/Courses:** Engineering and Technology; Physics; Design; Chemistry; Building and Construction; Biology.

Career Clusters: 15 Science, Technology, Engineering, and Mathematics; 16 Transportation, Distribution, and Logistics. **Career Pathways:** 15.1 Engineering and Technology; 16.6 Health, Safety, and Environmental Management.

Skills: Science; Mathematics; Systems Analysis; Operations Analysis; Management of Financial Resources; Programming; Quality Control Analysis; Systems Evaluation.

Work Environment: More often indoors than outdoors; sitting; using hands; noise; contaminants.

Job Specialization: Water/Wastewater Engineers

Design or oversee projects involving provision of fresh water, disposal of wastewater and sewage, or prevention of flood-related damage. Prepare environmental documentation for water resources, regulatory program compliance, data management and analysis, and fieldwork. Perform hydraulic modeling and pipeline design. Write technical reports or publications related to water resources development or water use efficiency. Review and critique proposals, plans, or designs related to water and wastewater treatment systems. Provide technical support on water resource or treatment issues to government agencies. Provide technical direction or supervision to junior engineers, engineering or computer-aided design (CAD) technicians, or other technical personnel. Identify design alternatives for the development of new water resources. Develop plans for new water resources or water efficiency programs. Design or select equipment for use in wastewater processing to ensure compliance with government standards. Conduct water quality studies to identify and characterize water pollutant sources. Perform mathematical modeling of underground or surface water resources, such as floodplains, ocean coastlines, streams, rivers, and wetlands. Perform hydrological analyses, using three-dimensional simulation software, to model the movement of water or forecast the dispersion of chemical pollutants in the water supply. Perform hydraulic analyses of water supply systems or water distribution networks to model flow characteristics, test for pressure losses, or to identify opportunities to mitigate risks and improve operational efficiency. Oversee the construction of decentralized and on-site wastewater treatment systems, including reclaimed water facilities. Gather and analyze water use data to forecast water demand.

Education/Training Required: Bachelor's degree. **Education and Training Program:** Environmental/Environmental Health Engineering. **Knowledge/Courses:** No data available.

Personality Type: No data available. **Career Cluster:** 15 Science, Technology, Engineering, and Mathematics. **Career Pathway:** 15.1 Engineering and Technology.

Skills: No data available.

Work Environment: No data available.

Investigative–E

Environmental Science and Protection Technicians, Including Health

❋ Personality Type: Investigative-Realistic-Conventional
❋ Annual Earnings: $41,380
❋ Earnings Growth Potential: Low (35.7%)
❋ Growth: 28.9%
❋ Annual Job Openings: 2,520
❋ Self-Employed: 1.7%

Considerations for Job Outlook: The continued growth of scientific and medical research and the development and manufacturing of technical products are expected to drive employment growth for these workers. Opportunities are expected to be best for graduates of applied science technology programs who are knowledgeable about equipment used in laboratories or production facilities.

Perform laboratory and field tests to monitor the environment and investigate sources of pollution, including those that affect health. Under direction of environmental scientists or specialists, may collect samples of gases, soil, water, and other materials for testing and take corrective actions as assigned. Collect samples of gases, soils, water, industrial wastewater, and asbestos products to conduct tests on pollutant levels and identify sources of pollution. Record test data, and prepare reports, summaries, and charts that interpret test results. Develop and implement programs for monitoring of environmental pollution and radiation. Discuss test results and analyses with customers. Set up equipment or stations to monitor and collect pollutants from sites such as smokestacks, manufacturing plants, or mechanical equipment. Maintain files, such as hazardous waste databases, chemical usage data, personnel exposure information, and diagrams showing equipment locations. Develop testing procedures or direct activities of workers in laboratory. Prepare samples or photomicrographs for testing and analysis. Calibrate microscopes, and test instru-

ments. Examine and analyze material for presence and concentration of contaminants such as asbestos, using variety of microscopes. Calculate amount of pollutant in samples or compute air pollution or gas flow in industrial processes, using chemical and mathematical formulas. Make recommendations to control or eliminate unsafe conditions at workplaces or public facilities. Weigh, analyze, and measure collected sample particles such as lead, coal dust, or rock to determine concentration of pollutants.

Education/Training Required: Associate degree. **Education and Training Programs:** Environmental Science; Environmental Studies; Physical Science Technologies/Technicians, Other; Science Technologies/Technicians, Other. **Knowledge/Courses:** Biology; Chemistry; Geography; Physics; Computers and Electronics; Building and Construction.

Career Clusters: 01 Agriculture, Food, and Natural Resources; 13 Manufacturing; 16 Transportation, Distribution, and Logistics. **Career Pathways:** 01.5 Natural Resources Systems; 13.2 Manufacturing Production Process Development; 16.6 Health, Safety, and Environmental Management.

Skills: Science; Equipment Maintenance; Troubleshooting; Operation and Control; Operations Analysis; Repairing; Equipment Selection; Mathematics.

Work Environment: More often outdoors than indoors; standing; using hands; noise; very hot or cold; bright or inadequate lighting; contaminants; hazardous conditions; hazardous equipment; minor burns, cuts, bites, or stings.

Environmental Scientists and Specialists, Including Health

- ❋ Personality Type: Investigative-Realistic-Conventional
- ❋ Annual Earnings: $61,700
- ❋ Earnings Growth Potential: Medium (38.7%)
- ❋ Growth: 27.9%
- ❋ Annual Job Openings: 4,840
- ❋ Self-Employed: 2.4%

Considerations for Job Outlook: A growing population and increased awareness of environmental concerns are expected to increase employment of environmental scientists. These workers should have good job prospects, particularly in state and local governments.

Conduct research or perform investigation for the purpose of identifying, abating, or eliminating sources of pollutants or hazards that affect either the environment or the health of the population. Using knowledge of various scientific disciplines, may collect, synthesize, study, report, and take action based on data derived from measurements or observations of air, food, soil, water, and other sources. Collect, synthesize, analyze, manage, and report environmental data such as pollution emission measurements, atmospheric monitoring measurements, meteorological and mineralogical information, and soil or water samples. Analyze data to determine validity, quality, and scientific significance, and to interpret correlations between human activities and environmental effects. Communicate scientific and technical information to the public, organizations, or internal audiences through oral briefings, written documents, workshops, conferences, training sessions, or public hearings. Provide scientific and technical guidance, support, coordination, and oversight to governmental agencies, environmental programs, industry, or the public. Process and review environmental permits, licenses, and related materials. Review and implement environmental technical standards, guidelines,

policies, and formal regulations that meet all appropriate requirements. Prepare charts or graphs from data samples, providing summary information on the environmental relevance of the data. Determine data-collection methods to be employed in research projects and surveys. Investigate and report on accidents affecting the environment. Research sources of pollution to determine their effects on the environment and to develop theories or methods of pollution abatement or control.

Education/Training Required: Master's degree. **Education and Training Programs:** Environmental Science; Environmental Studies. **Knowledge/Courses:** Biology; Geography; Chemistry; Physics; Law and Government; Engineering and Technology.

Career Clusters: 01 Agriculture, Food, and Natural Resources; 16 Transportation, Distribution, and Logistics. **Career Pathways:** 01.5 Natural Resources Systems; 16.6 Health, Safety, and Environmental Management.

Skills: Science; Programming; Reading Comprehension; Mathematics; Operations Analysis; Writing; Systems Analysis; Complex Problem Solving.

Work Environment: More often indoors than outdoors; sitting; noise.

Job Specialization: Climate Change Analysts

Research and analyze policy developments related to climate change. Make climate-related recommendations for actions such as legislation, awareness campaigns, or fundraising approaches. Write reports or academic papers to communicate findings of climate-related studies. Promote initiatives to mitigate climate change with government or environmental groups. Present climate-related information at public-interest, governmental, or other meetings. Present and defend proposals for climate change research projects. Prepare grant applications to obtain funding for programs related to climate change, environmental management, or sustainability. Gather and review climate-related studies from government agencies, research laboratories, and other organizations. Develop, or contribute to the development of, educational or outreach programs on the environment or climate change. Review existing policies or legislation to identify environmental impacts. Provide analytical support for policy briefs related to renewable energy, energy efficiency, or climate change. Prepare study reports, memoranda, briefs, testimonies, or other written materials to inform government or environmental groups on environmental issues such as climate change. Make legislative recommendations related to climate change or environmental management, based on climate change policies, principles, programs, practices, and processes. Research policies, practices, or procedures for climate or environmental management. Propose new or modified policies involving use of traditional and alternative fuels, transportation of goods, and other factors relating to climate and climate change.

Education/Training Required: Master's degree. **Education and Training Programs:** Environmental Science; Environmental Studies. **Knowledge/Courses:** No data available.

Personality Type: No data available. **Career Cluster:** 01 Agriculture, Food, and Natural Resources. **Career Pathway:** 01.5 Natural Resources Systems.

Skills: No data available.

Work Environment: No data available.

Job Specialization: Environmental Restoration Planners

Collaborate with field and biology staff to oversee the implementation of restoration projects and to develop new products. Process and synthesize complex scientific data into practical strategies for restoration, monitoring, or management. Notify regulatory or permitting agencies of deviations from implemented remediation plans. Develop environmental restoration project schedules and budgets.

Develop and communicate recommendations for landowners to maintain or restore environmental conditions. Create diagrams to communicate environmental remediation planning using geographic information systems (GIS), computer-aided design (CAD), or other mapping or diagramming software. Apply for permits required for the implementation of environmental remediation projects. Review existing environmental remediation designs. Supervise and provide technical guidance, training, or assistance to employees working in the field to restore habitats. Provide technical direction on environmental planning to energy engineers, biologists, geologists, or other professionals working to develop restoration plans or strategies. Plan or supervise environmental studies to achieve compliance with environmental regulations in construction, modification, operation, acquisition, or divestiture of facilities such as power plants. Inspect active remediation sites to ensure compliance with environmental or safety policies, standards, or regulations. Plan environmental restoration projects, using biological databases, environmental strategies, and planning software. Identify short- and long-term impacts of environmental remediation activities.

Education/Training Required: Master's degree. **Education and Training Programs:** Environmental Science; Environmental Studies. **Knowledge/Courses:** No data available.

Personality Type: No data available. **Career Cluster:** 01 Agriculture, Food, and Natural Resources. **Career Pathway:** 01.5 Natural Resources Systems.

Skills: No data available.

Work Environment: No data available.

Job Specialization: Industrial Ecologists

Study or investigate industrial production and natural ecosystems to achieve high production, sustainable resources, and environmental safety or protection. May apply principles and activities of natural ecosystems to develop models for industrial systems. Write ecological reports and other technical documents for publication in the research literature or in industrial or government reports. Recommend methods to protect the environment or minimize environmental damage. Investigate accidents affecting the environment to assess ecological impact. Investigate the adaptability of various animal and plant species to changed environmental conditions. Review industrial practices, such as the methods and materials used in construction or production, to identify potential liabilities and environmental hazards. Research sources of pollution to determine environmental impact or to develop methods of pollution abatement or control. Provide industrial managers with technical materials on environmental issues, regulatory guidelines, or compliance actions. Plan or conduct studies of the ecological implications of historic or projected changes in industrial processes or development. Plan or conduct field research on topics such as industrial production, industrial ecology, population ecology, and environmental production or sustainability. Monitor the environmental impact of development activities, pollution, or land degradation. Model alternative energy-investment scenarios to compare economic and environmental costs and benefits. Identify or develop strategies or methods to minimize the environmental impact of industrial production processes. Investigate the impact of changed land management or land use practices on ecosystems.

Education/Training Required: Master's degree. **Education and Training Programs:** Environmental Science; Environmental Studies. **Knowledge/ Courses:** No data available.

Personality Type: No data available. **Career Cluster:** 01 Agriculture, Food, and Natural Resources. **Career Pathway:** 01.5 Natural Resources Systems.

Skills: No data available.

Work Environment: No data available.

Geographers

❋ Personality Type: Investigative-Realistic-Artistic
❋ Annual Earnings: $72,800
❋ Earnings Growth Potential: High (41.7%)
❋ Growth: 26.0%
❋ Annual Job Openings: 100
❋ Self-Employed: 1.5%

Considerations for Job Outlook: Social scientists, other, are expected to have employment growth of 22 percent from 2008 to 2018, much faster than the average for all occupations. Job competition is expected.

Study nature and use of areas of Earth's surface, relating and interpreting interactions of physical and cultural phenomena. Conduct research on physical aspects of a region, including land forms, climates, soils, plants, and animals, and conduct research on the spatial implications of human activities within a given area, including social characteristics, economic activities, and political organization, as well as researching interdependence between regions at scales ranging from local to global. Create and modify maps, graphs, or diagrams, using geographical information software and related equipment and principles of cartography such as coordinate systems, longitude, latitude, elevation, topography, and map scales. Write and present reports of research findings. Develop, operate, and maintain Geographic Information Systems (GIS), including hardware, software, plotters, digitizers, printers, and video cameras. Locate and obtain existing geographic information databases. Analyze geographic distributions of physical and cultural phenomena on local, regional, continental, or global scales. Teach geography. Gather and compile geographic data from sources including censuses, field observations, satellite imagery, aerial photographs, and existing maps. Conduct fieldwork at outdoor sites. Study the economic, political, and cultural characteristics of a specific region's population. Provide consulting services in fields including

Investigative-G

resource development and management, business location and market area analysis, environmental hazards, regional cultural history, and urban social planning. Collect data on physical characteristics of specified areas, such as geological formations, climates, and vegetation, using surveying or meteorological equipment. Provide GIS support to the private and public sectors.

Education/Training Required: Master's degree. **Education and Training Program:** Geography. **Knowledge/Courses:** Geography; Sociology and Anthropology; History and Archeology; Philosophy and Theology; Foreign Language; Biology.

Career Cluster: 15 Science, Technology, Engineering, and Mathematics. **Career Pathway:** 15.2 Science and Mathematics.

Skills: Science; Writing; Systems Analysis; Systems Evaluation; Operations Analysis; Reading Comprehension; Active Learning; Instructing.

Work Environment: Indoors; sitting.

Geoscientists, Except Hydrologists and Geographers

- ❋ Personality Type: Investigative-Realistic
- ❋ Annual Earnings: $82,500
- ❋ Earnings Growth Potential: High (46.9%)
- ❋ Growth: 17.5%
- ❋ Annual Job Openings: 1,540
- ❋ Self-Employed: 2.4%

Considerations for Job Outlook: The need for energy services, environmental protection services, and responsible land and water management is expected to spur employment growth for these workers. Jobseekers who have a master's degree in geoscience should have excellent opportunities.

Study the composition, structure, and other physical aspects of Earth. May use knowledge of geology, physics, and mathematics in exploration for oil, gas, minerals, or underground water or in waste disposal, land reclamation, or other environmental problems. May study Earth's internal composition, atmospheres, and oceans and its magnetic, electrical, and gravitational forces. Includes mineralogists, crystallographers, paleontologists, stratigraphers, geodesists, and seismologists. Analyze and interpret geological, geochemical, and geophysical information from sources such as survey data, well logs, bore holes, and aerial photos. Locate and estimate probable natural gas, oil, and mineral ore deposits and underground water resources, using aerial photographs, charts, or research and survey results. Plan and conduct geological, geochemical, and geophysical field studies and surveys, sample collection, or drilling and testing programs used to collect data for research or application. Analyze and interpret geological data, using computer software. Search for and review research articles or environmental, historical, and technical reports. Assess ground and surface water movement to provide advice regarding issues such as waste management, route and site selection, and the restoration of contaminated sites. Prepare geological maps, cross-sectional diagrams, charts, and reports concerning mineral extraction, land use, and resource management, using results of field work and laboratory research. Investigate the composition, structure, and history of the Earth's crust through the collection, examination, measurement, and classification of soils, minerals, rocks, or fossil remains. Conduct geological and geophysical studies to provide information for use in regional development, site selection, and development of public works projects.

Education/Training Required: Master's degree. **Education and Training Programs:** Geochemistry; Geochemistry and Petrology; Geological and Earth Sciences/Geosciences, Other; Geology/Earth Science, General; Geophysics and Seismology; Oceanography, Chemical and Physical; Paleontology. **Knowledge/Courses:** Geography; Engineering and Technology; Physics; Chemistry; Mathematics; Design.

Career Cluster: 15 Science, Technology, Engineering, and Mathematics. **Career Pathway:** 15.2 Science and Mathematics.

Skills: Science; Reading Comprehension; Operations

Analysis; Mathematics; Writing; Systems Evaluation; Systems Analysis; Active Listening.

Work Environment: Indoors; sitting.

Industrial Engineers

- ❋ Personality Type: Investigative-Conventional-Enterprising
- ❋ Annual Earnings: $76,100
- ❋ Earnings Growth Potential: Low (34.7%)
- ❋ Growth: 14.2%
- ❋ Annual Job Openings: 8,540
- ❋ Self-Employed: 0.7%

Considerations for Job Outlook: Industrial engineers are expected to have employment growth of 14 percent from 2008 to 2018, faster than the average for all occupations. As firms look for new ways to reduce costs and raise productivity, they increasingly will turn to industrial engineers to develop more efficient processes and reduce costs, delays, and waste. This focus should lead to job growth for these engineers, even in some manufacturing industries with declining employment overall. Because their work is similar to that done in management occupations, many industrial engineers leave the occupation to become managers. Numerous openings will be created by the need to replace industrial engineers who transfer to other occupations or leave the labor force.

Design, develop, test, and evaluate integrated systems for managing industrial production processes, including human work factors, quality control, inventory control, logistics and material flow, cost analysis, and production coordination. Analyze statistical data and product specifications to determine standards and establish quality and reliability objectives of finished product. Develop manufacturing methods, labor-utilization standards, and cost-analysis systems to promote efficient staff and facility utilization. Recommend methods for improving utilization of personnel, material, and utilities. Plan and establish sequence of operations to fabricate and assemble parts or products and to promote efficient

utilization. Apply statistical methods and perform mathematical calculations to determine manufacturing processes, staff requirements, and production standards. Coordinate quality control objectives and activities to resolve production problems, maximize product reliability, and minimize cost. Confer with vendors, staff, and management personnel regarding purchases, procedures, product specifications, manufacturing capabilities, and project status. Draft and design layout of equipment, materials, and workspace to illustrate maximum efficiency, using drafting tools and computer. Review production schedules, engineering specifications, orders, and related information to obtain knowledge of manufacturing methods, procedures, and activities. Communicate with management and user personnel to develop production and design standards. Estimate production cost and effect of product design changes for management review, action, and control.

Education/Training Required: Bachelor's degree. **Education and Training Program:** Industrial Engineering. **Knowledge/Courses:** Engineering and Technology; Design; Production and Processing; Mechanical Devices; Physics; Mathematics.

Career Cluster: 15 Science, Technology, Engineering, and Mathematics. **Career Pathway:** 15.1 Engineering and Technology.

Skills: Management of Material Resources; Management of Financial Resources; Mathematics; Systems Evaluation; Systems Analysis; Reading Comprehension; Complex Problem Solving; Technology Design.

Work Environment: Indoors; sitting; noise; contaminants; hazardous equipment.

Job Specialization: Human Factors Engineers and Ergonomists

Design objects, facilities, and environments to optimize human well-being and overall system performance, applying theory, principles, and data regarding the relationship between humans

and respective technology. Investigate and analyze characteristics of human behavior and performance as it relates to the use of technology. Write, review, or comment on documents such as proposals, test plans, and procedures. Train users in task techniques or ergonomic principles. Review health, safety, accident, or worker compensation records to evaluate safety program effectiveness or to identify jobs with high incidents of injury. Provide human-factors technical expertise on topics such as advanced user-interface technology development and the role of human users in automated or autonomous sub-systems in advanced vehicle systems. Investigate theoretical or conceptual issues, such as the human design considerations of lunar landers or habitats. Estimate time and resource requirements for ergonomic or human-factors research or development projects. Conduct interviews or surveys of users or customers to collect information on topics such as requirements, needs, fatigue, ergonomics, and interface. Recommend workplace changes to improve health and safety, using knowledge of potentially harmful factors, such as heavy loads and repetitive motions. Provide technical support to clients through activities such as rearranging workplace fixtures to reduce physical hazards or discomfort and modifying task sequences to reduce cycle time. Prepare reports or presentations summarizing results or conclusions of human-factors engineering or ergonomics activities, such as testing, investigation, and validation.

Education/Training Required: Bachelor's degree. **Education and Training Program:** Industrial Engineering. **Knowledge/Courses:** No data available.

Personality Type: No data available. **Career Cluster:** 15 Science, Technology, Engineering, and Mathematics. **Career Pathway:** 15.1 Engineering and Technology.

Skills: No data available.

Work Environment: No data available.

Industrial-Organizational Psychologists

- ❋ Personality Type: Investigative-Enterprising-Artistic
- ❋ Annual Earnings: $87,330
- ❋ Earnings Growth Potential: High (43.6%)
- ❋ Growth: 26.1%
- ❋ Annual Job Openings: 130
- ❋ Self-Employed: 33.6%

Considerations for Job Outlook: Employment growth is expected due to increased emphasis on mental health in a variety of specializations, including school counseling, depression, and substance abuse. Job-seekers with a doctoral degree should have the best opportunities.

Apply principles of psychology to personnel, administration, management, sales, and marketing problems. Activities may include policy planning; employee screening, training, and development; and organizational development and analysis. May work with management to reorganize the work setting to improve worker productivity. Develop and implement employee selection and placement programs. Analyze job requirements and content to establish criteria for classification, selection, training, and other related personnel functions. Develop interview techniques, rating scales, and psychological tests used to assess skills, abilities, and interests for the purpose of employee selection, placement, and promotion. Advise management concerning personnel, managerial, and marketing policies and practices and their potential effects on organizational effectiveness and efficiency. Analyze data, using statistical methods and applications, to evaluate the outcomes and effectiveness of workplace programs. Assess employee performance. Observe and interview workers to obtain information about the physical, mental, and educational requirements of jobs as well as information about aspects such as job satisfaction. Write reports on research findings and implications to contribute to general knowledge and to suggest potential changes in organizational functioning. Facilitate organizational development and change. Identify training and development needs. Formulate and implement training programs, applying principles of learning and individual differences. Study organizational effectiveness, productivity, and efficiency, including the nature of workplace supervision and leadership.

Education/Training Required: Master's degree. **Education and Training Program:** Psychology, General. **Knowledge/Courses:** Personnel and Human Resources; Psychology; Sociology and Anthropology; Education and Training; Therapy and Counseling; Mathematics.

Career Cluster: 08 Health Science. **Career Pathway:** 08.1 Therapeutic Services.

Skills: Programming; Science; Mathematics; Systems Evaluation; Management of Personnel Resources; Learning Strategies; Operations Analysis; Systems Analysis.

Work Environment: Indoors; sitting.

Logisticians

Look for the job description among the Conventional jobs.

Management Analysts

- ❀ Personality Type: Investigative-Enterprising-Conventional
- ❀ Annual Earnings: $78,160
- ❀ Earnings Growth Potential: High (43.8%)
- ❀ Growth: 23.9%
- ❀ Annual Job Openings: 30,650
- ❀ Self-Employed: 25.8%

Considerations for Job Outlook: Organizations are expected to rely increasingly on outside expertise in an effort to maintain competitiveness and improve performance. Keen competition is expected.

Opportunities are expected to be best for those who have a graduate degree, specialized expertise, and ability in salesmanship and public relations.

Conduct organizational studies and evaluations, design systems and procedures, conduct work simplifications and measurement studies, and prepare operations and procedures manuals to assist management in operating more efficiently and effectively. Includes program analysts and management consultants. Gather and organize information on problems or procedures. Analyze data gathered and develop solutions or alternative methods of proceeding. Confer with personnel concerned to ensure successful functioning of newly implemented systems or procedures. Develop and implement records-management program for filing, protection, and retrieval of records, and assure compliance with program. Review forms and reports and confer with management and users about format, distribution, and purpose and to identify problems and improvements. Document findings of study, and prepare recommendations for implementation of new systems, procedures, or organizational changes. Interview personnel and conduct on-site observation to ascertain unit functions; work performed; and methods, equipment, and personnel used. Prepare manuals and train workers in use of new forms, reports, procedures, or equipment according to organizational policy. Design, evaluate, recommend, and approve changes of forms and reports. Plan study of work problems and procedures, such as organizational change, communications, information flow, integrated production methods, inventory control, or cost analysis. Recommend purchase of storage equipment, and design area layout to locate equipment in space available.

Education/Training Required: Work experience plus degree. **Education and Training Programs:** Business Administration and Management, General; Business/Commerce, General. **Knowledge/Courses:** Personnel and Human Resources; Clerical Practices; Sales and Marketing; Economics and Accounting; Customer and Personal Service; Administration and Management.

Investigative-M

Career Cluster: 04 Business, Management, and Administration. **Career Pathway:** 04.1 Management.

Skills: Operations Analysis; Systems Evaluation; Systems Analysis; Science; Judgment and Decision Making; Management of Material Resources; Writing; Management of Personnel Resources.

Work Environment: Indoors; sitting.

Market Research Analysts and Marketing Specialists

- ❋ Personality Type: Investigative-Enterprising-Conventional
- ❋ Annual Earnings: $60,570
- ❋ Earnings Growth Potential: High (44.9%)
- ❋ Growth: 28.1%
- ❋ Annual Job Openings: 13,730
- ❋ Self-Employed: 6.8%

Considerations for Job Outlook: Demand for market research is expected as businesses strive to increase sales and as governments rely on survey research to form public policy. Opportunities should be best for job-seekers who have a doctoral degree and strong quantitative skills.

Research market conditions in local, regional, or national areas to determine potential sales of a product or service. May gather information on competitors, prices, sales, and methods of marketing and distribution. May use survey results to create a marketing campaign based on regional preferences and buying habits. Collect and analyze data on customer demographics, preferences, needs, and buying habits to identify potential markets and factors affecting product demand. Prepare reports of findings, illustrating data graphically and translating complex findings into written text. Measure and assess customer and employee satisfaction. Forecast and track marketing and sales trends, analyzing collected data. Seek and provide information to help companies determine their position in the marketplace. Measure the effectiveness of marketing, ad-

vertising, and communications programs and strategies. Conduct research on consumer opinions and marketing strategies, collaborating with marketing professionals, statisticians, pollsters, and other professionals. Attend staff conferences to provide management with information and proposals concerning the promotion, distribution, design, and pricing of company products or services. Gather data on competitors, and analyze their prices, sales, and method of marketing and distribution. Monitor industry statistics, and follow trends in trade literature. Devise and evaluate methods and procedures for collecting data, such as surveys, opinion polls, or questionnaires, or arrange to obtain existing data. Develop and implement procedures for identifying advertising needs. Direct trained survey interviewers.

Education/Training Required: Bachelor's degree. **Education and Training Programs:** Apparel and Textile Marketing Management; Consumer Merchandising/Retailing Management; International Marketing; Marketing Research; Marketing, Other; Marketing/Marketing Management, General. **Knowledge/Courses:** Sales and Marketing; Clerical Practices; Sociology and Anthropology; Economics and Accounting; Personnel and Human Resources; Computers and Electronics.

Career Cluster: 04 Business, Management, and Administration; 14 Marketing Sales and Service; 15 Science, Technology, Engineering, and Mathematics. **Career Pathways:** 04.1 Management; 14.5 Marketing Information Management and Research; 15.2 Science and Mathematics.

Skills: Programming; Systems Analysis; Operations Analysis; Systems Evaluation; Reading Comprehension; Management of Financial Resources; Mathematics; Science.

Work Environment: Indoors; sitting.

Mathematicians

- ❋ Personality Type: Investigative-Conventional-Artistic
- ❋ Annual Earnings: $99,380
- ❋ Earnings Growth Potential: High (46.8%)
- ❋ Growth: 22.4%
- ❋ Annual Job Openings: 150
- ❋ Self-Employed: 0.0%

Considerations for Job Outlook: Technological advances are expected to expand applications of mathematics, leading to employment growth of mathematicians. Competition is expected to be keen. Jobseekers with a strong background in math and a related discipline should have the best prospects.

Conduct research in fundamental mathematics or in application of mathematical techniques to science, management, and other fields. Solve or direct solutions to problems in various fields by mathematical methods. Apply mathematical theories and techniques to the solution of practical problems in business, engineering, the sciences, or other fields. Develop computational methods for solving problems that occur in areas of science and engineering or that come from applications in business or industry. Maintain knowledge in the field by reading professional journals, talking with other mathematicians, and attending professional conferences. Perform computations, and apply methods of numerical analysis to data. Develop mathematical or statistical models of phenomena to be used for analysis or for computational simulation. Assemble sets of assumptions, and explore the consequences of each set. Address the relationships of quantities, magnitudes, and forms through the use of numbers and symbols. Develop new principles and new relationships between existing mathematical principles to advance mathematical science. Design, analyze, and decipher encryption systems designed to transmit military, political, financial, or law-enforcement-related information in code. Conduct research to extend mathematical knowledge in traditional areas, such as algebra, geometry, probability, and logic.

Education/Training Required: Doctoral degree. **Education and Training Programs:** Algebra and Number Theory; Analysis and Functional Analysis; Applied Mathematics, General; Applied Mathematics, Other; Computational Mathematics; Geometry/Geometric Analysis; Logic; Mathematical Statistics and Probability; Mathematics and Statistics, Other; Mathematics, General; Mathematics, Other; Topology and Foundations. **Knowledge/Courses:** Mathematics; Physics; Computers and Electronics; Engineering and Technology; English Language.

Career Cluster: 15 Science, Technology, Engineering, and Mathematics. **Career Pathway:** 15.2 Science and Mathematics.

Skills: Mathematics; Science; Active Learning; Programming; Reading Comprehension; Complex Problem Solving; Critical Thinking; Systems Analysis.

Work Environment: Indoors; sitting.

Mechanical Engineers

- ❋ Personality Type: Investigative-Realistic-Conventional
- ❋ Annual Earnings: $78,160
- ❋ Earnings Growth Potential: Low (35.3%)
- ❋ Growth: 6.0%
- ❋ Annual Job Openings: 7,570
- ❋ Self-Employed: 2.3%

Considerations for Job Outlook: Materials engineers are expected to have employment growth of 9 percent from 2008 to 2018, about as fast as the average for all occupations. Growth should result from increased use of composite and other nontraditional materials developed through biotechnology and nanotechnology research. As manufacturing firms contract for their materials engineering needs, most employment growth is expected in professional, scientific, and technical services industries.

Perform engineering duties in planning and designing tools, engines, machines, and other mechanically functioning equipment. Oversee in-

Investigative–M

stallation, operation, maintenance, and repair of such equipment as centralized heat, gas, water, and steam systems. Read and interpret blueprints, technical drawings, schematics, and computer-generated reports. Confer with engineers and other personnel to implement operating procedures, resolve system malfunctions, and provide technical information. Research and analyze customer design proposals, specifications, manuals, and other data to evaluate the feasibility, cost, and maintenance requirements of designs or applications. Specify system components or direct modification of products to ensure conformance with engineering design and performance specifications. Research, design, evaluate, install, operate, and maintain mechanical products, equipment, systems, and processes to meet requirements, applying knowledge of engineering principles. Investigate equipment failures and difficulties to diagnose faulty operation and to make recommendations to maintenance crew. Assist drafters in developing the structural design of products, using drafting tools, computer-assisted design (CAD), or drafting equipment and software. Provide feedback to design engineers on customer problems and needs. Oversee installation, operation, maintenance, and repair to ensure that machines and equipment are installed and functioning according to specifications. Conduct research that tests and analyzes the feasibility, design, operation, and performance of equipment, components, and systems. Recommend design modifications to eliminate machine or system malfunctions.

Education/Training Required: Bachelor's degree. **Education and Training Program:** Mechanical Engineering. **Knowledge/Courses:** Design; Engineering and Technology; Physics; Mechanical Devices; Production and Processing; Mathematics.

Career Cluster: 15 Science, Technology, Engineering, and Mathematics. **Career Pathway:** 15.1 Engineering and Technology.

Skills: Technology Design; Science; Mathematics; Installation; Operations Analysis; Programming; Quality Control Analysis; Troubleshooting.

Work Environment: Indoors; sitting; noise.

Job Specialization: Automotive Engineers

Develop new or improved designs for vehicle structural members, engines, transmissions, and other vehicle systems, using computer-assisted design technology. Direct building, modification, and testing of vehicle and components. Read current literature, attend meetings or conferences, and talk with colleagues to stay abreast of new technology and competitive products. Establish production or quality-control standards. Prepare and present technical or project-status reports. Develop or implement operating methods and procedures. Write, review, or maintain engineering documentation. Conduct research studies to develop new concepts in the field of automotive engineering. Coordinate production activities with other functional units such as procurement, maintenance, and quality control. Provide technical direction to other engineers or engineering support personnel. Perform failure, variation, or root cause analyses. Develop or integrate control feature requirements. Develop engineering specifications and cost estimates for automotive design concepts. Develop calibration methodologies, test methodologies, or tools. Conduct automotive design reviews. Calibrate vehicle systems, including control algorithms and other software systems. Build models for algorithm and control feature verification testing. Alter or modify designs to obtain specified functional and operational performance. Design or analyze automobile systems in areas such as aerodynamics, alternate fuels, ergonomics, hybrid power, brakes, transmissions, steering, calibration, safety, and diagnostics. Conduct or direct system-level automotive testing.

Education/Training Required: Bachelor's degreez. **Education and Training Program:** Mechanical Engineering. **Knowledge/Courses:** No data available.

Personality Type: No data available. **Career Cluster:** 15 Science, Technology, Engineering, and Mathematics. **Career Pathway:** 15.1 Engineering and Technology.

Skills: No data available.

Work Environment: No data available.

Job Specialization: Fuel Cell Engineers

Design, evaluate, modify, and construct fuel cell components and systems for transportation, stationary, or portable applications. Write technical reports or proposals related to engineering projects. Read current literature, attend meetings or conferences, and talk with colleagues to stay abreast of new technology and competitive products. Prepare test stations, instrumentation, or data acquisition systems for use in specific tests. Plan or implement cost-reduction or product-improvement projects in collaboration with other engineers, suppliers, support personnel, or customers. Coordinate engineering or test schedules with departments outside engineering, such as manufacturing. Validate design of fuel cells, fuel cell components, or fuel cell systems. Authorize the release of parts or subsystems for production. Simulate or model fuel cell, motor, or other system information using simulation software programs. Recommend or implement changes to fuel cell system design. Provide technical consultation or direction related to the development or production of fuel cell systems. Plan or conduct experiments to validate new materials, optimize startup protocols, reduce conditioning time, or examine contaminant tolerance. Manage hybrid system architecture, including sizing of components such as fuel cells, energy storage units, and electric drives, for fuel cell battery hybrids. Integrate electric drive subsystems with other vehicle systems to optimize performance or mitigate faults. Identify and define the vehicle and system-integration challenges for fuel cell vehicles.

Education/Training Required: Bachelor's degree. **Education and Training Program:** Mechanical Engineering. **Knowledge/Courses:** No data available.

Personality Type: No data available. **Career Cluster:** 15 Science, Technology, Engineering, and Mathematics. **Career Pathway:** 15.1 Engineering and Technology.

Skills: No data available.

Work Environment: No data available.

Medical and Clinical Laboratory Technologists

* Personality Type: Investigative-Realistic-Conventional
* Annual Earnings: $56,130
* Earnings Growth Potential: Low (30.9%)
* Growth: 11.9%
* Annual Job Openings: 5,330
* Self-Employed: 0.2%

Considerations for Job Outlook: Employment of these workers is expected to rise as the volume of laboratory tests continues to increase with population growth and the development of new tests. Excellent opportunities are expected.

Perform complex medical laboratory tests for diagnosis, treatment, and prevention of disease. May train or supervise staff. Conduct chemical analysis of bodily fluids, including blood, urine, and spinal fluid, to determine presence of normal and abnormal components. Analyze laboratory findings to check the accuracy of the results. Enter data from analysis of medical tests and clinical results into computer for storage. Operate, calibrate, and maintain equipment used in quantitative and qualitative analysis, such as spectrophotometers, calorimeters, flame photometers, and computer-controlled analyzers. Establish and monitor quality assurance programs and activities to ensure the accuracy of laboratory results. Set up, clean, and maintain laboratory equipment. Provide technical information about test results to physicians, family members, and researchers. Supervise, train, and direct lab assistants, medical and clinical laboratory technicians and technologists, and other medical laboratory workers engaged in laboratory testing. Collect and study blood samples to determine the number of cells, their morphology, or their blood group, blood type, and compatibility for transfusion purposes, using microscopic techniques. Analyze samples of biological material for chemical content or reaction. Cultivate, isolate, and assist in identifying microbial organisms, and perform various tests on these microorganisms.

Obtain, cut, stain, and mount biological material on slides for microscopic study and diagnosis, following standard laboratory procedures.

Education/Training Required: Bachelor's degree. **Education and Training Programs:** Clinical Laboratory Science/Medical Technology/Technologist; Clinical/Medical Laboratory Science and Allied Professions, Other; Cytogenetics/Genetics/Clinical Genetics Technology/Technologist; Cytotechnology/Cytotechnologist; Histologic Technology/Histotechnologist; Renal/Dialysis Technologist/Technician. **Knowledge/Courses:** Biology; Chemistry; Medicine and Dentistry; Mechanical Devices; Clerical Practices; Mathematics.

Career Cluster: 08 Health Science. **Career Pathway:** 08.2 Diagnostics Services.

Skills: Science; Equipment Selection; Equipment Maintenance; Quality Control Analysis; Programming; Troubleshooting; Operation Monitoring; Operation and Control.

Work Environment: Indoors; standing; using hands; repetitive motions; noise; contaminants; exposed to disease or infections; hazardous conditions.

Job Specialization: Cytogenetic Technologists

Analyze chromosomes found in biological specimens such as amniotic fluids, bone marrow, and blood to aid in the study, diagnosis, or treatment of genetic diseases. Develop and implement training programs for trainees, medical students, resident physicians or post-doctoral fellows. Stain slides to make chromosomes visible for microscopy. Summarize test results and report to appropriate authorities. Select or prepare specimens and media for cell cultures using aseptic techniques, knowledge of medium components, or cell nutritional requirements. Select banding methods to permit identification of chromosome pairs. Identify appropriate methods of specimen collection, preservation, or transport. Prepare slides of cell cultures following standard procedures. Select appropriate methods of

preparation and storage of media to maintain potential of hydrogen (pH), sterility, or ability to support growth. Harvest cell cultures using substances such as mitotic arrestants, cell releasing agents, and cell fixatives. Create chromosome images using computer imaging systems. Determine optimal time sequences and methods for manual or robotic cell harvests. Examine chromosomes found in biological specimens to detect abnormalities. Recognize and report abnormalities in the color, size, shape, composition, or pattern of cells. Communicate test results or technical information to patients, physicians, family members, or researchers. Prepare biological specimens such as amniotic fluids, bone marrow, tumors, chorionic villi, and blood for chromosome examinations.

Education/Training Required: Bachelor's degree. **Education and Training Programs:** Clinical Laboratory Science/Medical Technology/Technologist; Cytogenetics/Genetics/Clinical Genetics Technology/Technologist. **Knowledge/Courses:** Biology; Chemistry; Medicine and Dentistry; Education and Training.

Personality Type: Investigative-Realistic-Conventional. **Career Cluster:** 08 Health Science. **Career Pathway:** 08.2 Diagnostics Services.

Skills: Science; Reading Comprehension; Writing; Active Learning; Speaking; Mathematics; Instructing; Active Listening.

Work Environment: Indoors; sitting; using hands; repetitive motions; contaminants; exposed to disease or infections; hazardous conditions.

Job Specialization: Cytotechnologists

Stain, mount, and study cells to detect evidence of cancer, hormonal abnormalities, and other pathological conditions following established standards and practices. Examine cell samples to detect abnormalities in the color, shape, or size of cellular components and patterns. Examine specimens using microscopes to evaluate specimen quality.

Prepare and analyze samples, such as Papanicolaou (PAP) smear body fluids and fine needle aspirations (FNAs), to detect abnormal conditions. Provide patient clinical data or microscopic findings to assist pathologists in the preparation of pathology reports. Assist pathologists or other physicians to collect cell samples such as by FNA biopsies. Examine specimens to detect abnormal hormone conditions. Document specimens by verifying patients' and specimens' information. Maintain effective laboratory operations by adhering to standards of specimen collection, preparation, or laboratory safety. Perform karyotyping or organizing of chromosomes according to standardized ideograms. Prepare cell samples by applying special staining techniques, such as chromosomal staining, to differentiate cells or cell components. Submit slides with abnormal cell structures to pathologists for further examination. Adjust, maintain, or repair laboratory equipment such as microscopes. Assign tasks or coordinate task assignments to ensure adequate performance of laboratory activities. Attend continuing education programs that address laboratory issues.

Education/Training Required: Bachelor's degree. **Education and Training Programs:** Clinical Laboratory Science/Medical Technology/Technologist; Cytotechnology/Cytotechnologist. **Knowledge/Courses:** Biology; Medicine and Dentistry; Chemistry; Clerical Practices.

Personality Type: Investigative-Realistic. **Career Cluster:** 08 Health Science. **Career Pathway:** 08.2 Diagnostics Services.

Skills: Science; Reading Comprehension; Mathematics; Writing; Operation Monitoring; Judgment and Decision Making; Learning Strategies; Instructing.

Work Environment: Indoors; sitting; using hands; repetitive motions; contaminants; exposed to disease or infections; hazardous conditions.

Job Specialization: Histotechnologists and Histologic Technicians

Prepare histologic slides from tissue sections for microscopic examination and diagnosis by pathologists. May assist in research studies. Cut sections of body tissues for microscopic examination using microtomes. Embed tissue specimens into paraffin wax blocks, or infiltrate tissue specimens with wax. Freeze tissue specimens. Mount tissue specimens on glass slides. Stain tissue specimens with dyes or other chemicals to make cell details visible under microscopes. Examine slides under microscopes to ensure tissue preparation meets laboratory requirements. Identify tissue structures or cell components to be used in the diagnosis, prevention, or treatment of diseases. Operate computerized laboratory equipment to dehydrate, decalcify, or microincinerate tissue samples. Perform electron microscopy or mass spectrometry to analyze specimens. Perform procedures associated with histochemistry to prepare specimens for immunofluorescence or microscopy. Maintain laboratory equipment such as microscopes, mass spectrometers, microtomes, immunostainers, tissue processors, embedding centers, and water baths. Prepare or use prepared tissue specimens for teaching, research, or diagnostic purposes. Supervise histology laboratory activities. Teach students or other staff.

Education/Training Required: Associate degree. **Education and Training Programs:** Clinical Laboratory Science/Medical Technology/Technologist; Clinical/Medical Laboratory Science and Allied Professions, Other; Cytogenetics/Genetics/Clinical Genetics Technology/Technologist; Cytotechnology/Cytotechnologist; Histologic Technology/Histotechnologist; Renal/Dialysis Technologist/Technician. **Knowledge/Courses:** Biology; Chemistry; Medicine and Dentistry; Production and Processing; Mechanical Devices; Education and Training.

Investigative—M

Personality Type: Realistic-Investigative-Conventional. **Career Cluster:** 08 Health Science. **Career Pathway:** 08.2 Diagnostics Services.

Skills: Science; Equipment Maintenance; Equipment Selection; Repairing; Operation and Control; Troubleshooting; Mathematics; Quality Control Analysis.

Work Environment: Indoors; sitting; using hands; repetitive motions; contaminants; exposed to disease or infections; hazardous conditions.

Medical Scientists, Except Epidemiologists

- Personality Type: Investigative-Realistic-Artistic
- Annual Earnings: $76,700
- Earnings Growth Potential: High (45.8%)
- Growth: 40.4%
- Annual Job Openings: 6,620
- Self-Employed: 2.5%

Considerations for Job Outlook: New discoveries in biological and medical science are expected to create strong employment growth for these workers. Medical scientists with both doctoral and medical degrees should have the best opportunities.

Conduct research dealing with the understanding of human diseases and the improvement of human health. Engage in clinical investigation or other research, production, technical writing, or related activities. Conduct research to develop methodologies, instrumentation, and procedures for medical application, analyzing data and presenting findings. Plan and direct studies to investigate human or animal disease, preventive methods, and treatments for disease. Follow strict safety procedures when handling toxic materials to avoid contamination. Evaluate effects of drugs, gases, pesticides, parasites, and microorganisms at various levels. Teach principles of medicine and medical and laboratory procedures to physicians, residents, students, and technicians. Prepare and analyze organ, tissue, and cell samples to identify toxicity, bacteria, or microorganisms or to study cell structure. Standardize drug dosages, methods of immunization, and procedures for manufacture of drugs and medicinal compounds. Investigate cause, progress, life cycle, or mode of transmission of diseases or parasites. Confer with the health department, industry personnel, physicians, and others to develop health safety standards and public health-improvement programs. Study animal and human health and physiological processes. Consult with and advise physicians, educators, researchers, and others regarding medical applications of physics, biology, and chemistry. Use equipment such as atomic absorption spectrometers, electron microscopes, flow cytometers, and chromatography systems.

Education/Training Required: Doctoral degree. **Education and Training Programs:** Anatomy; Biochemistry; Biomedical Sciences, General; Biophysics; Biostatistics; Cardiovascular Science; Cell Physiology; Cell/Cellular Biology and Histology; Endocrinology; Environmental Toxicology; Epidemiology; Exercise Physiology; Human/Medical Genetics; Immunology; Medical Microbiology and Bacteriology; Medical Science; Molecular Biology; Molecular Pharmacology; Molecular Physiology; Molecular Toxicology; Neuropharmacology; Oncology and Cancer Biology; Pathology/Experimental Pathology; Pharmacology; Pharmacology and Toxicology; Pharmacology and Toxicology, Other; Physiology, General; Physiology, Pathology, and Related Sciences, Other; Reproductive Biology; Toxicology; Vision Science/Physiological Optics. **Knowledge/Courses:** Biology; Medicine and Dentistry; Chemistry; Communications and Media; Personnel and Human Resources; Mathematics.

Career Clusters: 08 Health Science; 15 Science, Technology, Engineering, and Mathematics. **Career Pathways:** 08.1 Therapeutic Services; 15.2 Science and Mathematics.

Skills: Science; Operations Analysis; Reading Comprehension; Mathematics; Systems Evaluation; Instructing; Complex Problem Solving; Systems Analysis.

Work Environment: Indoors; sitting; using hands.

Network and Computer Systems Administrators

- ✺ Personality Type: Investigative-Realistic-Conventional
- ✺ Annual Earnings: $69,160
- ✺ Earnings Growth Potential: Medium (38.7%)
- ✺ Growth: 23.2%
- ✺ Annual Job Openings: 13,550
- ✺ Self-Employed: 0.8%

Considerations for Job Outlook: Employment of these workers should grow as organizations increasingly use network technologies. Job prospects are expected to be excellent.

Install, configure, and support organizations' local area networks (LANs), wide area networks (WANs), and Internet systems or segments of network systems. Maintain network hardware and software. Monitor networks to ensure network availability to all system users, and perform necessary maintenance to support network availability. May supervise other network-support and client-server specialists and plan, coordinate, and implement network security measures. Perform data backups and disaster recovery operations. Maintain and administer computer networks and related computing environments including computer hardware, systems software, applications software, and all configurations. Plan, coordinate, and implement network security measures to protect data, software, and hardware. Operate master consoles to monitor the performance of computer systems and networks, and to coordinate computer network access and use. Perform routine network startup and shutdown procedures, and maintain control records. Design, configure, and test computer hardware, networking software, and operating system software. Recommend changes to improve systems and network configurations, and determine hardware or software requirements related to such changes. Confer with network users about how to solve existing system problems. Monitor network performance to determine whether adjustments need to be made, and to determine where changes will need to be made in the future. Train people in computer system use. Load computer tapes and disks, and install software and printer paper or forms. Gather data pertaining to customer needs, and use the information to identify, predict, interpret, and evaluate system and network requirements. Analyze equipment-performance records to determine the need for repair or replacement. Maintain logs related to network functions, as well as maintenance and repair records. Maintain an inventory of parts for emergency repairs.

Education/Training Required: Bachelor's degree. **Education and Training Programs:** Network and System Administration/Administrator; System, Networking, and LAN/WAN Management/Manager. **Knowledge/Courses:** Telecommunications; Computers and Electronics; Clerical Practices; Administration and Management; Engineering and Technology.

Career Cluster: 11 Information Technology. **Career Pathways:** 11.1 Network Systems; 11.2 Information Support Services; 11.4 Programming and Software Development.

Skills: Programming; Equipment Maintenance; Troubleshooting; Equipment Selection; Technology Design; Repairing; Installation; Quality Control Analysis.

Work Environment: Indoors; sitting; using hands; repetitive motions; noise.

Nuclear Engineers

- ✺ Personality Type: Investigative-Realistic-Conventional
- ✺ Annual Earnings: $99,920
- ✺ Earnings Growth Potential: Low (32.7%)
- ✺ Growth: 11.0%
- ✺ Annual Job Openings: 540
- ✺ Self-Employed: 0.0%

Investigative-N

Considerations for Job Outlook: Nuclear engineers are expected to have employment growth of 11 percent from 2008 to 2018, about as fast as the average for all occupations. Most job growth will be in research and development and engineering services. Although no commercial nuclear power plants have been built in the United States for many years, increased interest in nuclear power as an energy source will spur demand for nuclear engineers to research and develop new designs for reactors. They also will be needed to work in defense-related areas, to develop nuclear medical technology, and to improve and enforce waste management and safety standards. Nuclear engineers are expected to have good employment opportunities because the small number of nuclear engineering graduates is likely to be in rough balance with the number of job openings.

Conduct research on nuclear engineering problems or apply principles and theory of nuclear science to problems concerned with release, control, and utilization of nuclear energy and nuclear waste disposal. Examine accidents to obtain data that can be used to design preventive measures. Monitor nuclear facility operations to identify any design, construction, or operation practices that violate safety regulations and laws or that could jeopardize the safety of operations. Keep abreast of developments and changes in the nuclear field by reading technical journals and by independent study and research. Perform experiments that will provide information about acceptable methods of nuclear material usage, nuclear fuel reclamation, and waste disposal. Design and oversee construction and operation of nuclear reactors and power plants and nuclear-fuels reprocessing and reclamation systems. Design and develop nuclear equipment such as reactor cores, radiation shielding, and associated instrumentation and control mechanisms. Initiate corrective actions or order plant shutdowns in emergency situations. Recommend preventive measures to be taken in the handling of nuclear technology, based on data obtained from operations monitoring or from evaluation of test results. Write operational instructions to be used in nuclear plant operation and nuclear fuel and waste handling and disposal. Conduct tests of nuclear fuel behavior and cycles and performance of nuclear machinery and equipment to optimize performance of existing plants. Direct operating and maintenance activities of operational nuclear power plants to ensure efficiency and conformity to safety standards.

Education/Training Required: Bachelor's degree. **Education and Training Program:** Nuclear Engineering. **Knowledge/Courses:** Engineering and Technology; Physics; Design; Chemistry; Mathematics; Mechanical Devices.

Career Cluster: 15 Science, Technology, Engineering, and Mathematics. **Career Pathway:** 15.1 Engineering and Technology.

Skills: Operations Analysis; Science; Technology Design; Operation Monitoring; Mathematics; Troubleshooting; Quality Control Analysis; Systems Evaluation.

Work Environment: Indoors; sitting; exposed to radiation.

Operations Research Analysts

* Personality Type: Investigative-Conventional-Enterprising
* Annual Earnings: $70,960
* Earnings Growth Potential: High (43.7%)
* Growth: 22.0%
* Annual Job Openings: 3,220
* Self-Employed: 0.2%

Considerations for Job Outlook: As technology advances and companies further emphasize efficiency, demand for operations research analysis should continue to grow. Excellent opportunities are expected, especially for those who have an advanced degree.

Formulate and apply mathematical modeling and other optimizing methods, using a computer to develop and interpret information that assists management with decision making, policy formulation, or other managerial functions. May develop related software, service, or products.

Frequently concentrates on collecting and analyzing data and developing decision support software. May develop and supply optimal time, cost, or logistics networks for program evaluation, review, or implementation. Formulate mathematical or simulation models of problems, relating constants and variables, restrictions, alternatives, and conflicting objectives and their numerical parameters. Collaborate with others in the organization to ensure successful implementation of chosen problem solutions. Analyze information obtained from management in order to conceptualize and define operational problems. Perform validation and testing of models to ensure adequacy; reformulate models as necessary. Collaborate with senior managers and decision-makers to identify and solve a variety of problems and to clarify management objectives. Define data requirements; then gather and validate information, applying judgment and statistical tests. Study and analyze information about alternative courses of action in order to determine which plan will offer the best outcomes. Prepare management reports defining and evaluating problems and recommending solutions. Break systems into their component parts, assign numerical values to each component, and examine the mathematical relationships between them. Specify manipulative or computational methods to be applied to models. Observe the current system in operation, and gather and analyze information about each of the parts of component problems, using a variety of sources. Design, conduct, and evaluate experimental operational models in cases where models cannot be developed from existing data.

Education/Training Required: Master's degree. **Education and Training Programs:** Management Science; Management Sciences and Quantitative Methods, Other; Operations Research. **Knowledge/Courses:** Mathematics; Computers and Electronics; Engineering and Technology; Production and Processing; Economics and Accounting; Transportation.

Career Clusters: 04 Business, Management, and Administration; 15 Science, Technology, Engineering, and Mathematics. **Career Pathways:**

04.1 Management; 04.4 Business Analysis; 15.2 Science and Mathematics.

Skills: Operations Analysis; Mathematics; Science; Systems Evaluation; Programming; Systems Analysis; Complex Problem Solving; Active Learning.

Work Environment: Indoors; sitting.

Optometrists

- Personality Type: Investigative-Social-Realistic
- Annual Earnings: $94,990
- Earnings Growth Potential: High (47.8%)
- Growth: 24.4%
- Annual Job Openings: 2,010
- Self-Employed: 24.6%

Considerations for Job Outlook: An aging population and increasing insurance coverage for vision care are expected to lead to employment growth for optometrists. Excellent opportunities are expected.

Diagnose, manage, and treat conditions and diseases of the human eye and visual system. Examine eyes and visual systems, diagnose problems or impairments, prescribe corrective lenses, and provide treatment. May prescribe therapeutic drugs to treat specific eye conditions. Examine eyes, using observation, instruments, and pharmaceutical agents, to determine visual acuity and perception, focus, and coordination and to diagnose diseases and other abnormalities such as glaucoma or color blindness. Prescribe medications to treat eye diseases if state laws permit. Analyze test results and develop treatment plans. Prescribe, supply, fit, and adjust eyeglasses, contact lenses, and other vision aids. Educate and counsel patients on contact lens care, visual hygiene, lighting arrangements, and safety factors. Remove foreign bodies from eyes. Consult with and refer patients to ophthalmologist or other health-care practitioners if additional medical treatment is determined necessary. Provide patients undergoing eye surgeries such as cataract and laser vision correction, with pre- and post-operative

Investigative-O

care. Prescribe therapeutic procedures to correct or conserve vision. Provide vision therapy and low vision rehabilitation.

Education/Training Required: First professional degree. **Education and Training Program:** Optometry (OD). **Knowledge/Courses:** Medicine and Dentistry; Biology; Therapy and Counseling; Physics; Sales and Marketing; Economics and Accounting.

Career Cluster: 08 Health Science. **Career Pathway:** 08.1 Therapeutic Services.

Skills: Science; Reading Comprehension; Operations Analysis; Management of Financial Resources; Quality Control Analysis; Management of Material Resources; Operation and Control; Service Orientation.

Work Environment: Indoors; sitting; using hands; exposed to disease or infections.

Orthodontists

- Personality Type: Investigative-Realistic-Social
- Annual Earnings: 166,400+
- Earnings Growth Potential: (Cannot be calculated)
- Growth: 19.7%
- Annual Job Openings: 360
- Self-Employed: 28.1%

Considerations for Job Outlook: An increase in the elderly population who often need complicated dental work and expanded insurance coverage for dental procedures are expected to create job growth. Good prospects are expected from the need to replace the large number of dentists who are retiring.

Examine, diagnose, and treat dental malocclusions and oral cavity anomalies. Design and fabricate appliances to realign teeth and jaws to produce and maintain normal function and to improve appearance. Fit dental appliances in patients' mouths to alter the position and relationship of teeth and jaws and to realign teeth. Study diagnostic records such as medical/dental histories, plaster models of the teeth, photos of a patient's face and teeth, and X-rays to develop patient treatment plans. Diagnose teeth and jaw or other dental-facial abnormalities. Examine patients to assess abnormalities of jaw development, tooth position, and other dental-facial structures. Prepare diagnostic and treatment records. Adjust dental appliances periodically to produce and maintain normal function. Provide patients with proposed treatment plans and cost estimates. Instruct dental officers and technical assistants in orthodontic procedures and techniques. Coordinate orthodontic services with other dental and medical services. Design and fabricate appliances, such as space maintainers, retainers, and labial and lingual arch wires.

Education/Training Required: First professional degree. **Education and Training Programs:** Orthodontics Specialty; Orthodontics/Orthodontology. **Knowledge/Courses:** Medicine and Dentistry; Biology; Sales and Marketing; Economics and Accounting; Personnel and Human Resources; Customer and Personal Service.

Career Cluster: 08 Health Science. **Career Pathway:** 08.1 Therapeutic Services.

Skills: Science; Operations Analysis; Instructing; Active Learning; Reading Comprehension; Management of Personnel Resources; Writing; Operation Monitoring.

Work Environment: Indoors; sitting; using hands; bending or twisting the body; repetitive motions; exposed to radiation; exposed to disease or infections.

Petroleum Engineers

- Personality Type: Investigative-Realistic-Conventional
- Annual Earnings: $114,080
- Earnings Growth Potential: High (44.4%)
- Growth: 18.4%
- Annual Job Openings: 860
- Self-Employed: 0.4%

Considerations for Job Outlook: Petroleum engineers are expected to have employment growth of 18 percent from 2008 to 2018, faster than the average for all occupations. Petroleum engineers increasingly will be needed to develop new resources, as well as new methods of extracting more from existing sources. Excellent opportunities are expected for petroleum engineers because the number of job openings is likely to exceed the relatively small number of graduates. Petroleum engineers work around the world, and, in fact, the best employment opportunities may include some work in other countries.

Devise methods to improve oil and gas well production, and determine the need for new or modified tool designs. Oversee drilling, and offer t echnical advice to achieve economical and satisfactory progress. Assess costs and estimate the production capabilities and economic value of oil and gas wells to evaluate the economic viability of potential drilling sites. Monitor production rates and plan rework processes to improve production. Analyze data to recommend placement of wells and supplementary processes to enhance production. Specify and supervise well modification and stimulation programs to maximize oil and gas recovery. Direct and monitor the completion and evaluation of wells, well testing, or well surveys. Assist engineering and other personnel to solve operating problems. Develop plans for oil and gas field drilling and for product recovery and treatment. Maintain records of drilling and production operations. Confer with scientific, engineering, and technical personnel to resolve design, research, and testing problems. Write technical reports for engineering and management personnel. Evaluate findings to develop, design, or test equipment or processes. Assign work to staff to obtain maximum utilization of personnel. Interpret drilling and testing information for personnel. Design and implement environmental controls on oil and gas operations. Coordinate the installation, maintenance, and operation of mining and oil field equipment. Supervise the removal of drilling equipment, the removal of any waste, and the safe return of land to structural stability when wells or pockets are exhausted. Inspect oil and gas wells to determine that installations are completed.

Education/Training Required: Bachelor's degree. **Education and Training Program:** Petroleum Engineering. **Knowledge/Courses:** Engineering and Technology; Physics; Geography; Chemistry; Economics and Accounting; Design.

Career Cluster: 15 Science, Technology, Engineering, and Mathematics. **Career Pathway:** 15.1 Engineering and Technology.

Skills: Science; Systems Evaluation; Management of Financial Resources; Management of Material Resources; Mathematics; Technology Design; Operation Monitoring; Systems Analysis.

Work Environment: Indoors; sitting.

Pharmacists

- ❋ Personality Type: Investigative-Conventional-Social
- ❋ Annual Earnings: $111,570
- ❋ Earnings Growth Potential: Low (26.4%)
- ❋ Growth: 17.0%
- ❋ Annual Job Openings: 10,580
- ❋ Self-Employed: 0.6%

Considerations for Job Outlook: The increasing numbers of middle-aged and elderly people—who use more prescription drugs than younger people—should continue to spur employment growth for pharmacists. Job prospects are expected to be excellent.

Compound and dispense medications, following prescriptions issued by physicians, dentists, or other authorized medical practitioners. Review prescriptions to assure accuracy, to ascertain the needed ingredients, and to evaluate their suitability. Provide information and advice regarding drug interactions, side effects, dosage, and proper medication storage. Analyze prescribing trends to monitor patient compliance and to prevent excessive usage or harmful interactions. Order and purchase pharmaceutical supplies, medical supplies, and drugs, maintaining stock and storing and handling it properly. Maintain records such as pharmacy files; patient profiles; charge system files; inventories; control records for radioactive nuclei; and registries of poisons, narcotics, and controlled drugs. Provide specialized services to help patients manage conditions such as diabetes, asthma, smoking cessation, or high blood pressure. Advise customers on the selection of medication brands, medical equipment, and health-care supplies. Collaborate with other health-care professionals to plan, monitor, review, and evaluate the quality and effectiveness of drugs and drug regimens, providing advice on drug applications and characteristics. Compound and dispense medications as prescribed by doctors and dentists by calculating, weighing, measuring, and mixing ingredients, or oversee these activities. Offer health promotion and prevention activities—for example, training people to use devices such as blood-pressure or diabetes monitors. Refer patients to other health professionals and agencies when appropriate.

Education/Training Required: First professional degree. **Education and Training Programs:** Clinical, Hospital, and Managed Care Pharmacy (MS, PhD); Industrial and Physical Pharmacy and Cosmetic Sciences (MS, PhD); Medicinal and Pharmaceutical Chemistry (MS, PhD); Natural Products Chemistry and Pharmacognosy (MS, PhD); Pharmaceutics and Drug Design (MS, PhD); Pharmacoeconomics/Pharmaceutical Economics (MS, PhD); Pharmacy (PharmD [USA], PharmD or BS/BPharm [Canada]); Pharmacy Administration and Pharmacy Policy and Regulatory Affairs (MS, PhD); Pharmacy, Pharmaceutical Sciences, and Administration, Other. **Knowledge/Courses:** Biology; Medicine and Dentistry; Chemistry; Therapy and Counseling; Psychology; Clerical Practices.

Career Cluster: 08 Health Science. **Career Pathways:** 08.1 Therapeutic Services; 08.5 Biotechnology Research and Development.

Skills: Science; Operations Analysis; Reading Comprehension; Management of Material Resources; Active Listening; Writing; Instructing; Management of Financial Resources.

Work Environment: Indoors; standing; using hands; repetitive motions; exposed to disease or infections.

Physicians and Surgeons

- ❋ Personality Type: Investigative-Social-Realistic
- ❋ Annual Earnings: $165,279
- ❋ Earnings Growth Potential: Very high (55.2%)
- ❋ Growth: 21.8%
- ❋ Annual Job Openings: 26,050
- ❋ Self-Employed: 11.7%

Considerations for Job Outlook: Employment growth is expected to be tied to increases in the aging population and in new medical technologies that allow more maladies to be diagnosed and treated. Job prospects should be very good, particularly in underserved areas.

Job Specialization: Allergists and Immunologists

Diagnose, treat, and help prevent allergic diseases and disease processes affecting the immune system. Present research findings at national meetings or in peer-reviewed journals. Engage in self-directed learning and continuing education activities. Document patients' medical histories. Conduct laboratory or clinical research on allergy or immunology topics. Provide allergy or immunology consultation or education to physicians or other health-care providers. Prescribe medication such as antihistamines, antibiotics, and nasal, oral, topical, or inhaled glucocorticosteroids. Conduct physical examinations of patients. Order or perform diagnostic tests such as skin pricks and intradermal, patch, or delayed hypersensitivity tests. Educate patients about diagnoses, prognoses, or treatments. Interpret diagnostic test results to make appropriate differential diagnoses. Develop individualized treatment plans for patients, considering patient preferences, clinical data, or the risks and benefits of therapies. Coordinate the care of patients with other health-care professionals or support staff. Assess the risks and benefits of therapies for allergic and immunologic disorders. Provide therapies, such as allergen immunotherapy and immunoglobin therapy, to treat immune conditions. Perform allergen provocation tests such as nasal, conjunctival, bronchial, oral, food, and medication challenges. Diagnose or treat allergic or immunologic conditions.

Education/Training Required: First professional degree. **Education and Training Program:** Allergy and Immunology Residency Program. **Knowledge/Courses:** No data available.

Personality Type: Investigative-Social-Realistic. **Career Cluster:** 08 Health Science. **Career Pathway:** 08.1 Therapeutic Services.

Skills: No data available.

Work Environment: No data available.

Job Specialization: Anesthesiologists

Administer anesthetics during surgery or other medical procedures. Administer anesthetic or sedation during medical procedures, using local, intravenous, spinal, or caudal methods. Monitor patient before, during, and after anesthesia, and counteract adverse reactions or complications. Provide and maintain life support and airway management, and help prepare patients for emergency surgery. Record type and amount of anesthesia and patient condition throughout procedure. Examine patient; obtain medical history; and use diagnostic tests to determine risk during surgical, obstetrical, and other medical procedures. Position patient on operating table to maximize patient comfort and surgical accessibility. Decide when patients have recovered or stabilized enough to be sent to another room or ward or to be sent home following outpatient surgery. Coordinate administration of anesthetics with surgeons during operation. Confer with other medical professionals to determine type and method of anesthetic or sedation to render patient insensible to pain. Coordinate and direct work of nurses, medical technicians, and other health-care providers. Order laboratory tests, X-rays, and other diagnostic procedures. Diagnose illnesses, using examinations, tests,

and reports. Manage anesthesiological services, coordinating them with other medical activities and formulating plans and procedures. Provide medical care and consultation in many settings, prescribing medication and treatment and referring patients for surgery.

Education/Training Required: First professional degree. **Education and Training Program:** Medicine (MD). **Knowledge/Courses:** Medicine and Dentistry; Biology; Chemistry; Psychology; Physics; Therapy and Counseling.

Personality Type: Investigative-Realistic-Social. **Career Cluster:** 08 Health Science. **Career Pathway:** 08.1 Therapeutic Services.

Skills: Science; Operation Monitoring; Reading Comprehension; Operations Analysis; Operation and Control; Judgment and Decision Making; Time Management; Management of Personnel Resources.

Work Environment: Indoors; more often sitting than standing; using hands; noise; contaminants; exposed to radiation; exposed to disease or infections; hazardous conditions.

Job Specialization: Dermatologists

Diagnose, treat, and help prevent diseases or other conditions of the skin. Refer patients to other specialists, as needed. Record patients' health histories. Provide dermatologic consultation to other health professionals. Provide liposuction treatment to patients. Read current literature, talk with colleagues, and participate in professional organizations or conferences to keep abreast of developments in dermatology. Instruct interns or residents in diagnosis and treatment of dermatological diseases. Evaluate patients to determine eligibility for cosmetic procedures such as liposuction, laser resurfacing, and microdermabrasion. Conduct or order diagnostic tests such as chest radiographs (X-rays), microbiologic tests, and endocrinologic tests. Recommend diagnostic tests based on patients' histories and physical examination findings. Conduct clinical or basic research. Provide therapies such as intralesional steroids, chemical peels, and comodo removal to treat age spots, sun damage, rough skin, discolored skin, or oily skin. Provide dermabrasion or laser abrasion to treat atrophic scars, elevated scars, or other skin conditions. Prescribe hormonal agents or topical treatments such as contraceptives, spironolactone, antiandrogens, oral corticosteroids, retinoids, benzoyl peroxide, and antibiotics. Perform skin surgery to improve appearance, make early diagnoses, or control diseases such as skin cancer. Perform incisional biopsies to diagnose melanoma.

Education/Training Required: First professional degree. **Education and Training Program:** Dermatology Residency Program. **Knowledge/Courses:** No data available.

Personality Type: Investigative-Social-Realistic. **Career Cluster:** 08 Health Science. **Career Pathway:** 08.1 Therapeutic Services.

Skills: No data available.

Work Environment: No data available.

Job Specialization: Family and General Practitioners

Diagnose, treat, and help prevent diseases and injuries that commonly occur in the general population. Prescribe or administer treatment, therapy, medication, vaccination, and other specialized medical care to treat or prevent illness, disease, or injury. Order, perform, and interpret tests and analyze records, reports, and examination information to diagnose patients' condition. Monitor the patients' conditions and progress, and re-evaluate treatments as necessary. Explain procedures and discuss test results or prescribed treatments with patients. Collect, record, and maintain patient information, such as medical history, reports, and examination results. Advise patients and community members concerning diet, activity, hygiene, and disease prevention. Refer patients to medical specialists or other practitioners when necessary. Direct and coordinate activities of nurses, students, assistants, specialists,

therapists, and other medical staff. Coordinate work with nurses, social workers, rehabilitation therapists, pharmacists, psychologists, and other health-care providers. Deliver babies. Operate on patients to remove, repair, or improve functioning of diseased or injured body parts and systems. Plan, implement, or administer health programs or standards in hospital, business, or community for information, prevention, or treatment of injury or illness. Prepare reports for government or management of birth, death, and disease statistics; workforce evaluations; or medical status of individuals.

Education/Training Required: First professional degree. **Education and Training Programs:** Medicine (MD); Osteopathic Medicine/Osteopathy (DO). **Knowledge/Courses:** Medicine and Dentistry; Therapy and Counseling; Psychology; Biology; Customer and Personal Service; Sociology and Anthropology.

Personality Type: Investigative-Social. **Career Clusters:** 08 Health Science; 15 Science, Technology, Engineering, and Mathematics. **Career Pathways:** 08.1 Therapeutic Services; 15.2 Science and Mathematics.

Skills: Science; Judgment and Decision Making; Active Listening; Social Perceptiveness; Reading Comprehension; Complex Problem Solving; Writing; Management of Personnel Resources.

Work Environment: More often indoors than outdoors; sitting; exposed to disease or infections.

Job Specialization: Hospitalists

Provide inpatient care predominantly in settings such as medical wards, acute care units, intensive care units, rehabilitation centers, or emergency rooms. Manage and coordinate patient care throughout treatment. Refer patients to medical specialists, social services, or other professionals as appropriate. Participate in continuing education activities to maintain or enhance knowledge and skills. Direct, coordinate, or supervise the patient care activities of nursing or support staff.

Write patient discharge summaries, and send them to primary care physicians. Direct the operations of short-stay or specialty units. Train or supervise medical students, residents, or other health professionals. Prescribe medications or treatment regimens to hospital inpatients. Order or interpret the results of tests such as laboratory tests and radiographs (X-rays). Attend inpatient consultations in areas of specialty. Conduct discharge planning, and discharge patients. Diagnose, treat, or provide continuous care to hospital inpatients. Admit patients for hospital stays. Communicate with patients' primary care physicians upon admission, when treatment plans change, or at discharge to maintain continuity and quality of care.

Education/Training Required: First professional degree. **Education and Training Program:** Medicine (MD). **Knowledge/Courses:** Medicine and Dentistry; Therapy and Counseling; Biology; Psychology; Sociology and Anthropology; Chemistry.

Personality Type: Social-Investigative. **Career Cluster:** 08 Health Science. **Career Pathway:** 08.1 Therapeutic Services.

Skills: Science; Instructing; Social Perceptiveness; Reading Comprehension; Active Learning; Learning Strategies; Service Orientation; Systems Evaluation.

Work Environment: Indoors; standing; noise; contaminants; exposed to disease or infections.

Job Specialization: Internists, General

Diagnose and provide non-surgical treatment of diseases and injuries of internal organ systems. Provide care mainly for adults who have a wide range of problems associated with the internal organs. Treat internal disorders, such as hypertension; heart disease; diabetes; and problems of the lung, brain, kidney, and gastrointestinal tract. Analyze records, reports, test results, or examination information to diagnose medical condition of patient. Prescribe or administer medication, therapy, and other specialized medical care to treat or pre-

vent illness, disease, or injury. Provide and manage long-term, comprehensive medical care, including diagnosis and non-surgical treatment of diseases, for adult patients in an office or hospital. Manage and treat common health problems, such as infections, influenza, and pneumonia, as well as serious, chronic, and complex illnesses, in adolescents, adults, and the elderly. Monitor patients' conditions and progress, and re-evaluate treatments as necessary. Collect, record, and maintain patient information, such as medical history, reports, and examination results. Make diagnoses when different illnesses occur together or in situations where the diagnosis may be obscure. Explain procedures and discuss test results or prescribed treatments with patients. Advise patients and community members concerning diet, activity, hygiene, and disease prevention. Refer patient to medical specialist or other practitioner when necessary. Immunize patients to protect them from preventable diseases. Advise surgeon of a patient's risk status, and recommend appropriate intervention to minimize risk.

Education/Training Required: First professional degree. **Education and Training Program:** Medicine (MD). **Knowledge/Courses:** Medicine and Dentistry; Biology; Therapy and Counseling; Psychology; Chemistry; Education and Training.

Personality Type: Investigative-Social-Realistic. **Career Cluster:** 08 Health Science. **Career Pathway:** 08.1 Therapeutic Services.

Skills: Science; Operations Analysis; Reading Comprehension; Active Learning; Service Orientation; Complex Problem Solving; Writing; Systems Evaluation.

Work Environment: Indoors; standing; exposed to disease or infections.

Job Specialization: Neurologists

Diagnose, treat, and help prevent diseases and disorders of the nervous system. Participate in neuroscience research activities. Provide training to medical students or staff members. Participate

Investigative-P

in continuing education activities to maintain and expand competence. Supervise medical technicians in the performance of neurological diagnostic or therapeutic activities. Counsel patients or others on the background of neurological disorders, including risk factors, or genetic or environmental concerns. Interpret the results of neuroimaging studies such as Magnetic Resonance Imaging (MRI), Single Photon Emission Computed Tomography (SPECT), and Positron Emission Tomography (PET) scans. Refer patients to other health-care practitioners as necessary. Advise other physicians on the treatment of neurological problems. Prescribe or administer medications, such as anti-epileptic drugs, and monitor patients for behavioral and cognitive side effects. Prescribe or administer treatments such as transcranial magnetic stimulation, vagus nerve stimulation, and deep brain stimulation. Prepare, maintain, or review records that include patients' histories, neurological examination findings, treatment plans, or outcomes. Perform specialized treatments in areas such as sleep disorders, neuroimmunology, neurooncology, behavioral neurology, and neurogenetics. Order or interpret results of laboratory analyses of patients' blood or cerebrospinal fluid. Order supportive care services such as physical therapy, specialized nursing care, and social services.

Education/Training Required: First professional degree. **Education and Training Program:** Neurology Residency Program. **Knowledge/Courses:** No data available.

Personality Type: Investigative-Social-Realistic. **Career Cluster:** 08 Health Science. **Career Pathway:** 08.1 Therapeutic Services.

Skills: No data available.

Work Environment: No data available.

Job Specialization: Nuclear Medicine Physicians

Diagnose and treat diseases, using radioactive materials and techniques. May monitor radionuclide preparation, administration, and disposi-tion. Test dosage evaluation instruments and survey meters to ensure they are operating properly. Teach nuclear medicine, diagnostic radiology, or other specialties at graduate educational level. Schedule examinations and staff activities. Provide advice on the selection of nuclear medicine supplies or equipment. Monitor cleanup of radioactive spills to ensure that proper procedures are followed and that decontamination activities are conducted. Monitor handling of radioactive materials to ensure that established procedures are followed. Formulate plans and procedures for nuclear medicine departments. Direct the safe management and disposal of radioactive substances. Establish and enforce radiation protection standards for patients and staff. Advise other physicians of the clinical indications, limitations, assessments, or risks of diagnostic and therapeutic applications of radioactive materials. Conduct laboratory procedures, such as radioimmunoassay studies of blood or urine, using radionuclides. Review procedure requests and patients' medical histories to determine applicability of procedures and radioisotopes to be used. Prescribe radionuclides and dosages to be administered to individual patients. Prepare comprehensive interpretive reports of findings. Perform cardiovascular nuclear medicine procedures such as exercise testing and pharmacologic stress testing.

Education/Training Required: First professional degree. **Education and Training Program:** Nuclear Medicine Residency Program. **Knowledge/Courses:** Medicine and Dentistry; Biology; Physics; Chemistry; Therapy and Counseling; Personnel and Human Resources.

Personality Type: Investigative-Social. **Career Cluster:** 08 Health Science. **Career Pathway:** 08.1 Therapeutic Services.

Skills: Science; Reading Comprehension; Writing; Instructing; Active Learning; Learning Strategies; Critical Thinking; Social Perceptiveness.

Work Environment: Indoors; sitting; using hands; exposed to radiation; exposed to disease or infections.

Job Specialization: Obstetricians and Gynecologists

Diagnose, treat, and help prevent diseases of women, especially those affecting the reproductive system and the process of childbirth. Care for and treat women during prenatal, natal, and post-natal periods. Explain procedures and discuss test results or prescribed treatments with patients. Treat diseases of female organs. Monitor patients' condition and progress, and re-evaluate treatments as necessary. Perform cesarean sections or other surgical procedures as needed to preserve patients' health and deliver babies safely. Prescribe or administer therapy, medication, and other specialized medical care to treat or prevent illness, disease, or injury. Analyze records, reports, test results, or examination information to diagnose medical condition of patient. Collect, record, and maintain patient information, such as medical histories, reports, and examination results. Advise patients and community members concerning diet, activity, hygiene, and disease prevention. Refer patient to medical specialist or other practitioner when necessary. Consult with, or provide consulting services to, other physicians. Direct and coordinate activities of nurses, students, assistants, specialists, therapists, and other medical staff. Plan, implement, or administer health programs in hospitals, businesses, or communities for prevention and treatment of injuries or illnesses. Prepare government and organizational reports on birth, death, and disease statistics; workforce evaluations; or the medical status of individuals.

Education/Training Required: First professional degree. **Education and Training Program:** Medicine (MD). **Knowledge/Courses:** Medicine and Dentistry; Biology; Therapy and Counseling; Psychology; Customer and Personal Service; Chemistry.

Personality Type: Investigative-Social-Realistic. **Career Cluster:** 08 Health Science. **Career Pathway:** 08.1 Therapeutic Services.

Skills: Science; Reading Comprehension; Operations Analysis; Active Listening; Judgment and Decision Making; Active Learning; Learning Strategies; Instructing.

Work Environment: Indoors; standing; using hands; exposed to disease or infections.

Job Specialization: Ophthalmologists

Diagnose, treat, and help prevent diseases and injuries of the eyes and related structures. Provide ophthalmic consultation to other medical professionals. Refer patients for more specialized treatments when conditions exceed the experience, expertise, or scope of practice of practitioner. Instruct interns, residents, or others in ophthalmologic procedures and techniques. Develop or implement plans and procedures for ophthalmologic services. Educate patients about maintenance and promotion of healthy vision. Conduct clinical or laboratory-based research in ophthalmology. Collaborate with multidisciplinary teams of health professionals to provide optimal patient care. Provide or direct the provision of postoperative care. Document or evaluate patients' medical histories. Prescribe corrective lenses such as glasses and contact lenses. Prescribe or administer topical or systemic medications to treat ophthalmic conditions and to manage pain. Perform, order, or interpret the results of diagnostic or clinical tests. Develop treatment plans based on patients' histories and goals, the nature and severity of disorders, and treatment risks and benefits. Perform laser surgeries to alter, remove, reshape, or replace ocular tissue. Perform ophthalmic surgeries such as cataract, glaucoma, refractive, corneal, vitro-retinal, eye muscle, and oculoplastic surgeries. Prescribe ophthalmologic treatments or therapies such as chemotherapy, cryotherapy, and low vision therapy. Perform comprehensive examinations of the visual system to determine the nature or extent of ocular disorders.

Education/Training Required: First professional degree. **Education and Training Program:** Ophthalmology Residency Program. **Knowledge/Courses:** No data available.

Investigative-P

Personality Type: Investigative-Social-Realistic. **Career Cluster:** 08 Health Science. **Career Pathway:** 08.1 Therapeutic Services.

Skills: No data available.

Work Environment: No data available.

Job Specialization: Pathologists

Diagnose presence and stage of diseases, using laboratory techniques and patient specimens. Study the nature, cause, and development of diseases. May perform autopsies. Testify in depositions or trials as an expert witness. Review cases by analyzing autopsies, laboratory findings, or case investigation reports. Manage medical laboratories. Read current literature, talk with colleagues, or participate in professional organizations or conferences to keep abreast of developments in pathology. Develop or adopt new tests or instruments to improve diagnosis of diseases. Educate physicians, students, and other personnel in medical laboratory professions such as medical technology, cytotechnology, and histotechnology. Conduct research and present scientific findings. Perform autopsies to determine causes of deaths. Plan and supervise the work of the pathology staff, residents, or visiting pathologists. Obtain specimens by performing procedures such as biopsies and fine need aspirations (FNAs) of superficial nodules. Identify the etiology, pathogenesis, morphological change, and clinical significance of diseases. Diagnose infections, such as Hepatitis B and Acquired Immune Deficiency Syndrome (AIDS), by conducting tests to detect the antibodies that patients' immune systems make to fight such infections. Conduct genetic analyses of deoxyribonucleic acid (DNA) or chromosomes to diagnose small biopsies and cell samples. Write pathology reports summarizing analyses, results, and conclusions.

Education/Training Required: First professional degree. **Education and Training Program:** Pathology Residency Program. **Knowledge/ Courses:** Medicine and Dentistry; Biology; Chemistry; English Language; Personnel and Human Resources; Education and Training.

Personality Type: Investigative-Realistic. **Career Cluster:** 08 Health Science. **Career Pathway:** 08.2 Diagnostics Services.

Skills: Science; Reading Comprehension; Instructing; Management of Financial Resources; Management of Material Resources; Active Learning; Judgment and Decision Making; Complex Problem Solving.

Work Environment: Indoors; sitting; exposed to disease or infections.

Job Specialization: Pediatricians, General

Diagnose, treat, and help prevent children's diseases and injuries. Examine patients or order, perform, and interpret diagnostic tests to obtain information on medical condition and determine diagnosis. Examine children regularly to assess their growth and development. Prescribe or administer treatment, therapy, medication, vaccination, and other specialized medical care to treat or prevent illness, disease, or injury in infants and children. Collect, record, and maintain patient information, such as medical history, reports, and examination results. Advise patients, parents or guardians, and community members concerning diet, activity, hygiene, and disease prevention. Treat children who have minor illnesses, acute and chronic health problems, and growth and development concerns. Explain procedures and discuss test results or prescribed treatments with patients and parents or guardians. Monitor patients' condition and progress, and re-evaluate treatments as necessary. Plan and execute medical care programs to aid in the mental and physical growth and development of children and adolescents. Refer patient to medical specialist or other practitioner when necessary. Direct and coordinate activities of nurses, students, assistants, specialists, therapists, and other medical staff. Provide consulting services to other physicians. Plan, implement, or administer health programs or standards in hospital, business, or community for information, prevention, or treatment of injury or illness.

Education/Training Required: First professional degree. **Education and Training Program:** Medicine (MD). **Knowledge/Courses:** Medicine and Dentistry; Therapy and Counseling; Biology; Psychology; Chemistry; Sociology and Anthropology.

Personality Type: Investigative-Social. **Career Cluster:** 08 Health Science. **Career Pathway:** 08.1 Therapeutic Services.

Skills: Science; Operations Analysis; Reading Comprehension; Active Learning; Systems Evaluation; Judgment and Decision Making; Service Orientation; Speaking.

Work Environment: Indoors; standing; using hands; exposed to disease or infections.

Job Specialization: Physical Medicine and Rehabilitation Physicians

Diagnose and treat disorders requiring physiotherapy to provide physical, mental, and occupational rehabilitation. Instruct interns and residents in the diagnosis and treatment of temporary or permanent physically disabling conditions. Conduct physical tests such as functional capacity evaluations to determine injured workers' capabilities to perform the physical demands of their jobs. Assess characteristics of patients' pain such as intensity, location, and duration using standardized clinical measures. Monitor effectiveness of pain-management interventions such as medication and spinal injections. Examine patients to assess mobility, strength, communication, or cognition. Document examination results, treatment plans, and patients' outcomes. Diagnose or treat performance-related conditions such as sports injuries or repetitive motion injuries. Develop comprehensive plans for immediate and long-term rehabilitation including therapeutic exercise; speech and occupational therapy; counseling; cognitive retraining; patient, family or caregiver education; or community reintegration. Prescribe physical therapy to relax the muscles and improve strength. Coordinate physical medicine and rehabil-

itation services with other medical activities. Consult or coordinate with other rehabilitative professionals including physical and occupational therapists, rehabilitation nurses, speech pathologists, neuropsychologists, behavioral psychologists, social workers, or medical technicians.

Education/Training Required: First professional degree. **Education and Training Program:** Physical Medicine and Rehabilitation Residency Program. **Knowledge/Courses:** No data available.

Personality Type: Investigative-Social-Realistic. **Career Cluster:** 08 Health Science. **Career Pathway:** 08.1 Therapeutic Services.

Skills: No data available.

Work Environment: No data available.

Job Specialization: Preventive Medicine Physicians

Apply knowledge of general preventive medicine and public health issues to promote health care to groups or individuals and aid in the prevention or reduction of risk of disease, injury, disability, or death. May practice population-based medicine or diagnose and treat patients in the context of clinical health promotion and disease prevention. Teach or train medical staff regarding preventive medicine issues. Document or review comprehensive patients' histories with an emphasis on occupation or environmental risks. Prepare preventive health reports including problem descriptions, analyses, alternative solutions, and recommendations. Supervise or coordinate the work of physicians, nurses, statisticians, or other professional staff members. Deliver presentations to lay or professional audiences. Evaluate the effectiveness of prescribed risk-reduction measures or other interventions. Identify groups at risk for specific preventable diseases or injuries. Design or use surveillance tools, such as screening, lab reports, and vital records, to identify health risks. Direct public health education programs dealing with topics such as preventable diseases, injuries, nutrition, food service sanitation,

Investigative–P

water supply safety, sewage and waste disposal, insect control, and immunizations. Perform epidemiological investigations of acute and chronic diseases. Develop or implement interventions to address behavioral causes of diseases. Direct or manage prevention programs in specialty areas such as aerospace, occupational, infectious disease, and environmental medicine. Design, implement, or evaluate health-service delivery systems to improve the health of targeted populations.

Education/Training Required: First professional degree. **Education and Training Program:** Medicine (MD). **Knowledge/Courses:** Medicine and Dentistry; Biology; Therapy and Counseling; Sociology and Anthropology; Psychology; Philosophy and Theology.

Personality Type: Social-Investigative-Realistic. **Career Cluster:** 08 Health Science. **Career Pathway:** 08.1 Therapeutic Services.

Skills: Science; Reading Comprehension; Service Orientation; Complex Problem Solving; Systems Evaluation; Social Perceptiveness; Management of Personnel Resources; Instructing.

Work Environment: Indoors; sitting; exposed to disease or infections.

Job Specialization: Psychiatrists

Diagnose, treat, and help prevent disorders of the mind. Prescribe, direct, and administer psychotherapeutic treatments or medications to treat mental, emotional, or behavioral disorders. Analyze and evaluate patient data and test findings to diagnose nature and extent of mental disorders. Collaborate with physicians, psychologists, social workers, psychiatric nurses, or other professionals to discuss treatment plans and progress. Gather and maintain patient information and records, including social and medical histories obtained from patients, relatives, and other professionals. Design individualized care plans, using a variety of treatments. Counsel outpatients and other patients during office visits. Examine or conduct laboratory or diagnostic tests

on patients to provide information on general physical conditions and mental disorders. Advise and inform guardians, relatives, and significant others of patients' conditions and treatments. Teach, take continuing education classes, attend conferences and seminars, and conduct research and publish findings to increase understanding of mental, emotional, and behavioral states and disorders. Review and evaluate treatment procedures and outcomes of other psychiatrists and medical professionals. Prepare and submit case reports and summaries to government and mental health agencies. Serve on committees to promote and maintain community mental health services and delivery systems.

Education/Training Required: First professional degree. **Education and Training Program:** Medicine (MD). **Knowledge/Courses:** Therapy and Counseling; Medicine and Dentistry; Psychology; Biology; Sociology and Anthropology; Philosophy and Theology.

Personality Type: Investigative-Social-Artistic. **Career Cluster:** 08 Health Science. **Career Pathway:** 08.1 Therapeutic Services.

Skills: Science; Social Perceptiveness; Operations Analysis; Persuasion; Negotiation; Service Orientation; Instructing; Judgment and Decision Making.

Work Environment: Indoors; sitting; exposed to disease or infections.

Job Specialization: Radiologists

Examine and diagnose disorders and diseases, using X-rays and radioactive materials. May treat patients. Implement protocols in areas such as drugs, resuscitation, emergencies, power failures, and infection control. Treat malignant internal or external growths by exposure to radiation from radiographs (X-rays), high energy sources, or natural or synthetic radioisotopes. Serve as an offsite tele-radiologist for facilities that do not have on-site radiologists. Provide advice on types or quantities of radiology equipment needed to maintain facilities. Participate in research projects involving radiology. Participate in quality-improvement activities including discussions of areas where risk of error is high. Supervise and teach residents or medical students. Schedule examinations and assign radiologic personnel. Participate in continuing education activities to maintain and develop expertise. Develop treatment plans for radiology patients. Establish or enforce standards for protection of patients or personnel. Administer radiopaque substances by injection, orally, or as enemas to render internal structures and organs visible on X-ray films or fluoroscopic screens. Administer or maintain conscious sedation during and after procedures. Review or transmit images and information using picture archiving or communications systems. Interpret images using computer-aided detection or diagnosis systems. Recognize or treat complications during and after procedures, including blood pressure problems, pain, oversedation, or bleeding. Prepare comprehensive interpretive reports of findings.

Education/Training Required: First professional degree. **Education and Training Programs:** Diagnostic Radiology Residency Program; Radiologic Physics Residency Program. **Knowledge/Courses:** No data available.

Personality Type: Investigative-Realistic-Social. **Career Cluster:** 08 Health Science. **Career Pathway:** 08.2 Diagnostics Services.

Skills: No data available.

Work Environment: No data available.

Job Specialization: Sports Medicine Physicians

Diagnose, treat, and help prevent injuries that occur during sporting events, athletic training, and physical activities. Select and prepare medical equipment or medications to be taken to athletic competition sites. Provide coaches and therapists with assistance in selecting and fitting protective equipment. Advise against injured athletes returning to games or competition if resuming activity could lead to further injury. Observe and evaluate athletes' mental well-being. Participate in continuing education activities to improve and maintain knowledge

and skills. Develop and prescribe exercise programs such as off-season conditioning regimens. Advise athletes on how substances, such as herbal remedies, could affect drug testing results. Conduct research in the prevention or treatment of injuries or medical conditions related to sports and exercise. Advise athletes, trainers, or coaches to alter or cease sports practices that are potentially harmful. Attend games and competitions to provide evaluation and treatment of activity-related injuries or medical conditions. Record athletes' medical histories and perform physical examinations. Supervise the rehabilitation of injured athletes. Refer athletes for specialized consultation, physical therapy, or diagnostic testing. Record athletes' medical care information, and maintain medical records. Inform coaches, trainers, or other interested parties regarding the medical conditions of athletes. Provide education and counseling on illness and injury prevention. Prescribe orthotics, prosthetics, and adaptive equipment.

Education/Training Required: First professional degree. **Education and Training Program:** Orthopedic Sports Medicine Residency Program. **Knowledge/Courses:** No data available.

Personality Type: Investigative-Social-Realistic. **Career Cluster:** 08 Health Science. **Career Pathway:** 08.1 Therapeutic Services.

Skills: No data available.

Work Environment: No data available.

Job Specialization: Surgeons

Treat diseases, injuries, and deformities by invasive methods, such as manual manipulation, or by using instruments and appliances. Analyze patient's medical history, medication allergies, physical condition, and examination results to verify operation's necessity and to determine best procedure. Operate on patients to correct deformities, repair injuries, prevent and treat diseases, or improve or restore patients' functions. Follow established surgical techniques during the operation. Prescribe preoperative and postoperative treatments and procedures, such as sedatives, diets, antibiotics, and prepara-

Investigative-P

tion and treatment of the patient's operative area. Examine patient to provide information on medical condition and surgical risk. Diagnose bodily disorders and orthopedic conditions, and provide treatments, such as medicines and surgeries, in clinics, hospital wards, and operating rooms. Direct and coordinate activities of nurses, assistants, specialists, residents, and other medical staff. Provide consultation and surgical assistance to other physicians and surgeons. Refer patient to medical specialist or other practitioners when necessary. Examine instruments, equipment, and operating room to ensure sterility. Prepare case histories. Manage surgery services, including planning, scheduling and coordination, determination of procedures, and procurement of supplies and equipment. Conduct research to develop and test surgical techniques that can improve operating procedures and outcomes.

Education/Training Required: First professional degree. **Education and Training Program:** Medicine (MD). **Knowledge/Courses:** Medicine and Dentistry; Biology; Therapy and Counseling; Psychology; English Language; Customer and Personal Service.

Personality Type: Investigative-Realistic-Social. **Career Cluster:** 08 Health Science. **Career Pathway:** 08.1 Therapeutic Services.

Skills: Science; Reading Comprehension; Active Learning; Instructing; Judgment and Decision Making; Complex Problem Solving; Social Perceptiveness; Active Listening.

Work Environment: Indoors; standing; using hands; repetitive motions; exposed to disease or infections.

Job Specialization: Urologists

Diagnose, treat, and help prevent benign and malignant medical and surgical disorders of the genitourinary system and the renal glands. Teach or train medical and clinical staff. Document or review patients' histories. Provide urology consultation to physicians or other health-care professionals. Refer patients to specialists when condition exceeds experience, expertise, or scope of practice. Direct the work of nurses, residents, or other staff members to provide patient care. Treat urologic disorders using alternatives to traditional surgery such as extracorporeal shock wave lithotripsy, laparoscopy, and laser techniques. Treat lower urinary tract dysfunctions using equipment such as diathermy machines, catheters, cystoscopes, and radium emanation tubes. Prescribe or administer antibiotics, antiseptics, or compresses to treat infection or injury. Perform abdominal, pelvic, or retroperitoneal surgeries. Perform brachytherapy, cryotherapy, high-intensity focused ultrasound (HIFU), or photodynamic therapy to treat prostate or other cancers. Order and interpret the results of diagnostic tests, such as prostate-specific antigen (PSA) screening, to detect prostate cancer. Examine patients using equipment, such as radiograph (X-ray) machines and fluoroscopes, to determine the nature and extent of disorder or injury. Diagnose or treat diseases or disorders of genitourinary organs and tracts including erectile dysfunction (ED), infertility, incontinence, bladder cancer, prostate cancer, urethral stones, or premature ejaculation.

Education/Training Required: First professional degree. **Education and Training Program:** Urology Residency Program. **Knowledge/Courses:** No data available.

Personality Type: Investigative-Social-Realistic. **Career Cluster:** 08 Health Science. **Career Pathway:** 08.1 Therapeutic Services.

Skills: No data available.

Work Environment: No data available.

Job Specialization: Physicians and Surgeons, All Other

This occupation includes all physicians and surgeons not listed separately. Because this is a highly diverse occupation, no data is available for some information topics.

Education/Training Required: First professional degree. **Education and Training Program:** Medicine (MD).

Personality Type: No data available. **Career Clusters:** 08 Health Science; 10 Human Services. **Career Pathways:** 08.1 Therapeutic Services; 10.2 Counseling and Mental Health Services.

Physicists

* Personality Type: Investigative-Realistic
* Annual Earnings: $106,370
* Earnings Growth Potential: High (44.7%)
* Growth: 15.9%
* Annual Job Openings: 690
* Self-Employed: 0.0%

Considerations for Job Outlook: An increased focus on basic research, particularly that related to energy, is expected to drive employment growth for these workers. Prospects should be favorable for physicists in applied research, development, and related technical fields.

Conduct research into phases of physical phenomena, develop theories and laws on basis of observation and experiments, and devise methods to apply laws and theories to industry and other fields. Perform complex calculations as part of the analysis and evaluation of data, using computers. Describe and express observations and conclusions in mathematical terms. Analyze data from research conducted to detect and measure physical phenomena. Report experimental results by writing papers for scientific journals or by presenting information at scientific conferences. Design computer simulations to model physical data so that it can be better understood. Collaborate with other scientists in the design, development, and testing of experimental, industrial, or medical equipment, instrumentation, and procedures. Direct testing and monitoring of contamination of radioactive equipment and recording of personnel and plant-area radiation exposure data. Observe the structure and properties of matter and the transformation and propagation of energy, using equipment such as masers, lasers, and telescopes, in order to explore and identify the basic principles governing these phenomena. Develop theories and laws on the basis of observation and experiments, and apply these theories and laws to problems in areas such as nuclear energy, optics, and aerospace technology. Teach physics to students. Develop manufacturing, assembly, and fabrication processes of lasers, masers, and infrared and other light-emitting and light-sensitive devices.

Education/Training Required: Doctoral degree. **Education and Training Programs:** Acoustics; Astrophysics; Atomic/Molecular Physics; Condensed Matter and Materials Physics; Elementary Particle Physics; Health/Medical Physics; Nuclear Physics; Optics/Optical Sciences; Physics, General; Physics, Other; Plasma and High-Temperature Physics; Theoretical and Mathematical Physics. **Knowledge/Courses:** Physics; Mathematics; Engineering and Technology; Computers and Electronics; English Language; Telecommunications.

Career Clusters: 05 Education and Training; 15 Science, Technology, Engineering, and Mathematics. **Career Pathways:** 05.3 Teaching/Training; 15.2 Science and Mathematics.

Skills: Science; Programming; Mathematics; Technology Design; Active Learning; Reading Comprehension; Learning Strategies; Writing.

Work Environment: Indoors; sitting.

Political Scientists

* Personality Type: Investigative-Artistic-Social
* Annual Earnings: $107,420
* Earnings Growth Potential: Very high (54.6%)
* Growth: 19.4%
* Annual Job Openings: 280
* Self-Employed: 1.4%

Investigative-P

Considerations for Job Outlook: Political scientists are expected to experience employment growth especially in nonprofit, political lobbying, and civic organizations. Opportunities should be best for jobseekers who have an advanced degree.

Study the origin, development, and operation of political systems. Research a wide range of subjects, such as relations between the United States and foreign countries, the beliefs and institutions of foreign nations, or the politics of small towns or a major metropolis. May study topics such as public opinion, political decision making, and ideology. May analyze the structure and operation of governments, as well as various political entities. May conduct public opinion surveys, analyze election results, or analyze public documents. Teach political science. Disseminate research results through academic publications, written reports, or public presentations. Identify issues for research and analysis. Develop and test theories, using information from interviews, newspapers, periodicals, case law, historical papers, polls, and/or statistical sources. Maintain current knowledge of government policy decisions. Collect, analyze, and interpret data such as election results and public opinion surveys; report on findings, recommendations, and conclusions. Interpret and analyze policies; public issues; legislation; and the operations of governments, businesses, and organizations. Evaluate programs and policies, and make related recommendations to institutions and organizations. Write drafts of legislative proposals, and prepare speeches, correspondence, and policy papers for governmental use. Forecast political, economic, and social trends. Consult with and advise government officials, civic bodies, research agencies, the media, political parties, and others concerned with political issues. Provide media commentary and/or criticism related to public policy and political issues and events.

Education/Training Required: Master's degree. **Education and Training Programs:** American Government and Politics (United States); Canadian Government and Politics; International Relations and Affairs; International/Global Studies; Political

Science and Government, General; Political Science and Government, Other. **Knowledge/Courses:** History and Archeology; Law and Government; Philosophy and Theology; Sociology and Anthropology; Foreign Language; Geography.

Career Clusters: 07 Government and Public Administration; 15 Science, Technology, Engineering, and Mathematics. **Career Pathways:** 07.1 Governance; 15.2 Science and Mathematics.

Skills: Science; Speaking; Writing; Critical Thinking; Active Listening; Active Learning; Systems Analysis; Reading Comprehension.

Work Environment: Indoors; sitting.

Prosthodontists

- ❋ Personality Type: Investigative-Realistic
- ❋ Annual Earnings: $118,400
- ❋ Earnings Growth Potential: Very high (65.1%)
- ❋ Growth: 26.4%
- ❋ Annual Job Openings: 30
- ❋ Self-Employed: 27.9%

Considerations for Job Outlook: An increase in the elderly population—who often need complicated dental work—and expanded insurance coverage for dental procedures are expected to create job growth. Good prospects are expected from the need to replace the large number of dentists who are retiring.

Construct oral prostheses to replace missing teeth and other oral structures to correct natural and acquired deformation of mouth and jaws; to restore and maintain oral function, such as chewing and speaking; and to improve appearance. Replace missing teeth and associated oral structures with permanent fixtures, such as crowns and bridges, or removable fixtures, such as dentures. Fit prostheses to patients, making any necessary adjustments and modifications. Design and fabricate dental prostheses, or supervise dental technicians and laboratory bench workers who construct the devices. Measure and take impressions of patients' jaws and teeth to determine the shape and size of dental prostheses, using face bows, dental articulators, recording devices, and other materials. Collaborate with general dentists, specialists, and other health professionals to develop solutions to dental and oral health concerns. Repair, reline, and/or rebase dentures. Restore function and aesthetics to traumatic injury victims or to individuals with diseases or birth defects. Use bonding technology on the surface of the teeth to change tooth shape or to close gaps. Treat facial pain and jaw joint problems. Place veneers onto teeth to conceal defects. Bleach discolored teeth to brighten and whiten them.

Education/Training Required: First professional degree. **Education and Training Programs:** Prosthodontics Specialty; Prosthodontics/Prosthodontology (Cert., MS, PhD). **Knowledge/Courses:** Medicine and Dentistry; Biology; Chemistry; Psychology; Engineering and Technology; Sales and Marketing.

Career Cluster: 08 Health Science. **Career Pathway:** 08.1 Therapeutic Services.

Skills: Operations Analysis; Science; Technology Design; Social Perceptiveness; Service Orientation; Management of Personnel Resources; Learning Strategies; Instructing.

Work Environment: Indoors; more often sitting than standing; using hands; repetitive motions; noise; contaminants; cramped work space; exposed to radiation; exposed to disease or infections; hazardous conditions; hazardous equipment; minor burns, cuts, bites, or stings.

Psychologists, All Other

- ❋ Personality Type: Investigative-Social-Artistic
- ❋ Annual Earnings: $89,900
- ❋ Earnings Growth Potential: Very high (54.2%)
- ❋ Growth: 14.4%
- ❋ Annual Job Openings: 680
- ❋ Self-Employed: 32.8%

Considerations for Job Outlook: Employment growth is expected due to increased emphasis on mental health in a variety of specializations, including school counseling, depression, and substance abuse. Job-seekers with a doctoral degree should have the best opportunities.

This occupation includes all psychologists not listed separately. Because this is a highly diverse occupation, no data is available for some information topics.

Education/Training Required: Master's degree. **Education and Training Program:** Psychology, Other.

Career Clusters: 08 Health Science; 10 Human Services; 15 Science, Technology, Engineering, and Mathematics. **Career Pathways:** 08.1 Therapeutic Services; 10.2 Counseling and Mental Health Services; 15.2 Science and Mathematics.

Job Specialization: Neuropsychologists and Clinical Neuropsychologists

Apply theories and principles of neuropsychology to diagnose and treat disorders of higher cerebral functioning. Write or prepare detailed clinical neuropsychological reports using data from psychological or neuropsychological tests, self-report measures, rating scales, direct observations, or interviews. Provide psychotherapy, behavior therapy, or other counseling interventions to patients with neurological disorders. Provide education or counseling to individuals and families. Participate in educational programs, in-service training, or workshops to remain current in methods and techniques. Read current literature, talk with colleagues, and participate in professional organizations or conferences to keep abreast of developments in neuropsychology. Interview patients to obtain comprehensive medical histories. Identify and communicate risks associated with specific neurological surgical procedures such as epilepsy surgery. Educate and supervise practicum students, psychology interns, or hospital staff. Diagnose and treat conditions such as chemical dependency, alcohol de-

Investigative-P

pendency, Acquired Immune Deficiency Syndrome (AIDS) dementia, and environmental toxin exposure. Distinguish between psychogenic and neurogenic syndromes, two or more suspected etiologies of cerebral dysfunction, or between disorders involving complex seizures. Diagnose and treat neural and psychological conditions in medical and surgical populations such as patients with early dementing illness or chronic pain with a neurological basis. Design or implement rehabilitation plans for patients with cognitive dysfunction.

Education/Training Required: Doctoral degree. **Education and Training Program:** Physiological Psychology/Psychobiology. **Knowledge/Courses:** Therapy and Counseling; Psychology; Biology; Medicine and Dentistry; Sociology and Anthropology; Philosophy and Theology.

Personality Type: Investigative-Social-Artistic. **Career Cluster:** 15 Science, Technology, Engineering, and Mathematics. **Career Pathway:** 15.2 Science and Mathematics.

Skills: Science; Social Perceptiveness; Reading Comprehension; Active Learning; Writing; Learning Strategies; Systems Evaluation; Critical Thinking.

Work Environment: Indoors; sitting; using hands; exposed to disease or infections.

Social Scientists and Related Workers, All Other

- ❈ Personality Type: Investigative-Conventional-Realistic
- ❈ Annual Earnings: $74,620
- ❈ Earnings Growth Potential: High (41.8%)
- ❈ Growth: 22.5%
- ❈ Annual Job Openings: 2,380
- ❈ Self-Employed: 1.5%

Considerations for Job Outlook: Much faster than average employment growth is projected.

This occupation includes all social scientists and related workers not listed separately. Because this is a highly diverse occupation, no data is available for some information topics.

Education/Training Required: Master's degree. **Education and Training Program:** Social Sciences, Other.

Career Clusters: 10 Human Services; 15 Science, Technology, Engineering, and Mathematics. **Career Pathways:** 10.3 Family and Community Services; 15.2 Science and Mathematics.

Job Specialization: Transportation Planners

Prepare studies for proposed transportation projects. Gather, compile, and analyze data. Study the use and operation of transportation systems. Develop transportation models or simulations. Prepare or review engineering studies or specifications. Represent jurisdictions in the legislative and administrative approval of land development projects. Prepare necessary documents to obtain project approvals or permits. Direct urban traffic counting programs. Develop or test new methods and models of transportation analysis. Define or update information such as urban boundaries and classification of roadways. Analyze transportation-related consequences of federal and state legislative proposals. Analyze information from traffic counting programs. Review development plans for transportation system effects, infrastructure requirements, or compliance with applicable transportation regulations. Prepare reports and recommendations on transportation planning. Produce environmental documents, such as environmental assessments and environmental impact statements. Participate in public meetings or hearings to explain planning proposals, gather feedback from those affected by projects, or achieve consensus on project designs. Document and evaluate transportation project needs and costs. Develop design ideas for new or improved transport infrastructure, such as junction improvements, pedestrian projects, bus facilities, and car parking areas. Develop computer models to address transportation planning issues. Design transportation surveys to identify areas of public concern.

Education/Training Required: Master's degree. **Education and Training Program:** City/Urban, Community and Regional Planning. **Knowledge/ Courses:** Geography; Transportation; Law and Government; Design; History and Archeology; Sociology and Anthropology.

Personality Type: Investigative-Conventional-Realistic. **Career Cluster:** 15 Science, Technology, Engineering, and Mathematics. **Career Pathway:** 15.2 Science and Mathematics.

Skills: Systems Evaluation; Management of Material Resources; Mathematics; Operations Analysis; Systems Analysis; Management of Financial Resources; Technology Design; Complex Problem Solving.

Work Environment: Indoors; sitting.

Software Developers, Applications

- ❋ Personality Type: Investigative-Realistic-Conventional
- ❋ Annual Earnings: $87,790
- ❋ Earnings Growth Potential: Medium (38.1%)
- ❋ Growth: 34.0%
- ❋ Annual Job Openings: 21,840
- ❋ Self-Employed: 2.7%

Considerations for Job Outlook: Employment is expected to increase as businesses and other organizations continue to demand newer, more sophisticated software products. As a result of rapid growth, job prospects for software engineers should be excellent. The need to replace workers who leave the occupation is expected to generate numerous openings for programmers.

Develop, create, and modify general computer applications software or specialized utility programs. Analyze user needs, and develop software solutions. Design software or customize software for client use with the aim of optimizing operational efficiency. May analyze and design databases within an application area, working individually or coordinating database development as part of a team. Confer with systems analysts, engineers, programmers, and others to design system and to obtain information on project limitations and capabilities, performance requirements, and interfaces. Modify existing software to correct errors, allow it to adapt to new hardware, or improve its performance. Analyze user needs and software requirements to determine feasibility of design within time and cost constraints. Consult with customers about software system design and maintenance. Coordinate software system installation and monitor equipment functioning to ensure specifications are met. Design, develop, and modify software systems, using scientific analysis and mathematical models to predict and measure outcome and consequences of design. Develop and direct software system testing and validation procedures, programming, and documentation. Analyze information to determine, recommend, and plan computer specifications and layouts as well as peripheral equipment modifications. Supervise the work of programmers, technologists, technicians, and other engineering and scientific personnel. Obtain and evaluate information on factors such as reporting formats required, costs, and security needs to determine hardware configuration. Determine system performance standards. Train users to use new or modified equipment. Store, retrieve, and manipulate data for analysis of system capabilities and requirements. Specify power supply requirements and configuration.

Education/Training Required: Bachelor's degree. **Education and Training Programs:** Computer Graphics; Computer Science; Computer Software and Media Applications, Other; Data Modeling/ Warehousing and Database Administration; Modeling, Virtual Environments and Simulation; Web Page, Digital/Multimedia, and Information Resources Design. **Knowledge/Courses:** Computers and Electronics; Mathematics; Engineering and Technology; Design; English Language.

Career Cluster: 08 Health Science; 11 Information Technology; 13 Manufacturing; 15 Science, Technology, Engineering, and Mathematics. **Career Pathways:** 08.3 Health Informatics; 11.1 Network

Systems; 11.2 Information Support Services; 11.3 Interactive Media; 11.4 Programming and Software Development; 13.3 Maintenance, Installation, and Repair; 15.2 Science and Mathematics.

Skills: Programming; Troubleshooting; Technology Design; Systems Evaluation; Operations Analysis; Mathematics; Systems Analysis; Quality Control Analysis.

Work Environment: Indoors; sitting; repetitive motions.

Software Developers, Systems Software

- ✸ Personality Type: Investigative-Conventional-Realistic
- ✸ Annual Earnings: $94,180
- ✸ Earnings Growth Potential: Low (35.2%)
- ✸ Growth: 30.4%
- ✸ Annual Job Openings: 15,340
- ✸ Self-Employed: 2.7%

Considerations for Job Outlook: Employment is expected to increase as businesses and other organizations continue to demand newer, more sophisticated software products. As a result of rapid growth, job prospects for software engineers should be excellent. The need to replace workers who leave the occupation is expected to generate numerous openings for programmers.

Research, design, develop, and test operating systems—level software, compilers, and network distribution software for medical, industrial, military, communications, aerospace, business, scientific, and general computing applications. Set operational specifications, and formulate and analyze software requirements. Apply principles and techniques of computer science, engineering, and mathematical analysis. Modify existing software to correct errors, adapt it to new hardware, or upgrade interfaces and improve performance. Design and develop software systems, using scientific analy-

sis and mathematical models to predict and measure outcome and consequences of design. Consult with engineering staff to evaluate the interface between hardware and software, develop specifications and performance requirements, and resolve customer problems. Analyze information to determine, recommend, and plan installation of a new system or modification of an existing system. Develop and direct software system testing and validation procedures. Direct software programming and development of documentation. Consult with customers or other departments on project status, proposals, and technical issues such as software system design and maintenance. Advise customer about, or perform, maintenance of software system. Coordinate installation of software system. Monitor functioning of equipment to ensure system operates in conformance with specifications. Store, retrieve, and manipulate data for analysis of system capabilities and requirements. Confer with data processing and project managers to obtain information on limitations and capabilities for data processing projects. Prepare reports and correspondence concerning project specifications, activities, and status. Evaluate factors such as reporting formats required, cost constraints, and need for security restrictions to determine hardware configuration.

Education/Training Required: Bachelor's degree. **Education and Training Programs:** Computer Graphics; Computer Science; Computer Software and Media Applications, Other; Data Modeling/Warehousing and Database Administration; Modeling, Virtual Environments and Simulation; Web Page, Digital/Multimedia, and Information Resources Design. **Knowledge/Courses:** Computers and Electronics; Engineering and Technology; Design; Telecommunications; Mathematics; Communications and Media.

Career Cluster: 11 Information Technology. **Career Pathways:** 11.1 Network Systems; 11.2 Information Support Services; 11.3 Interactive Media; 11.4 Programming and Software Development.

Skills: Programming; Technology Design; Operations Analysis; Science; Equipment Selection; Quality Control Analysis; Systems Evaluation; Mathematics.

Work Environment: Indoors; sitting; repetitive motions.

Survey Researchers

* Personality Type: Investigative-Conventional-Enterprising
* Annual Earnings: $36,050
* Earnings Growth Potential: High (48.2%)
* Growth: 30.3%
* Annual Job Openings: 1,340
* Self-Employed: 6.7%

Considerations for Job Outlook: Demand for market research is expected as businesses strive to increase sales and as governments rely on survey research to form public policy. Opportunities should be best for job-seekers who have a doctoral degree and strong quantitative skills.

Design or conduct surveys. May supervise interviewers who conduct the survey in person or over the telephone. May present survey results to client. Prepare and present summaries and analyses of survey data, including tables, graphs, and fact sheets that describe survey techniques and results. Consult with clients in order to identify survey needs and any specific requirements, such as special samples. Analyze data from surveys, old records, and/or case studies, using statistical software programs. Review, classify, and record survey data in preparation for computer analysis. Conduct research in order to gather information about survey topics. Conduct surveys and collect data, using methods such as interviews, questionnaires, focus groups, market-analysis surveys, public opinion polls, literature reviews, and file reviews. Collaborate with other researchers in the planning, implementation, and evaluation of surveys. Direct and review the work of staff members, including survey support staff and interviewers who gather survey data. Monitor and evaluate survey progress and performance, using sample disposition reports and response rate calculations. Produce documentation of the questionnaire development process, data collection methods, sampling designs, and decisions related to sample statistical weighting. Determine and specify details of survey projects, including sources of information, procedures to be used, and the design of survey instruments and materials. Support, plan, and coordinate operations for single or multiple surveys. Direct updates and changes in survey implementation and methods.

Education/Training Required: Bachelor's degree. **Education and Training Programs:** Applied Economics; Business/Managerial Economics; Economics, General; Marketing Research. **Knowledge/Courses:** Sociology and Anthropology; Sales and Marketing; Personnel and Human Resources; Mathematics; Administration and Management; English Language.

Career Clusters: 04 Business, Management, and Administration; 14 Marketing, Sales, and Service; 15 Science, Technology, Engineering, and Mathematics. **Career Pathways:** 04.1 Management; 14.5 Marketing Information Management and Research; 15.2 Science and Mathematics.

Skills: Mathematics; Programming; Writing; Science; Learning Strategies; Management of Financial Resources; Complex Problem Solving; Operations Analysis.

Work Environment: Indoors; sitting.

Urban and Regional Planners

* Personality Type: Investigative-Enterprising-Artistic
* Annual Earnings: $63,040
* Earnings Growth Potential: Low (35.9%)
* Growth: 19.0%
* Annual Job Openings: 1,470
* Self-Employed: 0.0%

Considerations for Job Outlook: State and local governments are expected to hire urban and regional planners to help manage population growth and commercial development. Private businesses, mainly architecture and engineering firms, will also hire these workers to deal with storm water management, environmental regulation, and other concerns. Job prospects should be best for job-seekers with a master's degree.

Develop comprehensive plans and programs for use of land and physical facilities of local jurisdictions such as towns, cities, counties, and metropolitan areas. Design, promote, and administer government plans and policies affecting land use, zoning, public utilities, community facilities, housing, and transportation. Hold public meetings and confer with government, social scientists, lawyers, developers, the public, and special interest groups to formulate and develop land use or community plans. Recommend approval, denial, or conditional approval of proposals. Determine the effects of regulatory limitations on projects. Assess the feasibility of proposals, and identify necessary changes. Create, prepare, or requisition graphic and narrative reports on land use data, including land area maps overlaid with geographic variables such as population density. Conduct field investigations, surveys, impact studies, or other research to compile and analyze data on economic, social, regulatory, and physical factors affecting land use. Advise planning officials on project feasibility, cost-effectiveness, regulatory conformance, and possible alternatives. Discuss with planning officials the purpose of land use projects such as transportation, conservation, residential, commercial, industrial, and community service. Keep informed about economic and legal issues involved in zoning codes, building codes, and environmental regulations. Mediate community disputes, and assist in developing alternative plans and recommendations for programs or projects.

Education/Training Required: Master's degree. **Education and Training Program:** City/Urban, Community and Regional Planning. **Knowledge/ Courses:** Geography; History and Archeology; Transportation; Design; Law and Government; Building and Construction.

Career Cluster: 07 Government and Public Administration. **Career Pathway:** 07.4 Planning.

Skills: Systems Analysis; Operations Analysis; Management of Financial Resources; Science; Systems Evaluation; Judgment and Decision Making; Mathematics; Programming.

Work Environment: Indoors; sitting; noise.

Veterinarians

- ❋ Personality Type: Investigative-Realistic
- ❋ Annual Earnings: $82,040
- ❋ Earnings Growth Potential: Medium (39.2%)
- ❋ Growth: 32.9%
- ❋ Annual Job Openings: 3,020
- ❋ Self-Employed: 6.9%

Considerations for Job Outlook: Growth in the pet population and pet owners' increased willingness to pay for intensive veterinary care and treatment are projected to create significantly more jobs for veterinarians. Excellent job opportunities are expected.

Diagnose and treat diseases and dysfunctions of animals. May engage in a particular function, such as research and development, consultation, administration, technical writing, sale or production of commercial products, or rendering of technical services to commercial firms or other organizations. Includes veterinarians who inspect livestock. Examine animals to detect and determine the nature of diseases or injuries. Treat sick or injured animals by prescribing medication, setting bones, dressing wounds, or performing surgery. Inoculate animals against various diseases such as rabies and distemper. Collect body tissue, feces, blood, urine, or other body fluids for examination and analysis. Operate diagnostic equipment such as radiographic and ultrasound equipment, and interpret the resulting images. Advise animal owners regarding sanitary measures, feeding, and general care necessary to promote health of animals. Educate the public about diseases that can be spread from animals to humans. Train and supervise workers who handle and care for animals. Provide care to a wide range of animals, or specialize in a particular species, such as horses or exotic birds. Euthanize animals. Establish and conduct quarantine and testing procedures that prevent the spread of diseases to other animals or to humans and that comply with applicable government regulations. Conduct postmortem studies and analyses to determine the causes of animals' deaths. Perform administrative duties such as scheduling appointments, accepting payments from clients, and maintaining business records. Drive mobile clinic vans to farms so that health problems can be treated or prevented. Direct the overall operations of animal hospitals, clinics, or mobile services to farms.

Education/Training Required: First professional degree. **Education and Training Programs:** Comparative and Laboratory Animal Medicine; Laboratory Animal Medicine; Large Animal/ Food Animal and Equine Surgery and Medicine; Small/Companion Animal Surgery and Medicine; Theriogenology; Veterinary Anatomy; Veterinary Anesthesiology; Veterinary Dentistry; Veterinary Dermatology; Veterinary Emergency and Critical Care Medicine; Veterinary Infectious Diseases; Veterinary Internal Medicine; Veterinary Medicine; Veterinary Microbiology; Veterinary Microbiology and Immunobiology; Veterinary Nutrition; Veterinary Ophthalmology; Veterinary Pathology; Veterinary Pathology and Pathobiology; Veterinary Physiology; Veterinary Practice; Veterinary Preventive Medicine; Veterinary Preventive Medicine Epidemiology and Public Health; Veterinary Radiology; Veterinary Sciences/Veterinary Clinical Sciences, General; Veterinary Surgery; Veterinary Toxicology; Veterinary Toxicology and Pharmacology; Zoological Medicine; others. **Knowledge/Courses:** Medicine and Dentistry; Biology; Chemistry; Therapy and Counseling; Sales and Marketing; Personnel and Human Resources.

Career Clusters: 01 Agriculture, Food, and Natural Resources; 08 Health Science. **Career Pathways:** 01.3 Animal Systems; 08.1 Therapeutic Services.

Skills: Science; Operations Analysis; Reading Comprehension; Active Learning; Instructing; Service Orientation; Writing; Judgment and Decision Making.

Work Environment: Indoors; standing; using hands; noise; contaminants; exposed to radiation; exposed to disease or infections; minor burns, cuts, bites, or stings.

Investigative-V

Artistic Occupations

Adult Basic and Secondary Education and Literacy Teachers and Instructors

* Personality Type: Social-Artistic-Enterprising
* Annual Earnings: $46,530
* Earnings Growth Potential: High (41.8%)
* Growth: 15.1%
* Annual Job Openings: 2,920
* Self-Employed: 20.4%

Considerations for Job Outlook: As the need for educated workers increases, so will the need for teachers to instruct them. In addition, there should be employment growth for teachers to help immigrants and others improve their English-language skills. Opportunities should be favorable.

Teach or instruct out-of-school youths and adults in remedial education classes, preparatory classes for the General Educational Development test, literacy, or English as a Second Language. Teaching may or may not take place in a traditional educational institution. Adapt teaching methods and instructional materials to meet students' varying needs, abilities, and interests. Observe and evaluate students' work to determine progress, and make suggestions for improvement. Instruct students individually and in groups, using various teaching methods such as lectures, discussions, and demonstrations. Plan and conduct activities for a balanced program of instruction, demonstration, and work time that provides students with opportunities to observe, question, and investigate. Maintain accurate and complete student records as required by laws or administrative policies. Prepare materials and classrooms for class activities. Establish clear objectives for all lessons, units, and projects, and communicate those objectives to students. Conduct classes, workshops, and demonstrations to teach principles, techniques, or methods in subjects such as basic English-language skills, life skills, and workforce entry skills. Prepare students for further education by encouraging them to explore learning opportunities and to persevere with challenging tasks. Establish and enforce rules for behavior and procedures for maintaining order among the students for whom they are responsible. Provide information, guidance, and preparation for the General Equivalency Diploma (GED) examination. Assign and grade classwork and homework. Observe students to determine qualifications, limitations, abilities, interests, and other individual characteristics.

Education/Training Required: Bachelor's degree. **Education and Training Programs:** Adult and Continuing Education and Teaching; Adult Literacy Tutor/Instructor Training; Bilingual and Multilingual Education; Multicultural Education; Teaching English as a Second or Foreign Language/ESL Language Instructor. **Knowledge/Courses:** English Language; History and Archeology; Education and Training; Sociology and Anthropology; Geography; Foreign Language.

Career Cluster: 05 Education and Training. **Career Pathway:** 05.3 Teaching/Training.

Skills: Learning Strategies; Instructing; Writing; Reading Comprehension; Persuasion; Time Management; Social Perceptiveness; Negotiation.

Work Environment: Indoors; standing.

Advertising and Promotions Managers

* Personality Type: Enterprising-Artistic-Conventional
* Annual Earnings: $83,890
* Earnings Growth Potential: High (50.6%)
* Growth: –1.7%
* Annual Job Openings: 1,050
* Self-Employed: 16.6%

Considerations for Job Outlook: Job growth is expected to result from companies' need to distinguish their products and services in an increasingly competitive marketplace. Keen competition is expected.

Plan and direct advertising policies and programs or produce collateral materials, such as posters, contests, coupons, or giveaways, to create extra interest in the purchase of a product or service for a department, for an entire organization, or on an account basis. Prepare budgets and submit estimates for program costs as part of campaign plan development. Plan and prepare advertising and promotional material to increase sales of products or services, working with customers, company officials, sales departments, and advertising agencies. Assist with annual budget development. Inspect layouts and advertising copy, and edit scripts, audio and video materials, and other promotional material for adherence to specifications. Coordinate activities of departments, such as sales, graphic arts, media, finance, and research. Prepare and negotiate advertising and sales contracts. Identify and develop contacts for promotional campaigns and industry programs that meet identified buyer targets, such as dealers, distributors, or consumers. Gather and organize information to plan advertising campaigns. Confer with department heads or staff members to discuss topics such as contracts, selection of advertising media, or product to be advertised. Confer with clients to provide marketing or technical advice. Monitor and analyze sales promotion results to determine cost-effectiveness of promotion campaigns. Read trade journals and professional literature to stay informed on trends, innovations, and changes that affect media planning. Formulate plans to extend business with established accounts and to transact business as agent for advertising accounts.

Education/Training Required: Work experience plus degree. **Education and Training Programs:** Advertising; Marketing/Marketing Management, General; Public Relations/Image Management. **Knowledge/Courses:** Communications and Media; Fine Arts; Sales and Marketing; Telecommunications; English Language; Design.

Career Clusters: 04 Business, Management, and Administration; 14 Marketing, Sales, and Service. **Career Pathways:** 04.1 Management; 04.5 Marketing; 14.1 Management and Entrepreneurship.

Skills: Management of Financial Resources; Management of Personnel Resources; Operations Analysis; Systems Evaluation; Coordination; Negotiation; Management of Material Resources; Speaking.

Work Environment: Indoors; sitting.

Job Specialization: Green Marketers

Create and implement methods to market green products and services. Prepare renewable-energy communications in response to public relations or promotional inquiries. Monitor energy industry statistics or literature to identify trends. Maintain portfolios of marketing campaigns, strategies, and other marketing products or ideas. Generate or identify sales leads for green energy. Devise or evaluate methods and procedures for collecting data, such as surveys, opinion polls, and questionnaires. Conduct market simulations for wind, solar, or geothermal energy projects. Write marketing content for green energy websites, brochures, or other communication media. Revise existing marketing plans or campaigns for green products or services. Monitor energy market or regulatory conditions to identify buying or other business opportunities. Identify marketing channels for green energy products or services. Develop communications materials, advertisements, presentations, or public relations initiatives to promote awareness of, and participation in, green energy initiatives. Consult with clients to identify potential energy-efficiency opportunities or to promote green energy alternatives. Conduct energy-pricing analyses for specific clients or client groups. Conduct research on consumer opinions and marketing strategies related to green energy technologies. Attend or participate in conferences or meetings to promote green energy, environmental protection, or energy conservation. Analyze the effectiveness of marketing tactics or channels.

Education/Training Required: Work experience plus degree. **Education and Training Programs:** Advertising; Marketing/Marketing Management, General; Public Relations/Image Management. **Knowledge/Courses:** No data available.

Personality Type: No data available. **Career Clusters:** 04 Business, Management, and Administration; 14 Marketing, Sales, and Service. **Career Pathways:** 04.1 Management; 04.5 Marketing; 14.1 Management and Entrepreneurship.

Skills: No data available.

Work Environment: No data available.

Anthropologists and Archeologists

- ❀ Personality Type: Investigative-Artistic
- ❀ Annual Earnings: $54,230
- ❀ Earnings Growth Potential: High (42.3%)
- ❀ Growth: 28.0%
- ❀ Annual Job Openings: 450
- ❀ Self-Employed: 1.5%

Considerations for Job Outlook: Anthropologists are projected to have significant employment growth in the management, scientific, and technical consulting industry. Expected job growth for archaeologists is associated with large-scale construction projects that must comply with federal laws to preserve archaeological sites. Job competition is expected.

Job Specialization: Anthropologists

Research, evaluate, and establish public policy concerning the origins of humans; their physical, social, linguistic, and cultural development; and their behavior, as well as the cultures, organizations, and institutions they have created. Collect information, and make judgments through observation, interviews, and the review of documents. Plan and direct research to characterize and compare the economic, demographic, health-care, social, political, linguistic, and religious institutions of distinct cultural groups, communities, and organizations. Write about and present research findings for a variety of specialized and general audiences. Advise government agencies, private organizations, and communities regarding proposed programs, plans, and policies and their potential impacts on cultural institutions, organizations, and communities. Identify culturally specific beliefs and practices affecting health status and access to services for distinct populations and communities in collaboration with medical and public health officials. Build and use text-based database management systems to support the analysis of detailed first-hand observational records, or "field notes." Develop intervention procedures, utilizing techniques such as individual and focus group interviews, consultations, and participant observation of social interaction. Construct and test data collection methods. Explain the origins and physical, social, or cultural development of humans, including physical attributes, cultural traditions, beliefs, languages, resource-management practices, and settlement patterns.

Education/Training Required: Master's degree. **Education and Training Programs:** Anthropology; Archeology; Classics and Classical Languages, Literatures, and Linguistics, General; Physical and Biological Anthropology. **Knowledge/Courses:** Sociology and Anthropology; History and Archeology; Geography; Philosophy and Theology; Foreign Language; Communications and Media.

Personality Type: Investigative-Artistic. **Career Cluster:** 15 Science, Technology, Engineering, and Mathematics. **Career Pathway:** 15.2 Science and Mathematics.

Skills: Science; Writing; Systems Analysis; Operations Analysis; Speaking; Reading Comprehension; Active Learning; Instructing.

Work Environment: Indoors; sitting.

Job Specialization: Archeologists

Conduct research to reconstruct record of past human life and culture from human remains, artifacts, architectural features, and structures recovered through excavation, underwater recovery, or other means of discovery. Write, present, and publish reports that record site history, methodology, and artifact analysis results, along with recommendations for conserving and interpreting findings. Compare findings from one site with archeological data from other sites to find similarities or differences. Research, survey, or assess sites of past societies and cultures in search of answers to specific research questions. Study objects and structures recovered by excavation to identify, date, and authenticate them and to interpret their significance. Develop and test theories concerning the origin and development of past cultures. Consult site reports, existing artifacts, and topographic maps to identify archeological sites. Create a grid of each site, and draw and update maps of unit profiles, stratum surfaces, features, and findings. Record the exact locations and conditions of artifacts uncovered in diggings or surveys, using drawings and photographs as necessary. Assess archeological sites for resource management, development, or conservation purposes, and recommend methods for site protection. Describe artifacts' physical properties or attributes, such as the materials from which artifacts are made and their size, shape, function, and decoration. Teach archeology at colleges and universities. Collect artifacts made of stone, bone, metal, and other materials, placing them in bags and marking them to show where they were found.

Education/Training Required: Master's degree. **Education and Training Programs:** Anthropology; Archeology; Classics and Classical Languages, Literatures, and Linguistics, General; Physical and Biological Anthropology. **Knowledge/Courses:** History and Archeology; Sociology and Anthropology; Geography; Philosophy and Theology; Foreign Language; English Language.

Personality Type: Investigative-Realistic-Artistic. **Career Cluster:** 15 Science, Technology, Engineering, and Mathematics. **Career Pathway:** 15.2 Science and Mathematics.

Skills: Science; Reading Comprehension; Writing; Management of Personnel Resources; Programming; Learning Strategies; Mathematics; Active Learning.

Work Environment: More often indoors than outdoors; sitting; using hands.

Architects, Except Landscape and Naval

- ❋ Personality Type: Artistic-Investigative
- ❋ Annual Earnings: $72,550
- ❋ Earnings Growth Potential: Medium (40.9%)
- ❋ Growth: 16.2%
- ❋ Annual Job Openings: 4,680
- ❋ Self-Employed: 21.2%

Considerations for Job Outlook: Changing demographics, such as the population's aging and shifting to warmer states, should lead to employment growth for architects to design new buildings to accommodate these changes. Job competition should be keen.

Plan and design structures such as private residences, office buildings, theaters, factories, and other structural property. Prepare information regarding design, structure specifications, materials, color, equipment, estimated costs, or construction time. Consult with client to determine functional and spatial requirements of structure. Direct activities of workers engaged in preparing drawings and specification documents. Plan layout of project. Prepare contract documents for building contractors. Prepare scale drawings. Integrate engineering element into unified design. Conduct periodic on-site observation of work during construction to monitor compliance with plans. Administer construction contracts. Represent client in obtaining bids and awarding construction contracts. Prepare operating and maintenance manuals, studies, and reports.

Education/Training Required: Bachelor's degree. **Education and Training Programs:** Architectural History and Criticism, General; Architecture (BArch, BA/BS, MArch, MA/MS, PhD); Architecture and Related Services, Other; Environmental Design/Architecture. **Knowledge/Courses:** Design; Building and Construction; Engineering and Technology; Fine Arts; Sales and Marketing; Law and Government.

Career Cluster: 02 Architecture and Construction. **Career Pathway:** 02.1 Design/Pre-Construction.

Skills: Operations Analysis; Management of Financial Resources; Management of Material Resources; Mathematics; Science; Judgment and Decision Making; Quality Control Analysis; Negotiation.

Work Environment: Indoors; sitting; using hands; repetitive motions.

Architectural and Civil Drafters

Look for the job description among the Realistic jobs.

Architecture Teachers, Postsecondary

- ❋ Personality Type: Social-Artistic
- ❋ Annual Earnings: $73,500
- ❋ Earnings Growth Potential: High (43.2%)
- ❋ Growth: 15.1%
- ❋ Annual Job Openings: 200
- ❋ Self-Employed: 0.2%

Considerations for Job Outlook: Enrollments in postsecondary institutions are expected to continue rising as more people attend college and as workers return to school to update their skills. Opportunities for part-time or temporary positions should be favorable, but significant competition exists for tenure-track positions.

Teach courses in architecture and architectural design, such as architectural environmental design, interior architecture/design, and landscape architecture. Evaluate and grade students' work, including work performed in design studios. Prepare and deliver lectures to undergraduate and/or graduate students on topics such as architectural design methods, aesthetics and design, and structures and materials. Prepare course materials such as syllabi, homework assignments, and handouts. Initiate, facilitate, and moderate classroom discussions. Plan, evaluate, and revise curricula, course content, course materials, and methods of instruction. Keep abreast of developments in the field by reading current literature, talking with colleagues, and participating in professional conferences. Maintain student attendance records, grades, and other required records. Maintain regularly scheduled office hours to advise and assist students. Compile, administer, and grade examinations, or assign this work to others. Conduct research in a particular field of knowledge and publish findings in professional journals, books, and/or electronic media. Supervise undergraduate and/or graduate teaching, internship, and research work. Advise students on academic and vocational curricula and on career issues. Collaborate with colleagues to address teaching and research issues. Compile bibliographies of specialized materials for outside reading assignments. Serve on academic or administrative committees that deal with institutional policies, departmental matters, and academic issues. Participate in student recruitment, registration, and placement activities.

Education/Training Required: Doctoral degree. **Education and Training Programs:** Architectural Engineering; Architecture (BArch, BA/BS, MArch, MA/MS, PhD); City/Urban, Community and Regional Planning; Environmental Design/Architecture; Interior Architecture; Landscape Architecture (BS, BSLA, BLA, MSLA, MLA, PhD); Teacher Education and Professional Development, Specific Subject Areas, Other. **Knowledge/Courses:** Fine Arts; Design; Building and Construction; History and Archeology; Engineering and Technology; Philosophy and Theology.

Artistic-A

Career Clusters: 02 Architecture and Construction; 05 Education and Training; 15 Science, Technology, Engineering, and Mathematics. **Career Pathways:** 02.1 Design/Pre-Construction; 05.3 Teaching/Training; 15.1 Engineering and Technology.

Skills: Writing; Instructing; Learning Strategies; Reading Comprehension; Speaking; Mathematics; Active Learning; Complex Problem Solving.

Work Environment: Indoors; sitting.

Art Directors

❋ Personality Type: Artistic-Enterprising
❋ Annual Earnings: $80,630
❋ Earnings Growth Potential: High (46.9%)
❋ Growth: 11.7%
❋ Annual Job Openings: 2,870
❋ Self-Employed: 60.2%

Considerations for Job Outlook: Demand for digital and multimedia artwork is expected to drive growth. Competition should be keen for certain kinds of jobs.

Formulate design concepts and presentation approaches and direct workers engaged in art work, layout design, and copy writing for visual communications media, such as magazines, books, newspapers, and packaging. Formulate basic layout design or presentation approach, and specify material details, such as style and size of type, photographs, graphics, animation, video, and sound. Review and approve proofs of printed copy and art, and copy materials developed by staff members. Manage own accounts and projects, working within budget and scheduling requirements. Confer with creative, art, copy-writing, or production department heads to discuss client requirements and presentation concepts and to coordinate creative activities. Present final layouts to clients for approval. Confer with clients to determine objectives; budget; background information; and presentation approaches, styles, and techniques. Hire, train, and direct staff members who develop design concepts into art layouts or who

prepare layouts for printing. Work with creative directors to develop design solutions. Review illustrative material to determine if it conforms to standards and specifications. Attend photo shoots and printing sessions to ensure that the products needed are obtained. Create custom illustrations or other graphic elements. Mark up, paste, and complete layouts, and write typography instructions to prepare materials for typesetting or printing. Negotiate with printers and estimators to determine what services will be performed. Conceptualize and help design interfaces for multimedia games, products, and devices.

Education/Training Required: Work experience plus degree. **Education and Training Programs:** Graphic Design; Intermedia/Multimedia. **Knowledge/Courses:** Fine Arts; Design; Communications and Media; Production and Processing; Computers and Electronics; Administration and Management.

Career Cluster: 03 Arts, Audio/Video Technology, and Communications. **Career Pathway:** 03.3 Visual Arts.

Skills: Management of Financial Resources; Management of Material Resources; Operations Analysis; Coordination; Management of Personnel Resources; Systems Evaluation; Learning Strategies; Instructing.

Work Environment: Indoors; sitting; using hands; repetitive motions.

Art, Drama, and Music Teachers, Postsecondary

Look for the job description among the Social jobs.

Astronomers

* ❋ Personality Type: Investigative-Artistic-Realistic
* ❋ Annual Earnings: $87,260
* ❋ Earnings Growth Potential: High (44.2%)
* ❋ Growth: 15.6%
* ❋ Annual Job Openings: 70
* ❋ Self-Employed: 0.0%

Considerations for Job Outlook: An increased focus on basic research, particularly that related to energy, is expected to drive employment growth for these workers. Prospects should be favorable for astronomers in government and academia.

Observe, research, and interpret celestial and astronomical phenomena to increase basic knowledge and apply such information to practical problems. Study celestial phenomena, using a variety of ground-based and space-borne telescopes and scientific instruments. Analyze research data to determine its significance, using computers. Present research findings at scientific conferences and in papers written for scientific journals. Measure radio, infrared, gamma, and X-ray emissions from extraterrestrial sources. Develop theories based on personal observations or on observations and theories of other astronomers. Raise funds for scientific research. Collaborate with other astronomers to carry out research projects. Develop instrumentation and software for astronomical observation and analysis. Teach astronomy or astrophysics. Develop and modify astronomy-related programs for public presentation. Calculate orbits and determine sizes, shapes, brightness, and motions of different celestial bodies. Direct the operations of a planetarium.

Education/Training Required: Doctoral degree. **Education and Training Programs:** Astronomy; Astronomy and Astrophysics, Other; Astrophysics; Planetary Astronomy and Science. **Knowledge/Courses:** Physics; Mathematics; Computers and Electronics; Engineering and Technology; Chemistry; Education and Training.

Career Cluster: 15 Science, Technology, Engineering, and Mathematics. **Career Pathway:** 15.2 Science and Mathematics.

Skills: Science; Mathematics; Active Learning; Writing; Reading Comprehension; Technology Design; Operations Analysis; Management of Financial Resources.

Work Environment: More often outdoors than indoors; sitting.

Biochemists and Biophysicists

Look for the job description among the Investigative jobs.

Camera Operators, Television, Video, and Motion Picture

* ❋ Personality Type: Realistic-Artistic
* ❋ Annual Earnings: $40,390
* ❋ Earnings Growth Potential: High (49.7%)
* ❋ Growth: 9.2%
* ❋ Annual Job Openings: 890
* ❋ Self-Employed: 26.2%

Considerations for Job Outlook: Projected employment growth will be driven by increases in the motion picture and video industry; however, that growth should be tempered by automation in broadcasting. Competition is expected to be keen.

Operate television, video, or motion picture camera to photograph images or scenes for various purposes, such as TV broadcasts, advertising, video production, or motion pictures. Operate television or motion picture cameras to record scenes for television broadcasts, advertising, or motion pictures. Compose and frame each shot, applying the technical aspects of light, lenses, film, filters, and camera settings to achieve the effects sought by directors. Operate zoom lenses, changing images according to specifications and rehearsal instructions. Use cameras in any of several different camera mounts, such as stationary, track-mounted, or crane-mounted. Test, clean, and maintain equipment to ensure proper working condition. Adjust positions and controls of cameras, printers, and related equipment to change focus, exposure, and lighting. Gather and edit raw footage on location to send to television affiliates for broadcast, using electronic news-gathering or film-production equipment. Confer with directors, sound and lighting technicians, electricians, and other crew members to discuss assignments and determine filming sequences, desired effects, camera movements, and lighting requirements. Observe sets or locations for potential problems and to determine filming and lighting requirements. Instruct camera operators regarding camera setups, angles, distances, movement, variables, and cues for starting and stopping filming. Select and assemble cameras, accessories, equipment, and film stock to be used during filming, using knowledge of filming techniques, requirements, and computations.

Education/Training Required: Postsecondary vocational training. **Education and Training Programs:** Audiovisual Communications Technologies/Technicians, Other; Cinematography and Film/Video Production; Radio and Television Broadcasting Technology/Technician. **Knowledge/Courses:** Communications and Media; Telecommunications; Computers and Electronics; Engineering and Technology.

Career Cluster: 03 Arts, Audio/Video Technology, and Communications. **Career Pathways:** 03.1 Audio and Video Technology and Film; 03.5 Journalism and Broadcasting.

Skills: Equipment Selection; Operation and Control; Quality Control Analysis; Technology Design; Management of Material Resources; Operation Monitoring; Coordination; Operations Analysis.

Work Environment: More often indoors than outdoors; standing; using hands; repetitive motions; noise; bright or inadequate lighting.

Commercial and Industrial Designers

* Personality Type: Artistic-Enterprising-Realistic
* Annual Earnings: $58,230
* Earnings Growth Potential: High (43.0%)
* Growth: 9.0%
* Annual Job Openings: 1,760
* Self-Employed: 26.7%

Considerations for Job Outlook: An increase in demand for new and upgraded products should lead to job growth for these workers, but this growth is expected to be tempered by the use of design firms abroad. Keen competition is expected.

Develop and design manufactured products, such as cars, home appliances, and children's toys. Combine artistic talent with research on product use, marketing, and materials to create the most functional and appealing product design. Prepare sketches of ideas and detailed drawings, illustrations, artwork, or blueprints, using drafting instruments, paints and brushes, or computer-aided design equipment. Direct and coordinate the fabrication of models or samples and the drafting of working drawings and specification sheets from sketches. Modify and refine designs, using working models, to conform with customer specifications, production limitations, or changes in design trends. Coordinate the look and function of product lines. Confer with engineering, marketing, production, or sales departments, or with customers, to establish and evaluate design concepts for manufactured products. Present designs and reports to customers or design committees for approval, and discuss need for modification. Evaluate feasibility of design ideas based on factors such as appearance, safety, function, serviceability, budget, production costs/methods, and market characteristics. Read publications, attend showings, and study competing products and design styles and motifs to obtain perspective and generate design concepts. Research production specifications, costs, production materials, and manufacturing methods, and provide cost

Artistic-C

estimates and itemized production requirements. Design graphic material for use as ornamentation, illustration, or advertising on manufactured materials and packaging or containers.

Education/Training Required: Bachelor's degree. **Education and Training Programs:** Commercial and Advertising Art; Design and Applied Arts, Other; Design and Visual Communications, General; Industrial and Product Design. **Knowledge/Courses:** Design; Engineering and Technology; Mechanical Devices; Production and Processing; Physics; Fine Arts.

Career Cluster: 03 Arts, Audio/Video Technology, and Communications. **Career Pathways:** 03.1 Audio and Video Technology and Film; 03.3 Visual Arts.

Skills: Technology Design; Operations Analysis; Systems Evaluation; Science; Mathematics; Active Learning; Systems Analysis; Quality Control Analysis.

Work Environment: Indoors; sitting; using hands; noise.

Communications Teachers, Postsecondary

- ❋ Personality Type: Social-Artistic
- ❋ Annual Earnings: $60,300
- ❋ Earnings Growth Potential: High (44.5%)
- ❋ Growth: 15.1%
- ❋ Annual Job Openings: 800
- ❋ Self-Employed: 0.2%

Considerations for Job Outlook: Enrollments in postsecondary institutions are expected to continue rising as more people attend college and as workers return to school to update their skills. Opportunities for part-time or temporary positions should be favorable, but significant competition exists for tenure-track positions.

Teach courses in communications, such as organizational communications, public relations, **radio/television broadcasting, and journalism.** Evaluate and grade students' classwork, assignments, and papers. Prepare course materials such as syllabi, homework assignments, and handouts. Initiate, facilitate, and moderate classroom discussions. Prepare and deliver lectures to undergraduate or graduate students on topics such as public speaking, media criticism, and oral traditions. Compile, administer, and grade examinations, or assign this work to others. Maintain student attendance records, grades, and other required records. Plan, evaluate, and revise curricula, course content, course materials, and methods of instruction. Maintain regularly scheduled office hours to advise and assist students. Keep abreast of developments in the field by reading current literature, talking with colleagues, and participating in professional conferences. Advise students on academic and vocational curricula and on career issues. Supervise undergraduate or graduate teaching, internship, and research work. Select and obtain materials and supplies such as textbooks. Collaborate with colleagues to address teaching and research issues. Conduct research in a particular field of knowledge, and publish findings in professional journals, books, or electronic media. Participate in student recruitment, registration, and placement activities. Serve on academic or administrative committees that deal with institutional policies, departmental matters, and academic issues.

Education/Training Required: Doctoral degree. **Education and Training Programs:** Advertising; Broadcast Journalism; Communication, Journalism, and Related Programs, Other; Digital Communication and Media/Multimedia; Health Communication; Humanities/Humanistic Studies; Journalism; Journalism, Other; Mass Communication/Media Studies; Political Communication; Public Relations/Image Management; Radio and Television; Speech Communication and Rhetoric. **Knowledge/Courses:** Communications and Media; English Language; Sociology and Anthropology; Philosophy and Theology; Education and Training; History and Archeology.

Career Clusters: 03 Arts, Audio/Video Technology, and Communications; 04 Business, Management, and Administration; 05 Education and Training; 08 Health Science. **Career Pathways:** 03.5 Journalism and Broadcasting; 04.1 Management; 04.5 Marketing; 05.3 Teaching/Training; 08.3 Health Informatics.

Skills: Learning Strategies; Instructing; Speaking; Writing; Reading Comprehension; Active Learning; Active Listening; Critical Thinking.

Work Environment: Indoors; sitting.

Editors

- Personality Type: Artistic-Enterprising-Conventional
- Annual Earnings: $51,470
- Earnings Growth Potential: High (43.9%)
- Growth: –0.3%
- Annual Job Openings: 3,390
- Self-Employed: 12.1%

Considerations for Job Outlook: Projected job growth for these workers stems from increased use of online media and growing demand for web-based information. But print publishing is expected to continue weakening. Job competition should be keen.

Perform variety of editorial duties, such as laying out, indexing, and revising content of written materials, in preparation for final publication. Prepare, rewrite, and edit copy to improve readability, or supervise others who do this work. Read copy or proof to detect and correct errors in spelling, punctuation, and syntax. Allocate print space for story text, photos, and illustrations according to space parameters and copy significance, using knowledge of layout principles. Plan the contents of publications according to the publication's style, editorial policy, and publishing requirements. Verify facts, dates, and statistics, using standard reference sources. Review and approve proofs submitted by composing room prior to publication production. Develop story or content ideas, considering reader or audience appeal. Oversee publication production, including artwork, layout, computer typesetting, and printing, ensur-

ing adherence to deadlines and budget requirements. Confer with management and editorial staff members regarding placement and emphasis of developing news stories. Assign topics, events, and stories to individual writers or reporters for coverage. Read, evaluate, and edit manuscripts or other materials submitted for publication, and confer with authors regarding changes in content, style, organization, or publication. Monitor news-gathering operations to ensure utilization of all news sources, such as press releases, telephone contacts, radio, television, wire services, and other reporters.

Education/Training Required: Bachelor's degree. **Education and Training Programs:** Broadcast Journalism; Business/Corporate Communications; Communication, Journalism, and Related Programs, Other; English Language and Literature, General; Family and Consumer Sciences/Human Sciences Communication; Journalism; Mass Communication/Media Studies; Publishing. **Knowledge/Courses:** Communications and Media; History and Archeology; Fine Arts; Geography; English Language; Clerical Practices.

Career Clusters: 03 Arts, Audio/Video Technology, and Communications; 08 Health Science. **Career Pathways:** 03.5 Journalism and Broadcasting; 08.3 Health Informatics.

Skills: Writing; Reading Comprehension; Quality Control Analysis; Negotiation; Management of Personnel Resources; Time Management; Persuasion; Active Learning.

Work Environment: Indoors; sitting; using hands; repetitive motions; noise.

Fashion Designers

- Personality Type: Artistic-Enterprising-Realistic
- Annual Earnings: $64,530
- Earnings Growth Potential: High (49.6%)
- Growth: 0.8%
- Annual Job Openings: 720
- Self-Employed: 26.8%

Artistic-F

Considerations for Job Outlook: Some job growth is expected due to an increasing population; however, many jobs in apparel manufacturing will continue to move abroad. Competition should be keen.

Design clothing and accessories. Create original garments, or design garments that follow well-established fashion trends. May develop the line of color and kinds of materials. Examine sample garments on and off models, then modify designs to achieve desired effects. Determine prices for styles. Select materials and production techniques to be used for products. Draw patterns for articles designed, then cut patterns and cut material according to patterns, using measuring instruments and scissors. Design custom clothing and accessories for individuals, retailers, or theatrical, television, or film productions. Attend fashion shows and review garment magazines and manuals to gather information about fashion trends and consumer preferences. Develop a group of products and/or accessories, and market them through venues such as boutiques or mail-order catalogs. Test fabrics or oversee testing so that garment-care labels can be created. Visit textile showrooms to keep up to date on the latest fabrics. Sew together sections of material to form mockups or samples of garments or articles, using sewing equipment. Research the styles and periods of clothing needed for film or theatrical productions. Direct and coordinate workers involved in drawing and cutting patterns and constructing samples or finished garments. Purchase new or used clothing and accessory items as needed to complete designs. Provide sample garments to agents and sales representatives, and arrange for showings of sample garments at sales meetings or fashion shows. Identify target markets for designs, looking at factors such as age, gender, and socioeconomic status.

Education/Training Required: Associate degree. **Education and Training Programs:** Apparel and Textile Manufacture; Fashion and Fabric Consultant Training; Fashion/Apparel Design; Textile Science. **Knowledge/Courses:** Fine Arts; Design; Sales and Marketing; Production and Processing; Communications and Media; Administration and Management.

Career Clusters: 03 Arts, Audio/Video Technology, and Communications; 13 Manufacturing. **Career Pathways:** 03.3 Visual Arts; 13.2 Manufacturing Production Process Development.

Skills: Operations Analysis; Management of Financial Resources; Management of Material Resources; Systems Evaluation; Time Management; Negotiation; Persuasion; Social Perceptiveness.

Work Environment: Indoors; sitting; using hands; repetitive motions; noise; contaminants; cramped work space.

Film and Video Editors

* Personality Type: Artistic-Enterprising-Investigative
* Annual Earnings: $50,930
* Earnings Growth Potential: High (49.0%)
* Growth: 11.9%
* Annual Job Openings: 930
* Self-Employed: 26.3%

Considerations for Job Outlook: Projected employment growth will be driven by increases in the motion picture and video industry; however, that growth should be tempered by automation in broadcasting. Competition is expected to be keen.

Edit motion picture soundtracks, film, and video. Cut shot sequences to different angles at specific points in scenes, making each individual cut as fluid and seamless as possible. Study scripts to become familiar with production concepts and requirements. Edit films and videotapes to insert music, dialogue, and sound effects; to arrange films into sequences; and to correct errors, using editing equipment. Select and combine the most effective shots of each scene to form a logical and smoothly running story. Mark frames where a particular shot or piece of sound is to begin or end. Determine the specific audio and visual effects and music necessary to complete films. Verify key numbers and time codes on materials. Organize and string together raw footage into a continuous whole according to scripts or the instructions of directors and producers. Review assembled films or edited videotapes on screens or monitors to determine if corrections are necessary. Program computerized graphic effects. Review footage sequence by sequence to become familiar with it before assembling it into a final product. Set up and operate computer editing systems, electronic titling systems, video switching equipment, and digital video effects units to produce a final product. Record needed sounds, or obtain them from sound effects libraries. Confer with producers and directors concerning layout or editing approaches needed to increase dramatic or entertainment value of productions.

Education/Training Required: Bachelor's degree. **Education and Training Programs:** Audiovisual Communications Technologies/Technicians, Other; Cinematography and Film/Video Production; Communications Technology/Technician; Photojournalism; Radio and Television; Radio and Television Broadcasting Technology/Technician. **Knowledge/Courses:** Communications and Media; Fine Arts; Computers and Electronics; Production and Processing; Telecommunications; Sales and Marketing.

Career Cluster: 03 Arts, Audio/Video Technology, and Communications. **Career Pathways:** 03.1 Audio and Video Technology and Film; 03.5 Journalism and Broadcasting; 03.6 Telecommunications.

Skills: Technology Design; Programming; Time Management; Active Listening; Systems Evaluation; Operations Analysis; Persuasion; Systems Analysis.

Work Environment: Indoors; sitting; using hands; repetitive motions.

Foreign Language and Literature Teachers, Postsecondary

- ❋ Personality Type: Social-Artistic-Investigative
- ❋ Annual Earnings: $59,080
- ❋ Earnings Growth Potential: High (42.8%)
- ❋ Growth: 15.1%
- ❋ Annual Job Openings: 900
- ❋ Self-Employed: 0.2%

Considerations for Job Outlook: Enrollments in postsecondary institutions are expected to continue rising as more people attend college and as workers return to school to update their skills. Opportunities for part-time or temporary positions should be favorable, but significant competition exists for tenure-track positions.

Teach courses in foreign (i.e., other than English) languages and literature. Evaluate and grade students' classwork, assignments, and papers. Prepare course materials such as syllabi, homework assignments, and handouts. Initiate, facilitate, and moderate classroom discussions. Maintain student attendance records, grades, and other required records. Compile, administer, and grade examinations, or assign this work to others. Plan, evaluate, and revise curricula, course content, course materials, and methods of instruction. Prepare and deliver lectures to undergraduate and graduate students on topics such as how to speak and write a foreign language and the cultural aspects of areas where a particular language is used. Maintain regularly scheduled office hours to advise and assist students. Select and obtain materials and supplies such as textbooks. Keep abreast of developments in the field by reading current literature, talking with colleagues, and participating in professional organizations and activities. Advise students on academic and vocational curricula and on career issues. Conduct research in a particular field of knowledge, and publish findings in scholarly journals, books, and/or electronic media. Collaborate with colleagues to address teaching and research issues. Serve on academic or administrative committees that deal with institutional policies, departmental matters, and academic issues. Participate in student recruitment, registration, and placement activities.

Education/Training Required: Doctoral degree. **Education and Training Programs:** Ancient Near Eastern and Biblical Languages, Literatures, and Linguistics; Ancient/Classical Greek Language and Literature; Arabic Language and Literature; Celtic Languages, Literatures, and Linguistics; Chinese Language and Literature; Classics and Classical Languages, Literatures, and Linguistics, General;

Artistic-F

East Asian Languages, Literatures, and Linguistics, Other; Filipino/Tagalog Language and Literature; Foreign Languages and Literatures, General; Foreign Languages, Literatures, and Linguistics, Other; French Language and Literature; German Language and Literature; Germanic Languages, Literatures, and Linguistics, Other; Hebrew Language and Literature; Hindi Language and Literature; Italian Language and Literature; Japanese Language and Literature; Language Interpretation and Translation; Latin Language and Literature; Linguistics; Middle/Near Eastern and Semitic Languages, Literatures, and Linguistics, Other; others. **Knowledge/Courses:** Foreign Language; History and Archeology Philosophy and Theology; Sociology and Anthropology; English Language; Education and Training.

Career Cluster: 05 Education and Training. **Career Pathway:** 05.3 Teaching/Training.

Skills: Writing; Learning Strategies; Speaking; Instructing; Reading Comprehension; Active Listening; Active Learning; Monitoring.

Work Environment: Indoors; sitting.

Graphic Designers

- ❋ Personality Type: Artistic-Realistic-Enterprising
- ❋ Annual Earnings: $43,500
- ❋ Earnings Growth Potential: Medium (39.8%)
- ❋ Growth: 12.9%
- ❋ Annual Job Openings: 12,480
- ❋ Self-Employed: 26.3%

Considerations for Job Outlook: Advertising firms that specialize in digital and interactive designs are expected to drive growth, but declines in print publishing will temper this growth. Competition is expected to be keen.

Design or create graphics to meet specific commercial or promotional needs such as packaging, displays, or logos. May use a variety of media to achieve artistic or decorative effects. Create designs, concepts, and sample layouts based on knowledge of layout principles and esthetic design concepts. Determine size and arrangement of illustrative material and copy; and select style and size of type. Confer with clients to discuss and determine layout designs. Develop graphics and layouts for product illustrations, company logos, and Internet websites. Review final layouts, and suggest improvements as needed. Prepare illustrations or rough sketches of material, discussing them with clients or supervisors and making necessary changes. Use computer software to generate new images. Key information into computer equipment to create layouts for client or supervisor. Maintain archive of images, photos, or previous work products. Prepare notes and instructions for workers who assemble and prepare final layouts for printing. Draw and print charts, graphs, illustrations, and other artwork, using computer. Study illustrations and photographs to plan presentations of materials, products, or services. Research new software or design concepts. Mark up, paste, and assemble final layouts to prepare layouts for printer. Produce still and animated graphics for on-air and taped portions of television news broadcasts, using electronic video equipment. Photograp h layouts, using cameras, to make layout prints for supervisors or clients. Develop negatives and prints to produce layout photographs, using negative and print developing equipment and tools.

Education/Training Required: Bachelor's degree. **Education and Training Programs:** Agricultural Communication/Journalism; Commercial and Advertising Art; Computer Graphics; Design and Visual Communications, General; Graphic Design; Industrial and Product Design; Web Page, Digital/Multimedia and Information Resources Design. **Knowledge/Courses:** Fine Arts; Design; Communications and Media; Sales and Marketing; Sociology and Anthropology; Computers and Electronics.

Career Clusters: 03 Arts, Audio/Video Technology, and Communications; 11 Information Technology. **Career Pathways:** 03.1 Audio and Video Technology and Film; 03.3 Visual Arts; 11.1 Network Systems.

Skills: Operations Analysis; Technology Design; Negotiation; Management of Financial Resources; Time Management; Complex Problem Solving; Reading Comprehension; Writing.

Work Environment: Indoors; sitting; using hands; repetitive motions.

Hairdressers, Hairstylists, and Cosmetologists

* Personality Type: Artistic-Enterprising-Social
* Annual Earnings: $22,760
* Earnings Growth Potential: Low (28.2%)
* Growth: 20.1%
* Annual Job Openings: 21,950
* Self-Employed: 43.5%

Considerations for Job Outlook: A larger population and increasing demand for personal-appearance services, especially skin care, are expected to create jobs for these workers. Prospects should be good, especially for job-seekers who have formal training.

Provide beauty services, such as shampooing, cutting, coloring, and styling hair and massaging and treating scalp. May also apply makeup, dress wigs, perform hair removal, and provide nail and skin care services. Keep work stations clean, and sanitize tools such as scissors and combs. Cut, trim, and shape hair or hairpieces based on customers' instructions, hair type, and facial features, using clippers, scissors, trimmers, and razors. Analyze patrons' hair and other physical features to determine and recommend beauty treatment or suggest hairstyles. Schedule client appointments. Bleach, dye, or tint hair, using applicator or brush. Update and maintain customer-information records, such as beauty services provided. Shampoo, rinse, condition, and dry hair and scalp or hairpieces with water, liquid soap, or other solutions. Operate cash registers to receive payments from patrons. Demonstrate and sell hair-care products and cosmetics. Apply water, setting, straightening, or waving solutions to hair, and use curlers, rollers, hot combs, and curling irons to press and curl hair. Develop new styles and techniques. Comb, brush, and spray hair or wigs to set style. Shape eyebrows and remove facial hair, using depilatory cream, tweezers, electrolysis, or wax. Administer therapeutic medication, and advise patron to seek medical treatment for chronic or contagious scalp conditions. Massage and treat scalp for hygienic and remedial purposes, using hands, fingers, or vibrating equipment. Shave, trim, and shape beards and moustaches. Train or supervise other hairstylists, hairdressers, and assistants.

Education/Training Required: Postsecondary vocational training. **Education and Training Programs:** Cosmetology and Related Personal Grooming Arts, Other; Cosmetology, Barber/Styling, and Nail Instructor; Cosmetology/Cosmetologist Training, General; Electrolysis/Electrology and Electrolysis Technician Training; Hair Styling/Stylist and Hair Design; Make-Up Artist/Specialist Training; Permanent Cosmetics/Makeup and Tattooing; Salon/Beauty Salon Management/Manager Training. **Knowledge/Courses:** Chemistry; Sales and Marketing.

Career Cluster: 10 Human Services. **Career Pathway:** 10.4 Personal Care Services.

Skills: Service Orientation; Learning Strategies; Instructing; Equipment Selection; Operations Analysis.

Work Environment: Indoors; standing; using hands; bending or twisting the body; repetitive motions; contaminants; hazardous conditions; minor burns, cuts, bites, or stings.

Interior Designers

* Personality Type: Artistic-Enterprising
* Annual Earnings: $46,280
* Earnings Growth Potential: High (43.0%)
* Growth: 19.4%
* Annual Job Openings: 3,590
* Self-Employed: 26.7%

Artistic-I

Considerations for Job Outlook: A growing interest in interior design by both homeowners and businesses is expected to lead to employment increases in this occupation. Competition is expected to be keen, and job-seekers with formal training should have the best opportunities.

Plan, design, and furnish interiors of residential, commercial, or industrial buildings. Formulate design that is practical, aesthetic, and conducive to intended purposes, such as raising productivity, selling merchandise, or improving lifestyle. May specialize in a particular field, style, or phase of interior design. Estimate material requirements and costs, and present design to client for approval. Confer with client to determine factors affecting planning interior environments, such as budget, architectural preferences, and purpose and function. Advise client on interior design factors such as space planning, layout, utilization of furnishings or equipment, and color coordination. Select or design and purchase furnishings, artwork, and accessories. Formulate environmental plan to be practical, aesthetic, and conducive to intended purposes such as raising productivity or selling merchandise. Subcontract fabrication, installation, and arrangement of carpeting, fixtures, accessories, draperies, paint and wall coverings, artwork, furniture, and related items. Render design ideas in form of paste-ups or drawings. Plan and design interior environments for boats, planes, buses, trains, and other enclosed spaces.

Education/Training Required: Associate degree. **Education and Training Programs:** Facilities Planning and Management; Interior Architecture; Interior Design; Textile Science. **Knowledge/ Courses:** Design; Fine Arts; Building and Construction; Sales and Marketing; History and Archeology; Psychology.

Career Clusters: 02 Architecture and Construction; 03 Arts, Audio/Video Technology, and Communications; 13 Manufacturing; 14 Marketing, Sales, and Service. **Career Pathways:** 02.1 Design/ Pre-Construction; 03.3 Visual Arts; 13.3 Maintenance, Installation, and Repair; 14.2 Professional Sales and Marketing.

Skills: Management of Financial Resources; Operations Analysis; Management of Material Resources; Negotiation; Persuasion; Service Orientation; Coordination; Mathematics.

Work Environment: Indoors; sitting.

Interpreters and Translators

- ❋ Personality Type: Artistic-Social
- ❋ Annual Earnings: $43,300
- ❋ Earnings Growth Potential: High (47.0%)
- ❋ Growth: 22.2%
- ❋ Annual Job Openings: 2,340
- ❋ Self-Employed: 26.1%

Considerations for Job Outlook: Globalization and large increases in the number of nonnative English speakers in the United States are expected to lead to employment increases for these workers. Job prospects vary by specialty and language.

Translate or interpret written, oral, or sign language text into another language for others. Follow ethical codes that protect the confidentiality of information. Identify and resolve conflicts related to the meanings of words, concepts, practices, or behaviors. Proofread, edit, and revise translated materials. Translate messages simultaneously or consecutively into specified languages orally or by using hand signs, maintaining message content, context, and style as much as possible. Check translations of technical terms and terminology to ensure that they are accurate and remain consistent throughout translation revisions. Read written materials such as legal documents, scientific works, or news reports, and rewrite material into specified languages. Refer to reference materials such as dictionaries, lexicons, encyclopedias, and computerized terminology banks as needed to ensure translation accuracy. Compile terminology and information to be used in translations, including technical terms such as those for legal or medical material. Adapt translations to students' cognitive and grade levels, collaborating with educational team members as necessary. Listen to speakers' statements to determine meanings and to prepare translations, using electronic listening systems as necessary. Check original texts or confer with authors to ensure that translations retain the content, meaning, and feeling of the original material.

Education/Training Required: Long-term on-the-job training. **Education and Training Programs:** American Sign Language (ASL); Ancient Near Eastern and Biblical Languages, Literatures, and Linguistics; Ancient/Classical Greek Language and Literature; Arabic Language and Literature; Celtic Languages, Literatures, and Linguistics; Chinese Language and Literature; Classics and Classical Languages, Literatures, and Linguistics, General; East Asian Languages, Literatures, and Linguistics, Other; Education/Teaching of Individuals with Hearing Impairments, Including Deafness; Foreign Languages and Literatures, General; Foreign Languages, Literatures, and Linguistics, Other; French Language and Literature; German Language and Literature; Germanic Languages, Literatures, and Linguistics, Other; Hebrew Language and Literature; Hindi Language and Literature; Italian Language and Literature; Japanese Language and Literature; Language Interpretation and Translation; Latin Language and Literature; Linguistics; Middle/Near Eastern and Semitic Languages, Literatures, and Linguistics, Other; others. **Knowledge/Courses:** Foreign Language; English Language; Geography; Sociology and Anthropology; Communications and Media; Computers and Electronics.

Career Clusters: 05 Education and Training; 10 Human Services. **Career Pathways:** 05.3 Teaching/Training; 10.5 Consumer Services Career.

Skills: Writing; Reading Comprehension; Active Listening; Speaking; Social Perceptiveness; Service Orientation; Learning Strategies; Monitoring.

Work Environment: Indoors; sitting; repetitive motions.

Kindergarten Teachers, Except Special Education

Look for the job description among the Social jobs.

Landscape Architects

- ❀ Personality Type: Artistic-Investigative-Realistic
- ❀ Annual Earnings: $62,090
- ❀ Earnings Growth Potential: Medium (40.6%)
- ❀ Growth: 19.6%
- ❀ Annual Job Openings: 980
- ❀ Self-Employed: 21.3%

Considerations for Job Outlook: Employment should grow as new construction and redevelopment create more opportunities for these workers. Opportunities should be good, but entry-level jobseekers should expect keen competition for openings in large firms.

Plan and design land areas for such projects as parks and other recreational facilities; airports; highways; hospitals; schools; land subdivisions; and commercial, industrial, and residential sites. Prepare site plans, specifications, and cost estimates for land development, coordinating arrangement of existing and proposed land features and structures. Confer with clients, engineering personnel, and architects on overall program. Compile and analyze data on conditions such as location, drainage, and placement of structures for environmental reports and landscaping plans. Inspect landscape work to ensure compliance with specifications, approve quality of materials and work, and advise client and construction personnel.

Education/Training Required: Bachelor's degree. **Education and Training Programs:** Environmental Design/Architecture; Landscape Architecture (BS, BSLA, BLA, MSLA, MLA, PhD). **Knowledge/**

Artistic-L

Courses: Design; Geography; Building and Construction; Fine Arts; Biology; History and Archeology.

Career Cluster: 02 Architecture and Construction. **Career Pathway:** 02.1 Design/Pre-Construction.

Skills: Operations Analysis; Science; Management of Financial Resources; Systems Evaluation; Management of Material Resources; Management of Personnel Resources; Systems Analysis; Persuasion.

Work Environment: More often indoors than outdoors; sitting.

Makeup Artists, Theatrical and Performance

- ❋ Personality Type: Artistic-Realistic
- ❋ Annual Earnings: $38,130
- ❋ Earnings Growth Potential: Very high (53.5%)
- ❋ Growth: 17.0%
- ❋ Annual Job Openings: 90
- ❋ Self-Employed: 32.1%

Considerations for Job Outlook: Steady growth in the entertainment industry should result in increased employment for these workers. Competition should be keen. Job openings will be concentrated in areas that have many media production companies, such as Los Angeles and New York.

Apply makeup to performers to reflect period, setting, and situation of their role. Confer with stage or motion picture officials and performers in order to determine desired effects. Duplicate work precisely in order to replicate characters' appearances on a daily basis. Establish budgets, and work within budgetary limits. Apply makeup to enhance and/or alter the appearance of people appearing in productions such as movies. Alter or maintain makeup during productions as necessary to compensate for lighting changes or to achieve continuity of effect. Select desired makeup shades from stock, or mix oil, grease, and coloring in order to achieve specific color effects. Cleanse and tone the skin in order to prepare it for makeup application. Assess performers' skin-type in order to ensure that make-up will not cause break-outs or skin irritations. Analyze a script, noting events that affect each character's appearance, so that plans can be made for each scene. Requisition or acquire needed materials for special effects, including wigs, beards, and special cosmetics. Write makeup sheets, and take photos in order to document specific looks and the products that were used to achieve the looks. Examine sketches, photographs, and plaster models in order to obtain desired character image depiction. Attach prostheses to performers and apply makeup in order to create special features or effects such as scars, aging, or illness. Evaluate environmental characteristics such as venue size and lighting plans in order to determine makeup requirements.

Education/Training Required: Postsecondary vocational training. **Education and Training Programs:** Cosmetology/Cosmetologist Training, General; Make-Up Artist/Specialist Training; Permanent Cosmetics/Makeup and Tattooing. **Knowledge/Courses:** Fine Arts; Chemistry; Design; Sales and Marketing; Personnel and Human Resources; Psychology.

Career Cluster: 10 Human Services. **Career Pathway:** 10.4 Personal Care Services.

Skills: Management of Financial Resources; Management of Material Resources; Operations Analysis; Equipment Selection; Active Learning; Technology Design; Coordination; Quality Control Analysis.

Work Environment: More often indoors than outdoors; standing; using hands; repetitive motions; bright or inadequate lighting; contaminants; cramped work space.

Marriage and Family Therapists

* Personality Type: Social-Artistic-Investigative
* Annual Earnings: $45,720
* Earnings Growth Potential: High (47.8%)
* Growth: 14.5%
* Annual Job Openings: 950
* Self-Employed: 5.9%

Considerations for Job Outlook: Increasing demand for services provided by counselors is expected to result in employment growth. But growth will vary by specialty and will be faster for mental health, substance abuse and behavioral disorder, and rehabilitation counselors than for counselors of other specialties. Opportunities should be favorable, particularly in rural areas.

Diagnose and treat mental and emotional disorders, whether cognitive, affective, or behavioral, within the context of marriage and family systems. Apply psychotherapeutic and family systems theories and techniques in the delivery of professional services to individuals, couples, and families for the purpose of treating such diagnosed nervous and mental disorders. Ask questions that will help clients identify their feelings and behaviors. Counsel clients on concerns such as unsatisfactory relationships, divorce and separation, child rearing, home management, and financial difficulties. Encourage individuals and family members to develop and use skills and strategies for confronting their problems in a constructive manner. Maintain case files that include activities, progress notes, evaluations, and recommendations. Collect information about clients, using techniques such as testing, interviewing, discussion, and observation. Develop and implement individualized treatment plans addressing family relationship problems. Determine whether clients should be counseled or referred to other specialists in such fields as medicine, psychiatry, and legal aid. Confer with clients in order to develop plans for post-treatment activities. Confer with other counselors to analyze individual cases and to coordinate counseling services. Follow up on results of counseling programs and clients' adjustments to determine effectiveness of programs. Provide instructions to clients on how to obtain help with legal, financial, and other personal issues. Contact doctors, schools, social workers, juvenile counselors, law enforcement personnel, and others to gather information in order to make recommendations to courts for the resolution of child custody or visitation disputes.

Education/Training Required: Master's degree. **Education and Training Programs:** Clinical Pastoral Counseling/Patient Counseling; Marriage and Family Therapy/Counseling; Social Work. **Knowledge/Courses:** Therapy and Counseling; Psychology; Philosophy and Theology; Sociology and Anthropology; Medicine and Dentistry; Customer and Personal Service.

Career Cluster: 10 Human Services. **Career Pathways:** 10.2 Counseling and Mental Health Services; 10.3 Family and Community Services.

Skills: Social Perceptiveness; Science; Operations Analysis; Active Listening; Service Orientation; Systems Evaluation; Systems Analysis; Speaking.

Work Environment: Indoors; sitting.

Merchandise Displayers and Window Trimmers

* Personality Type: Artistic-Enterprising-Realistic
* Annual Earnings: $25,960
* Earnings Growth Potential: Low (32.9%)
* Growth: 7.1%
* Annual Job Openings: 3,220
* Self-Employed: 26.7%

Considerations for Job Outlook: About average employment growth is projected.

Plan and erect commercial displays, such as those in windows and interiors of retail stores and at trade exhibitions. Take photographs of displays and signage. Plan and erect commercial displays to entice and appeal to customers. Place prices and descriptive signs on backdrops, fixtures, merchandise, or floor. Change or rotate window displays, interior display areas, and signage to reflect changes in inventory or promotion. Obtain plans from display designers or display managers, and discuss their implementation with clients or supervisors. Develop ideas or plans for merchandise displays or window decorations. Consult with advertising and sales staff to determine type of merchandise to be featured and time and place for each display. Arrange properties, furniture, merchandise, backdrops, and other accessories as shown in prepared sketches. Construct or assemble displays and display components from fabric, glass, paper, and plastic according to specifications, using hand tools and woodworking power tools. Collaborate with others to obtain products and other display items. Use computers to produce signage. Dress mannequins for displays. Maintain props and mannequins, inspecting them for imperfections and applying preservative coatings as necessary. Select themes, lighting, colors, and props to be used. Attend training sessions and corporate planning meetings to obtain new ideas for product launches. Instruct sales staff in color-coordination of clothing racks and counter displays. Store, pack, and maintain records of props and display items.

Education/Training Required: Moderate-term on-the-job training. **Education and Training Program:** Commercial and Advertising Art. **Knowledge/Courses:** Sales and Marketing; Design; Administration and Management.

Career Cluster: 14 Marketing, Sales, and Service. **Career Pathway:** 14.2 Professional Sales and Marketing.

Skills: No data available.

Work Environment: More often indoors than outdoors; standing; climbing; walking and running; kneeling, crouching, stooping, or crawling; using hands; bending or twisting the body; repetitive motions; contaminants; cramped work space; high places.

Middle School Teachers, Except Special and Career/Technical Education

Look for the job description among the Social jobs.

Multimedia Artists and Animators

- ❋ Personality Type: Artistic-Investigative
- ❋ Annual Earnings: $58,510
- ❋ Earnings Growth Potential: High (42.2%)
- ❋ Growth: 14.2%
- ❋ Annual Job Openings: 2,890
- ❋ Self-Employed: 60.1%

Considerations for Job Outlook: Demand for digital and multimedia artwork is expected to drive growth. Competition should be keen for certain kinds of jobs. Multimedia artists and animators should have better opportunities than other artists.

Create special effects, animation, or other visual images, using film, video, computers, or other electronic tools and media, for use in products or creations such as computer games, movies, music videos, and commercials. Design complex graphics and animation, using independent judgment, creativity, and computer equipment. Create two-dimensional and three-dimensional images depicting objects in motion or illustrating a process, using computer animation or modeling programs. Make objects or characters appear lifelike by manipulating light, color, texture, shadow, and transparency or manipulating static images to give the illusion of motion. Apply story development, directing, cinematography, and editing to animation to create storyboards that show the flow of the animation and map out key scenes and characters. Assemble, typeset, scan, and produce digital camera-ready art or film negatives and printer's proofs. Script, plan, and create animated narrative sequences under tight deadlines, using computer software and hand-drawing techniques. Create basic designs, drawings, and illustrations for product labels, cartons, direct mail, or television. Create pen-and-paper images to be scanned, edited, colored, textured, or animated by computer. Develop briefings, brochures, multimedia presentations, webpages, promotional products, technical illustrations, and computer artwork for use in products, technical manuals, literature, newsletters, and slide shows. Use models to simulate the behavior of animated objects in the finished sequence. Create and install special effects as required by the script, mixing chemicals and fabricating needed parts from wood, metal, plaster, and clay.

Education/Training Required: Bachelor's degree. **Education and Training Programs:** Animation, Interactive Technology, Video Graphics and Special Effects; Drawing; Graphic Design; Intermedia/Multimedia; Painting; Printmaking; Web Page, Digital/Multimedia and Information Resources Design. **Knowledge/Courses:** Fine Arts; Communications and Media; Design; Computers and Electronics; Sales and Marketing; English Language.

Career Clusters: 03 Arts, Audio/Video Technology, and Communications; 11 Information Technology. **Career Pathways:** 03.1 Audio and Video Technology and Film; 03.2 Printing Technology; 03.3 Visual Arts; 11.1 Network Systems.

Skills: Technology Design; Programming; Management of Financial Resources; Coordination; Management of Material Resources; Negotiation; Active Listening; Systems Evaluation.

Work Environment: Indoors; sitting; using hands; repetitive motions.

Museum Technicians and Conservators

- ❋ Personality Type: Realistic-Artistic
- ❋ Annual Earnings: $37,310
- ❋ Earnings Growth Potential: Low (34.5%)
- ❋ Growth: 25.6%
- ❋ Annual Job Openings: 610
- ❋ Self-Employed: 1.9%

Considerations for Job Outlook: Employment growth for museum technicians should be strong as museum attendance levels remain high. Keen competition is expected.

Prepare specimens, such as fossils, skeletal parts, lace, and textiles, for museum collection and exhibits. May restore documents or install, arrange, and exhibit materials. Install, arrange, assemble, and prepare artifacts for exhibition, ensuring the artifacts' safety, reporting their status and condition, and identifying and correcting any problems with the setup. Coordinate exhibit installations, assisting with design; constructing displays, dioramas, display cases, and models; and ensuring the availability of necessary materials. Determine whether objects need repair, and choose the safest and most effective method of repair. Clean objects, such as paper, textiles, wood, metal, glass, rock, pottery, and furniture, using cleansers, solvents, soap solutions, and polishes. Prepare artifacts for storage and shipping. Supervise and work with volunteers. Present public programs and tours. Specialize in particular materials or types of object, such as documents and books, paintings, decorative arts, textiles, metals, or architectural materials. Recommend preservation procedures, such as control of temperature and humidity, to curatorial and building staff. Classify and assign registration numbers to artifacts, and supervise inventory control. Direct and supervise curatorial and technical staff in the handling, mounting, care, and storage of art objects. Perform on-site fieldwork, which may involve interviewing people, inspecting and identifying artifacts, note-taking, viewing sites and collections, and repainting exhibition spaces.

Education/Training Required: Bachelor's degree. **Education and Training Programs:** Art History, Criticism and Conservation; Museology/Museum Studies; Public/Applied History. **Knowledge/ Courses:** Fine Arts; History and Archeology; Chemistry; Design; English Language; Clerical Practices.

Career Clusters: 03 Arts, Audio/Video Technology, and Communications; 15 Science, Technology, Engineering, and Mathematics. **Career Pathways:** 03.1 Audio and Video Technology and Film; 15.2 Science and Mathematics.

Skills: Science; Technology Design; Writing; Installation; Quality Control Analysis; Management of Material Resources; Systems Evaluation; Systems Analysis.

Work Environment: Indoors; sitting; using hands; noise; contaminants.

Music Directors and Composers

- ❋ Personality Type: Artistic-Enterprising
- ❋ Annual Earnings: $45,970
- ❋ Earnings Growth Potential: Very high (52.8%)
- ❋ Growth: 10.0%
- ❋ Annual Job Openings: 1,620
- ❋ Self-Employed: 36.2%

Considerations for Job Outlook: Most new wage-and-salary jobs are expected to be in religious organizations. Self-employed musicians should have slower than average employment growth. Keen competition is expected for full-time positions.

Job Specialization: Music Directors

Direct and conduct instrumental or vocal performances by musical groups such as orchestras or choirs. Study scores to learn the music in detail, and to develop interpretations. Consider such factors as ensemble size and abilities, availability of scores, and the need for musical variety in order to select music to be performed. Use gestures to shape the music being played, communicating desired tempo, phrasing, tone, color, pitch, volume, and other performance aspects. Engage services of composers to write scores. Plan and implement fund-raising and promotional activities. Coordinate and organize tours, or hire touring companies to arrange concert dates, venues, accommodations, and transportation for longer tours. Confer with clergy to select music for church services. Transcribe musical compositions and melodic lines to adapt them to a particular group, or to create a particular musical style. Audition and select performers for musical presentations. Meet with composers to discuss interpretations of their works. Conduct guest soloists in addition to ensemble members. Collaborate with music librarians to ensure availability of scores. Assign and review staff work in such areas as scoring, arranging, copying music, and vocal coaching. Position members within groups to obtain balance among instrumental or vocal sections. Plan and schedule rehearsals and performances, and arrange details such as locations, accompanists, and instrumentalists. Meet with soloists and concertmasters to discuss and prepare for performances.

Education/Training Required: Work experience plus degree. **Education and Training Programs:** Conducting; Music Performance, General; Music Theory and Composition; Music, Other; Musicology and Ethnomusicology; Religious/Sacred Music; Voice and Opera. **Knowledge/Courses:** Fine Arts; Philosophy and Theology; Education and Training; History and Archeology; Communications and Media; Personnel and Human Resources.

Personality Type: Artistic-Enterprising-Social. **Career Clusters:** 03 Arts, Audio/Video Technology, and Communications; 10 Human Services. **Career Pathways:** 03.4 Performing Arts; 10.2 Counseling and Mental Health Services.

Skills: Instructing; Management of Personnel Resources; Systems Evaluation; Monitoring; Systems Analysis; Learning Strategies; Persuasion; Management of Financial Resources.

Work Environment: Sitting; standing.

Job Specialization: Music Composers and Arrangers

Write and transcribe musical scores. Copy parts from scores for individual performers. Transpose music from one voice or instrument to another to accommodate particular musicians. Use computers and synthesizers to compose, orchestrate, and arrange music. Write changes directly into compositions, or use computer software to make changes. Confer with producers and directors to define the nature and placement of film or television music. Guide musicians during rehearsals, performances, or recording sessions. Study original pieces of music to become familiar with them prior to making any changes. Study films or scripts to determine how musical scores can be used to create desired effects or moods. Write music for commercial mediums, including advertising jingles or film soundtracks. Accept commissions to create music for special occasions. Arrange music composed by others, changing the music to achieve desired effects. Write musical scores for orchestras, bands, choral groups, or individual instrumentalists or vocalists, using knowledge of music theory and of instrumental and vocal capabilities. Score compositions so that they are consistent with instrumental and vocal capabilities such as ranges and keys, using knowledge of music theory. Apply elements of music theory to create musical and tonal structures, including harmonies and melodies. Collaborate with other colleagues such as copyists to complete final scores.

Education/Training Required: Work experience plus degree. **Education and Training Programs:** Conducting; Music Performance, General; Music Theory and Composition; Music, Other; Musicology and Ethnomusicology; Religious/Sacred Music; Voice and Opera. **Knowledge/Courses:** Fine Arts; Communications and Media; Computers and Electronics; Sales and Marketing; Production and Processing; Design.

Personality Type: Artistic-Enterprising. **Career Cluster:** 03 Arts, Audio/Video Technology, and Communications. **Career Pathway:** 03.4 Performing Arts.

Skills: Operations Analysis; Writing; Coordination; Active Listening; Complex Problem Solving; Speaking.

Work Environment: Indoors; sitting; using hands; repetitive motions.

Philosophy and Religion Teachers, Postsecondary

- ❀ Personality Type: Social-Artistic-Investigative
- ❀ Annual Earnings: $62,330
- ❀ Earnings Growth Potential: High (46.4%)
- ❀ Growth: 15.1%
- ❀ Annual Job Openings: 600
- ❀ Self-Employed: 0.2%

Considerations for Job Outlook: Enrollments in postsecondary institutions are expected to continue rising as more people attend college and as workers return to school to update their skills. Opportunities for part-time or temporary positions should be favorable, but significant competition exists for tenure-track positions.

Teach courses in philosophy, religion, and theology. Evaluate and grade students' classwork, assignments, and papers. Initiate, facilitate, and moderate classroom discussions. Prepare and deliver lectures to undergraduate and graduate students on topics such as ethics, logic, and contemporary religious thought. Prepare course materials such as syllabi, homework assignments, and handouts. Compile, administer, and grade examinations, or assign this work to others. Keep abreast of developments in the field by reading current literature, talking with colleagues, and participating in professional conferences. Maintain student attendance records, grades, and other required records. Plan, evaluate, and revise curricula, course content, course materials, and methods of instruction. Maintain regularly scheduled office hours to advise and assist students. Select and obtain materials and supplies such as textbooks. Advise students on academic and vocational curricula and on career issues. Conduct research in a particular field of knowledge, and publish findings in professional journals, books, or electronic media. Perform administrative duties such as serving as department head. Serve on academic or administrative committees that deal with institutional policies, departmental matters, and academic issues. Collaborate with colleagues to address teaching and research issues. Participate in campus and community events. Participate in student recruitment, registration, and placement activities.

Education/Training Required: Doctoral degree. **Education and Training Programs:** Bible/Biblical Studies; Buddhist Studies; Christian Studies; Divinity/Ministry (BD, MDiv.); Ethics; Hindu Studies; Humanities/Humanistic Studies; Missions/Missionary Studies and Missiology; Pastoral Counseling and Specialized Ministries, Other; Pastoral Studies/Counseling; Philosophy; Philosophy and Religious Studies, Other; Philosophy, Other; Pre-Theology/Pre-Ministerial Studies; Rabbinical Studies (M.H.L./Rav); Religion/Religious Studies; Religious Education; Religious/Sacred Music; Talmudic Studies; Theological and Ministerial Studies, Other; Theology and Religious Vocations, Other; Theology/Theological Studies. **Knowledge/Courses:** Philosophy and Theology; History and Archeology; Foreign Language; English Language; Communications and Media; Education and Training.

Career Clusters: 05 Education and Training; 10 Human Services. **Career Pathways:** 05.3 Teaching/Training; 10.2 Counseling and Mental Health Services.

Skills: Writing; Learning Strategies; Reading Comprehension; Speaking; Instructing; Active Learning; Active Listening; Critical Thinking.

Work Environment: Indoors; sitting.

Photographers

- ❋ Personality Type: Artistic-Realistic
- ❋ Annual Earnings: $29,130
- ❋ Earnings Growth Potential: Medium (40.4%)
- ❋ Growth: 11.5%
- ❋ Annual Job Openings: 4,800
- ❋ Self-Employed: 60.1%

Considerations for Job Outlook: Employment for some photographers is expected to increase as online publication of magazines expands, but other photographers are expected to be adversely affected by amateur photography and increased use of copyright-free photos. Competition should be keen.

Photograph persons, subjects, merchandise, or other commercial products. May develop negatives and produce finished prints. Take pictures of individuals, families, and small groups, either in studio or on location. Adjust apertures, shutter speeds, and camera focus based on a combination of factors such as lighting, field depth, subject motion, film type, and film speed. Use traditional or digital cameras, along with a variety of equipment such as tripods, filters, and flash attachments. Create artificial light, using flashes and reflectors. Determine desired images and picture composition; select and adjust subjects, equipment, and lighting to achieve desired effects. Scan photographs into computers for editing, storage, and electronic transmission. Test equipment prior to use to ensure that it is in good working order. Review sets of photographs to select the best work. Estimate or measure light levels, distances, and numbers of exposures needed, using measuring devices and formulas. Manipulate and enhance scanned or digital images to create desired effects, using computers and specialized software. Perform maintenance tasks necessary to keep equipment working properly. Perform general office duties such as scheduling appointments, keeping books, and ordering supplies. Consult with clients or advertising staff and study assignments to determine project goals, locations, and equipment needs. Select and assemble equipment and required background properties according to subjects, materials, and conditions.

Education/Training Required: Long-term on-the-job training. **Education and Training Programs:** Commercial Photography; Film/Video and Photographic Arts, Other; Photography; Photojournalism; Visual and Performing Arts, General. **Knowledge/Courses:** Sales and Marketing; Fine Arts; Clerical Practices; Customer and Personal Service; Communications and Media; Production and Processing.

Career Cluster: 03 Arts, Audio/Video Technology, and Communications. **Career Pathways:** 03.1 Audio and Video Technology and Film; 03.3 Visual Arts; 03.5 Journalism and Broadcasting.

Skills: Operations Analysis; Science; Management of Personnel Resources; Technology Design; Operation and Control; Social Perceptiveness; Operation Monitoring; Negotiation.

Work Environment: More often indoors than outdoors; sitting; using hands.

Political Scientists

Look for the job description among the Investigative jobs.

Preschool Teachers, Except Special Education

Look for the job description among the Social jobs.

Producers and Directors

- ❋ Personality Type: Enterprising-Artistic-Conventional
- ❋ Annual Earnings: $68,440
- ❋ Earnings Growth Potential: Very high (53.0%)

- ❋ Growth: 9.8%
- ❋ Annual Job Openings: 4,040
- ❋ Self-Employed: 20.1%

Considerations for Job Outlook: Employment growth is expected to be driven by expanding film and television operations and an increase in production of online and mobile video content. Keen competition is expected.

Job Specialization: Producers

Plan and coordinate various aspects of radio, television, stage, or motion picture production, such as selecting script; coordinating writing, directing, and editing; and arranging financing. Coordinate the activities of writers, directors, managers, and other personnel throughout the production process. Monitor post-production processes to ensure accurate completion of all details. Perform management activities such as budgeting, scheduling, planning, and marketing. Determine production size, content, and budget, establishing details such as production schedules and management policies. Compose and edit scripts or provide screenwriters with story outlines from which scripts can be written. Conduct meetings with staff to discuss production progress and to ensure production objectives are attained. Resolve personnel problems that arise during the production process by acting as liaisons between dissenting parties when necessary. Produce shows for special occasions, such as holidays or testimonials. Edit and write news stories from information collected by reporters. Write and submit proposals to bid on contracts for projects. Hire directors, principal cast members, and key production staff members. Arrange financing for productions. Select plays, scripts, books, or ideas to be produced. Review film, recordings, or rehearsals to ensure conformance to production and broadcast standards. Perform administrative duties such as preparing operational reports, distributing rehearsal call sheets and script copies, and arranging for rehearsal quarters. Obtain and distribute costumes, props, music, and studio equipment needed to complete productions.

Artistic-P

Education/Training Required: Work experience plus degree. **Education and Training Programs:** Cinematography and Film/Video Production; Directing and Theatrical Production; Drama and Dramatics/Theatre Arts, General; Dramatic/Theatre Arts and Stagecraft, Other; Film/Cinema/Video Studies; Radio and Television. **Knowledge/Courses:** Communications and Media; Fine Arts; Philosophy and Theology; Sociology and Anthropology; History and Archeology; Geography.

Personality Type: Enterprising-Artistic. **Career Cluster:** 03 Arts, Audio/Video Technology, and Communications. **Career Pathways:** 03.4 Performing Arts; 03.5 Journalism and Broadcasting.

Skills: Management of Financial Resources; Management of Material Resources; Coordination; Management of Personnel Resources; Persuasion; Time Management; Negotiation; Monitoring.

Work Environment: Indoors; sitting.

Job Specialization: Directors—Stage, Motion Pictures, Television, and Radio

Interpret script, conduct rehearsals, and direct activities of cast and technical crew for stage, motion pictures, television, or radio programs. Direct live broadcasts, films and recordings, or non-broadcast programming for public entertainment or education. Supervise and coordinate the work of camera, lighting, design, and sound crew members. Study and research scripts to determine how they should be directed. Cut and edit film or tape to integrate component parts into desired sequences. Collaborate with film and sound editors during the post-production process as films are edited and soundtracks are added. Confer with technical directors, managers, crew members, and writers to discuss details of production, such as photography, script, music, sets, and costumes. Plan details such as framing, composition, camera movement, sound, and actor movement for each shot or scene. Communicate to actors the approach, characterization, and movement needed for each scene in such a way that re-

hearsals and takes are minimized. Establish pace of programs and sequences of scenes according to time requirements and cast and set accessibility. Choose settings and locations for films and determine how scenes will be shot in these settings. Identify and approve equipment and elements required for productions, such as scenery, lights, props, costumes, choreography, and music. Compile scripts, program notes, and other material related to productions. Perform producers' duties such as securing financial backing, establishing and administering budgets, and recruiting cast and crew.

Education/Training Required: Work experience plus degree. **Education and Training Programs:** Cinematography and Film/Video Production; Directing and Theatrical Production; Drama and Dramatics/Theatre Arts, General; Dramatic/Theatre Arts and Stagecraft, Other; Film/Cinema/Video Studies; Radio and Television. **Knowledge/Courses:** Communications and Media; Fine Arts; Telecommunications; Production and Processing; Computers and Electronics; Engineering and Technology.

Personality Type: Enterprising-Artistic. **Career Cluster:** 03 Arts, Audio/Video Technology, and Communications. **Career Pathways:** 03.4 Performing Arts; 03.5 Journalism and Broadcasting.

Skills: Management of Personnel Resources; Management of Material Resources; Negotiation; Persuasion; Coordination; Speaking; Instructing; Time Management.

Work Environment: Indoors; sitting; using hands; repetitive motions; noise.

Job Specialization: Program Directors

Direct and coordinate activities of personnel engaged in preparation of radio or television station program schedules and programs such as sports or news. Plan and schedule programming and event coverage based on broadcast length; time availability; and other factors such as community needs, ratings data, and viewer demographics. Monitor and review programming to ensure that schedules are met, guidelines are adhered to, and performances are of adequate quality. Direct and coordinate activities of personnel engaged in broadcast news, sports, or programming. Check completed program logs for accuracy and conformance with FCC rules and regulations, and resolve program log inaccuracies. Establish work schedules, and assign work to staff members. Coordinate activities between departments such as news and programming. Perform personnel duties such as hiring staff and evaluating work performance. Evaluate new and existing programming for suitability and to assess the need for changes, using information such as audience surveys and feedback. Develop budgets for programming and broadcasting activities, and monitor expenditures to ensure that they remain within budgetary limits. Confer with directors and production staff to discuss issues such as production and casting problems, budgets, policies, and news coverage. Select, acquire, and maintain programs, music, films, and other needed materials, and obtain legal clearances for their use as necessary. Monitor network transmissions for advisories concerning daily program schedules, program content, special feeds, or program changes. Develop promotions for current programs and specials.

Education/Training Required: Work experience plus degree. **Education and Training Programs:** Cinematography and Film/Video Production; Directing and Theatrical Production; Drama and Dramatics/Theatre Arts, General; Dramatic/Theatre Arts and Stagecraft, Other; Film/Cinema/Video Studies; Radio and Television. **Knowledge/Courses:** Telecommunications; Communications and Media; Clerical Practices; Computers and Electronics; Personnel and Human Resources; Engineering and Technology.

Personality Type: Enterprising-Conventional-Artistic. **Career Cluster:** 03 Arts, Audio/Video Technology, and Communications. **Career Pathways:** 03.4 Performing Arts; 03.5 Journalism and Broadcasting.

Skills: Management of Financial Resources;

Management of Material Resources; Operations Analysis; Management of Personnel Resources; Systems Evaluation; Systems Analysis; Instructing; Time Management.

Work Environment: Indoors; sitting; noise.

Job Specialization: Talent Directors

Audition and interview performers to select most appropriate talent for parts in stage, television, radio, or motion picture productions. Review performer information such as photos, resumes, voice tapes, videos, and union membership in order to decide whom to audition for parts. Read scripts and confer with producers in order to determine the types and numbers of performers required for a given production. Select performers for roles, or submit lists of suitable performers to producers or directors for final selection. Audition and interview performers in order to match their attributes to specific roles or to increase the pool of available acting talent. Maintain talent files that include information such as performers' specialties, past performances, and availability. Prepare actors for auditions by providing scripts and information about roles and casting requirements. Serve as liaisons between directors, actors, and agents. Attend or view productions in order to maintain knowledge of available actors. Negotiate contract agreements with performers, with agents, or between performers and agents or production companies. Contact agents and actors in order to provide notification of audition and performance opportunities and to set up audition times. Hire and supervise workers who help locate people with specified attributes and talents. Arrange for and/or design screen tests or auditions for prospective performers. Locate performers or extras for crowd and background scenes and stand-ins or photo doubles for actors by direct contact or through agents.

Education/Training Required: Long-term on-the-job training. **Education and Training Programs:** Cinematography and Film/Video Production; Directing and Theatrical Production; Drama and Dramatics/Theatre Arts, General; Dramatic/Theatre Arts and Stagecraft, Other; Film/Cinema/Video Studies; Radio and Television. **Knowledge/Courses:** Fine Arts; Communications and Media; Clerical Practices; Sales and Marketing; Computers and Electronics; Telecommunications.

Personality Type: Enterprising-Artistic. **Career Cluster:** 03 Arts, Audio/Video Technology, and Communications. **Career Pathways:** 03.4 Performing Arts; 03.5 Journalism and Broadcasting.

Skills: Negotiation; Persuasion; Management of Personnel Resources; Speaking; Social Perceptiveness; Reading Comprehension; Monitoring; Management of Financial Resources.

Work Environment: Indoors; sitting; noise.

Job Specialization: Technical Directors/Managers

Coordinate activities of technical departments, such as taping, editing, engineering, and maintenance, to produce radio or television programs. Direct technical aspects of newscasts and other productions, checking and switching between video sources and taking responsibility for the on-air product, including camera shots and graphics. Test equipment to ensure proper operation. Monitor broadcasts to ensure that programs conform to station or network policies and regulations. Observe pictures through monitors, and direct camera and video staff concerning shading and composition. Act as liaisons between engineering and production departments. Supervise and assign duties to workers engaged in technical control and production of radio and television programs. Schedule use of studio and editing facilities for producers and engineering and maintenance staff. Confer with operations directors to formulate and maintain fair and attainable technical policies for programs. Operate equipment to produce programs or broadcast live programs from remote locations. Train workers in use of equipment such as switchers, cameras, monitors, microphones, and lights. Switch between video sources in a studio or on multi-camera remotes, using equipment such

as switchers, video slide projectors, and video effects generators. Set up and execute video transitions and special effects such as fades, dissolves, cuts, keys, and supers, using computers to manipulate pictures as necessary. Collaborate with promotions directors to produce on-air station promotions.

Education/Training Required: Long-term on-the-job training. **Education and Training Programs:** Cinematography and Film/Video Production; Directing and Theatrical Production; Drama and Dramatics/Theatre Arts, General; Dramatic/Theatre Arts and Stagecraft, Other; Film/Cinema/Video Studies; Radio and Television. **Knowledge/Courses:** Communications and Media; Telecommunications; Fine Arts; Engineering and Technology; Production and Processing; Computers and Electronics.

Personality Type: Enterprising-Realistic-Conventional. **Career Cluster:** 03 Arts, Audio/Video Technology, and Communications. **Career Pathways:** 03.1 Audio and Video Technology and Film; 03.4 Performing Arts; 03.5 Journalism and Broadcasting.

Skills: Equipment Selection; Monitoring; Management of Personnel Resources; Coordination; Systems Analysis; Operation and Control; Instructing; Operation Monitoring.

Work Environment: Indoors; sitting; using hands.

Public Relations and Fundraising Managers

Look for the job description among the Enterprising jobs.

Public Relations Specialists

Look for the job description among the Enterprising jobs.

Recreational Therapists

* Personality Type: Social-Artistic
* Annual Earnings: $39,410
* Earnings Growth Potential: Medium (37.5%)
* Growth: 14.6%
* Annual Job Openings: 1,160
* Self-Employed: 0.1%

Considerations for Job Outlook: Employment growth for recreational therapists is expected to continue as the population ages and better medical technology increases the survival rates of people who become injured or ill.

Plan, direct, or coordinate medically approved recreation programs for patients in hospitals, nursing homes, or other institutions. Activities include sports, trips, dramatics, social activities, and arts and crafts. May assess a patient condition and recommend appropriate recreational activity. Observe, analyze, and record patients' participation, reactions, and progress during treatment sessions, modifying treatment programs as needed. Develop treatment plan to meet needs of patient, based on needs assessment, patient interests, and objectives of therapy. Encourage clients with special needs and circumstances to acquire new skills and get involved in health-promoting leisure activities, such as sports, games, arts and crafts, and gardening. Counsel and encourage patients to develop leisure activities. Confer with members of treatment team to plan and evaluate therapy programs. Conduct therapy sessions to improve patients' mental and physical well-being. Instruct patient in activities and techniques, such as sports, dance, music, art, or relaxation techniques, designed to meet their specific physical or psychological needs. Obtain information from medical records, medical staff, family members, and the patients themselves to assess patients' capabilities, needs, and interests. Plan, organize, direct, and participate in treatment programs and activities to facilitate patients' rehabilitation, help them integrate into the community, and prevent further medical problems. Prepare and submit reports and charts to treatment team to reflect patients' reactions and evidence of progress or regression.

Education/Training Required: Bachelor's degree. **Education and Training Program:** Therapeutic Recreation/Recreational Therapy. **Knowledge/ Courses:** Therapy and Counseling; Psychology; Sociology and Anthropology; Philosophy and Theology; Medicine and Dentistry; Fine Arts.

Career Cluster: 08 Health Science. **Career Pathway:** 08.3 Health Informatics.

Skills: Service Orientation; Operations Analysis; Social Perceptiveness; Science; Persuasion; Negotiation; Coordination; Learning Strategies.

Work Environment: Indoors; standing; exposed to disease or infections.

Job Specialization: Art Therapists

Plan or conduct art therapy sessions or programs to improve clients' physical, cognitive, or emotional well-being. Analyze data to determine the effectiveness of treatments or therapy approaches. Analyze or synthesize client data to draw conclusions or make recommendations for art therapy. Assess client needs or disorders, using drawing, painting, sculpting, or other artistic processes. Communicate client assessment findings and recommendations in oral, written, audio, video, or other forms. Conduct art therapy sessions, providing guided self-expression experiences to help clients recover from or cope with cognitive, emotional, or physical impairments. Confer with other professionals on client's treatment team to develop, coordinate, or integrate treatment plans. Customize art therapy programs for specific client populations, such as those in schools, nursing homes, wellness centers, prisons, shelters, or hospitals. Design art therapy sessions or programs to meet client's goals or objectives. Develop individualized treatment plans that incorporate studio art therapy, counseling, or psychotherapy techniques. Establish goals or objectives for art therapy sessions in consul-

Artistic-R

tation with clients or site administrators. Instruct individuals or groups in the use of art media, such as paint, clay, or yarn. Interpret the artistic creations of clients to assess their functioning, needs, or progress. Observe and document client reactions, progress, or other outcomes related to art therapy. Photograph or videotape client artwork for inclusion in client records or for promotional purposes.

Education/Training Required: Master's degree. **Education and Training Program:** Art Therapy/Therapist Training. **Knowledge/Courses:** No data available.

Personality Type: No data available. **Career Cluster:** 08 Health Science. **Career Pathway:** 08.1 Therapeutic Services.

Skills: No data available.

Work Environment: No data available.

Job Specialization: Music Therapists

Plan, organize, or direct medically prescribed music therapy activities designed to positively influence patients' psychological or behavioral status. Adapt existing or create new music therapy assessment instruments or procedures to meet an individual client's needs. Analyze data to determine the effectiveness of specific treatments or therapy approaches. Analyze or synthesize client data to draw conclusions or make recommendations for therapy. Assess client functioning levels, strengths, and areas of need in terms of perceptual, sensory, affective, communicative, musical, or other abilities. Communicate client assessment findings and recommendations in oral, written, audio, video, or other forms. Confer with professionals on client's treatment team to develop, coordinate, or integrate treatment plans. Customize treatment programs for specific client populations, such as hospice, psychiatric, or obstetrics populations. Design music therapy experiences to meet client's goals or objectives. Engage clients in music experiences to identify client responses to different styles of music, types of mu-

sical experiences, such as improvising or listening, or elements of music, such as tempo or harmony. Establish client goals or objectives for music therapy treatment, considering client needs, capabilities, interests, overall therapeutic program, coordination of treatment, or length of treatment. Gather diagnostic data from sources such as case documentation, observations of clients, or interviews of clients or family members. Improvise instrumentally, vocally, or physically to meet client's therapeutic needs.

Education/Training Required: Bachelor's degree. **Education and Training Program:** Music Therapy/Therapist Training. **Knowledge/Courses:** No data available.

Personality Type: No data available. **Career Cluster:** 08 Health Science. **Career Pathway:** 08.1 Therapeutic Services.

Skills: No data available.

Work Environment: No data available.

Secondary School Teachers, Except Special and Career/Technical Education

- ❋ Personality Type: Social-Artistic-Enterprising
- ❋ Annual Earnings: $53,230
- ❋ Earnings Growth Potential: Low (34.2%)
- ❋ Growth: 8.9%
- ❋ Annual Job Openings: 41,240
- ❋ Self-Employed: 0.0%

Considerations for Job Outlook: Enrollment from 2008 to 2018 is expected to grow more slowly than in recent years. Prospects are usually better in urban and rural areas, for bilingual teachers, and for math and science teachers.

Instruct students in secondary public or private schools in one or more subjects at the secondary level, such as English, mathematics, or social studies. May be designated according to subject

matter specialty, such as typing instructors, commercial teachers, or English teachers. Establish
and enforce rules for behavior and procedures for
maintaining order among the students for whom
they are responsible. Instruct through lectures, discussions, and demonstrations in one or more subjects such as English, mathematics, or social studies. Establish clear objectives for all lessons, units,
and projects, and communicate those objectives to
students. Prepare, administer, and grade tests and
assignments to evaluate students' progress. Prepare
materials and classrooms for class activities. Adapt
teaching methods and instructional materials to
meet students' varying needs and interests. Assign
and grade classwork and homework. Maintain accurate and complete student records as required by
laws, district policies, and administrative regulations. Enforce all administration policies and rules
governing students. Observe and evaluate students'
performance, behavior, social development, and
physical health. Plan and conduct activities for a balanced program of instruction, demonstration, and
work time that provides students with opportunities to observe, question, and investigate. Prepare
students for later grades by encouraging them to explore learning opportunities and to persevere with
challenging tasks. Guide and counsel students with
adjustment and/or academic problems or special academic interests. Instruct and monitor students in the
use and care of equipment and materials to prevent
injuries and damage.

Education/Training Required: Bachelor's degree.
Education and Training Programs: Agricultural
Teacher Education; Art Teacher Education; Biology
Teacher Education; Business Teacher Education;
Chemistry Teacher Education; Computer Teacher
Education; Drama and Dance Teacher Education;
Driver and Safety Teacher Education; English/
Language Arts Teacher Education; Family and
Consumer Sciences/Home Economics Teacher
Education; Foreign Language Teacher Education;
French Language Teacher Education; Geography
Teacher Education; German Language Teacher
Education; Health Occupations Teacher Education;
Health Teacher Education; History Teacher Edu-

cation; Junior High/Intermediate/Middle School
Education and Teaching; Latin Teacher Education;
Mathematics Teacher Education; Music Teacher
Education; Physical Education Teaching and
Coaching; Physics Teacher Education; Reading
Teacher Education; Sales and Marketing Operations/
Marketing and Distribution Teacher Education;
Science Teacher Education; Secondary Education
and Teaching; Social Science Teacher Education;
Social Studies Teacher Education; Spanish Language
Teacher Education; Speech Teacher Education;
Teacher Education, Multiple Levels; Technology
Teacher Education/Industrial Arts Teacher Edu-
cation; others. **Knowledge/Courses:** History and
Archeology; Philosophy and Theology; Sociology
and Anthropology; Fine Arts; Education and
Training; Therapy and Counseling.

Career Cluster: 05 Education and Training. **Career
Pathway:** 05.3 Teaching/Training.

Skills: Learning Strategies; Systems Evaluation;
Instructing; Social Perceptiveness; Service Orien-
tation; Writing; Speaking; Judgment and Decision
Making.

Work Environment: Indoors; standing.

Self-Enrichment Education Teachers

*Look for the job description among the Social
jobs.*

Set and Exhibit Designers

* Personality Type: Artistic-Realistic
* Annual Earnings: $46,680
* Earnings Growth Potential: High (45.2%)
* Growth: 16.6%
* Annual Job Openings: 510
* Self-Employed: 26.2%

Considerations for Job Outlook: Faster than average employment growth is projected.

Design special exhibits and movie, television, and theater sets. May study scripts, confer with directors, and conduct research to determine appropriate architectural styles. Examine objects to be included in exhibits to plan where and how to display them. Acquire, or arrange for acquisition of, specimens or graphics required to complete exhibits. Prepare rough drafts and scale working drawings of sets, including floor plans, scenery, and properties to be constructed. Confer with clients and staff to gather information about exhibit space, proposed themes and content, timelines, budgets, materials, and promotion requirements. Estimate set- or exhibit-related costs, including materials, construction, and rental of props or locations. Develop set designs based on evaluation of scripts, budgets, research information, and available locations. Direct and coordinate construction, erection, or decoration activities to ensure that sets or exhibits meet design, budget, and schedule requirements. Inspect installed exhibits for conformance to specifications and satisfactory operation of special effects components. Plan for location-specific issues such as space limitations, traffic flow patterns, and safety concerns. Submit plans for approval, and adapt plans to serve intended purposes or to conform to budget or fabrication restrictions. Prepare preliminary renderings of proposed exhibits, including detailed construction, layout, and material specifications and diagrams relating to aspects such as special effects and lighting. Select and purchase lumber and hardware necessary for set construction.

Education/Training Required: Bachelor's degree. **Education and Training Programs:** Design and Applied Arts, Other; Design and Visual Communications, General; Illustration; Technical Theatre/Theatre Design and Technology. **Knowledge/Courses:** Fine Arts; Design; History and Archeology; Communications and Media; Sociology and Anthropology; Computers and Electronics.

Career Cluster: 03 Arts, Audio/Video Technology, and Communications. **Career Pathways:** 03.1 Audio and Video Technology and Film; 03.3 Visual Arts; 03.4 Performing Arts.

Skills: Management of Financial Resources; Operations Analysis; Management of Material Resources; Mathematics; Equipment Selection; Management of Personnel Resources; Time Management; Technology Design.

Work Environment: Indoors; sitting; using hands.

Sociologists

- ❋ Personality Type: Investigative-Artistic-Social
- ❋ Annual Earnings: $72,360
- ❋ Earnings Growth Potential: Medium (39.2%)
- ❋ Growth: 22.0%
- ❋ Annual Job Openings: 200
- ❋ Self-Employed: 0.0%

Considerations for Job Outlook: Employment growth of sociologists in a variety of fields is tied to expected demand for their research and analytical skills. Opportunities should be best for job-seekers who have an advanced degree.

Study human society and social behavior by examining the groups and social institutions that people form, as well as various social, religious, political, and business organizations. May study the behavior and interaction of groups, trace their origin and growth, and analyze the influence of group activities on individual members. Analyze and interpret data in order to increase the understanding of human social behavior. Prepare publications and reports containing research findings. Plan and conduct research to develop and test theories about societal issues such as crime, group relations, poverty, and aging. Collect data about the attitudes, values, and behaviors of people in groups, using observation, interviews, and review of documents. Develop, implement, and evaluate methods of data collection, such as questionnaires or interviews. Teach sociology. Direct work of statistical clerks, statisticians, and others who compile and evaluate research data. Consult with and advise individuals such as administrators, social workers, and legislators regarding social issues and policies, as well as the implications of research findings. Collaborate with research workers in other disciplines. Develop approaches to the solution of groups' problems based on research findings in sociology and related disciplines. Observe group interactions and role affiliations to collect data, identify problems, evaluate progress, and determine the need for additional change. Develop problem-intervention procedures, utilizing techniques such as interviews, consultations, role-playing, and participant observation of group interactions.

Education/Training Required: Master's degree. **Education and Training Programs:** Criminology; Demography and Population Studies; Sociology; Urban Studies/Affairs. **Knowledge/Courses:** Sociology and Anthropology; Philosophy and Theology; History and Archeology; Psychology; English Language; Mathematics.

Career Clusters: 10 Human Services; 15 Science, Technology, Engineering, and Mathematics. **Career Pathways:** 10.3 Family and Community Services; 15.2 Science and Mathematics.

Skills: Science; Reading Comprehension; Writing; Speaking; Mathematics; Active Listening; Active Learning; Operations Analysis.

Work Environment: Indoors; sitting.

Special Education Teachers, Middle School

Look for the job description among the Social jobs.

Substance Abuse and Behavioral Disorder Counselors

- Personality Type: Social-Artistic-Investigative
- Annual Earnings: $38,120

- Earnings Growth Potential: Low (35.2%)
- Growth: 21.0%
- Annual Job Openings: 3,550
- Self-Employed: 6.0%

Considerations for Job Outlook: Increasing demand for services provided by counselors is expected to result in employment growth. But growth will vary by specialty and will be faster for mental health, substance abuse and behavioral disorder, and rehabilitation counselors than for counselors of other specialties. Opportunities should be favorable, particularly in rural areas.

Counsel and advise individuals with alcohol; tobacco; drug; or other problems, such as gambling and eating disorders. May counsel individuals, families, or groups or engage in prevention programs. Counsel clients and patients individually and in group sessions to assist in overcoming dependencies, adjusting to life, and making changes. Complete and maintain accurate records and reports regarding the patients' histories and progress, services provided, and other required information. Develop client treatment plans based on research, clinical experience, and client histories. Review and evaluate clients' progress in relation to measurable goals described in treatment and care plans. Interview clients, review records, and confer with other professionals to evaluate individuals' mental and physical condition and to determine their suitability for participation in a specific program. Intervene as advocate for clients or patients to resolve emergency problems in crisis situations. Provide clients or family members with information about addiction issues and about available services and programs, making appropriate referrals when necessary. Modify treatment plans to comply with changes in client status. Coordinate counseling efforts with mental health professionals and other health professionals such as doctors, nurses, and social workers. Attend training sessions to increase knowledge and skills. Plan and implement follow-up and aftercare programs for clients to be discharged from treatment programs. Conduct chemical-dependency program orientation sessions.

Artistic-S

Counsel family members to assist them in understanding, dealing with, and supporting clients or patients.

Education/Training Required: Bachelor's degree. **Education and Training Programs:** Clinical/Medical Social Work; Mental and Social Health Services and Allied Professions, Other; Substance Abuse/Addiction Counseling. **Knowledge/Courses:** Therapy and Counseling; Psychology; Sociology and Anthropology; Philosophy and Theology; Education and Training; Clerical Practices.

Career Clusters: 08 Health Science; 10 Human Services. **Career Pathways:** 08.1 Therapeutic Services; 08.3 Health Informatics; 10.2 Counseling and Mental Health Services.

Skills: Social Perceptiveness; Service Orientation; Persuasion; Learning Strategies; Active Listening; Negotiation; Monitoring; Systems Analysis.

Work Environment: Indoors; sitting.

Technical Writers

- ❊ Personality Type: Artistic-Investigative-Conventional
- ❊ Annual Earnings: $63,280
- ❊ Earnings Growth Potential: High (41.3%)
- ❊ Growth: 18.2%
- ❊ Annual Job Openings: 1,680
- ❊ Self-Employed: 2.0%

Considerations for Job Outlook: Fast growth is expected because of the need for technical writers to explain an increasing number of scientific and technical products. Prospects should be good, especially for workers with strong technical and communication skills. Competition will be keen for some jobs.

Write technical materials, such as equipment manuals, appendices, or operating and maintenance instructions. May assist in layout work. Organize material and complete writing assignment according to set standards regarding order, clarity, conciseness, style, and terminology. Maintain records and files of work and revisions. Edit, standardize, or make changes to material prepared by other writers or establishment personnel. Confer with customer representatives, vendors, plant executives, or publisher to establish technical specifications and to determine subject material to be developed for publication. Review published materials, and recommend revisions or changes in scope, format, content, and methods of reproduction and binding. Select photographs, drawings, sketches, diagrams, and charts to illustrate material. Study drawings, specifications, mockups, and product samples to integrate and delineate technology, operating procedure, and production sequence and detail. Interview production and engineering personnel and read journals and other material to become familiar with product technologies and production methods. Observe production, developmental, and experimental activities to determine operating procedure and detail. Arrange for typing, duplication, and distribution of material. Assist in laying out material for publication. Analyze developments in specific field to determine need for revisions in previously published materials and development of new material. Review manufacturer's and trade catalogs, drawings, and other data relative to operation, maintenance, and service of equipment.

Education/Training Required: Bachelor's degree. **Education and Training Programs:** Business/Corporate Communications; Speech Communication and Rhetoric. **Knowledge/Courses:** Communications and Media; Clerical Practices; English Language; Computers and Electronics; Education and Training; Engineering and Technology.

Career Clusters: 03 Arts, Audio/Video Technology, and Communications; 04 Business, Management, and Administration. **Career Pathways:** 03.5 Journalism and Broadcasting; 04.5 Marketing.

Skills: Writing; Reading Comprehension; Active Learning; Speaking; Operations Analysis; Critical Thinking; Active Listening; Complex Problem Solving.

Work Environment: Indoors; sitting; using hands; repetitive motions.

Training and Development Specialists

Look for the job description among the Social jobs.

Writers and Authors

- ❀ Personality Type: Artistic-Enterprising-Investigative
- ❀ Annual Earnings: $55,420
- ❀ Earnings Growth Potential: High (48.4%)
- ❀ Growth: 14.8%
- ❀ Annual Job Openings: 5,420
- ❀ Self-Employed: 69.4%

Considerations for Job Outlook: Projected job growth for these workers stems from increased use of online media and growing demand for web-based information. But print publishing is expected to continue weakening. Job competition should be keen.

Job Specialization: Copy Writers

Write advertising copy for use by publication or broadcast media to promote sale of goods and services. Write advertising copy for use by publication, broadcast, or Internet media to promote the sale of goods and services. Present drafts and ideas to clients. Discuss the product, advertising themes and methods, and any changes that should be made in advertising copy with the client. Consult with sales, media, and marketing representatives to obtain information on product or service, and discuss style and length of advertising copy. Vary language and tone of messages based on product and medium. Edit or rewrite existing copy as necessary, and submit copy for approval by supervisor. Write to customers in their terms and on their level so that the advertiser's sales message is more readily received. Write articles; bulletins; sales letters; speeches; and other related informative, marketing, and promotional material. Invent names for products, and write

the slogans that appear on packaging, brochures, and other promotional material. Review advertising trends, consumer surveys, and other data regarding marketing of goods and services to determine the best way to promote products. Develop advertising campaigns for a wide range of clients, working with an advertising agency's creative director and art director to determine the best way to present advertising information. Conduct research and interviews to determine which of a product's selling features should be promoted.

Education/Training Required: Bachelor's degree. **Education and Training Programs:** Broadcast Journalism; Business/Corporate Communications; Communication, Journalism, and Related Programs, Other; Family and Consumer Sciences/Human Sciences Communication; Journalism; Mass Communication/Media Studies; Playwriting and Screenwriting; Speech Communication and Rhetoric. **Knowledge/Courses:** Sales and Marketing; Communications and Media; English Language; Clerical Practices; Computers and Electronics; Administration and Management.

Personality Type: Enterprising-Artistic. **Career Cluster:** 03 Arts, Audio/Video Technology, and Communications. **Career Pathway:** 03.5 Journalism and Broadcasting.

Skills: Writing; Persuasion; Reading Comprehension; Negotiation; Operations Analysis; Active Listening; Management of Personnel Resources; Speaking.

Work Environment: Indoors; sitting.

Job Specialization: Poets, Lyricists and Creative Writers

Create original written works, such as scripts, essays, prose, poetry, or song lyrics, for publication or performance. Revise written material to meet personal standards and to satisfy needs of clients, publishers, directors, or producers. Choose subject matter and suitable form to express personal feelings, experiences, or ideas or to narrate stories or events. Plan project arrangements or outlines, and organize

Artistic-W

material accordingly. Prepare works in appropriate format for publication, and send them to publishers or producers. Follow appropriate procedures to get copyrights for completed work. Write fiction or nonfiction prose such as short stories, novels, biographies, articles, descriptive or critical analyses, and essays. Develop factors such as themes, plots, characterizations, psychological analyses, historical environments, action, and dialogue to create material. Confer with clients, editors, publishers, or producers to discuss changes or revisions to written material. Conduct research to obtain factual information and authentic detail, using sources such as newspaper accounts, diaries, and interviews. Write narrative, dramatic, lyric, or other types of poetry for publication. Attend book launches and publicity events, or conduct public readings. Write words to fit musical compositions, including lyrics for operas, musical plays, and choral works. Adapt text to accommodate musical requirements of composers and singers. Teach writing classes. Write humorous material for publication or for performances such as comedy routines, gags, and comedy shows.

Education/Training Required: Bachelor's degree. **Education and Training Programs:** Broadcast Journalism; Business/Corporate Communications; Communication, Journalism, and Related Programs, Other; Family and Consumer Sciences/Human Sciences Communication; Journalism; Mass Communication/Media Studies; Playwriting and Screenwriting; Speech Communication and Rhetoric. **Knowledge/Courses:** Fine Arts; Communications and Media; Philosophy and Theology; Sociology and Anthropology; Sales and Marketing; History and Archeology.

Personality Type: Artistic-Investigative. **Career Cluster:** 03 Arts, Audio/Video Technology, and Communications. **Career Pathway:** 03.4 Performing Arts.

Skills: Writing; Reading Comprehension; Active Learning; Persuasion; Management of Financial Resources; Active Listening; Social Perceptiveness; Negotiation.

Work Environment: Indoors; sitting; using hands; repetitive motions.

Social Occupations

Adult Basic and Secondary Education and Literacy Teachers and Instructors

Look for the job description among the Artistic jobs.

Agricultural Sciences Teachers, Postsecondary

- ❋ Personality Type: Social-Investigative-Realistic
- ❋ Annual Earnings: $78,370
- ❋ Earnings Growth Potential: High (46.9%)
- ❋ Growth: 15.1%
- ❋ Annual Job Openings: 300
- ❋ Self-Employed: 0.2%

Considerations for Job Outlook: Enrollments in postsecondary institutions are expected to continue rising as more people attend college and as workers return to school to update their skills. Opportunities for part-time or temporary positions should be favorable, but significant competition exists for tenure-track positions.

Teach courses in the agricultural sciences, including agronomy, dairy sciences, fisheries management, horticultural sciences, poultry sciences, range management, and agricultural soil conservation. Prepare course materials such as syllabi, homework assignments, and handouts. Evaluate and grade students' classwork, laboratory work, assignments, and papers. Keep abreast of developments in agriculture by reading current literature, talking with colleagues, and participating in professional conferences. Prepare and deliver lectures to undergraduate and/or graduate students on topics such as crop production, plant genetics, and soil chemistry. Initiate, facilitate, and moderate classroom discussions. Conduct research in a particular field of knowledge, and publish findings in professional journals, books, and/or electronic media. Supervise laboratory sessions and fieldwork, and coordinate laboratory operations. Supervise undergraduate and/or graduate teaching, internship, and research work. Compile, administer, and grade examinations, or assign this work to others. Advise students on academic and vocational curricula and on career issues. Plan, evaluate, and revise curricula, course content, course materials, and methods of instruction. Maintain student attendance records, grades, and other required records. Write grant proposals to procure external research funding. Collaborate with colleagues to address teaching and research issues. Maintain regularly scheduled office hours in order to advise and assist students. Participate in student recruitment, registration, and placement activities. Select and obtain materials and supplies such as textbooks and laboratory equipment.

Education/Training Required: Doctoral degree. **Education and Training Programs:** Agribusiness/Agricultural Business Operations; Agricultural and Food Products Processing; Agricultural and Horticultural Plant Breeding; Agricultural Animal Breeding; Agricultural Business and Management, General; Agricultural Economics; Agricultural Mechanization, General; Agricultural Power Machinery Operation; Agricultural Production Operations, General; Agricultural Teacher Education; Agricultural/Farm Supplies Retailing and Wholesaling; Agriculture, General; Animal Health; Animal Nutrition; Animal Training; Animal/Livestock Husbandry and Production; Applied Horticulture/Horticulture Operations, General; Aquaculture; Crop Production; Dairy Science; Equestrian/Equine Studies; Farm/Farm and Ranch Management; Food Science; Greenhouse Operations and Management; Horticultural Science; International Agriculture; Landscaping and Groundskeeping; Livestock Management; Ornamental Horticulture; Plant Nursery Operations and Management; Plant Protection and Integrated Pest Management; Plant Sciences, General; Poultry Science; Range Science and Management; Soil

Science and Agronomy, General; Turf and Turfgrass Management; others. **Knowledge/Courses:** Biology; Food Production; Education and Training; Geography; Mathematics; Chemistry.

Career Clusters: 01 Agriculture, Food, and Natural Resources; 05 Education and Training. **Career Pathways:** 01.1 Food Products and Processing Systems; 01.2 Plant Systems; 01.3 Animal Systems; 01.4 Power Structure and Technical Systems; 01.7 Agribusiness Systems; 05.3 Teaching/Training.

Skills: Instructing; Science; Writing; Speaking; Reading Comprehension; Learning Strategies; Active Learning; Active Listening.

Work Environment: Indoors; sitting.

Architecture Teachers, Postsecondary

Look for the job description among the Artistic occupations.

Art, Drama, and Music Teachers, Postsecondary

- ❀ Personality Type: Social-Artistic
- ❀ Annual Earnings: $62,040
- ❀ Earnings Growth Potential: High (46.5%)
- ❀ Growth: 15.1%
- ❀ Annual Job Openings: 2,500
- ❀ Self-Employed: 0.2%

Considerations for Job Outlook: Enrollments in postsecondary institutions are expected to continue rising as more people attend college and as workers return to school to update their skills. Opportunities for part-time or temporary positions should be favorable, but significant competition exists for tenure-track positions.

Teach courses in drama; music; and the arts, including fine and applied art, such as painting and sculpture, or design and crafts. Evaluate and grade students' classwork, performances, projects, assignments, and papers. Explain and demonstrate artistic techniques. Prepare students for performances, exams, or assessments. Prepare and deliver lectures to undergraduate or graduate students on topics such as acting techniques, fundamentals of music, and art history. Organize performance groups, and direct their rehearsals. Prepare course materials such as syllabi, homework assignments, and handouts. Initiate, facilitate, and moderate classroom discussions. Keep abreast of developments in the field by reading current literature, talking with colleagues, and participating in professional conferences. Advise students on academic and vocational curricula and on career issues. Maintain student attendance records, grades, and other required records. Conduct research in a particular field of knowledge, and publish findings in professional journals, books, or electronic media. Supervise undergraduate and/or graduate teaching, internship, and research work. Plan, evaluate, and revise curricula, course content, course materials, and methods of instruction. Maintain regularly scheduled office hours to advise and assist students. Compile, administer, and grade examinations, or assign this work to others. Participate in student recruitment, registration, and placement activities. Select and obtain materials and supplies such as textbooks and performance pieces.

Education/Training Required: Doctoral degree. **Education and Training Programs:** Art History, Criticism and Conservation; Art, General; Ceramic Arts and Ceramics; Cinematography and Film/Video Production; Commercial Photography; Conducting; Crafts/Craft Design, Folk Art and Artisanry; Dance, General; Design and Visual Communications, General; Directing and Theatrical Production; Drama and Dramatics/Theatre Arts, General; Fashion/Apparel Design; Fiber, Textile and Weaving Arts; Film/Cinema/Video Studies; Fine/Studio Arts, General; Graphic Design; Humanities/Humanistic Studies; Industrial and Product Design; Interior Design; Intermedia/Multimedia; Jazz/Jazz Studies; Keyboard Instruments; Metal and Jewelry Arts; Music History, Literature, and Theory;

Music Pedagogy; Music Performance, General; Music Theory and Composition; Musicology and Ethnomusicology; Painting; Photography; Playwriting and Screenwriting; Printmaking; Sculpture; Stringed Instruments; Technical Theatre/Theatre Design and Technology; Theatre Literature, History and Criticism; Visual and Performing Arts, General; Voice and Opera; others. **Knowledge/Courses:** Fine Arts; Philosophy and Theology; History and Archeology; Education and Training; Communications and Media; Sociology and Anthropology.

Career Clusters: 03 Arts, Audio/Video Technology, and Communications; 05 Education and Training. **Career Pathways:** 03.1 Audio and Video Technology and Film; 03.2 Printing Technology; 03.3 Visual Arts; 03.4 Performing Arts; 05.3 Teaching/Training.

Skills: Instructing; Learning Strategies; Speaking; Reading Comprehension; Time Management; Writing; Active Learning; Management of Material Resources.

Work Environment: Indoors; standing; using hands.

Athletic Trainers

- ❋ Personality Type: Social-Realistic-Investigative
- ❋ Annual Earnings: $41,600
- ❋ Earnings Growth Potential: Medium (38.1%)
- ❋ Growth: 36.9%
- ❋ Annual Job Openings: 1,150
- ❋ Self-Employed: 0.7%

Considerations for Job Outlook: Employment growth is expected to be concentrated in the healthcare industry, as athletic training is increasingly used to prevent illness and injury. Job prospects for athletic trainers should also be good in high schools. Keen competition is expected for positions with professional and college sports teams.

Evaluate, advise, and treat athletes to assist recovery from injury, avoid injury, or maintain peak physical fitness. Conduct an initial assessment of an athlete's injury or illness to provide emergency or continued care and to determine whether he or she should be referred to physicians for definitive diagnosis and treatment. Care for athletic injuries, using physical therapy equipment, techniques, and medication. Evaluate athletes' readiness to play, and provide participation clearances when necessary and warranted. Apply protective or injury-preventive devices such as tape, bandages, or braces to body parts such as ankles, fingers, or wrists. Assess and report the progress of recovering athletes to coaches and physicians. Collaborate with physicians to develop and implement comprehensive rehabilitation programs for athletic injuries. Advise athletes on the proper use of equipment. Plan and implement comprehensive athletic-injury and illness-prevention programs. Develop training programs and routines designed to improve athletic performance. Travel with athletic teams to be available at sporting events. Instruct coaches, athletes, parents, medical personnel, and community members in the care and prevention of athletic injuries. Inspect playing fields to locate any items that could injure players. Conduct research and provide instruction on subject matter related to athletic training or sports medicine. Recommend special diets to improve athletes' health, increase their stamina, or alter their weight. Massage body parts to relieve soreness, strains, and bruises.

Education/Training Required: Bachelor's degree. **Education and Training Program:** Athletic Training/Trainer. **Knowledge/Courses:** Medicine and Dentistry; Therapy and Counseling; Biology; Psychology; Customer and Personal Service; Clerical Practices.

Career Cluster: 08 Health Science. **Career Pathway:** 08.2 Diagnostics Services.

Skills: Learning Strategies; Quality Control Analysis; Service Orientation; Instructing; Social Perceptiveness; Science; Monitoring; Systems Evaluation.

Work Environment: More often indoors than outdoors; standing; using hands; exposed to disease or infections.

Atmospheric, Earth, Marine, and Space Sciences Teachers, Postsecondary

- ❋ Personality Type: Social-Investigative
- ❋ Annual Earnings: $82,840
- ❋ Earnings Growth Potential: High (46.9%)
- ❋ Growth: 15.1%
- ❋ Annual Job Openings: 300
- ❋ Self-Employed: 0.2%

Considerations for Job Outlook: Enrollments in postsecondary institutions are expected to continue rising as more people attend college and as workers return to school to update their skills. Opportunities for part-time or temporary positions should be favorable, but significant competition exists for tenure-track positions.

Teach courses in the physical sciences, except chemistry and physics. Conduct research in a particular field of knowledge, and publish findings in professional journals, books, and/or electronic media. Write grant proposals to procure external research funding. Keep abreast of developments in the field by reading current literature, talking with colleagues, and participating in professional conferences. Supervise undergraduate and/or graduate teaching, internships, and research work. Prepare and deliver lectures to undergraduate and/or graduate students on topics such as structural geology, micrometeorology, and atmospheric thermodynamics. Supervise laboratory work and fieldwork. Evaluate and grade students' classwork, assignments, and papers. Prepare course materials such as syllabi, homework assignments, and handouts. Collaborate with colleagues to address teaching and research issues. Compile, administer, and grade examinations, or assign this work to others. Plan, evaluate, and revise curricula, course content, course materials, and methods of instruction. Initiate, facilitate, and moderate classroom discussions. Maintain regularly scheduled office hours to advise and assist students. Advise students on academic and vocational curricula and on career issues. Maintain student atten-

dance records, grades, and other required records. Participate in student recruitment, registration, and placement activities. Perform administrative duties such as serving as department head.

Education/Training Required: Doctoral degree. **Education and Training Programs:** Acoustics; Astronomy; Astrophysics; Atmospheric Chemistry and Climatology; Atmospheric Physics and Dynamics; Atmospheric Sciences and Meteorology, General; Atmospheric Sciences and Meteorology, Other; Atomic/Molecular Physics; Condensed Matter and Materials Physics; Elementary Particle Physics; Geochemistry; Geochemistry and Petrology; Geological and Earth Sciences/Geosciences, Other; Geology/Earth Science, General; Geophysics and Seismology; Hydrology and Water Resources Science; Meteorology; Nuclear Physics; Oceanography, Chemical and Physical; Optics/Optical Sciences; Paleontology; Physics Teacher Education; Physics, Other; Planetary Astronomy and Science; Plasma and High-Temperature Physics; Science Teacher Education/General Science Teacher Education; Theoretical and Mathematical Physics. **Knowledge/Courses:** Chemistry; Physics; Geography; Education and Training; Biology; Mathematics.

Career Clusters: 05 Education and Training; 15 Science, Technology, Engineering, and Mathematics. **Career Pathways:** 05.3 Teaching/Training; 15.2 Science and Mathematics.

Skills: Science; Writing; Mathematics; Learning Strategies; Reading Comprehension; Speaking; Active Listening; Systems Evaluation.

Work Environment: Indoors; sitting.

Biological Science Teachers, Postsecondary

- ❋ Personality Type: Social-Investigative
- ❋ Annual Earnings: $72,700
- ❋ Earnings Growth Potential: High (44.5%)
- ❋ Growth: 15.1%

❋ Annual Job Openings: 1,700
❋ Self-Employed: 0.2%

Considerations for Job Outlook: Enrollments in postsecondary institutions are expected to continue rising as more people attend college and as workers return to school to update their skills. Opportunities for part-time or temporary positions should be favorable, but significant competition exists for tenure-track positions.

Teach courses in biological sciences. Prepare and deliver lectures to undergraduate and/or graduate students on topics such as molecular biology, marine biology, and botany. Evaluate and grade students' classwork, laboratory work, assignments, and papers. Prepare course materials such as syllabi, homework assignments, and handouts. Compile, administer, and grade examinations, or assign this work to others. Supervise students' laboratory work. Keep abreast of developments in the field by reading current literature, talking with colleagues, and participating in professional conferences. Maintain student attendance records, grades, and other required records. Initiate, facilitate, and moderate classroom discussions. Plan, evaluate, and revise curricula, course content, course materials, and methods of instruction. Advise students on academic and vocational curricula and on career issues. Maintain regularly scheduled office hours to advise and assist students. Supervise undergraduate and/or graduate teaching, internships, and research work. Select and obtain materials and supplies such as textbooks and laboratory equipment. Collaborate with colleagues to address teaching and research issues. Conduct research in a particular field of knowledge, and publish findings in professional journals, books, and/or electronic media. Serve on academic or administrative committees that deal with institutional policies, departmental matters, and academic issues.

Education/Training Required: Doctoral degree. **Education and Training Programs:** Anatomy; Animal Physiology; Biochemistry; Biological and Biomedical Sciences, Other; Biology/Biological Sciences, General; Biometry/Biometrics; Biophysics; Biotechnology; Botany/Plant Biology; Cell/Cellular Biology and Histology; Ecology; Ecology, Evolution, Systematics and Population Biology, Other; Entomology; Evolutionary Biology; Immunology; Marine Biology and Biological Oceanography; Microbiology, General; Molecular Biology; Nutrition Sciences; Parasitology; Pathology/Experimental Pathology; Pharmacology; Plant Genetics; Plant Pathology/Phytopathology; Plant Physiology; Radiation Biology/Radiobiology; Toxicology; Virology; Zoology/Animal Biology. **Knowledge/Courses:** Biology; Chemistry; Education and Training; Geography; Physics; English Language.

Career Clusters: 01 Agriculture, Food, and Natural Resources; 05 Education and Training; 15 Science, Technology, Engineering, and Mathematics. **Career Pathways:** 01.5 Natural Resources Systems; 05.3 Teaching/Training; 15.2 Science and Mathematics.

Skills: Science; Writing; Reading Comprehension; Instructing; Speaking; Learning Strategies; Active Learning; Active Listening.

Work Environment: Indoors; sitting.

Business Teachers, Postsecondary

❋ Personality Type: Social-Enterprising-Investigative
❋ Annual Earnings: $73,760
❋ Earnings Growth Potential: Very high (53.0%)
❋ Growth: 15.1%
❋ Annual Job Openings: 2,000
❋ Self-Employed: 0.2%

Considerations for Job Outlook: Enrollments in postsecondary institutions are expected to continue rising as more people attend college and as workers return to school to update their skills. Opportunities for part-time or temporary positions should be favorable, but significant competition exists for tenure-track positions.

Teach courses in business administration and management, such as accounting, finance, human resources, labor relations, marketing, and operations research. Prepare and deliver lectures to undergraduate and/or graduate students on topics such as financial accounting, principles of marketing, and operations management. Evaluate and grade students' classwork, assignments, and papers. Compile, administer, and grade examinations, or assign this work to others. Prepare course materials such as syllabi, homework assignments, and handouts. Maintain student attendance records, grades, and other required records. Initiate, facilitate, and moderate classroom discussions. Plan, evaluate, and revise curricula, course content, course materials, and methods of instruction. Keep abreast of developments in the field by reading current literature, talking with colleagues, and participating in professional organizations and conferences. Maintain regularly scheduled office hours to advise and assist students. Conduct research in a particular field of knowledge, and publish findings in professional journals, books, and/or electronic media. Advise students on academic and vocational curricula and on career issues. Select and obtain materials and supplies such as textbooks. Collaborate with colleagues to address teaching and research issues. Collaborate with members of the business community to improve programs, develop new programs, and provide student access to learning opportunities such as internships. Participate in student recruitment, registration, and placement activities. Serve on academic or administrative committees that deal with institutional policies, departmental matters, and academic issues. Participate in campus and community events.

Education/Training Required: Doctoral degree. **Education and Training Programs:** Accounting; Actuarial Science; Business Administration and Management, General; Business Statistics; Business Teacher Education; Business/Commerce, General; Business/Corporate Communications; Entrepreneurship/Entrepreneurial Studies; Finance, General; Financial Planning and Services; Franchising and Franchise Operations; Human Resources Management/Personnel Administration,

General; Insurance; International Business/Trade/Commerce; International Finance; International Marketing; Investments and Securities; Labor and Industrial Relations; Logistics, Materials, and Supply Chain Management; Management Science; Marketing Research; Marketing/Marketing Management, General; Operations Management and Supervision; Organizational Behavior Studies; Public Finance; Purchasing, Procurement/Acquisitions and Contracts Management. **Knowledge/Courses:** Sociology and Anthropology; Education and Training; Communications and Media; Sales and Marketing; Economics and Accounting; English Language.

Career Clusters: 04 Business, Management, and Administration; 05 Education and Training; 06 Finance; 14 Marketing, Sales, and Service. **Career Pathways:** 04.1 Management; 04.2 Business, Financial Management, and Accounting; 04.3 Human Resources; 04.5 Marketing; 05.3 Teaching/Training; 06.1 Financial and Investment Planning; 06.4 Insurance Services; 14.1 Management and Entrepreneurship; 14.5 Marketing Information Management and Research.

Skills: Writing; Learning Strategies; Instructing; Speaking; Reading Comprehension; Active Learning; Mathematics; Critical Thinking.

Work Environment: Indoors; sitting.

Chemistry Teachers, Postsecondary

* Personality Type: Social-Investigative-Realistic
* Annual Earnings: $70,520
* Earnings Growth Potential: High (41.9%)
* Growth: 15.1%
* Annual Job Openings: 600
* Self-Employed: 0.2%

Considerations for Job Outlook: Enrollments in postsecondary institutions are expected to continue rising as more people attend college and as workers return to school to update their skills. Opportunities for part-time or temporary positions should be favorable, but significant competition exists for tenure-track positions.

Teach courses pertaining to the chemical and physical properties and compositional changes of substances. Work may include instruction in the methods of qualitative and quantitative chemical analysis. Includes both teachers primarily engaged in teaching and those who do a combination of both teaching and research. Prepare and deliver lectures to undergraduate and/or graduate students on topics such as organic chemistry, analytical chemistry, and chemical separation. Supervise students' laboratory work. Evaluate and grade students' classwork, laboratory performance, assignments, and papers. Compile, administer, and grade examinations, or assign this work to others. Maintain student attendance records, grades, and other required records. Prepare course materials such as syllabi, homework assignments, and handouts. Maintain regularly scheduled office hours to advise and assist students. Plan, evaluate, and revise curricula, course content, course materials, and methods of instruction. Supervise undergraduate and/or graduate teaching, internships, and research work. Keep abreast of developments in the field by reading current literature, talking with colleagues, and participating in professional conferences. Initiate, facilitate, and moderate classroom discussions. Select and obtain materials and supplies such as textbooks and laboratory equipment. Conduct research in a particular field of knowledge, and publish findings in professional journals, books, and/or electronic media. Advise students on academic and vocational curricula and on career issues. Collaborate with colleagues to address teaching and research issues. Serve on academic or administrative committees that deal with institutional policies, departmental matters, and academic issues.

Education/Training Required: Doctoral degree. **Education and Training Programs:** Analytical Chemistry; Chemical Physics; Chemistry, General; Chemistry, Other; Geochemistry; Inorganic Chemistry; Organic Chemistry; Physical Chemistry; Poly-mer Chemistry. **Knowledge/Courses:** Chemistry; Physics; Biology; Education and Training; Mathematics; Computers and Electronics.

Career Cluster: 15 Science, Technology, Engineering, and Mathematics. **Career Pathway:** 15.2 Science and Mathematics.

Skills: Science; Writing; Speaking; Instructing; Reading Comprehension; Learning Strategies; Active Learning; Operations Analysis.

Work Environment: Indoors; sitting; contaminants; hazardous conditions.

Chiropractors

- ❋ Personality Type: Social-Investigative-Realistic
- ❋ Annual Earnings: $67,200
- ❋ Earnings Growth Potential: Very high (52.0%)
- ❋ Growth: 19.5%
- ❋ Annual Job Openings: 1,820
- ❋ Self-Employed: 44.5%

Considerations for Job Outlook: Projected growth stems from increasing consumer demand for alternative health care. Job prospects for new chiropractors are expected to be good, especially for those who enter a multidisciplined practice.

Adjust spinal column and other articulations of the body to correct abnormalities of the human body believed to be caused by interference with the nervous system. Examine patients to determine nature and extent of disorders. Manipulate spines or other involved areas. May utilize supplementary measures such as exercise, rest, water, light, heat, and nutritional therapy. Diagnose health problems by reviewing patients' health and medical histories; questioning, observing, and examining patients; and interpreting X-rays. Maintain accurate case histories of patients. Evaluate the functioning of the neuromuscularskeletal system and the spine, using systems of chiropractic diagnosis.

Social-C

Perform a series of manual adjustments to spines, or other articulations of the body, to correct musculoskeletal systems. Obtain and record patients' medical histories. Advise patients about recommended courses of treatment. Consult with and refer patients to appropriate health practitioners when necessary. Analyze X-rays to locate the sources of patients' difficulties and to rule out fractures or diseases as sources of problems. Counsel patients about nutrition, exercise, sleeping habits, stress management, and other matters. Arrange for diagnostic X-rays to be taken. Suggest and apply the use of supports such as straps, tapes, bandages, and braces if necessary.

Education/Training Required: First professional degree. **Education and Training Program:** Chiropractic (DC). **Knowledge/Courses:** Medicine and Dentistry; Therapy and Counseling; Biology; Psychology; Personnel and Human Resources; Sales and Marketing.

Career Cluster: 08 Health Science. **Career Pathway:** 08.1 Therapeutic Services.

Skills: Science; Service Orientation; Operations Analysis; Management of Financial Resources; Writing; Reading Comprehension; Systems Evaluation; Time Management.

Work Environment: Indoors; standing; using hands; bending or twisting the body; repetitive motions; exposed to disease or infections.

Coaches and Scouts

- ❋ Personality Type: Social-Enterprising-Realistic
- ❋ Annual Earnings: $28,340
- ❋ Earnings Growth Potential: High (42.2%)
- ❋ Growth: 24.8%
- ❋ Annual Job Openings: 9,920
- ❋ Self-Employed: 16.2%

Considerations for Job Outlook: Employment is expected to grow as more people participate in organized sports. Opportunities should be best for part-time umpires, referees, and other sports officials at the high school level.

Instruct or coach groups or individuals in the fundamentals of sports. Demonstrate techniques and methods of participation. May evaluate athletes' strengths and weaknesses as possible recruits or to improve the athletes' technique to prepare them for competition. Plan, organize, and conduct practice sessions. Provide training direction, encouragement, and motivation to prepare athletes for games, competitive events, or tours. Identify and recruit potential athletes, arranging and offering incentives such as athletic scholarships. Plan strategies and choose team members for individual games or sports seasons. Plan and direct physical conditioning programs that will enable athletes to achieve maximum performance. Adjust coaching techniques based on the strengths and weaknesses of athletes. File scouting reports that detail player assessments, provide recommendations on athlete recruitment, and identify locations and individuals to be targeted for future recruitment efforts. Keep records of athlete, team, and opposing team performance. Instruct individuals or groups in sports rules, game strategies, and performance principles such as specific ways of moving the body, hands, and feet in order to achieve desired results. Analyze the strengths and weaknesses of opposing teams to develop game strategies. Evaluate athletes' skills and review performance records to determine their fitness and potential in a particular area of athletics. Keep abreast of changing rules, techniques, technologies, and philosophies relevant to their sport. Monitor athletes' use of equipment to ensure safe and proper use. Explain and enforce safety rules and regulations. Develop and arrange competition schedules and programs.

Education/Training Required: Long-term on-the-job training. **Education and Training Programs:** Health and Physical Education, General; Physical Education Teaching and Coaching; Sport and Fitness Administration/Management. **Knowledge/Courses:** Education and Training; Therapy and Counseling; Sales and Marketing; Personnel and Human Resources; Psychology; English Language.

Career Cluster: 05 Education and Training. **Career Pathways:** 05.1 Administration and Administrative Support; 05.3 Teaching/Training.

Skills: Management of Personnel Resources; Instructing; Systems Evaluation; Monitoring; Management of Material Resources; Negotiation; Learning Strategies; Persuasion.

Work Environment: Indoors; standing; noise; very hot or cold.

Communications Teachers, Postsecondary

Look for the job description among the Artistic jobs.

Compliance Officers

Look for the job description among the Conventional jobs.

Computer Science Teachers, Postsecondary

- ❋ Personality Type: Social-Investigative-Conventional
- ❋ Annual Earnings: $70,300
- ❋ Earnings Growth Potential: High (48.5%)
- ❋ Growth: 15.1%
- ❋ Annual Job Openings: 1,000
- ❋ Self-Employed: 0.2%

Considerations for Job Outlook: Enrollments in postsecondary institutions are expected to continue rising as more people attend college and as workers return to school to update their skills. Opportunities for part-time or temporary positions should be favorable, but significant competition exists for tenure-track positions.

Teach courses in computer science. May specialize in a field of computer science, such as the design and function of computers or operations and research analysis. Evaluate and grade students' classwork, laboratory work, assignments, and papers. Maintain student attendance records, grades, and other required records. Prepare and deliver lectures to undergraduate and/or graduate students on topics such as programming, data structures, and software design. Prepare course materials such as syllabi, homework assignments, and handouts. Compile, administer, and grade examinations, or assign this work to others. Keep abreast of developments in the field by reading current literature, talking with colleagues, and participating in professional conferences. Initiate, facilitate, and moderate classroom discussions. Plan, evaluate, and revise curricula, course content, course materials, and methods of instruction. Supervise students' laboratory work. Maintain regularly scheduled office hours to advise and assist students. Select and obtain materials and supplies such as textbooks and laboratory equipment. Conduct research in a particular field of knowledge, and publish findings in professional journals, books, and/or electronic media. Advise students on academic and vocational curricula and on career issues. Participate in student recruitment, registration, and placement activities. Collaborate with colleagues to address teaching and research issues. Serve on academic or administrative committees that deal with institutional policies, departmental matters, and academic issues. Act as advisers to student organizations. Supervise undergraduate and/or graduate teaching, internship, and research work. Perform administrative duties such as serving as department head.

Education/Training Required: Doctoral degree. **Education and Training Programs:** Computer and Information Sciences, General; Computer Programming/Programmer, General; Computer Science; Computer Systems Analysis/Analyst; Information Science/Studies. **Knowledge/Courses:** Computers and Electronics; Engineering and Technology; Education and Training; Telecommunications; Design; English Language.

Career Clusters: 05 Education and Training; 11 Information Technology. **Career Pathways:** 05.3 Teaching/Training; 11.1 Network Systems; 11.2

Social-C

Information Support Services; 11.4 Programming and Software Development.

Skills: Programming; Learning Strategies; Instructing; Writing; Speaking; Reading Comprehension; Active Learning; Mathematics.

Work Environment: Indoors; sitting; repetitive motions.

Computer Systems Analysts

Look for the job description among the Investigative jobs.

Customer Service Representatives

- ❋ Personality Type: Social-Enterprising-Conventional
- ❋ Annual Earnings: $30,460
- ❋ Earnings Growth Potential: Low (35.8%)
- ❋ Growth: 17.7%
- ❋ Annual Job Openings: 110,840
- ❋ Self-Employed: 0.4%

Considerations for Job Outlook: Businesses are expected to place increasing emphasis on customer relations, resulting in increased employment for these workers. Prospects are expected to be good, particularly for job-seekers who are fluent in more than one language.

Interact with customers to provide information in response to inquiries about products and services and to handle and resolve complaints. Confer with customers by telephone or in person to provide information about products and services, to take orders or cancel accounts, or to obtain details of complaints. Keep records of customer interactions and transactions, recording details of inquiries, complaints, and comments, as well as actions taken. Resolve customers' service or billing complaints by performing activities such as exchanging merchandise, refunding money, and adjusting bills. Check to

ensure that appropriate changes were made to resolve customers' problems. Contact customers to respond to inquiries or to notify them of claim-investigation results and any planned adjustments. Refer unresolved customer grievances to designated departments for further investigation. Determine charges for services requested, collect deposits or payments, or arrange for billing. Complete contract forms, prepare change of address records, and issue service-discontinuance orders, using computers. Obtain and examine all relevant information to assess validity of complaints and to determine possible causes, such as extreme weather conditions, that could increase utility bills. Solicit sale of new or additional services or products. Review insurance policy terms to determine whether a particular loss is covered by insurance. Review claims adjustments with dealers, examining parts claimed to be defective and approving or disapproving dealers' claims.

Education/Training Required: Moderate-term on-the-job training. **Education and Training Programs:** Customer Service Support/Call Center/Teleservice Operation; Receptionist Training. **Knowledge/Courses:** Clerical Practices; Customer and Personal Service; English Language.

Career Cluster: 04 Business, Management, and Administration. **Career Pathway:** 04.6 Administrative and Information Support.

Skills: Service Orientation; Persuasion; Negotiation; Active Listening; Speaking; Reading Comprehension.

Work Environment: Indoors; sitting; using hands; repetitive motions; noise.

Job Specialization: Patient Representatives

Assist patients in obtaining services, understanding policies, and making health-care decisions. Explain policies, procedures, or services to patients using medical or administrative knowledge. Coordinate communication between patients, family members, medical staff, administrative staff, or regulatory agencies. Investigate and direct patient inquiries or complaints to appropriate medical staff members, and follow up to ensure satisfactory resolution. Interview patients or their representatives to identify problems relating to care. Refer patients to appropriate health-care services or resources. Analyze patients' abilities to pay to determine charges on a sliding scale. Collect and report data on topics such as patient encounters and inter-institutional problems, making recommendations for change when appropriate. Develop and distribute newsletters, brochures, or other printed materials to share information with patients or medical staff. Teach patients to use home health-care equipment. Identify and share research, recommendations, or other information regarding legal liabilities, risk management, or quality of care. Read current literature, talk with colleagues, continue education, or participate in professional organizations or conferences to keep abreast of developments in the field. Maintain knowledge of community services and resources available to patients. Provide consultation or training to volunteers or staff on topics such as guest relations, patients' rights, and medical issues.

Education/Training Required: Bachelor's degree. **Education and Training Programs:** Customer Service Support/Call Center/Teleservice Operation; Receptionist Training. **Knowledge/Courses:** Therapy and Counseling; Psychology; Customer and Personal Service; Sociology and Anthropology; Philosophy and Theology; Medicine and Dentistry.

Personality Type: Social-Enterprising. **Career Cluster:** 04 Business, Management, and Administration. **Career Pathway:** 04.6 Administrative and Information Support.

Skills: Service Orientation; Persuasion; Social Perceptiveness; Negotiation; Systems Evaluation; Instructing; Critical Thinking; Systems Analysis.

Work Environment: Indoors; sitting; noise; exposed to disease or infections.

Dental Hygienists

- ✴ Personality Type: Social-Realistic-Conventional
- ✴ Annual Earnings: $68,250
- ✴ Earnings Growth Potential: Low (34.1%)
- ✴ Growth: 36.1%
- ✴ Annual Job Openings: 9,840
- ✴ Self-Employed: 0.1%

Considerations for Job Outlook: An increase in the number of older people and a growing emphasis on preventative dental care are expected to create jobs. To meet increased demand, dental hygienists will perform some services previously done by dentists. Job prospects should be favorable but will vary by geographic location.

Clean teeth, and examine oral areas, head, and neck for signs of oral disease. May educate patients on oral hygiene, take and develop X-rays, or apply fluoride or sealants. Clean calcareous deposits, accretions, and stains from teeth and beneath margins of gums, using dental instruments. Feel and visually examine gums for sores and signs of disease. Chart conditions of decay and disease for diagnosis and treatment by dentist. Feel lymph nodes under patient's chin to detect swelling or tenderness that could indicate presence of oral cancer. Apply fluorides and other cavity-preventing agents to arrest dental decay. Examine gums, using probes, to locate periodontal recessed gums and signs of gum disease. Expose and develop X-ray film. Provide clinical services and health education to improve and maintain oral health of schoolchildren. Remove excess cement from coronal surfaces of teeth. Make impressions for study casts. Place, carve, and finish amalgam restorations. Administer local anesthetic agents. Conduct dental health clinics for community groups to augment services of dentist. Remove sutures and dressings. Place and remove rubber dams, matrices, and temporary restorations.

Education/Training Required: Associate degree. **Education and Training Program:** Dental

Social-D

Hygiene/Hygienist. **Knowledge/Courses:** Medicine and Dentistry; Psychology; Therapy and Counseling; Chemistry; Biology; Sales and Marketing.

Career Cluster: 08 Health Science. **Career Pathway:** 08.1 Therapeutic Services.

Skills: Science; Troubleshooting; Service Orientation; Writing; Instructing; Coordination; Operation Monitoring; Active Learning.

Work Environment: Indoors; sitting; using hands; bending or twisting the body; repetitive motions; noise; contaminants; exposed to radiation; exposed to disease or infections.

Economics Teachers, Postsecondary

- ❀ Personality Type: Social-Investigative
- ❀ Annual Earnings: $83,370
- ❀ Earnings Growth Potential: High (50.5%)
- ❀ Growth: 15.1%
- ❀ Annual Job Openings: 400
- ❀ Self-Employed: 0.2%

Considerations for Job Outlook: Enrollments in postsecondary institutions are expected to continue rising as more people attend college and as workers return to school to update their skills. Opportunities for part-time or temporary positions should be favorable, but significant competition exists for tenure-track positions.

Teach courses in economics. Prepare and deliver lectures to undergraduate and/or graduate students on topics such as econometrics, price theory, and macroeconomics. Prepare course materials such as syllabi, homework assignments, and handouts. Evaluate and grade students' classwork, assignments, and papers. Compile, administer, and grade examinations, or assign this work to others. Keep abreast of developments in the field by reading current literature, talking with colleagues, and participating in professional conferences. Maintain student attendance records, grades, and other required records. Initiate, facilitate, and moderate classroom discus-sions. Maintain regularly scheduled office hours in order to advise and assist students. Select and obtain materials and supplies such as textbooks. Plan, evaluate, and revise curricula, course content, course materials, and methods of instruction. Conduct research in a particular field of knowledge, and publish findings in professional journals, books, and/or electronic media. Supervise undergraduate and/or graduate teaching, internship, and research work. Advise students on academic and vocational curricula and on career issues. Serve on academic or administrative committees that deal with institutional policies, departmental matters, and academic issues. Collaborate with colleagues to address teaching and research issues. Compile bibliographies of specialized materials for outside reading assignments.

Education/Training Required: Doctoral degree. **Education and Training Programs:** Applied Economics; Business/Managerial Economics; Development Economics and International Development; Econometrics and Quantitative Economics; Economics, General; Economics, Other; Humanities/Humanistic Studies; International Economics; Social Science Teacher Education. **Knowledge/Courses:** Economics and Accounting; History and Archeology; Mathematics; Geography; English Language; Law and Government.

Career Clusters: 04 Business, Management, and Administration; 15 Science, Technology, Engineering, and Mathematics. **Career Pathways:** 04.1 Management; 15.2 Science and Mathematics.

Skills: Science; Operations Analysis; Learning Strategies; Instructing; Mathematics; Active Learning; Writing; Speaking.

Work Environment: Indoors; sitting.

Education Teachers, Postsecondary

- ❀ Personality Type: Social-Artistic-Investigative
- ❀ Annual Earnings: $59,140
- ❀ Earnings Growth Potential: High (45.0%)

❊ Growth: 15.1%

❊ Annual Job Openings: 1,800

❊ Self-Employed: 0.2%

Considerations for Job Outlook: Enrollments in postsecondary institutions are expected to continue rising as more people attend college and as workers return to school to update their skills. Opportunities for part-time or temporary positions should be favorable, but significant competition exists for tenure-track positions.

Teach courses pertaining to education, such as counseling, curriculum, guidance, instruction, teacher education, and teaching English as a second language. Prepare course materials such as syllabi, homework assignments, and handouts. Prepare and deliver lectures to undergraduate and/or graduate students on topics such as children's literature, learning and development, and reading instruction. Initiate, facilitate, and moderate classroom discussions. Evaluate and grade students' classwork, assignments, and papers. Plan, evaluate, and revise curricula, course content, course materials, and methods of instruction. Supervise students' fieldwork, internship, and research work. Keep abreast of developments in the field by reading current literature, talking with colleagues, and participating in professional conferences. Advise students on academic and vocational curricula and on career issues. Maintain regularly scheduled office hours to advise and assist students. Maintain student attendance records, grades, and other required records. Collaborate with colleagues to address teaching and research issues. Compile, administer, and grade examinations, or assign this work to others. Conduct research in a particular field of knowledge, and publish findings in professional journals, books, or electronic media. Select and obtain materials and supplies such as textbooks. Participate in student recruitment, registration, and placement activities. Advise and instruct teachers employed in school systems by providing activities such as in-service seminars.

Education/Training Required: Doctoral degree. **Education and Training Programs:** Agricultural Teacher Education; Art Teacher Education; Biology Teacher Education; Business Teacher Education; Chemistry Teacher Education; Computer Teacher Education; Drama and Dance Teacher Education; Driver and Safety Teacher Education; Education, General; English/Language Arts Teacher Education; Family and Consumer Sciences/Home Economics Teacher Education; Foreign Language Teacher Education; French Language Teacher Education; Geography Teacher Education; German Language Teacher Education; Health Occupations Teacher Education; Health Teacher Education; History Teacher Education; Humanities; Mathematics Teacher Education; Music Teacher Education; Physical Education Teaching and Coaching; Physics Teacher Education; Reading Teacher Education; Marketing and Distribution Teacher Education; Science Teacher Education; Social Science Teacher Education; Social Studies Teacher Education; Spanish Language Teacher Education; Speech Teacher Education; Technical Teacher Education; Technology Teacher Education/Industrial Arts Teacher Education; Trade and Industrial Teacher Education; others. **Knowledge/Courses:** Sociology and Anthropology; Education and Training; Psychology; Therapy and Counseling; English Language; Philosophy and Theology.

Career Cluster: 05 Education and Training. **Career Pathway:** 05.3 Teaching/Training.

Skills: Writing; Speaking; Learning Strategies; Reading Comprehension; Instructing; Active Listening; Science; Monitoring.

Work Environment: Indoors; sitting.

Elementary School Teachers, Except Special Education

❊ Personality Type: Social-Artistic-Conventional

❊ Annual Earnings: $51,660

❊ Earnings Growth Potential: Low (33.4%)

❊ Growth: 15.8%

❊ Annual Job Openings: 59,650

❊ Self-Employed: 0.0%

Social-E

Considerations for Job Outlook: Enrollment from 2008 to 2018 is expected to grow more slowly than in recent years. Prospects are usually better in urban and rural areas, for bilingual teachers, and for math and science teachers.

Teach pupils in public or private schools at the elementary level basic academic, social, and other formative skills. Establish and enforce rules for behavior and procedures for maintaining order among the students for whom they are responsible. Observe and evaluate students' performance, behavior, social development, and physical health. Prepare materials and classrooms for class activities. Adapt teaching methods and instructional materials to meet students' varying needs and interests. Plan and conduct activities for a balanced program of instruction, demonstration, and work time that provides students with opportunities to observe, question, and investigate. Instruct students individually and in groups, using various teaching methods such as lectures, discussions, and demonstrations. Establish clear objectives for all lessons, units, and projects, and communicate those objectives to students. Assign and grade classwork and homework. Read books to entire classes or small groups. Prepare, administer, and grade tests and assignments in order to evaluate students' progress. Confer with parents or guardians, teachers, counselors, and administrators to resolve students' behavioral and academic problems. Meet with parents and guardians to discuss their children's progress and to determine their priorities for their children and their resource needs. Prepare students for later grades by encouraging them to explore learning opportunities and to persevere with challenging tasks. Maintain accurate and complete student records as required by laws, district policies, and administrative regulations.

Education/Training Required: Bachelor's degree. **Education and Training Programs:** Elementary Education and Teaching; Teacher Education, Multiple Levels. **Knowledge/Courses:** History and Archeology; Geography; Philosophy and Theology; Sociology and Anthropology; Fine Arts; Therapy and Counseling.

Career Cluster: 05 Education and Training. **Career Pathway:** 05.3 Teaching/Training.

Skills: Learning Strategies; Social Perceptiveness; Monitoring; Systems Evaluation; Service Orientation; Writing; Instructing; Systems Analysis.

Work Environment: Indoors; standing; noise.

Engineering Teachers, Postsecondary

- Personality Type: Social-Investigative-Realistic
- Annual Earnings: $89,670
- Earnings Growth Potential: High (49.0%)
- Growth: 15.1%
- Annual Job Openings: 1,000
- Self-Employed: 0.2%

Considerations for Job Outlook: Enrollments in postsecondary institutions are expected to continue rising as more people attend college and as workers return to school to update their skills. Opportunities for part-time or temporary positions should be favorable, but significant competition exists for tenure-track positions.

Teach courses pertaining to the application of physical laws and principles of engineering for the development of machines, materials, instruments, processes, and services. Includes teachers of subjects such as chemical, civil, electrical, industrial, mechanical, mineral, and petroleum engineering. Includes both teachers primarily engaged in teaching and those who do a combination of both teaching and research. Prepare and deliver lectures to undergraduate and/or graduate students on topics such as mechanics, hydraulics, and robotics. Keep abreast of developments in the field by reading current literature, talking with colleagues, and participating in professional conferences. Supervise undergraduate and/or graduate teaching, internship, and research work. Evaluate and grade students' classwork, laboratory work, assignments, and papers. Conduct research in a particular field of knowledge, and publish findings in professional journals, books, and/or electronic media. Prepare course materials such as syllabi, homework assignments, and handouts. Compile, administer, and grade examinations, or assign this work to others. Write grant proposals to procure external research funding. Supervise students' laboratory work. Initiate, facilitate, and moderate class discussions. Maintain regularly scheduled office hours to advise and assist students. Plan, evaluate, and revise curricula, course content, course materials, and methods of instruction. Advise students on academic and vocational curricula and on career issues. Maintain student attendance records, grades, and other required records. Collaborate with colleagues to address teaching and research issues. Select and obtain materials and supplies such as textbooks and laboratory equipment. Participate in student recruitment, registration, and placement activities.

Education/Training Required: Doctoral degree. **Education and Training Programs:** Aerospace, Aeronautical, and Astronautical/Space Engineering; Agricultural Engineering; Architectural Engineering; Bioengineering and Biomedical Engineering; Ceramic Sciences and Engineering; Chemical Engineering; Civil Engineering, General; Computer Engineering, General; Computer Hardware Engineering; Computer Software Engineering; Construction Engineering; Electrical and Electronics Engineering; Engineering Mechanics; Engineering Physics/Applied Physics; Engineering Science; Engineering, General; Environmental/Environmental Health Engineering; Forest Engineering; Geological/Geophysical Engineering; Geotechnical and Geoenvironmental Engineering; Industrial Engineering; Manufacturing Engineering; Materials Engineering; Mechanical Engineering; Metallurgical Engineering; Mining and Mineral Engineering; Naval Architecture and Marine Engineering; Nuclear Engineering; Ocean Engineering; Petroleum Engineering; Polymer/Plastics Engineering; Structural Engineering; Surveying Engineering; Systems Engineering; Textile Sciences and Engineering; Transportation and Highway Engineering; Water Resources Engineering; others. **Knowledge/Courses:** Physics; Engineering and

Technology; Design; Mathematics; Chemistry; Education and Training.

Career Clusters: 02 Architecture and Construction; 05 Education and Training; 11 Information Technology; 15 Science, Technology, Engineering, and Mathematics. **Career Pathways:** 02.1 Design/Pre-Construction; 05.3 Teaching/Training; 11.4 Programming and Software Development; 15.1 Engineering and Technology; 15.2 Science and Mathematics.

Skills: Mathematics; Science; Instructing; Reading Comprehension; Writing; Learning Strategies; Speaking; Operations Analysis.

Work Environment: Indoors; sitting.

English Language and Literature Teachers, Postsecondary

- ❋ Personality Type: Social-Artistic-Investigative
- ❋ Annual Earnings: $60,400
- ❋ Earnings Growth Potential: High (45.6%)
- ❋ Growth: 15.1%
- ❋ Annual Job Openings: 2,000
- ❋ Self-Employed: 0.2%

Considerations for Job Outlook: Enrollments in postsecondary institutions are expected to continue rising as more people attend college and as workers return to school to update their skills. Opportunities for part-time or temporary positions should be favorable, but significant competition exists for tenure-track positions.

Teach courses in English language and literature, including linguistics and comparative literature. Initiate, facilitate, and moderate classroom discussions. Evaluate and grade students' classwork, assignments, and papers. Prepare course materials such as syllabi, homework assignments, and handouts. Prepare and deliver lectures to undergraduate and graduate students on topics such as poetry, novel structure, and translation and adaptation. Maintain

Social-E

student attendance records, grades, and other required records. Plan, evaluate, and revise curricula, course content, course materials, and methods of instruction. Compile, administer, and grade examinations, or assign this work to others. Maintain regularly scheduled office hours in order to advise and assist students. Keep abreast of developments in the field by reading current literature, talking with colleagues, and participating in professional conferences. Select and obtain materials and supplies such as textbooks. Advise students on academic and vocational curricula and on career issues. Conduct research in a particular field of knowledge, and publish findings in professional journals, books, or electronic media. Collaborate with colleagues to address teaching and research issues. Serve on academic or administrative committees that deal with institutional policies, departmental matters, and academic issues. Participate in campus and community events. Participate in student recruitment, registration, and placement activities. Compile bibliographies of specialized materials for outside reading assignments.

Education/Training Required: Doctoral degree. **Education and Training Programs:** Comparative Literature; English Language and Literature, General; English Language and Literature/Letters, Other; Humanities/Humanistic Studies. **Knowledge/Courses:** Philosophy and Theology; Fine Arts; English Language; Communications and Media; History and Archeology; Sociology and Anthropology.

Career Clusters: 03 Arts, Audio/Video Technology, and Communications; 05 Education and Training. **Career Pathways:** 03.5 Journalism and Broadcasting; 05.3 Teaching/Training.

Skills: Learning Strategies; Writing; Instructing; Reading Comprehension; Speaking; Judgment and Decision Making; Active Listening; Active Learning.

Work Environment: Indoors; sitting.

Fitness Trainers and Aerobics Instructors

* Personality Type: Social-Realistic-Enterprising

* Annual Earnings: $31,090
* Earnings Growth Potential: High (45.1%)
* Growth: 29.4%
* Annual Job Openings: 12,380
* Self-Employed: 9.2%

Considerations for Job Outlook: Employment growth for these workers is expected due to increased concern about health and physical fitness. People who have degrees in fitness-related subjects should have better opportunities, and trainers who incorporate new technology and wellness issues as part of their services may be more sought after.

Instruct or coach groups or individuals in exercise activities and the fundamentals of sports. Demonstrate techniques and methods of participation. Explain and enforce safety rules and regulations governing sports, recreational activities, and the use of exercise equipment. Offer alternatives during classes to accommodate different levels of fitness. Plan routines, choose appropriate music, and choose different movements for each set of muscles, depending on participants' capabilities and limitations. Observe participants, and inform them of corrective measures necessary for skill improvement. Teach proper breathing techniques used during physical exertion. Teach and demonstrate use of gymnastic and training equipment such as trampolines and weights. Instruct participants in maintaining exertion levels to maximize benefits from exercise routines. Maintain fitness equipment. Conduct therapeutic, recreational, or athletic activities. Monitor participants' progress, and adapt programs as needed. Evaluate individuals' abilities, needs, and physical conditions, and develop suitable training programs to meet any special requirements. Plan physical education programs to promote development of participants' physical attributes and social skills. Provide students with information and resources regarding nutrition, weight control, and lifestyle issues. Administer emergency first aid, wrap injuries, treat minor chronic disabilities, or refer injured persons to physicians. Advise clients about proper clothing and shoes.

Education/Training Required: Postsecondary vocational training. **Education and Training**

Programs: Health and Physical Education, General; Physical Education Teaching and Coaching; Sport and Fitness Administration/Management. **Knowledge/Courses:** Education and Training; Therapy and Counseling; Psychology; Customer and Personal Service; Medicine and Dentistry; Biology.

Career Cluster: 05 Education and Training. **Career Pathways:** 05.3 Teaching/Training; 05.1 Administration and Administrative Support.

Skills: Learning Strategies; Service Orientation; Operations Analysis; Instructing; Social Perceptiveness; Technology Design; Systems Evaluation; Persuasion.

Work Environment: Indoors; standing; walking and running; bending or twisting the body; repetitive motions.

Foreign Language and Literature Teachers, Postsecondary

Look for the job description among the Artistic occupations.

Health Specialties Teachers, Postsecondary

- ❋ Personality Type: Social-Investigative
- ❋ Annual Earnings: $85,270
- ❋ Earnings Growth Potential: Very high (52.7%)
- ❋ Growth: 15.1%
- ❋ Annual Job Openings: 4,000
- ❋ Self-Employed: 0.2%

Considerations for Job Outlook: Enrollments in postsecondary institutions are expected to continue rising as more people attend college and as workers return to school to update their skills. Opportunities for part-time or temporary positions should be favorable, but significant competition exists for tenure-track positions.

Teach courses in health specialties, such as veterinary medicine, dentistry, pharmacy, therapy, laboratory technology, and public health. Initiate, facilitate, and moderate classroom discussions. Keep abreast of developments in the field by reading current literature, talking with colleagues, and participating in professional conferences. Compile, administer, and grade examinations, or assign this work to others. Evaluate and grade students' classwork, assignments, and papers. Prepare course materials such as syllabi, homework assignments, and handouts. Prepare and deliver lectures to undergraduate or graduate students on topics such as public health, stress management, and worksite health promotion. Plan, evaluate, and revise curricula, course content, course materials, and methods of instruction. Supervise undergraduate or graduate teaching, internship, and research work. Conduct research in a particular field of knowledge, and publish findings in professional journals, books, or electronic media. Collaborate with colleagues to address teaching and research issues. Supervise laboratory sessions. Maintain student attendance records, grades, and other required records. Maintain regularly scheduled office hours in order to advise and assist students. Advise students on academic and vocational curricula and on career issues. Participate in student recruitment, registration, and placement activities. Write grant proposals to procure external research funding. Serve on academic or administrative committees that deal with institutional policies, departmental matters, and academic issues.

Education/Training Required: Doctoral degree. **Education and Training Programs:** Art Therapy; Asian Bodywork Therapy; Audiology and Speech-Language Pathology; Biostatistics; Blood Bank Technology Specialist Training; Cardiovascular Technology; Chiropractic; Clinical Laboratory Science/Medical Technology; Clinical Laboratory Assistant Training; Clinical Laboratory Technician; Cytotechnology; Dance Therapy; Dental Assisting; Dental Hygiene; Dental Laboratory Technology; Dentistry; Diagnostic Medical Sonography and Ultrasound Technician Training; Electrocardiograph Technology; Emergency Medical Technology; Environmental Health; Medical Radiologic Technology; Music Therapy; Nuclear Medical Technology; Occupational Health and Industrial Hygiene; Occupational Therapist Assistant Training; Occupational Therapy; Orthotist/Prosthetist; Pharmacy; Pharmacy Technician Training; Physical Therapy Assistant Training; Physical Therapy; Physician Assistant Training; Respiratory Care Therapy; Speech-Language Pathology; Surgical Technology; Therapeutic Recreation/Recreational Therapy; Veterinary Medicine; Veterinary Clinical Sciences, General; Veterinary Technology; Vocational Rehabilitation Counseling; others. **Knowledge/Courses:** Medicine and Dentistry; Biology; Education and Training; Therapy and Counseling; Sociology and Anthropology; Psychology.

Career Clusters: 05 Education and Training; 08 Health Science; 15 Science, Technology, Engineering, and Mathematics. **Career Pathways:** 05.3 Teaching/Training; 08.1 Therapeutic Services; 08.2 Diagnostics Services; 08.3 Health Informatics; 08.5 Biotechnology Research and Development; 15.2 Science and Mathematics.

Skills: Science; Writing; Instructing; Reading Comprehension; Active Listening; Speaking; Learning Strategies; Active Learning.

Work Environment: Indoors; sitting; exposed to disease or infections.

Healthcare Social Workers

- ❋ Personality Type: Social-Investigative
- ❋ Annual Earnings: $47,230
- ❋ Earnings Growth Potential: Medium (37.6%)
- ❋ Growth: 22.4%
- ❋ Annual Job Openings: 6,590
- ❋ Self-Employed: 2.2%

Considerations for Job Outlook: The rapidly increasing elderly population is expected to spur demand for social services. Job prospects should be favorable because of the need to replace the many workers who are leaving the occupation permanently.

Provide persons, families, or vulnerable populations with the psychosocial support needed to cope with chronic, acute, or terminal illnesses such as Alzheimer's, cancer, or AIDS. Services include advising family caregivers, providing patient education and counseling, and making necessary referrals for other social services. Advocate for clients or patients to resolve crises. Collaborate with other professionals to evaluate patients' medical or physical condition and to assess client needs. Refer patients, clients, or families to community resources to assist in recovery from mental or physical illnesses and to provide access to services such as financial assistance, legal aid, housing, job placement, or education. Counsel clients and patients in individual and group sessions to help them overcome dependencies, recover from illnesses, and adjust to life. Use consultation data and social work experience to plan and coordinate client or patient care and rehabilitation, following through to ensure service efficacy. Plan discharge from care facility to home or other care facility. Organize support groups or counsel family members to assist them in understanding, dealing with, and supporting clients or patients. Modify treatment plans to comply with changes in clients' statuses. Monitor, evaluate, and record client progress according to measurable goals described in treatment and care plans. Identify environmental impediments to client or patient progress through interviews and review of patient records. Supervise and direct other workers providing services to clients or patients. Develop or advise on social policy and assist in community development. Investigate child abuse or neglect cases, and take authorized protective action when necessary.

Education/Training Required: Bachelor's degree. **Education and Training Program:** Clinical/Medical Social Work. **Knowledge/Courses:** Therapy and Counseling; Sociology and Anthropology; Psychology; Philosophy and Theology; Customer and Personal Service; Medicine and Dentistry.

Career Cluster: 10 Human Services. **Career Pathway:** 10.2 Counseling and Mental Health Services.

Skills: Social Perceptiveness; Science; Operations Analysis; Service Orientation; Learning Strategies; Active Listening; Writing; Systems Evaluation.

Work Environment: Indoors; sitting; noise; exposed to disease or infections.

Instructional Coordinators

- Personality Type: Social-Investigative-Artistic
- Annual Earnings: $58,830
- Earnings Growth Potential: High (43.1%)
- Growth: 23.2%
- Annual Job Openings: 6,060
- Self-Employed: 2.9%

Considerations for Job Outlook: Continued efforts to improve educational standards are expected to result in more new jobs for these workers. Opportunities should be best for job-seekers who train teachers to use classroom technology and who have experience in reading, mathematics, and science.

Develop instructional material, coordinate educational content, and incorporate current technology in specialized fields that provide guidelines to educators and instructors for developing curricula and conducting courses. Conduct or participate in workshops, committees, and conferences designed to promote the intellectual, social, and physical welfare of students. Plan and conduct teacher training programs and conferences dealing with new classroom procedures, instructional materials and equipment, and teaching aids. Advise teaching and administrative staff in curriculum development, use of materials and equipment, and implementation of state and federal programs and procedures. Recommend, order, or authorize purchase of instructional materials, supplies, equipment, and visual aids designed to meet student educational needs and district standards. Interpret and enforce provisions of state education codes and rules as well as regulations of state education boards. Confer with members of educational committees and advisory groups to obtain knowledge of subject areas and to relate curriculum materials to specific subjects, individual student needs, and occupational areas. Organize production and design of curriculum materials. Research, evaluate, and prepare recommendations on curricula, instructional methods, and materials for school systems. Observe work of teaching staff to evaluate performance and to recommend changes that could strengthen teaching skills. Develop instructional materials to be used by educators and instructors. Prepare grant proposals, budgets, and program policies and goals, or assist in their preparation.

Education/Training Required: Master's degree. **Education and Training Programs:** Curriculum and Instruction; Educational/Instructional Technology. **Knowledge/Courses:** Education and Training; Therapy and Counseling; Philosophy and Theology; Sociology and Anthropology; Personnel and Human Resources; Psychology.

Career Cluster: 05 Education and Training. **Career Pathways:** 05.1 Administration and Administrative Support; 05.3 Teaching/Training.

Skills: Learning Strategies; Systems Evaluation; Instructing; Management of Material Resources; Negotiation; Writing; Management of Personnel Resources; Systems Analysis.

Work Environment: Indoors; standing.

Job Specialization: Instructional Designers and Technologists

Develop instructional materials and products, and assist in the technology-based redesign of courses. Assist faculty in learning about, becoming proficient in, and applying instructional technology. Observe and provide feedback on instructional techniques, presentation methods, or instructional aids. Edit instructional materials, such as books, simulation exercises, lesson plans, instructor guides, and tests. Develop measurement tools to evaluate the effectiveness of instruction or training interventions. Develop instructional materials, such as lesson plans, handouts, or examinations. Define instructional, learning, or performance objectives. Assess effectiveness and efficiency of instruction according to ease of instructional technology use and student learning, knowledge transfer, and satisfaction. Analyze performance data to determine effectiveness of instructional systems, courses, or instructional materials. Research and evaluate emerging instructional technologies or methods. Recommend instructional methods, such as individual or group instruction, self-study, lectures, demonstrations, simulation exercises, and role-playing, appropriate for content and learner characteristics. Recommend changes to curricula or delivery methods, based on information such as instructional effectiveness data, current or future performance requirements, feasibility, and costs. Provide technical support to clients in the implementation of designed instruction or in task analyses and instructional systems design.

Education/Training Required: Bachelor's degree. **Education and Training Programs:** Curriculum and Instruction; Educational/Instructional Technology. **Knowledge/Courses:** No data available.

Personality Type: No data available. **Career Cluster:** 05 Education and Training. **Career Pathways:** 05.1 Administration and Administrative Support; 05.3 Teaching/Training.

Skills: No data available.

Work Environment: No data available.

Kindergarten Teachers, Except Special Education

- ❋ Personality Type: Social-Artistic
- ❋ Annual Earnings: $48,800
- ❋ Earnings Growth Potential: Low (35.0%)
- ❋ Growth: 15.0%
- ❋ Annual Job Openings: 6,300
- ❋ Self-Employed: 1.6%

Considerations for Job Outlook: Enrollment from 2008 to 2018 is expected to grow more slowly than in recent years. Prospects are usually better in urban and rural areas, for bilingual teachers, and for math and science teachers.

Teach elemental natural and social science, personal hygiene, music, art, and literature to children from 4 to 6 years of age. Promote physical, mental, and social development. May be required to hold state certification. Teach basic skills such as color, shape, number, and letter recognition; personal hygiene; and social skills. Establish and enforce rules for behavior and policies and procedures to maintain order among students. Observe and evaluate children's performance, behavior, social development, and physical health. Instruct students individually and in groups, adapting teaching methods to meet students' varying needs and interests. Read books to entire classes or to small groups. Demonstrate activities to children. Provide a variety of materials and resources for children to explore, manipulate, and use, both in learning activities and in imaginative play. Plan and conduct activities for a balanced program of instruction, demonstration, and work time that provides students with opportunities to observe, question, and investigate. Confer with parents or guardians, other teachers, counselors, and administrators to resolve students' behavioral and academic problems. Prepare children for later grades by encouraging them to explore learning opportunities and to persevere with challenging tasks. Establish clear objectives for all lessons, units, and projects, and communicate those objectives to children. Prepare and implement remedial programs for students requiring extra help. Meet with parents and guardians to discuss their children's progress and to determine their priorities for their children and their resource needs.

Education/Training Required: Bachelor's degree. **Education and Training Program:** Early Childhood Education and Teaching. **Knowledge/Courses:** Philosophy and Theology; Fine Arts; Geography; Sociology and Anthropology; Psychology; Education and Training.

Career Cluster: 05 Education and Training. **Career Pathway:** 05.3 Teaching/Training.

Skills: Learning Strategies; Negotiation; Social Perceptiveness; Technology Design; Service Orientation; Active Listening; Management of Personnel Resources; Active Learning.

Work Environment: Indoors; standing.

Law Teachers, Postsecondary

- ✳ Personality Type: Social-Investigative-Enterprising
- ✳ Annual Earnings: $94,260
- ✳ Earnings Growth Potential: Very high (65.0%)
- ✳ Growth: 15.1%
- ✳ Annual Job Openings: 400
- ✳ Self-Employed: 0.2%

Considerations for Job Outlook: Enrollments in postsecondary institutions are expected to continue rising as more people attend college and as workers return to school to update their skills. Opportunities for part-time or temporary positions should be favorable, but significant competition exists for tenure-track positions.

Teach courses in law. Evaluate and grade students' classwork, assignments, papers, and oral presentations. Compile, administer, and grade examinations, or assign this work to others. Prepare and deliver lectures to undergraduate or graduate students on topics such as civil procedure, contracts, and torts. Initiate, facilitate, and moderate classroom discussions. Prepare course materials such as syllabi, homework assignments, and handouts. Keep abreast of developments in the field by reading current literature, talking with colleagues, and participating in professional conferences. Plan, evaluate, and revise curricula, course content, course materials, and methods of instruction. Maintain regularly scheduled office hours to advise and assist students. Conduct research in a particular field of knowledge, and publish findings in professional journals, books, or electronic media. Advise students on academic and vocational curricula and on career issues. Supervise undergraduate and/

or graduate teaching, internship, and research work. Select and obtain materials and supplies such as textbooks. Maintain student attendance records, grades, and other required records. Serve on academic or administrative committees that deal with institutional policies, departmental matters, and academic issues. Perform administrative duties such as serving as department head. Collaborate with colleagues to address teaching and research issues. Participate in student recruitment, registration, and placement activities.

Education/Training Required: First professional degree. **Education and Training Program:** Law (LL.B, J.D.). **Knowledge/Courses:** Law and Government; Education and Training; History and Archeology; English Language; Communications and Media; Philosophy and Theology.

Career Clusters: 05 Education and Training; 12 Law, Public Safety, Corrections, and Security. **Career Pathways:** 05.3 Teaching/Training; 12.5 Legal Services.

Skills: Speaking; Writing; Active Learning; Reading Comprehension; Learning Strategies; Instructing; Active Listening; Critical Thinking.

Work Environment: Indoors; sitting.

Licensed Practical and Licensed Vocational Nurses

- ✳ Personality Type: Social-Realistic
- ✳ Annual Earnings: $40,380
- ✳ Earnings Growth Potential: Low (26.5%)
- ✳ Growth: 20.6%
- ✳ Annual Job Openings: 39,130
- ✳ Self-Employed: 1.2%

Considerations for Job Outlook: An aging population is expected to boost demand for nursing services. Job prospects are expected to be very good, especially in employment settings that serve older populations.

Social-L

Care for ill, injured, convalescent, or disabled persons in hospitals, nursing homes, clinics, private homes, group homes, and similar institutions. May work under the supervision of a registered nurse. Licensing required. Administer prescribed medications or start intravenous fluids, recording times and amounts on patients' charts. Observe patients, charting and reporting changes in patients' conditions, such as adverse reactions to medication or treatment, and taking any necessary actions. Provide basic patient care and treatments such as taking temperatures or blood pressures, dressing wounds, treating bedsores, giving enemas or douches, rubbing with alcohol, massaging, or performing catheterizations. Sterilize equipment and supplies, using germicides, sterilizer, or autoclave. Answer patients' calls, and determine how to assist them. Work as part of a health-care team to assess patient needs, plan and modify care, and implement interventions. Measure and record patients' vital signs, such as height, weight, temperature, blood pressure, pulse, and respiration. Collect samples such as blood, urine, and sputum from patients, and perform routine laboratory tests on samples. Prepare patients for examinations, tests, or treatments, and explain procedures. Assemble and use equipment such as catheters, tracheotomy tubes, and oxygen suppliers. Evaluate nursing intervention outcomes, conferring with other health-care team members as necessary. Record food and fluid intake and output. Help patients with bathing, dressing, maintaining personal hygiene, moving in bed, or standing and walking. Apply compresses, ice bags, and hot water bottles. Inventory and requisition supplies and instruments.

Education/Training Required: Postsecondary vocational training. **Education and Training Program:** Licensed Practical/Vocational Nurse Training. **Knowledge/Courses:** Psychology; Medicine and Dentistry; Therapy and Counseling; Biology; Philosophy and Theology; Customer and Personal Service.

Career Cluster: 08 Health Science. **Career Pathway:** 08.1 Therapeutic Services.

Skills: Science; Social Perceptiveness; Service

Orientation; Operation and Control; Persuasion; Negotiation; Speaking; Operations Analysis.

Work Environment: Indoors; standing; walking and running; using hands; repetitive motions; noise; contaminants; cramped work space; exposed to disease or infections.

Marriage and Family Therapists

Look for the job description among the Artistic occupations.

Mathematical Science Teachers, Postsecondary

* Personality Type: Social-Investigative-Artistic
* Annual Earnings: $65,710
* Earnings Growth Potential: High (46.4%)
* Growth: 15.1%
* Annual Job Openings: 1,000
* Self-Employed: 0.2%

Considerations for Job Outlook: Enrollments in postsecondary institutions are expected to continue rising as more people attend college and as workers return to school to update their skills. Opportunities for part-time or temporary positions should be favorable, but significant competition exists for tenure-track positions.

Teach courses pertaining to mathematical concepts, statistics, and actuarial science and to the application of original and standardized mathematical techniques in solving specific problems and situations. Evaluate and grade students' classwork, assignments, and papers. Compile, administer, and grade examinations, or assign this work to others. Prepare and deliver lectures to undergraduate and/or graduate students on topics such as linear algebra, differential equations, and discrete mathematics. Prepare course materials such as syllabi, homework assignments, and handouts. Maintain student attendance records, grades, and other required records. Maintain regularly scheduled office hours to advise and assist students. Plan, evaluate, and revise curricula, course content, course materials, and methods of instruction. Initiate, facilitate, and moderate classroom discussions. Select and obtain materials and supplies such as textbooks. Keep abreast of developments in the field by reading current literature, talking with colleagues, and participating in professional conferences. Advise students on academic and vocational curricula and on career issues. Collaborate with colleagues to address teaching and research issues. Serve on academic or administrative committees that deal with institutional policies, departmental matters, and academic issues. Participate in student recruitment, registration, and placement activities. Perform administrative duties such as serving as department head. Conduct research in a particular field of knowledge, and publish findings in books, professional journals, and/or electronic media.

Education/Training Required: Doctoral degree. **Education and Training Programs:** Algebra and Number Theory; Analysis and Functional Analysis; Applied Mathematics, General; Business Statistics; Geometry/Geometric Analysis; Logic; Mathematical Statistics and Probability; Mathematics and Statistics, Other; Mathematics, General; Mathematics, Other; Statistics, General; Topology and Foundations. **Knowledge/Courses:** Mathematics; Education and Training; Physics; Computers and Electronics; English Language; Sociology and Anthropology.

Career Cluster: 15 Science, Technology, Engineering, and Mathematics. **Career Pathway:** 15.2 Science and Mathematics.

Skills: Mathematics; Writing; Instructing; Learning Strategies; Reading Comprehension; Active Learning; Speaking; Critical Thinking.

Work Environment: Indoors; sitting; using hands.

Medical Assistants

- ❋ Personality Type: Social-Conventional-Realistic
- ❋ Annual Earnings: $28,860
- ❋ Earnings Growth Potential: Low (27.9%)
- ❋ Growth: 33.9%
- ❋ Annual Job Openings: 21,780
- ❋ Self-Employed: 0.0%

Considerations for Job Outlook: Technological advances in medicine and the aging of the population will create demand for health care, and doctors are expected to hire more assistants in response. Prospects should be excellent, especially for job-seekers with certification.

Perform administrative and certain clinical duties under the direction of physicians. Administrative duties may include scheduling appointments, maintaining medical records, billing, and coding for insurance purposes. Clinical duties may include taking and recording vital signs and medical histories, preparing patients for examination, drawing blood, and administering medications as directed by physician. Record patients' medical history, vital statistics, and information such as test results in medical records. Prepare treatment rooms for patient examinations, keeping the rooms neat and clean. Interview patients to obtain medical information, and measure their vital signs, weights, and heights. Authorize drug refills, and provide prescription information to pharmacies. Clean and sterilize instruments, and dispose of contaminated supplies. Prepare and administer medications as directed by a physician. Show patients to examination rooms, and prepare them for the physician. Explain treatment procedures, medications, diets, and physicians' instructions to patients. Help physicians examine and treat patients, handing them instruments and materials or performing such tasks as giving injections or removing sutures. Collect blood, tissue, or other laboratory specimens, log the specimens, and prepare them for testing. Perform routine laboratory tests and sample analyses. Contact medical facilities

Social-M

or departments to schedule patients for tests or admission. Operate X-ray, electrocardiogram (EKG), and other equipment to administer routine diagnostic tests. Change dressings on wounds. Set up medical laboratory equipment. Perform general office duties such as answering telephones, taking dictation, or completing insurance forms. Greet and log in patients arriving at office or clinic. Schedule appointments for patients. Inventory and order medical, lab, or office supplies and equipment.

Education/Training Required: Moderate-term on-the-job training. **Education and Training Programs:** Allied Health and Medical Assisting Services, Other; Anesthesiologist Assistant Training; Chiropractic Assistant/Technician Training; Medical Administrative/Executive Assistant and Medical Secretary Training; Medical Insurance Coding Specialist/Coder Training; Medical Office Assistant/Specialist Training; Medical Office Management/Administration; Medical Reception/Receptionist; Medical/Clinical Assistant Training; Ophthalmic Technician/Technologist Training; Optometric Technician/Assistant Training; Orthoptics/Orthoptist. **Knowledge/Courses:** Medicine and Dentistry; Clerical Practices; Psychology; Therapy and Counseling; Customer and Personal Service; Public Safety and Security.

Career Cluster: 08 Health Science. **Career Pathways:** 08.2 Diagnostics Services; 08.3 Health Informatics.

Skills: Service Orientation; Active Listening; Science; Speaking; Social Perceptiveness; Negotiation; Operation Monitoring; Monitoring.

Work Environment: Indoors; standing; walking and running; using hands; repetitive motions; exposed to disease or infections.

Mental Health and Substance Abuse Social Workers

* Personality Type: Social-Investigative-Artistic
* Annual Earnings: $38,600
* Earnings Growth Potential: Low (34.7%)
* Growth: 19.5%
* Annual Job Openings: 6,130
* Self-Employed: 2.2%

Considerations for Job Outlook: The rapidly increasing elderly population is expected to spur demand for social services. Job prospects should be favorable because of the need to replace the many workers who are leaving the occupation permanently.

Assess and treat individuals with mental, emotional, or substance abuse problems, including abuse of alcohol, tobacco, and/or other drugs. Activities may include individual and group therapy, crisis intervention, case management, client advocacy, prevention, and education. Counsel clients in individual and group sessions to assist them in dealing with substance abuse, mental and physical illness, poverty, unemployment, or physical abuse. Interview clients, review records, and confer with other professionals to evaluate mental or physical condition of client or patient. Collaborate with counselors, physicians, and nurses to plan and coordinate treatment, drawing on social work experience and patient needs. Monitor, evaluate, and record client progress with respect to treatment goals. Refer patient, client, or family to community resources for housing or treatment to assist in recovery from mental or physical illness, following through to ensure service efficacy. Counsel and aid family members to assist them in understanding, dealing with, and supporting the client or patient. Modify treatment plans according to changes in client status. Plan and conduct programs to prevent substance abuse, to combat social problems, or to improve health and counseling services in community. Supervise and direct other workers who provide services to clients or patients. Develop or advise on social policy and assist in community development. Conduct social research to advance knowledge in the social work field.

Education/Training Required: Master's degree. **Education and Training Program:** Clinical/Medical Social Work. **Knowledge/Courses:** Therapy and Counseling; Psychology; Sociology and

Anthropology; Philosophy and Theology; Customer and Personal Service; Education and Training.

Career Cluster: 10 Human Services. **Career Pathway:** 10.2 Counseling and Mental Health Services.

Skills: Social Perceptiveness; Science; Operations Analysis; Service Orientation; Learning Strategies; Active Learning; Persuasion; Negotiation.

Work Environment: Indoors; sitting; repetitive motions; noise; exposed to disease or infections.

Mental Health Counselors

- ❀ Personality Type: Social-Investigative-Artistic
- ❀ Annual Earnings: $38,150
- ❀ Earnings Growth Potential: Medium (36.6%)
- ❀ Growth: 24.0%
- ❀ Annual Job Openings: 5,010
- ❀ Self-Employed: 6.1%

Considerations for Job Outlook: Increasing demand for services provided by counselors is expected to result in employment growth. But growth will vary by specialty and will be faster for mental health, substance abuse and behavioral disorder, and rehabilitation counselors than for counselors of other specialties. Opportunities should be favorable, particularly in rural areas.

Counsel with emphasis on prevention. Work with individuals and groups to promote optimum mental health. May help individuals deal with addictions and substance abuse; family, parenting, and marital problems; suicide; stress management; problems with self-esteem; and issues associated with aging and mental and emotional health. Maintain confidentiality of records relating to clients' treatment. Guide clients in the development of skills and strategies for dealing with their problems. Encourage clients to express their feelings and discuss what is happening in their lives, and help

them to develop insight into themselves and their relationships. Prepare and maintain all required treatment records and reports. Counsel clients and patients, individually and in group sessions, to assist in overcoming dependencies, adjusting to life, and making changes. Collect information about clients through interviews, observation, and tests. Act as client advocates to coordinate required services or to resolve emergency problems in crisis situations. Develop and implement treatment plans based on clinical experience and knowledge. Collaborate with other staff members to perform clinical assessments and develop treatment plans. Evaluate clients' physical or mental condition based on review of client information. Meet with families, probation officers, police, and other interested parties to exchange necessary information during the treatment process. Refer patients, clients, or family members to community resources or to specialists as necessary. Evaluate the effectiveness of counseling programs and clients' progress in resolving identified problems and moving towards defined objectives. Counsel family members to assist them in understanding, dealing with, and supporting clients or patients.

Education/Training Required: Master's degree. **Education and Training Programs:** Clinical/Medical Social Work; Mental and Social Health Services and Allied Professions, Other; Mental Health Counseling/Counselor; Substance Abuse/Addiction Counseling. **Knowledge/Courses:** Therapy and Counseling; Psychology; Sociology and Anthropology; Philosophy and Theology; Customer and Personal Service; Medicine and Dentistry.

Career Clusters: 08 Health Science; 10 Human Services. **Career Pathways:** 08.3 Health Informatics; 10.2 Counseling and Mental Health Services.

Skills: Science; Social Perceptiveness; Active Listening; Operations Analysis; Service Orientation; Systems Evaluation; Persuasion; Systems Analysis.

Work Environment: Indoors; sitting.

Social-N

Middle School Teachers, Except Special and Career/Technical Education

- Personality Type: Social-Artistic
- Annual Earnings: $51,960
- Earnings Growth Potential: Low (32.7%)
- Growth: 15.3%
- Annual Job Openings: 25,110
- Self-Employed: 0.0%

Considerations for Job Outlook: Enrollment from 2008 to 2018 is expected to grow more slowly than in recent years. Prospects are usually better in urban and rural areas, for bilingual teachers, and for math and science teachers.

Teach students in public or private schools in one or more subjects at the middle, intermediate, or junior high level, which falls between elementary and senior high school as defined by applicable state laws and regulations. Establish and enforce rules for behavior and procedures for maintaining order among the students for whom they are responsible. Adapt teaching methods and instructional materials to meet students' varying needs and interests. Instruct through lectures, discussions, and demonstrations in one or more subjects such as English, mathematics, or social studies. Prepare, administer, and grade tests and assignments to evaluate students' progress. Establish clear objectives for all lessons, units, and projects, and communicate these objectives to students. Plan and conduct activities for a balanced program of instruction, demonstration, and work time that provides students with opportunities to observe, question, and investigate. Maintain accurate, complete, and correct student records as required by laws, district policies, and administrative regulations. Observe and evaluate students' performance, behavior, social development, and physical health. Assign lessons, and correct homework. Prepare materials and classrooms for class activities. Enforce all administration policies and rules governing students. Confer with parents or guardians, oth-er teachers, counselors, and administrators to resolve students' behavioral and academic problems. Prepare students for later grades by encouraging them to explore learning opportunities and to persevere with challenging tasks.

Education/Training Required: Bachelor's degree. **Education and Training Programs:** Art Teacher Education; Computer Teacher Education; English/Language Arts Teacher Education; Family and Consumer Sciences/Home Economics Teacher Education; Foreign Language Teacher Education; Health Occupations Teacher Education; Health Teacher Education; History Teacher Education; Junior High/Intermediate/Middle School Education and Teaching; Mathematics Teacher Education; Music Teacher Education; Physical Education Teaching and Coaching; Reading Teacher Education; Science Teacher Education/General Science Teacher Education; Social Science Teacher Education; Social Studies Teacher Education; Teacher Education and Professional Development, Specific Subject Areas, Other; Technology Teacher Education/Industrial Arts Teacher Education. **Knowledge/Courses:** History and Archeology; Education and Training; Sociology and Anthropology; Fine Arts; Philosophy and Theology; English Language.

Career Cluster: 05 Education and Training. **Career Pathway:** 05.3 Teaching/Training.

Skills: Learning Strategies; Instructing; Negotiation; Writing; Social Perceptiveness; Reading Comprehension; Active Listening; Active Learning.

Work Environment: Indoors; standing; noise.

Museum Technicians and Conservators

Look for the job description among the Artistic occupations.

Nursing Instructors and Teachers, Postsecondary

- ❈ Personality Type: Social-Investigative
- ❈ Annual Earnings: $62,390
- ❈ Earnings Growth Potential: Medium (38.1%)
- ❈ Growth: 15.1%
- ❈ Annual Job Openings: 1,500
- ❈ Self-Employed: 0.2%

Considerations for Job Outlook: Enrollments in postsecondary institutions are expected to continue rising as more people attend college and as workers return to school to update their skills. Opportunities for part-time or temporary positions should be favorable, but significant competition exists for tenure-track positions.

Demonstrate and teach patient care in classroom and clinical units to nursing students. Includes both teachers primarily engaged in teaching and those who do a combination of both teaching and research. Initiate, facilitate, and moderate classroom discussions. Prepare and deliver lectures to undergraduate or graduate students on topics such as pharmacology, mental health nursing, and community health-care practices. Keep abreast of developments in the field by reading current literature, talking with colleagues, and participating in professional conferences. Prepare course materials such as syllabi, homework assignments, and handouts. Supervise students' laboratory and clinical work. Evaluate and grade students' classwork, laboratory and clinic work, assignments, and papers. Collaborate with colleagues to address teaching and research issues. Plan, evaluate, and revise curricula, course content, course materials, and methods of instruction. Assess clinical education needs and patient and client teaching needs, utilizing a variety of methods. Compile, administer, and grade examinations, or assign this work to others. Advise students on academic and vocational curricula and on career issues. Maintain student attendance records, grades, and other required records. Maintain regularly scheduled office hours to advise and assist students. Supervise undergraduate or graduate teaching, internship, and research work. Conduct research in a particular field of knowledge, and publish findings in professional journals, books, and/or electronic media. Participate in student recruitment, registration, and placement activities.

Education/Training Required: Doctoral degree. **Education and Training Program:** Pre-Nursing Studies. **Knowledge/Courses:** Therapy and Counseling; Biology; Sociology and Anthropology; Medicine and Dentistry; Education and Training; Psychology.

Career Clusters: 05 Education and Training; 08 Health Science. **Career Pathways:** 05.3 Teaching/Training; 08.1 Therapeutic Services.

Skills: Instructing; Science; Learning Strategies; Reading Comprehension; Writing; Speaking; Active Learning; Social Perceptiveness.

Work Environment: Indoors; sitting; exposed to disease or infections.

Occupational Therapists

- ❈ Personality Type: Social-Investigative
- ❈ Annual Earnings: $72,320
- ❈ Earnings Growth Potential: Low (32.4%)
- ❈ Growth: 25.6%
- ❈ Annual Job Openings: 4,580
- ❈ Self-Employed: 7.0%

Considerations for Job Outlook: Employment growth for occupational therapists should continue as the population ages and better medical technology increases the survival rates of people who become injured or ill. Job opportunities are expected be good.

Assess, plan, organize, and participate in rehabilitative programs that help restore vocational, homemaking, and daily living skills, as well as general independence, to disabled persons. Plan, organize, and conduct occupational therapy programs in hospital, institutional, or community settings to help rehabilitate those impaired because of illness, injury, or psychological or developmental problems. Test and evaluate patients' physical and mental abilities, and analyze medical data to determine realistic rehabilitation goals for patients. Select activities that will help individuals learn work and life-management skills within limits of their mental and physical capabilities. Evaluate patients' progress, and prepare reports that detail progress. Complete and maintain necessary records. Train caregivers to provide for the needs of patients during and after therapies. Recommend changes in patients' work or living environments, consistent with their needs and capabilities. Develop and participate in health promotion programs, group activities, or discussions to promote client health, facilitate social adjustment, alleviate stress, and prevent physical or mental disability. Consult with rehabilitation team to select activity programs, and coordinate occupational therapy with other therapeutic activities. Plan and implement programs and social activities to help patients learn work and school skills and adjust to handicaps. Design and create, or requisition, special supplies and equipment such as splints, braces and computer-aided adaptive equipment. Conduct research in occupational therapy.

Education/Training Required: Master's degree. **Education and Training Program:** Occupational Therapy/Therapist. **Knowledge/Courses:** Therapy and Counseling; Psychology; Sociology and Anthropology; Medicine and Dentistry; Biology; Philosophy and Theology.

Career Cluster: 08 Health Science. **Career Pathway:** 08.1 Therapeutic Services.

Skills: Operations Analysis; Science; Service Orientation; Social Perceptiveness; Active Listening; Writing; Learning Strategies; Persuasion.

Work Environment: Indoors; standing; using hands; bending or twisting the body; exposed to disease or infections.

Job Specialization: Low Vision Therapists, Orientation and Mobility Specialists, and Vision Rehabilitation Therapists

Provide therapy to patients with visual impairments to improve their functioning in daily life activities. May train patients in activities such as computer use, communication skills, or home management skills. Teach cane skills including cane use with a guide, diagonal techniques, and two-point touches. Refer clients to services, such as eye care, health care, rehabilitation, and counseling, to enhance visual and life functioning or when condition exceeds scope of practice. Provide consultation, support, or education to groups such as parents and teachers. Participate in professional development activities such as reading literature, continuing education, attending conferences, and collaborating with colleagues. Obtain, distribute, or maintain low-vision devices. Design instructional programs to improve communication using devices such as slates and styluses, braillers, keyboards, adaptive handwriting devices, talking book machines, digital books, and optical character readers (OCRs). Collaborate with specialists, such as rehabilitation counselors, speech pathologists, and occupational therapists, to provide client solutions. Administer tests and interpret test results to develop rehabilitation plans for clients. Train clients to read or write Braille. Teach clients to travel independently using a variety of actual or simulated travel situations or exercises. Train clients to use tactile, auditory, kinesthetic, olfactory, and proprioceptive information. Train clients to use adaptive equipment such as large print, reading stands, lamps, writing implements, software, and electronic devices. Monitor clients' progress to determine whether changes in rehabilitation plans are needed.

Education/Training Required: Master's degree. **Education and Training Program:** Occupational Therapy/Therapist. **Knowledge/Courses:** Therapy and Counseling; Psychology; Sociology and Anthropology; Education and Training; Transportation; Medicine and Dentistry.

Personality Type: Social-Investigative-Realistic. **Career Cluster:** 08 Health Science. **Career Pathway:** 08.1 Therapeutic Services.

Skills: Technology Design; Learning Strategies; Writing; Social Perceptiveness; Negotiation; Service Orientation; Reading Comprehension; Active Learning.

Work Environment: More often outdoors than indoors; standing.

Occupational Therapy Assistants

* Personality Type: Social-Realistic
* Annual Earnings: $51,010
* Earnings Growth Potential: Low (35.1%)
* Growth: 29.8%
* Annual Job Openings: 1,180
* Self-Employed: 2.1%

Considerations for Job Outlook: Employment growth for occupational therapist assistants should continue as the population ages and better medical technology increases the survival rates of people who become injured or ill. Job prospects should be very good for assistants who have credentials.

Assist occupational therapists in providing occupational therapy treatments and procedures. May, in accordance with state laws, assist in development of treatment plans, carry out routine functions, direct activity programs, and document the progress of treatments. Generally requires formal training. Observe and record patients' progress, attitudes, and behavior, and maintain this information in client records. Maintain and promote a positive attitude toward clients and their treatment programs. Monitor patients' performance in therapy activities, providing encouragement. Select therapy activities to fit patients' needs and capabilities. Instruct, or assist in instructing, patients and families in home programs, basic living skills, and the care and use of adaptive equipment. Evaluate the daily living skills and capacities of physically, developmentally, or emotionally disabled clients. Aid patients in dressing and grooming themselves. Implement, or assist occupational therapists with implementing, treatment plans designed to help clients function independently. Report to supervisors, verbally or in writing, on patients' progress, attitudes, and behavior. Alter treatment programs to obtain better results if treatment is not having the intended effect. Work under the direction of occupational therapists to plan, implement, and administer educational, vocational, and recreational programs that restore and enhance performance in individuals with functional impairments. Design, fabricate, and repair assistive devices, and make adaptive changes to equipment and environments. Assemble, clean, and maintain equipment and materials for patient use. Teach patients how to deal constructively with their emotions.

Education/Training Required: Associate degree. **Education and Training Program:** Occupational Therapist Assistant Training. **Knowledge/Courses:** Psychology; Therapy and Counseling; Philosophy and Theology; Medicine and Dentistry; Sociology and Anthropology; Education and Training.

Career Cluster: 08 Health Science. **Career Pathway:** 08.1 Therapeutic Services.

Skills: Learning Strategies; Social Perceptiveness; Negotiation; Service Orientation; Instructing; Persuasion; Operation Monitoring; Writing.

Work Environment: Indoors; standing; using hands; noise; exposed to disease or infections.

Philosophy and Religion Teachers, Postsecondary

Look for the job description among the Artistic occupations.

Physical Therapist Assistants

- ❀ Personality Type: Social-Realistic-Investigative
- ❀ Annual Earnings: $49,690
- ❀ Earnings Growth Potential: Medium (37.5%)
- ❀ Growth: 33.3%
- ❀ Annual Job Openings: 3,050
- ❀ Self-Employed: 1.3%

Considerations for Job Outlook: Projected growth stems from an expected increase in the elderly population and better medical technology that increases the survival rates of people who become injured or ill. Job opportunities should be good in settings that treat the elderly.

Assist physical therapists in providing physical therapy treatments and procedures. May, in accordance with state laws, assist in the development of treatment plans, carry out routine functions, document the progress of treatment, and modify specific treatments in accordance with patient status and within the scope of treatment plans established by physical therapists. Generally requires formal training. Instruct, motivate, safeguard, and assist patients as they practice exercises and functional activities. Observe patients during treatments to compile and evaluate data on their responses and progress, and provide results to physical therapists in person or through progress notes. Confer with physical therapy staffs or others to discuss and evaluate patient information for planning, modifying, and coordinating treatment. Transport patients to and from treatment areas, lifting and transferring them according to positioning requirements. Secure patients into or onto therapy equipment. Administer active and passive manual therapeutic exercises; therapeutic massages; aquatic physical therapy; and heat, light, sound, and electrical modality treatments such as ultrasound. Communicate with or instruct caregivers and family members on patient therapeutic activities and treatment plans. Measure patients' ranges-of-joint motion, body parts, and vital signs to determine effects of treatments or for patient evaluations. Monitor operation of equipment, and record use of equipment and administration of treatment. Fit patients for orthopedic braces, prostheses, and supportive devices such as crutches. Train patients in the use of orthopedic braces, prostheses, or supportive devices. Clean work areas, and check and store equipment after treatments. Assist patients to dress; undress; or put on and remove supportive devices such as braces, splints, and slings.

Education/Training Required: Associate degree. **Education and Training Program:** Physical Therapy Technician/Assistant Training. **Knowledge/Courses:** Therapy and Counseling; Medicine and Dentistry; Psychology; Biology; Customer and Personal Service; Education and Training.

Career Cluster: 08 Health Science. **Career Pathway:** 08.1 Therapeutic Services.

Skills: Service Orientation; Quality Control Analysis; Social Perceptiveness; Science; Speaking; Learning Strategies; Reading Comprehension; Systems Evaluation.

Work Environment: Indoors; standing; walking and running; exposed to disease or infections.

Physical Therapists

- ❀ Personality Type: Social-Investigative-Realistic
- ❀ Annual Earnings: $76,310
- ❀ Earnings Growth Potential: Low (29.7%)
- ❀ Growth: 30.3%
- ❀ Annual Job Openings: 7,860
- ❀ Self-Employed: 8.0%

Considerations for Job Outlook: Employment of physical therapists is expected to increase as the population ages and as better medical technology increases survival rates of people who become injured or ill. Job opportunities should be good in settings that treat primarily the elderly.

Assess, plan, organize, and participate in rehabilitative programs that improve mobility, relieve pain, increase strength, and decrease or prevent deformity of patients suffering from disease or injury. Perform and document initial exams, evaluating data to identify problems and determine diagnoses prior to interventions. Plan, prepare, and carry out individually designed programs of physical treatment to maintain, improve, or restore physical functioning; alleviate pain; and prevent physical dysfunction in patients. Record prognoses, treatments, responses, and progresses in patients' charts, or enter information into computers. Identify and document goals, anticipated progresses, and plans for reevaluation. Evaluate effects of treatments at various stages, and adjust treatments to achieve maximum benefits. Administer manual exercises, massages, or traction to help relieve pain, increase patient strength, or decrease or prevent deformity or crippling. Test and measure patients' strength, motor development and function, sensory perception, functional capacity, and respiratory and circulatory efficiency, and record data. Instruct patients and families in treatment procedures to be continued at home. Confer with patients, medical practitioners, and appropriate others to plan, implement, and assess intervention programs. Review physicians' referrals and patients' medical records to help determine diagnoses and physical therapy treatments required. Obtain patients' informed consent to proposed interventions. Discharge patients from physical therapy when goals or projected outcomes have been attained, and provide for appropriate follow-up care or referrals.

Education/Training Required: Master's degree. **Education and Training Programs:** Kinesiotherapy/Kinesiotherapist; Physical Therapy/Therapist. **Knowledge/Courses:** Therapy and Counseling; Medicine and Dentistry; Psychology; Education and Training; Biology; Customer and Personal Service.

Career Cluster: 08 Health Science. **Career Pathway:** 08.3 Health Informatics.

Skills: Science; Operations Analysis; Service Orientation; Persuasion; Instructing; Time Management; Social Perceptiveness; Reading Comprehension.

Work Environment: Indoors; standing; exposed to disease or infections.

Physician Assistants

- Personality Type: Social-Investigative-Realistic
- Annual Earnings: $86,410
- Earnings Growth Potential: Low (33.5%)
- Growth: 39.0%
- Annual Job Openings: 4,280
- Self-Employed: 1.4%

Considerations for Job Outlook: Employment growth for these workers should be driven by an aging population and by health-care providers' increasing use of physician assistants to contain costs. Opportunities should be good, particularly in underserved areas.

Under the supervision of physicians, provide health-care services typically performed by a physician. Conduct complete physicals, provide treatment, and counsel patients. May, in some cases, prescribe medication. Must graduate from an accredited educational program for physician assistants. Examine patients to obtain information about their physical conditions. Obtain, compile, and record patient medical data, including health history, progress notes, and results of physical examinations. Interpret diagnostic test results for deviations from normal. Make tentative diagnoses and decisions about management and treatment of patients. Prescribe therapy or medication with physician approval. Administer or order diagnostic tests, such as X-ray, electrocardiogram, and laboratory tests. Instruct and counsel patients about prescribed therapeutic regimens, normal growth and development, family planning, emotional problems of daily living, and health maintenance. Perform therapeutic procedures such as injections, immunizations, suturing and wound care, and infection management. Provide physicians with assistance during surgery or

Social-P

complicated medical procedures. Visit and observe patients on hospital rounds or house calls, updating charts, ordering therapy, and reporting back to physicians. Supervise and coordinate activities of technicians and technical assistants. Order medical and laboratory supplies and equipment.

Education/Training Required: Master's degree. **Education and Training Program:** Physician Assistant Training. **Knowledge/Courses:** Medicine and Dentistry; Biology; Therapy and Counseling; Psychology; Chemistry; Sociology and Anthropology.

Career Cluster: 08 Health Science. **Career Pathway:** 08.2 Diagnostics Services.

Skills: Science; Instructing; Service Orientation; Judgment and Decision Making; Social Perceptiveness; Reading Comprehension; Operations Analysis; Systems Evaluation.

Work Environment: Indoors; standing; using hands; exposed to disease or infections.

Job Specialization: Anesthesiologist Assistants

Assist anesthesiologists in the administration of anesthesia for surgical and non-surgical procedures. Monitor patient status and provide patient care during surgical treatment. Verify availability of operating room supplies, medications, and gases. Provide clinical instruction, supervision, or training to staff in areas such as anesthesia practices. Collect samples or specimens for diagnostic testing. Participate in seminars, workshops, or other professional activities to keep abreast of developments in anesthesiology. Collect and document patients' preanesthetic health histories. Provide airway management interventions including tracheal intubation, fiber optics, or ventilary support. Respond to emergency situations by providing cardiopulmonary resuscitation (CPR), basic cardiac life support (BLS), advanced cardiac life support (ACLS), or pediatric advanced life support (PALS). Monitor and document patients' progress during post-anesthesia period. Pretest and calibrate anesthesia delivery systems

and monitors. Assist anesthesiologists in monitoring of patients including electrocardiogram (EKG), direct arterial pressure, central venous pressure, arterial blood gas, hematocrit, or routine measurement of temperature, respiration, blood pressure, and heart rate. Assist in the provision of advanced life support techniques including those procedures using high-frequency ventilation or intra-arterial cardiovascular assistance devices. Assist anesthesiologists in performing anesthetic procedures such as epidural and spinal injections.

Education/Training Required: Master's degree. **Education and Training Program:** Physician Assistant Training. **Knowledge/Courses:** No data available.

Personality Type: Realistic-Social-Investigative. **Career Cluster:** 08 Health Science. **Career Pathway:** 08.2 Diagnostics Services.

Skills: No data available.

Work Environment: No data available.

Physicians and Surgeons

Look for the job description among the Investigative jobs.

Physics Teachers, Postsecondary

- ❋ Personality Type: Social-Investigative
- ❋ Annual Earnings: $77,610
- ❋ Earnings Growth Potential: High (44.4%)
- ❋ Growth: 15.1%
- ❋ Annual Job Openings: 400
- ❋ Self-Employed: 0.2%

Considerations for Job Outlook: Enrollments in postsecondary institutions are expected to continue rising as more people attend college and as workers return to school to update their skills. Opportunities for part-time or temporary positions should be favorable, but significant competition exists for tenure-track positions.

Teach courses pertaining to the laws of matter and energy. Includes both teachers primarily engaged in teaching and those who do a combination of both teaching and research. Evaluate and grade students' classwork, laboratory work, assignments, and papers. Prepare and deliver lectures to undergraduate and/or graduate students on topics such as quantum mechanics, particle physics, and optics. Compile, administer, and grade examinations, or assign this work to others. Maintain student attendance records, grades, and other required records. Supervise students' laboratory work. Prepare course materials such as syllabi, homework assignments, and handouts. Maintain regularly scheduled office hours to advise and assist students. Supervise undergraduate and/or graduate teaching, internship, and research work. Keep abreast of developments in the field by reading current literature, talking with colleagues, and participating in professional conferences. Plan, evaluate, and revise curricula, course content, course materials, and methods of instruction. Initiate, facilitate, and moderate classroom discussions. Conduct research in a particular field of knowledge, and publish findings in professional journals, books, and/or electronic media. Advise students on academic and vocational curricula and on career issues. Select and obtain materials and supplies such as textbooks and laboratory equipment. Collaborate with colleagues to address teaching and research issues. Participate in student recruitment, registration, and placement activities.

Education/Training Required: Doctoral degree. **Education and Training Programs:** Acoustics; Atomic/Molecular Physics; Condensed Matter and Materials Physics; Elementary Particle Physics; Nuclear Physics; Optics/Optical Sciences; Physics, General; Physics, Other; Plasma and High-Temperature Physics; Theoretical and Mathematical Physics. **Knowledge/Courses:** Physics; Mathematics; Engineering and Technology; Geography; Computers and Electronics; Design.

Career Cluster: 15 Science, Technology, Engineering, and Mathematics. **Career Pathway:**

15.2 Science and Mathematics.

Skills: Science; Writing; Reading Comprehension; Speaking; Mathematics; Learning Strategies; Instructing; Active Learning.

Work Environment: Indoors; sitting.

Political Science Teachers, Postsecondary

- ❋ Personality Type: Social-Enterprising-Artistic
- ❋ Annual Earnings: $70,540
- ❋ Earnings Growth Potential: High (48.9%)
- ❋ Growth: 15.1%
- ❋ Annual Job Openings: 500
- ❋ Self-Employed: 0.2%

Considerations for Job Outlook: Enrollments in postsecondary institutions are expected to continue rising as more people attend college and as workers return to school to update their skills. Opportunities for part-time or temporary positions should be favorable, but significant competition exists for tenure-track positions.

Teach courses in political science, international affairs, and international relations. Initiate, facilitate, and moderate classroom discussions. Prepare and deliver lectures to undergraduate or graduate students on topics such as classical political thought, international relations, and democracy and citizenship. Evaluate and grade students' classwork, assignments, and papers. Compile, administer, and grade examinations, or assign this work to others. Prepare course materials such as syllabi, homework assignments, and handouts. Keep abreast of developments in the field by reading current literature, talking with colleagues, and participating in professional conferences. Plan, evaluate, and revise curricula, course content, course materials, and methods of instruction. Maintain student attendance records, grades, and other required records. Maintain regularly scheduled office hours in order to advise and assist students. Advise students on academic and vo-

Social-P

cational curricula and on career issues. Select and obtain materials and supplies such as textbooks. Conduct research in a particular field of knowledge, and publish findings in professional journals, books, and electronic media. Supervise undergraduate and graduate teaching, internship, and research work. Collaborate with colleagues to address teaching and research issues. Serve on academic or administrative committees that deal with institutional policies, departmental matters, and academic issues. Participate in student recruitment, registration, and placement activities.

Education/Training Required: Doctoral degree. **Education and Training Programs:** American Government and Politics (United States); Humanities/Humanistic Studies; International Relations and Affairs; Political Science and Government, General; Political Science and Government, Other; Social Science Teacher Education. **Knowledge/Courses:** Philosophy and Theology; History and Archeology; Sociology and Anthropology; Law and Government; Geography; Communications and Media.

Career Clusters: 05 Education and Training; 07 Government and Public Administration; 15 Science, Technology, Engineering, and Mathematics. **Career Pathways:** 05.3 Teaching/Training; 07.1 Governance; 07.4 Planning; 15.2 Science and Mathematics.

Skills: Science; Writing; Speaking; Learning Strategies; Instructing; Operations Analysis; Reading Comprehension; Active Learning.

Work Environment: Indoors; sitting.

Preschool Teachers, Except Special Education

- Personality Type: Social-Artistic
- Annual Earnings: $25,700
- Earnings Growth Potential: Low (33.1%)
- Growth: 19.0%
- Annual Job Openings: 17,830
- Self-Employed: 1.4%

Considerations for Job Outlook: Continued emphasis on early childhood education is increasing the employment of preschool teachers. The need to replace workers who leave the occupation permanently should create good job opportunities.

Instruct children (normally up to 5 years of age) in activities designed to promote social, physical, and intellectual growth needed for primary school in preschool, day care center, or other child development facility. May be required to hold state certification. Provide a variety of materials and resources for children to explore, manipulate, and use, both in learning activities and in imaginative play. Attend to children's basic needs by feeding them, dressing them, and changing their diapers. Establish and enforce rules for behavior and procedures for maintaining order. Read books to entire classes or to small groups. Teach basic skills such as color, shape, number, and letter recognition; personal hygiene; and social skills. Organize and lead activities designed to promote physical, mental, and social development, such as games, arts and crafts, music, storytelling, and field trips. Observe and evaluate children's performance, behavior, social development, and physical health. Meet with parents and guardians to discuss their children's progress and needs, determine their priorities for their children, and suggest ways that they can promote learning and development. Identify children showing signs of emotional, developmental, or health-related problems, and discuss them with supervisors, parents or guardians, and child development specialists. Enforce all administration policies and rules governing students. Prepare materials and classrooms for class activities. Serve meals and snacks in accordance with nutritional guidelines. Teach proper eating habits and personal hygiene. Assimilate arriving children to the school environment by greeting them, helping them remove outerwear, and selecting activities of interest to them.

Education/Training Required: Postsecondary vocational training. **Education and Training Programs:** Child Care and Support Services Management; Early Childhood Education and

Teaching. **Knowledge/Courses:** Philosophy and Theology; Therapy and Counseling; Sociology and Anthropology; Geography; Customer and Personal Service; Psychology.

Career Clusters: 05 Education and Training; 10 Human Services. **Career Pathways:** 05.3 Teaching/Training; 10.1 Early Childhood Development and Services.

Skills: Learning Strategies; Social Perceptiveness; Service Orientation; Coordination; Monitoring; Time Management; Negotiation; Complex Problem Solving.

Work Environment: Indoors; standing; noise.

Probation Officers and Correctional Treatment Specialists

* Personality Type: Social-Enterprising-Conventional
* Annual Earnings: $47,200
* Earnings Growth Potential: Low (34.5%)
* Growth: 19.3%
* Annual Job Openings: 4,180
* Self-Employed: 0.3%

Considerations for Job Outlook: Many states are expected to emphasize alternatives to incarceration, such as probation. As a result, employment growth should be strong for these workers. Opportunities should be excellent.

Provide social services to assist in rehabilitation of law offenders in custody or on probation or parole. Make recommendations for actions involving formulation of rehabilitation plan and treatment of offender, including conditional release and education and employment stipulations. Prepare and maintain case folder for each assigned inmate or offender. Write reports describing offenders' progress. Inform offenders or inmates of requirements of conditional release, such as office visits, restitution payments, or educational and employment stipulations. Discuss with offenders how such issues

as drug and alcohol abuse and anger management problems might have played roles in their criminal behavior. Gather information about offenders' backgrounds by talking to offenders, their families and friends, and other people who have relevant information. Develop rehabilitation programs for assigned offenders or inmates, establishing rules of conduct, goals, and objectives. Develop liaisons and networks with other parole officers; community agencies; and staff in correctional institutions, psychiatric facilities, and after-care agencies to make plans for helping offenders with life adjustments. Arrange for medical, mental health, or substance abuse treatment services according to individual needs and court orders. Provide offenders or inmates with assistance in matters concerning detainers, sentences in other jurisdictions, writs, and applications for social assistance. Arrange for post-release services such as employment, housing, counseling, education, and social activities. Recommend remedial action or initiate court action when terms of probation or parole are not complied with.

Education/Training Required: Bachelor's degree. **Education and Training Program:** Social Work. **Knowledge/Courses:** Therapy and Counseling; Sociology and Anthropology; Psychology; Law and Government; Public Safety and Security; Philosophy and Theology.

Career Cluster: 10 Human Services. **Career Pathway:** 10.3 Family and Community Services.

Skills: Social Perceptiveness; Service Orientation; Persuasion; Negotiation; Monitoring; Active Listening; Speaking; Reading Comprehension.

Work Environment: Indoors; sitting; exposed to disease or infections.

Producers and Directors

Look for the job description among the Artistic occupations.

Psychology Teachers, Postsecondary

- ❋ Personality Type: Social-Investigative-Artistic
- ❋ Annual Earnings: $67,330
- ❋ Earnings Growth Potential: High (46.8%)
- ❋ Growth: 15.1%
- ❋ Annual Job Openings: 1,000
- ❋ Self-Employed: 0.2%

Considerations for Job Outlook: Enrollments in postsecondary institutions are expected to continue rising as more people attend college and as workers return to school to update their skills. Opportunities for part-time or temporary positions should be favorable, but significant competition exists for tenure-track positions.

Teach courses in psychology, such as child, clinical, and developmental psychology and psychological counseling. Prepare and deliver lectures to undergraduate and/or graduate students on topics such as abnormal psychology, cognitive processes, and work motivation. Evaluate and grade students' classwork, laboratory work, assignments, and papers. Initiate, facilitate, and moderate classroom discussions. Compile, administer, and grade examinations, or assign this work to others. Keep abreast of developments in the field by reading current literature, talking with colleagues, and participating in professional conferences. Prepare course materials such as syllabi, homework assignments, and handouts. Plan, evaluate, and revise curricula, course content, course materials, and methods of instruction. Maintain student attendance records, grades, and other required records. Supervise undergraduate and/or graduate teaching, internship, and research work. Maintain regularly scheduled office hours to advise and assist students. Conduct research in a particular field of knowledge, and publish findings in professional journals, books, and electronic media. Advise students on academic and vocational curricula and on career issues. Select and obtain materials and supplies such as textbooks. Collaborate with colleagues to address teaching and research issues. Serve on academic or administrative committees that deal with institutional policies, departmental matters, and academic issues. Compile bibliographies of specialized materials for outside reading assignments.

Education/Training Required: Doctoral degree. **Education and Training Programs:** Humanities/Humanistic Studies; Marriage and Family Therapy/Counseling; Psychology Teacher Education; Psychology, General; Psychology, Other; Social Science Teacher Education. **Knowledge/Courses:** Psychology; Therapy and Counseling; Philosophy and Theology; Sociology and Anthropology; Education and Training; Biology.

Career Clusters: 05 Education and Training; 08 Health Science; 10 Human Services; 12 Law, Public Safety, Corrections, and Security. **Career Pathways:** 05.3 Teaching/Training; 08.1 Therapeutic Services; 10.2 Counseling and Mental Health Services; 12.1 Correction Services.

Skills: Science; Learning Strategies; Writing; Social Perceptiveness; Speaking; Instructing; Reading Comprehension; Active Learning.

Work Environment: Indoors; sitting.

Radiation Therapists

- ❋ Personality Type: Social-Realistic-Conventional
- ❋ Annual Earnings: $74,980
- ❋ Earnings Growth Potential: Low (32.0%)
- ❋ Growth: 27.1%
- ❋ Annual Job Openings: 690
- ❋ Self-Employed: 0.0%

Considerations for Job Outlook: The increasing number of elderly people, who are more likely than younger people to need radiation treatment, is expected to lead to employment growth for these workers. Prospects are expected to be good; job-seekers with a bachelor's degree should have the best opportunities.

Provide radiation therapy to patients as pre-scribed by radiologists according to established practices and standards. Duties may include reviewing prescriptions and diagnoses; acting as liaisons with physicians and supportive care personnel; preparing equipment such as immobilization, treatment, and protection devices; and maintaining records, reports, and files. May assist in dosimetry procedures and tumor localization. Position patients for treatment with accuracy according to prescription. Administer prescribed doses of radiation to specific body parts, using radiation therapy equipment according to established practices and standards. Check radiation therapy equipment to ensure proper operation. Review prescriptions, diagnoses, patient charts, and identification. Follow principles of radiation protection for patients, radiation therapists, and others. Maintain records, reports, and files as required, including such information as radiation dosages, equipment settings, and patients' reactions. Conduct most treatment sessions independently, in accordance with long-term treatment plans and under general direction of patients' physicians. Enter data into computers, and set controls to operate and adjust equipment and regulate dosages. Observe and reassure patients during treatments, and report unusual reactions to physicians or turn equipment off if unexpected adverse reactions occur. Calculate actual treatment dosages delivered during each session. Check for side effects such as skin irritation, nausea, and hair loss to assess patients' reaction to treatment. Prepare and construct equipment such as immobilization, treatment, and protection devices. Educate, prepare, and reassure patients and their families by answering questions, providing physical assistance, and reinforcing physicians' advice regarding treatment reactions and post-treatment care.

Education/Training Required: Associate degree. **Education and Training Program:** Medical Radiologic Technology/Science—Radiation Therapist. **Knowledge/Courses:** Medicine and Dentistry; Biology; Physics; Psychology; Philosophy and Theology; Therapy and Counseling.

Career Cluster: 08 Health Science. **Career Pathway:** 08.2 Diagnostics Services.

Skills: Operation and Control; Equipment Selection; Equipment Maintenance; Science; Quality Control Analysis; Operation Monitoring; Troubleshooting; Operations Analysis.

Work Environment: Indoors; standing; walking and running; using hands; bending or twisting the body; repetitive motions; contaminants; exposed to radiation; exposed to disease or infections.

Recreational Therapists

Look for the job description among the Artistic occupations.

Registered Nurses

* Personality Type: Social-Investigative
* Annual Earnings: $64,690
* Earnings Growth Potential: Low (31.7%)
* Growth: 22.2%
* Annual Job Openings: 103,900
* Self-Employed: 0.6%

Considerations for Job Outlook: Employment growth for registered nurses will be driven by the medical needs of an aging population. In addition, registered nurses are expected to provide more primary care as a low-cost alternative to physician-provided care. Job opportunities should be excellent.

Assess patient health problems and needs, develop and implement nursing care plans, and maintain medical records. Administer nursing care to ill, injured, convalescent, or disabled patients. May advise patients on health maintenance and disease prevention or provide case management. Licensing or registration required. Includes advance practice nurses such as nurse practitioners, clinical nurse specialists, certified nurse midwives, and certified registered nurse anesthetists. Advanced practice nursing is practiced by RNs who have specialized formal, post-basic education and who function in highly autonomous and

specialized roles. Maintain accurate, detailed reports and records. Monitor, record, and report symptoms and changes in patients' conditions. Record patients' medical information and vital signs. Modify patient treatment plans as indicated by patients' responses and conditions. Consult and coordinate with health-care team members to assess, plan, implement, and evaluate patient care plans. Order, interpret, and evaluate diagnostic tests to identify and assess patient's condition. Monitor all aspects of patient care, including diet and physical activity. Direct and supervise less-skilled nursing or health-care personnel, or supervise a particular unit. Prepare patients for, and assist with, examinations and treatments. Observe nurses and visit patients to ensure proper nursing care. Assess the needs of individuals, families, or communities, including assessment of individuals' home or work environments, to identify potential health or safety problems. Instruct individuals, families, and other groups on topics such as health education, disease prevention, and childbirth, and develop health improvement programs. Prepare rooms, sterile instruments, equipment, and supplies, and ensure that stock of supplies is maintained. Inform physician of patient's condition during anesthesia. Administer local, inhalation, intravenous, and other anesthetics. Provide health care, first aid, immunizations, and assistance in convalescence and rehabilitation in locations such as schools, hospitals, and industry.

Education/Training Required: Associate degree. **Education and Training Programs:** Adult Health Nurse/Nursing; Clinical Nurse Specialist Training; Critical Care Nursing; Family Practice Nurse/Nursing; Maternal/Child Health and Neonatal Nurse/Nursing; Nurse Anesthetist Training; Nurse Midwife/Nursing Midwifery; Nursing Science; Occupational and Environmental Health Nursing; Pediatric Nurse/Nursing; Perioperative/Operating Room and Surgical Nurse/Nursing; Psychiatric/Mental Health Nurse/Nursing; Public Health/Community Nurse/Nursing; Registered Nursing/Registered Nurse Training. **Knowledge/Courses:** Psychology; Medicine and Dentistry; Therapy and Counseling; Biology; Philosophy and Theology; Sociology and Anthropology.

Career Cluster: 08 Health Science. **Career Pathway:** 08.1 Therapeutic Services.

Skills: Science; Social Perceptiveness; Quality Control Analysis; Service Orientation; Learning Strategies; Coordination; Management of Material Resources; Instructing.

Work Environment: Indoors; standing; walking and running; using hands; exposed to disease or infections.

Job Specialization: Acute Care Nurses

Provide advanced nursing care for patients with acute conditions such as heart attacks, respiratory distress syndrome, or shock. May care for pre- and post-operative patients or perform advanced, invasive diagnostic or therapeutic procedures. Analyze the indications, contraindications, risk complications, and cost-benefit tradeoffs of therapeutic interventions. Diagnose acute or chronic conditions that could result in rapid physiological deterioration or life-threatening instability. Distinguish between normal and abnormal developmental and age-related physiological and behavioral changes in acute, critical, and chronic illness. Manage patients' pain relief and sedation by providing pharmacologic and non-pharmacologic interventions, monitoring patients' responses, and changing care plans accordingly. Interpret information obtained from electrocardiograms (EKGs) or radiographs (X-rays). Perform emergency medical procedures, such as basic cardiac life support (BLS), advanced cardiac life support (ACLS), and other condition-stabilizing interventions. Assess urgent and emergent health conditions using both physiologically and technologically derived data. Adjust settings on patients' assistive devices such as temporary pacemakers. Assess the impact of illnesses or injuries on patients' health, function, growth, development, nutrition, sleep, rest, quality of life, or family, social, and educational relationships. Collaborate with members of multidisciplinary health-care teams to plan, manage, or assess patient treatments. Discuss illnesses and treatments with patients and family members.

Education/Training Required: Associate degree. **Education and Training Program:** Critical Care Nursing. **Knowledge/Courses:** Therapy and Counseling; Medicine and Dentistry; Psychology; Biology; Sociology and Anthropology; Philosophy and Theology.

Personality Type: Social-Investigative-Realistic. **Career Cluster:** 08 Health Science. **Career Pathway:** 08.1 Therapeutic Services.

Skills: Science; Social Perceptiveness; Reading Comprehension; Operation Monitoring; Service Orientation; Systems Evaluation; Operation and Control; Active Learning.

Work Environment: Indoors; standing; walking and running; using hands; noise; contaminants; cramped work space; exposed to radiation; exposed to disease or infections.

Job Specialization: Advanced Practice Psychiatric Nurses

Provide advanced nursing care for patients with psychiatric disorders. May provide psychotherapy under the direction of a psychiatrist. Teach classes in mental health topics such as stress reduction. Participate in activities aimed at professional growth and development including conferences or continuing education activities. Direct or provide home health services. Monitor the use and status of medical and pharmaceutical supplies. Develop practice protocols for mental health problems based on review and evaluation of published research. Develop, implement, or evaluate programs such as outreach activities, community mental health programs, and crisis situation response activities. Treat patients for routine physical health problems. Write prescriptions for psychotropic medications as allowed by state regulations and collaborative practice agreements. Refer patients requiring more specialized or complex treatment to psychiatrists, primary care physicians, or other medical specialists. Provide routine physical health screenings to detect or monitor problems such as heart disease and diabetes. Participate in treatment team conferences regarding diagnosis or treat-

ment of difficult cases. Interpret diagnostic or laboratory tests such as electrocardiograms (EKGs) and renal functioning tests. Evaluate patients' behavior to formulate diagnoses or assess treatments. Develop and implement treatment plans. Monitor patients' medication usage and results. Educate patients and family members about mental health and medical conditions, preventive health measures, medications, or treatment plans.

Education/Training Required: Master's degree. **Education and Training Program:** Psychiatric/Mental Health Nurse Training/Nursing. **Knowledge/Courses:** Therapy and Counseling; Psychology; Medicine and Dentistry; Sociology and Anthropology; Philosophy and Theology; Biology.

Personality Type: Social-Investigative. **Career Cluster:** 08 Health Science. **Career Pathway:** 08.1 Therapeutic Services.

Skills: Social Perceptiveness; Science; Negotiation; Service Orientation; Systems Evaluation; Persuasion; Learning Strategies; Reading Comprehension.

Work Environment: Indoors; sitting; exposed to disease or infections.

Job Specialization: Clinical Nurse Specialists

Plan, direct, or coordinate daily patient care activities in a clinical practice. Ensure adherence to established clinical policies, protocols, regulations, and standards. Coordinate or conduct educational programs or in-service training sessions on topics such as clinical procedures. Observe, interview, and assess patients to identify care needs. Evaluate the quality and effectiveness of nursing practice or organizational systems. Provide direct care by performing comprehensive health assessments, developing differential diagnoses, conducting specialized tests, or prescribing medications or treatments. Provide specialized direct and indirect care to inpatients and outpatients within a designated specialty such as obstetrics, neurology, oncology, or neonatal care. Maintain departmental policies, pro-

Social-R

cedures, objectives, or infection control standards. Collaborate with other health-care professionals and service providers to ensure optimal patient care. Develop nursing service philosophies, goals, policies, priorities, or procedures. Develop, implement, or evaluate standards of nursing practice in specialty area such as pediatrics, acute care, and geriatrics. Develop or assist others in development of care and treatment plans. Make clinical recommendations to physicians, other health-care providers, insurance companies, patients, or health-care organizations. Plan, evaluate, or modify treatment programs based on information gathered by observing and interviewing patients, or by analyzing patient records. Present clients with information required to make informed health-care and treatment decisions.

Education/Training Required: Master's degree. **Education and Training Program:** Clinical Nurse Specialist Training. **Knowledge/Courses:** Medicine and Dentistry; Biology; Therapy and Counseling; Psychology; Sociology and Anthropology; Philosophy and Theology.

Personality Type: Enterprising-Social-Conventional. **Career Cluster:** 08 Health Science. **Career Pathways:** 08.1 Therapeutic Services; 08.3 Health Informatics.

Skills: Science; Operations Analysis; Instructing; Service Orientation; Negotiation; Persuasion; Judgment and Decision Making; Active Learning.

Work Environment: Indoors; standing; using hands; noise; contaminants; exposed to radiation; exposed to disease or infections.

Job Specialization: Critical Care Nurses

Provide advanced nursing care for patients in critical or coronary care units. Identify patients' age-specific needs, and alter care plans as necessary to meet those needs. Provide post-mortem care. Evaluate patients' vital signs and laboratory data to determine emergency intervention needs. Perform approved therapeutic or diagnostic procedures based upon patients' clinical status. Administer blood and blood products, monitoring patients for signs and symptoms related to transfusion reactions. Administer medications intravenously, by injection, orally, through gastric tubes, or by other methods. Advocate for patients' and families' needs, or provide emotional support for patients and their families. Set up and monitor medical equipment and devices such as cardiac monitors, mechanical ventilators and alarms, oxygen delivery devices, transducers, and pressure lines. Monitor patients' fluid intake and output to detect emerging problems such as fluid and electrolyte imbalances. Monitor patients for changes in status and indications of conditions such as sepsis or shock, and institute appropriate interventions. Assess patients' pain levels and sedation requirements. Assess patients' psychosocial status and needs including areas such as sleep patterns, anxiety, grief, anger, and support systems. Collaborate with other health-care professionals to develop and revise treatment plans based on identified needs and assessment data. Collect specimens for laboratory tests. Compile and analyze data obtained from monitoring or diagnostic tests.

Education/Training Required: Associate degree. **Education and Training Program:** Critical Care Nursing. **Knowledge/Courses:** Medicine and Dentistry; Biology; Psychology; Therapy and Counseling; Sociology and Anthropology; Philosophy and Theology.

Personality Type: Social-Investigative-Realistic. **Career Cluster:** 08 Health Science. **Career Pathway:** 08.1 Therapeutic Services.

Skills: Science; Social Perceptiveness; Operation and Control; Quality Control Analysis; Operation Monitoring; Service Orientation; Monitoring; Active Learning.

Work Environment: Indoors; standing; walking and running; using hands; bending or twisting the body; noise; contaminants; cramped work space; exposed to radiation; exposed to disease or infections.

Rehabilitation Counselors

- ❋ Personality Type: Social-Investigative
- ❋ Annual Earnings: $32,350
- ❋ Earnings Growth Potential: Low (35.8%)
- ❋ Growth: 18.9%
- ❋ Annual Job Openings: 5,070
- ❋ Self-Employed: 5.7%

Considerations for Job Outlook: Increasing demand for services provided by counselors is expected to result in employment growth. But growth will vary by specialty and will be faster for mental health, substance abuse and behavioral disorder, and rehabilitation counselors than for counselors of other specialties. Opportunities should be favorable, particularly in rural areas.

Counsel individuals to maximize the independence and employability of persons coping with personal, social, and vocational difficulties that result from birth defects, illness, disease, accidents, or the stress of daily life. Coordinate activities for residents of care and treatment facilities. Assess client needs, and design and implement rehabilitation programs that may include personal and vocational counseling, training, and job placement. Monitor and record clients' progress in order to ensure that goals and objectives are met. Confer with clients to discuss their options and goals so that rehabilitation programs and plans for accessing needed services can be developed. Prepare and maintain records and case files, including documentation such as clients' personal and eligibility information, services provided, narratives of client contacts, and relevant correspondence. Arrange for physical, mental, academic, vocational, and other evaluations to obtain information for assessing clients' needs and developing rehabilitation plans. Analyze information from interviews, educational and medical records, consultation with other professionals, and diagnostic evaluations to assess clients' abilities, needs, and eligibility for services. Develop rehabilitation plans that fit clients' aptitudes, education levels, physical abilities, and career goals. Maintain close contact with clients during job training and placements to resolve problems and evaluate placement adequacy. Locate barriers to client employment, such as inaccessible work sites, inflexible schedules, and transportation problems, and work with clients to develop strategies for overcoming these barriers. Develop and maintain relationships with community referral sources such as schools and community groups. Arrange for on-site job coaching or assistive devices such as specially equipped wheelchairs in order to help clients adapt to work or school environments.

Education/Training Required: Master's degree. **Education and Training Programs:** Assistive/Augmentative Technology and Rehabilitation Engineering; Vocational Rehabilitation Counseling/Counselor. **Knowledge/Courses:** Therapy and Counseling; Psychology; Philosophy and Theology; Education and Training; Personnel and Human Resources; Sociology and Anthropology.

Career Cluster: 08 Health Science. **Career Pathway:** 08.3 Health Informatics.

Skills: Operations Analysis; Social Perceptiveness; Systems Analysis; Service Orientation; Science; Systems Evaluation; Learning Strategies; Monitoring.

Work Environment: More often indoors than outdoors; sitting; walking and running.

Respiratory Therapists

- ❋ Personality Type: Social-Investigative-Realistic
- ❋ Annual Earnings: $54,280
- ❋ Earnings Growth Potential: Low (26.3%)
- ❋ Growth: 20.9%
- ❋ Annual Job Openings: 4,140
- ❋ Self-Employed: 0.0%

Considerations for Job Outlook: Growth of the elderly population is expected to increase employment for these workers, especially as they take on additional duties related to case management, disease prevention, and emergency care. Opportunities are expected to be very good.

Social-R

Assess, treat, and care for patients with breathing disorders. Assume primary responsibility for all respiratory care modalities, including the supervision of respiratory therapy technicians. Initiate and conduct therapeutic procedures; maintain patient records; and select, assemble, check, and operate equipment. Set up and operate devices such as mechanical ventilators, therapeutic gas-administration apparatus, environmental control systems, and aerosol generators, following specified parameters of treatment. Provide emergency care, including artificial respiration, external cardiac massage, and assistance with cardiopulmonary resuscitation. Determine requirements for treatment, such as type, method, and duration of therapy; precautions to be taken; and medication and dosages, compatible with physicians' orders. Monitor patient's physiological responses to therapy, such as vital signs, arterial blood gases, and blood chemistry changes, and consult with physician if adverse reactions occur. Read prescription, measure arterial blood gases, and review patient information to assess patient condition. Work as part of a team of physicians, nurses, and other health-care professionals to manage patient care. Enforce safety rules, and ensure careful adherence to physicians' orders. Maintain charts that contain patients' pertinent identification and therapy information. Inspect, clean, test, and maintain respiratory therapy equipment to ensure equipment is functioning safely and efficiently, ordering repairs when necessary. Educate patients and their families about their conditions, and teach appropriate disease management techniques, such as breathing exercises and the use of medications and respiratory equipment. Explain treatment procedures to patients to gain cooperation and allay fears.

Education/Training Required: Associate degree. **Education and Training Program:** Respiratory Care Therapy/Therapist. **Knowledge/Courses:** Medicine and Dentistry; Biology; Customer and Personal Service; Therapy and Counseling; Psychology; Chemistry.

Career Cluster: 08 Health Science. **Career Pathway:** 08.1 Therapeutic Services.

Skills: Science; Repairing; Equipment Maintenance; Operation and Control; Equipment Selection; Quality Control Analysis; Operation Monitoring; Service Orientation.

Work Environment: Indoors; standing; walking and running; using hands; repetitive motions; contaminants; exposed to radiation; exposed to disease or infections.

Secondary School Teachers, Except Special and Career/Technical Education

Look for the job description among the Artistic occupations.

Self-Enrichment Education Teachers

- ❀ Personality Type: Social-Artistic-Enterprising
- ❀ Annual Earnings: $36,340
- ❀ Earnings Growth Potential: High (48.3%)
- ❀ Growth: 32.0%
- ❀ Annual Job Openings: 12,030
- ❀ Self-Employed: 17.3%

Considerations for Job Outlook: Demand for self-enrichment education will increase as more people embrace lifelong learning or seek to acquire or improve skills that make them more attractive to prospective employers. Opportunities should be favorable.

Teach or instruct courses othe r than those that normally lead to an occupational objective or degree. Courses may include self-improvement, non-vocational, and nonacademic subjects. Teaching may or may not take place in a traditional educational institution. Adapt teaching methods and instructional materials to meet students' varying needs and interests. Conduct classes, workshops, and demonstrations, and provide individual instruction to teach topics and skills such as cooking, dancing, writing, physical fitness, photography, personal finance, and flying. Monitor students' performance to make suggestions for improvement and to ensure that they satisfy course standards, training requirements, and objectives. Observe students to determine qualifications, limitations, abilities, interests, and other individual characteristics. Instruct students individually and in groups, using various teaching methods such as lectures, discussions, and demonstrations. Establish clear objectives for all lessons, units, and projects, and communicate those objectives to students. Instruct and monitor students in use and care of equipment and materials to prevent injury and damage. Prepare students for further development by encouraging them to explore learning opportunities and to persevere with challenging tasks. Prepare materials and classrooms for class activities. Enforce policies and rules governing students. Plan and conduct activities for a balanced program of instruction, demonstration, and work time that provides students with opportunities to observe, question, and investigate. Prepare instructional program objectives, outlines, and lesson plans. Maintain accurate and complete student records as required by administrative policy.

Education/Training Required: Work experience in a related occupation. **Education and Training Program:** Adult and Continuing Education and Teaching. **Knowledge/Courses:** Education and Training; Fine Arts; Communications and Media; Customer and Personal Service; Sales and Marketing; English Language.

Career Cluster: 05 Education and Training. **Career Pathway:** 05.3 Teaching/Training.

Skills: Learning Strategies; Operations Analysis; Instructing; Writing; Speaking; Service Orientation; Reading Comprehension; Monitoring.

Work Environment: Indoors; standing; repetitive motions.

Sociologists

Look for the job description among the Artistic occupations.

Special Education Teachers, Middle School

- ✳ Personality Type: Social-Artistic
- ✳ Annual Earnings: $53,440
- ✳ Earnings Growth Potential: Low (32.0%)
- ✳ Growth: 18.1%
- ✳ Annual Job Openings: 4,410
- ✳ Self-Employed: 0.2%

Considerations for Job Outlook: Employment of these teachers is expected to rise as more students qualify for special education services. Excellent job prospects are expected.

Teach middle school subjects to educationally and physically handicapped students. Includes teachers who specialize and work with audibly and visually handicapped students and those who teach basic academic and life-processes skills to the mentally impaired. Establish and enforce rules for behavior and policies and procedures to maintain order among students. Maintain accurate and complete student records, and prepare reports on children and activities, as required by laws, district policies, and administrative regulations. Prepare materials and classrooms for class activities. Confer with parents, administrators, testing specialists, social workers, and professionals to develop individual educational plans designed to promote students' educational, physical, and social development. Develop and implement strategies to meet the needs of students with a variety of handicapping conditions. Teach socially acceptable behavior, employing techniques such as behavior modification and positive reinforcement. Modify the general education curriculum for special-needs students based upon a variety of instructional techniques and instructional technology. Employ special educational strategies and techniques during instruction to improve the development of sensory- and perceptual-motor skills, language, cognition, and memory. Confer with parents or guardians, other teachers, counselors, and administrators to resolve students' behavioral and academic problems. Instruct through lectures, discussions, and demonstrations in one or more subjects, such as

Social-T

English, mathematics, or social studies. Coordinate placement of students with special needs into mainstream classes.

Education/Training Required: Bachelor's degree. **Education and Training Program:** Education/ Teaching of Individuals in Junior High/Middle School Special Education Programs. **Knowledge/ Courses:** Therapy and Counseling; History and Archeology; Psychology; Education and Training; Geography; Philosophy and Theology.

Career Cluster: 05 Education and Training. **Career Pathway:** 05.3 Teaching/Training.

Skills: Learning Strategies; Instructing; Time Management; Social Perceptiveness; Negotiation; Systems Evaluation; Persuasion; Coordination.

Work Environment: Indoors; standing.

Speech-Language Pathologists

- ❋ Personality Type: Social-Investigative-Artistic
- ❋ Annual Earnings: $66,920
- ❋ Earnings Growth Potential: Low (35.8%)
- ❋ Growth: 18.5%
- ❋ Annual Job Openings: 4,380
- ❋ Self-Employed: 9.0%

Considerations for Job Outlook: The aging population, better medical technology that increases the survival rates of people who become injured or ill, and growing enrollments in elementary and secondary schools are expected to increase employment of these workers. Job prospects are expected to be favorable.

Assess and treat persons with speech, language, voice, and fluency disorders. May select alternative communication systems and teach their use. May perform research related to speech and language problems. Monitor patients' progress and adjust treatments accordingly. Evaluate hearing and speech/language test results and medical or background information to diagnose and plan treatment for speech, language, fluency, voice, and swallowing disorders. Administer hearing or speech and language evaluations, tests, or examinations to patients to collect information on type and degree of impairments, using written and oral tests and special instruments. Record information on the initial evaluation, treatment, progress, and discharge of clients. Develop and implement treatment plans for problems such as stuttering, delayed language, swallowing disorders, and inappropriate pitch or harsh voice problems based on own assessments and recommendations of physicians, psychologists, or social workers. Develop individual or group programs in schools to deal with speech or language problems. Instruct clients in techniques for more effective communication, including sign language, lip reading, and voice improvement. Teach clients to control or strengthen tongue, jaw, face muscles, and breathing mechanisms. Develop speech exercise programs to reduce disabilities. Consult with and advise educators or medical staff on speech or hearing topics, such as communication strategies or speech and language stimulation. Instruct patients and family members in strategies to cope with or avoid communication-related misunderstandings.

Education/Training Required: Master's degree. **Education and Training Programs:** Audiology/ Audiologist and Speech-Language Pathology/ Pathologist; Communication Disorders Sciences and Services, Other; Communication Disorders, General; Communication Sciences and Disorders, General; Speech-Language Pathology/Pathologist. **Knowledge/Courses:** Therapy and Counseling; English Language; Psychology; Sociology and Anthropology; Education and Training; Medicine and Dentistry.

Career Cluster: 08 Health Science. **Career Pathway:** 08.1 Therapeutic Services.

Skills: Science; Learning Strategies; Social Perceptiveness; Writing; Monitoring; Active Learning; Systems Evaluation; Operations Analysis.

Work Environment: Indoors; sitting; noise; exposed to disease or infections.

Substance Abuse and Behavioral Disorder Counselors

Look for the job description among the Artistic occupations.

Training and Development Specialists

- ❋ Personality Type: Social-Artistic-Conventional
- ❋ Annual Earnings: $54,160
- ❋ Earnings Growth Potential: High (42.6%)
- ❋ Growth: 23.3%
- ❋ Annual Job Openings: 10,710
- ❋ Self-Employed: 1.6%

Considerations for Job Outlook: Efforts to recruit and retain employees, the growing importance of employee training, and new legal standards are expected to increase employment of these workers. College graduates and those with certification should have the best opportunities.

Conduct training and development programs for employees. Keep up with developments in area of expertise by reading current journals, books, and magazine articles. Present information, using a variety of instructional techniques and formats such as role playing, simulations, team exercises, group discussions, videos, and lectures. Schedule classes based on availability of classrooms, equipment, and instructors. Organize and develop, or obtain, training-procedure manuals and guides and course materials such as handouts and visual materials. Offer specific training programs to help workers maintain or improve job skills. Monitor, evaluate, and record training activities and program effectiveness. Attend meetings and seminars to obtain information for use in training programs, or to inform management of training-program status. Coordinate recruitment and placement of training-program participants. Evaluate training materials prepared by instructors, such as outlines, text, and handouts. Develop

alternative training methods if expected improvements are not seen. Assess training needs through surveys, interviews with employees, focus groups, or consultation with managers, instructors, or customer representatives. Screen, hire, and assign workers to positions based on qualifications. Select and assign instructors to conduct training. Devise programs to develop executive potential among employees in lower-level positions.

Education/Training Required: Work experience plus degree. **Education and Training Program:** Human Resources Development. **Knowledge/Courses:** Education and Training; Sociology and Anthropology; Sales and Marketing; Clerical Practices; Personnel and Human Resources; Psychology.

Career Clusters: 04 Business, Management, and Administration; 05 Education and Training. **Career Pathway:** 04.3 Human Resources; 5.3 Teaching/Training

Skills: Operations Analysis; Learning Strategies; Science; Instructing; Systems Evaluation; Management of Material Resources; Writing; Management of Financial Resources.

Work Environment: Indoors; sitting.

Vocational Education Teachers, Postsecondary

- ❋ Personality Type: Social-Realistic
- ❋ Annual Earnings: $48,210
- ❋ Earnings Growth Potential: High (42.3%)
- ❋ Growth: 15.1%
- ❋ Annual Job Openings: 4,000
- ❋ Self-Employed: 0.2%

Considerations for Job Outlook: Enrollments in postsecondary institutions are expected to continue rising as more people attend college and as workers return to school to update their skills. Opportunities for part-time or temporary positions should be favorable, but significant competition exists for tenure-track positions.

Social-V

Teach or instruct vocational or occupational subjects at the postsecondary level (but at less than the baccalaureate) to students who have graduated or left high school. Includes correspondence school instructors; industrial, commercial, and government training instructors; and adult education teachers and instructors who prepare persons to operate industrial machinery and equipment and transportation and communications equipment. Teaching may take place in public or private schools whose primary business is education or in a school associated with an organization whose primary business is other than education. Supervise and monitor students' use of tools and equipment. Observe and evaluate students' work to determine progress, provide feedback, and make suggestions for improvement. Present lectures and conduct discussions to increase students' knowledge and competence, using visual aids such as graphs, charts, videotapes, and slides. Administer oral, written, or performance tests to measure progress and to evaluate training effectiveness. Prepare reports and maintain records such as student grades, attendance rolls, and training activity details. Supervise independent or group projects, field placements, laboratory work, or other training. Determine training needs of students or workers. Provide individualized instruction and tutorial or remedial instruction. Conduct on-the-job training, classes, or training sessions to teach and demonstrate principles, techniques, procedures, and methods of designated subjects. Develop curricula, and plan course content and methods of instruction. Prepare outlines of instructional programs and training schedules, and establish course goals. Integrate academic and vocational curricula so that students can obtain a variety of skills. Develop teaching aids such as instructional software, multimedia visual aids, or study materials. Select and assemble books, materials, supplies, and equipment for training, courses, or projects. Advise students on course selection, career decisions, and other academic and vocational concerns.

Education/Training Required: Work experience in a related occupation. **Education and Training Programs:** Agricultural Teacher Education; Business Teacher Education; Health Occupations Teacher Education; Sales and Marketing Operations/Marketing and Distribution Teacher Education; Teacher Education and Professional Development, Specific Subject Areas, Other; Technical Teacher Education; Technology Teacher Education/Industrial Arts Teacher Education; Trade and Industrial Teacher Education. **Knowledge/Courses:** Education and Training; Therapy and Counseling; Psychology; Personnel and Human Resources; Sociology and Anthropology; English Language.

Career Cluster: 05 Education and Training. **Career Pathway:** 05.3 Teaching/Training.

Skills: Learning Strategies; Instructing; Speaking; Operations Analysis; Monitoring; Writing; Active Learning; Reading Comprehension.

Work Environment: Indoors; standing; walking and running; using hands; repetitive motions.

Enterprising Occupations

Administrative Services Managers

- ❋ Personality Type: Enterprising-Conventional
- ❋ Annual Earnings: $77,890
- ❋ Earnings Growth Potential: High (46.8%)
- ❋ Growth: 12.5%
- ❋ Annual Job Openings: 8,660
- ❋ Self-Employed: 0.2%

Considerations for Job Outlook: Employment of these workers is projected to increase as companies strive to maintain, secure, and efficiently operate their facilities. Competition should be keen for top managers; better opportunities are expected at the entry level.

Plan, direct, or coordinate supportive services of an organization, such as recordkeeping, mail distribution, telephone operator/receptionist, and other office support services. May oversee facilities planning and maintenance and custodial operations. Monitor the facility to ensure that it remains safe, secure, and well-maintained. Direct or coordinate the supportive services department of a business, agency, or organization. Set goals and deadlines for the department. Prepare and review operational reports and schedules to ensure accuracy and efficiency. Analyze internal processes, and recommend and implement procedural or policy changes to improve operations such as supply changes or the disposal of records. Acquire, distribute, and store supplies. Plan, administer, and control budgets for contracts, equipment, and supplies. Oversee construction and renovation projects to improve efficiency and to ensure that facilities meet environmental, health, and security standards and comply with government regulations. Hire and terminate clerical and administrative personnel. Oversee the maintenance and repair of machinery, equipment, and electrical and mechanical systems. Manage leasing of facility space. Participate in architectural and engineering planning and design, including space and installation management. Conduct classes to teach procedures to staff. Dispose of, or oversee the disposal of, surplus or unclaimed property.

Education/Training Required: Work experience plus degree. **Education and Training Programs:** Business Administration and Management, General; Business/Commerce, General; Medical Staff Services Technology/Technician; Medical/Health Management and Clinical Assistant/Specialist Training; Public Administration; Purchasing, Procurement/Acquisitions and Contracts Management; Transportation/Mobility Management. **Knowledge/Courses:** Clerical Practices; Economics and Accounting; Personnel and Human Resources; Customer and Personal Service; Sales and Marketing; Administration and Management.

Career Clusters: 04 Business, Management, and Administration; 07 Government and Public Administration. **Career Pathways:** 04.1 Management; 07.1 Governance.

Skills: Management of Financial Resources; Management of Material Resources; Management of Personnel Resources; Negotiation; Coordination; Time Management; Social Perceptiveness; Service Orientation.

Work Environment: Indoors; sitting.

Advertising and Promotions Managers

Look for the job description among the Artistic occupations.

Agents and Business Managers of Artists, Performers, and Athletes

* Personality Type: Enterprising-Social
* Annual Earnings: $63,130
* Earnings Growth Potential: Very high (59.7%)
* Growth: 22.4%
* Annual Job Openings: 1,010
* Self-Employed: 45.8%

Considerations for Job Outlook: Much faster than average employment growth is projected.

Represent and promote artists, performers, and athletes to prospective employers. May handle contract negotiation and other business matters for clients. Manage business and financial affairs for clients, such as arranging travel and lodging, selling tickets, and directing marketing and advertising activities. Obtain information about and/or inspect performance facilities, equipment, and accommodations to ensure that they meet specifications. Negotiate with managers, promoters, union officials, and other persons regarding clients' contractual rights and obligations. Advise clients on financial and legal matters such as investments and taxes. Hire trainers or coaches to advise clients on performance matters such as training techniques or performance presentations. Prepare periodic accounting statements for clients. Keep informed of industry trends and deals. Develop contacts with individuals and organizations, and apply effective strategies and techniques to ensure clients' success. Confer with clients to develop strategies for their careers and to explain actions taken on their behalf. Conduct auditions or interviews in order to evaluate potential clients. Schedule promotional or performance engagements for clients. Arrange meetings concerning issues involving clients. Collect fees, commissions, or other payments according to contract terms.

Education/Training Required: Work experience plus degree. **Education and Training Program:** Purchasing, Procurement/Acquisitions and Contracts Management. **Knowledge/Courses:** Fine Arts; Sales and Marketing; Communications and Media; Clerical Practices; Customer and Personal Service; Economics and Accounting.

Career Clusters: 03 Arts, Audio/Video Technology, and Communications; 04 Business, Management, and Administration. **Career Pathways:** 03.1 Audio and Video Technology and Film; 04.1 Management.

Skills: Negotiation; Persuasion; Management of Financial Resources; Service Orientation; Judgment and Decision Making; Speaking; Management of Personnel Resources; Time Management.

Work Environment: Indoors; sitting.

Air Traffic Controllers

* Personality Type: Enterprising-Conventional
* Annual Earnings: $108,040
* Earnings Growth Potential: High (49.6%)
* Growth: 13.1%
* Annual Job Openings: 1,230
* Self-Employed: 0.0%

Considerations for Job Outlook: More controllers are expected to be needed to handle increasing air traffic. Competition for admission to the FAA Academy—the usual first step in employment as an air traffic controller—is expected to remain keen.

Control air traffic on and within vicinity of airport and movement of air traffic between altitude sectors and control centers according to established procedures and policies. Authorize, regulate, and control commercial airline flights according to government or company regulations to expedite and ensure flight safety. Issue landing and take-off authorizations and instructions. Monitor and direct the movement of aircraft within an assigned air space and on the ground at airports to minimize delays and maximize safety. Monitor aircraft within a specific airspace, using radar, computer equipment, and visual references. Inform pilots about nearby planes as well as potentially hazardous conditions such as weather, speed and direction of wind, and visibility problems. Provide flight path changes or directions to emergency landing fields for pilots traveling in bad weather or in emergency situations. Alert airport emergency services in cases of emergency and when aircraft are experiencing difficulties. Direct pilots to runways when space is available, or direct them to maintain a traffic pattern until there is space for them to land. Transfer control of departing flights to traffic control centers and accept control of arriving flights. Direct ground traffic, including taxiing aircraft, maintenance and baggage vehicles, and airport workers. Determine the timing and procedures for flight vector changes. Maintain radio and telephone contact with adjacent control towers, terminal control units, and other area control centers in order to coordinate aircraft movement. Contact pilots by radio to provide meteorological, navigational, and other information. Initiate and coordinate searches for missing aircraft. Check conditions and traffic at different altitudes in response to pilots' requests for altitude changes. Relay to control centers such air traffic information as courses, altitudes, and expected arrival times.

Education/Training Required: Long-term on-the-job training. **Education and Training Program:** Air Traffic Controller Training. **Knowledge/Courses:** Transportation; Geography; Telecommunications; Public Safety and Security; Physics; Education and Training.

Career Cluster: 16 Transportation, Distribution, and Logistics. **Career Pathway:** 16.1 Transportation Operations.

Skills: Complex Problem Solving; Operation Monitoring; Operations Analysis; Judgment and Decision Making; Monitoring; Coordination; Systems Analysis; Active Learning.

Work Environment: Indoors; sitting; using hands; repetitive motions; noise.

Architectural and Engineering Managers

* Personality Type: Enterprising-Realistic-Investigative
* Annual Earnings: $119,260
* Earnings Growth Potential: Low (35.1%)
* Growth: 6.2%
* Annual Job Openings: 4,870
* Self-Employed: 0.6%

Considerations for Job Outlook: Employment is expected to grow along with that of the scientists and engineers these workers supervise. Prospects should be better in the rapidly growing areas of environmental and biomedical engineering and medical and environmental sciences.

Plan, direct, or coordinate activities or research and development in such fields as architecture and engineering. Coordinate and direct projects, making detailed plans to accomplish goals and directing the integration of technical activities. Consult or negotiate with clients to prepare project specifications. Present and explain proposals, reports, and findings to clients. Direct, review, and approve product design and changes. Recruit employees; assign, direct, and evaluate their work; and oversee the development and maintenance of staff competence. Perform administrative functions such as reviewing and writing reports, approving expenditures, enforcing rules, and making decisions about the purchase of materials or services. Prepare budgets, bids, and contracts, and direct the negotiation of research contracts. Analyze technology, resource needs, and market demand to plan and assess the feasibility of projects. Confer with management, production, and marketing staff to discuss project specifications and procedures. Review and recommend or approve contracts and cost estimates. Develop and implement policies, standards, and procedures for the engineering and technical work performed in the department, service, laboratory, or firm. Plan and direct the installation, testing, operation, maintenance, and repair of facilities and equipment. Administer highway planning, construction, and maintenance. Confer with and report to officials and the public to provide information and solicit support for projects. Set scientific and technical goals within broad outlines provided by top management.

Education/Training Required: Work experience plus degree. **Education and Training Programs:** Aerospace, Aeronautical, and Astronautical/Space Engineering; Agricultural Engineering; Architectural Engineering; Architecture; Bioengineering and Biomedical Engineering; Ceramic Sciences and Engineering; Chemical Engineering; City/Urban, Community and Regional Planning; Civil Engineering, General; Computer Engineering, General; Computer Hardware Engineering; Computer Software Engineering; Construction Engineering; Electrical and Electronics Engineering; Engineering Mechanics; Engineering Physics/Applied Physics; Engineering Science; Engineering, General; Environmental Design; Environmental/Environmental Health Engineering; Forest Engineering; Geological Engineering; Geotechnical and Geoenvironmental Engineering; Industrial Engineering; Interior Architecture; Landscape Architecture; Manufacturing Engineering; Materials Engineering; Mechanical Engineering; Metallurgical Engineering; Mining and Mineral Engineering; Naval Architecture and Marine Engineering; Nuclear Engineering; Ocean Engineering; Petroleum Engineering; Polymer/Plastics Engineering; Structural Engineering; Surveying Engineering; Systems Engineering; Textile Sciences and Engineering; Transportation and Highway Engineering; Water Resources Engineering; others. **Knowledge/Courses:** Engineering and Technology; Design; Physics; Building and Construction; Computers and Electronics; Mathematics.

Career Clusters: 02 Architecture and Construction; 11 Information Technology; 15 Science, Technology, Engineering, and Mathematics. **Career Pathways:** 02.1 Design/Pre-Construction; 11.4 Programming and Software Development; 15.1 Engineering and Technology; 15.2 Science and Mathematics.

Skills: Operations Analysis; Management of Financial Resources; Management of Material Resources; Science; Mathematics; Management of Personnel Resources; Systems Evaluation; Systems Analysis.

Work Environment: Indoors; sitting; noise.

Job Specialization: Biofuels/Biodiesel Technology and Product Development Managers

Define, plan, or execute biofuel/biodiesel research programs that evaluate alternative feedstock and process technologies with near-term commercial potential. Develop lab scale models of industrial-scale processes, such as fermentation. Develop computational tools or approaches to improve biofuels research-and-development activities. Develop carbohydrates arrays and associated methods for screening enzymes involved in biomass conversion. Provide technical or scientific guidance to technical staff in the conduct of biofuels research or development. Prepare, or oversee the preparation of, experimental plans for biofuels research or development. Prepare biofuels research-and-development reports for senior management or technical professionals. Perform protein functional analysis and engineering for processing of feedstock and creation of biofuels. Develop separation processes to recover biofuels. Develop methods to recover ethanol or other fuels from complex bioreactor liquid and gas streams. Develop methods to estimate the efficiency of biomass pretreatments. Design or execute solvent- or product-recovery experiments in laboratory or field settings. Design or conduct applied biodiesel or biofuels research projects on topics such as transport, thermodynamics, mixing, filtration, distillation, fermentation, extraction, and separation. Design chemical-conversion processes, such as etherification, esterification, interesterification, transesterification, distillation, hydrogenation, oxidation or reduction of fats and oils, and vegetable oil refining. Conduct experiments on biomass or pretreatment technologies.

Education/Training Required: Work experience plus degree. **Education and Training Programs:**

Agricultural Engineering; Bioengineering and Biomedical Engineering; Chemical Engineering; Engineering, Other; Manufacturing Engineering. **Knowledge/Courses:** No data available.

Personality Type: No data available. **Career Cluster:** 15 Science, Technology, Engineering, and Mathematics. **Career Pathways:** 15.1 Engineering and Technology; 15.2 Science and Mathematics.

Skills: No data available.

Work Environment: No data available.

Business Operations Specialists, All Other

Look for the job description among the Conventional jobs.

Captains, Mates, and Pilots of Water Vessels

Look for the job description among the Realistic jobs.

Chief Executives

- ❋ Personality Type: Enterprising-Conventional
- ❋ Annual Earnings: $165,080
- ❋ Earnings Growth Potential: Very high (54.5%)
- ❋ Growth: –1.4%
- ❋ Annual Job Openings: 11,250
- ❋ Self-Employed: 21.6%

Considerations for Job Outlook: The number of top executives is expected to remain steady, but employment may be adversely affected by consolidation and mergers. Keen competition is expected.

Determine and formulate policies and provide the overall direction of companies or private and public sector organizations within the guidelines set up by a board of directors or similar governing body. Plan, direct, or coordinate operational activities at the highest level of management with the help of subordinate executives and staff managers. Direct and coordinate an organization's financial and budget activities in order to fund operations, maximize investments, and increase efficiency. Confer with board members, organization officials, and staff members to discuss issues, coordinate activities, and resolve problems. Analyze operations to evaluate performance of a company and its staff in meeting objectives and to determine areas of potential cost reduction, program improvement, or policy change. Direct, plan, and implement policies, objectives, and activities of organizations or businesses in order to ensure continuing operations, to maximize returns on investments, and to increase productivity. Prepare budgets for approval, including those for funding and implementation of programs. Direct and coordinate activities of businesses or departments concerned with production, pricing, sales, and/or distribution of products. Negotiate or approve contracts and agreements with suppliers, distributors, federal and state agencies, and other organizational entities. Review reports submitted by staff members in order to recommend approval or to suggest changes. Appoint department heads or managers, and assign or delegate responsibilities to them. Direct human resources activities, including the approval of human resource plans and activities, the selection of directors and other high-level staff, and establishment and organization of major departments.

Education/Training Required: Work experience plus degree. **Education and Training Programs:** Business Administration and Management, General; Business/Commerce, General; Entrepreneurship/Entrepreneurial Studies; International Business/Trade/Commerce; International Relations and Affairs; Public Administration; Public Administration and Social Service Professions, Other; Public Policy Analysis, General; Transportation/Mobility Management. **Knowledge/Courses:** Economics and

Accounting; Administration and Management; Sales and Marketing; Personnel and Human Resources; Law and Government; Medicine and Dentistry.

Career Clusters: 04 Business, Management, and Administration; 07 Government and Public Administration; 10 Human Services; 16 Transportation, Distribution, and Logistics. **Career Pathways:** 04.1 Management; 07.1 Governance; 07.3 Foreign Service; 07.6 Regulation; 10.3 Family and Community Services; 16.2 Logistics, Planning, and Management Services.

Skills: Management of Financial Resources; Management of Material Resources; Management of Personnel Resources; Systems Evaluation; Systems Analysis; Judgment and Decision Making; Persuasion; Monitoring.

Work Environment: Indoors; sitting.

Job Specialization: Chief Sustainability Officers

Communicate and coordinate with management, shareholders, customers, and employees to address sustainability issues. Enact or oversee a corporate sustainability strategy. Identify educational, training, or other development opportunities for sustainability employees or volunteers. Identify and evaluate pilot projects or programs to enhance the sustainability research agenda. Conduct sustainability- or environment-related risk assessments. Create and maintain sustainability program documents, such as schedules and budgets. Write project proposals, grant applications, or other documents to pursue funding for environmental initiatives. Supervise employees or volunteers working on sustainability projects. Write and distribute financial or environmental-impact reports. Review sustainability program objectives, progress, or status to ensure compliance with policies, standards, regulations, or laws. Formulate or implement sustainability campaign or marketing strategies. Research environmental-sustainability issues, concerns, or stakeholder interests. Evaluate and approve proposals for sustainability

projects, considering factors such as cost effectiveness, technical feasibility, and integration with other initiatives. Develop sustainability reports, presentations, or proposals for supplier, employee, academia, media, government, public interest, or other groups. Develop, or oversee the development of, sustainability-evaluation or monitoring systems. Develop, or oversee the development of, marketing or outreach media for sustainability projects or events. Develop methodologies to assess the viability or success of sustainability initiatives.

Education/Training Required: Work experience plus degree. **Education and Training Programs:** Business Administration and Management, General; Business/Commerce, General; Entrepreneurship/Entrepreneurial Studies; International Business/Trade/Commerce; International Relations and Affairs; Public Administration; Public Administration and Social Service Professions, Other; Public Policy Analysis, General; Transportation/Mobility Management. **Knowledge/Courses:** No data available.

Personality Type: No data available. **Career Clusters:** 04 Business, Management, and Administration; 07 Government and Public Administration; 16 Transportation, Distribution, and Logistics. **Career Pathways:** 04.1 Management; 07.1 Governance; 16.2 Logistics, Planning, and Management Services.

Skills: No data available.

Work Environment: No data available.

Compensation and Benefits Managers

* Personality Type: Enterprising-Conventional-Social
* Annual Earnings: $89,270
* Earnings Growth Potential: High (41.6%)
* Growth: 8.5%
* Annual Job Openings: 1,210
* Self-Employed: 0.6%

Considerations for Job Outlook: Efforts to recruit and retain employees, the growing importance of employee training, and new legal standards are expected to increase employment of these workers. College graduates and those with certification should have the best opportunities.

Plan, direct, or coordinate compensation and benefits activities and staff of an organization. Advise management on such matters as equal employment opportunity, sexual harassment, and discrimination. Direct preparation and distribution of written and verbal information to inform employees of benefits, compensation, and personnel policies. Administer, direct, and review employee benefit programs, including the integration of benefit programs following mergers and acquisitions. Plan and conduct new employee orientations to foster positive attitude toward organizational objectives. Plan, direct, supervise, and coordinate work activities of subordinates and staff relating to employment, compensation, labor relations, and employee relations. Identify and implement benefits to increase the quality of life for employees, by working with brokers and researching benefits issues. Design, evaluate, and modify benefits policies to ensure that programs are current, competitive, and in compliance with legal requirements. Analyze compensation policies, government regulations, and prevailing wage rates to develop competitive compensation plan. Formulate policies, procedures, and programs for recruitment, testing, placement, classification, orientation, benefits and compensation, and labor and industrial relations. Mediate between benefits providers and employees, such as by assisting in handling employees' benefits-related questions or taking suggestions.

Education/Training Required: Work experience plus degree. **Education and Training Program:** Human Resources Management/Personnel Administration, General. **Knowledge/Courses:** Personnel and Human Resources; Economics and Accounting; Administration and Management; Mathematics; Law and Government; Communications and Media.

Career Cluster: 04 Business, Management, and Administration. **Career Pathway:** 04.3 Human Resources.

Skills: Management of Financial Resources; Operations Analysis; Systems Evaluation; Systems Analysis; Management of Personnel Resources; Time Management; Management of Material Resources; Negotiation.

Work Environment: Indoors; sitting.

Computer and Information Systems Managers

- ❈ Personality Type: Enterprising-Conventional-Investigative
- ❈ Annual Earnings: $115,780
- ❈ Earnings Growth Potential: Medium (38.3%)
- ❈ Growth: 16.9%
- ❈ Annual Job Openings: 9,710
- ❈ Self-Employed: 3.3%

Considerations for Job Outlook: New applications of technology in the workplace should continue to drive demand for IT services, fueling employment growth of these managers. Job prospects are expected to be excellent.

Plan, direct, or coordinate activities in such fields as electronic data processing, information systems, systems analysis, and computer programming. Review project plans to plan and coordinate project activity. Manage backup, security, and user help systems. Develop and interpret organizational goals, policies, and procedures. Develop computer information resources, providing for data security and control, strategic computing, and disaster recovery. Consult with users, management, vendors, and technicians to assess computing needs and system requirements. Stay abreast of advances in technology. Meet with department heads, managers, supervisors, vendors, and others to solicit cooperation and resolve problems. Provide users with technical support for computer problems. Recruit, hire, train, and supervise staff, or participate in staffing decisions. Evaluate data-processing proposals to assess project feasibility

Enterprising-C

and requirements. Review and approve all systems charts and programs prior to their implementation. Control operational budget and expenditures. Direct daily operations of department, analyzing workflow, establishing priorities, developing standards, and setting deadlines. Assign and review the work of systems analysts, programmers, and other computer-related workers. Evaluate the organization's technology use and needs, and recommend improvements such as hardware and software upgrades. Prepare and review operational reports or project progress reports. Purchase necessary equipment.

Education/Training Required: Work experience plus degree. **Education and Training Programs:** Computer and Information Sciences, General; Computer Science; Information Resources Management/CIO Training; Information Science/Studies; Knowledge Management; Management Information Systems, General; Network and System Administration/Administrator; Operations Management and Supervision. **Knowledge/Courses:** Telecommunications; Computers and Electronics; Economics and Accounting; Production and Processing; Personnel and Human Resources; Administration and Management.

Career Clusters: 04 Business, Management, and Administration; 11 Information Technology. **Career Pathways:** 04.1 Management; 04.4 Business Analysis; 11.1 Network Systems; 11.2 Information Support Services.

Skills: Management of Financial Resources; Management of Material Resources; Programming; Equipment Selection; Systems Evaluation; Troubleshooting; Repairing; Operations Analysis.

Work Environment: Indoors; sitting; using hands.

Construction Managers

- ❋ Personality Type: Enterprising-Realistic-Conventional
- ❋ Annual Earnings: $83,860
- ❋ Earnings Growth Potential: Medium (40.1%)
- ❋ Growth: 17.2%
- ❋ Annual Job Openings: 13,770
- ❋ Self-Employed: 60.9%

Considerations for Job Outlook: As population and the number of businesses grow, building activity is expected to increase, which in turn will boost employment of construction managers. Prospects should be best for jobseekers who have a bachelor's or higher degree in a construction-related discipline, plus construction experience.

Plan, direct, coordinate, or budget, usually through subordinate supervisory personnel, activities concerned with the construction and maintenance of structures, facilities, and systems. Participate in the conceptual development of a construction project, and oversee its organization, scheduling, and implementation. Schedule the project in logical steps, and budget time required to meet deadlines. Confer with supervisory personnel, owners, contractors, and design professionals to discuss and resolve matters such as work procedures, complaints, and construction problems. Prepare contracts, and negotiate revisions, changes, and additions to contractual agreements with architects, consultants, clients, suppliers, and subcontractors. Prepare and submit budget estimates and progress and cost-tracking reports. Interpret and explain plans and contract terms to administrative staff, workers, and clients, representing the owner or developer. Plan, organize, and direct activities concerned with the construction and maintenance of structures, facilities, and systems. Take actions to deal with the results of delays, bad weather, or emergencies at construction sites. Inspect and review projects to monitor compliance with building and safety codes and other regulations. Study job specifications to determine appropriate construction methods. Select, contract, and oversee workers who complete specific pieces of the project, such as painting or plumbing. Obtain all necessary permits and licenses. Direct and supervise workers. Develop and implement quality control programs. Investigate damage, accidents, or delays at construction sites to ensure that proper procedures are being carried out. Determine labor requirements, and dispatch workers to construction sites.

Education/Training Required: Bachelor's degree. **Education and Training Programs:** Business Administration and Management, General; Business/Commerce, General; Construction Engineering Technology/Technician; Operations Management and Supervision. **Knowledge/Courses:** Building and Construction; Design; Engineering and Technology; Mechanical Devices; Administration and Management; Personnel and Human Resources.

Career Clusters: 02 Architecture and Construction; 04 Business, Management, and Administration. **Career Pathways:** 02.2 Construction; 04.1 Management.

Skills: Management of Financial Resources; Management of Material Resources; Operations Analysis; Management of Personnel Resources; Negotiation; Mathematics; Persuasion; Systems Evaluation.

Work Environment: More often outdoors than indoors; sitting; noise; contaminants; hazardous equipment.

Customer Service Representatives

Look for the job description among the Social jobs.

Detectives and Criminal Investigators

- ❋ Personality Type: Enterprising-Conventional-Realistic
- ❋ Annual Earnings: $68,820
- ❋ Earnings Growth Potential: High (43.5%)
- ❋ Growth: 16.6%
- ❋ Annual Job Openings: 4,160
- ❋ Self-Employed: 1.1%

Considerations for Job Outlook: Population growth is the main source of demand for police services. Overall, opportunities in local police departments should be favorable for qualified applicants.

Job Specialization: Criminal Investigators and Special Agents

Investigate alleged or suspected criminal violations of federal, state, or local laws to determine if evidence is sufficient to recommend prosecution. Record evidence and documents, using equipment such as cameras and photocopy machines. Obtain and verify evidence by interviewing and observing suspects and witnesses or by analyzing records. Examine records to locate links in chains of evidence or information. Prepare reports that detail investigation findings. Determine scope, timing, and direction of investigations. Collaborate with other offices and agencies to exchange information and coordinate activities. Testify before grand juries concerning criminal activity investigations. Analyze evidence in laboratories or in the field. Investigate organized crime, public corruption, financial crime, copyright infringement, civil rights violations, bank robbery, extortion, kidnapping, and other violations of federal or state statutes. Identify case issues and evidence needed, based on analysis of charges, complaints, or allegations of law violations. Obtain and use search and arrest warrants. Serve subpoenas or other official papers. Collaborate with other authorities on activities such as surveillance, transcription, and research. Develop relationships with informants to obtain information related to cases. Search for and collect evidence such as fingerprints, using investigative equipment. Collect and record physical information about arrested suspects, including fingerprints, height and weight measurements, and photographs.

Education/Training Required: Work experience in a related occupation. **Education and Training Programs:** Criminal Justice/Police Science; Criminalistics and Criminal Science. **Knowledge/Courses:** Public Safety and Security; Psychology; Law and Government; Customer and Personal Service; Sociology and Anthropology; Therapy and Counseling.

Personality Type: Enterprising-Investigative. **Career Cluster:** 12 Law, Public Safety, Corrections, and Security. **Career Pathway:** 12.4 Law Enforcement Services.

Enterprising–D

Skills: Negotiation; Science; Complex Problem Solving; Persuasion; Judgment and Decision Making; Speaking; Critical Thinking; Social Perceptiveness.

Work Environment: Indoors; sitting; noise; very hot or cold; contaminants; exposed to disease or infections.

Job Specialization: Immigration and Customs Inspectors

Investigate and inspect persons, common carriers, goods, and merchandise arriving in or departing from the United States or moving between states to detect violations of immigration and customs laws and regulations. Examine immigration applications, visas, and passports and interview persons to determine eligibility for admission, residence, and travel in the United States. Detain persons found to be in violation of customs or immigration laws, and arrange for legal action such as deportation. Locate and seize contraband or undeclared merchandise and vehicles, aircraft, or boats that contain such merchandise. Interpret and explain laws and regulations to travelers, prospective immigrants, shippers, and manufacturers. Inspect cargo, baggage, and personal articles entering or leaving U.S. for compliance with revenue laws and U.S. Customs Service regulations. Record and report job-related activities, findings, transactions, violations, discrepancies, and decisions. Institute civil and criminal prosecutions, and cooperate with other law enforcement agencies in the investigation and prosecution of those in violation of immigration or customs laws. Testify regarding decisions at immigration appeals or in federal court. Determine duty and taxes to be paid on goods. Collect samples of merchandise for examination, appraisal, or testing. Investigate applications for duty refunds, and petition for remission or mitigation of penalties when warranted.

Education/Training Required: Work experience in a related occupation. **Education and Training Programs:** Criminal Justice/Police Science; Criminalistics and Criminal Science. **Knowledge/ Courses:** Public Safety and Security; Law and

Government; Foreign Language; Geography; Customer and Personal Service; Philosophy and Theology.

Personality Type: Conventional-Enterprising-Realistic. **Career Cluster:** 12 Law, Public Safety, Corrections, and Security. **Career Pathway:** 12.4 Law Enforcement Services.

Skills: Active Listening; Persuasion; Negotiation; Operation and Control; Speaking; Social Perceptiveness; Time Management; Judgment and Decision Making.

Work Environment: More often outdoors than indoors; more often sitting than standing; using hands; repetitive motions; noise; very hot or cold; bright or inadequate lighting; contaminants; cramped work space; exposed to radiation; hazardous equipment.

Job Specialization: Intelligence Analysts

Gather, analyze, and evaluate information from a variety of sources, such as law enforcement databases, surveillance, intelligence networks, and geographic information systems. Use data to anticipate and prevent organized crime activities, such as terrorism. Predict future gang, organized crime, or terrorist activity, using analyses of intelligence data. Study activities relating to narcotics, money laundering, gangs, auto theft rings, terrorism, or other national security threats. Design, use, or maintain databases and software applications, such as geographic information systems (GIS) mapping and artificial intelligence tools. Establish criminal profiles to aid in connecting criminal organizations with their members. Evaluate records of communications, such as telephone calls, to plot activity and determine the size and location of criminal groups and members. Gather and evaluate information, using tools such as aerial photographs, radar equipment, or sensitive radio equipment. Gather intelligence information by field observation, confidential information sources, or public records. Gather, analyze, correlate, or evaluate information from a variety of resources, such as law enforcement databases.

Link or chart suspects to criminal organizations or events to determine activities and interrelationships. Operate cameras, radios, or other surveillance equipment to intercept communications or document activities. Prepare comprehensive written reports, presentations, maps, or charts based on research, collection, and analysis of intelligence data. Prepare plans to intercept foreign communications transmissions. Study the assets of criminal suspects to determine the flow of money from or to targeted groups.

Education/Training Required: Work experience plus degree. **Education and Training Programs:** Criminal Justice/Police Science; Criminalistics and Criminal Science. **Knowledge/Courses:** No data available.

Personality Type: No data available. **Career Cluster:** 12 Law, Public Safety, Corrections, and Security. **Career Pathway:** 12.4 Law Enforcement Services.

Skills: No data available.

Work Environment: No data available.

Job Specialization: Police Detectives

Conduct investigations to prevent crimes or solve criminal cases. Provide testimony as witnesses in court. Secure deceased bodies, and obtain evidence from them, preventing bystanders from tampering with bodies prior to medical examiners' arrival. Examine crime scenes to obtain clues and evidence such as loose hairs, fibers, clothing, or weapons. Obtain evidence from suspects. Record progress of investigations, maintain informational files on suspects, and submit reports to commanding officers or magistrates to authorize warrants. Check victims for signs of life such as breathing and pulse. Prepare charges or responses to charges, or information for court cases, according to formalized procedures. Obtain facts or statements from complainants, witnesses, and accused persons, and record interviews, using recording devices. Prepare and serve search and arrest warrants. Note, mark, and photograph

locations of objects found such as footprints, tire tracks, bullets, and bloodstains, and take measurements of each scene. Question individuals or observe persons and establishments to confirm information given to patrol officers. Preserve, process, and analyze items of evidence obtained from crime scenes and suspects, placing them in proper containers and destroying evidence no longer needed. Secure persons at scenes, keeping witnesses from conversing or leaving scenes before investigators arrive. Take photographs from all angles of relevant parts of crime scenes, including entrance and exit routes and streets and intersections.

Education/Training Required: Work experience in a related occupation. **Education and Training Programs:** Criminal Justice/Police Science; Criminalistics and Criminal Science. **Knowledge/Courses:** Public Safety and Security; Law and Government; Psychology; Therapy and Counseling; Customer and Personal Service; Philosophy and Theology.

Personality Type: Enterprising-Investigative. **Career Cluster:** 12 Law, Public Safety, Corrections, and Security. **Career Pathway:** 12.4 Law Enforcement Services.

Skills: Science; Negotiation; Operation and Control; Social Perceptiveness; Operation Monitoring; Service Orientation; Active Learning; Critical Thinking.

Work Environment: More often outdoors than indoors; sitting; noise; very hot or cold; contaminants; exposed to disease or infections.

Job Specialization: Police Identification and Records Officers

Collect evidence at crime scene, classify and identify fingerprints, and photograph evidence for use in criminal and civil cases. Photograph crime or accident scenes for evidence records. Analyze and process evidence at crime scenes and in the laboratory, wearing protective equipment and using powders and chemicals. Look for trace evidence, such as

Enterprising-E

fingerprints, hairs, fibers, or shoe impressions, using alternative light sources when necessary. Dust selected areas of crime scene, and lift latent fingerprints, adhering to proper preservation procedures. Testify in court, and present evidence. Package, store, and retrieve evidence. Serve as technical advisor and coordinate with other law enforcement workers to exchange information on crime-scene collection activities. Perform emergency work during off-hours. Submit evidence to supervisors. Process film and prints from crime or accident scenes. Identify, classify, and file fingerprints, using systems such as the Henry Classification system.

Education/Training Required: Work experience in a related occupation. **Education and Training Programs:** Criminal Justice/Police Science; Criminalistics and Criminal Science. **Knowledge/ Courses:** Public Safety and Security; Law and Government; Chemistry; Customer and Personal Service; Clerical Practices; Telecommunications.

Personality Type: Conventional-Realistic-Investigative. **Career Cluster:** 12 Law, Public Safety, Corrections, and Security. **Career Pathway:** 12.4 Law Enforcement Services.

Skills: Operation and Control; Speaking; Negotiation; Operation Monitoring; Critical Thinking; Active Listening; Persuasion; Technology Design.

Work Environment: Indoors; sitting; using hands; noise; contaminants; exposed to disease or infections; hazardous conditions.

Education Administrators, Elementary and Secondary School

* Personality Type: Enterprising-Social-Conventional
* Annual Earnings: $86,970
* Earnings Growth Potential: Low (33.0%)
* Growth: 8.6%
* Annual Job Openings: 8,880
* Self-Employed: 4.7%

Considerations for Job Outlook: Increasing student enrollments are expected to drive employment growth for these workers. Prospects are expected to be good.

Plan, direct, or coordinate the academic, clerical, or auxiliary activities of public or private elementary or secondary-level schools. Review and approve new programs, or recommend modifications to existing programs, submitting program proposals for school board approval as necessary. Prepare, maintain, or oversee the preparation and maintenance of attendance, activity, planning, or personnel reports and records. Confer with parents and staff to discuss educational activities, policies, and student behavioral or learning problems. Prepare and submit budget requests and recommendations, or grant proposals to solicit program funding. Direct and coordinate school maintenance services and the use of school facilities. Counsel and provide guidance to students regarding personal, academic, vocational, or behavioral issues. Organize and direct committees of specialists, volunteers, and staff to provide technical and advisory assistance for programs. Teach classes or courses to students. Advocate for new schools to be built or for existing facilities to be repaired or remodeled. Plan and develop instructional methods and content for educational, vocational, or student activity programs. Develop partnerships with businesses, communities, and other organizations to help meet identified educational needs and to provide school-to-work programs. Direct and coordinate activities of teachers, administrators, and support staff at schools, public agencies, and institutions.

Education/Training Required: Work experience plus degree. **Education and Training Programs:** Educational Administration and Supervision, Other; Educational Leadership and Administration, General; Educational, Instructional, and Curriculum Supervision; Elementary and Middle School Administration/Principalship; Secondary School Administration/Principalship. **Knowledge/ Courses:** Therapy and Counseling; Education and Training; Philosophy and Theology; Sociology and Anthropology; Personnel and Human Resources; History and Archeology.

Career Cluster: 05 Education and Training. **Career Pathway:** 05.1 Administration and Administrative Support.

Skills: Management of Financial Resources; Management of Material Resources; Learning Strategies; Management of Personnel Resources; Systems Evaluation; Systems Analysis; Persuasion; Negotiation.

Work Environment: Indoors; sitting; noise.

Farmers, Ranchers, and Other Agricultural Managers

- ❋ Personality Type: Enterprising-Realistic-Conventional
- ❋ Annual Earnings: $60,750
- ❋ Earnings Growth Potential: Very high (51.8%)
- ❋ Growth: 5.9%
- ❋ Annual Job Openings: 6,490
- ❋ Self-Employed: No data available.

Considerations for Job Outlook: As farm productivity increases and consolidation continues, a decline in the number of farmers and ranchers is expected. Agricultural managers at larger, well-financed operations should have better prospects. Small, local farming offers the best entry-level opportunities.

Job Specialization: Aquacultural Managers

Direct and coordinate, through subordinate supervisory personnel, activities of workers engaged in fish hatchery production for corporations, cooperatives, or other owners. Grow fish and shellfish as cash crops or for release into freshwater or saltwater. Supervise and train aquaculture and fish hatchery support workers. Collect and record growth, production, and environmental data. Conduct and supervise stock examinations in order to identify diseases or parasites. Account for and disburse funds. Devise and participate in activities to improve fish hatching and growth rates, and to prevent disease in hatcheries. Monitor environments to ensure maintenance of optimum conditions for aquatic life. Direct and monitor trapping and spawning of fish, egg incubation, and fry rearing, applying knowledge of management and fish culturing techniques. Coordinate the selection and maintenance of brood stock. Direct and monitor the transfer of mature fish to lakes, ponds, streams, or commercial tanks. Determine, administer, and execute policies relating to operations administration and standards, and facility maintenance. Collect information regarding techniques for fish collection and fertilization, spawn incubation, and treatment of spawn and fry. Determine how to allocate resources, and how to respond to unanticipated problems such as insect infestation, drought, and fire. Operate and maintain cultivating and harvesting equipment. Confer with biologists, fish pathologists, and other fishery personnel to obtain data concerning fish habits, diseases, food, and environmental requirements. Prepare reports required by state and federal laws.

Education/Training Required: Work experience plus degree. **Education and Training Program:** Aquaculture. **Knowledge/Courses:** Food Production; Biology; Engineering and Technology; Building and Construction; Chemistry; Mechanical Devices.

Personality Type: Enterprising-Realistic-Conventional. **Career Cluster:** 01 Agriculture, Food, and Natural Resources. **Career Pathways:** 01.1 Food Products and Processing Systems; 01.2 Plant Systems; 01.3 Animal Systems.

Skills: Science; Management of Financial Resources; Equipment Maintenance; Operations Analysis; Repairing; Systems Analysis; Quality Control Analysis; Management of Material Resources.

Work Environment: More often outdoors than indoors; standing; using hands; noise; very hot or cold; contaminants.

Job Specialization: Farm and Ranch Managers

Plan, direct, or coordinate the management or operation of farms, ranches, greenhouses, aquacultural operations, nurseries, timber tracts, or other agricultural establishments. May hire, train, or supervise farm workers or contract for services to carry out the day-to-day activities of the managed operation. May engage in or supervise planting, cultivating, harvesting, financial, or marketing activities. Change processes such as drying, grading, storing, or shipping to improve efficiency or profitability. Determine types or quantities of crops or livestock to be raised, according to factors such as market conditions, federal programs or incentives, or soil conditions. Direct crop production operations, such as planning, tilling, planting, fertilizing, cultivating, spraying, or harvesting. Direct the breeding or raising of stock, such as cattle, poultry, or honeybees, using recognized breeding practices to ensure stock improvement. Evaluate marketing or sales alternatives for farm or ranch products. Hire, train, or supervise workers engaged in planting, cultivating, irrigating, harvesting, or marketing crops, or in raising livestock. Inspect farm or ranch structures, such as buildings, fences, or roads, ordering repair or maintenance activities, as needed. Maintain financial, operational, production, or employment records for farms or ranches. Monitor activities such as irrigation, chemical application, harvesting, milking, breeding, or grading to ensure adherence to safety regulations or standards. Monitor pasture or grazing land use to ensure that livestock are properly fed or that conservation methods, such as rotational grazing, are used. Negotiate with buyers for the sale, storage, or shipment of crops or livestock. Obtain financing necessary for purchases of machinery, land, supplies, or livestock. Operate or oversee the operations of dairy farms that produce bulk milk.

Education/Training Required: Work experience in a related occupation. **Education and Training Program:** Farm/Farm and Ranch Management. **Knowledge/Courses:** No data available.

Personality Type: No data available. **Career Cluster:** 01 Agriculture, Food, and Natural Resources. **Career Pathways:** 01.2 Plant Systems; 01.3 Animal Systems.

Skills: No data available.

Work Environment: No data available.

Job Specialization: Nursery and Greenhouse Managers

Plan, organize, direct, control, and coordinate activities of workers engaged in propagating, cultivating, and harvesting horticultural specialties, such as trees, shrubs, flowers, mushrooms, and other plants. Manage nurseries that grow horticultural plants for sale to trade or retail customers, for display or exhibition, or for research. Identify plants as well as problems such as diseases, weeds, and insect pests. Tour work areas to observe work being done, to inspect crops, and to evaluate plant and soil conditions. Assign work schedules and duties to nursery or greenhouse staff, and supervise their work. Determine plant growing conditions, such as greenhouses, hydroponics, or natural settings, and set planting and care schedules. Apply pesticides and fertilizers to plants. Hire employees, and train them in gardening techniques. Select and purchase seeds, plant nutrients, disease control chemicals, and garden and lawn care equipment. Determine types and quantities of horticultural plants to be grown, based on budgets, projected sales volumes, and/or executive directives. Explain and enforce safety regulations and policies. Position and regulate plant irrigation systems, and program environmental and irrigation control computers. Inspect facilities and equipment for signs of disrepair, and perform necessary maintenance work. Coordinate clerical, recordkeeping, inventory, requisitioning, and marketing activities. Prepare soil for planting, and plant or transplant seeds, bulbs, and cuttings. Confer with horticultural personnel in order to plan facility renovations or additions. Cut and prune trees, shrubs, flowers, and plants.

Education/Training Required: Work experience plus degree. **Education and Training Programs:**

Greenhouse Operations and Management; Landscaping and Groundskeeping; Ornamental Horticulture; Plant Nursery Operations and Management. **Knowledge/Courses:** Biology; Production and Processing; Sales and Marketing; Chemistry; Personnel and Human Resources; Design.

Personality Type: Enterprising-Realistic-Conventional. **Career Cluster:** 01 Agriculture, Food, and Natural Resources. **Career Pathway:** 01.2 Plant Systems.

Skills: Management of Material Resources; Management of Financial Resources; Science; Management of Personnel Resources; Instructing; Negotiation; Operation and Control; Persuasion.

Work Environment: More often outdoors than indoors; standing; walking and running; kneeling, crouching, stooping, or crawling; noise; very hot or cold; contaminants; hazardous conditions; minor burns, cuts, bites, or stings.

Financial Examiners

- ❀ Personality Type: Enterprising-Conventional
- ❀ Annual Earnings: $74,940
- ❀ Earnings Growth Potential: High (42.4%)
- ❀ Growth: 41.2%
- ❀ Annual Job Openings: 1,600
- ❀ Self-Employed: 0.0%

Considerations for Job Outlook: Much faster than average employment growth is projected.

Enforce or ensure compliance with laws and regulations governing financial and securities institutions and financial and real estate transactions. May examine, verify correctness of, or establish authenticity of records. Investigate activities of institutions in order to enforce laws and regulations and to ensure legality of transactions and operations or financial solvency. Review and analyze new, proposed, or revised laws, regulations, policies, and procedures in order to interpret their meaning and determine

their impact. Plan, supervise, and review work of assigned subordinates. Recommend actions to ensure compliance with laws and regulations or to protect solvency of institutions. Examine the minutes of meetings of directors, stockholders, and committees in order to investigate the specific authority extended at various levels of management. Prepare reports, exhibits, and other supporting schedules that detail an institution's safety and soundness, compliance with laws and regulations, and recommended solutions to questionable financial conditions. Review balance sheets, operating income and expense accounts, and loan documentation in order to confirm institution assets and liabilities. Review audit reports of internal and external auditors in order to monitor adequacy of scope of reports or to discover specific weaknesses in internal routines. Train other examiners in the financial examination process. Establish guidelines for procedures and policies that comply with new and revised regulations and direct their implementation.

Education/Training Required: Bachelor's degree. **Education and Training Programs:** Accounting; Taxation. **Knowledge/Courses:** Economics and Accounting; Law and Government; Clerical Practices; Mathematics; English Language; Administration and Management.

Career Clusters: 04 Business, Management, and Administration; 07 Government and Public Administration. **Career Pathways:** 04.2 Business, Financial Management, and Accounting; 07.5 Revenue and Taxation.

Skills: Management of Personnel Resources; Active Learning; Systems Evaluation; Learning Strategies; Systems Analysis; Mathematics; Writing; Programming.

Work Environment: Indoors; sitting.

Financial Managers

- ❀ Personality Type: Enterprising-Conventional
- ❀ Annual Earnings: $103,910
- ❀ Earnings Growth Potential: High (46.0%)

* Growth: 7.6%
* Annual Job Openings: 13,820
* Self-Employed: 5.3%

Considerations for Job Outlook: Business expansion and globalization will require financial expertise, which is expected to drive employment growth for these managers. Job growth, however, is expected to be tempered by mergers and downsizing. Keen competition is expected.

Job Specialization: Financial Managers, Branch or Department

Direct and coordinate financial activities of workers in a branch, office, or department of an establishment, such as branch bank, brokerage firm, risk and insurance department, or credit department. Establish and maintain relationships with individual and business customers and provide assistance with problems these customers may encounter. Examine, evaluate, and process loan applications. Plan, direct, and coordinate the activities of workers in branches, offices, or departments of such establishments as branch banks, brokerage firms, risk and insurance departments, or credit departments. Oversee the flow of cash and financial instruments. Recruit staff members and oversee training programs. Network within communities to find and attract new business. Approve or reject, or coordinate the approval and rejection of, lines of credit and commercial, real estate, and personal loans. Prepare financial and regulatory reports required by laws, regulations, and boards of directors. Establish procedures for custody and control of assets, records, loan collateral, and securities in order to ensure safekeeping. Review collection reports to determine the status of collections and the amounts of outstanding balances. Prepare operational and risk reports for management analysis. Evaluate financial reporting systems, accounting and collection procedures, and investment activities, and make recommendations for changes to procedures, operating systems, budgets, and other financial control functions. Plan,

direct, and coordinate risk and insurance programs of establishments to control risks and losses. Submit delinquent accounts to attorneys or outside agencies for collection.

Education/Training Required: Work experience plus degree. **Education and Training Programs:** Accounting and Business/Management; Accounting and Finance; Credit Management; Finance and Financial Management Services, Other; Finance, General; International Finance; Public Finance. **Knowledge/Courses:** Economics and Accounting; Sales and Marketing; Personnel and Human Resources; Clerical Practices; Customer and Personal Service; Mathematics.

Personality Type: Enterprising-Conventional. **Career Clusters:** 04 Business, Management, and Administration; 06 Finance. **Career Pathways:** 04.2 Business, Financial Management, and Accounting; 06.1 Financial and Investment Planning.

Skills: Management of Financial Resources; Management of Personnel Resources; Persuasion; Service Orientation; Systems Evaluation; Learning Strategies; Time Management; Monitoring.

Work Environment: Indoors; sitting.

Job Specialization: Treasurers and Controllers

Direct financial activities, such as planning, procurement, and investments, for all or part of an organization. Prepare and file annual tax returns, or prepare financial information so that outside accountants can complete tax returns. Prepare or direct preparation of financial statements, business activity reports, financial position forecasts, annual budgets, and/or reports required by regulatory agencies. Supervise employees performing financial reporting, accounting, billing, collections, payroll, and budgeting duties. Delegate authority for the receipt, disbursement, banking, protection, and custody of funds, securities, and financial instruments. Maintain current knowledge of organizational policies and procedures, federal and state policies and directives, and current accounting standards. Conduct or coordinate audits of company accounts and financial transactions to ensure compliance with state and federal requirements and statutes. Receive and record requests for disbursements; authorize disbursements in accordance with policies and procedures. Monitor financial activities and details such as reserve levels to ensure that all legal and regulatory requirements are met. Monitor and evaluate the performance of accounting and other financial staff; recommend and implement personnel actions such as promotions and dismissals. Develop and maintain relationships with banking, insurance, and non-organizational accounting personnel in order to facilitate financial activities.

Education/Training Required: Work experience plus degree. **Education and Training Programs:** Accounting and Business/Management; Accounting and Finance; Credit Management; Finance and Financial Management Services, Other; Finance, General; International Finance; Public Finance. **Knowledge/Courses:** Economics and Accounting; Administration and Management; Personnel and Human Resources; Law and Government; Mathematics; English Language.

Personality Type: Conventional-Enterprising. **Career Clusters:** 04 Business, Management, and Administration; 06 Finance. **Career Pathways:** 04.2 Business, Financial Management, and Accounting; 06.1 Financial and Investment Planning.

Skills: Management of Financial Resources; Management of Material Resources; Systems Analysis; Operations Analysis; Judgment and Decision Making; Management of Personnel Resources; Systems Evaluation; Mathematics.

Work Environment: Indoors; sitting.

Financial Specialists, All Other

Look for the job description among the Conventional jobs.

First-Line Supervisors of Fire Fighting and Prevention Workers

❋ Personality Type: Enterprising-Realistic
❋ Annual Earnings: $68,240
❋ Earnings Growth Potential: Medium (39.3%)
❋ Growth: 8.2%
❋ Annual Job Openings: 3,250
❋ Self-Employed: 0.0%

Considerations for Job Outlook: Most job growth will stem from the conversion of volunteer fire fighting positions into paid positions. Job-seekers are expected to face keen competition. Those who have completed some fire fighter education at a community college and have EMT or paramedic certification should have the best prospects.

Job Specialization: Forest Fire Fighting and Prevention Supervisors

Supervise fire fighters who control and suppress fires in forests or vacant public land. Communicate fire details to superiors, subordinates, and interagency dispatch centers, using two-way radios. Serve as working leader of an engine, hand, helicopter, or prescribed fire crew of three or more firefighters. Maintain fire suppression equipment in good condition, checking equipment periodically to ensure that it is ready for use. Evaluate size, location, and condition of forest fires in order to request and dispatch crews and position equipment so fires can be contained safely and effectively. Operate wildland fire engines and hoselays. Direct and supervise prescribed burn projects, and prepare post-burn reports analyzing burn conditions and results. Monitor prescribed burns to ensure that they are conducted safely and effectively. Identify staff training and development needs to ensure that appropriate training can be arranged. Maintain knowledge of forest fire laws and fire prevention techniques and tactics. Recommend equipment modifications or new equipment purchases. Perform administrative duties such as compiling and maintaining records, completing forms, preparing reports, and composing correspondence. Recruit and hire forest fire-fighting personnel. Train workers in such skills as parachute jumping, fire suppression, aerial observation, and radio communication, both in the classroom and on the job. Review and evaluate employee performance.

Education/Training Required: Work experience in a related occupation. **Education and Training Programs:** Fire Prevention and Safety Technology/ Technician; Fire Services Administration. **Knowledge/Courses:** Public Safety and Security; Building and Construction; Mechanical Devices; Customer and Personal Service; Personnel and Human Resources; Transportation.

Personality Type: Enterprising-Realistic-Conventional. **Career Cluster:** 12 Law, Public Safety, Corrections, and Security. **Career Pathway:** 12.2 Emergency and Fire Management Services.

Skills: Operations Analysis; Equipment Maintenance; Operation and Control; Management of Personnel Resources; Coordination; Operation Monitoring; Monitoring; Equipment Selection.

Work Environment: Outdoors; standing; walking and running; using hands; noise; very hot or cold; bright or inadequate lighting; contaminants; cramped work space; hazardous equipment; minor burns, cuts, bites, or stings.

Job Specialization: Municipal Fire Fighting and Prevention Supervisors

Supervise fire fighters who control and extinguish municipal fires, protect life and property, and conduct rescue efforts. Assign firefighters to jobs at strategic locations to facilitate rescue of persons and maximize application of extinguishing agents. Provide emergency medical services as required, and perform light to heavy rescue functions at emergencies. Assess nature and extent of fire, condition of building, danger to adjacent buildings, and water supply status to determine crew or company require-

ments. Instruct and drill fire department personnel in assigned duties, including firefighting, medical care, hazardous materials response, fire prevention, and related subjects. Evaluate the performance of assigned firefighting personnel. Direct the training of firefighters, assigning of instructors to training classes, and providing of supervisors with reports on training progress and status. Prepare activity reports listing fire call locations, actions taken, fire types and probable causes, damage estimates, and situation dispositions. Maintain required maps and records. Attend in-service training classes to remain current in knowledge of codes, laws, ordinances, and regulations. Evaluate fire station procedures to ensure efficiency and enforcement of departmental regulations. Direct firefighters in station maintenance duties, and participate in these duties. Compile and maintain equipment and personnel records, including accident reports. Direct investigation of cases of suspected arson, hazards, and false alarms, and submit reports outlining findings.

Education/Training Required: Work experience in a related occupation. **Education and Training Programs:** Fire Prevention and Safety Technology/ Technician; Fire Services Administration. **Knowledge/Courses:** Building and Construction; Public Safety and Security; Medicine and Dentistry; Mechanical Devices; Chemistry; Personnel and Human Resources.

Personality Type: Enterprising-Realistic-Social. **Career Cluster:** 12 Law, Public Safety, Corrections, and Security. **Career Pathway:** 12.2 Emergency and Fire Management Services.

Skills: Operation and Control; Science; Equipment Selection; Repairing; Equipment Maintenance; Quality Control Analysis; Management of Personnel Resources; Systems Analysis.

Work Environment: More often outdoors than indoors; standing; using hands; noise; very hot or cold; bright or inadequate lighting; contaminants; cramped work space; exposed to disease or infections; high places; hazardous conditions; hazardous equipment; minor burns, cuts, bites, or stings.

First-Line Supervisors of Landscaping, Lawn Service, and Groundskeeping Workers

- Personality Type: Enterprising-Realistic-Conventional
- Annual Earnings: $41,860
- Earnings Growth Potential: Low (35.6%)
- Growth: 14.9%
- Annual Job Openings: 5,600
- Self-Employed: 50.4%

Considerations for Job Outlook: Demand for lawn care and landscaping services is expected to grow, resulting in employment growth for these workers. Job prospects are expected to be good. Opportunities for year-round work should be best in regions with temperate climates.

Plan, organize, direct, or coordinate activities of workers engaged in landscaping or groundskeeping activities such as planting and maintaining ornamental trees, shrubs, flowers, and lawns and applying fertilizers, pesticides, and other chemicals, according to contract specifications. May also coordinate activities of workers engaged in terracing hillsides, building retaining walls, constructing pathways, installing patios, and similar activities in following a landscape design plan. Work may involve reviewing contracts to ascertain service, machine, and work force requirements; answering inquiries from potential customers regarding methods, material, and price ranges; and preparing estimates according to labor, material, and machine costs. Establish and enforce operating procedures and work standards that will ensure adequate performance and personnel safety. Inspect completed work to ensure conformance to specifications, standards, and contract requirements. Direct activities of workers who perform duties such as landscaping, cultivating lawns, or pruning trees and shrubs. Schedule work for crews depending on work priorities, crew and equipment availability, and weather conditions. Plant and maintain vegetation through activities such as mulching, fertilizing, watering, mowing, and pruning. Monitor project activities to ensure that instructions are followed, deadlines are met, and schedules are maintained. Train workers in tasks such as transplanting and pruning trees and shrubs, finishing cement, using equipment, and caring for turf. Provide workers with assistance in performing duties as necessary to meet deadlines. Inventory supplies of tools, equipment, and materials to ensure that sufficient supplies are available and items are in usable condition. Confer with other supervisors to coordinate work activities with those of other departments or units. Perform personnel-related activities such as hiring workers, evaluating staff performance, and taking disciplinary actions when performance problems occur. Direct or perform mixing and application of fertilizers, insecticides, herbicides, and fungicides. Review contracts or work assignments to determine service, machine, and workforce requirements for jobs.

Education/Training Required: Work experience in a related occupation. **Education and Training Programs:** Landscaping and Groundskeeping; Ornamental Horticulture; Turf and Turfgrass Management. **Knowledge/Courses:** Mechanical Devices; Building and Construction; Design; Biology; Chemistry; Education and Training.

Career Cluster: 01 Agriculture, Food, and Natural Resources. **Career Pathway:** 01.2 Plant Systems.

Skills: Operation and Control; Repairing; Equipment Maintenance; Operation Monitoring; Management of Financial Resources; Management of Material Resources; Troubleshooting; Quality Control Analysis.

Work Environment: More often outdoors than indoors; standing; walking and running; using hands; noise; very hot or cold; bright or inadequate lighting; contaminants; hazardous equipment; minor burns, cuts, bites, or stings.

First-Line Supervisors of Mechanics, Installers, and Repairers

* Personality Type: Enterprising-Conventional-Realistic
* Annual Earnings: $59,150
* Earnings Growth Potential: Medium (39.2%)
* Growth: 4.2%
* Annual Job Openings: 13,650
* Self-Employed: 0.4%

Considerations for Job Outlook: Slower than average employment growth is projected.

Supervise and coordinate the activities of mechanics, installers, and repairers. Determine schedules, sequences, and assignments for work activities, based on work priority, quantity of equipment, and skill of personnel. Monitor employees' work levels, and review work performance. Monitor tool and part inventories and the condition and maintenance of shops to ensure adequate working conditions. Recommend or initiate personnel actions such as hires, promotions, transfers, discharges, and disciplinary measures. Investigate accidents and injuries, and prepare reports of findings. Compile operational and personnel records such as time and production records, inventory data, repair and maintenance statistics, and test results. Develop, implement, and evaluate maintenance policies and procedures. Counsel employees about work-related issues, and assist employees to correct job-skill deficiencies. Examine objects, systems, or facilities, and analyze information to determine needed installations, services, or repairs. Conduct or arrange for worker training in safety, repair, and maintenance techniques, operational procedures, or equipment use. Inspect and monitor work areas, examine tools and equipment, and provide employee safety training to prevent, detect, and correct unsafe conditions or violations of procedures and safety rules. Inspect, test, and measure completed work, using devices such as hand tools and gauges to verify conformance to standards and repair requirements. Requisition materials and supplies such as tools, equipment, and replacement parts.

Education/Training Required: Work experience in a related occupation. **Education and Training Program:** Operations Management and Supervision. **Knowledge/Courses:** Mechanical Devices; Personnel and Human Resources; Production and Processing; Building and Construction; Engineering and Technology; Economics and Accounting.

Career Cluster: 13 Manufacturing. **Career Pathway:** 13.1 Production.

Skills: Repairing; Management of Financial Resources; Equipment Maintenance; Troubleshooting; Management of Material Resources; Equipment Selection; Quality Control Analysis; Operation and Control.

Work Environment: More often indoors than outdoors; standing; noise; contaminants; hazardous conditions.

First-Line Supervisors of Non-Retail Sales Workers

* Personality Type: Enterprising-Conventional-Social
* Annual Earnings: $68,880
* Earnings Growth Potential: High (46.2%)
* Growth: 4.8%
* Annual Job Openings: 12,950
* Self-Employed: 45.6%

Considerations for Job Outlook: Limited job growth is expected as retailers increase the responsibilities of existing sales worker supervisors and as the retail industry grows slowly overall. Competition is expected. Job-seekers with college degrees and retail experience should have the best prospects.

Directly supervise and coordinate activities of sales workers other than retail sales workers. May

perform duties such as budgeting, accounting, and personnel work in addition to supervisory duties. Listen to and resolve customer complaints regarding services, products, or personnel. Monitor sales staff performance to ensure that goals are met. Hire, train, and evaluate personnel. Confer with company officials to develop methods and procedures to increase sales, expand markets, and promote business. Direct and supervise employees engaged in sales, inventory-taking, reconciling cash receipts, or performing specific services such as pumping gasoline for customers. Provide staff members with assistance in performing difficult or complicated duties. Plan and prepare work schedules, and assign employees to specific duties. Attend company meetings to exchange product information and coordinate work activities with other departments. Prepare sales and inventory reports for management and budget departments. Formulate pricing policies on merchandise according to profitability requirements. Examine merchandise to ensure correct pricing and display, and ensure that it functions as advertised. Analyze details of sales territories to assess their growth potential and to set quotas. Visit retailers and sales representatives to promote products and gather information. Keep records pertaining to purchases, sales, and requisitions. Coordinate sales promotion activities, and prepare merchandise displays and advertising copy. Prepare rental or lease agreements, specifying charges and payment procedures for use of machinery, tools, or other items.

Education/Training Required: Work experience in a related occupation. **Education and Training Programs:** Business, Management, Marketing, and Related Support Services, Other; General Merchandising, Sales, and Related Marketing Operations, Other; Special Products Marketing Operations; Specialized Merchandising, Sales, and Marketing Operations, Other. **Knowledge/Courses:** Sales and Marketing; Economics and Accounting; Personnel and Human Resources; Administration and Management; Mathematics; Clerical Practices.

Career Cluster: 14 Marketing, Sales, and Service. **Career Pathway:** 14.2 Professional Sales and

Marketing.

Skills: Management of Financial Resources; Management of Material Resources; Systems Evaluation; Instructing; Negotiation; Management of Personnel Resources; Persuasion; Monitoring.

Work Environment: Indoors; noise.

First-Line Supervisors of Office and Administrative Support Workers

- ✳ Personality Type: Enterprising-Conventional-Social
- ✳ Annual Earnings: $47,460
- ✳ Earnings Growth Potential: Medium (39.2%)
- ✳ Growth: 11.0%
- ✳ Annual Job Openings: 48,900
- ✳ Self-Employed: 1.4%

Considerations for Job Outlook: Employment growth is expected to be tempered by technological advances that increase the productivity of—and thus decrease the need for—these workers and the workers they supervise. Keen competition is expected.

Supervise and coordinate the activities of clerical and administrative support workers. Resolve customer complaints, and answer customers' questions regarding policies and procedures. Supervise the work of office, administrative, or customer service employees to ensure adherence to quality standards, deadlines, and proper procedures, correcting errors or problems. Provide employees with guidance in handling difficult or complex problems and in resolving escalated complaints or disputes. Implement corporate and departmental policies, procedures, and service standards in conjunction with management. Discuss job performance problems with employees to identify causes and issues and to work on resolving problems. Train and instruct employees in job duties and company policies, or arrange for training to be provided. Evaluate employees' job performance and conformance to regulations, and recommend appropriate personnel action. Recruit, interview, and select employees. Review records and reports pertaining to activities such as production, payroll, and shipping to verify details, monitor work activities, and evaluate performance. Interpret and communicate work procedures and company policies to staff. Prepare and issue work schedules, deadlines, and duty assignments of office or administrative staff. Maintain records pertaining to inventory, personnel, orders, supplies, and machine maintenance. Compute figures such as balances, totals, and commissions.

Education/Training Required: Work experience in a related occupation. **Education and Training Programs:** Agricultural Business Technology; Customer Service Management; Medical Staff Services Technology/Technician; Medical/Health Management and Clinical Assistant/Specialist Training; Office Management and Supervision. **Knowledge/Courses:** Clerical Practices; Economics and Accounting; Administration and Management; Personnel and Human Resources; Customer and Personal Service; Education and Training.

Career Clusters: 01 Agriculture, Food, and Natural Resources; 04 Business, Management, and Administration; 08 Health Science. **Career Pathways:** 01.1 Food Products and Processing Systems; 04.1 Management; 08.3 Health Informatics.

Skills: Management of Financial Resources; Management of Material Resources; Negotiation; Monitoring; Management of Personnel Resources; Learning Strategies; Persuasion; Time Management.

Work Environment: Indoors; sitting; noise.

First-Line Supervisors of Personal Service Workers

* Personality Type: Enterprising-Conventional-Social
* Annual Earnings: $35,290
* Earnings Growth Potential: Medium (37.9%)
* Growth: 15.4%
* Annual Job Openings: 9,080
* Self-Employed: 37.8%

Considerations for Job Outlook: Faster than average employment growth is projected.

Supervise and coordinate activities of personal service workers such as flight attendants, hairdressers, or caddies. Requisition necessary supplies, equipment, and services. Inform workers about interests and special needs of specific groups. Participate in continuing education to stay abreast of industry trends and developments. Meet with managers and other supervisors to stay informed of changes affecting operations. Collaborate with staff members to plan and develop programs of events, schedules of activities, or menus. Train workers in proper operational procedures and functions, and explain company policies. Furnish customers with information on events and activities. Resolve customer complaints regarding worker performance and services rendered. Analyze and record personnel and operational data, and write related activity reports. Observe and evaluate workers' appearance and performance to ensure quality service and compliance with specifications. Inspect work areas and operating equipment to ensure conformance to established standards in areas such as cleanliness and maintenance. Direct and coordinate the activities of workers such as flight attendants, hotel staff, or hair stylists. Assign work schedules, following work requirements, to ensure quality and timely delivery of service. Apply customer/guest feedback to service improvement efforts. Direct marketing, advertising, and other customer recruitment efforts. Take disciplinary action to address performance problems. Recruit and hire staff members.

Education/Training Required: Work experience in a related occupation. **Education and Training Program:** Business, Management, Marketing, and Related Support Services, Other. **Knowledge/Courses:** Psychology; Therapy and Counseling; Education and Training; Philosophy and Theology; Public Safety and Security; Medicine and Dentistry.

Career Cluster: 04 Business, Management, and Administration. **Career Pathway:** 04.1 Management.

Skills: Management of Personnel Resources; Time

Management; Management of Financial Resources; Operation Monitoring; Negotiation; Management of Material Resources; Service Orientation; Systems Evaluation.

Work Environment: Indoors; standing; walking and running; using hands; noise; contaminants.

Job Specialization: Spa Managers

Plan, direct, or coordinate activities of a spa facility. Coordinate programs, schedule and direct staff, and oversee financial activities. Inform staff of job responsibilities, performance expectations, client service standards, or corporate policies and guidelines. Plan or direct spa services and programs. Train staff in the use or sale of products, programs, or activities. Assess employee performance, and suggest ways to improve work. Check spa equipment to ensure proper functioning. Coordinate facility schedules to maximize usage and efficiency. Develop staff service or retail goals, and guide staff in goal achievement. Establish spa budgets and financial goals. Inventory products, and order new supplies. Monitor operations to ensure compliance with applicable health, safety, or hygiene standards. Perform accounting duties, such as recording daily cash flow, preparing bank deposits, or generating financial statements. Recruit, interview, or hire employees. Respond to customer inquiries or complaints. Schedule staff, or supervise scheduling. Verify staff credentials, such as educational and certification requirements. Develop or implement marketing strategies. Direct facility maintenance or repair. Maintain client databases. Participate in continuing education classes to maintain current knowledge of industry. Schedule guest appointments. Sell products, services, or memberships.

Education/Training Required: Work experience in a related occupation. **Education and Training Program:** Resort Management. **Knowledge/ Courses:** No data available.

Personality Type: Enterprising-Conventional-Social. **Career Cluster:** 04 Business, Management, and Administration. **Career Pathway:** 04.1 Management.

Skills: No data available.

Work Environment: No data available.

First-Line Supervisors of Police and Detectives

- ❋ Personality Type: Enterprising-Social-Conventional
- ❋ Annual Earnings: $78,260
- ❋ Earnings Growth Potential: Medium (40.4%)
- ❋ Growth: 8.1%
- ❋ Annual Job Openings: 5,050
- ❋ Self-Employed: 0.0%

Considerations for Job Outlook: Population growth is the main source of demand for police services. Overall, opportunities in local police departments should be favorable for qualified applicants.

Supervise and coordinate activities of members of police force. Supervise and coordinate the investigation of criminal cases, offering guidance and expertise to investigators, and ensuring that procedures are conducted in accordance with laws and regulations. Maintain logs, prepare reports, and direct the preparation, handling, and maintenance of departmental records. Explain police operations to subordinates to assist them in performing their job duties. Cooperate with court personnel and officials from other law enforcement agencies, and testify in court as necessary. Review contents of written orders to ensure adherence to legal requirements. Investigate and resolve personnel problems within organization and charges of misconduct against staff. Direct collection, preparation, and handling of evidence and personal property of prisoners. Inform personnel of changes in regulations and policies, implications of new or amended laws, and new techniques of police work. Train staff in proper police work procedures. Monitor and evaluate the job performance of subordinates, and authorize promotions and transfers. Prepare work schedules, and assign duties to subordinates. Conduct raids, and order detention of witnesses and suspects for questioning. Discipline staff members for violation of departmental rules and regulations. Develop, implement, and revise departmental policies and procedures. Inspect facilities, supplies, vehicles, and equipment to ensure conformance to standards. Requisition and issue equipment and supplies.

Education/Training Required: Work experience in a related occupation. **Education and Training Programs:** Corrections; Criminal Justice/Law Enforcement Administration; Criminal Justice/Safety Studies. **Knowledge/Courses:** Public Safety and Security; Law and Government; Psychology; Sociology and Anthropology; Therapy and Counseling; Personnel and Human Resources.

Career Cluster: 12 Law, Public Safety, Corrections, and Security. **Career Pathways:** 12.1 Correction Services; 12.4 Law Enforcement Services.

Skills: Management of Financial Resources; Management of Personnel Resources; Persuasion; Management of Material Resources; Monitoring; Learning Strategies; Time Management; Instructing.

Work Environment: More often indoors than outdoors; sitting; noise; very hot or cold; bright or inadequate lighting; contaminants; hazardous equipment.

General and Operations Managers

- ❋ Personality Type: Enterprising-Conventional-Social
- ❋ Annual Earnings: $94,400
- ❋ Earnings Growth Potential: High (49.9%)
- ❋ Growth: –0.1%
- ❋ Annual Job Openings: 50,220
- ❋ Self-Employed: 0.9%

Considerations for Job Outlook: The number of top executives is expected to remain steady, but employment may be adversely affected by consolidation and mergers. Keen competition is expected.

Plan, direct, or coordinate the operations of companies or public- and private-sector organizations. Duties and responsibilities include formulating policies, managing daily operations, and planning the use of materials and human resources, but are too diverse and general in nature to be classified in any one functional area of management or administration, such as personnel, purchasing, or administrative services. Includes owners and managers who head small business establishments whose duties are primarily managerial. Oversee activities directly related to making products or providing services. Direct and coordinate activities of businesses or departments concerned with the production, pricing, sales, or distribution of products. Review financial statements, sales and activity reports, and other performance data to measure productivity and goal achievement and to determine areas needing cost reduction and program improvement. Manage staff, preparing work schedules and assigning specific duties. Direct and coordinate organization's financial and budget activities to fund operations, maximize investments, and increase efficiency. Establish and implement departmental policies, goals, objectives, and procedures, conferring with board members, organization officials, and staff members as necessary. Determine staffing requirements, and interview, hire, and train new employees, or oversee those personnel processes. Plan and direct activities such as sales promotions, coordinating with other department heads as required. Determine goods and services to be sold, and set prices and credit terms based on forecasts of customer demand. Monitor businesses and agencies to ensure that they efficiently and effectively provide needed services while staying within budgetary limits. Locate, select, and procure merchandise for resale, representing management in purchase negotiations. Perform sales floor work such as greeting and assisting customers, stocking shelves, and taking inventory.

Education/Training Required: Work experience plus degree. **Education and Training Programs:** Business Administration and Management, General; Entrepreneurship/Entrepreneurial Studies; International Business/Trade/Commerce; Public

Administration. **Knowledge/Courses:** Economics and Accounting; Personnel and Human Resources; Administration and Management; Sales and Marketing; Building and Construction; Clerical Practices.

Career Clusters: 04 Business, Management, and Administration; 07 Government and Public Administration. **Career Pathways:** 04.1 Management; 07.1 Governance.

Skills: Management of Material Resources; Management of Financial Resources; Operations Analysis; Management of Personnel Resources; Negotiation; Systems Analysis; Coordination; Systems Evaluation.

Work Environment: Indoors; more often sitting than standing; noise.

Human Resources Managers

* Personality Type: Enterprising-Social-Conventional
* Annual Earnings: $99,180
* Earnings Growth Potential: Medium (37.9%)
* Growth: 9.6%
* Annual Job Openings: 4,140
* Self-Employed: 0.6%

Considerations for Job Outlook: Efforts to recruit and retain employees, the growing importance of employee training, and new legal standards are expected to increase employment of these workers. College graduates and those with certification should have the best opportunities.

Plan, direct, and coordinate human resource management activities of an organization to maximize the strategic use of human resources and maintain functions such as employee compensation, recruitment, personnel policies, and regulatory compliance. Administer compensation, benefits and performance management systems, and safety and recreation programs. Identify staff vacancies, and recruit, interview, and select applicants. Allocate human resources, ensuring appropriate matches between personnel. Provide current and prospective employees with information about policies, job duties, working conditions, wages, opportunities for promotion, and employee benefits. Perform difficult staffing duties, including dealing with understaffing, refereeing disputes, firing employees, and administering disciplinary procedures. Advise managers on organizational policy matters such as equal employment opportunity and sexual harassment, and recommend needed changes. Analyze and modify compensation and benefits policies to establish competitive programs and ensure compliance with legal requirements. Plan and conduct new employee orientation to foster positive attitude toward organizational objectives. Serve as a link between management and employees by handling questions, interpreting and administering contracts, and helping resolve work-related problems. Plan, direct, supervise, and coordinate work activities of subordinates and staff relating to employment, compensation, labor relations, and employee relations. Analyze training needs to design employee development, language training, and health and safety programs.

Education/Training Required: Work experience plus degree. **Education and Training Program:** Human Resources Management/Personnel Administration, General. **Knowledge/Courses:** Personnel and Human Resources; Therapy and Counseling; Sociology and Anthropology; Psychology; Clerical Practices; Administration and Management.

Career Cluster: 04 Business, Management, and Administration. **Career Pathway:** 04.3 Human Resources.

Skills: Management of Financial Resources; Management of Personnel Resources; Management of Material Resources; Systems Evaluation; Negotiation; Systems Analysis; Persuasion; Learning Strategies.

Work Environment: Indoors; sitting.

Human Resources Specialists

- ❋ Personality Type: Enterprising-Social-Conventional
- ❋ Annual Earnings: $52,690
- ❋ Earnings Growth Potential: High (44.9%)
- ❋ Growth: 27.9%
- ❋ Annual Job Openings: 11,230
- ❋ Self-Employed: 1.6%

Considerations for Job Outlook: Efforts to recruit and retain employees, the growing importance of employee training, and new legal standards are expected to increase employment of these workers. College graduates and those with certification should have the best opportunities.

Recruit and place workers. Address employee relations issues, such as harassment allegations, work complaints, or other employee concerns. Analyze employment-related data, and prepare required reports. Conduct exit interviews, and ensure that necessary employment-termination paperwork is completed. Conduct reference or background checks on job applicants. Confer with management to develop or implement personnel policies or procedures. Contact job applicants to inform them of the status of their applications. Develop or implement recruiting strategies to meet current or anticipated staffing needs. Hire employees and process hiring-related paperwork. Inform job applicants of details such as duties and responsibilities, compensation, benefits, schedules, working conditions, or promotion opportunities. Interpret and explain human resources policies, procedures, laws, standards, or regulations. Interview job applicants to obtain information on work history, training, education, or job skills. Maintain and update human resources documents, such as organizational charts, employee handbooks or directories, or performance evaluation forms. Maintain current knowledge of Equal Employment Opportunity (EEO) and affirmative action guidelines and laws, such as the Americans with Disabilities Act (ADA). Perform searches for qualified job candidates, using sources such as computer databases, networking, Internet recruiting resources, media advertisements, job fairs, recruiting firms, or employee referrals.

Education/Training Required: Bachelor's degree. **Education and Training Programs:** Human Resources Management/Personnel Administration, General; Labor and Industrial Relations. **Knowledge/Courses:** Personnel and Human Resources; Sales and Marketing; Clerical Practices; Law and Government; Customer and Personal Service; Communications and Media.

Career Cluster: 04 Business, Management, and Administration. **Career Pathway:** 04.3 Human Resources.

Skills: Science; Service Orientation; Social Perceptiveness; Speaking; Operations Analysis; Management of Personnel Resources; Writing; Active Listening.

Work Environment: Indoors; sitting; repetitive motions.

Insurance Sales Agents

- ❋ Personality Type: Enterprising-Conventional-Social
- ❋ Annual Earnings: $46,770
- ❋ Earnings Growth Potential: High (44.5%)
- ❋ Growth: 11.9%
- ❋ Annual Job Openings: 15,260
- ❋ Self-Employed: 22.4%

Considerations for Job Outlook: Projected employment increases stem from the growth and aging of the population. But these increases will be tempered by insurance carriers attempting to contain costs by relying on independent agents rather than employees. Job opportunities should be best for college graduates with good interpersonal skills.

Sell life, property, casualty, health, automotive, or other types of insurance. May refer clients to independent brokers, work as independent broker, or be employed by an insurance company. Call on policyholders to deliver and explain policy, to analyze insurance program and suggest additions or changes, or to change beneficiaries. Calculate premiums, and establish payment method. Customize insurance programs to suit individual customers, often covering a variety of risks. Sell various types of insurance policies to businesses and individuals on behalf of insurance companies, including automobile, fire, life, property, medical, and dental insurance or specialized policies such as marine, farm/crop, and medical malpractice. Interview prospective clients to obtain data about their financial resources and needs and the physical condition of the person or property to be insured and to discuss any existing coverage. Seek out new clients and develop clientele by networking to find new customers and generate lists of prospective clients. Explain features, advantages, and disadvantages of various policies to promote sale of insurance plans. Contact underwriter, and submit forms to obtain binder coverage. Ensure that policy requirements are fulfilled, including any necessary medical examinations and the completion of appropriate forms. Confer with clients to obtain and provide information when claims are made on a policy. Perform administrative tasks, such as maintaining records and handling policy renewals. Select company that offers type of coverage requested by client to underwrite policy.

Education/Training Required: Bachelor's degree. **Education and Training Program:** Insurance. **Knowledge/Courses:** Sales and Marketing; Economics and Accounting; Customer and Personal Service; Clerical Practices; Law and Government; Computers and Electronics.

Career Cluster: 06 Finance. **Career Pathway:** 06.4 Insurance Services.

Skills: Negotiation; Persuasion; Service Orientation; Active Listening; Speaking; Systems Analysis; Active Learning; Systems Evaluation.

Work Environment: Indoors; sitting.

Lawyers

- ❋ Personality Type: Enterprising-Investigative
- ❋ Annual Earnings: $112,760
- ❋ Earnings Growth Potential: Very high (52.0%)
- ❋ Growth: 13.0%
- ❋ Annual Job Openings: 24,040
- ❋ Self-Employed: 26.2%

Considerations for Job Outlook: Growth in both population and business activity is expected to result in more civil disputes and criminal cases and, thus, employment growth for lawyers. This growth is expected to be constrained, however, as paralegals and other workers perform some of the tasks previously done by lawyers. Keen competition is expected.

Represent clients in criminal and civil litigation and other legal proceedings, draw up legal documents, and manage or advise clients on legal transactions. May specialize in a single area or may practice broadly in many areas of law. Advise clients concerning business transactions, claim liability, advisability of prosecuting or defending lawsuits, or legal rights and obligations. Interpret laws, rulings, and regulations for individuals and businesses. Analyze the probable outcomes of cases, using knowledge of legal precedents. Present and summarize cases to judges and juries. Gather evidence to formulate defense or to initiate legal actions by such means as interviewing clients and witnesses to ascertain the facts of a case. Evaluate findings and develop strategies and arguments in preparation for presentation of cases. Represent clients in court or before government agencies. Examine legal data to determine advisability of defending or prosecuting lawsuit. Select jurors, argue motions, meet with judges, and question witnesses during the course of a trial. Present evidence to defend clients or prosecute defendants in criminal or civil litigation. Study Constitution, statutes, decisions, regulations, and ordinances of quasi-judicial bodies to determine ramifications for cases. Prepare and draft legal doc-

Enterprising-L

uments, such as wills, deeds, patent applications, mortgages, leases, and contracts. Prepare legal briefs and opinions, and file appeals in state and federal courts of appeal. Negotiate settlements of civil disputes. Confer with colleagues with specialties in appropriate areas of legal issue to establish and verify bases for legal proceedings.

Education/Training Required: First professional degree. **Education and Training Programs:** Advanced Legal Research/Studies, General (LL.M., M.C.L., M.L.I., M.S.L., J.S.D./S.J.D.); American/ U.S. Law/Legal Studies/Jurisprudence (LL.M., M.C.J., J.S.D./S.J.D.); Banking, Corporate, Finance, and Securities Law (LL.M., J.S.D./S.J.D.); Canadian Law/Legal Studies/Jurisprudence (LL.M., M.C.J., J.S.D./S.J.D.); Comparative Law (LL.M., M.C.L., J.S.D./S.J.D.); Energy, Environment, and Natural Resources Law (LL.M., M.S., J.S.D./S.J.D.); Health Law (LL.M., M.J., J.S.D./S.J.D.); International Business, Trade, and Tax Law (LL.M., J.S.D./ S.J.D.); International Law and Legal Studies (LL.M., J.S.D./S.J.D.); Law (LL.B, J.D.); Legal Professions and Studies, Other; Legal Research and Advanced Professional Studies, Other; Legal Studies, General; Pre-Law Studies; Programs for Foreign Lawyers (LL.M., M.C.L.); Tax Law/Taxation (LL.M., J.S.D./S.J.D.). **Knowledge/Courses:** Law and Government; English Language; Personnel and Human Resources; Customer and Personal Service; Economics and Accounting; Administration and Management.

Career Cluster: 12 Law, Public Safety, Corrections, and Security. **Career Pathway:** 12.5 Legal Services.

Skills: Persuasion; Negotiation; Speaking; Writing; Critical Thinking; Judgment and Decision Making; Active Learning; Active Listening.

Work Environment: Indoors; sitting.

Managers, All Other

- ❀ Personality Type: Enterprising-Conventional
- ❀ Annual Earnings: $96,450

- ❀ Earnings Growth Potential: High (48.2%)
- ❀ Growth: 7.3%
- ❀ Annual Job Openings: 29,750
- ❀ Self-Employed: 57.1%

Considerations for Job Outlook: About average employment growth is projected.

This occupation includes all managers not listed separately. Because this is a highly diverse occupation, no data is available for some information topics.

Education/Training Required: Work experience in a related occupation. **Education and Training Program:** Business/Commerce, General.

Career Clusters: 03 Arts, Audio/Video Technology, and Communications; 04 Business, Management, and Administration; 07 Government and Public Administration; 09 Hospitality and Tourism; 10 Human Services; 16 Transportation, Distribution, and Logistics. **Career Pathways:** 03.1 Audio and Video Technology and Film; 03.4 Performing Arts; 04.1 Management; 04.2 Business, Financial Management, and Accounting; 07.1 Governance; 07.7 Public Management and Administration; 09.3 Travel and Tourism; 10.3 Family and Community Services; 16.2 Logistics, Planning, and Management Services.

Job Specialization: Brownfield Redevelopment Specialists and Site Managers

Participate in planning and directing cleanup and redevelopment of contaminated properties for reuse. Does not include properties sufficiently contaminated to qualify as Superfund sites. Review or evaluate environmental-remediation project proposals. Review or evaluate designs for contaminant treatment or disposal facilities. Provide training on hazardous-material or waste-cleanup procedures and technologies. Provide expert witness testimony on issues such as soil, air, or water contamination and associated cleanup measures. Prepare reports or presentations to communicate brownfield redevelopment needs, status, or progress. Negotiate contracts for services or materials needed for environmental remediation. Prepare and submit permit applications for demolition, cleanup, remediation, or construction projects. Maintain records of decisions, actions, and progress related to environmental-redevelopment projects. Inspect sites to assess environmental damage or monitor cleanup progress. Plan or implement brownfield redevelopment projects to ensure safety, quality, and compliance with applicable standards or requirements. Identify environmental-contamination sources. Estimate costs for environmental cleanup and remediation of land-redevelopment projects. Develop or implement plans for revegetation of brownfield sites. Design or implement plans for surface- or ground-water remediation. Design or implement plans for structural demolition and debris removal. Design or implement measures to improve the water, air, and soil quality of military test sites, abandoned mine land, or other contaminated sites. Design or conduct environmental-restoration studies.

Education/Training Required: Bachelor's degree. **Education and Training Program:** Hazardous Materials Management and Waste Technology/Technician. **Knowledge/Courses:** No data available.

Personality Type: No data available. **Career Cluster:** 04 Business, Management, and Administration. **Career Pathways:** 04.1 Management; 04.2 Business, Financial Management, and Accounting.

Skills: No data available.

Work Environment: No data available.

Job Specialization: Compliance Managers

Plan, direct, or coordinate activities of an organization to ensure compliance with ethical or regulatory standards. Verify that software technology is in place to adequately provide oversight and monitoring in all required areas. Serve as a confidential point of contact for employees to communicate with management, seek clarification on issues or dilemmas,

or report irregularities. Maintain documentation of compliance activities such as complaints received and investigation outcomes. Consult with corporate attorneys as necessary to address difficult legal-compliance issues. Discuss emerging compliance issues with management or employees. Collaborate with human resources departments to ensure the implementation of consistent disciplinary action strategies in cases of compliance standard violations. Advise internal management or business partners on the implementation and operation of compliance programs. Review communications such as securities sales advertising to ensure there are no violations of standards or regulations. Provide employee training on compliance-related topics, policies, or procedures. Report violations of compliance or regulatory standards to duly authorized enforcement agencies as appropriate or required. Provide assistance to internal and external auditors in compliance reviews. Prepare management reports regarding compliance operations and progress. Oversee internal reporting systems such as corporate compliance hotlines, and inform employees about these systems. Monitor compliance systems to ensure their effectiveness.

Education/Training Required: Work experience plus degree. **Education and Training Program:** Business Administration and Management, General. **Knowledge/Courses:** No data available.

Personality Type: Conventional-Enterprising-Realistic. **Career Clusters:** 04 Business, Management, and Administration; 07 Government and Public Administration. **Career Pathways:** 04.1 Management; 04.2 Business, Financial Management, and Accounting; 07.1 Governance.

Skills: No data available.

Work Environment: No data available.

Job Specialization: Investment Fund Managers

Plan, direct, or coordinate investment strategy or operations for a large pool of liquid assets supplied by institutional investors or individual investors. Prepare for and respond to regulatory inquiries. Verify regulatory compliance of transaction reporting. Hire and evaluate staff. Direct activities of accounting or operations departments. Develop, implement, or monitor security valuation policies. Attend investment briefings or consult financial media to stay abreast of relevant investment markets. Review offering documents or marketing materials to ensure regulatory compliance. Perform or evaluate research, such as detailed company and industry analyses, to inform financial forecasting, decision making, or valuation. Present investment information, such as product risks, fees, and fund performance statistics. Monitor financial or operational performance of individual investments to ensure that portfolios meet risk goals. Monitor regulatory or tax law changes to ensure fund compliance or to capitalize on development opportunities. Meet with investors to determine investment goals or to discuss investment strategies. Identify group and individual target investors for a specific fund. Develop, or direct development of, offering documents or marketing materials. Evaluate the potential of new product developments or market opportunities according to factors such as business plans, technologies, and market potential. Develop and implement fund investment policies and strategies. Select and direct the execution of trades. Analyze acquisitions to ensure conformance with strategic goals or regulatory requirements.

Education/Training Required: Work experience plus degree. **Education and Training Program:** Investments and Securities. **Knowledge/Courses:** No data available.

Personality Type: Enterprising-Conventional. **Career Cluster:** 04 Business, Management, and Administration. **Career Pathways:** 04.1 Management; 04.2 Business, Financial Management, and Accounting.

Skills: No data available.

Work Environment: No data available.

Job Specialization: Loss Prevention Managers

Plan and direct policies, procedures, or systems to prevent the loss of assets. Determine risk exposure or potential liability, and develop risk control measures. Review loss-prevention exception reports and cash discrepancies to ensure adherence to guidelines. Perform cash audits and deposit investigations to fully account for store cash. Provide recommendations and solutions in crisis situations such as workplace violence, protests, and demonstrations. Monitor and review paperwork procedures and systems to prevent error-related shortages. Maintain databases such as bad check logs, reports on multiple offenders, and alarm activation lists. Investigate or interview individuals suspected of shoplifting or internal theft. Direct installation of covert surveillance equipment, such as security cameras. Advise retail establishments on development of loss-investigation procedures. Visit stores to ensure compliance with company policies and procedures. Verify correct use and maintenance of physical security systems, such as closed-circuit television, merchandise tags, and burglar alarms. Train loss-prevention staff, retail managers, or store employees on loss control and prevention measures. Supervise surveillance, detection, or criminal processing related to theft and criminal cases. Recommend improvements in loss-prevention programs, staffing, scheduling, or training. Perform or direct inventory investigations in response to shrink results outside of acceptable ranges. Hire or supervise loss-prevention staff. Maintain documentation of all loss-prevention activity.

Education/Training Required: Bachelor's degree. **Education and Training Program:** Security and Loss Prevention Services. **Knowledge/Courses:** No data available.

Personality Type: Enterprising-Conventional. **Career Cluster:** 04 Business, Management, and Administration. **Career Pathways:** 04.1 Management; 04.2 Business, Financial Management, and Accounting.

Skills: No data available.

Work Environment: No data available.

Job Specialization: Regulatory Affairs Managers

Plan, direct, or coordinate production activities of an organization to ensure compliance with regulations and standard operating procedures. Direct the preparation and submission of regulatory agency applications, reports, or correspondence. Review all regulatory agency submission materials to ensure timeliness, accuracy, comprehensiveness, and compliance with regulatory standards. Provide regulatory guidance to departments or development project teams regarding design, development, evaluation, or marketing of products. Formulate or implement regulatory affairs policies and procedures to ensure that regulatory compliance is maintained or enhanced. Manage activities such as audits, regulatory agency inspections, and product recalls. Communicate regulatory information to multiple departments, and ensure that information is interpreted correctly. Develop regulatory strategies and implementation plans for the preparation and submission of new products. Provide responses to regulatory agencies regarding product information or issues. Maintain current knowledge of relevant regulations including proposed and final rules. Investigate product complaints, and prepare documentation and submissions to appropriate regulatory agencies as necessary. Review materials such as marketing literature and user manuals to ensure that regulatory agency requirements are met. Implement or monitor complaint processing systems to ensure effective and timely resolution of all complaint investigations. Represent organizations before domestic or international regulatory agencies on major policy matters or decisions regarding company products.

Education/Training Required: Work experience plus degree. **Education and Training Program:** Business Administration and Management, General. **Knowledge/Courses:** Biology; Medicine and Dentistry; Law and Government; Chemistry; Clerical Practices; Personnel and Human Resources.

Personality Type: Enterprising - Conventional. **Career Clusters:** 04 Business, Management, and Administration; 07 Government and Public Ad-

ministration. **Career Pathways:** 04.1 Management; 04.2 Business, Financial Management, and Accounting; 07.1 Governance; 07.6 Regulation.

Skills: Operations Analysis; Management of Personnel Resources; Systems Evaluation; Systems Analysis; Negotiation; Coordination; Science; Writing.

Work Environment: Indoors; sitting.

Job Specialization: Security Managers

Direct an organization's security functions, including physical security and safety of employees, facilities, and assets. Write or review security-related documents, such as incident reports, proposals, and tactical or strategic initiatives. Train subordinate security professionals or other organization members in security rules and procedures. Plan security for special and high-risk events. Review financial reports to ensure efficiency and quality of security operations. Develop budgets for security operations. Order security-related supplies and equipment as needed. Coordinate security operations or activities with public law enforcement, fire, and other agencies. Attend meetings, professional seminars, or conferences to keep abreast of changes in executive legislative directives or new technologies impacting security operations. Assist in emergency management and contingency planning. Arrange for or perform executive protection activities. Respond to medical emergencies, bomb threats, fire alarms, or intrusion alarms, following emergency response procedures. Recommend security procedures for security call centers, operations centers, domains, asset classification systems, system acquisition, system development, system maintenance, access control, program models, or reporting tools. Prepare reports or make presentations on internal investigations, losses, or violations of regulations, policies, and procedures. Identify, investigate, or resolve security breaches.

Education/Training Required: Work experience plus degree. **Education and Training Program:** Security and Loss Prevention Services. **Knowledge/**

Enterprising-M

Courses: No data available.

Personality Type: No data available. **Career Cluster:** 04 Business, Management, and Administration. **Career Pathways:** 04.1 Management; 04.2 Business, Financial Management, and Accounting.

Skills: No data available.

Work Environment: No data available.

Job Specialization: Supply Chain Managers

Direct, or coordinate production, purchasing, warehousing, distribution, or financial forecasting services and activities to limit costs and improve accuracy, customer service, and safety. Examine existing procedures and opportunities for streamlining activities to meet product distribution needs. Direct the movement, storage, and processing of inventory. Select transportation routes to maximize economy by combining shipments and consolidating warehousing and distribution. Diagram supply chain models to help facilitate discussions with customers. Develop material costs forecasts or standard cost lists. Assess appropriate material handling equipment needs and staffing levels to load, unload, move, or store materials. Appraise vendor manufacturing ability through on-site visits and measurements. Negotiate prices and terms with suppliers, vendors, or freight forwarders. Monitor supplier performance to assess ability to meet quality and delivery requirements. Monitor forecasts and quotas to identify changes or to determine their effect on supply chain activities. Meet with suppliers to discuss performance metrics, to provide performance feedback, or to discuss production forecasts or changes. Implement new or improved supply chain processes. Collaborate with other departments, such as procurement, engineering, and quality assurance, to identify or qualify new suppliers. Document physical supply chain processes, such as workflows, cycle times, position responsibilities, and system flows. Develop and implement procedures or systems to evaluate and select suppliers. Design and implement plant warehousing strategies for production materi-

als or finished products. Confer with supply chain planners to forecast demand or create supply plans that ensure availability of materials and products.

Education/Training Required: Work experience plus degree. **Education and Training Program:** Logistics, Materials, and Supply Chain Management. **Knowledge/Courses:** Production and Processing; Transportation; Economics and Accounting; Administration and Management; Geography; Sales and Marketing.

Personality Type: Enterprising-Conventional. **Career Clusters:** 04 Business, Management, and Administration; 09 Hospitality and Tourism; 10 Human Services; 16 Transportation, Distribution, and Logistics. **Career Pathways:** 04.1 Management; 04.2 Business, Financial Management, and Accounting; 09.3 Travel and Tourism; 10.3 Family and Community Services; 16.2 Logistics, Planning, and Management Services.

Skills: Management of Material Resources; Management of Financial Resources; Systems Evaluation; Negotiation; Monitoring; Management of Personnel Resources; Systems Analysis; Complex Problem Solving.

Work Environment: Indoors; sitting.

Job Specialization: Wind Energy Operations Managers

Manage wind field operations, including personnel, maintenance activities, financial activities, and planning. Train, or coordinate the training of, employees in operations, safety, environmental issues, or technical issues. Track and maintain records for wind operations, such as site performance, downtime events, parts usage, and substation events. Provide technical support to wind field customers, employees, or subcontractors. Manage warranty repair or replacement services. Order parts, tools, or equipment needed to maintain, restore, or improve wind field operations. Maintain operations records, such as work orders, site inspection forms, or other documentation. Negotiate or review and approve wind farm contracts. Recruit or select wind operations employees, contractors, or subcontractors. Monitor and maintain records of daily facility operations. Estimate costs associated with operations, including repairs and preventive maintenance. Establish goals, objectives, or priorities for wind field operations. Develop relationships and communicate with customers, site managers, developers, land owners, authorities, utility representatives, or residents. Develop processes and procedures for wind operations, including transitioning from construction to commercial operations. Prepare wind field operational budgets. Supervise employees or subcontractors to ensure quality of work or adherence to safety regulations or policies. Oversee the maintenance of wind field equipment or structures, such as towers, transformers, electrical collector systems, roadways, and other site assets.

Education/Training Required: Work experience plus degree. **Education and Training Program:** Energy Management and Systems Technology/Technician. **Knowledge/Courses:** No data available.

Personality Type: No data available. **Career Cluster:** 04 Business, Management, and Administration. **Career Pathways:** 04.1 Management; 04.2 Business, Financial Management, and Accounting.

Skills: No data available.

Work Environment: No data available.

Job Specialization: Wind Energy Project Managers

Lead or manage the development and evaluation of potential wind energy business opportunities, including environmental studies, permitting, and proposals. May also manage construction of projects. Supervise the work of subcontractors or consultants to ensure quality and conformance to specifications or budgets. Prepare requests for proposals (RFPs) for wind project construction or equipment acquisition. Manage site assessments or environmental studies for wind fields. Lead or support negotiations involving tax agreements or abatements, power

purchase agreements, land use, or interconnection agreements. Update schedules, estimates, forecasts, or budgets for wind projects. Review or evaluate proposals or bids to make recommendations regarding awarding of contracts. Provide verbal or written project status reports to project teams, management, subcontractors, customers, or owners. Review civil design, engineering, or construction technical documentation to ensure compliance with applicable government or industrial codes, standards, requirements, or regulations. Provide technical support for the design, construction, or commissioning of wind farm projects. Prepare wind project documentation, including diagrams or layouts. Manage wind project costs to stay within budget limits. Develop scope of work for wind project functions, such as design, site assessment, environmental studies, surveying, and field support services. Coordinate or direct development, energy assessment, engineering, or construction activities to ensure that wind project needs and objectives are met.

Education/Training Required: Work experience plus degree. **Education and Training Program:** Energy Management and Systems Technology/Technician. **Knowledge/Courses:** No data available.

Personality Type: No data available. **Career Cluster:** 04 Business, Management, and Administration. **Career Pathways:** 04.1 Management; 04.2 Business, Financial Management, and Accounting.

Skills: No data available.

Work Environment: No data available.

Marketing Managers

- ❊ Personality Type: Enterprising-Conventional
- ❊ Annual Earnings: $112,800
- ❊ Earnings Growth Potential: High (48.8%)
- ❊ Growth: 12.5%
- ❊ Annual Job Openings: 5,970
- ❊ Self-Employed: 4.1%

Enterprising-M

Considerations for Job Outlook: Job growth is expected to result from companies' need to distinguish their products and services in an increasingly competitive marketplace. Keen competition is expected.

Determine the demand for products and services offered by firms and their competitors, and identify potential customers. Develop pricing strategies with the goal of maximizing firms' profits or shares of the market while ensuring that firms' customers are satisfied. Oversee product development or monitor trends that indicate the need for new products and services. Formulate, direct, and coordinate marketing activities and policies to promote products and services, working with advertising and promotion managers. Identify, develop, and evaluate marketing strategies, based on knowledge of establishment objectives, market characteristics, and cost and markup factors. Direct the hiring, training, and performance evaluations of marketing and sales staff, and oversee their daily activities. Evaluate the financial aspects of product development, such as budgets, expenditures, research and development appropriations, and return-on-investment and profit-loss projections. Develop pricing strategies, balancing firm objectives and customer satisfaction. Compile lists describing product or service offerings. Initiate market research studies, and analyze their findings. Use sales forecasting and strategic planning to ensure the sale and profitability of products, lines, or services, analyzing business developments and monitoring market trends. Coordinate and participate in promotional activities and trade shows, working with developers, advertisers, and production managers to market products and services. Consult with buying personnel to gain advice regarding the types of products or services expected to be in demand. Conduct economic and commercial surveys to identify potential markets for products and services. Select products and accessories to be displayed at trade or special production shows.

Education/Training Required: Work experience plus degree. **Education and Training Programs:** Apparel and Textile Marketing Management; Consumer Merchandising/Retailing Management;

International Marketing; Marketing Research; Marketing, Other; Marketing/Marketing Management, General. **Knowledge/Courses:** Sales and Marketing; Customer and Personal Service; Personnel and Human Resources; Communications and Media; Economics and Accounting; Sociology and Anthropology.

Career Cluster: 14 Marketing, Sales, and Service. **Career Pathways:** 14.1 Management and Entrepreneurship; 14.2 Professional Sales and Marketing; 14.5 Marketing Information Management and Research.

Skills: Management of Financial Resources; Operations Analysis; Persuasion; Management of Material Resources; Negotiation; Management of Personnel Resources; Systems Evaluation; Systems Analysis.

Work Environment: Indoors; sitting.

Medical and Health Services Managers

- ✸ Personality Type: Enterprising-Conventional-Social
- ✸ Annual Earnings: $84,270
- ✸ Earnings Growth Potential: Medium (39.1%)
- ✸ Growth: 16.0%
- ✸ Annual Job Openings: 9,940
- ✸ Self-Employed: 6.0%

Considerations for Job Outlook: The health-care industry is expected to continue growing and diversifying, requiring managers increasingly to run business operations. Opportunities should be good, especially for jobseekers who have work experience in health care and strong business-management skills.

Plan, direct, or coordinate medicine and health services in hospitals, clinics, managed care organizations, public health agencies, or similar organizations. Conduct and administer fiscal operations, including accounting, planning budgets, authorizing expenditures, establishing rates for services, and coordinating financial reporting. Direct, supervise, and evaluate work activities of medical, nursing, technical, clerical, service, maintenance, and other personnel. Maintain communication between governing boards, medical staff, and department heads by attending board meetings and coordinating interdepartmental functioning. Review and analyze facility activities and data to aid planning as well as cash and risk management, and to improve service utilization. Plan, implement, and administer programs and services in a health-care or medical facility, including personnel administration, training, and coordination of medical, nursing, and physical plant staff. Direct or conduct recruitment, hiring, and training of personnel. Establish work schedules and assignments for staff, according to workload, space, and equipment availability. Maintain awareness of advances in medicine, computerized diagnostic and treatment equipment, data processing technology, government regulations, health insurance changes, and financing options. Monitor the use of diagnostic services, inpatient beds, facilities, and staff to ensure effective use of resources and assess the need for additional staff, equipment, and services.

Education/Training Required: Work experience plus degree. **Education and Training Programs:** Community Health and Preventive Medicine; Health and Medical Administrative Services, Other; Health Information/Medical Records Administration/Administrator; Health Services Administration; Health Unit Manager/Ward Supervisor Training; Health/Health Care Administration/Management; Hospital and Health Care Facilities Administration/Management; Public Health, General. **Knowledge/Courses:** Economics and Accounting; Personnel and Human Resources; Administration and Management; Sales and Marketing; Medicine and Dentistry; Law and Government.

Career Cluster: 08 Health Science. **Career Pathways:** 08.1 Therapeutic Services; 08.2 Diagnostics Services; 08.3 Health Informatics.

Skills: Management of Financial Resources; Operations Analysis; Management of Material Resources; Science; Management of Personnel Resources; Systems Evaluation; Coordination; Time Management.

Work Environment: Indoors; sitting; exposed to disease or infections.

Natural Sciences Managers

- ❋ Personality Type: Enterprising-Investigative
- ❋ Annual Earnings: $116,020
- ❋ Earnings Growth Potential: High (42.0%)
- ❋ Growth: 15.5%
- ❋ Annual Job Openings: 2,010
- ❋ Self-Employed: 0.0%

Considerations for Job Outlook: Employment is expected to grow along with that of the scientists and engineers these workers supervise. Prospects should be better in the rapidly growing areas of environmental and biomedical engineering and medical and environmental sciences.

Plan, direct, or coordinate activities in such fields as life sciences, physical sciences, mathematics, and statistics and research and development in these fields. Confer with scientists, engineers, regulators, and others to plan and review projects and to provide technical assistance. Develop client relationships and communicate with clients to explain proposals, present research findings, establish specifications, or discuss project status. Plan and direct research, development, and production activities. Prepare project proposals. Design and coordinate successive phases of problem analysis, solution proposals, and testing. Review project activities, and prepare and review research, testing, and operational reports. Hire, supervise, and evaluate engineers, technicians, researchers, and other staff. Determine scientific and technical goals within broad outlines provided by top management, and make detailed plans to accomplish these goals. Develop and implement policies, standards, and procedures for the architectural, scientific, and technical work performed

Enterprising-N

to ensure regulatory compliance and operations enhancement. Develop innovative technology, and train staff for its implementation. Provide for stewardship of plant and animal resources and habitats, studying land use; monitoring animal populations; and providing shelter, resources, and medical treatment for animals. Conduct own research in field of expertise. Recruit personnel, and oversee the development and maintenance of staff competence. Advise and assist in obtaining patents or meeting other legal requirements.

Education/Training Required: Work experience plus degree. **Education and Training Programs:** Acoustics; Analytical Chemistry; Anatomy; Animal Genetics; Animal Physiology; Astronomy; Astrophysics; Atmospheric Chemistry and Climatology; Atmospheric Physics and Dynamics; Atmospheric Sciences and Meteorology, General; Atomic Physics; Biochemistry; Biological and Physical Sciences; Biology, General; Biometry; Biophysics; Biopsychology; Biostatistics; Biotechnology; Botany; Cell Biology and Histology; Chemistry, General; Ecology; Elementary Particle Physics; Entomology; Evolutionary Biology; Geochemistry; Geochemistry and Petrology; Geology/Earth Science, General; Geophysics and Seismology; Hydrology and Water Resources Science; Inorganic Chemistry; Marine Biology and Biological Oceanography; Meteorology; Microbiology, General; Molecular Biology; Natural Sciences; Nuclear Physics; Nutrition Sciences; Oceanography, Chemical and Physical; Optics; Organic Chemistry; Paleontology; Parasitology; Pathology; Pharmacology; Physical Chemistry; Physical Sciences; Physics, General; Planetary Astronomy and Science; Plant Genetics; Plant Pathology; Plant Physiology; Plasma and High-Temperature Physics; Polymer Chemistry; Radiation Biology; Science, Technology, and Society; Theoretical and Mathematical Physics; Toxicology; Virology; Zoology; others. **Knowledge/Courses:** Biology; Chemistry; Engineering and Technology; Law and Government; Administration and Management; Physics.

Career Clusters: 04 Business, Management, and Administration; 15 Science, Technology, Engineering, and Mathematics. **Career Pathways:** 04.2 Business, Financial Management, and Accounting; 04.4 Business Analysis; 15.2 Science and Mathematics.

Skills: Science; Operations Analysis; Management of Financial Resources; Technology Design; Management of Personnel Resources; Mathematics; Time Management; Reading Comprehension.

Work Environment: Indoors; sitting; noise.

Job Specialization: Clinical Research Coordinators

Plan, direct, or coordinate clinical research projects. Direct the activities of workers engaged in clinical research projects to ensure compliance with protocols and overall clinical objectives. May evaluate and analyze clinical data. Solicit industry-sponsored trials through contacts and professional organizations. Review scientific literature, participate in continuing education activities, or attend conferences and seminars to maintain current knowledge of clinical-studies affairs and issues. Register protocol patients with appropriate statistical centers as required. Prepare for or participate in quality assurance audits conducted by study sponsors, federal agencies, or specially designated review groups. Participate in preparation and management of research budgets and monetary disbursements. Perform specific protocol procedures such as interviewing subjects, taking vital signs, and performing electrocardiograms. Interpret protocols, and advise treating physicians on appropriate dosage modifications or treatment calculations based on patient characteristics. Develop advertising and other informational materials to be used in subject recruitment. Contact industry representatives to ensure equipment and software specifications necessary for successful study completion. Confer with health-care professionals to determine the best recruitment practices for studies. Track enrollment status of subjects, and document dropout information such as dropout causes and subject contact efforts. Review proposed study protocols to evaluate factors such as sample collection processes, data management plans, and potential subject risks.

Education/Training Required: Work experience in a related occupation. **Education and Training Programs:** Biometry/Biometrics; Biostatistics; Biotechnology; Cell/Cellular Biology and Anatomical Sciences, Other; Immunology; Medical Microbiology and Bacteriology; Microbiology, General; Nutrition Sciences; Parasitology; Pathology/Experimental Pathology; Pharmacology; Statistics, General; Toxicology; Virology. **Knowledge/Courses:** Medicine and Dentistry; Biology; Administration and Management; Clerical Practices; English Language; Law and Government.

Personality Type: Enterprising-Investigative-Conventional. **Career Cluster:** 15 Science, Technology, Engineering, and Mathematics. **Career Pathway:** 15.2 Science and Mathematics.

Skills: Management of Material Resources; Science; Management of Financial Resources; Management of Personnel Resources; Coordination; Active Learning; Systems Evaluation; Negotiation.

Work Environment: Indoors; sitting.

Job Specialization: Water Resource Specialists

Design or implement programs and strategies related to water resource issues, such as supply, quality, and regulatory compliance issues. Supervise teams of workers who capture water from wells and rivers. Review or evaluate designs for water detention facilities, storm drains, flood control facilities, or other hydraulic structures. Negotiate for water rights with communities or water facilities to meet water supply demands. Perform hydrologic, hydraulic, or water quality modeling. Compile water resource data, using geographic information systems (GIS) or global position systems (GPS) software. Compile and maintain documentation on the health of a body of water. Write proposals, project reports, informational brochures, or other documents on wastewater purification, water supply and demand, or other water resource subjects. Recommend new or revised policies, procedures, or regulations to support water resource or conservation goals. Provide technical expertise to assist communities in the development or implementation of storm water monitoring or other water programs. Present water resource proposals to government, public interest groups, or community groups. Identify methods for distributing purified wastewater into rivers, streams, or oceans. Monitor water use, demand, or quality in a particular geographic area. Identify and characterize specific causes or sources of water pollution. Develop plans to protect watershed health or rehabilitate watersheds. Develop or implement standardized water monitoring and assessment methods.

Education/Training Required: Work experience plus degree. **Education and Training Programs:** Geochemistry; Geological and Earth Sciences/Geosciences, Other; Geology/Earth Science, General; Hydrology and Water Resources Science; Oceanography, Chemical and Physical. **Knowledge/Courses:** No data available.

Personality Type: No data available. **Career Cluster:** 15 Science, Technology, Engineering, and Mathematics. **Career Pathway:** 15.2 Science and Mathematics.

Skills: No data available.

Work Environment: No data available.

Personal Financial Advisors

- ⊛ Personality Type: Enterprising-Conventional-Social
- ⊛ Annual Earnings: $64,750
- ⊛ Earnings Growth Potential: High (49.6%)
- ⊛ Growth: 30.1%
- ⊛ Annual Job Openings: 8,530
- ⊛ Self-Employed: 29.3%

Considerations for Job Outlook: Employment growth for these workers is projected as large numbers of baby boomers retire and need advice on managing their retirement accounts. In addition, widespread transition from traditional pension plans to individually managed retirement savings programs should also create jobs. Keen competition is expected in this relatively high-paying occupation.

Advise clients on financial plans, using knowledge of tax and investment strategies, securities, insurance, pension plans, and real estate. Duties include assessing clients' assets, liabilities, cash flows, insurance coverages, tax statuses, and financial objectives to establish investment strategies. Prepare and interpret for clients information such as investment performance reports, financial document summaries, and income projections. Recommend strategies clients can use to achieve their financial goals and objectives, including specific recommendations in such areas as cash management, insurance coverage, and investment planning. Build and maintain client bases, keeping current client plans up-to-date and recruiting new clients on an ongoing basis. Devise debt liquidation plans that include payoff priorities and timelines. Implement financial-planning recommendations, or refer clients to someone who can assist them with plan implementation. Interview clients to determine their current incomes, expenses, insurance coverages, tax statuses, financial objectives, risk tolerances, and other information needed to develop financial plans. Monitor financial market trends to ensure that plans are effective, and to identify any necessary updates. Explain and document for clients the types of services that are to be provided, and the responsibilities to be taken by personal financial advisors. Explain to individuals and groups the details of financial assistance available to college and university students, such as loans, grants, and scholarships. Guide clients in the gathering of information such as bank account records, income tax returns, life and disability insurance records, pension plan information, and wills.

Education/Training Required: Bachelor's degree. **Education and Training Programs:** Finance, General; Financial Planning and Services. **Knowledge/Courses:** Economics and Accounting; Sales

and Marketing; Law and Government; Customer and Personal Service; Mathematics; Computers and Electronics.

Career Cluster: 06 Finance. **Career Pathway:** 06.1 Financial and Investment Planning.

Skills: Operations Analysis; Management of Financial Resources; Mathematics; Persuasion; Service Orientation; Speaking; Writing; Reading Comprehension.

Work Environment: Indoors; sitting.

Police and Sheriff's Patrol Officers

- ✷ Personality Type: Enterprising-Realistic-Social
- ✷ Annual Earnings: $53,540
- ✷ Earnings Growth Potential: Medium (40.8%)
- ✷ Growth: 8.7%
- ✷ Annual Job Openings: 22,790
- ✷ Self-Employed: 0.0%

Considerations for Job Outlook: Population growth is the main source of demand for police services. Overall, opportunities in local police departments should be favorable for qualified applicants.

Job Specialization: Police Patrol Officers

Patrol assigned areas to enforce laws and ordinances, regulate traffic, control crowds, prevent crime, and arrest violators. Provide for public safety by maintaining order, responding to emergencies, protecting people and property, enforcing motor vehicle and criminal laws, and promoting good community relations. Monitor, note, report, and investigate suspicious persons and situations, safety hazards, and unusual or illegal activity in patrol area. Record facts to prepare reports that document incidents and activities. Identify, pursue, and arrest suspects and perpetrators of criminal acts. Patrol specific areas on foot, horseback, or motorized conveyance, responding promptly to calls for assistance. Review facts of incidents to determine whether criminal acts or statute violations were involved. Investigate traffic accidents and other accidents to determine causes and to determine whether crimes have been committed. Render aid to accident victims and other persons requiring first aid for physical injuries. Testify in court to present evidence or act as witness in traffic and criminal cases. Photograph or draw diagrams of crime or accident scenes, and interview principals and eyewitnesses. Relay complaint and emergency-request information to appropriate agency dispatchers. Evaluate complaint and emergency-request information to determine response requirements. Process prisoners, and prepare and maintain records of prisoner bookings and prisoner statuses during booking and pre-trial processes. Monitor traffic to ensure motorists observe traffic regulations and exhibit safe driving procedures.

Education/Training Required: Long-term on-the-job training. **Education and Training Programs:** Criminal Justice/Police Science; Criminalistics and Criminal Science. **Knowledge/Courses:** Psychology; Public Safety and Security; Law and Government; Customer and Personal Service; Therapy and Counseling; Sociology and Anthropology.

Personality Type: Realistic-Enterprising-Conventional. **Career Cluster:** 12 Law, Public Safety, Corrections, and Security. **Career Pathway:** 12.4 Law Enforcement Services.

Skills: Negotiation; Persuasion; Service Orientation; Operation and Control; Social Perceptiveness; Active Listening; Critical Thinking; Coordination.

Work Environment: More often outdoors than indoors; sitting; using hands; noise; very hot or cold; bright or inadequate lighting; contaminants; exposed to disease or infections; hazardous equipment; minor burns, cuts, bites, or stings.

Job Specialization: Sheriffs and Deputy Sheriffs

Enforce law and order in rural or unincorporated districts, or serve legal processes of courts. May patrol courthouse, guard court or grand jury, or escort defendants. Drive vehicles or patrol specific areas to detect law violators, issue citations, and make arrests. Investigate illegal or suspicious activities. Verify that the proper legal charges have been made against law offenders. Execute arrest warrants, locating and taking persons into custody. Record daily activities, and submit logs and other related reports and paperwork to appropriate authorities. Patrol and guard courthouses, grand jury rooms, or assigned areas to provide security, enforce laws, maintain order, and arrest violators. Notify patrol units to take violators into custody or to provide needed assistance or medical aid. Place people in protective custody. Serve statements of claims, subpoenas, summonses, jury summonses, orders to pay alimony, and other court orders. Take control of accident scenes to maintain traffic flow, to assist accident victims, and to investigate causes. Question individuals entering secured areas to determine their business, directing and re-routing individuals as necessary. Transport or escort prisoners and defendants en route to courtrooms, prisons or jails, attorneys' offices, or medical facilities. Locate and confiscate real or personal property, as directed by court order. Manage jail operations, and tend to jail inmates.

Education/Training Required: Long-term on-the-job training. **Education and Training Programs:** Criminal Justice/Police Science; Criminalistics and Criminal Science. **Knowledge/Courses:** Public Safety and Security; Law and Government; Telecommunications; Psychology; Therapy and Counseling; Philosophy and Theology.

Personality Type: Enterprising-Realistic-Social. **Career Cluster:** 12 Law, Public Safety, Corrections, and Security. **Career Pathways:** 12.3 Security and Protective Services; 12.4 Law Enforcement Services.

Skills: Negotiation; Social Perceptiveness; Persuasion; Service Orientation; Management of

Personnel Resources; Critical Thinking; Time Management; Reading Comprehension.

Work Environment: More often outdoors than indoors; sitting; using hands; repetitive motions; noise; very hot or cold; bright or inadequate lighting; contaminants; cramped work space; exposed to disease or infections; hazardous equipment.

Producers and Directors

Look for the job description among the Artistic jobs.

Property, Real Estate, and Community Association Managers

- ✽ Personality Type: Enterprising-Conventional
- ✽ Annual Earnings: $51,480
- ✽ Earnings Growth Potential: High (49.1%)
- ✽ Growth: 8.4%
- ✽ Annual Job Openings: 7,800
- ✽ Self-Employed: 45.9%

Considerations for Job Outlook: Job growth is expected to be driven, in part, by a growing population and increasing use of third-party management companies for residential property oversight. Opportunities should be best for jobseekers who have a college degree and earn professional designation.

Plan, direct, or coordinate selling, buying, leasing, or governance activities of commercial, industrial, or residential real estate properties. Meet with prospective tenants to show properties, explain terms of occupancy, and provide information about local areas. Direct collection of monthly assessments; rental fees; and deposits and payment of insurance premiums, mortgage, taxes, and incurred operating expenses. Inspect grounds, facilities, and equipment routinely to determine necessity of repairs or main-tenance. Investigate complaints, disturbances, and violations, and resolve problems, following management rules and regulations. Manage and oversee operations, maintenance, administration, and improvement of commercial, industrial, or residential properties. Plan, schedule, and coordinate general maintenance, major repairs, and remodeling or construction projects for commercial or residential properties. Negotiate the sale, lease, or development of property, and complete or review appropriate documents and forms. Maintain records of sales, rental or usage activity, special permits issued, maintenance and operating costs, or property availability. Determine and certify the eligibility of prospective tenants, following government regulations. Prepare detailed budgets and financial reports for properties. Direct and coordinate the activities of staff and contract personnel, and evaluate their performance. Maintain contact with insurance carriers, fire and police departments, and other agencies to ensure protection and compliance with codes and regulations.

Education/Training Required: Bachelor's degree. **Education and Training Program:** Real Estate. **Knowledge/Courses:** Sales and Marketing; Clerical Practices; Economics and Accounting; Building and Construction; Administration and Management; Customer and Personal Service.

Career Cluster: 14 Marketing, Sales, and Service. **Career Pathway:** 14.2 Professional Sales and Marketing.

Skills: Management of Financial Resources; Negotiation; Management of Personnel Resources; Operations Analysis; Persuasion; Management of Material Resources; Service Orientation; Writing.

Work Environment: More often indoors than outdoors; sitting.

Public Relations and Fundraising Managers

* Personality Type: Enterprising-Artistic
* Annual Earnings: $91,810
* Earnings Growth Potential: High (45.8%)
* Growth: 12.9%
* Annual Job Openings: 2,060
* Self-Employed: 0.0%

Considerations for Job Outlook: Job growth is expected to result from companies' need to distinguish their products and services in an increasingly competitive marketplace. Keen competition is expected.

Plan and direct public relations programs designed to create and maintain a favorable public image for employer or client, or, if engaged in fundraising, plan and direct activities to solicit and maintain funds for special projects and nonprofit organizations. Identify main client groups and audiences, and determine the best way to communicate publicity information to them. Write interesting and effective press releases, prepare information for media kits, and develop and maintain company Internet or intranet webpages. Develop and maintain the company's corporate image and identity, which includes the use of logos and signage. Manage communications budgets. Manage special events such as sponsorship of races, parties introducing new products, or other activities the firm supports to gain public attention through the media without advertising directly. Draft speeches for company executives, and arrange interviews and other forms of contact for them. Assign, supervise, and review the activities of public relations staff. Evaluate advertising and promotion programs for compatibility with public relations efforts. Establish and maintain effective working relationships with local and municipal government officials and media representatives. Confer with labor relations managers to develop internal communications that keep employees informed of company activities. Direct activities of external agencies, establishments, and departments that develop and implement communication strategies and infor-

mation programs. Formulate policies and procedures related to public information programs, working with public relations executives. Respond to requests for information about employers' activities or status.

Education/Training Required: Work experience plus degree. **Education and Training Program:** Public Relations/Image Management. **Knowledge/Courses:** Sales and Marketing; Communications and Media; Customer and Personal Service; Personnel and Human Resources; English Language; Administration and Management.

Career Cluster: 04 Business, Management, and Administration. **Career Pathway:** 04.1 Management.

Skills: Management of Financial Resources; Persuasion; Management of Material Resources; Negotiation; Management of Personnel Resources; Systems Evaluation; Systems Analysis; Coordination.

Work Environment: Indoors; sitting.

Public Relations Specialists

* Personality Type: Enterprising-Artistic-Social
* Annual Earnings: $52,090
* Earnings Growth Potential: High (41.3%)
* Growth: 24.0%
* Annual Job Openings: 13,130
* Self-Employed: 4.5%

Considerations for Job Outlook: As the business environment becomes increasingly globalized, the need for good public relations and communications is growing rapidly. Opportunities should be best for workers with knowledge of more than one language.

Engage in promoting or creating goodwill for individuals, groups, or organizations by writing or selecting favorable publicity material and releasing it through various communications media. May prepare and arrange displays and make speeches. Prepare or edit organizational publications for internal and external audiences, including employee newsletters and stockholders' reports. Respond to requests for information from the media, or designate another appropriate spokesperson or information source. Establish and maintain cooperative relationships with representatives of community, consumer, employee, and public interest groups. Plan and direct development and communication of informational programs to maintain favorable public and stockholder perceptions of an organization's accomplishments and agenda. Confer with production and support personnel to produce or coordinate production of advertisements and promotions. Arrange public appearances, lectures, contests, or exhibits for clients to increase product and service awareness and to promote goodwill. Study the objectives, promotional policies, and needs of organizations to develop public relations strategies that will influence public opinion or promote ideas, products, and services. Consult with advertising agencies or staff to arrange promotional campaigns in all types of media for products, organizations, or individuals. Confer with other managers to identify trends and key group interests and concerns or to provide advice on business decisions. Coach client representatives in effective communication with the public and with employees. Prepare and deliver speeches to further public relations objectives.

Education/Training Required: Bachelor's degree. **Education and Training Programs:** Family and Consumer Sciences/Human Sciences Communication; Health Communication; Political Communication; Public Relations/Image Management; Speech Communication and Rhetoric. **Knowledge/Courses:** Communications and Media; Sales and Marketing; English Language; Geography; Computers and Electronics; Customer and Personal Service.

Career Clusters: 03 Arts, Audio/Video Technology, and Communications; 04 Business, Management, and Administration; 08 Health Science; 10 Human Services. **Career Pathways:** 03.5 Journalism and Broadcasting; 04.1 Management; 08.3 Health Informatics; 10.5 Consumer Services Career.

Skills: Operations Analysis; Social Perceptiveness; Negotiation; Writing; Systems Evaluation; Speaking; Persuasion; Time Management.

Work Environment: Indoors; sitting.

Real Estate Sales Agents

* Personality Type: Enterprising-Conventional
* Annual Earnings: $40,030
* Earnings Growth Potential: High (48.9%)
* Growth: 16.2%
* Annual Job Openings: 12,830
* Self-Employed: 58.3%

Considerations for Job Outlook: A growing population is expected to require the services of real estate agents, creating more jobs for these workers. People who are well-trained, ambitious, and socially and professionally active in their communities should have the best prospects.

Rent, buy, or sell property for clients. Perform duties such as studying property listings, interviewing prospective clients, accompanying clients to property site, discussing conditions of sale, and drawing up real estate contracts. Includes agents who represent buyer. Present purchase offers to sellers for consideration. Confer with escrow companies, lenders, home inspectors, and pest control operators to ensure that terms and conditions of purchase agreements are met before closing dates. Interview clients to determine what kinds of properties they are seeking. Prepare documents such as representation contracts, purchase agreements, closing statements, deeds, and leases. Coordinate property closings, overseeing signing of documents and disbursement of funds. Act as an intermediary in negotiations between buyers and sellers, generally representing one or the other. Promote sales of properties through advertisements, open houses, and participation in multiple listing services. Compare a property with similar properties that have recently sold to determine its competitive market price. Coordinate appointments to show homes to prospective buyers. Generate lists of properties that are compatible with buyers' needs and financial resources. Display commercial, industrial, agricultural, and residential properties to clients, and explain their features. Arrange for title searches to determine whether clients have clear property titles. Review plans for new construction with clients, enumerating and recommending available options and features. Answer clients' questions regarding construction work, financing, maintenance, repairs, and appraisals.

Education/Training Required: Postsecondary vocational training. **Education and Training Program:** Real Estate. **Knowledge/Courses:** Sales and Marketing; Customer and Personal Service; Law and Government; Building and Construction; Economics and Accounting; Computers and Electronics.

Career Cluster: 14 Marketing, Sales, and Service. **Career Pathway:** 14.2 Professional Sales and Marketing.

Skills: Negotiation; Persuasion; Service Orientation; Systems Evaluation; Judgment and Decision Making; Mathematics; Speaking; Coordination.

Work Environment: More often indoors than outdoors; sitting.

Registered Nurses

Look for the job description among the Social jobs.

Sales Engineers

- ❋ Personality Type: Enterprising-Realistic-Investigative
- ❋ Annual Earnings: $87,390
- ❋ Earnings Growth Potential: Medium (40.6%)
- ❋ Growth: 8.8%
- ❋ Annual Job Openings: 3,500
- ❋ Self-Employed: 0.0%

Considerations for Job Outlook: Projected job growth will stem from the increasing variety and technical nature of goods and services to be sold. Competition is expected. Prospects should be best for job-seekers with excellent interpersonal skills and communication, math, and science aptitude.

Sell business goods or services, the selling of which requires a technical background equivalent to a baccalaureate degree in engineering. Plan and modify product configurations to meet customer needs. Confer with customers and engineers to assess equipment needs and to determine system requirements. Collaborate with sales teams to understand customer requirements, to promote the sale of company products, and to provide sales support. Secure and renew orders, and arrange delivery. Develop, present, or respond to proposals for specific customer requirements, including request for proposal responses and industry-specific solutions. Sell products requiring extensive technical expertise and support for installation and use, such as material-handling equipment, numerical-control machinery, and computer systems. Diagnose problems with installed equipment. Prepare and deliver technical presentations that explain products or services to customers and prospective customers. Recommend improved materials or machinery to customers, documenting how such changes will lower costs or increase production. Provide technical and non-technical support and services to clients or other staff members regarding the use, operation, and maintenance of equipment. Research and identify potential customers for products or services. Visit prospective buyers at commercial, industrial, or other establishments to show samples or catalogs and to inform them about product pricing, availability, and advantages. Create sales or service contracts for products or services. Arrange for demonstrations or trial installations of equipment.

Education/Training Required: Bachelor's degree. **Education and Training Program:** Selling Skills and Sales Operations. **Knowledge/Courses:** Sales and Marketing; Engineering and Technology; Design; Physics; Computers and Electronics; Customer and Personal Service.

Career Cluster: 14 Marketing, Sales, and Service. **Career Pathway:** 14.2 Professional Sales and Marketing.

Skills: Technology Design; Persuasion; Negotiation; Systems Evaluation; Systems Analysis; Troubleshooting; Active Learning; Judgment and Decision Making.

Work Environment: Indoors; sitting; repetitive motions.

Sales Managers

- ✳ Personality Type: Enterprising-Conventional
- ✳ Annual Earnings: $98,530
- ✳ Earnings Growth Potential: High (49.3%)
- ✳ Growth: 14.9%
- ✳ Annual Job Openings: 12,660
- ✳ Self-Employed: 4.2%

Considerations for Job Outlook: Job growth is expected to result from companies' need to distinguish their products and services in an increasingly competitive marketplace. Keen competition is expected.

Direct the actual distribution or movement of products or services to customers. Coordinate sales distribution by establishing sales territories, quotas, and goals, and establish training programs for sales representatives. Analyze sales statistics gathered by staff to determine sales potential and inventory requirements and monitor customer preferences. Resolve customer complaints regarding sales and service. Oversee regional and local sales managers and their staffs. Plan and direct staffing, training, and performance evaluations to develop and control sales and service programs. Determine price schedules and discount rates. Review operational records and reports to project sales, and determine profitability. Monitor customer preferences to determine focus of sales efforts. Prepare budgets, and approve budget expenditures. Confer or consult with department heads to plan advertising services and to secure information

on equipment and customer specifications. Direct and coordinate activities involving sales of manufactured products, services, commodities, real estate, or other subjects of sale. Confer with potential customers regarding equipment needs, and advise customers on types of equipment to purchase. Direct foreign sales and service outlets of an organization. Advise dealers and distributors on policies and operating procedures to ensure functional effectiveness of businesses. Visit franchised dealers to stimulate interest in establishment or expansion of leasing programs. Direct clerical staff to keep records of export correspondence, bid requests, and credit collections and to maintain current information on tariffs, licenses, and restrictions. Direct, coordinate, and review activities in sales and service accounting and recordkeeping and in receiving and shipping operations.

Education/Training Required: Work experience plus degree. **Education and Training Programs:** Business Administration and Management, General; Business/Commerce, General; Consumer Merchandising/Retailing Management; Marketing, Other; Marketing/Marketing Management, General. **Knowledge/Courses:** Sales and Marketing; Personnel and Human Resources; Economics and Accounting; Administration and Management; Customer and Personal Service; Psychology.

Career Clusters: 04 Business, Management, and Administration; 10 Human Services; 14 Marketing, Sales, and Service. **Career Pathways:** 04.1 Management; 10.5 Consumer Services Career; 14.1 Management and Entrepreneurship; 14.4 Marketing Communications and Promotion.

Skills: Management of Financial Resources; Management of Personnel Resources; Management of Material Resources; Systems Evaluation; Persuasion; Monitoring; Negotiation; Systems Analysis.

Work Environment: Indoors; sitting.

Sales Representatives, Services, All Other

- ❈ Personality Type: Enterprising-Conventional
- ❈ Annual Earnings: $50,620
- ❈ Earnings Growth Potential: High (49.2%)
- ❈ Growth: 13.9%
- ❈ Annual Job Openings: 22,810
- ❈ Self-Employed: 3.7%

Considerations for Job Outlook: Faster than average employment growth is projected.

This occupation includes all services sales representatives not listed separately. Because this is a highly diverse occupation, no data is available for some information topics.

Education/Training Required: Work experience in a related occupation. **Education and Training Program:** Selling Skills and Sales Operations.

Career Cluster: 14 Marketing, Sales, and Service. **Career Pathway:** 14.2 Professional Sales and Marketing.

Job Specialization: Energy Brokers

Purchase or sell energy for customers. Contact prospective buyers or sellers of power to arrange transactions. Create product packages based on assessment of customers' or potential customers' needs. Educate customers, and answer customer questions related to the buying or selling of energy, energy markets, or alternative energy sources. Explain contracts and related documents to customers. Forecast energy supply and demand to minimize the cost of meeting load demands and to maximize the value of supply resources. Negotiate prices and contracts for energy sales or purchases. Price energy based on market conditions. Analyze customer bills and utility rate structures to select optimal rate structures for customers. Develop and deliver proposals or presentations on topics such as the purchase and sale of energy. Facilitate the delivery or receipt of wholesale power or retail load scheduling. Monitor the flow of energy in response to changes in consumer demand.

Education/Training Required: Work experience in a related occupation. **Education and Training Program:** Specialized Merchandising, Sales, and Marketing Operations, Other. **Knowledge/Courses:** No data available.

Personality Type: Enterprising-Conventional. **Career Cluster:** 14 Marketing, Sales, and Service. **Career Pathway:** 14.2 Professional Sales and Marketing.

Skills: No data available.

Work Environment: No data available.

Sales Representatives, Wholesale and Manufacturing, Technical and Scientific Products

- ❈ Personality Type: Enterprising-Conventional
- ❈ Annual Earnings: $73,710
- ❈ Earnings Growth Potential: High (50.2%)
- ❈ Growth: 9.7%
- ❈ Annual Job Openings: 14,230
- ❈ Self-Employed: 3.6%

Considerations for Job Outlook: Continued expansion in the variety and number of goods sold is expected to lead to additional jobs for these workers. Prospects should be best for jobseekers with a college degree, technical expertise, and interpersonal skills.

Sell goods for wholesalers or manufacturers where technical or scientific knowledge is required in such areas as biology, engineering, chemistry, and electronics that is normally obtained from at least two years of postsecondary education. Contact new and existing customers to discuss their needs and to explain how these needs could be met by specific products and services. Answer customers' questions about products, prices, availability,

Enterprising-S

product uses, and credit terms. Quote prices, credit terms, and other bid specifications. Emphasize product features based on analyses of customers' needs and on technical knowledge of product capabilities and limitations. Negotiate prices and terms of sales and service agreements. Maintain customer records, using automated systems. Identify prospective customers by using business directories, following leads from existing clients, participating in organizations and clubs, and attending trade shows and conferences. Prepare sales contracts for orders obtained, and submit orders for processing. Select the correct products, or assist customers in making product selections based on customers' needs, product specifications, and applicable regulations. Collaborate with colleagues to exchange information such as selling strategies and marketing information. Prepare sales presentations and proposals that explain product specifications and applications. Provide customers with ongoing technical support. Demonstrate and explain the operation and use of products. Inform customers of estimated delivery schedules, service contracts, warranties, or other information pertaining to purchased products.

Education/Training Required: Work experience in a related occupation. **Education and Training Programs:** Business, Management, Marketing, and Related Support Services, Other; Selling Skills and Sales Operations. **Knowledge/Courses:** Sales and Marketing; Customer and Personal Service; Production and Processing; Administration and Management; Transportation; Computers and Electronics.

Career Cluster: 14 Marketing, Sales, and Service. **Career Pathway:** 14.2 Professional Sales and Marketing.

Skills: Persuasion; Negotiation; Management of Financial Resources; Management of Material Resources; Active Listening; Speaking; Reading Comprehension; Operations Analysis.

Work Environment: Indoors; sitting.

Job Specialization: Solar Sales Representatives and Assessors

Contact new or existing customers to determine their solar equipment needs, suggest systems or equipment, or estimate costs. Generate solar energy customer leads to develop new accounts. Prepare proposals, quotes, contracts, or presentations for potential solar customers. Select solar energy products, systems, or services for customers based on electrical energy requirements, site conditions, price, or other factors. Assess sites to determine suitability for solar equipment, using equipment such as tape measures, compasses, and computer software. Calculate potential solar resources or solar solar-array production for a particular site, considering issues such as climate, shading, and roof orientation. Create customized energy energy-management packages to satisfy customer needs. Develop marketing or strategic plans for sales territories. Gather information from prospective customers to identify their solar energy needs. Prepare or review detailed design drawings, specifications, or lists related to solar installations. Provide customers with information such as quotes, orders, sales, shipping, warranties, credit, funding options, incentives, or tax rebates. Provide technical information about solar power, solar systems, equipment, and services to potential customers or dealers. Take quote requests or orders from dealers or customers. Demonstrate use of solar and related equipment to customers or dealers.

Education/Training Required: Work experience in a related occupation. **Education and Training Programs:** Business, Management, Marketing, and Related Support Services, Other; Selling Skills and Sales Operations. **Knowledge/Courses:** No data available.

Personality Type: No data available. **Career Cluster:** 14 Marketing, Sales, and Service. **Career Pathway:** 14.2 Professional Sales and Marketing.

Skills: No data available.

Work Environment: No data available.

Securities, Commodities, and Financial Services Sales Agents

❀ Personality Type: Enterprising-Conventional

❀ Annual Earnings: $70,190

❀ Earnings Growth Potential: Very high (55.4%)

❀ Growth: 9.3%

❀ Annual Job Openings: 12,680

❀ Self-Employed: 15.4%

Considerations for Job Outlook: Consolidation of the financial industry is expected to inhibit employment growth. Individuals' ability to manage their own investments online is likely to reduce the need for brokers. Job competition should be keen.

Job Specialization: Sales Agents, Financial Services

Sell financial services such as loan, tax, and securities counseling to customers of financial institutions and business establishments. Determine customers' financial-services needs, and prepare proposals to sell services that address these needs. Contact prospective customers to present information and explain available services. Sell services and equipment, such as trusts, investments, and check-processing services. Prepare forms or agreements to complete sales. Develop prospects from current commercial customers, referral leads, and sales and trade meetings. Review business trends in order to advise customers regarding expected fluctuations. Make presentations on financial services to groups to attract new clients. Evaluate costs and revenue of agreements to determine continued profitability.

Education/Training Required: Bachelor's degree. **Education and Training Programs:** Business and Personal/Financial Services Marketing Operations; Financial Planning and Services; Investments and Securities. **Knowledge/Courses:** Sales and Marketing; Economics and Accounting; Customer and Personal Service; Law and Government; Mathematics; Personnel and Human Resources.

Personality Type: Enterprising-Conventional. **Career Cluster:** 06 Finance. **Career Pathway:** 06.1 Financial and Investment Planning.

Skills: Persuasion; Systems Evaluation; Negotiation; Service Orientation; Mathematics; Active Learning; Speaking; Systems Analysis.

Work Environment: Indoors; sitting.

Job Specialization: Sales Agents, Securities and Commodities

Buy and sell securities in investment and trading firms, and develop and implement financial plans for individuals, businesses, and organizations. Complete sales order tickets, and submit for processing of client-requested transactions. Interview clients to determine clients' assets, liabilities, cash flow, insurance coverage, tax status, and financial objectives. Record transactions accurately, and keep clients informed about transactions. Develop financial plans based on analysis of clients' financial status, and discuss financial options with clients. Review all securities transactions to ensure accuracy of information, and ensure that trades conform to regulations of governing agencies. Offer advice on the purchase or sale of particular securities. Relay buy-or-sell orders to securities exchanges or to firm trading departments. Identify potential clients, using advertising campaigns, mailing lists, and personal contacts. Review financial periodicals, stock and bond reports, business publications, and other material to identify potential investments for clients and to keep abreast of trends affecting market conditions. Contact prospective customers to determine customer needs, present information, and explain available services. Prepare documents needed to implement plans selected by clients. Analyze market conditions to determine optimum times to execute securities transactions. Explain stock market terms and trading practices to clients. Inform and advise concerned parties regarding fluctuations and securities transactions affecting plans or accounts. Calculate costs for billings and commissions purposes.

Education/Training Required: Bachelor's degree. **Education and Training Programs:** Business and Personal/Financial Services Marketing Operations; Financial Planning and Services; Investments and Securities. **Knowledge/Courses:** Economics and Accounting; Customer and Personal Service; Sales and Marketing; Clerical Practices; Law and Government; Mathematics.

Personality Type: Enterprising-Conventional. **Career Cluster:** 06 Finance. **Career Pathway:** 06.1 Financial and Investment Planning.

Skills: Systems Analysis; Persuasion; Systems Evaluation; Management of Financial Resources; Reading Comprehension; Judgment and Decision Making; Negotiation; Service Orientation.

Work Environment: Indoors; sitting.

Job Specialization: Securities and Commodities Traders

Buy and sell securities and commodities to transfer debt, capital, or risk. Establish and negotiate unit prices and terms of sale. Buy or sell stocks, bonds, commodity futures, foreign currencies, or other securities at stock exchanges on behalf of investment dealers. Agree on buying or selling prices at optimal levels for clients. Make bids and offers to buy or sell securities. Analyze target companies and investment opportunities to inform investment decisions. Develop and maintain supplier and customer relationships. Devise trading, option, and hedge strategies. Identify opportunities, and develop channels for purchase or sale of securities or commodities. Inform other traders, managers, or customers of market conditions, including volume, price, competition, and dynamics. Monitor markets and positions. Process paperwork for special orders, including margin and option purchases. Receive sales order tickets, and inspect forms to determine accuracy of information. Report all positions or trading results. Review securities transactions to ensure conformance to regulations. Track and analyze factors that affect price movement, such as trade policies, weather conditions, political developments, and

supply-and-demand changes. Write and sign sales order confirmation forms to record and approve security transactions. Audit accounts, and correct errors. Make transportation arrangements for sold or purchased commodities. Prepare financial reports, such as reviews of portfolio positions. Reconcile account-related statements, such as quarterly and annual statements and confirmations.

Education/Training Required: Bachelor's degree. **Education and Training Programs:** Business and Personal/Financial Services Marketing Operations; Financial Planning and Services; Investments and Securities. **Knowledge/Courses:** No data available.

Personality Type: Enterprising-Conventional. **Career Cluster:** 06 Finance. **Career Pathway:** 06.1 Financial and Investment Planning.

Skills: No data available.

Work Environment: No data available.

Social and Community Service Managers

❋ Personality Type: Enterprising-Social
❋ Annual Earnings: $57,950
❋ Earnings Growth Potential: Medium (40.8%)
❋ Growth: 13.8%
❋ Annual Job Openings: 4,820
❋ Self-Employed: 3.1%

Considerations for Job Outlook: Faster than average employment growth is projected.

Plan, organize, or coordinate the activities of a social service program or community outreach organization. Oversee the program or organization's budget and policies regarding participant involvement, program requirements, and benefits. Work may involve directing social workers, counselors, or probation officers. Establish and maintain relationships with other agencies and organizations in the community to meet community needs and to ensure that services are not duplicated. Prepare and maintain records and reports, such as budgets, personnel records, or training manuals. Direct activities of professional and technical staff members and volunteers. Evaluate the work of staff and volunteers to ensure that programs are of appropriate quality and that resources are used effectively. Establish and oversee administrative procedures to meet objectives set by boards of directors or senior management. Participate in the determination of organizational policies regarding such issues as participant eligibility, program requirements, and program benefits. Research and analyze member or community needs to determine program directions and goals. Speak to community groups to explain and interpret agency purposes, programs, and policies. Recruit, interview, and hire or sign up volunteers and staff. Represent organizations in relations with governmental and media institutions. Plan and administer budgets for programs, equipment, and support services. Analyze proposed legislation, regulations, or rule changes to determine how agency services could be impacted. Act as consultants to agency staff and other community programs regarding the interpretation of program-related federal, state, and county regulations and policies. Implement and evaluate staff training programs.

Education/Training Required: Bachelor's degree. **Education and Training Programs:** Business Administration and Management, General; Business, Management, Marketing, and Related Support Services, Other; Business/Commerce, General; Community Organization and Advocacy; Entrepreneurship/Entrepreneurial Studies; Human Services, General; Non-Profit/Public/Organizational Management; Public Administration. **Knowledge/Courses:** Therapy and Counseling; Psychology; Sociology and Anthropology; Philosophy and Theology; Personnel and Human Resources; Customer and Personal Service.

Career Clusters: 04 Business, Management, and Administration; 07 Government and Public Administration; 10 Human Services. **Career Pathways:** 04.1 Management; 07.1 Governance; 07.7

Public Management and Administration; 10.3 Family and Community Services.

Skills: Management of Financial Resources; Management of Personnel Resources; Management of Material Resources; Systems Evaluation; Operations Analysis; Social Perceptiveness; Systems Analysis; Learning Strategies.

Work Environment: Indoors; sitting.

Supervisors of Construction and Extraction Workers

* Personality Type: Enterprising-Realistic-Conventional
* Annual Earnings: $58,680
* Earnings Growth Potential: Medium (38.3%)
* Growth: 15.4%
* Annual Job Openings: 24,220
* Self-Employed: 19.0%

Considerations for Job Outlook: Faster than average employment growth is projected.

Directly supervise and coordinate activities of construction or extraction workers. Examine and inspect work progress, equipment, and construction sites to verify safety and to ensure that specifications are met. Read specifications such as blueprints to determine construction requirements and to plan procedures. Estimate material and worker requirements to complete jobs. Supervise, coordinate, and schedule the activities of construction or extractive workers. Confer with managerial and technical personnel, other departments, and contractors in order to resolve problems and to coordinate activities. Coordinate work activities with other construction project activities. Locate, measure, and mark site locations and placement of structures and equipment, using measuring and marking equipment. Order or requisition materials and supplies. Record information such as personnel, production, and operational data on specified forms and reports. Assign work to

Enterprising-S

employees based on material and worker requirements of specific jobs. Provide assistance to workers engaged in construction or extraction activities, using hand tools and equipment. Train workers in construction methods, operation of equipment, safety procedures, and company policies. Analyze worker and production problems, and recommend solutions such as improving production methods or implementing motivational plans. Arrange for repairs of equipment and machinery. Suggest or initiate personnel actions such as promotions, transfers, and hires.

Education/Training Required: Work experience in a related occupation. **Education and Training Programs:** Blasting/Blaster; Building/Construction Finishing, Management, and Inspection, Other; Building/Construction Site Management/Manager; Building/Home/Construction Inspection/Inspector; Building/Property Maintenance; Carpentry/Carpenter; Concrete Finishing/Concrete Finisher; Construction Trades, Other; Drywall Installation/Drywaller; Electrical and Power Transmission Installation/Installer, General; Electrical and Power Transmission Installers, Other; Electrician; Glazier Training; Lineworker; Masonry/Mason Training; Painting/Painter and Wall Coverer Training; Plumbing Technology/Plumber; Roofer Training; Well Drilling/Driller. **Knowledge/Courses:** Building and Construction; Mechanical Devices; Design; Engineering and Technology; Production and Processing; Public Safety and Security.

Career Cluster: 02 Architecture and Construction. **Career Pathway:** 02.2 Construction.

Skills: Equipment Selection; Management of Personnel Resources; Equipment Maintenance; Operation and Control; Quality Control Analysis; Operations Analysis; Management of Material Resources; Troubleshooting.

Work Environment: Outdoors; standing; using hands; noise; very hot or cold; bright or inadequate lighting; contaminants; hazardous equipment.

Job Specialization: Solar Energy Installation Managers

Direct work crews installing residential or commercial solar photovoltaic or thermal systems. Plan and coordinate installations of photovoltaic (PV) solar and solar thermal systems to ensure conformance to codes. Supervise solar installers, technicians, and subcontractors for solar installation projects to ensure compliance with safety standards. Assess potential solar installation sites to determine feasibility and design requirements. Assess system performance or functionality at the system, subsystem, and component levels. Coordinate or schedule building inspections for solar installation projects. Monitor work of contractors and subcontractors to ensure projects conform to plans, specifications, schedules, or budgets. Perform start-up of systems for testing or customer implementation. Provide technical assistance to installers, technicians, or other solar professionals in areas such as solar electric systems, solar thermal systems, electrical systems, and mechanical systems. Visit customer sites to determine solar system needs, requirements, or specifications. Develop and maintain system architecture, including all piping, instrumentation, or process flow diagrams. Estimate materials, equipment, and personnel needed for residential or commercial solar installation projects. Evaluate subcontractors or subcontractor bids for quality, cost, and reliability. Identify means to reduce costs, minimize risks, or increase efficiency of solar installation projects. Prepare solar installation project proposals, quotes, budgets, or schedules.

Education/Training Required: Work experience in a related occupation. **Education and Training Programs:** Blasting/Blaster; Building/Construction Finishing, Management, and Inspection, Other; Building/Construction Site Management/Manager; Building/Home/Construction Inspection/Inspector; Building/Property Maintenance; Carpentry/Carpenter; Concrete Finishing/Concrete Finisher; Construction Trades, Other; Drywall Installation/Drywaller; Electrical and Power Transmission Installation/Installer, General; Electrical and

Power Transmission Installers, Other; Electrician; Glazier Training; Lineworker; Masonry/Mason Training; Painting/Painter and Wall Coverer Training; Plumbing Technology/Plumber; Roofer Training; Well Drilling/Driller. **Knowledge/ Courses:** No data available.

Personality Type: No data available. **Career Cluster:** 02 Architecture and Construction. **Career Pathway:** 02.2 Construction.

Skills: No data available.

Work Environment: No data available.

Training and Development Managers

- ❋ Personality Type: Enterprising-Social
- ❋ Annual Earnings: $89,170
- ❋ Earnings Growth Potential: High (43.4%)
- ❋ Growth: 11.9%
- ❋ Annual Job Openings: 1,010
- ❋ Self-Employed: 0.6%

Considerations for Job Outlook: Efforts to recruit and retain employees, the growing importance of employee training, and new legal standards are expected to increase employment of these workers. College graduates and those with certification should have the best opportunities.

Plan, direct, or coordinate the training and development activities and staff of organizations. Conduct orientation sessions, and arrange on-the-job training for new hires. Evaluate instructor performance and the effectiveness of training programs, providing recommendations for improvement. Develop testing and evaluation procedures. Conduct or arrange for ongoing technical training and personal development classes for staff members. Confer with management and conduct surveys to identify training needs based on projected production processes, changes, and other

factors. Develop and organize training manuals, multimedia visual aids, and other educational materials. Plan, develop, and provide training and staff development programs, using knowledge of the effectiveness of methods such as classroom training, demonstrations, on-the-job training, meetings, conferences, and workshops. Analyze training needs to develop new training programs or modify and improve existing programs. Review and evaluate training and apprenticeship programs for compliance with government standards. Train instructors and supervisors in techniques and skills for training and dealing with employees. Coordinate established courses with technical and professional courses provided by community schools, and designate training procedures. Prepare training budget for department or organization.

Education/Training Required: Work experience plus degree. **Education and Training Program:** Human Resources Development. **Knowledge/ Courses:** Education and Training; Personnel and Human Resources; Sociology and Anthropology; Sales and Marketing; Therapy and Counseling; English Language.

Career Clusters: 04 Business, Management, and Administration. **Career Pathway:** 04.3 Human Resources.

Skills: Management of Financial Resources; Learning Strategies; Management of Personnel Resources; Instructing; Systems Evaluation; Management of Material Resources; Speaking; Systems Analysis.

Work Environment: Indoors; sitting.

Writers and Authors

Look for the job description among the Artistic jobs.

Conventional Occupations

Accountants and Auditors

- ❀ Personality Type: Conventional-Enterprising-Investigative
- ❀ Annual Earnings: $61,690
- ❀ Earnings Growth Potential: Medium (36.9%)
- ❀ Growth: 21.6%
- ❀ Annual Job Openings: 49,750
- ❀ Self-Employed: 8.1%

Considerations for Job Outlook: An increase in the number of businesses, a more stringent regulatory environment, and increased corporate accountability are expected to drive job growth for accountants and auditors. Opportunities should be favorable; job-seekers with professional certification, especially a CPA, should have the best prospects.

Job Specialization: Accountants

Analyze financial information and prepare financial reports to determine or maintain record of assets, liabilities, profit and loss, tax liability, or other financial activities within an organization. Prepare, examine, or analyze accounting records, financial statements, or other financial reports to assess accuracy, completeness, and conformance to reporting and procedural standards. Compute taxes owed, and prepare tax returns, ensuring compliance with payment, reporting, or other tax requirements. Analyze business operations, trends, costs, revenues, financial commitments, and obligations to project future revenues and expenses or to provide advice. Report to management regarding the finances of establishment. Establish tables of accounts, and assign entries to proper accounts. Develop, maintain, and analyze budgets, preparing periodic reports that compare budgeted costs to actual costs. Develop, implement, modify, and document recordkeeping and

accounting systems, making use of current computer technology. Prepare forms and manuals for accounting and bookkeeping personnel, and direct their work activities. Survey operations to ascertain accounting needs and to recommend, develop, or maintain solutions to business and financial problems. Work as Internal Revenue Service (IRS) agents. Advise management about issues such as resource utilization, tax strategies, and the assumptions underlying budget forecasts. Provide internal and external auditing services for businesses or individuals. Advise clients in areas such as compensation, employee health-care benefits, the design of accounting or data processing systems, or long-range tax or estate plans.

Education/Training Required: Bachelor's degree. **Education and Training Programs:** Accounting; Accounting and Business/Management; Accounting and Computer Science; Accounting and Finance; Auditing; Taxation. **Knowledge/Courses:** Economics and Accounting; Clerical Practices; Mathematics; Computers and Electronics; Personnel and Human Resources; Administration and Management.

Personality Type: Conventional-Enterprising. **Career Cluster:** 04 Business, Management, and Administration. **Career Pathway:** 04.2 Business, Financial Management, and Accounting.

Skills: Operations Analysis; Mathematics; Systems Analysis; Management of Financial Resources; Systems Evaluation; Critical Thinking; Judgment and Decision Making; Negotiation.

Work Environment: Indoors; sitting; repetitive motions.

Job Specialization: Auditors

Examine and analyze accounting records to determine financial status of establishment, and prepare financial reports concerning operating procedures. Collect and analyze data to detect deficient controls; duplicated effort; extravagance; fraud; or non-compliance with laws, regulations, and management policies. Prepare detailed reports on audit findings. Supervise auditing of establishments, and determine scope of investigation required. Report to management about asset utilization and audit results, and recommend changes in operations and financial activities. Inspect account books and accounting systems for efficiency, effectiveness, and use of accepted accounting procedures to record transactions. Examine records and interview workers to ensure recording of transactions and compliance with laws and regulations. Examine and evaluate financial and information systems, recommending controls to ensure system reliability and data integrity. Review data about material assets, net worth, liabilities, capital stock, surplus, income, and expenditures. Confer with company officials about financial and regulatory matters. Examine whether the organization's objectives are reflected in its management activities and whether employees understand the objectives. Prepare, analyze, and verify annual reports, financial statements, and other records, using accepted accounting and statistical procedures to assess financial condition and facilitate financial planning. Inspect cash on hand, notes receivable and payable, negotiable securities, and canceled checks to confirm records are accurate.

Education/Training Required: Bachelor's degree. **Education and Training Programs:** Accounting; Accounting and Business/Management; Accounting and Computer Science; Accounting and Finance; Auditing; Taxation. **Knowledge/Courses:** Economics and Accounting; Administration and Management; Personnel and Human Resources; Law and Government; Computers and Electronics; Mathematics.

Personality Type: Conventional-Enterprising-Investigative. **Career Cluster:** 04 Business, Management, and Administration. **Career Pathway:** 04.2 Business, Financial Management, and Accounting.

Skills: Systems Evaluation; Systems Analysis; Management of Financial Resources; Mathematics; Programming; Writing; Operations Analysis; Management of Personnel Resources.

Work Environment: Indoors; sitting.

Actuaries

* Personality Type: Conventional-Investigative-Enterprising
* Annual Earnings: $87,650
* Earnings Growth Potential: Medium (39.4%)
* Growth: 21.3%
* Annual Job Openings: 1,000
* Self-Employed: 0.0%

Considerations for Job Outlook: Employment growth is projected as industries not traditionally associated with actuaries, such as financial services and consulting, employ these workers to assess risk. Keen competition is expected.

Analyze statistical data, such as mortality, accident, sickness, disability, and retirement rates, and construct probability tables to forecast risk and liability for payment of future benefits. May ascertain premium rates required and cash reserves necessary to ensure payment of future benefits. Ascertain premium rates required and cash reserves and liabilities necessary to ensure payment of future benefits. Analyze statistical information to estimate mortality, accident, sickness, disability, and retirement rates. Design, review, and help administer insurance, annuity, and pension plans, determining financial soundness and calculating premiums. Collaborate with programmers, underwriters, accountants, claims experts, and senior management to help companies develop plans for new lines of business or for improving existing business. Determine or help determine company policy, and explain complex technical matters to company executives, government officials, shareholders, policyholders, or the public. Testify before public agencies on proposed legislation affecting businesses. Provide advice to clients on a contract basis, working as a consultant. Testify in court as expert witness or to provide legal evidence on matters such as the value of potential lifetime earnings of a person who is disabled or killed in an accident. Construct probability tables for events such as fires, natural disasters, and unemployment, based on analysis of statistical data and other pertinent information. Determine policy contract provisions for each type of insurance. Manage credit, and help price corporate security offerings. Provide expertise to help financial institutions manage risks and maximize returns associated with investment products or credit offerings.

Education/Training Required: Work experience plus degree. **Education and Training Program:** Actuarial Science. **Knowledge/Courses:** Economics and Accounting; Mathematics; Computers and Electronics; Administration and Management; Personnel and Human Resources; Sales and Marketing.

Career Cluster: 06 Finance. **Career Pathway:** 06.4 Insurance Services.

Skills: Mathematics; Management of Financial Resources; Systems Evaluation; Systems Analysis; Programming; Operations Analysis; Judgment and Decision Making; Complex Problem Solving.

Work Environment: Indoors; sitting.

Bill and Account Collectors

* Personality Type: Conventional-Enterprising
* Annual Earnings: $31,310
* Earnings Growth Potential: Low (31.9%)
* Growth: 19.3%
* Annual Job Openings: 15,690
* Self-Employed: 0.9%

Considerations for Job Outlook: New jobs are projected to be created in industries in which delinquent accounts are common, such as health care and financial services. Opportunities also should be favorable. Job-seekers who have related experience should have the best prospects.

Locate and notify customers of delinquent accounts by mail, telephone, or personal visit to solicit payment. Duties include receiving payment and posting amount to customer's account, preparing statements to credit department if customer fails to respond, initiating repossession proceedings or service disconnection, and keeping records of collection and status of accounts. Receive payments, and post amounts paid to customer accounts. Locate and monitor overdue accounts, using computers and a variety of automated systems. Record information about financial status of customers and status of collection efforts. Confer with customers by telephone or in person to determine reasons for overdue payments and to review the terms of sales, service, or credit contracts. Advise customers of necessary actions and strategies for debt repayment. Persuade customers to pay amounts due on credit accounts, damage claims, or nonpayable checks or to return merchandise. Sort and file correspondence, and perform miscellaneous clerical duties such as answering correspondence and writing reports. Perform various administrative functions for assigned accounts, such as recording address changes and purging the records of deceased customers. Arrange for debt repayment, or establish repayment schedules based on customers' financial situations. Negotiate credit extensions when necessary. Trace delinquent customers to new addresses by inquiring at post offices, telephone companies, or credit bureaus or through the questioning of neighbors. Notify credit departments, order merchandise repossession or service disconnection, and turn over account records to attorneys when customers fail to respond to collection attempts.

Education/Training Required: Short-term on-the-job training. **Education and Training Program:** Banking and Financial Support Services. **Knowledge/Courses:** Clerical Practices; Economics and Accounting; Customer and Personal Service; Law and Government; Computers and Electronics.

Career Cluster: 06 Finance. **Career Pathway:** 06.3 Banking and Related Services.

Skills: Persuasion; Negotiation; Speaking; Active Listening; Social Perceptiveness; Mathematics; Writing; Critical Thinking.

Work Environment: Indoors; sitting; using hands; repetitive motions; noise.

Billing and Posting Clerks

* Personality Type: Conventional-Enterprising
* Annual Earnings: $32,170
* Earnings Growth Potential: Low (30.8%)
* Growth: 15.3%
* Annual Job Openings: 16,760
* Self-Employed: 1.7%

Considerations for Job Outlook: Employment growth is projected to stem from an increasing number of transactions, especially in the rapidly growing health-care industry. Prospects should be good.

Job Specialization: Billing, Cost, and Rate Clerks

Compile data, compute fees and charges, and prepare invoices for billing purposes. Duties include computing costs and calculating rates for goods, services, and shipment of goods; posting data; and keeping other relevant records. May involve use of computer or typewriter, calculator, and adding and bookkeeping machines. Verify accuracy of billing data, and revise any errors. Operate typing, adding, calculating, and billing machines. Prepare itemized statements, bills, or invoices, and record amounts due for items purchased or services rendered. Review documents such as purchase orders, sales tickets, charge slips, or hospital records to compute fees and charges due. Perform bookkeeping work, including posting data and keeping other records concerning costs of goods and services and the shipment of goods. Keep records of invoices and support documents. Resolve discrepancies in accounting records. Type billing documents, shipping labels, credit memoranda, and credit forms, using typewriters or computers. Contact customers to obtain or relay account information. Compute credit terms, discounts, shipment charges, and rates for goods and services to complete billing documents. Answer mail and telephone inquiries regarding rates, routing, and procedures. Track accumulated hours and dollar amounts charged to each client job to calculate client fees for professional services such as legal and accounting services. Review compiled data on operating costs and revenues to set rates. Compile reports of cost factors, such as labor, production, storage, and equipment. Consult sources such as rate books, manuals, and insurance company representatives to determine specific charges and information such as rules, regulations, and government tax and tariff information.

Education/Training Required: Moderate-term on-the-job training. **Education and Training Program:** Accounting Technology/Technician and Bookkeeping. **Knowledge/Courses:** Clerical Practices; Economics and Accounting; Computers and Electronics.

Personality Type: Conventional-Enterprising. **Career Cluster:** 04 Business, Management, and Administration. **Career Pathway:** 04.2 Business, Financial Management, and Accounting.

Skills: Programming; Mathematics; Active Listening; Service Orientation.

Work Environment: Indoors; sitting.

Job Specialization: Statement Clerks

Prepare and distribute bank statements to customers, answer inquiries, and reconcile discrepancies in records and accounts. Encode and cancel checks, using bank machines. Take orders for imprinted checks. Compare previously prepared bank statements with canceled checks, and reconcile discrepancies. Verify signatures and required information on checks. Post stop-payment notices to prevent payment of protested checks. Maintain files of canceled checks and customers' signatures. Match statements with batches of canceled checks by account numbers. Weigh envelopes containing statements to determine correct postage, and affix postage using stamps or metering equipment. Load machines with statements, cancelled checks, and envelopes to prepare statements for distribution to customers, or stuff envelopes by hand. Retrieve checks returned to customers in error, adjusting customer accounts and answering inquiries about errors as necessary. Route statements for mailing or over-the-counter delivery to customers. Monitor equipment to ensure proper operation. Fix minor problems, such as equipment jams, and notify repair personnel of major equipment problems.

Education/Training Required: Moderate-term on-the-job training. **Education and Training Program:** Accounting Technology/Technician and Bookkeeping. **Knowledge/Courses:** Economics and Accounting; Clerical Practices; Administration and Management.

Personality Type: Conventional-Enterprising-Social. **Career Cluster:** 04 Business, Management, and Administration. **Career Pathway:** 04.2 Business, Financial Management, and Accounting.

Skills: Programming.

Work Environment: Indoors; sitting; repetitive motions.

Bookkeeping, Accounting, and Auditing Clerks

- ❋ Personality Type: Conventional-Enterprising
- ❋ Annual Earnings: $34,030
- ❋ Earnings Growth Potential: Medium (37.5%)
- ❋ Growth: 10.3%
- ❋ Annual Job Openings: 46,040
- ❋ Self-Employed: 6.3%

Considerations for Job Outlook: Overall economic expansion will result in more financial transactions and other activities requiring recordkeeping, leading to expected employment growth for these workers. Job openings will be plentiful, including many opportunities for temporary and part-time work.

Compute, classify, and record numerical data to keep financial records complete. Perform any combination of routine calculating, posting, and

verifying duties to obtain primary financial data for use in maintaining accounting records. May also check the accuracy of figures, calculations, and postings pertaining to business transactions recorded by other workers. Operate computers programmed with accounting software to record, store, and analyze information. Check figures, postings, and documents for correct entry, mathematical accuracy, and proper codes. Comply with federal, state, and company policies, procedures, and regulations. Debit, credit, and total accounts on computer spreadsheets and databases, using specialized accounting software. Classify, record, and summarize numerical and financial data to compile and keep financial records, using journals and ledgers or computers. Calculate, prepare, and issue bills, invoices, account statements, and other financial statements according to established procedures. Code documents according to company procedures. Compile statistical, financial, accounting, or auditing reports and tables pertaining to such matters as cash receipts, expenditures, accounts payable and receivable, and profits and losses. Operate 10-key calculators, typewriters, and copy machines to perform calculations and produce documents. Access computerized financial information to answer general questions as well as those related to specific accounts. Reconcile or note and report discrepancies found in records. Perform financial calculations such as amounts due, interest charges, balances, discounts, equity, and principal. Perform general office duties such as filing, answering telephones, and handling routine correspondence.

Education/Training Required: Moderate-term on-the-job training. **Education and Training Programs:** Accounting and Related Services, Other; Accounting Technology/Technician and Bookkeeping. **Knowledge/Courses:** Economics and Accounting; Clerical Practices; Mathematics; Computers and Electronics.

Career Cluster: 04 Business, Management, and Administration. **Career Pathway:** 04.2 Business, Financial Management, and Accounting.

Skills: Management of Financial Resources; Mathematics; Active Listening; Reading Comprehension; Time Management; Writing; Speaking.

Work Environment: Indoors; sitting; using hands; repetitive motions.

Budget Analysts

- ❋ Personality Type: Conventional-Enterprising-Investigative
- ❋ Annual Earnings: $68,200
- ❋ Earnings Growth Potential: Low (34.2%)
- ❋ Growth: 15.1%
- ❋ Annual Job Openings: 2,230
- ❋ Self-Employed: 0.0%

Considerations for Job Outlook: Projected employment growth will be driven by the continued demand for financial analysis in both the public and the private sectors. Job seekers with a master's degree should have the best prospects.

Examine budget estimates for completeness, accuracy, and conformance with procedures and regulations. Analyze budgeting and accounting reports for the purpose of maintaining expenditure controls. Direct the preparation of regular and special budget reports. Consult with managers to ensure that budget adjustments are made in accordance with program changes. Match appropriations for specific programs with appropriations for broader programs, including items for emergency funds. Provide advice and technical assistance with cost analysis, fiscal allocation, and budget preparation. Summarize budgets, and submit recommendations for the approval or disapproval of funds requests. Seek new ways to improve efficiency and increase profits. Review operating budgets to analyze trends affecting budget needs. Perform cost-benefit analyses to compare operating programs, review financial requests, or explore alternative financing methods. Interpret budget directives, and establish policies for carrying out directives. Compile and analyze accounting records and other data to determine the financial resources required to implement a program.

Testify before examining and fund-granting authorities, clarifying and promoting the proposed budgets.

Education/Training Required: Bachelor's degree. **Education and Training Programs:** Accounting; Finance, General. **Knowledge/Courses:** Economics and Accounting; Clerical Practices; Administration and Management; Mathematics; Personnel and Human Resources; Law and Government.

Career Clusters: 04 Business, Management, and Administration; 06 Finance. **Career Pathways:** 04.2 Business, Financial Management, and Accounting; 06.1 Financial and Investment Planning.

Skills: Management of Financial Resources; Operations Analysis; Systems Analysis; Mathematics; Management of Material Resources; Systems Evaluation; Judgment and Decision Making; Active Learning.

Work Environment: Indoors; sitting; repetitive motions.

Business Operations Specialists, All Other

- ❋ Personality Type: Conventional-Enterprising-Realistic
- ❋ Annual Earnings: $62,450
- ❋ Earnings Growth Potential: High (45.8%)
- ❋ Growth: 11.5%
- ❋ Annual Job Openings: 36,830
- ❋ Self-Employed: 0.6%

Considerations for Job Outlook: About average employment growth is projected.

This occupation includes all business operations specialists not listed separately. Because this is a highly diverse occupation, no data is available for some information topics.

Education/Training Required: Bachelor's degree. **Education and Training Program:** Business Administration and Management, General.

Conventional-B

Career Cluster: 04 Business, Management, and Administration. **Career Pathway:** 04.1 Management.

Job Specialization: Business Continuity Planners

Develop, maintain, and implement business continuity and disaster-recovery strategies and solutions. Perform risk analyses. Act as a coordinator for recovery efforts in emergency situations. Write reports to summarize testing activities, including descriptions of goals, planning, scheduling, execution, results, analysis, conclusions, and recommendations. Maintain and update organization information technology applications and network systems blueprints. Interpret government regulations and applicable codes to ensure compliance. Identify individual or transaction targets to direct intelligence collection. Establish, maintain, or test call trees to ensure appropriate communication during disaster. Design or implement products and services to mitigate risk, or facilitate use of technology-based tools and methods. Create business continuity and disaster recovery budgets. Create or administer training and awareness presentations or materials. Attend professional meetings, read literature, and participate in training or other educational offerings to keep abreast of new developments and technologies related to disaster recovery and business continuity. Test documented disaster recovery strategies and plans. Review existing disaster recovery, crisis management, or business continuity plans. Recommend or implement methods to monitor, evaluate, or enable resolution of safety, operations, or compliance interruptions. Prepare reports summarizing operational results, financial performance, or accomplishments of specified objectives, goals, or plans.

Education/Training Required: Work experience plus degree. **Education and Training Program:** Business Administration and Management, General. **Knowledge/Courses:** Public Safety and Security; Telecommunications; Administration and Management; Communications and Media; Geography; Economics and Accounting.

Personality Type: No data available. **Career Cluster:** 04 Business, Management, and Administration. **Career Pathway:** 04.1 Management.

Skills: Management of Financial Resources; Management of Material Resources; Complex Problem Solving; Systems Analysis; Systems Evaluation; Judgement and Decision Making; Operations Analysis; Critical Thinking.

Work Environment: Indoors; sitting.

Job Specialization: Customs Brokers

Prepare customs documentation, and ensure that shipments meet all applicable laws to facilitate the import and export of goods. Determine and track duties and taxes payable, and process payments on behalf of client. Sign documents under a power of attorney. Represent clients in meetings with customs officials, and apply for duty refunds and tariff reclassifications. Coordinate transportation and storage of imported goods. Sign documents on behalf of clients, using powers of attorney. Provide advice on transportation options, types of carriers, or shipping routes. Post bonds for the products being imported, or assist clients in obtaining bonds. Insure cargo against loss, damage, or pilferage. Obtain line releases for frequent shippers of low-risk commodities, high-volume entries, or multiple-container loads. Contract with freight forwarders for destination services. Arrange for transportation, warehousing, or product distribution of imported or exported products. Suggest best methods of packaging or labeling products. Request or compile necessary import documentation, such as customs invoices, certificates of origin, and cargo-control documents. Stay abreast of changes in import or export laws or regulations by reading current literature, attending meetings or conferences, or conferring with colleagues. Quote duty and tax rates on goods to be imported, based on federal tariffs and excise taxes. Prepare papers for shippers to appeal duty charges. Pay, or arrange for payment of, taxes and duties on shipments. Monitor or trace the location of goods.

Maintain relationships with customs brokers in other ports to expedite clearing of cargo. Inform importers and exporters of steps to reduce duties and taxes. Confer with officials in various agencies to facilitate clearance of goods through customs and quarantine. Classify goods according to tariff coding system.

Education/Training Required: Postsecondary vocational training. **Education and Training Program:** Traffic, Customs, and Transportation Clerk/Technician Training. **Knowledge/Courses:** Clerical Practices; Geography; Transportation; Sales and Marketing; Law and Government; Economics and Accounting.

Personality Type: Enterprising-Conventional. **Career Cluster:** 04 Business, Management, and Administration. **Career Pathway:** 04.1 Management.

Skills: Management of Financial Resources; Management of Material Resources; Negotiation; Programming; Mathematics; Management of Personnel Resources; Writing; Systems Analysis.

Work Environment: Indoors; sitting.

Job Specialization: Energy Auditors

Conduct energy audits of buildings, building systems, and process systems. May also conduct investment-grade audits of buildings or systems. Identify and prioritize energy-saving measures. Prepare audit reports containing energy analysis results and recommendations for energy cost savings. Inspect or evaluate building envelopes, mechanical systems, electrical systems, or process systems to determine the energy consumption of each system. Collect and analyze field data related to energy usage. Perform tests such as blower-door tests to locate air leaks. Calculate potential for energy savings. Educate customers on energy efficiency, or answer questions on topics such as the costs of running household appliances and the selection of energy-efficient appliances. Recommend energy-efficient technologies or alternate energy sources. Prepare job specification sheets for home energy improvements such as at-

tic insulation, window retrofits, and heating system upgrades. Quantify energy consumption to establish baselines for energy use and need. Identify opportunities to improve the operation, maintenance, or energy efficiency of building or process systems. Analyze technical feasibility of energy-saving measures using knowledge of engineering, energy production, energy use, construction, maintenance, system operation, or process systems. Analyze energy bills including utility rates or tariffs to gather historical energy-usage data.

Education/Training Required: Associate degree. **Education and Training Program:** Energy Management and Systems Technology/Technician. **Knowledge/Courses:** Building and Construction; Physics; Sales and Marketing; Design; Clerical Practices; Mechanical Devices.

Personality Type: Conventional-Enterprising. **Career Cluster:** 04 Business, Management, and Administration. **Career Pathway:** 04.1 Management.

Skills: Operations Analysis; Science; Systems Evaluation; Systems Analysis; Mathematics; Management of Financial Resources; Operation and Control; Writing.

Work Environment: More often outdoors than indoors; standing; using hands; very hot or cold; bright or inadequate lighting; contaminants; cramped work space; high places.

Job Specialization: Online Merchants

Plan, direct, or coordinate retail activities of businesses operating online. May perform duties such as preparing business strategies, buying merchandise, managing inventory, implementing marketing activities, fulfilling and shipping online orders, and balancing financial records. Participate in online forums and conferences to stay abreast of online retailing trends, techniques, and security threats. Upload digital media, such as photos, video, or scanned images to online storefront, auction sites, or other shopping websites. Order or purchase merchandise to maintain optimal inventory levels. Maintain inventory of shipping supplies, such as boxes, labels, tape, bubble wrap, loose packing materials, and tape guns. Integrate online retailing strategy with physical and catalogue retailing operations. Determine and set product prices. Disclose merchant information and terms and policies of transactions in online and offline materials. Deliver e-mail confirmation of completed transactions and shipment. Create, manage, and automate orders and invoices using order management and invoicing software. Create and maintain database of customer accounts. Create and distribute offline promotional material, such as brochures, pamphlets, business cards, stationary, and signage. Collaborate with search engine shopping specialists to place marketing content in desired online locations. Cancel orders based on customer requests or problems with inventory or delivery. Transfer digital media, such as music, video, and software, to customers via the Internet. Select and purchase technical web services, such as web hosting services, online merchant accounts, shopping cart software, payment gateway software, and spyware.

Education/Training Required: Work experience in a related occupation. **Education and Training Program:** E-Commerce/Electronic Commerce. **Knowledge/Courses:** No data available.

Personality Type: Enterprising-Conventional-Realistic. **Career Cluster:** 14 Marketing, Sales, and Service. **Career Pathway:** 14.2 Professional Sales and Marketing.

Skills: No data available.

Work Environment: No data available.

Job Specialization: Security Management Specialists

Conduct security assessments for organizations, and design security systems and processes. May specialize in areas such as physical security, personnel security, and information security. May work in fields such as health care, banking, gam-ing, security engineering, or manufacturing.** Prepare documentation for case reports or court proceedings. Review design drawings or technical documents for completeness, correctness, or appropriateness. Monitor tapes or digital recordings to identify the source of losses. Interview witnesses or suspects to identify persons responsible for security breaches, establish losses, pursue prosecutions, or obtain restitution. Budget and schedule security design work. Develop conceptual designs of security systems. Respond to emergency situations on an on-call basis. Train personnel in security procedures or use of security equipment. Prepare, maintain, or update security procedures, security system drawings, or related documentation. Monitor the work of contractors in the design, construction, and startup phases of security systems. Inspect security design features, installations, or programs to ensure compliance with applicable standards or regulations. Inspect fire, intruder detection, or other security systems. Engineer, install, maintain, or repair security systems, programmable logic controls, or other security-related electronic systems. Recommend improvements in security systems or procedures. Develop or review specifications for design or construction of security systems. Design security policies, programs, or practices to ensure adequate security relating to issues such as protection of assets, alarm response, and access card use.

Education/Training Required: Bachelor's degree. **Education and Training Program:** Security and Loss Prevention Services. **Knowledge/Courses:** No data available.

Personality Type: Realistic-Investigative-Conventional. **Career Cluster:** 04 Business, Management, and Administration. **Career Pathway:** 04.1 Management.

Skills: No data available.

Work Environment: No data available.

Job Specialization: Sustainability Specialists

Address organizational sustainability issues, such as waste stream management, green building practices, and green procurement plans. Review and revise sustainability proposals or policies. Research or review regulatory, technical, or market issues related to sustainability. Identify or investigate violations of natural resources, waste management, recycling, or other environmental policies. Identify or create new sustainability indicators. Write grant applications, rebate applications, or project proposals to secure funding for sustainability projects. Provide technical or administrative support for sustainability programs or issues. Identify or procure needed resources to implement sustainability programs or projects. Create or maintain plans or other documents related to sustainability projects. Develop reports or presentations to communicate the effectiveness of sustainability initiatives. Create marketing or outreach media, such as brochures or websites, to communicate sustainability issues, procedures, or objectives. Collect information about waste stream management or green building practices to inform decision-makers. Assess or propose sustainability initiatives, considering factors such as cost effectiveness, technical feasibility, and acceptance. Monitor or track sustainability indicators, such as energy usage, natural resource usage, waste generation, and recycling. Develop sustainability project goals, objectives, initiatives, or strategies in collaboration with other sustainability professionals.

Education/Training Required: Bachelor's degree. **Education and Training Program:** Business Administration and Management, General. **Knowledge/Courses:** No data available.

Personality Type: No data available. **Career Cluster:** 04 Business, Management, and Administration. **Career Pathway:** 04.1 Management.

Skills: No data available.

Work Environment: No data available.

Cargo and Freight Agents

- ❋ Personality Type: Conventional-Enterprising
- ❋ Annual Earnings: $37,150
- ❋ Earnings Growth Potential: Medium (40.5%)
- ❋ Growth: 23.9%
- ❋ Annual Job Openings: 4,030
- ❋ Self-Employed: 0.3%

Considerations for Job Outlook: More agents should be needed to handle the growing number of shipments resulting from expected increases in cargo traffic. Job prospects should be good.

Expedite and route movement of incoming and outgoing cargo and freight shipments in airline, train, and trucking terminals and shipping docks. Take orders from customers, and arrange pickup of freight and cargo for delivery to loading platform. Prepare and examine bills of lading to determine shipping charges and tariffs. Negotiate and arrange transport of goods with shipping or freight companies. Notify consignees, passengers, or customers of the arrival of freight or baggage, and arrange for delivery. Advise clients on transportation and payment methods. Prepare manifests showing baggage, mail, and freight weights and number of passengers on airplanes, and transmit data to destinations. Determine method of shipment, and prepare bills of lading, invoices, and other shipping documents. Check import/export documentation to determine cargo contents, and classify goods into different fee or tariff groups using a tariff coding system. Estimate freight or postal rates, and record shipment costs and weights. Enter shipping information into a computer by hand or by using a handheld scanner that reads bar codes on goods. Retrieve stored items, and trace lost shipments as necessary. Pack goods for shipping, using tools such as staplers, strapping machines, and hammers. Direct delivery trucks to shipping doors or designated marshalling areas, and help load and unload goods safely. Inspect and count items received, and check them against invoices or other documents, recording shortages and rejecting damaged goods. Install straps, braces, and padding to loads to prevent shifting or damage during shipment. Keep records of all goods shipped, received, and stored. Coordinate and supervise activities of workers engaged in packing and shipping merchandise. Arrange insurance coverage for goods.

Education/Training Required: Moderate-term on-the-job training. **Education and Training Program:** General Office Occupations and Clerical Services. **Knowledge/Courses:** Transportation; Geography; Customer and Personal Service; Clerical Practices; Administration and Management.

Career Cluster: 04 Business, Management, and Administration. **Career Pathway:** 04.6 Administrative and Information Support.

Skills: Negotiation; Service Orientation; Time Management; Mathematics; Speaking; Systems Evaluation; Persuasion; Critical Thinking.

Work Environment: Indoors; sitting; repetitive motions.

Job Specialization: Freight Forwarders

Research rates, routings, or modes of transport for shipment of products. Maintain awareness of regulations affecting the international movement of cargo. Make arrangements for additional services such as storage and inland transportation. Select shipment routes, based on nature of goods shipped, transit times, or security needs. Determine efficient and cost-effective methods of moving goods from one location to another. Reserve necessary space on ships, aircraft, trains, or trucks. Arrange delivery or storage of goods at destinations. Arrange for special transport of sensitive cargoes, such as livestock, food, and medical supplies. Assist clients in obtaining insurance reimbursements. Calculate weight, volume, or cost of goods to be moved. Complete shipping documentation, such as including bills of lading, packing lists, dock receipts, and certificates of origin. Consolidate loads with a common destina-

tion to reduce costs to individual shippers. Inform clients of factors such as shipping options, timelines, transfers, and regulations affecting shipments. Keep records of goods dispatched and received. Maintain current knowledge of relevant legislation, political situations, or other factors that could affect freight shipping. Monitor and record locations of goods in transit. Negotiate shipping rates with freight carriers. Obtain or arrange cargo insurance. Pay, or arrange for payment of, freight and insurance fees, or other charges. Prepare invoices and cost quotations for freight transportation. Recommend or arrange appropriate merchandise packing methods, according to climate, terrain, weight, nature of goods, or costs. Verify proper packaging and labeling of exported goods.

Education/Training Required: Moderate-term on-the-job training. **Education and Training Program:** General Office Occupations and Clerical Services. **Knowledge/Courses:** No data available.

Personality Type: Conventional-Enterprising. **Career Cluster:** 04 Business, Management, and Administration. **Career Pathway:** 04.6 Administrative and Information Support.

Skills: No data available.

Work Environment: No data available.

Claims Adjusters, Examiners, and Investigators

- ❋ Personality Type: Conventional-Enterprising
- ❋ Annual Earnings: $58,620
- ❋ Earnings Growth Potential: Medium (39.1%)
- ❋ Growth: 7.1%
- ❋ Annual Job Openings: 9,560
- ❋ Self-Employed: 1.6%

Considerations for Job Outlook: Job growth for adjusters and claims examiners should grow along with the growth of the health-care industry. Employment growth for insurance investigators should be tempered by productivity increases associated with the Internet. Keen competition is expected for investigator jobs.

Job Specialization: Claims Examiners, Property and Casualty Insurance

Review settled insurance claims to determine that payments and settlements have been made in accordance with company practices and procedures. Report overpayments, underpayments, and other irregularities. Confer with legal counsel on claims requiring litigation. Investigate, evaluate, and settle claims, applying technical knowledge and human relations skills to effect fair and prompt disposal of cases and to contribute to a reduced loss ratio. Pay and process claims within designated authority level. Adjust reserves or provide reserve recommendations to ensure that reserve activities are consistent with corporate policies. Enter claim payments, reserves, and new claims on computer system, inputting concise yet sufficient file documentation. Resolve complex severe exposure claims, using high-service-oriented file handling. Maintain claim files such as records of settled claims and an inventory of claims requiring detailed analysis. Verify and analyze data used in settling claims to ensure that claims are valid and that settlements are made according to company practices and procedures. Examine claims investigated by insurance adjusters, further investigating questionable claims to determine whether to authorize payments. Present cases, and participate in their discussion at claim committee meetings. Contact or interview claimants, doctors, medical specialists, or employers to get additional information. Confer with legal counsel on claims requiring litigation. Report overpayments, underpayments, and other irregularities. Communicate with reinsurance brokers to obtain information necessary for processing claims. Supervise claims adjusters to ensure that adjusters have followed proper methods.

Education/Training Required: Long-term on-the-job training. **Education and Training Programs:**

Health/Medical Claims Examiner Training; Insurance. **Knowledge/Courses:** Customer and Personal Service; Law and Government; Building and Construction; Administration and Management; English Language; Clerical Practices.

Personality Type: Conventional-Enterprising. **Career Cluster:** 06 Finance. **Career Pathway:** 06.4 Insurance Services.

Skills: Negotiation; Persuasion; Service Orientation; Reading Comprehension; Writing; Critical Thinking; Management of Financial Resources; Mathematics.

Work Environment: Indoors; sitting; repetitive motions; noise.

Job Specialization: Insurance Adjusters, Examiners, and Investigators

Investigate, analyze, and determine the extent of insurance company's liability concerning personal, casualty, or property loss or damages, and attempt to effect settlement with claimants. Correspond with or interview medical specialists, agents, witnesses, or claimants to compile information. Calculate benefit payments, and approve payment of claims within a certain monetary limit. Interview or correspond with claimant and witnesses, consult police and hospital records, and inspect property damage to determine extent of liability. Investigate and assess damage to property. Examine claims forms and other records to determine insurance coverage. Analyze information gathered by investigation, and report findings and recommendations. Negotiate claim settlements, and recommend litigation when settlement cannot be negotiated. Collect evidence to support contested claims in court. Prepare report of findings of investigation. Interview or correspond with agents and claimants to correct errors or omissions and to investigate questionable claims. Refer questionable claims to investigator or claims adjuster for investigation or settlement. Examine titles to property to determine validity, and act as company agent in transactions with property owners. Obtain credit information from banks and other credit services. Communicate with former associates to verify employment record and to obtain background information regarding persons or businesses applying for credit.

Education/Training Required: Long-term on-the-job training. **Education and Training Programs:** Health/Medical Claims Examiner Training; Insurance. **Knowledge/Courses:** Customer and Personal Service; Clerical Practices; Building and Construction; English Language; Law and Government; Mathematics.

Personality Type: Conventional-Enterprising. **Career Cluster:** 06 Finance. **Career Pathway:** 06.4 Insurance Services.

Skills: Management of Financial Resources; Negotiation; Mathematics; Critical Thinking; Active Listening; Speaking; Reading Comprehension; Writing.

Work Environment: Indoors; sitting; repetitive motions.

Compensation, Benefits, and Job Analysis Specialists

- ❋ Personality Type: Conventional-Enterprising
- ❋ Annual Earnings: $57,000
- ❋ Earnings Growth Potential: Medium (37.4%)
- ❋ Growth: 23.6%
- ❋ Annual Job Openings: 6,050
- ❋ Self-Employed: 1.6%

Considerations for Job Outlook: Efforts to recruit and retain employees, the growing importance of employee training, and new legal standards are expected to increase employment of these workers. College graduates and those with certification should have the best opportunities.

Conduct programs of compensation and benefits

and job analysis for employer. May specialize in specific areas, such as position classification and pension programs. Evaluate job positions, determining classification, exempt or non-exempt status, and salary. Ensure company compliance with federal and state laws, including reporting requirements. Advise managers and employees on state and federal employment regulations, collective agreements, benefit and compensation policies, personnel procedures, and classification programs. Plan, develop, evaluate, improve, and communicate methods and techniques for selecting, promoting, compensating, evaluating, and training workers. Provide advice on the resolution of classification and salary complaints. Prepare occupational classifications, job descriptions, and salary scales. Assist in preparing and maintaining personnel records and handbooks. Prepare reports, such as organization and flow charts, and career path reports, to summarize job analysis and evaluation and compensation analysis information. Administer employee insurance, pension, and savings plans, working with insurance brokers and plan carriers. Negotiate collective agreements on behalf of employers or workers, and mediate labor disputes and grievances. Develop, implement, administer, and evaluate personnel and labor relations programs, including performance appraisal, affirmative action, and employment equity programs. Perform multifactor data and cost analyses that may be used in areas such as support of collective bargaining agreements.

Education/Training Required: Bachelor's degree. **Education and Training Program:** Human Resources Management/Personnel Administration, General. **Knowledge/Courses:** Personnel and Human Resources; Economics and Accounting; Law and Government; Administration and Management; Mathematics; English Language.

Career Cluster: 04 Business, Management, and Administration. **Career Pathway:** 04.3 Human Resources.

Skills: Operations Analysis; Science; Systems Analysis; Mathematics; Programming; Systems Evaluation; Management of Financial Resources; Speaking.

Work Environment: Indoors; sitting.

Compliance Officers

* Personality Type: Conventional-Enterprising-Investigative
* Annual Earnings: $58,720
* Earnings Growth Potential: High (41.2%)
* Growth: 31.0%
* Annual Job Openings: 10,850
* Self-Employed: 1.4%

Considerations for Job Outlook: Much faster than average employment growth is projected.

Job Specialization: Coroners

Direct activities such as autopsies, pathological and toxicological analyses, and inquests relating to the investigation of deaths occurring within a legal jurisdiction to determine cause of death or to fix responsibility for accidental, violent, or unexplained deaths. Perform medico-legal examinations and autopsies, conducting preliminary examinations of the body in order to identify victims, to locate signs of trauma, and to identify factors that would indicate time of death. Inquire into the cause, manner, and circumstances of human deaths, and establish the identities of deceased persons. Direct activities of workers who conduct autopsies, perform pathological and toxicological analyses, and prepare documents for permanent records. Complete death certificates, including the assignment of a cause and manner of death. Observe and record the positions and conditions of bodies and of related evidence. Collect and document any pertinent medical history information. Observe, record, and preserve any objects or personal property related to deaths, including objects such as medication containers and suicide notes. Complete reports and forms required to finalize cases. Remove or supervise removal of bodies from death scenes, using the proper equipment and supplies, and arrange for transportation to morgues. Testify at inquests, hearings, and court trials. Interview persons present at death scenes to obtain information useful in determining the manner of death. Provide information concerning the circumstances of death to relatives of the deceased. Locate and document information regarding the next of kin, including their relationship to the deceased and the status of notification attempts.

Education/Training Required: Work experience in a related occupation. **Education and Training Program:** Public Administration. **Knowledge/Courses:** Medicine and Dentistry; Biology; Psychology; Therapy and Counseling; Chemistry; Law and Government.

Personality Type: Investigative-Realistic-Conventional. **Career Cluster:** 12 Law, Public Safety, Corrections, and Security. **Career Pathway:** 12.6 Inspection Services.

Skills: Science; Social Perceptiveness; Speaking; Critical Thinking; Management of Personnel Resources; Writing; Learning Strategies; Instructing.

Work Environment: More often indoors than outdoors; sitting; using hands; contaminants; exposed to disease or infections; hazardous equipment.

Job Specialization: Environmental Compliance Inspectors

Inspect and investigate sources of pollution to protect the public and environment and ensure conformance with federal, state, and local regulations and ordinances. Determine the nature of code violations and actions to be taken; issue written notices of violation; and participate in enforcement hearings as necessary. Examine permits, licenses, applications, and records to ensure compliance with licensing requirements. Prepare, organize, and maintain inspection records. Interview individuals to determine the nature of suspected violations and to obtain evidence of violations. Prepare written, oral, tabular, and graphic reports summarizing requirements and regulations, including enforcement and chain of custody documentation. Monitor follow-up actions in cases where violations were found, and review compliance-monitoring reports. Investigate complaints and suspected violations regarding illegal

Conventional-C

dumping, pollution, pesticides, product quality, or labeling laws. Inspect waste pretreatment, treatment, and disposal facilities and systems for conformance to federal, state, or local regulations. Inform individuals and groups of pollution control regulations and inspection findings, and explain how problems can be corrected. Determine sampling locations and methods, and collect water or wastewater samples for analysis, preserving samples with appropriate containers and preservation methods. Verify that hazardous chemicals are handled, stored, and disposed of in accordance with regulations. Research and keep informed of pertinent information and developments in areas such as EPA laws and regulations.

Education/Training Required: Long-term on-the-job training. **Education and Training Program:** Natural Resources Management and Policy, Other. **Knowledge/Courses:** Biology; Chemistry; Law and Government; Geography; Physics; Engineering and Technology.

Personality Type: Conventional-Investigative-Realistic. **Career Clusters:** 07 Government and Public Administration; 12 Law, Public Safety, Corrections, and Security; 16 Transportation, Distribution, and Logistics. **Career Pathways:** 07.6 Regulation; 12.6 Inspection Services; 16.6 Health, Safety, and Environmental Management.

Skills: Quality Control Analysis; Science; Programming; Troubleshooting; Mathematics; Reading Comprehension; Writing; Active Learning.

Work Environment: More often indoors than outdoors; sitting; contaminants.

Job Specialization: Equal Opportunity Representatives and Officers

Monitor and evaluate compliance with equal opportunity laws, guidelines, and policies to ensure that employment practices and contracting arrangements give equal opportunity without regard to race, religion, color, national origin, sex, age, or disability. Investigate employment practices and alleged violations of laws to document and correct discriminatory factors. Interpret civil rights laws and equal opportunity regulations for individuals and employers. Study equal opportunity complaints to clarify issues. Meet with persons involved in equal opportunity complaints to verify case information and to arbitrate and settle disputes. Coordinate, monitor, and revise complaint procedures to ensure timely processing and review of complaints. Prepare reports of selection, survey, and other statistics and recommendations for corrective action. Conduct surveys and evaluate findings to determine whether systematic discrimination exists. Develop guidelines for nondiscriminatory employment practices, and monitor their implementation and impact. Review company contracts to determine actions required to meet governmental equal opportunity provisions. Counsel newly hired members of minority and disadvantaged groups, informing them about details of civil rights laws. Provide information, technical assistance, and training to supervisors, managers, and employees on topics such as employee supervision, hiring, grievance procedures, and staff development. Verify that all job descriptions are submitted for review and approval and that descriptions meet regulatory standards. Act as liaisons between minority placement agencies and employers or between job search committees and other equal opportunity administrators.

Education/Training Required: Long-term on-the-job training. **Education and Training Program:** Public Administration and Social Service Professions, Other. **Knowledge/Courses:** Law and Government; Personnel and Human Resources; Clerical Practices; English Language; Customer and Personal Service; Administration and Management.

Personality Type: Social-Enterprising-Conventional. **Career Cluster:** 12 Law, Public Safety, Corrections, and Security. **Career Pathway:** 12.6 Inspection Services.

Skills: Persuasion; Reading Comprehension; Active Listening; Active Learning; Programming; Negotiation; Writing; Speaking.

Work Environment: Indoors; sitting; repetitive motions.

Job Specialization: Government Property Inspectors and Investigators

Investigate or inspect government property to ensure compliance with contract agreements and government regulations. Prepare correspondence, reports of inspections or investigations, and recommendations for action. Inspect government-owned equipment and materials in the possession of private contractors to ensure compliance with contracts and regulations and to prevent misuse. Examine records, reports, and documents to establish facts and detect discrepancies. Inspect manufactured or processed products to ensure compliance with contract specifications and legal requirements. Locate and interview plaintiffs, witnesses, or representatives of business or government to gather facts relevant to inspections or alleged violations. Recommend legal or administrative action to protect government property. Submit samples of products to government laboratories for testing as required. Coordinate with and assist law enforcement agencies in matters of mutual concern. Testify in court or at administrative proceedings concerning findings of investigations. Collect, identify, evaluate, and preserve case evidence. Monitor investigations of suspected offenders to ensure that they are conducted in accordance with constitutional requirements. Investigate applications for special licenses or permits, as well as alleged violations of licenses or permits.

Education/Training Required: Long-term on-the-job training. **Education and Training Program:** Building/Home/Construction Inspection/Inspector. **Knowledge/Courses:** Building and Construction; Engineering and Technology; Public Safety and Security; Mechanical Devices; Transportation; Computers and Electronics.

Personality Type: Conventional-Enterprising-Realistic. **Career Cluster:** 12 Law, Public Safety, Corrections, and Security. **Career Pathway:** 12.6 Inspection Services.

Skills: Quality Control Analysis; Programming; Persuasion; Operation and Control; Writing; Systems Evaluation; Speaking; Judgment and Decision Making.

Work Environment: More often outdoors than indoors; sitting; noise; very hot or cold; contaminants.

Job Specialization: Licensing Examiners and Inspectors

Examine, evaluate, and investigate eligibility for, conformity with, or liability under licenses or permits. Issue licenses to individuals meeting standards. Evaluate applications, records, and documents in order to gather information about eligibility or liability issues. Administer oral, written, road, or flight tests to license applicants. Score tests and observe equipment operation and control in order to rate ability of applicants. Advise licensees and other individuals or groups concerning licensing, permit, or passport regulations. Warn violators of infractions or penalties. Prepare reports of activities, evaluations, recommendations, and decisions. Prepare correspondence to inform concerned parties of licensing decisions and of appeals processes. Confer with and interview officials, technical or professional specialists, and applicants in order to obtain information or to clarify facts relevant to licensing decisions. Report law or regulation violations to appropriate boards and agencies. Visit establishments to verify that valid licenses and permits are displayed and that licensing standards are being upheld.

Education/Training Required: Long-term on-the-job training. **Education and Training Program:** Public Administration and Social Service Professions, Other. **Knowledge/Courses:** Clerical Practices; Customer and Personal Service; Law and Government; Foreign Language; Psychology; Public Safety and Security.

Personality Type: Conventional-Enterprising. **Career Cluster:** 12 Law, Public Safety, Corrections, and Security. **Career Pathway:** 12.6 Inspection Services.

Conventional-C

Skills: Quality Control Analysis; Judgment and Decision Making; Social Perceptiveness; Speaking; Operation Monitoring; Service Orientation; Systems Evaluation; Negotiation.

Work Environment: More often indoors than outdoors; sitting; using hands; repetitive motions; contaminants.

Job Specialization: Regulatory Affairs Specialists

Coordinate and document internal regulatory processes, such as internal audits, inspections, license renewals, or registrations. May compile and prepare materials for submission to regulatory agencies. Coordinate, prepare, or review regulatory submissions for domestic or international projects. Provide technical review of data or reports that will be incorporated into regulatory submissions to assure scientific rigor, accuracy, and clarity of presentation. Review product promotional materials, labeling, batch records, specification sheets, or test methods for compliance with applicable regulations and policies. Maintain current knowledge base of existing and emerging regulations, standards, or guidance documents. Interpret regulatory rules or rule changes and ensure that they are communicated through corporate policies and procedures. Advise project teams on subjects such as premarket regulatory requirements, export and labeling requirements, and clinical study compliance issues. Determine the types of regulatory submissions or internal documentation that are required in situations such as proposed device changes and labeling changes. Prepare or maintain technical files as necessary to obtain and sustain product approval. Coordinate efforts associated with the preparation of regulatory documents or submissions. Prepare or direct the preparation of additional information or responses as requested by regulatory agencies. Analyze product complaints, and make recommendations regarding their reportability. Escort government inspectors during inspections, and provide post-inspection follow-up information as requested.

Education/Training Required: Work experi-ence in a related occupation. **Education and Training Program:** Business Administration and Management, General. **Knowledge/Courses:** Law and Government; Biology; Medicine and Dentistry; Clerical Practices; English Language; Chemistry.

Personality Type: Conventional-Enterprising. **Career Cluster:** 12 Law, Public Safety, Corrections, and Security. **Career Pathway:** 12.6 Inspection Services.

Skills: Systems Analysis; Systems Evaluation; Judgment and Decision Making; Persuasion; Writing; Speaking; Coordination; Reading Comprehension.

Work Environment: Indoors; sitting.

Computer Occupations, All Other

Look for the job description among the Investigative jobs.

Cost Estimators

- Personality Type: Conventional-Enterprising
- Annual Earnings: $57,860
- Earnings Growth Potential: High (41.1%)
- Growth: 25.3%
- Annual Job Openings: 10,360
- Self-Employed: 2.0%

Considerations for Job Outlook: Projected employment gains will be driven primarily by increased construction and repair activity, particularly that related to infrastructure. Jobseekers with a degree or extensive experience should have the best opportunities. In manufacturing, jobseekers who have a degree and are familiar with cost estimation software should have the best prospects.

Prepare cost estimates for product manufacturing, construction projects, or services to aid management in bidding on or determining prices of

products or services. May specialize according to particular service performed or type of product manufactured. Consult with clients, vendors, personnel in other departments, or construction foremen to discuss and formulate estimates and resolve issues. Analyze blueprints and other documentation to prepare time, cost, materials, and labor estimates. Prepare estimates for use in selecting vendors or subcontractors. Confer with engineers, architects, owners, contractors, and subcontractors on changes and adjustments to cost estimates. Prepare estimates used by management for purposes such as planning, organizing, and scheduling work. Prepare cost and expenditure statements and other necessary documentation at regular intervals for the duration of the project. Assess cost-effectiveness of products, projects, or services, tracking actual costs relative to bids as projects develop. Set up cost-monitoring and cost-reporting systems and procedures. Conduct special studies to develop and establish standard hour and related cost data or to effect cost reductions. Review material and labor requirements to decide whether it is more cost-effective to produce or purchase components. Prepare and maintain a directory of suppliers, contractors, and subcontractors. Establish and maintain tendering processes, and conduct negotiations. Visit sites, and record information about access, drainage and topography, and availability of services such as water and electricity.

Education/Training Required: Bachelor's degree. **Education and Training Programs:** Business Administration and Management, General; Business/Commerce, General; Construction Engineering; Construction Engineering Technology/ Technician; Manufacturing Engineering; Materials Engineering; Mechanical Engineering. **Knowledge/ Courses:** Engineering and Technology; Mathematics; Economics and Accounting; Building and Construction; Design; Computers and Electronics.

Career Clusters: 02 Architecture and Construction; 04 Business, Management, and Administration; 13 Manufacturing; 15 Science, Technology, Engineering, and Mathematics. **Career Pathways:** 02.2 Construction; 04.1 Management; 13.1 Production; 15.1 Engineering and Technology.

Skills: Management of Financial Resources; Management of Material Resources; Mathematics; Programming; Systems Analysis; Persuasion; Active Learning; Active Listening.

Work Environment: Indoors; sitting.

Court Reporters

- ❋ Personality Type: Conventional-Enterprising
- ❋ Annual Earnings: $47,700
- ❋ Earnings Growth Potential: High (46.1%)
- ❋ Growth: 18.3%
- ❋ Annual Job Openings: 710
- ❋ Self-Employed: 14.0%

Considerations for Job Outlook: The continuing need for transcripts of legal proceedings, the growing demand for TV and other broadcast captioning, and the need to provide translating services for the deaf and the hard of hearing are expected to create jobs. Prospects should be excellent.

Use verbatim methods and equipment to capture, store, retrieve, and transcribe pretrial and trial proceedings or other information. Includes stenocaptioners who operate computerized stenographic captioning equipment to provide captions of live or prerecorded broadcasts for hearing-impaired viewers. Take notes in shorthand, or use a stenotype or shorthand machine that prints letters on a paper tape. Provide transcripts of proceedings upon request of judges, lawyers, or the public. Record verbatim proceedings of courts, legislative assemblies, committee meetings, and other proceedings, using computerized recording equipment, electronic stenograph machines, or stenomasks. Transcribe recorded proceedings in accordance with established formats. Ask speakers to clarify inaudible statements. File a legible transcript of records of a court case with the court clerk's office. File and store shorthand notes of court session. Respond to requests during court sessions to read portions of the proceedings already recorded. Record depositions and other proceedings for attorneys. Verify accura-

Conventional-C

cy of transcripts by checking copies against original records of proceedings and accuracy of rulings by checking with judges. Record symbols on computer disks or CD-ROM; then translate and display them as text in computer-aided transcription process.

Education/Training Required: Postsecondary vocational training. **Education and Training Program:** Court Reporting/Court Reporter. **Knowledge/Courses:** Clerical Practices; English Language; Computers and Electronics; Law and Government.

Career Cluster: 12 Law, Public Safety, Corrections, and Security. **Career Pathway:** 12.5 Legal Services.

Skills: Active Listening; Writing.

Work Environment: Indoors; sitting; using hands; repetitive motions.

Court, Municipal, and License Clerks

- ❋ Personality Type: Conventional-Enterprising
- ❋ Annual Earnings: $34,390
- ❋ Earnings Growth Potential: Low (35.0%)
- ❋ Growth: 8.2%
- ❋ Annual Job Openings: 4,460
- ❋ Self-Employed: 1.5%

Considerations for Job Outlook: About average employment growth is projected.

Job Specialization: Court Clerks

Perform clerical duties in court of law; prepare docket of cases to be called; secure information for judges; and contact witnesses, attorneys, and litigants to obtain information for court. Prepare dockets or calendars of cases to be called, using typewriters or computers. Record case dispositions, court orders, and arrangements made for payment of court fees. Answer inquiries from the general public regarding judicial procedures, court appearances, trial dates, adjournments, outstanding warrants, summonses, subpoenas, witness fees, and payment of fines. Prepare and issue orders of the court, including probation orders, release documentation, sentencing information, and summonses. Prepare documents recording the outcomes of court proceedings. Instruct parties about timing of court appearances. Explain procedures or forms to parties in cases or to the general public. Search files and contact witnesses, attorneys, and litigants to obtain information for the court. Follow procedures to secure courtrooms and exhibits such as money, drugs, and weapons. Amend indictments when necessary, and endorse indictments with pertinent information. Read charges and related information to the court, and, if necessary, record defendants' pleas. Swear in jury members, interpreters, witnesses, and defendants. Collect court fees or fines, and record amounts collected. Direct support staff in handling of paperwork processed by clerks' offices. Examine legal documents submitted to courts for adherence to laws or court procedures. Prepare and mark all applicable court exhibits and evidence.

Education/Training Required: Short-term on-the-job training. **Education and Training Program:** General Office Occupations and Clerical Services. **Knowledge/Courses:** Clerical Practices; Law and Government; Computers and Electronics.

Personality Type: Conventional-Enterprising-Realistic. **Career Cluster:** 04 Business, Management, and Administration. **Career Pathway:** 04.6 Administrative and Information Support.

Skills: Reading Comprehension; Writing; Negotiation; Active Listening; Time Management; Speaking; Service Orientation.

Work Environment: Indoors; sitting; using hands; repetitive motions; noise.

Job Specialization: License Clerks

Issue licenses or permits to qualified applicants. Obtain necessary information, record data, advise applicants on requirements, collect fees, and

Conventional-C

issue licenses. **May conduct oral, written, visual, or performance testing.** Collect prescribed fees for licenses. Code information on license applications for entry into computers. Evaluate information on applications to verify completeness and accuracy and to determine whether applicants are qualified to obtain desired licenses. Answer questions and provide advice to the public regarding licensing policies, procedures, and regulations. Maintain records of applications made and licensing fees collected. Question applicants to obtain required information, such as name, address, and age, and record data on prescribed forms. Update operational records and licensing information, using computer terminals. Inform customers by mail or telephone of additional steps they need to take to obtain licenses. Perform routine data entry and other office support activities, including creating, sorting, photocopying, distributing, and filing documents. Stock counters with adequate supplies of forms, film, licenses, and other required materials. Enforce canine licensing regulations, contacting non-compliant owners in person or by mail to inform them of the required regulations and potential enforcement actions. Assemble photographs with printed license information to produce completed documents. Prepare bank deposits, and take them to banks. Operate specialized photographic equipment to obtain photographs for drivers' licenses and photo identification cards.

Education/Training Required: Short-term on-the-job training. **Education and Training Program:** General Office Occupations and Clerical Services. **Knowledge/Courses:** Clerical Practices; Customer and Personal Service; Law and Government; Computers and Electronics.

Personality Type: Conventional-Enterprising. **Career Cluster:** 04 Business, Management, and Administration. **Career Pathway:** 04.6 Administrative and Information Support.

Skills: Service Orientation.

Work Environment: Indoors; sitting; using hands; repetitive motions; noise.

Job Specialization: Municipal Clerks

Draft agendas and bylaws for town or city council, record minutes of council meetings, answer official correspondence, keep fiscal records and accounts, and prepare reports on civic needs. Participate in the administration of municipal elections, including preparation and distribution of ballots, appointment and training of election officers, and tabulation and certification of results. Record and edit the minutes of meetings; then distribute them to appropriate officials and staff members. Plan and direct the maintenance, filing, safekeeping, and computerization of all municipal documents. Issue public notification of all official activities and meetings. Maintain and update documents such as municipal codes and city charters. Prepare meeting agendas and packets of related information. Prepare ordinances, resolutions, and proclamations so that they can be executed, recorded, archived, and distributed. Respond to requests for information from the public, other municipalities, state officials, and state and federal legislative offices. Maintain fiscal records and accounts. Perform budgeting duties, including assisting in budget preparation, expenditure review, and budget administration. Perform general office duties such as taking and transcribing dictation, typing and proofreading correspondence, distributing and filing official forms, and scheduling appointments. Coordinate and maintain office-tracking systems for correspondence and follow-up actions. Research information in the municipal archives upon request of public officials and private citizens. Perform contract administration duties, assisting with bid openings and the awarding of contracts.

Education/Training Required: Short-term on-the-job training. **Education and Training Program:** General Office Occupations and Clerical Services. **Knowledge/Courses:** Clerical Practices; Law and Government; Economics and Accounting; English Language; Personnel and Human Resources; Administration and Management.

Personality Type: Conventional-Enterprising. **Career Cluster:** 04 Business, Management, and Administration. **Career Pathway:** 04.6 Administrative and Information Support.

Skills: Management of Financial Resources; Writing; Reading Comprehension; Speaking; Active Listening; Critical Thinking; Service Orientation; Coordination.

Work Environment: Indoors; sitting.

Credit Analysts

- ❈ Personality Type: Conventional-Enterprising
- ❈ Annual Earnings: $58,850
- ❈ Earnings Growth Potential: Medium (39.2%)
- ❈ Growth: 15.0%
- ❈ Annual Job Openings: 2,430
- ❈ Self-Employed: 0.0%

Considerations for Job Outlook: Faster than average employment growth is projected.

Analyze current credit data and financial statements of individuals or firms to determine the degree of risk involved in extending credit or lending money. Prepare reports with this credit information for use in decision-making. Evaluate customer records, and recommend payment plans based on earnings, savings data, payment history, and purchase activity. Confer with credit association and other business representatives to exchange credit information. Complete loan applications, including credit analyses and summaries of loan requests, and submit to loan committees for approval. Generate financial ratios, using computer programs, to evaluate customers' financial status. Review individual or commercial customer files to identify and select delinquent accounts for collection. Compare liquidity, profitability, and credit histories of establishments being evaluated with those of similar establishments in the same industries and geographic locations. Consult with customers to resolve complaints and verify financial and credit transactions. Analyze financial data such as income growth, quality of management, and market share to determine expected

profitability of loans.

Education/Training Required: Bachelor's degree. **Education and Training Programs:** Accounting; Credit Management; Finance, General. **Knowledge/Courses:** Economics and Accounting; Clerical Practices; Mathematics; Law and Government; English Language.

Career Clusters: 04 Business, Management, and Administration; 06 Finance. **Career Pathways:** 04.2 Business, Financial Management, and Accounting; 06.1 Financial and Investment Planning; 06.2 Business Financial Management; 06.3 Banking and Related Services.

Skills: Mathematics; Programming; Systems Evaluation; Management of Financial Resources; Critical Thinking; Operations Analysis; Active Learning; Systems Analysis.

Work Environment: Indoors; sitting; repetitive motions.

Database Administrators

- ❈ Personality Type: Conventional-Investigative
- ❈ Annual Earnings: $73,490
- ❈ Earnings Growth Potential: High (43.4%)
- ❈ Growth: 20.3%
- ❈ Annual Job Openings: 4,440
- ❈ Self-Employed: 0.6%

Considerations for Job Outlook: Employment of these workers should grow as organizations increasingly collect and organize data. Job prospects are expected to be excellent.

Coordinate changes to computer databases; test and implement the databases, applying knowledge of database management systems. May plan, coordinate, and implement security measures to safeguard computer databases. Develop standards and guidelines to guide the use and acquisition of software and to protect vulnerable information. Modify existing databases and database management systems, or direct programmers and analysts to make changes. Test programs or databases, correct errors, and make necessary modifications. Plan, coordinate, and implement security measures to safeguard information in computer files against accidental or unauthorized damage, modification, or disclosure. Approve, schedule, plan, and supervise the installation and testing of new products and improvements to computer systems such as the installation of new databases. Train users, and answer questions. Establish and calculate optimum values for database parameters, using manuals and calculator. Specify users and user access levels for each segment of database. Develop data model describing data elements and how they are used, following procedures and using pen, template, or computer software. Develop methods for integrating different products so they work properly together such as customizing commercial databases to fit specific needs. Review project requests describing database user needs to estimate time and cost required to accomplish project. Review procedures in database-management system manuals for making changes to database. Work as part of a project team to coordinate database development and determine project scope and limitations.

Education/Training Required: Bachelor's degree. **Education and Training Program:** Data Modeling/ Warehousing and Database Administration. **Knowledge/Courses:** Computers and Electronics; Telecommunications; Clerical Practices; Communications and Media; Engineering and Technology; Mathematics.

Career Cluster: 11 Information Technology. **Career Pathways:** 04.4 Business Analysis; 11.2 Information Support Services; 11.4 Programming and Software Development.

Skills: Programming; Technology Design; Troubleshooting; Systems Evaluation; Operations Analysis; Management of Financial Resources; Systems Analysis; Mathematics.

Work Environment: Indoors; sitting; using hands; repetitive motions; noise.

Dental Assistants

- ❋ Personality Type: Conventional-Realistic-Social
- ❋ Annual Earnings: $33,470
- ❋ Earnings Growth Potential: Low (32.2%)
- ❋ Growth: 35.7%
- ❋ Annual Job Openings: 16,100
- ❋ Self-Employed: 0.0%

Considerations for Job Outlook: An aging population and increased emphasis on preventative dental care will create more demand for dental services, and dentists are expected to hire more assistants to perform routine tasks. Job prospects should be excellent.

Assist dentist, set up patient and equipment, and keep records. Prepare patient, sterilize and disinfect instruments, set up instrument trays, prepare materials, and assist dentist during dental procedures. Expose dental diagnostic X-rays. Record treatment information in patient records. Take and record medical and dental histories and vital signs of patients. Provide postoperative instructions prescribed by dentist. Assist dentist in management of medical and dental emergencies. Pour, trim, and polish study casts. Instruct patients in oral hygiene and plaque-control programs. Make preliminary impressions for study casts and occlusal registrations for mounting study casts. Clean and polish removable appliances. Clean teeth, using dental instruments. Apply protective coating of fluoride to teeth. Fabricate temporary restorations and custom impressions from preliminary impressions. Schedule appointments, prepare bills, and receive payment for dental services; complete insurance forms; and maintain records, manually or using computer.

Education/Training Required: Moderate-term on-the-job training. **Education and Training Program:** Dental Assisting/Assistant. **Knowledge/Courses:** Medicine and Dentistry; Customer and Personal Service; Psychology; Sales and Marketing.

Conventional-D

Career Cluster: 08 Health Science. **Career Pathway:** 08.1 Therapeutic Services.

Skills: Repairing; Equipment Maintenance; Operation Monitoring; Equipment Selection; Science; Service Orientation; Operation and Control; Quality Control Analysis.

Work Environment: Indoors; standing; walking and running; using hands; bending or twisting the body; repetitive motions; contaminants; exposed to radiation; exposed to disease or infections; hazardous conditions.

Detectives and Criminal Investigators

Look for the job description among the Enterprising jobs.

Executive Secretaries and Executive Administrative Assistants

- Personality Type: Conventional-Enterprising
- Annual Earnings: $43,520
- Earnings Growth Potential: Low (34.0%)
- Growth: 12.8%
- Annual Job Openings: 41,920
- Self-Employed: 1.3%

Considerations for Job Outlook: Projected employment growth varies by occupational specialty. Faster than average growth is expected for medical secretaries and legal secretaries; average growth for executive secretaries and administrative assistants; and slower than average growth for secretaries other than legal, medical, or executive, who account for most of the workers in these specialties. Many opportunities are expected.

Provide high-level administrative support by conducting research; preparing statistical reports; handling information requests; and performing clerical functions such as preparing correspondence, receiving visitors, arranging conference calls, and scheduling meetings. May also train and supervise lower-level clerical staff. Manage and maintain executives' schedules. Prepare invoices, reports, memos, letters, financial statements, and other documents, using word-processing, spreadsheet, database, or presentation software. Open, sort, and distribute incoming correspondence, including faxes and e-mail. Read and analyze incoming memos, submissions, and reports to determine their significance and plan their distribution. File and retrieve corporate documents, records, and reports. Greet visitors, and determine whether they should be given access to specific individuals. Prepare responses to correspondence containing routine inquiries. Perform general office duties such as ordering supplies, maintaining records-management systems, and performing basic bookkeeping work. Prepare agendas and make arrangements for committee, board, and other meetings. Make travel arrangements for executives. Conduct research, compile data, and prepare papers for consideration and presentation by executives, committees, and boards of directors. Compile, transcribe, and distribute minutes of meetings. Attend meetings to record minutes. Coordinate and direct office services, such as records and budget preparation, personnel, and housekeeping, to aid executives. Meet with individuals, special-interest groups, and others on behalf of executives, committees, and boards of directors. Set up and oversee administrative policies and procedures for offices or organizations. Supervise and train other clerical staff.

Education/Training Required: Work experience in a related occupation. **Education and Training Programs:** Administrative Assistant and Secretarial Science, General; Executive Assistant/Executive Secretary Training; Medical Administrative/Executive Assistant and Medical Secretary Training. **Knowledge/Courses:** Clerical Practices; Personnel and Human Resources.

Career Clusters: 04 Business, Management, and Administration; 08 Health Science. **Career Pathways:** 04.6 Administrative and Information Support; 08.3 Health Informatics.

Skills: Service Orientation; Programming; Active Listening; Writing; Speaking; Time Management; Reading Comprehension; Monitoring.

Work Environment: Indoors; sitting; repetitive motions; noise.

Financial Analysts

- ❋ Personality Type: Conventional-Investigative-Enterprising
- ❋ Annual Earnings: $74,350
- ❋ Earnings Growth Potential: Medium (40.2%)
- ❋ Growth: 19.8%
- ❋ Annual Job Openings: 9,520
- ❋ Self-Employed: 4.6%

Considerations for Job Outlook: As investments become more numerous and complex, these workers will be needed for their expertise. Keen competition for openings is expected; jobseekers with a graduate degree and certification should have the best opportunities.

Conduct quantitative analyses of information affecting investment programs of public or private institutions. Assemble spreadsheets and draw charts and graphs used to illustrate technical reports, using computer. Analyze financial information to produce forecasts of business, industry, and economic conditions for use in making investment decisions. Maintain knowledge and stay abreast of developments in the fields of industrial technology, business, finance, and economic theory. Interpret data affecting investment programs, such as price, yield, stability, future trends in investment risks, and economic influences. Monitor fundamental economic, industrial, and corporate developments through the analysis of information obtained from financial publications and services, investment banking firms, govern-ment agencies, trade publications, company sources, and personal interviews. Recommend investments and investment timing to companies, investment firm staff, or the investing public. Determine the prices at which securities should be syndicated and offered to the public. Prepare plans of action for investment based on financial analyses. Evaluate and compare the relative quality of various securities in a given industry. Present oral and written reports on general economic trends, individual corporations, and entire industries. Contact brokers and purchase investments for companies according to company policy. Collaborate with investment bankers to attract new corporate clients to securities firms.

Education/Training Required: Bachelor's degree. **Education and Training Programs:** Accounting and Business/Management; Accounting and Finance; Finance, General. **Knowledge/Courses:** Economics and Accounting; Mathematics; Law and Government; Clerical Practices; Administration and Management; English Language.

Career Clusters: 04 Business, Management, and Administration; 06 Finance. **Career Pathways:** 04.2 Business, Financial Management, and Accounting; 06.1 Financial and Investment Planning; 06.2 Business Financial Management.

Skills: Systems Analysis; Mathematics; Systems Evaluation; Management of Financial Resources; Operations Analysis; Writing; Active Learning; Judgment and Decision Making.

Work Environment: Indoors; sitting.

Financial Managers

Look for the job description among the Enterprising jobs.

Financial Specialists, All Other

- ❋ Personality Type: Conventional-Investigative-Enterprising

Conventional-F

❋ Annual Earnings: $60,980
❋ Earnings Growth Potential: High (41.0%)
❋ Growth: 10.5%
❋ Annual Job Openings: 4,320
❋ Self-Employed: 0.9%

Considerations for Job Outlook: About average employment growth is projected.

This occupation includes all financial specialists not listed separately. Because this is a highly diverse occupation, no data is available for some information topics.

Education/Training Required: Bachelor's degree. **Education and Training Program:** Finance and Financial Management Services, Other.

Career Cluster: 06 Finance. **Career Pathway:** 06.1 Financial and Investment Planning.

Job Specialization: Financial Quantitative Analysts

Develop quantitative financial products used to inform individuals and financial institutions engaged in saving, lending, investing, borrowing, or managing risk. Investigate methods for financial analysis to create mathematical models used to develop improved analytical tools and advanced financial investment instruments. Write requirements documentation for use by software developers. Provide application or analytical support to researchers and traders on such issues as valuations and data. Identify, track, and maintain metrics for trading-system operations. Collaborate in the development and testing of new analytical software to ensure compliance with user requirements, specification, or scope. Research new products or analytics to determine their usefulness. Maintain and modify all analytic models in use. Produce written summaries of research results. Interpret results of analytical procedures. Develop core analytical capabilities or model libraries, using advanced statistical, quantitative, and econometric techniques. Define and recommend model specifications or data-collection

methods. Consult financial industry personnel, such as traders, to determine the need for new or improved analytical applications. Confer with other financial engineers and analysts to understand trading strategies, market dynamics, and trading system performance to inform development of quantitative techniques. Collaborate with product development teams to research, model, validate, or implement quantitative structured solutions for new or expanded markets. Research and develop analytical tools to address issues such as portfolio construction and optimization, performance measurement, attribution, profit-and-loss measurement, and pricing models.

Education/Training Required: Master's degree. **Education and Training Program:** Financial Planning and Services. **Knowledge/Courses:** No data available.

Personality Type: Investigative-Conventional. **Career Cluster:** 06 Finance. **Career Pathway:** 06.1 Financial and Investment Planning.

Skills: No data available.

Work Environment: No data available.

Job Specialization: Fraud Examiners, Investigators, and Analysts

Obtain evidence, take statements, produce reports, and testify to findings regarding resolution of fraud allegations. May coordinate fraud detection and prevention activities. Maintain knowledge of current events and trends in such areas as money laundering and criminal tools and techniques. Train others in fraud detection and prevention techniques. Research or evaluate new technologies for use in fraud detection systems. Prepare evidence for presentation in court. Obtain and serve subpoenas. Negotiate with responsible parties to arrange for recovery of losses due to fraud. Conduct field surveillance to gather case-related information. Arrest individuals to be charged with fraud. Testify in court regarding investigation findings. Advise businesses or agencies on ways to improve fraud detection. Review reports of suspected fraud to determine need for further investigation. Prepare written reports of investigation findings. Recommend actions in fraud cases. Lead, or participate in, fraud investigation teams. Interview witnesses or suspects, and take statements. Design, implement, or maintain fraud-detection tools or procedures. Gather financial documents related to investigations. Evaluate business operations to identify risk areas for fraud. Document all investigative activities. Create and maintain logs, records, or databases of information about fraudulent activity. Coordinate investigative efforts with law enforcement officers and attorneys. Conduct in-depth investigations of suspicious financial activity, such as suspected money-laundering efforts.

Education/Training Required: Work experience plus degree. **Education and Training Program:** Financial Forensics and Fraud Investigation. **Knowledge/Courses:** Law and Government; Economics and Accounting; Psychology; Personnel and Human Resources; Sociology and Anthropology; Public Safety and Security.

Personality Type: Enterprising-Investigative-Conventional. **Career Cluster:** 06 Finance. **Career Pathway:** 06.1 Financial and Investment Planning.

Skills: Writing; Negotiation; Active Listening; Speaking; Reading Comprehension; Systems Evaluation; Persuasion; Critical Thinking.

Work Environment: Indoors; sitting.

Job Specialization: Investment Underwriters

Intermediate between corporate issuers of securities and clients regarding private equity investments. Underwrite the issuance of securities to provide capital for client growth. Negotiate and structure the terms of mergers and acquisitions. Structure marketing campaigns to find buyers for new securities. Supervise, train, or mentor junior team members. Assess companies as investments for clients by examining company facilities. Prepare all materials for transactions and execution of deals. Perform securities valuation and pricing. Determine desirability of deals to develop solutions to financial problems or to assess the financial and capital impact of transactions, using financial modeling. Develop and maintain client relationships. Evaluate capital needs of clients, and assess market conditions to inform structuring of financial packages. Create client presentations of plan details. Coordinate due-diligence processes and the negotiation and execution of purchase and sale agreements. Collaborate on projects with teams of other professionals, such as lawyers, accountants, and public relations experts. Confer with clients to restructure debt, refinance debt, or raise new debt. Analyze financial and operational performance of companies facing financial difficulties to identify and recommend remedies. Advise clients on aspects of capitalization, such as amounts, sources, and timing. Intermediate between corporate issuers of new securities and the general public. Structure and negotiate deals, such as corporate mergers, sales, and acquisitions. Arrange financing of deals from sources such as financial institutions, agencies, and public or private companies.

Education/Training Required: Work experience in a related occupation. **Education and Training Program:** Financial Planning and Services. **Knowledge/Courses:** No data available.

Personality Type: Conventional-Enterprising. **Career Cluster:** 06 Finance. **Career Pathway:** 06.1 Financial and Investment Planning.

Skills: No data available.

Work Environment: No data available.

Job Specialization: Risk Management Specialists

Analyze and make decisions on risk-management issues by identifying, measuring, and managing operational and enterprise risks for an organization. Provide statistical modeling advice to other departments. Review and draft risk disclosures for offer documents. Meet with clients to answer queries on such subjects as risk exposure, market scenarios, and values-at-risk calculations. Maintain input and data quality of risk-management systems. Develop contingency plans to deal with emergencies. Devise scenario analyses reflecting possible severe market events. Consult financial literature to ensure use of the latest models and statistical techniques. Track, measure, and report on aspects of market risk for traded issues. Analyze new legislation to determine impact on risk exposure. Recommend ways to control or reduce risk. Produce reports and presentations that outline findings, explain risk positions, and recommend changes. Plan, and contribute to development of, risk-management systems. Gather risk-related data from internal or external resources. Develop and implement risk-assessment models and methodologies. Document, and ensure communication of, key risks. Devise systems and processes to monitor validity of risk-modeling outputs. Conduct statistical analyses to quantify risk, using statistical analysis software and econometric models. Identify key risks and mitigating factors of potential investments, such as asset types and values, legal and ownership structures, professional reputations, customer bases, or industry segments.

Education/Training Required: Work experience plus degree. **Education and Training Program:** Financial Planning and Services. **Knowledge/Courses:** Economics and Accounting; Mathematics; Law and Government; Administration and Management; Computers and Electronics; Personnel and Human Resources.

Personality Type: Conventional-Enterprising-Investigative. **Career Cluster:** 06 Finance. **Career Pathway:** 06.1 Financial and Investment Planning.

Skills: Mathematics; Programming; Systems Analysis; Management of Financial Resources; Systems Evaluation; Management of Material Resources; Writing; Reading Comprehension.

Work Environment: Indoors; sitting.

Insurance Underwriters

* Personality Type: Conventional-Enterprising-Investigative
* Annual Earnings: $59,290
* Earnings Growth Potential: Medium (38.1%)
* Growth: –4.1%
* Annual Job Openings: 3,000
* Self-Employed: 0.0%

Considerations for Job Outlook: Productivity increases, such as automatic underwriting, have limited employment of these workers. But this factor should be partially offset by an increased emphasis on underwriting to boost revenues and counteract decreasing returns on investments. Good job prospects are expected.

Review individual applications for insurance to evaluate degree of risk involved and determine acceptance of applications. Examine documents to determine degree of risk from such factors as applicant financial standing and value and condition of property. Decline excessive risks. Write to field representatives, medical personnel, and others to obtain further information, quote rates, or explain company underwriting policies. Evaluate possibility of losses due to catastrophe or excessive insurance. Decrease value of policy when risk is substandard and specify applicable endorsements, or apply rating to ensure safe profitable distribution of risks, using reference materials. Review company records to determine amount of insurance in force on single risk or group of closely related risks. Authorize reinsurance of policy when risk is high.

Education/Training Required: Bachelor's degree. **Education and Training Program:** Insurance. **Knowledge/Courses:** Medicine and Dentistry; Economics and Accounting; Clerical Practices; Therapy and Counseling; Sales and Marketing; Biology.

Career Cluster: 06 Finance. **Career Pathway:** 06.4 Insurance Services.

Skills: Judgment and Decision Making; Writing; Active Listening; Service Orientation; Mathematics; Systems Evaluation; Speaking; Critical Thinking.

Work Environment: Indoors; sitting; repetitive motions.

Interviewers, Except Eligibility and Loan

* Personality Type: Conventional-Enterprising-Social
* Annual Earnings: $28,820
* Earnings Growth Potential: Low (33.6%)
* Growth: 15.6%
* Annual Job Openings: 9,210
* Self-Employed: 0.6%

Considerations for Job Outlook: Growth in market research and health-care industries is expected to generate jobs for interviewers. Prospects should be good.

Interview persons by telephone, by mail, in person, or by other means for the purpose of completing forms, applications, or questionnaires. Ask specific questions, record answers, and assist persons with completing form. May sort, classify, and file forms. Ask questions in accordance with instructions to obtain various specified information such as person's name, address, age, religious preference, and state of residency. Identify and resolve inconsistencies in interviewees' responses by means of appropriate questioning or explanation. Compile, record, and code results and data from interview or survey, using computer or specified form. Review data obtained from interview for completeness and accuracy. Contact individuals to be interviewed at home, place of business, or field location by telephone, by mail, or in person. Assist individuals in filling out applications or questionnaires. Ensure payment for services by verifying benefits with the person's insurance provider or working out financing options. Identify and report problems in obtaining valid data. Explain survey objectives and procedures to interviewees, and interpret survey questions to help interviewees' comprehension. Perform patient services, such as answering the telephone and assisting patients with financial and medical questions. Prepare reports to provide answers in response to specific problems. Locate and list addresses and households. Perform other office duties as needed, such as telemarketing and customer-service inquiries, billing patients, and receiving payments. Meet with supervisor daily to submit completed assignments and discuss progress.

Education/Training Required: Short-term on-the-job training. **Education and Training Program:** Receptionist Training. **Knowledge/Courses:** Clerical Practices; Customer and Personal Service; Communications and Media.

Career Cluster: 04 Business, Management, and Administration. **Career Pathway:** 04.6 Administrative and Information Support.

Skills: Active Listening; Speaking; Programming; Writing; Persuasion; Instructing; Social Perceptiveness; Negotiation.

Work Environment: Indoors; sitting; using hands; repetitive motions; noise.

Judicial Law Clerks

* Personality Type: Conventional-Investigative
* Annual Earnings: $39,780
* Earnings Growth Potential: High (41.9%)
* Growth: 13.9%
* Annual Job Openings: 1,080
* Self-Employed: 14.0%

Considerations for Job Outlook: Faster than average employment growth is projected.

Assist judges in court or by conducting research or preparing legal documents. Attend court sessions to hear oral arguments or record necessary case information. Communicate with counsel regarding case management or procedural requirements.

Confer with judges concerning legal questions, construction of documents, or granting of orders. Draft or proofread judicial opinions, decisions, or citations. Keep abreast of changes in the law, and inform judges when cases are affected by such changes. Participate in conferences or discussions between trial attorneys and judges. Prepare briefs, legal memoranda, or statements of issues involved in cases, including appropriate suggestions or recommendations. Research laws, court decisions, documents, opinions, briefs, or other information related to cases before the court. Review complaints, petitions, motions, or pleadings that have been filed to determine issues involved or basis for relief. Review dockets of pending litigation to ensure adequate progress. Verify that all files, complaints, or other papers are available and in the proper order. Compile court-related statistics. Coordinate judges' meeting and appointment schedules. Enter information into computerized court calendar, filing, or case-management systems. Maintain judges' law libraries by assembling or updating appropriate documents. Perform courtroom duties, including calling calendars, administering oaths, and swearing in jury panels and witnesses. Prepare periodic reports on court proceedings, as required.

Education/Training Required: First professional degree. **Education and Training Programs:** Advanced Legal Research/Studies, General (LL.M., M.C.L., M.L.I., M.S.L., J.S.D./S.J.D.); American/U.S. Law/Legal Studies/Jurisprudence (LL.M., M.C.J., J.S.D./S.J.D.); Banking, Corporate, Finance, and Securities Law (LL.M., J.S.D./S.J.D.); Canadian Law/Legal Studies/Jurisprudence (LL.M., M.C.J., J.S.D./S.J.D.); Comparative Law (LL.M., M.C.L., J.S.D./S.J.D.); Energy, Environment, and Natural Resources Law (LL.M., M.S., J.S.D./S.J.D.); Health Law (LL.M., M.J., J.S.D./S.J.D.); International Business, Trade, and Tax Law (LL.M., J.S.D./S.J.D.); International Law and Legal Studies (LL.M., J.S.D./S.J.D.); Law (LL.B, J.D.); Legal Professions and Studies, Other; Legal Research and Advanced Professional Studies, Other; Legal Studies, General; Pre-Law Studies; Programs for Foreign Lawyers (LL.M., M.C.L.); Tax Law/Taxation (LL.M., J.S.D./S.J.D.). **Knowledge/Courses:** Law and Government; Clerical Practices; English Language;

Administration and Management.

Career Cluster: 12 Law, Public Safety, Corrections, and Security. **Career Pathway:** 12.5 Legal Services.

Skills: Critical Thinking; Reading Comprehension; Writing; Active Listening; Active Learning; Speaking; Persuasion; Negotiation.

Work Environment: Indoors; sitting; repetitive motions.

Legal Secretaries

- ❋ Personality Type: Conventional-Enterprising
- ❋ Annual Earnings: $41,500
- ❋ Earnings Growth Potential: Medium (36.5%)
- ❋ Growth: 18.4%
- ❋ Annual Job Openings: 8,380
- ❋ Self-Employed: 1.4%

Considerations for Job Outlook: Projected employment growth varies by occupational specialty. Faster than average growth is expected for medical secretaries and legal secretaries; average growth for executive secretaries and administrative assistants; and slower than average growth for secretaries other than legal, medical, or executive, who account for most of the workers in these specialties. Many opportunities are expected.

Perform secretarial duties, utilizing legal terminology, procedures, and documents. Prepare legal papers and correspondence, such as summonses, complaints, motions, and subpoenas. May also assist with legal research. Prepare and process legal documents and papers, such as summonses, subpoenas, complaints, appeals, motions, and pretrial agreements. Mail, fax, or arrange for delivery of legal correspondence to clients, witnesses, and court officials. Receive and place telephone calls. Schedule and make appointments. Make photocopies of correspondence, documents, and other printed matter. Organize and maintain law libraries, documents, and case files. Assist attorneys in collecting information such as employment, medical, and other records. Attend legal meetings, such as client interviews, hearings, or depositions, and take notes. Draft and type office memos. Review legal publications and perform database searches to identify laws and court decisions relevant to pending cases. Submit articles and information from searches to attorneys for review and approval for use. Complete various forms such as accident reports, trial and courtroom requests, and applications for clients.

Education/Training Required: Associate degree. **Education and Training Program:** Legal Administrative Assistant/Secretary Training. **Knowledge/Courses:** Clerical Practices; Law and Government; Computers and Electronics; English Language; Customer and Personal Service.

Career Cluster: 12 Law, Public Safety, Corrections, and Security. **Career Pathway:** 12.5 Legal Services.

Skills: Writing; Reading Comprehension; Active Listening; Programming; Service Orientation; Speaking.

Work Environment: Indoors; sitting; using hands; repetitive motions.

Librarians

- ❋ Personality Type: Conventional-Social-Enterprising
- ❋ Annual Earnings: $54,500
- ❋ Earnings Growth Potential: Medium (38.4%)
- ❋ Growth: 7.8%
- ❋ Annual Job Openings: 5,450
- ❋ Self-Employed: 0.3%

Considerations for Job Outlook: Growth in the number of librarians is expected to be limited by government budget constraints and the increasing use of electronic resources. Although many openings are expected, there will be competition for jobs in some regions.

Administer libraries and perform related library services. Work in a variety of settings, including public libraries, schools, colleges and universities, museums, corporations, government agencies, law firms, non-profit organizations, and healthcare providers. Tasks may include selecting, acquiring, cataloguing, classifying, circulating, and maintaining library materials and furnishing reference, bibliographical, and readers' advisory services. May perform in-depth, strategic research and synthesize, analyze, edit, and filter information. May set up or work with databases and information systems to catalogue and access information. Search standard reference materials, including online sources and the Internet, to answer patrons' reference questions. Analyze patrons' requests to determine needed information, and assist in furnishing or locating that information. Teach library patrons to search for information by using databases. Keep records of circulation and materials. Supervise budgeting, planning, and personnel activities. Check books in and out of the library. Explain use of library facilities, resources, equipment, and services, and provide information about library policies. Review and evaluate resource material, such as book reviews and catalogs, to select and order print, audiovisual, and electronic resources. Code, classify, and catalog books, publications, films, audiovisual aids, and other library materials based on subject matter or standard library-classification systems. Locate unusual or unique information in response to specific requests. Direct and train library staff in duties such as receiving, shelving, researching, cataloging, and equipment use. Respond to customer complaints, taking action as necessary. Organize collections of books, publications, documents, audiovisual aids, and other reference materials for convenient access. Develop library policies and procedures. Evaluate materials to determine outdated or unused items to be discarded. Develop information access aids such as indexes and annotated bibliographies, webpages, electronic pathfinders, and online tutorials.

Education/Training Required: Master's degree. **Education and Training Programs:** Library and Information Science; Library Science, Other; School Librarian/School Library Media Specialist.

Conventional-L

Knowledge/Courses: History and Archeology; Sociology and Anthropology; Philosophy and Theology; Clerical Practices; Education and Training; English Language.

Career Cluster: 05 Education and Training. **Career Pathways:** 05.2 Professional Support Services; 05.3 Teaching/Training.

Skills: Management of Material Resources; Service Orientation; Operations Analysis; Instructing; Negotiation; Management of Financial Resources; Writing; Systems Evaluation.

Work Environment: Indoors; sitting; repetitive motions.

Life, Physical, and Social Science Technicians, All Other

Look for the job description among the Realistic jobs.

Loan Officers

* Personality Type: Conventional-Enterprising-Social
* Annual Earnings: $56,490
* Earnings Growth Potential: High (45.2%)
* Growth: 10.1%
* Annual Job Openings: 6,880
* Self-Employed: 3.7%

Considerations for Job Outlook: Overall economic expansion and population growth are expected to increase employment of these workers. However, increased automation through the use of the Internet loan application will temper employment growth. Good job opportunities are expected.

Evaluate, authorize, or recommend approval of commercial, real estate, or credit loans. Advise borrowers on financial status and methods of payments. Includes mortgage loan officers and agents, collection analysts, loan servicing officers, and loan underwriters. Meet with applicants to obtain information for loan applications and to answer questions about the process. Approve loans within specified limits, and refer loan applications outside those limits to management for approval. Analyze applicants' financial status, credit, and property evaluations to determine feasibility of granting loans. Explain to customers the different types of loans and credit options that are available, as well as the terms of those services. Obtain and compile copies of loan applicants' credit histories, corporate financial statements, and other financial information. Review and update credit and loan files. Review loan agreements to ensure that they are complete and accurate according to policy. Compute payment schedules. Stay abreast of new types of loans and other financial services and products to better meet customers' needs. Submit applications to credit analysts for verification and recommendation. Handle customer complaints, and take appropriate action to resolve them. Work with clients to identify their financial goals and to find ways of reaching those goals. Confer with underwriters to aid in resolving mortgage application problems. Negotiate payment arrangements with customers who have delinquent loans. Market bank products to individuals and firms, promoting bank services that may meet customers' needs. Supervise loan personnel. Set credit policies, credit lines, procedures, and standards in conjunction with senior managers.

Education/Training Required: Bachelor's degree. **Education and Training Programs:** Credit Management; Finance, General. **Knowledge/Courses:** Sales and Marketing; Economics and Accounting; Customer and Personal Service; Law and Government; Clerical Practices; Mathematics.

Career Cluster: 06 Finance. **Career Pathways:** 06.3 Banking and Related Services; 06.1 Financial and Investment Planning.

Skills: Service Orientation; Mathematics; Judgment and Decision Making; Speaking; Negotiation; Active Listening; Critical Thinking; Reading Comprehension.

Work Environment: More often indoors than outdoors; sitting.

Logisticians

- ❋ Personality Type: Conventional-Enterprising-Investigative
- ❋ Annual Earnings: $70,800
- ❋ Earnings Growth Potential: Medium (38.5%)
- ❋ Growth: 19.5%
- ❋ Annual Job Openings: 4,190
- ❋ Self-Employed: 0.0%

Considerations for Job Outlook: Faster than average employment growth is projected.

Analyze and coordinate the logistical functions of a firm or organization. Responsible for the entire life cycle of a product, including acquisition, distribution, internal allocation, delivery, and final disposal of resources. Maintain and develop positive business relationships with a customer's key personnel involved in or directly relevant to a logistics activity. Develop an understanding of customers' needs, and take actions to ensure that such needs are met. Direct availability and allocation of materials, supplies, and finished products. Collaborate with other departments as necessary to meet customer requirements, to take advantage of sales opportunities, or, in the case of shortages, to minimize negative impacts on a business. Protect and control proprietary materials. Review logistics performance with customers against targets, benchmarks, and service agreements. Develop and implement technical project-management tools such as plans, schedules, and responsibility and compliance matrices. Direct team activities, establishing task priorities, scheduling and tracking work assignments, providing guidance, and ensuring the availability of resources. Report project plans, progress, and results. Direct and support the compilation and analysis of technical source data necessary for product development. Explain proposed solutions to customers, management, or other interested parties through written proposals and oral presentations.

Provide project-management services, including the provision and analysis of technical data. Develop proposals that include documentation for estimates.

Education/Training Required: Bachelor's degree. **Education and Training Programs:** Logistics, Materials, and Supply Chain Management; Operations Management and Supervision; Transportation/Mobility Management. **Knowledge/Courses:** Telecommunications; Geography; Computers and Electronics; Economics and Accounting; Administration and Management; Public Safety and Security.

Career Clusters: 04 Business, Management, and Administration; 16 Transportation, Distribution, and Logistics. **Career Pathways:** 04.1 Management; 16.2 Logistics, Planning, and Management Services.

Skills: Operations Analysis; Management of Personnel Resources; Programming; Coordination; Monitoring; Systems Evaluation; Persuasion; Systems Analysis.

Work Environment: Indoors; sitting.

Job Specialization: Logistics Analysts

Analyze product delivery or supply-chain processes to identify or recommend changes. May manage route activity including invoicing, electronic bills, and shipment tracing. Identify opportunities for inventory reductions. Monitor industry standards, trends, or practices to identify developments in logistics planning or execution. Enter logistics-related data into databases. Develop and maintain payment systems to ensure accuracy of vendor payments. Determine packaging requirements. Develop and maintain freight-rate databases for use by supply-chain departments to determine the most economical modes of transportation. Contact potential vendors to determine material availability. Contact carriers for rates or schedules. Communicate with and monitor service providers, such as ocean carriers, air freight forwarders, global consolidators, customs brokers, and trucking companies. Track product flow

Conventional-L

from origin to final delivery. Write or revise standard operating procedures for logistics processes. Review procedures such as distribution and inventory management to ensure maximum efficiency and minimum cost. Recommend improvements to existing or planned logistics processes. Provide ongoing analyses in areas such as transportation costs, parts procurement, back orders, and delivery processes. Prepare reports on logistics performance measures. Manage systems to ensure that pricing structures adequately reflect logistics costing. Monitor inventory transactions at warehouse facilities to assess receiving, storage, shipping, or inventory integrity. Maintain databases of logistics information. Maintain logistics records in accordance with corporate policies.

Education/Training Required: Bachelor's degree. **Education and Training Programs:** Logistics, Materials, and Supply Chain Management; Operations Management and Supervision; Transportation/Mobility Management. **Knowledge/Courses:** Transportation; Geography; Computers and Electronics; Production and Processing; Mathematics; Engineering and Technology.

Personality Type: Conventional-Enterprising-Investigative. **Career Clusters:** 04 Business, Management, and Administration; 16 Transportation, Distribution, and Logistics. **Career Pathways:** 04.1 Management; 16.3 Warehousing and Distribution Center Operations.

Skills: Mathematics; Systems Analysis; Systems Evaluation; Management of Financial Resources; Programming; Technology Design; Management of Material Resources; Active Learning.

Work Environment: Indoors; sitting.

Job Specialization: Logistics Engineers

Design and analyze operational solutions for projects such as transportation optimization, network modeling, process and methods analysis, cost containment, capacity enhancement, routing and shipment optimization, and information management. Propose logistics solutions for customers. Prepare production strategies and conceptual designs for production facilities. Interview key staff or tour facilities to identify efficiency-improvement, cost-reduction, or service-delivery opportunities. Direct the work of logistics analysts. Design plant distribution centers. Develop specifications for equipment, tools, facility layouts, or material-handling systems. Review contractual commitments, customer specifications, or related information to determine logistics and support requirements. Prepare or validate documentation on automated logistics or maintenance-data reporting and management-information systems. Identify cost-reduction and process-improvement opportunities. Identify or develop business rules and standard operating procedures to streamline operating processes. Develop metrics, internal analysis tools, or key performance indicators for business units within logistics. Develop and maintain cost estimates, forecasts, or cost models. Determine feasibility of designing new facilities or modifying existing facilities, based on such factors as cost, available space, schedule, technical requirements, and ergonomics. Determine logistics support requirements, such as facility details, staffing needs, and safety or maintenance plans. Conduct logistics studies and analyses, such as time studies, zero-base analyses, rate analyses, network analyses, flow-path analyses, and supply chain analyses.

Education/Training Required: Bachelor's degree. **Education and Training Programs:** Logistics, Materials, and Supply Chain Management; Operations Management and Supervision; Transportation/Mobility Management. **Knowledge/Courses:** Engineering and Technology; Design; Transportation; Telecommunications; Mechanical Devices; Production and Processing.

Personality Type: Investigative-Conventional-Realistic. **Career Clusters:** 04 Business, Management, and Administration; 16 Transportation, Distribution, and Logistics. **Career Pathways:** 04.1 Management; 16.2 Logistics, Planning, and Management Services.

Skills: Equipment Selection; Programming; Systems Evaluation; Operations Analysis; Systems Analysis; Management of Material Resources; Mathematics; Management of Financial Resources.

Work Environment: Indoors; sitting.

Managers, All Other

Look for the job description among the Enterprising jobs.

Medical Records and Health Information Technicians

- ❋ Personality Type: Conventional-Enterprising
- ❋ Annual Earnings: $32,350
- ❋ Earnings Growth Potential: Low (34.3%)
- ❋ Growth: 20.3%
- ❋ Annual Job Openings: 7,030
- ❋ Self-Employed: 0.0%

Considerations for Job Outlook: Employment of these workers is expected to grow as the number of elderly—a demographic group with a higher incidence of injury and illness—increases. Job prospects should be best for technicians who have strong skills in technology and computer software.

Compile, process, and maintain medical records of hospital and clinic patients in a manner consistent with medical, administrative, ethical, legal, and regulatory requirements of the heath-care system. Protect the security of medical records to ensure that confidentiality is maintained. Review records for completeness, accuracy, and compliance with regulations. Retrieve patient medical records for physicians, technicians, or other medical personnel. Release information to persons and agencies according to regulations. Plan, develop, maintain, and operate a variety of health record indexes and storage and retrieval systems to collect, classify, store, and analyze information. Enter data such as demographic characteristics, history and extent of disease, diagnostic procedures, and treatment into computer. Process and prepare business and government forms. Compile and maintain patients' medical records to document condition and treatment and to provide data for research or cost-control and care-improvement efforts. Process patient admission and discharge documents. Assign the patient to diagnosis-related groups (DRGs), using appropriate computer software. Transcribe medical reports. Identify, compile, abstract, and code patient data, using standard classification systems. Resolve or clarify codes and diagnoses with conflicting, missing, or unclear information by consulting with doctors or others or by participating in the coding team's regular meetings. Compile medical-care and census data for statistical reports on diseases treated, surgeries performed, or use of hospital beds. Post medical insurance billings. Train medical records staff.

Education/Training Required: Associate degree. **Education and Training Programs:** Health Information/Medical Records Technology/Technician; Medical Insurance Coding Specialist/Coder Training. **Knowledge/Courses:** Clerical Practices; Law and Government.

Career Cluster: 08 Health Science. **Career Pathway:** 08.3 Health Informatics.

Skills: No data available.

Work Environment: Indoors; sitting; using hands; repetitive motions; exposed to disease or infections.

Medical Secretaries

- ❋ Personality Type: Conventional-Social
- ❋ Annual Earnings: $30,530
- ❋ Earnings Growth Potential: Low (30.5%)
- ❋ Growth: 26.6%
- ❋ Annual Job Openings: 18,900
- ❋ Self-Employed: 1.4%

Conventional-M

Considerations for Job Outlook: Projected employment growth varies by occupational specialty. Faster than average growth is expected for medical secretaries and legal secretaries; average growth for executive secretaries and administrative assistants; and slower than average growth for secretaries other than legal, medical, or executive, who account for most of the workers in these specialties. Many opportunities are expected.

Perform secretarial duties, using specific knowledge of medical terminology and hospital, clinical, or laboratory procedures. Answer telephones, and direct calls to appropriate staff. Schedule and confirm patient diagnostic appointments, surgeries, and medical consultations. Greet visitors, ascertain purpose of visit, and direct them to appropriate staff. Operate office equipment, such as voice mail messaging systems, and use word processing, spreadsheet, and other software applications to prepare reports, invoices, financial statements, letters, case histories, and medical records. Complete insurance and other claim forms. Interview patients to complete documents, case histories, and forms such as intake and insurance forms. Receive and route messages and documents such as laboratory results to appropriate staff. Compile and record medical charts, reports, and correspondence, using typewriter or personal computer. Transmit correspondence and medical records by mail, e-mail, or fax. Maintain medical records, technical library documents, and correspondence files. Perform various clerical and administrative functions, such as ordering and maintaining an inventory of supplies. Perform bookkeeping duties, such as credits and collections, preparing and sending financial statements and bills, and keeping financial records. Transcribe recorded messages and practitioners' diagnoses and recommendations into patients' medical records. Arrange hospital admissions for patients.

Education/Training Required: Moderate-term on-the-job training. **Education and Training Programs:** Medical Administrative/Executive Assistant and Medical Secretary Training; Medical Insurance Specialist/Medical Biller Training; Medical Office Assistant/Specialist Training.

Knowledge/Courses: Clerical Practices; Medicine and Dentistry; Customer and Personal Service; Computers and Electronics; Economics and Accounting.

Career Cluster: 08 Health Science. **Career Pathways:** 08.3 Health Informatics; 08.1 Therapeutic Services.

Skills: Service Orientation; Active Listening; Speaking.

Work Environment: Indoors; sitting; repetitive motions; exposed to disease or infections.

Occupational Health and Safety Technicians

* Personality Type: Conventional-Realistic
* Annual Earnings: $45,330
* Earnings Growth Potential: Medium (39.2%)
* Growth: 14.5%
* Annual Job Openings: 520
* Self-Employed: 0.7%

Considerations for Job Outlook: Fast growth is expected as some employers contain costs by hiring more technicians and fewer specialists to ensure workplace safety in response to changing hazards, regulations, public expectations, and technology.

Collect data on work environments for analysis by occupational health and safety specialists. Implement and conduct evaluation of programs designed to limit chemical, physical, biological, and ergonomic risks to workers. Maintain all required records and documentation. Supply, operate, and maintain personal protective equipment. Verify that safety equipment such as hearing protection and respirators is available to employees, and monitor their use of such equipment to ensure proper fit and use. Evaluate situations where a worker has refused to work on the grounds that danger or potential harm exists, and determine how such situations should be handled. Prepare and calibrate equipment used to collect and analyze samples. Test workplaces for environmental hazards such as exposure to radiation, chemical and biological hazards, and excessive noise. Prepare and review specifications and orders for the purchase of safety equipment, ensuring that proper features are present and that items conform to health and safety standards. Report the results of environmental contaminant analyses, and recommend corrective measures to be applied. Review physicians' reports, and conduct worker studies in order to determine whether specific instances of disease or illness are job-related. Examine credentials, licenses, or permits to ensure compliance with licensing requirements. Conduct fire drills, and inspect fire-suppression systems and portable fire systems to ensure that they are in working order. Educate the public about health issues, and enforce health legislation in order to prevent diseases, to promote health, and to help people understand health protection procedures and regulations.

Education/Training Required: Bachelor's degree. **Education and Training Programs:** Environmental Health; Occupational Health and Industrial Hygiene; Radiation Protection/Health Physics Technician Training. **Knowledge/Courses:** Building and Construction; Chemistry; Public Safety and Security; Engineering and Technology; Physics; Education and Training.

Career Cluster: 08 Health Science. **Career Pathways:** 08.1 Therapeutic Services; 08.3 Health Informatics.

Skills: Science; Operation and Control; Operation Monitoring; Reading Comprehension; Writing; Active Listening; Monitoring; Systems Evaluation.

Work Environment: More often outdoors than indoors; standing; noise; contaminants; high places; hazardous conditions; hazardous equipment.

Office Clerks, General

* Personality Type: Conventional-Enterprising-Realistic
* Annual Earnings: $26,610
* Earnings Growth Potential: Low (35.1%)
* Growth: 11.9%
* Annual Job Openings: 77,090
* Self-Employed: 0.4%

Considerations for Job Outlook: Employment growth is expected to be spurred by new technology that allows these clerks to perform tasks previously done by specialists. Numerous opportunities are expected.

Perform duties too varied and diverse to be classified in any specific office clerical occupation requiring limited knowledge of office management systems and procedures. Clerical duties may be assigned in accordance with the office procedures of individual establishments and may include a combination of answering telephones, bookkeeping, typing or word processing, stenography, office machine operation, and filing. Collect, count, and disburse money; do basic bookkeeping; and complete banking transactions. Communicate with customers, employees, and other individuals to answer questions, disseminate or explain information, take orders, and address complaints. Answer telephones, direct calls, and take messages. Compile, copy, sort, and file records of office activities, business transactions, and other activities. Complete and mail bills, contracts, policies, invoices, or checks. Operate office machines such as photocopiers and scanners, facsimile machines, voice mail systems, and personal computers. Compute, record, and proofread data and other information, such as records or reports. Maintain and update filing, inventory, mailing, and database systems, either manually or using a computer. Open, sort, and route incoming mail; answer correspondence; and prepare outgoing mail. Review files, records, and other documents to obtain information to respond to requests. Deliver messages, and run errands. Inventory and order materials, supplies, and services. Complete work schedules, manage calendars, and arrange appointments. Process and prepare documents such as business or government forms and expense reports. Monitor and direct the work of lower-level clerks. Type, format, proofread, and edit correspondence and other documents from notes or dictating machines, using computers or typewriters. Count, weigh, measure, or organize materials.

Education/Training Required: Short-term on-the-job training. **Education and Training Program:** General Office Occupations and Clerical Services. **Knowledge/Courses:** Clerical Practices; Customer and Personal Service; Computers and Electronics.

Career Cluster: 04 Business, Management, and Administration. **Career Pathway:** 04.6 Administrative and Information Support.

Skills: Management of Material Resources; Service Orientation; Active Listening; Management of Financial Resources; Reading Comprehension; Speaking.

Work Environment: Indoors; sitting; repetitive motions.

Paralegals and Legal Assistants

- ✳ Personality Type: Conventional-Investigative-Enterprising
- ✳ Annual Earnings: $46,680
- ✳ Earnings Growth Potential: Medium (36.9%)
- ✳ Growth: 28.1%
- ✳ Annual Job Openings: 10,400
- ✳ Self-Employed: 3.2%

Considerations for Job Outlook: Increased demand for accessible, cost-efficient legal services is expected to increase employment for paralegals, who may perform more tasks previously done by lawyers. Keen competition is expected. Experienced, formally trained paralegals should have the best job prospects.

Assist lawyers by researching legal precedent, investigating facts, or preparing legal documents. Conduct research to support a legal proceeding, to formulate a defense, or to initiate legal action. Prepare legal documents, including briefs, pleadings, appeals, wills, contracts, and real estate closing statements. Prepare affidavits or other docu-

ments, maintain document file, and file pleadings with court clerk. Gather and analyze research data, such as statutes; decisions; and legal articles, codes, and documents. Investigate facts and law of cases to determine causes of action and to prepare cases. Call upon witnesses to testify at hearing. Direct and coordinate law office activity, including delivery of subpoenas. Arbitrate disputes between parties, and assist in real estate closing process. Keep and monitor legal volumes to ensure that law library is up to date. Appraise and inventory real and personal property for estate planning.

Education/Training Required: Associate degree. **Education and Training Program:** Legal Assistant/Paralegal Training. **Knowledge/Courses:** Clerical Practices; Law and Government; English Language; Computers and Electronics; Communications and Media.

Career Cluster: 12 Law, Public Safety, Corrections, and Security. **Career Pathway:** 12.5 Legal Services.

Skills: Writing; Active Listening; Speaking; Service Orientation.

Work Environment: Indoors; sitting; repetitive motions.

Pharmacy Technicians

- ✳ Personality Type: Conventional-Realistic
- ✳ Annual Earnings: $28,400
- ✳ Earnings Growth Potential: Low (30.1%)
- ✳ Growth: 30.6%
- ✳ Annual Job Openings: 18,200
- ✳ Self-Employed: 0.2%

Considerations for Job Outlook: Growth in the population of middle-aged and elderly people—who use more prescription drugs than younger people—should spur employment increases for these workers. Job prospects are expected to be good.

Prepare medications under the direction of a pharmacist. May measure, mix, count out, label, and record amounts and dosages of medications. Receive written prescription or refill requests, and verify that information is complete and accurate. Maintain proper storage and security conditions for drugs. Answer telephones, responding to questions or requests. Fill bottles with prescribed medications, and type and affix labels. Assist customers by answering simple questions, locating items, or referring them to the pharmacist for medication information. Price and file prescriptions that have been filled. Clean and help maintain equipment and work areas, and sterilize glassware according to prescribed methods. Establish and maintain patient profiles, including lists of medications taken by individual patients. Order, label, and count stock of medications, chemicals, and supplies, and enter inventory data into computer. Receive and store incoming supplies, verify quantities against invoices, and inform supervisors of stock needs and shortages. Transfer medication from vials to the appropriate number of sterile disposable syringes, using aseptic techniques. Under pharmacist supervision, add measured drugs or nutrients to intravenous solutions under sterile conditions to prepare intravenous (IV) packs. Supply and monitor robotic machines that dispense medicine into containers, and label the containers. Prepare and process medical insurance claim forms and records. Mix pharmaceutical preparations according to written prescriptions. Operate cash registers to accept payment from customers.

Education/Training Required: Moderate-term on-the-job training. **Education and Training Program:** Pharmacy Technician/Assistant Training. **Knowledge/Courses:** Medicine and Dentistry; Clerical Practices; Computers and Electronics; Customer and Personal Service; Chemistry; Mathematics.

Career Cluster: 08 Health Science. **Career Pathway:** 08.1 Therapeutic Services.

Skills: Management of Financial Resources; Service Orientation; Science; Mathematics; Programming; Active Listening.

Work Environment: Indoors; standing; walking and running; using hands; repetitive motions; exposed to disease or infections.

Police, Fire, and Ambulance Dispatchers

* Personality Type: Conventional-Realistic-Enterprising
* Annual Earnings: $35,370
* Earnings Growth Potential: Medium (36.9%)
* Growth: 17.8%
* Annual Job Openings: 3,840
* Self-Employed: 0.0%

Considerations for Job Outlook: The growing and aging population will increase demand for emergency services, leading to employment increases for these dispatchers. Job opportunities should be favorable.

Receive complaints from public concerning crimes and police emergencies. Broadcast orders to police patrol units in vicinity of complaint to investigate. Operate radio, telephone, or computer equipment to receive reports of fires and medical emergencies, and relay information or orders to proper officials. Question callers about their locations and the nature of their problems to determine types of response needed. Receive incoming telephone or alarm system calls regarding emergency and nonemergency police and fire service, emergency ambulance service, information, and after-hours calls for departments within a city. Determine response requirements and relative priorities of situations, and dispatch units in accordance with established procedures. Record details of calls, dispatches, and messages. Enter, update, and retrieve information from teletype networks and computerized data systems regarding such things as wanted persons, stolen property, vehicle registration, and stolen vehicles. Maintain access to and security of highly sensitive materials. Relay information and messages to and from emergency sites, to law enforcement agencies, and to all other individuals or groups requiring notification. Scan status charts and computer screens, and contact emergency response field units to determine emergency units available for dispatch.

Observe alarm registers and scan maps to determine whether a specific emergency is in the dispatch service area. Maintain files of information relating to emergency calls such as personnel rosters and emergency call-out and pager files. Monitor various radio frequencies such as those used by public works departments, school security, and civil defense to keep apprised of developing situations. Learn material, and pass required tests for certification.

Education/Training Required: Moderate-term on-the-job training. **Education and Training Programs:** No related CIP programs; this job is learned through moderate-term on-the-job training. **Knowledge/Courses:** Telecommunications; Customer and Personal Service; Clerical Practices; Law and Government; Public Safety and Security; Psychology.

Career Cluster: 12 Law, Public Safety, Corrections, and Security. **Career Pathway:** 12.3 Security and Protective Services.

Skills: Active Listening; Critical Thinking; Persuasion; Social Perceptiveness; Service Orientation; Operation and Control; Programming; Operations Analysis.

Work Environment: Indoors; sitting; using hands; repetitive motions; noise; contaminants.

Postal Service Mail Carriers

- ❋ Personality Type: Conventional-Realistic
- ❋ Annual Earnings: $53,860
- ❋ Earnings Growth Potential: Low (28.5%)
- ❋ Growth: –1.1%
- ❋ Annual Job Openings: 10,720
- ❋ Self-Employed: 0.0%

Considerations for Job Outlook: Declining mail volume, along with automation, is expected to offset employment growth driven by the need to provide mail-delivery services to a growing population. Keen competition is expected. Opportunities are expected to be best in areas experiencing population growth.

Sort mail for delivery. Deliver mail on established routes by vehicle or on foot. Obtain signed receipts for registered, certified, and insured mail; collect associated charges; and complete any necessary paperwork. Sort mail for delivery, arranging it in delivery sequence. Deliver mail to residences and business establishments along specified routes by walking and/or driving, using a combination of satchels, carts, cars, and small trucks. Return to the post office with mail collected from homes, businesses, and public mailboxes. Turn in money and receipts collected along mail routes. Sign for cash-on-delivery and registered mail before leaving post offices. Record address changes, and redirect mail for those addresses. Hold mail for customers who are away from delivery locations. Bundle mail in preparation for delivery or transportation to relay boxes. Leave notices telling patrons where to collect mail that could not be delivered. Meet schedules for the collection and return of mail. Return incorrectly addressed mail to senders. Maintain accurate records of deliveries. Answer customers' questions about postal services and regulations. Provide customers with change-of-address cards and other forms. Report any unusual circumstances concerning mail delivery, including the condition of street letter boxes. Register, certify, and insure parcels and letters. Travel to post offices to pick up the mail for routes and/or pick up mail from postal relay boxes. Enter change of address orders into computers that process forwarding address stickers.

Education/Training Required: Short-term on-the-job training. **Education and Training Program:** General Office Occupations and Clerical Services. **Knowledge/Courses:** Transportation; Public Safety and Security.

Career Cluster: 04 Business, Management, and Administration. **Career Pathway:** 04.6 Administrative and Information Support.

Skills: Operation and Control.

Work Environment: More often outdoors than indoors; standing; walking and running; using hands; bending or twisting the body; repetitive motions; noise; very hot or cold; bright or inadequate lighting; contaminants; minor burns, cuts, bites, or stings.

Production, Planning, and Expediting Clerks

- ❋ Personality Type: Conventional-Enterprising
- ❋ Annual Earnings: $42,220
- ❋ Earnings Growth Potential: Medium (39.5%)
- ❋ Growth: 1.5%
- ❋ Annual Job Openings: 7,410
- ❋ Self-Employed: 0.5%

Considerations for Job Outlook: Job openings are expected to arise from the need to replace workers who leave the occupation. Opportunities should be limited in manufacturing but better in industries with faster growth, such as wholesale trade and warehousing.

Coordinate and expedite the flow of work and materials within or between departments of an establishment according to production schedules, inventory levels, costs, and production problems. Examine documents, materials, and products, and monitor work processes to assess completeness, accuracy, and conformance to standards and specifications. Review documents such as production schedules, work orders, and staffing tables to determine personnel and materials requirements, and material priorities. Revise production schedules when required due to design changes, labor or material shortages, backlogs, or other interruptions, collaborating with management, marketing, sales, production, and engineering. Confer with department supervisors and other personnel to assess progress and discuss needed changes. Confer with establishment personnel, vendors, and customers to coordinate production and shipping activities, and to resolve complaints or eliminate delays. Record production data, including volume produced, consumption of raw materials, and quality control measures. Requisition and maintain inventories of materials and supplies necessary to meet production demands. Calculate figures such as required amounts of labor and materials, manufacturing costs, and wages, using pricing schedules, adding machines, calculators, or computers. Distribute production schedules and work orders to departments. Compile information such as production rates and progress, materials inventories, materials used, and customer information, so that status reports can be completed.

Education/Training Required: Moderate-term on-the-job training. **Education and Training Program:** Parts, Warehousing, and Inventory Management Operations. **Knowledge/Courses:** Production and Processing; Clerical Practices; Computers and Electronics; Administration and Management; Mathematics; Customer and Personal Service.

Career Cluster: 16 Transportation, Distribution, and Logistics. **Career Pathway:** 16.3 Warehousing and Distribution Center Operations.

Skills: Management of Material Resources; Negotiation; Management of Financial Resources; Reading Comprehension; Persuasion; Time Management; Speaking.

Work Environment: Indoors; sitting; noise; contaminants.

Purchasing Agents, Except Wholesale, Retail, and Farm Products

- ❋ Personality Type: Conventional-Enterprising
- ❋ Annual Earnings: $56,580
- ❋ Earnings Growth Potential: Medium (38.0%)
- ❋ Growth: 13.9%
- ❋ Annual Job Openings: 11,860
- ❋ Self-Employed: 1.4%

Considerations for Job Outlook: Almost all of the growth is expected to be for purchasing agents, except wholesale, retail, and farm products, as more companies demand a greater number of goods and services.

Purchase machinery, equipment, tools, parts, supplies, or services necessary for the operation of an establishment. Purchase raw or semi-finished materials for manufacturing. Purchase the highest-quality merchandise at the lowest possible price and in correct amounts. Prepare purchase orders, solicit bid proposals, and review requisitions for goods and services. Research and evaluate suppliers based on price, quality, selection, service, support, availability, reliability, production and distribution capabilities, and the supplier's reputation and history. Analyze price proposals, financial reports, and other data and information to determine reasonable prices. Monitor and follow applicable laws and regulations. Negotiate, or renegotiate, and administer contracts with suppliers, vendors, and other representatives. Monitor shipments to ensure that goods come in on time, and trace shipments and follow up on undelivered goods in the event of problems. Confer with staff, users, and vendors to discuss defective or unacceptable goods or services and determine corrective action. Evaluate and monitor contract performance to ensure compliance with contractual obligations and to determine need for changes. Maintain and review computerized or manual records of items purchased, costs, delivery, product performance, and inventories. Review catalogs, industry periodicals, directories, trade journals, and Internet sites and consult with other department personnel to locate necessary goods and services. Study sales records and inventory levels of current stock to develop strategic purchasing programs that facilitate employee access to supplies.

Education/Training Required: Long-term on-the-job training. **Education and Training Programs:** Insurance; Merchandising and Buying Operations; Sales, Distribution, and Marketing Operations, General. **Knowledge/Courses:** Economics and Accounting; Transportation; Law and Government; Production and Processing; Clerical Practices; Administration and Management.

Career Cluster: 14 Marketing, Sales, and Service. **Career Pathway:** 14.3 Buying and Merchandising.

Skills: Management of Financial Resources; Management of Material Resources; Negotiation; Persuasion; Active Learning; Operations Analysis; Judgment and Decision Making; Complex Problem Solving.

Work Environment: Sitting.

Receptionists and Information Clerks

- ❋ Personality Type: Conventional-Enterprising-Social
- ❋ Annual Earnings: $25,240
- ❋ Earnings Growth Potential: Low (30.4%)
- ❋ Growth: 15.2%
- ❋ Annual Job Openings: 48,020
- ❋ Self-Employed: 0.8%

Considerations for Job Outlook: Although technology makes these workers more productive, many new jobs are expected as clerical work is consolidated and involves more tasks. Employment growth is expected in offices of physicians and other health practitioners and in the legal services, personal care services, construction, and management and technical consulting industries. Plentiful opportunities are expected.

Answer inquiries and obtain information for general public, customers, visitors, and other interested parties. Provide information regarding activities conducted at establishment and location of departments, offices, and employees within organization. Operate telephone switchboard to answer, screen, and forward calls, providing information, taking messages, and scheduling appointments. Receive payments, and record receipts for services. Perform administrative support tasks such as proofreading, transcribing handwritten information, and operating calculators or computers to work with pay records, invoices, balance sheets, and other documents. Greet persons entering establishment, determine nature and purpose of visit, and direct or escort them to specific destinations. Hear and resolve complaints from customers and public. File and maintain records. Transmit information or documents to customers, using computer, mail, or facsimile machine. Schedule appointments, and maintain and update appointment calendars. Analyze data to determine answers to questions from customers or members of the public. Provide information about establishment such as location of departments or offices, employees within the organization, or services provided. Keep a current record of staff members' whereabouts and availability. Collect, sort, distribute, and prepare mail, messages, and courier deliveries. Calculate and quote rates for tours, stocks, insurance policies, or other products and services. Take orders for merchandise or materials, and send them to the proper departments to be filled. Process and prepare memos, correspondence, travel vouchers, or other documents.

Education/Training Required: Short-term on-the-job training. **Education and Training Programs:** General Office Occupations and Clerical Services; Health Unit Coordinator/Ward Clerk Training; Medical Reception/Receptionist; Receptionist Training. **Knowledge/Courses:** Clerical Practices; Customer and Personal Service; Computers and Electronics; Communications and Media.

Career Clusters: 04 Business, Management, and Administration; 08 Health Science. **Career Pathways:** 04.6 Administrative and Information Support; 08.3 Health Informatics.

Skills: Service Orientation; Speaking; Active Listening.

Work Environment: Indoors; sitting; using hands; repetitive motions.

Sales Representatives, Wholesale and Manufacturing, Except Technical and Scientific Products

- ❋ Personality Type: Conventional-Enterprising
- ❋ Annual Earnings: $52,440
- ❋ Earnings Growth Potential: High (48.6%)

- ❋ Growth: 6.6%
- ❋ Annual Job Openings: 45,790
- ❋ Self-Employed: 3.7%

Considerations for Job Outlook: Continued expansion in the variety and number of goods sold is expected to lead to additional jobs for these workers. Prospects should be best for jobseekers with a college degree, technical expertise, and interpersonal skills.

Sell goods for wholesalers or manufacturers to businesses or groups of individuals. Work requires substantial knowledge of items sold. Answer customers' questions about products, prices, availability, product uses, and credit terms. Recommend products to customers based on customers' needs and interests. Contact regular and prospective customers to demonstrate products, explain product features, and solicit orders. Estimate or quote prices, credit or contract terms, warranties, and delivery dates. Consult with clients after sales or contract signings to resolve problems and to provide ongoing support. Prepare drawings, estimates, and bids that meet specific customer needs. Provide customers with product samples and catalogs. Identify prospective customers by using business directories, following leads from existing clients, participating in organizations and clubs, and attending trade shows and conferences. Arrange and direct delivery and installation of products and equipment. Monitor market conditions; product innovations; and competitors' products, prices, and sales. Negotiate details of contracts and payments, and prepare sales contracts and order forms. Perform administrative duties, such as preparing sales budgets and reports, keeping sales records, and filing expense account reports. Obtain credit information about prospective customers. Forward orders to manufacturers. Check stock levels, and reorder merchandise as necessary. Plan, assemble, and stock product displays in retail stores, or make recommendations to retailers regarding product displays, promotional programs, and advertising.

Education/Training Required: Work experience in a related occupation. **Education and Training Programs:** Apparel and Accessories Marketing

Conventional-S

Operations; Business, Management, Marketing, and Related Support Services, Other; Fashion Merchandising; General Merchandising, Sales, and Related Marketing Operations, Other; Insurance; Sales, Distribution, and Marketing Operations, General; Special Products Marketing Operations; Specialized Merchandising, Sales, and Marketing Operations, Other. **Knowledge/Courses:** Sales and Marketing; Economics and Accounting; Customer and Personal Service; Transportation; Mathematics; Production and Processing.

Career Cluster: 14 Marketing, Sales, and Service. **Career Pathways:** 14.2 Professional Sales and Marketing; 14.3 Buying and Merchandising.

Skills: Negotiation; Persuasion; Service Orientation; Operations Analysis; Critical Thinking; Social Perceptiveness; Active Listening; Speaking.

Work Environment: Outdoors; more often sitting than standing; walking and running; noise; contaminants.

Secretaries and Administrative Assistants, Except Legal, Medical, and Executive

- ❋ Personality Type: Conventional-Enterprising
- ❋ Annual Earnings: $30,830
- ❋ Earnings Growth Potential: Medium (36.1%)
- ❋ Growth: 4.6%
- ❋ Annual Job Openings: 36,550
- ❋ Self-Employed: 1.3%

Considerations for Job Outlook: Projected employment growth varies by occupational specialty. Faster than average growth is expected for medical secretaries and legal secretaries; average growth for executive secretaries and administrative assistants; and slower than average growth for secretaries other than legal, medical, or executive, who account for most of the workers in these specialties. Many opportunities are expected.

Perform routine clerical and administrative functions such as drafting correspondence, scheduling appointments, organizing and maintaining paper and electronic files, or providing information to callers. Operate office equipment such as fax machines, copiers, and phone systems, and use computers for spreadsheet, word-processing, database management, and other applications. Answer telephones, and give information to callers, take messages, or transfer calls to appropriate individuals. Greet visitors and callers, handle their inquiries, and direct them to the appropriate persons according to their needs. Set up and maintain paper and electronic filing systems for records, correspondence, and other material. Locate and attach appropriate files to incoming correspondence requiring replies. Open, read, route, and distribute incoming mail and other material, and prepare answers to routine letters. Complete forms in accordance with company procedures. Make copies of correspondence and other printed material. Review work done by others to check for correct spelling and grammar, ensure that company format policies are followed, and recommend revisions. Compose, type, and distribute meeting notes, routine correspondence, and reports. Learn to operate new office technologies as they are developed and implemented. Maintain scheduling and event calendars. Schedule and confirm appointments for clients, customers, or supervisors. Manage projects, and contribute to committee and team work. Mail newsletters, promotional material, and other information. Order and dispense supplies. Conduct searches to find needed information, using such sources as the Internet.

Education/Training Required: Moderate-term on-the-job training. **Education and Training Programs:** Administrative Assistant and Secretarial Science, General; Executive Assistant/Executive Secretary Training. **Knowledge/Courses:** Clerical Practices; Customer and Personal Service; Economics and Accounting; Computers and Electronics; English Language; Personnel and Human Resources.

Career Cluster: 04 Business, Management, and Administration. **Career Pathway:** 04.6 Administrative and Information Support.

Skills: Service Orientation; Management of Financial Resources; Writing; Time Management; Management of Material Resources; Active Listening; Reading Comprehension; Speaking.

Work Environment: Indoors; sitting; repetitive motions.

Social and Human Service Assistants

- ❋ Personality Type: Conventional-Social-Enterprising
- ❋ Annual Earnings: $28,200
- ❋ Earnings Growth Potential: Low (33.4%)
- ❋ Growth: 22.6%
- ❋ Annual Job Openings: 15,390
- ❋ Self-Employed: 0.3%

Considerations for Job Outlook: As the elderly population grows, demand for the services provided by these workers is expected to increase. Opportunities are expected to be excellent, particularly for job-seekers with some postsecondary education, such as a certificate or associate degree in a related subject.

Assist professionals from a wide variety of fields such as psychology, rehabilitation, or social work to provide client services, as well as support for families. May assist clients in identifying available benefits and social and community services and help clients obtain them. May assist social workers with developing, organizing, and conducting programs to prevent and resolve problems relevant to substance abuse, human relationships, rehabilitation, or adult daycare. Keep records and prepare reports for owner or management concerning visits with clients. Submit reports, and review reports or problems with superior. Interview individuals and family members to compile information on social, educational, criminal, institutional, or drug histories. Provide information and refer individuals to public or private agencies or community services for assistance. Consult with supervisors concerning programs for individual families. Advise clients regarding food stamps, child care, food, money management, sanitation, or housekeeping. Oversee day-to-day group activities of residents in institution. Visit individuals in homes or attend group meetings to provide information on agency services, requirements, and procedures. Monitor free, supplementary meal program to ensure cleanliness of facility and that eligibility guidelines are met for persons receiving meals. Meet with youth groups to acquaint them with consequences of delinquent acts. Assist in planning of food budgets, using charts and sample budgets. Transport and accompany clients to shopping areas or to appointments, using automobiles. Assist in locating housing for displaced individuals. Observe and discuss meal preparation, and suggest alternate methods of food preparation. Observe clients' food selections, and recommend alternative economical and nutritional food choices. Explain rules established by owner or management, such as sanitation and maintenance requirements or parking regulations.

Education/Training Required: Moderate-term on-the-job training. **Education and Training Program:** Mental and Social Health Services and Allied Professions, Other. **Knowledge/Courses:** Therapy and Counseling; Philosophy and Theology; Psychology; Customer and Personal Service; Sociology and Anthropology; Clerical Practices.

Career Cluster: 08 Health Science. **Career Pathway:** 08.1 Therapeutic Services.

Skills: Social Perceptiveness; Service Orientation; Active Listening; Science; Speaking; Learning Strategies; Systems Analysis; Persuasion.

Work Environment: Indoors; sitting.

Social Science Research Assistants

- ❋ Personality Type: Conventional-Investigative
- ❋ Annual Earnings: $37,230

- ❋ Earnings Growth Potential: High (42.6%)
- ❋ Growth: 17.8%
- ❋ Annual Job Openings: 1,270
- ❋ Self-Employed: 1.5%

Considerations for Job Outlook: Faster than average employment growth is projected.

Assist social scientists in laboratory, survey, and other social research. May perform publication activities, laboratory analysis, quality control, or data management. Normally these individuals work under the direct supervision of social scientists and assist in those activities that are more routine. Code data in preparation for computer entry. Provide assistance in the design of survey instruments such as questionnaires. Prepare, manipulate, and manage extensive databases. Prepare tables, graphs, fact sheets, and written reports summarizing research results. Obtain informed consent of research subjects and/or their guardians. Edit and submit protocols and other required research documentation. Screen potential subjects in order to determine their suitability as study participants. Conduct Internet-based and library research. Supervise the work of survey interviewers. Perform descriptive and multivariate statistical analyses of data, using computer software. Recruit and schedule research participants. Develop and implement research quality control procedures. Track research participants, and perform any necessary follow-up tasks. Verify the accuracy and validity of data entered in databases; correct any errors. Track laboratory supplies and expenses such as participant reimbursement. Provide assistance with the preparation of project-related reports, manuscripts, and presentations. Present research findings to groups of people. Perform needs assessments and/or consult with clients in order to determine the types of research and information that are required. Allocate and manage laboratory space and resources. Design and create special programs for tasks such as statistical analysis and data entry and cleaning.

Education/Training Required: Associate degree. **Education and Training Program:** Social Sciences, General. **Knowledge/Courses:** Psychology;

Sociology and Anthropology; Clerical Practices; Computers and Electronics; English Language; Communications and Media.

Career Cluster: 10 Human Services. **Career Pathway:** 10.3 Family and Community Services.

Skills: Programming; Science; Mathematics; Reading Comprehension; Quality Control Analysis; Management of Financial Resources; Operations Analysis; Technology Design.

Work Environment: Indoors; sitting.

Job Specialization: City and Regional Planning Aides

Compile data from various sources, such as maps, reports, and field and file investigations, for use by city planner in making planning studies. Participate in and support team planning efforts. Prepare reports, using statistics, charts, and graphs, to illustrate planning studies in areas such as population, land use, or zoning. Research, compile, analyze, and organize information from maps, reports, investigations, and books for use in reports and special projects. Provide and process zoning and project permits and applications. Respond to public inquiries and complaints. Serve as liaison between planning department and other departments and agencies. Inspect sites, and review plans for minor development permit applications. Conduct interviews, surveys, and site inspections concerning factors that affect land usage, such as zoning, traffic flow, and housing. Prepare, maintain, and update files and records, including land use data and statistics. Prepare, develop, and maintain maps and databases. Perform clerical duties such as composing, typing, and proofreading documents; scheduling appointments and meetings; handling mail; and posting public notices. Perform code enforcement tasks.

Education/Training Required: Associate degree. **Education and Training Program:** Social Sciences, General. **Knowledge/Courses:** Geography; History and Archeology; Design; Law and Government; Building and Construction; Sociology and Anthropology.

Personality Type: Conventional-Realistic. **Career Cluster:** 10 Human Services. **Career Pathway:** 10.3 Family and Community Services.

Skills: Science; Systems Analysis; Negotiation; Mathematics; Writing; Systems Evaluation; Speaking; Operations Analysis.

Work Environment: Indoors; sitting.

Statisticians

- ❋ Personality Type: Conventional-Investigative
- ❋ Annual Earnings: $72,830
- ❋ Earnings Growth Potential: High (46.3%)
- ❋ Growth: 13.1%
- ❋ Annual Job Openings: 960
- ❋ Self-Employed: 2.8%

Considerations for Job Outlook: As data processing becomes faster and more efficient, employers are expected to need statisticians to analyze data. Projected employment growth for biostatisticians is related to the need for workers who can conduct research and clinical trials.

Engage in the development of mathematical theory, or apply statistical theory and methods to collect, organize, interpret, and summarize numerical data to provide usable information. May specialize in fields such as bio-statistics, agricultural statistics, business statistics, economic statistics, or other fields. Report results of statistical analyses, including information in the form of graphs, charts, and tables. Process large amounts of data for statistical modeling and graphic analysis, using computers. Identify relationships and trends in data, as well as any factors that could affect the results of research. Analyze and interpret statistical data in order to identify significant differences in relationships among sources of information. Prepare data for processing by organizing information, checking for any inaccuracies, and adjusting and weighting the raw data. Evaluate the statistical methods and procedures used to obtain data in order to ensure valid-ity, applicability, efficiency, and accuracy. Evaluate sources of information in order to determine any limitations in terms of reliability or usability. Plan data-collection methods for specific projects, and determine the types and sizes of sample groups to be used. Design research projects that apply valid scientific techniques, and utilize information obtained from baselines or historical data in order to structure uncompromised and efficient analyses. Develop an understanding of fields to which statistical methods are to be applied in order to determine whether methods and results are appropriate. Supervise and provide instructions for workers collecting and tabulating data. Apply sampling techniques or utilize complete enumeration bases in order to determine and define groups to be surveyed.

Education/Training Required: Master's degree. **Education and Training Programs:** Applied Mathematics, General; Biostatistics; Business Statistics; Mathematical Statistics and Probability; Mathematics, General; Statistics, General; Statistics, Other. **Knowledge/Courses:** Mathematics; Computers and Electronics; English Language; Law and Government; Education and Training.

Career Clusters: 04 Business, Management, and Administration; 15 Science, Technology, Engineering, and Mathematics. **Career Pathways:** 04.2 Business Financial Management and Accounting; 15.2 Science and Mathematics.

Skills: Programming; Mathematics; Science; Operations Analysis; Active Learning; Reading Comprehension; Critical Thinking; Learning Strategies.

Work Environment: Indoors; sitting; using hands; repetitive motions.

Job Specialization: Biostatisticians

Develop and apply biostatistical theory and methods to the study of life sciences. Write research proposals or grant applications for submission to external bodies. Teach graduate or continuing education courses or seminars in biostatistics.

Conventional-S

Read current literature, attend meetings or conferences, and talk with colleagues to keep abreast of methodological or conceptual developments in fields such as biostatistics, pharmacology, life sciences, and social sciences. Prepare statistical data for inclusion in reports to data monitoring committees, federal regulatory agencies, managers, or clients. Prepare articles for publication or presentation at professional conferences. Calculate sample size requirements for clinical studies. Determine project plans, timelines, or technical objectives for statistical aspects of biological research studies. Assign work to biostatistical assistants or programmers. Write program code to analyze data using statistical analysis software. Write detailed analysis plans and descriptions of analyses and findings for research protocols or reports. Plan or direct research studies related to life sciences. Prepare tables and graphs to present clinical data or results. Monitor clinical trials or experiments to ensure adherence to established procedures or to verify the quality of data collected. Draw conclusions or make predictions based on data summaries or statistical analyses. Develop or use mathematical models to track changes in biological phenomena such as the spread of infectious diseases. Design surveys to assess health issues.

Education/Training Required: Master's degree. **Education and Training Programs:** Applied Mathematics, General; Biostatistics; Business Statistics; Mathematical Statistics and Probability; Mathematics, General; Statistics, General; Statistics, Other. **Knowledge/Courses:** Mathematics; Biology; Computers and Electronics; Medicine and Dentistry; English Language; Education and Training.

Personality Type: Investigative-Conventional. **Career Cluster:** 15 Science, Technology, Engineering, and Mathematics. **Career Pathway:** 15.2 Science and Mathematics.

Skills: Programming; Science; Mathematics; Writing; Reading Comprehension; Operations Analysis; Active Learning; Instructing.

Work Environment: Indoors; sitting.

Job Specialization: Clinical Data Managers

Apply knowledge of health care and database management to analyze clinical data, and to identify and report trends. Read technical literature and participate in continuing education or professional associations to maintain awareness of current database technology and best practices. Provide support and information to functional areas such as marketing, clinical monitoring, and medical affairs. Prepare appropriate formatting to datasets as requested. Evaluate processes and technologies, and suggest revisions to increase productivity and efficiency. Develop technical specifications for data management programming, and communicate needs to information technology staff. Develop or select specific software programs for various research scenarios. Contribute to the compilation, organization, and production of protocols, clinical study reports, regulatory submissions, or other controlled documentation. Write work instruction manuals, data capture guidelines, or standard operating procedures. Track the flow of work forms including in-house data flow or electronic forms transfer. Train staff on technical procedures or software program usage. Supervise the work of data-management project staff. Prepare data analysis listings and activity, performance, or progress reports. Perform quality control audits to ensure accuracy, completeness, or proper usage of clinical systems and data. Monitor work productivity or quality to ensure compliance with standard operating procedures.

Education/Training Required: Bachelor's degree. **Education and Training Programs:** Applied Mathematics, General; Biostatistics; Business Statistics; Mathematical Statistics and Probability; Mathematics, General; Statistics, General; Statistics, Other. **Knowledge/Courses:** Medicine and Dentistry; Biology; Clerical Practices; Administration and Management; Computers and Electronics.

Personality Type: Conventional-Investigative. **Career Cluster:** 15 Science, Technology, Engineering, and Mathematics. **Career Pathway:** 15.2 Science and Mathematics.

Skills: Programming; Mathematics; Operations Analysis; Technology Design; Systems Evaluation; Systems Analysis; Instructing; Monitoring.

Work Environment: Indoors; sitting; repetitive motions.

Surveying and Mapping Technicians

- ❋ Personality Type: Conventional-Realistic
- ❋ Annual Earnings: $37,900
- ❋ Earnings Growth Potential: Medium (38.1%)
- ❋ Growth: 20.4%
- ❋ Annual Job Openings: 2,940
- ❋ Self-Employed: 5.6%

Considerations for Job Outlook: Increasing demand for geographic information should be the main source of employment growth. Jobseekers with a bachelor's degree and strong technical skills should have favorable prospects.

Job Specialization: Mapping Technicians

Calculate mapmaking information from field notes, and draw and verify accuracy of topographical maps. Check all layers of maps to ensure accuracy, identifying and marking errors and making corrections. Determine scales, line sizes, and colors to be used for hard copies of computerized maps, using plotters. Monitor mapping work and the updating of maps to ensure accuracy, the inclusion of new and/or changed information, and compliance with rules and regulations. Identify and compile database information to create maps in response to requests. Produce and update overlay maps to show information boundaries, water locations, and topographic features on various base maps and at different scales. Trace contours and topographic details to generate maps that denote specific land and property locations and geographic attributes. Lay out and match aerial photographs in sequences in which they were taken, and identify any areas missing from pho-

tographs. Compare topographical features and contour lines with images from aerial photographs, old maps, and other reference materials to verify the accuracy of their identification. Compute and measure scaled distances between reference points to establish relative positions of adjoining prints and enable the creation of photographic mosaics. Research resources such as survey maps and legal descriptions to verify property lines and to obtain information needed for mapping. Form three-dimensional images of aerial photographs taken from different locations, using mathematical techniques and plotting instruments.

Education/Training Required: Moderate-term on-the-job training. **Education and Training Programs:** Geographic Information Science and Cartography; Surveying Technology/Surveying. **Knowledge/Courses:** Geography; Design; Computers and Electronics; Engineering and Technology; Mathematics; Clerical Practices.

Personality Type: Conventional-Realistic. **Career Clusters:** 07 Government and Public Administration; 13 Manufacturing. **Career Pathways:** 07.1 Governance; 13.3 Maintenance, Installation, and Repair.

Skills: Programming; Mathematics; Quality Control Analysis; Management of Personnel Resources; Learning Strategies; Instructing; Operation and Control; Writing.

Work Environment: Indoors; sitting; using hands; repetitive motions.

Job Specialization: Surveying Technicians

Adjust and operate surveying instruments such as theodolite and electronic distance-measuring equipment, and compile notes, make sketches, and enter data into computers. Perform calculations to determine Earth curvature corrections, atmospheric impacts on measurements, traverse closures and adjustments, azimuths, level runs, and placement of markers. Record survey measurements and descriptive data using notes, drawings, sketches, and inked tracings. Search for section corners, property irons, and survey points. Position and hold the vertical rods, or targets, that theodolite operators use for sighting to measure angles, distances, and elevations. Lay out grids, and determine horizontal and vertical controls. Compare survey computations with applicable standards to determine adequacy of data. Set out and recover stakes, marks, and other monumentation. Conduct surveys to ascertain the locations of natural features and man-made structures on Earth's surface, underground, and underwater, using electronic distance-measuring equipment and other surveying instruments. Direct and supervise work of subordinate members of surveying parties. Compile information necessary to stake projects for construction, using engineering plans. Prepare topographic and contour maps of land surveyed, including site features and other relevant information, such as charts, drawings, and survey notes. Place and hold measuring tapes when electronic distance-measuring equipment is not used. Collect information needed to carry out new surveys using source maps, previous survey data, photographs, computer records, and other relevant information.

Education/Training Required: Moderate-term on-the-job training. **Education and Training Programs:** Geographic Information Science and Cartography; Surveying Technology/Surveying. **Knowledge/Courses:** Geography; Design; Building and Construction; Mathematics; Law and Government; Engineering and Technology.

Personality Type: Realistic-Conventional. **Career Clusters:** 02 Architecture and Construction; 07 Government and Public Administration. **Career Pathways:** 02.1 Design/Pre-Construction; 07.1 Governance.

Skills: Equipment Maintenance; Operation and Control; Repairing; Science; Equipment Selection; Mathematics; Troubleshooting; Operation Monitoring.

Work Environment: More often outdoors than indoors; standing; walking and running; using hands;

noise; very hot or cold; contaminants; hazardous equipment; minor burns, cuts, bites, or stings.

Tax Examiners and Collectors, and Revenue Agents

* Personality Type: Conventional-Enterprising
* Annual Earnings: $49,360
* Earnings Growth Potential: Medium (40.2%)
* Growth: 13.0%
* Annual Job Openings: 3,520
* Self-Employed: 2.3%

Considerations for Job Outlook: Employment growth of revenue agents and tax collectors should remain strong. The federal government is expected to increase its tax enforcement efforts, but demand for these workers' services is expected to be adversely affected by the automation of examiners' tasks and outsourcing of collection duties to private agencies.

Determine tax liability or collect taxes from individuals or business firms according to prescribed laws and regulations. Collect taxes from individuals or businesses according to prescribed laws and regulations. Maintain knowledge of tax code changes and of accounting procedures and theory to properly evaluate financial information. Maintain records for each case, including contacts, telephone numbers, and actions taken. Confer with taxpayers or their representatives to discuss the issues, laws, and regulations involved in returns and to resolve problems with returns. Contact taxpayers by mail or telephone to address discrepancies and to request supporting documentation. Send notices to taxpayers when accounts are delinquent. Notify taxpayers of any overpayment or underpayment, and either issue a refund or request further payment. Conduct independent field audits and investigations of income tax returns to verify information or to amend tax liabilities. Review filed tax returns to determine whether claimed tax credits and deductions are allowed by law. Review selected tax returns to determine the nature and extent of audits to be performed on them. Enter tax return information into computers for processing. Examine accounting systems and records to determine whether accounting methods used were appropriate and in compliance with statutory provisions. Process individual and corporate income tax returns and sales and excise tax returns. Impose payment deadlines on delinquent taxpayers and monitor payments to ensure that deadlines are met.

Education/Training Required: Bachelor's degree. **Education and Training Programs:** Accounting; Taxation. **Knowledge/Courses:** Economics and Accounting; Customer and Personal Service; Law and Government; Clerical Practices; Mathematics; Computers and Electronics.

Career Cluster: 07 Government and Public Administration. **Career Pathway:** 07.5 Revenue and Taxation.

Skills: Mathematics; Reading Comprehension; Active Listening; Active Learning; Negotiation; Speaking; Persuasion; Learning Strategies.

Work Environment: Indoors; sitting; repetitive motions.

Conventional-T

APPENDIX A

Occupations Ordered by Personality Codes

The job titles here are taken from the SOC taxonomy, which is what I use in the lists in Part III and to order the job descriptions within each personality type in Part IV. However, I use the O*NET database to match jobs to personality types, following the RIASEC codes assigned by the U.S. Department of Labor.

The SOC and O*NET-SOC taxonomies don't match precisely, so I made the following adjustments in the tables that follow:

❋ When a SOC title is linked to only one O*NET-SOC title, I use the RIASEC rating of the O*NET-SOC title.

❋ When a SOC title is linked to more than one O*NET-SOC title that has RIASEC ratings, I use the *average* of the RIASEC ratings of the related O*NET-SOC titles, and I follow the practices of the O*NET developers for ordering the primary and secondary personality types.

Other publishers may not create the exact same set of linkages between personality codes and occupations. For example, some sales jobs that are coded as Social by Psychological Assessment Resources, Inc., the publisher of the *Self-Directed Search,* are coded as Enterprising by O*NET.

Realistic

Personality Code	Job
RI	Physical Scientists, All Other
RIE	Commercial Pilots
RIC	Audio and Video Equipment Technicians
RIC	Biological Technicians
RIC	Civil Engineers
RIC	Computer User Support Specialists
RIC	Electrical Power-Line Installers and Repairers
RIC	Electricians
RIC	Environmental Engineering Technicians
RIC	Health Technologists and Technicians, All Other
RIC	Industrial Machinery Mechanics
RIC	Medical and Clinical Laboratory Technicians
RIC	Medical Equipment Repairers
RA	Museum Technicians and Conservators
RS	Firefighters
RS	Radiologic Technologists
RSI	Cardiovascular Technologists and Technicians
RSC	Surgical Technologists
RE	Cement Masons and Concrete Finishers
REC	Captains, Mates, and Pilots of Water Vessels
REC	Correctional Officers and Jailers
RC	Boilermakers
RC	Construction Laborers
RC	Drywall and Ceiling Tile Installers
RC	Heating, Air Conditioning, and Refrigeration Mechanics and Installers
RC	Heavy and Tractor-Trailer Truck Drivers
RC	Mobile Heavy Equipment Mechanics, Except Engines
RC	Plumbers, Pipefitters, and Steamfitters
RC	Refuse and Recyclable Material Collectors
RC	Security and Fire Alarm Systems Installers
RC	Water and Wastewater Treatment Plant and System Operators
RCI	Airline Pilots, Copilots, and Flight Engineers
RCI	Brickmasons and Blockmasons
RCI	Carpenters
RCI	Cartographers and Photogrammetrists
RCI	Civil Engineering Technicians
RCI	Construction and Building Inspectors
RCI	Life, Physical, and Social Science Technicians, All Other
RCI	Maintenance and Repair Workers, General
RCI	Operating Engineers and Other Construction Equipment Operators
RCI	Surveyors
RCI	Transportation Inspectors
RCA	Architectural and Civil Drafters
RCA	Tile and Marble Setters
RCE	Ship Engineers

Investigative

Personality Code	Job
IR	Aerospace Engineers
IR	Atmospheric and Space Scientists
IR	Biomedical Engineers
IR	Electrical Engineers
IR	Electronics Engineers, Except Computer
IR	Engineers, All Other

IR	Geoscientists, Except Hydrologists and Geographers
IR	Physicists
IR	Prosthodontists
IR	Veterinarians
IRA	Biological Scientists, All Other
IRA	Geographers
IRA	Medical Scientists, Except Epidemiologists
IRS	Dentists, General
IRS	Orthodontists
IRC	Computer and Information Research Scientists
IRC	Computer Hardware Engineers
IRC	Environmental Engineers
IRC	Environmental Science and Protection Technicians, Including Health
IRC	Environmental Scientists and Specialists, Including Health
IRC	Mechanical Engineers
IRC	Medical and Clinical Laboratory Technologists
IRC	Network and Computer Systems Administrators
IRC	Nuclear Engineers
IRC	Petroleum Engineers
IRC	Software Developers, Applications
IA	Anthropologists and Archeologists
IAR	Astronomers
IAR	Biochemists and Biophysicists
IAS	Political Scientists
IAS	Sociologists
IS	Audiologists
ISR	Diagnostic Medical Sonographers
ISR	Optometrists
ISR	Physicians and Surgeons
ISA	Clinical, Counseling, and School Psychologists
ISA	Psychologists, All Other
IEA	Industrial-Organizational Psychologists
IEA	Urban and Regional Planners

IEC	Management Analysts
IEC	Market Research Analysts and Marketing Specialists
ICR	Computer Network Architects
ICR	Computer Occupations, All Other
ICR	Computer Systems Analysts
ICR	Social Scientists and Related Workers, All Other
ICR	Software Developers, Systems Software
ICA	Mathematicians
ICS	Pharmacists
ICE	Industrial Engineers
ICE	Operations Research Analysts
ICE	Survey Researchers

Artistic

Personality Code	Job
AR	Makeup Artists, Theatrical and Performance
AR	Photographers
AR	Set and Exhibit Designers
ARE	Graphic Designers
AI	Architects, Except Landscape and Naval
AI	Multimedia Artists and Animators
AIR	Landscape Architects
AIC	Technical Writers
AS	Interpreters and Translators
AE	Art Directors
AE	Interior Designers
AE	Music Directors and Composers
AER	Commercial and Industrial Designers
AER	Fashion Designers
AEI	Film and Video Editors
AEI	Writers and Authors
AES	Hairdressers, Hairstylists, and Cosmetologists
AEC	Editors

Social

Personality Code	Job
SR	Licensed Practical and Licensed Vocational Nurses
SR	Occupational Therapy Assistants
SR	Vocational Education Teachers, Postsecondary
SRI	Athletic Trainers
SRI	Physical Therapist Assistants
SRE	Fitness Trainers and Aerobics Instructors
SRC	Dental Hygienists
SRC	Radiation Therapists
SI	Atmospheric, Earth, Marine, and Space Sciences Teachers, Postsecondary
SI	Biological Science Teachers, Postsecondary
SI	Economics Teachers, Postsecondary
SI	Health Specialties Teachers, Postsecondary
SI	Healthcare Social Workers
SI	Nursing Instructors and Teachers, Postsecondary
SI	Occupational Therapists
SI	Physics Teachers, Postsecondary
SI	Registered Nurses
SI	Rehabilitation Counselors
SIR	Agricultural Sciences Teachers, Postsecondary
SIR	Chemistry Teachers, Postsecondary
SIR	Chiropractors
SIR	Engineering Teachers, Postsecondary
SIR	Physical Therapists
SIR	Physician Assistants
SIR	Respiratory Therapists
SIA	Instructional Coordinators
SIA	Mathematical Science Teachers, Postsecondary
SIA	Mental Health and Substance Abuse Social Workers
SIA	Mental Health Counselors
SIA	Psychology Teachers, Postsecondary
SIA	Speech-Language Pathologists
SIE	Law Teachers, Postsecondary
SIC	Computer Science Teachers, Postsecondary
SA	Architecture Teachers, Postsecondary
SA	Art, Drama, and Music Teachers, Postsecondary
SA	Communications Teachers, Postsecondary
SA	Kindergarten Teachers, Except Special Education
SA	Middle School Teachers, Except Special and Career/Technical Education
SA	Preschool Teachers, Except Special Education
SA	Recreational Therapists
SA	Special Education Teachers, Middle School
SAI	Education Teachers, Postsecondary
SAI	English Language and Literature Teachers, Postsecondary
SAI	Foreign Language and Literature Teachers, Postsecondary
SAI	Marriage and Family Therapists
SAI	Philosophy and Religion Teachers, Postsecondary
SAI	Substance Abuse and Behavioral Disorder Counselors
SAE	Adult Basic and Secondary Education and Literacy Teachers and Instructors
SAE	Secondary School Teachers, Except Special and Career/Technical Education

Personality Code	Job
SAE	Self-Enrichment Education Teachers
SAC	Elementary School Teachers, Except Special Education
SAC	Training and Development Specialists
SER	Coaches and Scouts
SEI	Business Teachers, Postsecondary
SEA	Political Science Teachers, Postsecondary
SEC	Customer Service Representatives
SEC	Probation Officers and Correctional Treatment Specialists
SCR	Medical Assistants

Enterprising

Personality Code	Job
ER	First-Line Supervisors of Fire Fighting and Prevention Workers
ERI	Architectural and Engineering Managers
ERI	Sales Engineers
ERS	Police and Sheriff's Patrol Officers
ERC	Construction Managers
ERC	Farmers, Ranchers, and Other Agricultural Managers
ERC	First-Line Supervisors of Landscaping, Lawn Service, and Groundskeeping Workers
ERC	Supervisors of Construction and Extraction Workers
EI	Lawyers
EI	Natural Sciences Managers
EA	Public Relations and Fundraising Managers
EAS	Public Relations Specialists
EAC	Advertising and Promotions Managers
EAC	Producers and Directors
ES	Agents and Business Managers of Artists, Performers, and Athletes

Personality Code	Job
ES	Social and Community Service Managers
ES	Training and Development Managers
ESC	Education Administrators, Elementary and Secondary School
ESC	First-Line Supervisors of Police and Detectives
ESC	Human Resources Managers
ESC	Human Resources Specialists
EC	Administrative Services Managers
EC	Air Traffic Controllers
EC	Chief Executives
EC	Financial Examiners
EC	Financial Managers
EC	Managers, All Other
EC	Marketing Managers
EC	Property, Real Estate, and Community Association Managers
EC	Real Estate Sales Agents
EC	Sales Managers
EC	Sales Representatives, Services, All Other
EC	Sales Representatives, Wholesale and Manufacturing, Technical and Scientific Products
EC	Securities, Commodities, and Financial Services Sales Agents
ECR	Detectives and Criminal Investigators
ECR	First-Line Supervisors of Mechanics, Installers, and Repairers
ECI	Computer and Information Systems Managers
ECS	Compensation and Benefits Managers
ECS	First-Line Supervisors of Non-Retail Sales Workers
ECS	First-Line Supervisors of Office and Administrative Support Workers

ECS	First-Line Supervisors of Personal Service Workers
ECS	General and Operations Managers
ECS	Insurance Sales Agents
ECS	Medical and Health Services Managers
ECS	Personal Financial Advisors

Conventional

Personality Code	Job
CR	Occupational Health and Safety Technicians
CR	Pharmacy Technicians
CR	Postal Service Mail Carriers
CR	Surveying and Mapping Technicians
CRS	Dental Assistants
CRE	Police, Fire, and Ambulance Dispatchers
CI	Database Administrators
CI	Judicial Law Clerks
CI	Social Science Research Assistants
CI	Statisticians
CIE	Actuaries
CIE	Financial Analysts
CIE	Financial Specialists, All Other
CIE	Paralegals and Legal Assistants
CS	Medical Secretaries
CSE	Librarians
CSE	Social and Human Service Assistants
CE	Bill and Account Collectors
CE	Billing and Posting Clerks
CE	Bookkeeping, Accounting, and Auditing Clerks
CE	Cargo and Freight Agents
CE	Claims Adjusters, Examiners, and Investigators
CE	Compensation, Benefits, and Job Analysis Specialists
CE	Cost Estimators

CE	Court Reporters
CE	Court, Municipal, and License Clerks
CE	Credit Analysts
CE	Executive Secretaries and Executive Administrative Assistants
CE	Legal Secretaries
CE	Medical Records and Health Information Technicians
CE	Production, Planning, and Expediting Clerks
CE	Purchasing Agents, Except Wholesale, Retail, and Farm Products
CE	Sales Representatives, Wholesale and Manufacturing, Except Technical and Scientific Products
CE	Secretaries and Administrative Assistants, Except Legal, Medical, and Executive
CE	Tax Examiners and Collectors, and Revenue Agents
CER	Business Operations Specialists, All Other
CER	Office Clerks, General
CEI	Accountants and Auditors
CEI	Budget Analysts
CEI	Compliance Officers
CEI	Insurance Underwriters
CEI	Logisticians
CES	Interviewers, Except Eligibility and Loan
CES	Loan Officers
CES	Receptionists and Information Clerks

APPENDIX B

Definitions of Skills and Knowledge/ Courses Referenced in This Book

Definitions of Skills

Skill Name	Definition
Active Learning	Working with new material or information to grasp its implications.
Active Listening	Listening to what other people are saying and asking questions as appropriate.
Complex Problem Solving	Identifying complex problems, reviewing the options, and implementing solutions.
Coordination	Adjusting actions in relation to others' actions.
Critical Thinking	Using logic and analysis to identify the strengths and weaknesses of different approaches.
Equipment Maintenance	Performing routine maintenance and determining when and what kind of maintenance is needed.
Equipment Selection	Determining the kind of tools and equipment needed to do a job.
Installation	Installing equipment, machines, wiring, or programs to meet specifications.
Instructing	Teaching others how to do something.
Judgment and Decision Making	Weighing the relative costs and benefits of a potential action.
Learning Strategies	Using multiple approaches when learning or teaching new things.
Management of Financial Resources	Determining how money will be spent to get the work done and accounting for these expenditures.

(continued)

(continued)

Definitions of Skills

Skill Name	Definition
Management of Material Resources	Obtaining and seeing to the appropriate use of equipment, facilities, and materials needed to do certain work.
Management of Personnel Resources	Motivating, developing, and directing people as they work; identifying the best people for the job.
Mathematics	Using mathematics to solve problems.
Monitoring	Assessing how well one is doing when learning or doing something.
Negotiation	Bringing others together and trying to reconcile differences.
Operation and Control	Controlling operations of equipment or systems.
Operation Monitoring	Watching gauges, dials, or other indicators to make sure a machine is working properly.
Operations Analysis	Analyzing needs and product requirements to create a design.
Persuasion	Persuading others to approach things differently.
Programming	Writing computer programs for various purposes.
Quality Control Analysis	Evaluating the quality or performance of products, services, or processes.
Reading Comprehension	Understanding written sentences and paragraphs in work-related documents.
Repairing	Repairing machines or systems, using the needed tools.
Science	Using scientific methods to solve problems.
Service Orientation	Actively looking for ways to help people.
Social Perceptiveness	Being aware of others' reactions and understanding why they react the way they do.
Speaking	Talking to others to effectively convey information.
Systems Analysis	Determining how a system should work and how changes will affect outcomes.
Systems Evaluation	Looking at many indicators of system performance and taking into account their accuracy.
Technology Design	Generating or adapting equipment and technology to serve user needs.
Time Management	Managing one's own time and the time of others.

Definitions of Skills

Skill Name	Definition
Troubleshooting	Determining what is causing an operating error and deciding what to do about it.
Writing	Communicating effectively with others in writing as indicated by the needs of the audience.

Definitions of Knowledge/Courses

Knowledge/Course Name	Definition
Administration and Management	Knowledge of principles and processes involved in business and organizational planning, coordination, and execution, includimg strategic planning, resource allocation, manpower modeling, leadership techniques, and production methods.
Biology	Knowledge of plant and animal living tissue, cells, organisms, and entities, including their functions, interdependencies, and interactions with each other and the environment.
Building and Construction	Knowledge of materials, methods, and the appropriate tools to construct objects, structures, and buildings.
Chemistry	Knowledge of the composition, structure, and properties of substances and of the chemical processes and transformations that they undergo, including uses of chemicals and their interactions, danger signs, production techniques, and disposal methods.
Clerical Studies	Knowledge of administrative and clerical procedures and systems such as word-processing systems, filing and records-management systems, stenography and transcription, forms, design principles, and other office procedures and terminology.
Communications and Media	Knowledge of media production, communication, and dissemination techniques and methods, including alternative ways to inform and entertain via written, oral, and visual media.
Computers and Electronics	Knowledge of electric circuit boards, processors, chips, and computer hardware and software, including applications and programming.

(continued)

(continued)

Definitions of Knowledge/Courses

Knowledge/Course Name	Definition
Customer and Personal Service	Knowledge of principles and processes for providing customer and personal services, including needs-assessment techniques, quality service standards, alternative delivery systems, and customer-satisfaction evaluation techniques.
Design	Knowledge of design techniques, principles, tools, and instruments involved in the production and use of precision technical plans, blueprints, drawings, and models.
Economics and Accounting	Knowledge of economic and accounting principles and practices, the financial markets, banking, and the analysis and reporting of financial data.
Education and Training	Knowledge of instructional methods and training techniques, including curriculum-design principles, learning theory, group and individual teaching techniques, design of individual development plans, and test design principles.
Engineering and Technology	Knowledge of equipment, tools, and mechanical devices and their uses to produce motion, light, power, technology, and other applications.
English Language	Knowledge of the structure and content of the English language, including the meaning and spelling of words, rules of composition, and grammar.
Fine Arts	Knowledge of theory and techniques required to produce, compose, and perform works of music, dance, visual arts, drama, and sculpture.
Food Production	Knowledge of techniques and equipment for planting, growing, and harvesting of food for consumption, including crop rotation methods, animal husbandry, and food storage/handling techniques.
Foreign Language	Knowledge of the structure and content of a foreign (non-English) language, including the meaning and spelling of words, rules of composition and grammar, and pronunciation.
Geography	Knowledge of various methods for describing the location and distribution of land, sea, and air masses, including their physical locations, relationships, and characteristics.
History and Archeology	Knowledge of past historical events and their causes, indicators, and impact on particular civilizations and cultures.

Definitions of Knowledge/Courses

Knowledge/Course Name	Definition
Law and Government	Knowledge of laws, legal codes, court procedures, precedents, government regulations, executive orders, agency rules, and the democratic political process.
Mathematics	Knowledge of numbers and their operations and interrelationships, including arithmetic, algebra, geometry, calculus, and statistics and their applications.
Mechanical Devices	Knowledge of machines and tools, including their designs, uses, benefits, repair, and maintenance.
Medicine and Dentistry	Knowledge of the information and techniques needed to diagnose and treat injuries, diseases, and deformities, including symptoms, treatment alternatives, drug properties and interactions, and preventive health-care measures.
Personnel and Human Resources	Knowledge of policies and practices involved in personnel/human resource functions, including recruitment, selection, training, and promotion regulations and procedures; compensation and benefits packages; labor relations and negotiation strategies; and personnel information systems.
Philosophy and Theology	Knowledge of different philosophical systems and religions, including their basic principles, values, ethics, ways of thinking, customs, and practices and their impact on human culture.
Physics	Knowledge and prediction of physical principles, laws, and applications, including air, water, material dynamics, light, atomic principles, heat, electric theory, earth formations, and meteorological and related natural phenomena.
Production and Processing	Knowledge of inputs, outputs, raw materials, waste, quality control, costs, and techniques for maximizing the manufacture and distribution of goods.
Psychology	Knowledge of human behavior and performance, mental processes, psychological research methods, and the assessment and treatment of behavioral and affective disorders.
Public Safety and Security	Knowledge of weaponry; public safety; security operations, rules, regulations, precautions, and prevention; and the protection of people, data, and property.
Sales and Marketing	Knowledge of principles and methods involved in showing, promoting, and selling products or services, including marketing strategies and tactics, product demonstration and sales techniques, and sales control systems.

(continued)

(continued)

Definitions of Knowledge/Courses

Knowledge/Course Name	Definition
Sociology and Anthropology	Knowledge of group behavior and dynamics; societal trends and influences; and cultures and their history, migrations, ethnicity, and origins.
Telecommunications	Knowledge of transmission, broadcasting, switching, control, and operation of telecommunications systems.
Therapy and Counseling	Knowledge of information and techniques needed to rehabilitate physical and mental ailments and to provide career guidance, including alternative treatments, rehabilitation equipment and its proper use, and methods to evaluate treatment effects.
Transportation	Knowledge of principles and methods for moving people or goods by air, rail, sea, or road, including their relative costs, advantages, and limitations.

Appendix C

Resources for Further Exploration

The facts and pointers in this book provide a good beginning to the subject of jobs that may be well suited to your personality. If you want additional details, I suggest you consult some of the resources listed here.

Facts About Careers

Occupational Outlook Handbook (or the *OOH*) (JIST): Updated every two years by the U.S. Department of Labor, this book provides descriptions for almost 350 major jobs covering more than 85 percent of the workforce.

Enhanced Occupational Outlook Handbook (JIST): Includes all descriptions in the *OOH* plus descriptions of more-specialized jobs from the Occupational Information Network (O*NET) and Dictionary of Occupational Titles—a total of more than 6,000 job descriptions.

*O*NET Dictionary of Occupational Titles* (JIST): The only printed source of the 950 jobs described in the U.S. Department of Labor's Occupational Information Network database. It covers all the jobs in the book you're now reading, but it offers more topics than we were able to fit here.

Career Decision Making and Planning

Overnight Career Choice, by Laurence Shatkin, Ph.D., and Michael Farr (JIST): This book can help you choose a career goal based on a variety of criteria, including skills, interests, and values. It is part of the *Help in a Hurry* series, so it is designed to produce quick results.

The Sequel: How to Change Your Career Without Starting Over, by Laurence Shatkin, Ph.D. (JIST): If you have several years of work experience, this book can help you identify jobs you can transition to that will take advantage of the work-related knowledge and contacts you have accumulated.

Job Hunting

Same-Day Resume, by Louise M. Kursmark (JIST): Learn how to write an effective resume in an hour. This book includes dozens of sample resumes from professional writers and even offers advice on cover letters, online resumes, and more.

Find a Job Through Social Networking, by Diane Crompton and Ellen Sautter (JIST): Social networking is more than a fun way to pass time. Discover how to launch your social networking efforts and gain advice for maximizing LinkedIn, Twitter, blogs, and other sites. Learn how to find jobs, seek advice, research employers, build a network, and create online portfolios and blogs. Additional guidance and worksheets help you develop and communicate your personal brands online.

Job Banks by Occupation. This is a set of links offered by America's Career InfoNet, a Career OneStop site. At www.acinet.org, find the Career Tools box, click Career Resource Library, and then click Job & Resume Banks. The Job Banks by Occupation link leads you to groups of jobs such as "Healthcare Practitioners and Technical Occupations" and "Legal Occupations," which in turn lead you to more specific job titles and occupation-specific job-listing sites maintained by various organizations.

INDEX

number of occupations/workers with, 23
older workers, best jobs for, 77–79
personality codes, jobs ordered by, 453
rural workers, best jobs for, 113
self-employed workers, best jobs for, 89–90
urban workers, best jobs for, 111–112
women, best jobs for, 99–100
young workers, best jobs for, 67–69
assessments
Personality Type Inventory, 27–36
websites for, 24–25
associate degree, 121, 126–127
Astronomers, 44, 51, 77, 78, 100, 101, 111, 112, 132, 274, 453
Athletic Trainers, 46, 56, 80, 81, 101, 102, 113, 114, 129, 305, 454
Atmospheric and Space Scientists, 43, 98, 99, 110, 128, 197, 452
Atmospheric, Earth, Marine, and Space Sciences Teachers, Postsecondary, 46, 52, 70, 79, 81, 114, 132, 306, 454
Audio and Video Equipment Technicians, 41, 65, 66, 87, 95, 97, 124, 151–152, 452
Audiologists, 42, 55, 76, 77, 97, 110, 132, 197–198, 453
Auditors, 400–401. *See also* Accountants and Auditors
Automotive Engineers, 238. *See also* Mechanical Engineers
Aviation Inspectors, 192–193. *See also* Transportation Inspectors

B

bachelor's degree, 121, 127–129
Bill and Account Collectors, 49, 58, 63, 72, 73, 105, 122, 402–403, 456
Billing and Posting Clerks, 49, 63, 105, 118, 119, 123, 403–404, 456
Billing, Cost, and Rate Clerks, 403. *See also* Billing and Posting Clerks
Biochemical Engineers, 220. *See also* Engineers, All Other
Biochemists and Biophysicists, 42, 43, 51, 55, 56, 132, 136, 143, 198–199, 453
Biofuels/Biodiesel Technology and Product Development Managers, 352–353. *See also* Architectural and Engineering Managers
Bioinformatics Scientists, 199–200. *See also* Biological Scientists, All Other

Biological Science Teachers, Postsecondary, 45, 52, 70, 79, 81, 132, 143, 306–307, 454
Biological Scientists, All Other, 42, 110, 111, 132, 135, 142, 199–201, 453
Biological Technicians, 40, 55, 65, 66, 129, 152–153, 452
Biology knowledge area, 459
Biomedical Engineers, 42, 55, 98, 99, 110, 127, 134, 201–202, 452
Biostatisticians, 445–446. *See also* Statisticians
Boilermakers, 41, 50, 54, 95, 96, 124, 153, 452
Bookkeeping, Accounting, and Auditing Clerks, 49, 63, 84, 86, 104, 105, 123, 404–405, 456
Brickmasons and Blockmasons, 40, 65, 66, 87, 95, 96, 108, 109, 124, 153–154, 452
Brownfield Redevelopment Specialists and Site Managers, 376–377. *See also* Managers, All Other
Budget Analysts, 49, 53, 128, 405, 456
Building and Construction knowledge area, 459
Business Continuity Planners, 406. *See also* Business Operations Specialists, All Other
Business Intelligence Analysts, 207–208. *See also* Computer Occupations, All Other
Business Operations Specialists, All Other, 40, 47, 48, 50, 53, 59, 62, 63, 74, 75, 82, 83, 85, 124, 125, 126, 128, 130, 405–409, 456
Business Teachers, Postsecondary, 45, 52, 70, 79, 81, 132, 143, 307–308, 455

C

Camera Operators, Television, Video, and Motion Picture, 44, 67, 69, 89, 90, 100, 101, 111, 112, 126, 274–275
Captains, Mates, and Pilots of Water Vessels, 40, 47, 50, 57, 74, 75, 83, 84, 95, 96, 103, 104, 108, 109, 116, 117, 124, 145, 154–156, 452
Cardiovascular Technologists and Technicians, 40, 50, 54, 94, 126, 156–157, 452
career choice, relationship with personality types, 19–20
Career Interests Game, 24
Cargo and Freight Agents, 49, 58, 72, 73, 106, 123, 409–410, 456
Carpenters, 40, 59, 65, 66, 87, 95, 96, 108, 109, 124, 157–159, 452
Cartographers and Photogrammetrists, 41, 50, 54, 74, 75, 95, 96, 107, 108, 129, 159, 452
Cement Masons and Concrete Finishers, 41, 59, 65, 66, 95, 97, 108, 109, 123, 160, 452

Q

R

X–Z